THE SOUTH AFRICAN WAR

The Anglo-Boer War 1899-1902

THE SOUTH AFRICAN WAR

The Anglo-Boer War 1899-1902

General Editor: Peter Warwick
Advisory Editor: Professor S.B. Spies

First published in Great Britain 1980 by
Longman Group Limited,
Longman House,
Burnt Mill, Harlow, Essex

Created, designed and produced by
Trewin Copplestone Books Ltd, London

British Library Cataloguing in Publication Data
The South African war.
1. South African War, 1899-1902
I. Warwick, Peter
968'.204 DT930

ISBN 0-582-78526-X

Printed in Great Britain by Garden City Press, Letchworth.

Contents

The Contributors

Peter Richardson BA, PhD
Queen Elizabeth House, University of Oxford

Jean Jacques Van-Helten BA, MA, M Phil
Institute of Commonwealth Studies, University of London

Andrew N. Porter MA, PhD
Lecturer in History, King's College, London

Howard Bailes BA, PhD
Department of War Studies, King's College, London

Fransjohan Pretorius MA, Drs Litt
Lecturer in History, University of South Africa

William Nasson MA
Gonville and Caius College, Cambridge

Brian Willan MA, PhD
School of Oriental and African Studies, University of London

S. B. Spies MA, PhD
Professor of History, University of South Africa

Peter Warwick BA, D Phil
Africa and Caribbean Division, Longman Group Ltd, formerly Centre for Southern African Studies, University of York

M. D. Blanch B Soc Sci, PhD
Curator, Clifton Park Museum, Rotherham

Bernard Porter MA, PhD
Senior Lecturer in History, University of Hull

Albert Grundlingh MA
Lecturer in History, University of South Africa

Margaret Blunden MA
Lecturer in Systems, Open University

Malvern van Wyk Smith MA, B Litt, PhD
Professor of English, Rhodes University, Grahamstown

Henry S. Wilson BA, B Litt
Senior Lecturer in History, University of York

S. E. Katzenellenbogen BA, D Phil
Lecturer in Economic History, University of Manchester

Ronald Hyam MA, PhD
Fellow of Magdalene College, Cambridge

Irving Hexham MA, PhD
Assistant Professor (Philosophy of Religion), Regent College, Vancouver

GENERAL INTRODUCTION

Peter Warwick

The South African War 1899–1902 (variously known as the Anglo-Boer War or Boer War, or to Afrikaners as the English War, *die Engelseoorlog*, or the Second War of Freedom, *Tweede Vryheidsoorlog*) continues to generate considerable interest among authors and readers alike, fascinated by a conflict that embodied human drama, tragedy, heroism and military and political folly on a grand scale. Scarcely a year passes without a new book about the war rolling off the printing presses. Yet a serious weakness in most recent histories of the war has been their failure to take full account of the research conducted by historians working in university departments both in Britain and South Africa. This book has been specially written to provide those who wish to read more deeply about the war with a selection of essays that contain recent research findings on the period, and that, collectively, comprise a detailed, thematic history for those reading about the war for the first time.

The book is organized in three parts: the advent of war, the war itself, and its aftermath. Each part is opened by a short narrative account of the period under review. The chapters that follow deal with both the military and political history of the war, and, above all, with its social history, an element that has often been neglected in the past. Because of the importance attached to examining the social history of the war, and because there is a wealth of contemporary photographic material available, the book is extensively illustrated. Photographic journalism in many respects came of age during the war, and though very few action shots of engagements were possible at the time because film was slow, lenses of poor quality and cameras and equipment extremely cumbersome, the photographs of the war that survive nonetheless help to provide an authentic and more intimate understanding of the conditions and way of life of those who took part.

The collection opens with two essays that explore the background to the war and the character of the imperial 'problem' that confronted Britain as a consequence of the discovery of gold in unprecedented quantity on the Witwatersrand in 1886. In Chapter One Peter Richardson and Jean Jacques Van-Helten discuss the structure of the early mining industry on the Rand, the implications of the mineral revolution for the whole of the southern African economy, and the difficulties faced by the industry as a result of the geological character of the Rand goldfield and the nature of the control exercised over the industry by the government of the South African Republic. Gold mining on the Rand, particularly the recovery of gold-bearing ore from deep-levels, was a capital-intensive, speculative and acutely cost-sensitive industry. During the 1890s many of the leading members of the industrial community in the Transvaal became convinced that unless the government of the republic was removed, and a new regime installed that was more amenable to mining interests and more capable of enforcing the legislation that the industry needed to achieve optimum profits and production, the development of gold mining on the Rand would be handicapped for many years to come.

Andrew Porter in Chapter Two examines the implications of the mineral revolution in southern Africa for British imperial policy, and shows how the political authority that accrued to President Kruger's government as a result of the shift northward of the centre of economic activity in South Africa threatened to undermine Britain's pre-eminent influence in the subcontinent. As Dr Porter remarks, the discovery of gold 'for the first time made it economically desirable that the Transvaal should be drawn permanently into the British empire, [but] also reduced the likelihood of such an occurrence'. Dr Porter traces the course of British diplomacy with the South African Republic from the Drifts crisis in 1895 to the final breakdown of Anglo-Boer relations and the declaration of war on 11 October 1899, and in particular discusses the roles of Chamberlain and Milner in imperial policy-making, revealing the extent to which they were concerned throughout to gain the confidence and support of British public opinion.

The twelve essays in Part Two deal with the war. In Chapter Three Howard Bailes examines the conflict from the point of view of a military historian. Concentrating on the British side of the war, and treating in greatest depth the period of conventional military activity before the onset of the guerrilla war, Bailes discusses the character of the two competing armies, analyses some of the most important engagements of the war, and examines the ways in which strategy and tactics developed as the campaign unfolded. Fransjohan Pretorius in Chapter Four looks at the nature of the Boers' military system, and in particular at the outlook and duties of ordinary burghers serving on commando. He investigates such issues as the attitudes of commando fighters to the war, discipline, absenteeism, social distinction on commando, and the diet and health of members of the Boer forces. In Chapter Five William Nasson examines the ways in which rank and file British soldiers responded to army life in South Africa – for them an unfamiliar and often hostile environment. The focus of attention in both Pretorius' 'Life on Commando' and Nasson's 'Tommy Atkins in South Africa' is on individual participants in the war rather than the system of which they were a part, and both contributors have made extensive use of personal diaries, letters and memoirs written by those who became drawn into the conflict. Nasson concludes that most rank and file members of the British army 'found life in South Africa tedious, dreary and boring . . . the great majority of working class soldiers were unflagging in their wish for a speedy return home.'

Brian Willan in Chapter Six examines the siege of Mafeking from the point of view of the townspeople of Mafeking, rather than, as is customary, from the standpoint of the military participants in the siege or of the host of overseas war correspondents, eager for a good story, who succeeded in making their way into the town before the investment began. A very different view of life inside the besieged town emerges, one in which the tedium, frustrations, deprivations and sufferings of the ordinary residents of Mafeking, both white and black, assume most significance. Fresh light is also shed on the character and achievements of the siege's most renowned personality, Baden-Powell, whom many townspeople found overbearing, impatient and truculent, and whose actions on numerous occasions were deemed by the local community to be ill-considered and excessively theatrical.

The implications of the war for women are discussed by S. B. Spies in Chapter Seven. Women have been regarded as the conflict's most obvious victims in view of the appalling death rate that occurred among Boer civilians interned in British concentration camps, though their role in the war was by no means confined to passive subjection to male military and political dominance. Professor Spies discusses the roles of Boer women as combatants, military advisors, farm managers in their menfolk's absence, and peace emissaries. The plight of Uitlander women, and the activities of British women from the middle and upper classes as nurses and relief workers, and as members of the anti-war and humanitarian movements, are issues also dealt with in the chapter.

A remarkable feature of the historiography of the South African War is the way in which the involvement of South Africa's black population has been 'written out' of accounts of the conflict. At the beginning of the war the British and Boers tacitly agreed that the involvement of Africans and coloureds in the fighting should be confined to non-combatant categories of military employment. Yet, in spite of attempts by both sides to conceal the extent of African participation in the war, it is clear that at least 10 000, and possibly as many as 30 000, armed blacks accompanied the British forces by the end of the war, and that on a number of occasions during the war the Boers also employed Africans and coloureds in combatant roles. Thousands of blacks were also engaged by both sides as scouts, waggon drivers, labourers and servants. In Chapter Eight a survey is made by Peter Warwick of the involvement of black people in the war, their attitudes towards the fighting, and the ways in which they were affected by the war.

In Chapters Nine and Ten the focus of attention turns from South Africa to Britain. M. D. Blanch examines the ways in which British society responded to the war, paying particular attention to the attitudes of ordinary working people. Dr Blanch reveals how prevalent were ideas of nationalism, imperialism and militarism in British society during the closing years of the nineteenth century, and how working people were exposed to these values, especially in the schools. The response of ordinary people to the South African War can only be understood by identifying influences such as these that were at work in shaping 'popular' opinion at the time. Dr Blanch then discusses the extent of popular enthusiasm for the war, and the ways in which attitudes changed as the war passed through its various military phases. Military recruitment statistics and voting patterns in the 'khaki election' of September 1900 and in local elections throughout the war are analysed, and an examination made of crowd demonstrations and music hall patriotism.

In Chapter Ten Bernard Porter discusses the outlook and influence on official policy of the pro-

Boers in Britain. The pro-Boer movement was essentially political in nature, its most prominent members political journalists and backbench MPs (among them two future prime ministers, Lloyd George and Ramsay MacDonald). The pro-Boers were united in believing that the war was unjustified and immoral, that war had been forced on the Boer republics, that government policy had been perniciously manipulated by capitalist interests, and that the war should therefore be stopped at once. The intellectual basis of the pro-Boers case, however, did not spring from a coherent political philosophy; indeed, in Dr Porter's words, the pro-Boer platform was one shared by 'old-fashioned Liberalism looking for guidance to a golden age in the past, and the newer socialist fashion, whose golden age was yet to come'. Opponents of the war in Britain were not 'pro-Boer' in the strict sense of the phrase; very few pro-Boers wanted Britain to be defeated, and most opponents of the war were unsympathetic to the Boers' cause. Most pro-Boers were not even anti-imperialist; they merely believed that the empire should be organized on the basis of consent rather than military force. During the first year of the war the pro-Boers' path was a lonely and difficult one to follow, though as the war dragged on without any sign of coming to an end, and as the ruthlessness of British military policy drew increasing criticism both at home and abroad, the movement grew in confidence, the pro-Boers' case assumed greater poignancy, and the arguments of those who wished to stop the war at once gained a wider measure of support.

In the same way that there were those people in Britain who came to espouse the view that it was time to call a halt to military operations and to negotiate peace terms without delay once the republics had been annexed and the war had entered upon its ruthless and distasteful irregular phase, so too there were those Boers who came to believe that their forces were incapable of winning the war, and that, in order to ensure the survival of their own people, the commandos remaining in the field should lay down their arms and accept, however temporarily, British rule. In Chapter Eleven Albert Grundlingh traces the origins and development of the abortive burgher peace movement and shows how, with British encouragement, by the end of the war almost 4 000 surrendered Boers came to take up arms with the British forces. It becomes clear from Grundlingh's research that Afrikaner society at the turn of the century was much less homogeneous, socially and politically, than has often been portrayed in the past, and that the majority of rank and file collaborators during the war were members of a disgruntled, landless and underprivileged pre-war class within Afrikaner society.

Margaret Blunden in Chapter Twelve examines the reaction to the war of the Anglican clergy in South Africa, whose general – though not universal – support for the war was widely used by members of the British government as an endorsement of their South African policy. Clergymen nonetheless responded to the war 'in a bewildering variety of ways', writes Mrs Blunden. One of the most interesting and distinctive views put forward by some clergy of the Anglican Church was that the war was justified on the grounds of advancing the interests of those Africans living under Boer rule. Few churchmen, however, paid much attention to the post-war aspirations of African people, and when the war was over many warned against moving too quickly on the issue of extending African liberties, believing (with some justification) that white colonial society was not yet prepared to accept meaningful changes in the status of black people. In her chapter Mrs Blunden also compares the supportive role played by the Anglican Church on the British side with that performed by the Dutch Reformed Church on the side of the Boers.

The poetry of the South African War is discussed by Malvern van Wyk Smith in Chapter Thirteen. Professor van Wyk Smith writes: 'Compared to any of its predecessors, the South African War was a remarkably literary war. . . . Popular song, broadside ballad, brief lyric or blank verse epic – all were attempted, by labourers and academics, from costermongers to established authors, and their work may be found in penny pamphlet and sumptuous poetry review alike.' Afrikaner verse, written both at the time and later, as well as poems written by European onlookers, are also dealt with in the chapter. From a historian's point of view, South African War verse sheds light on the attitudes of contemporary observers to the issues raised by the war and the manner of its conduct, and, more importantly, provides a further insight into the experiences and outlook of those who took part in the war, in much the same way as the poetry of the First World War sheds light on the attitudes and emotions of some of those who participated in that conflict. Indeed, Professor van Wyk Smith concludes that some poems written during the South African War – T. W. H. Crosland's 'Slain' is a good example – show strong similarities to that of Owen and other poets of the First World War, and that poems such as 'Slain' provide 'thought-provoking evidence that during the South African conflict war poetry came a long way towards poetry of the pity of war'.

Finally in the second part of the book, Henry S. Wilson provides an account of how the South African War was perceived in a country not directly involved in the conflict – the United States. The extent to which the issues at stake in the war were discussed in newspapers and in political circles in America bears testimony to the way in which the South African conflict attracted world-wide interest. This was inevitable, for at the turn of the century Britain was the pre-eminent world 'super power', and the widespread interest generated by her military intervention in South Africa may be compared to that attracted by the United States' own military involvement in South-east Asia during the 1960s.

The three essays in the final part of the book deal with the years immediately following the conclusion of peace. In Chapter Fifteen S. E. Katzenellenbogen examines in detail Britain's reconstruction programme in the Transvaal, which was designed to consolidate the gains supposedly achieved by the war, and to lay the foundations of a British-dominated colony that would become the political and economic centre of a federation of the white settler colonies of South Africa – a federation that would represent a loyal and stable component of the British imperial system. Dr Katzenellenbogen discusses the nature of the post-war British design, so closely associated with its principal architect, Lord Milner, and explains why, after a period of only three years, the scheme collapsed. Ronald Hyam in Chapter Sixteen analyses the South African policy of the new Liberal government in Britain, and shows how between 1906 and 1910 self-government under Afrikaner leadership was restored to the former Boer republics, and how South African union was achieved in circumstances very different from those originally envisaged by Milner and Chamberlain.

In the final chapter of the book Irving Hexham examines some of the religious, cultural and intellectual influences upon the birth of modern Afrikaner nationalism in the aftermath of the war with Britain. In particular Dr Hexham discusses the work of the churches in the reconstruction of Boer society, the resistance to British domination revealed in the Christian-National Education Movement, the cultural revival associated with the Second Afrikaans Language Movement, and the growth in popularity of nationalist political theories among Afrikaners. These influences, together with disillusionment with the conciliatory approach towards Britain and English-speaking South Africans pursued by Afrikaner political leaders such as Botha and Smuts, and their failure to grapple with the very serious social problems created by the pauperization of a large section of Afrikaner society, led to the foundation in January 1914 of the National Party under the leadership of J. B. M. Hertzog.

The essays in the book provide a concise summary of many of the major themes of recent historical enquiry on the war. It is hoped that by providing a modest statement of the current state of knowledge about the period, by identifying areas in which further enquiry is needed, and by advancing conclusions with which not all readers will necessarily agree, research on the war will be stimulated. In particular there is a need for a detailed reassessment of the influence of the war upon social formation in South Africa, and a need for local studies of the ways in which particular communities, both in Britain and South Africa, were affected by, and responded to, the circumstances of war. Research and writing on the war should not be left only to professional historians. Archival material on the war is voluminous, much of it to be found in local archives and record offices. In Britain, for example, regimental archives could be used as a primary source for studies revealing how local soldiers interpreted the issues at stake in the war, and how they lived and fought in a country 6 000 miles away from home. Local archival sources and past editions of provincial newspapers could be used to provide an account of how different social and political groups in a particular town responded to the declaration of war and to the course of events in South Africa, and an assessment made of the depth and nature of local support for the war during its various phases. In South Africa much more information is needed about the experiences of particular communities, both white and black, throughout the region. Details are required about how communities responded to the issues raised by the war, the roles performed by residents in the war effort (however menial and insignificant these may appear at first sight), how people's livelihoods were affected by the prevailing conditions of war, and how relationships between local white and black communities, and between Dutch- and English-speaking residents, developed during the period immediately before, during and after the war.

Finally, I would like to thank all the authors, who assisted me in many ways in the construction of this book. In particular I am indebted to Burridge Spies for his advice – constantly sought and generously given – throughout the project. Tom Lodge kindly gave up valuable research and writing time to locate many of the photographs from South African sources.

PART ONE

ADVENT OF WAR

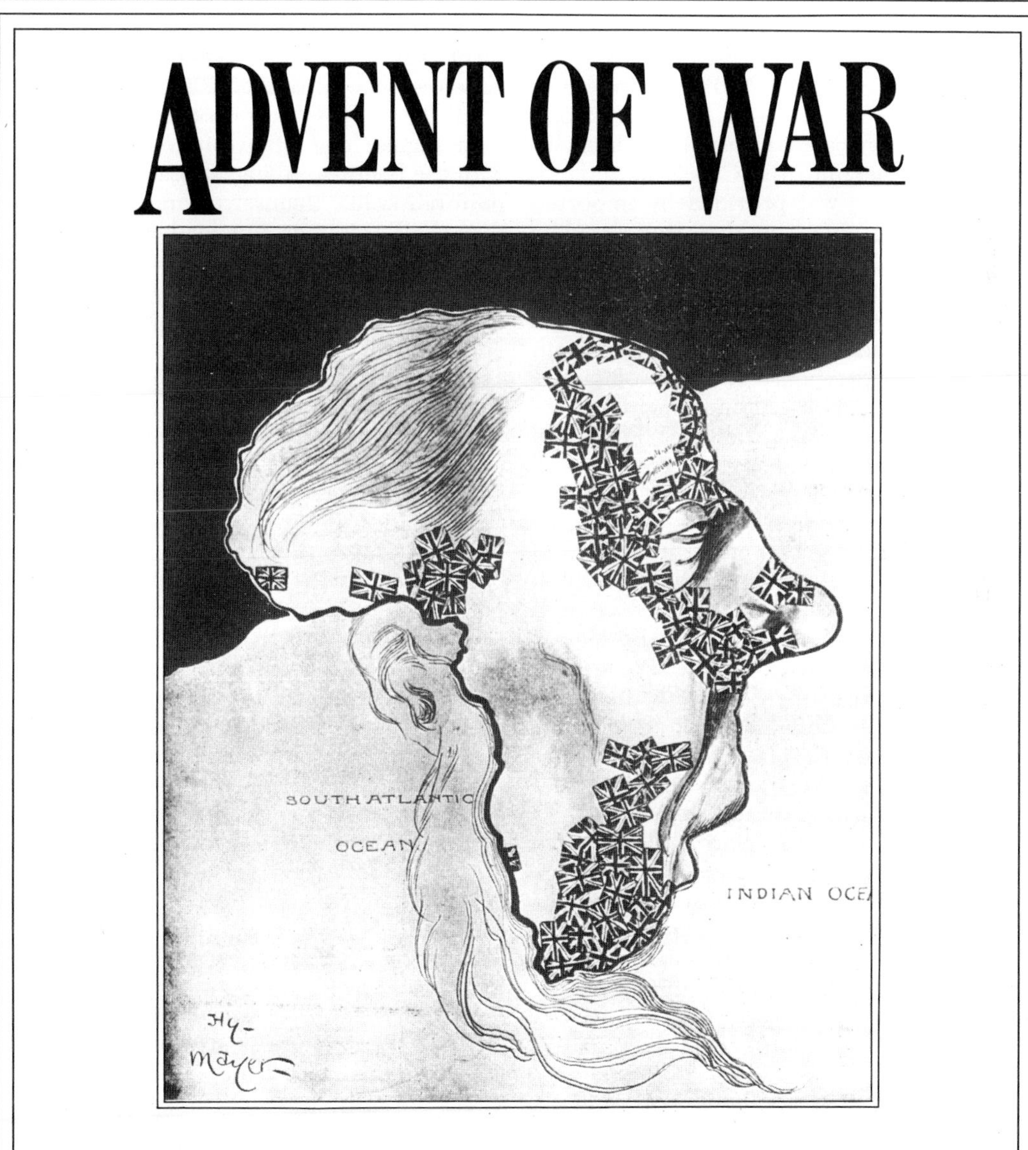

Radio-carbon dating has indicated that iron age settlements in South Africa date back at least to the fifth century AD. It was a millennium later, however, before Europeans first reached the southern tip of the African continent when the Portuguese voyager Bartholomew Dias rounded the Cape of Good Hope in 1488. Permanent white settlement began soon after 1652, the year in which the Dutch East India Company established a revictualling station at the Cape for its passing sailing vessels engaged in trade with India and the Spice Islands. Over the course of the next fifty years or more Dutch, German and French Huguenot settlers, the forbears of the Afrikaner (or Boer) people, arrived at the Cape to found a colony whose economy was based on cereal farming, viticulture and, further into the Cape's hinterland, stockraising. Labour was provided by imported slaves and the indigenous Khoikhoi people, and by the progeny of unions between white settlers, their slaves and the Khoikhoi, whose descendants now make up South Africa's two million coloured (mixed-race) population. During the eighteenth century, largely in response to the Company's close regulation of their livelihoods, many settlers progressively moved away from Cape Town and its environs to establish a dispersed, pastoral and patriarchal frontier society – a society based on individualism, companionship with one's own kind, freedom from government control, and strict observance of the Calvinist faith of the Dutch Reformed Church.

In 1795, following the invasion of the United Netherlands by the French revolutionary armies, British forces occupied the Cape with the agreement of the House of Orange, thereby ending the period of Dutch East India Company administration. Britain's initial occupation of the Cape lasted only until 1803, but three years later her forces again took control of the colony, largely for strategic reasons, and her possession of the Cape was ratified in 1815 by the peace treaties that ended the Napoleonic wars. Britain embarked at once upon the creation of a colony that was British in character as well as in name. In 1807 the slave trade was ended (the institution of slavery was abolished in 1834). Measures were introduced to regularize the administration of the colony, reform its legal system and encourage British immigration and the use of the English language. Many of the British reforms were deeply resented by Afrikaner settlers, especially by those living far into the Cape's interior, who had grown accustomed to the casual, remote and sometimes corrupt administration of a trading company. Attempts by Britain to stabilize the colony's frontiers and control and restrict landholding were regarded by the settlers as an affront to their pioneering way of life. The Afrikaner community was further alienated by the extension of liberties to coloured people, who were given legally-defined rights as workers, access to the courts and the right to own land in the colony. Activities on behalf of the coloured community by some of the early missionaries to South Africa, such as James Read and John Philip of the London Missionary Society, threatened further to turn upside down the world the Afrikaners knew. Their disillusionment was made more complete by the British government's apparent lack of concern for the predicament of settlers on the eastern frontier in their regular and often bitter clashes over land with the Bantu-speaking Xhosa people, who were pastoralists like themselves, more densely settled than the Khoisan groups further west, and better organized from a military point of view than the other indigenous groups the settlers had hitherto encountered in the subcontinent.

For many Afrikaners the final straw came in 1836 when Queen Adelaide Province between the Keiskamma and Kei rivers was handed back to the Xhosa. The possibility of moving as a group further into the interior away from British control had already been discussed among the frontier communities, and within weeks of the decision to abandon Queen Adelaide Province families had begun to sell their farms, form themselves into organized parties, and set out with their coloured servants to trek north beyond the Orange River and away from a government that seemed oppressive, wrong-headed and insensitive to their aspirations. While many Afrikaners chose to stay in the Cape, other families joined the exodus, so that the Voortrekkers, as the members of the Great Trek became known, eventually numbered some 6 000 whites. Further northward emigration took place during the following decades. The Voortrekkers dispersed across the high veld, clashing with Mzilikazi's Ndebele people who were driven north beyond the Limpopo River. The main body of trekkers led by Piet Retief moved eastwards across the Drakensberg mountains into the rich grasslands of Natal, controlled by the Zulu. The Zulu king, Dingane, was keenly aware of the military threat posed by the emigrants, and arranged the murder of Retief and his immediate companions at his kraal in February 1838; but on 16 December the reinforced Voortrekkers led by Andries Pretorius inflicted a crushing defeat on the Zulu army at the Battle of Blood River, and the trekker republic of Natalia was proclaimed. Its independence was short-lived, for soon afterwards Britain occupied Durban (Port Natal), and in 1842 its hinterland was annexed to the British Crown. Many of the settlers returned across the Drakensberg once more to begin a new life.

The emigrant communities eventually came together in two republics: the South African Republic (or Transvaal), between the Vaal and Limpopo rivers; and the Orange Free State, between the Orange River and the Vaal. Their independence was eventually recognized by Britain in 1852 and 1854. Although during this period each republic assumed the trappings of a modern state, with constitutions derived from Europe and America, an office of president and an all-white parliament (Volksraad), the Afrikaner states in practice were composed of widely dispersed farming communities that effectively controlled their own affairs. The republics remained extremely poor, compelled to compete with African societies for land and livestock, and only communicating with the outside world by the long ox-waggon routes passing through the British colonies to the coast.

Meanwhile in the south economic development began to gather pace with the expansion of sheep farming for the world market in the Cape, and the growth of sugar plantations in Natal worked by indentured Indian labour. The economy of the Cape Colony was further boosted after 1867 by the revenue and trade that resulted from diamond mining in Griqualand West. Responsible government was granted to the Cape in 1872. By contrast, the South African Republic was bankrupt and scarcely able to generate the resources needed to cope with the military threat posed by the Pedi, Zulu and other African societies of the interior. The republic's poverty and consequent political vulnerability enabled Disraeli's Conservative government to annex the Transvaal in 1877; annexation was looked upon by the Colonial Secretary of the time, Lord Carnarvon, as an important step towards achieving a loyal, self-governing federation of the South African colonies that would take responsibility for its own defence. In this way it was hoped that British strategic and economic interests in the region would be safeguarded, the direct involvement of Britain in South African affairs lessened, and the cost to the British taxpayer of imperial defence reduced. British forces defeated the Pedi and Zulu, a programme of administrative and financial reforms was instituted in the Transvaal, and the machinery to achieve federation was embodied in the South Africa Act, approved by the British Parliament in 1877. But Britain underestimated the spirit of independence of the majority of Afrikaners in the Transvaal, who, led by Paul Kruger, rose in rebellion in December 1880. The Transvaal War (also known as the First Boer War or the First War of Freedom) was a much shorter, less ruthless and less devastating conflict than the war that would ultimately follow in 1899. The Boers' military victory at Majuba in February 1881 prompted Gladstone's Liberal government to abandon the previous Conservative administration's federation policy, and by the Pretoria Convention signed in August 1881 the Transvaal was granted 'complete self-government, subject to the suzerainty of Her Majesty Queen Victoria'.

The phrasing of the preamble to the Pretoria Convention had important implications for the conduct of Anglo-Boer diplomacy during the late 1890s. Suzerainty was a word without precise meaning. Lord Kimberley, Gladstone's Colonial Secretary at the time, later explained that the word had been used as 'a convenient mode of expressing generally that certain stipulations existed in the Convention which limited the sovereignty of the Transvaal State', the most important of these being that Britain maintained control of the Transvaal's external relations and had the right of veto over legislation affecting the republic's black population. The Pretoria Convention was replaced in 1884 by the London Convention, which made no mention of suzerainty, restored to the Transvaal the name South African Republic, removed the British right of veto over 'native' legislation, and contained only one specific prohibition, namely, that 'The South African Republic will conclude no treaty or engagement with any State or nation other than the Orange Free State, nor with any native tribe to the eastward or westward of the Republic, until the same has been approved by Her Majesty the Queen.' During the 1890s the imperial government maintained that British suzerainty over the republic still existed since it had not been expressly withdrawn by the later agreement (this was a somewhat tenuous argument to say the least, for Lord Derby, the then Colonial Secretary, had himself crossed out the entire preamble mentioning suzerainty from his working copy of the 1881 document when the London Convention was being prepared). Conversely, the government of the South African Republic insisted that it retained full control over its internal affairs and that British claims to suzerainty were spurious. At the time the conventions were drawn up, however, the suzerainty issue generated relatively little concern among British officials responsible for South African affairs.[1]

The discovery of immense gold deposits on the Witwatersrand in 1886, and the subsequent rapid development of gold mining, revolutionized the affairs of the South African Republic, as well as of southern Africa as a whole. Johannesburg became a boom town with the arrival of a new cosmopolitan industrial community, the Uitlanders (or 'Foreigners'), many of whose members were British, and whose numbers threatened to swamp the republic's Afrikaner population. The relative size of the Uitlander and Afrikaner populations was the subject of much discussion during the late 1890s, and since no census was taken before the war precise statistics are unavailable for scrutiny. It does seem probable, however, that in January 1899 there were more Afrikaners than Uitlanders, but there may have been more Uitlander than Afrikaner adult males because the proportion of adult males was much larger among the new immigrants.[2] Whatever the precise demographic details, the political implications of the Uitlander presence were clear enough. In 1890 Kruger's government responded by restricting the Uitlander franchise for presidential and Volksraad elections to naturalized citizens who had lived in the republic for fourteen years. To accommodate Uitlander interests a 'Second Volksraad' was created, to be elected by naturalized citizens of more than two years' residence. But the issues this supplementary body could discuss were limited, and any legislation originating in the Second Volksraad required the approval of the Volksraad itself before becoming law. Though relatively few Uitlanders were genuinely concerned about the franchise question, and only a small proportion of Uitlanders chose to become citizens of the republic, the issue nonetheless assumed a central role in Anglo-Boer diplomacy after 1896.

Gold created for the Transvaal a new source of abundant wealth. The revenue derived from mining swelled the republic's treasury, customs' receipts soared and land values rose enormously, especially along the Witwatersrand and in the neighbourhood of the industrial area. Those Afrikaners who benefited most from the new economic climate were members of the powerful, though by no means cohesive, oligarchy of notable families who used their domination of the machinery of government and the opportunities offered by rapid industrialization to speculate in land and industrial concessions. In one of President Kruger's most successful investments he purchased Geduld-Springs farm for £700 shortly after the gold discoveries, and after buying the half share of his son-in-law, Frikkie Eloff, for £3 000 in 1891, sold the farm to the Springs Real Estate Company for £107 700.[3] Other prominent Afrikaner families, such as the Bothas, prospered through progressive commercial farming. Although different members believed greater or lesser assistance should be given to mining development, the Afrikaner oligarchy as a group sought to modernize the republic within a political system which it controlled.

However, at the same time that the economic policies of Kruger's government were enabling prominent Afrikaners to benefit from modernization, a serious 'poor white' problem in the Transvaal countryside was also emerging, largely as a consequence of population pressure on available land brought about by the progressive subdivision of farms, the closure of the frontier and the extensive speculative operations of land companies. The government of the republic seemed powerless to arrest the gradual pauperization of a section of its own Afrikaner population, and by the time war broke out in 1899 Afrikaner society in the Transvaal was already highly stratified.[4] Another aspect of modernization in the republic was of more immediate political consequence. The industrial policies of Kruger's government raised mining costs substantially, and this was especially the case in so far as the granting of numerous industrial concessions (or monopolies) was concerned. The concessions governing rail transport and the manufacture of dynamite and liquor particularly affected the mining industry and became a deep source of grievance between the Chamber of Mines and the government. The inability of the state to provide and enforce labour legislation that would make it possible for the mines to reduce substantially the wages of their African workforce became a further source of discontent within the industry.[5] Particularly adversely affected by the republic's industrial and labour policies were those companies more dependent than others on working the lowest grades of ore, whose operations were made marginal by the inadequacy of state aid to the industry, and the increasing number of companies that after 1895 became involved in the deep-level extraction of gold, a capital-intensive and cost-sensitive operation that depended on a continuous and assured flow of investment. To enable deep-level production to prosper it became clear to many mining executives that a much closer relationship between the industry and the state needed to be cemented, and that this was only likely to be achieved by a change of regime in the Transvaal.

Following the Transvaal War, and in particular after the gold discoveries, Kruger's government sought to extend the republic's frontiers. When expansion westwards was blocked by the incorporation of Bechuanaland in the British empire in 1885, efforts were made to come to an agreement with the Ndebele chief, Lobengula, with a view to eventual northward expansion beyond the Limpopo River. Kruger's representative, however, was unable to compete with the intense activity of Cecil Rhodes and his agents who succeeded in persuading Lobengula to append his mark to a document that gave the British High Commissioner control over his treaty-making and powers to grant mining concessions. Rhodes, a vigorous imperialist, the most successful Kimberley diamond magnate who had important, though at the time much less profitable, interests in gold mining too, and who in 1890 became Prime Minister of the Cape Colony, was granted a Royal Charter by the British government for his British South Africa Company to administer the region north of the Limpopo on Britain's behalf. Inspired by a desire to pave the way for future British colonial expansion in the interior, and by the expectation of discovering a 'second Rand', Rhodes from 1890 organized the conquest and initial white settlement of the region that became Rhodesia (Zimbabwe). Following Rhodes's colonization of the north the South African Republic still had one avenue of possible territorial expansion left open to it—eastwards towards the Indian Ocean. Kruger was intent upon obtaining for his landlocked state an outlet to the sea that did not depend on the routes to the harbours of the British colonies, but protracted negotiations to acquire territory to the east of the republic ultimately foundered in 1895 when the British government annexed Tongaland.

Denied territorial expansion, the government of the South African Republic concentrated its efforts on achieving greater commercial autonomy and on winning the support of Britain's industrial and colonial rivals. In 1895 the construction of a railway from the Rand to the Mozambican port of Lourenço Marques (Maputo) was completed, thereby providing the republic with the prospect of directing the bulk of its trade along it and away from the recently completed railways to Durban and the Cape ports. The new wealth of the Transvaal, and the attraction of European capital to the republic, enabled Kruger's government to forge closer relations with a number of overseas governments, in particular those of Holland and Germany.

For those British officials, colonists and industrialists who wished to see Britain's role in South African affairs more firmly secured and her influence consolidated, the political and economic implications of the gold discoveries had reached worrying proportions by the mid-1890s. The Transvaal had become the new economic centre of South Africa. The second Rand that Rhodes had hoped to discover north of the Limpopo to counter-balance the wealth of the Transvaal had failed to materialize. Federation of the coastal colonies and republics under British auspices now seemed out of the question, and Britain's main industrial rival, Germany, had begun to take an uncomfortably close interest in the affairs of the Transvaal. In these circumstances the important British naval base on the Cape peninsula seemed to some much less secure. In the republic itself British immigrants were denied a meaningful voice in the government of the country, and mining companies, especially those beginning to extract gold from deep-levels, were handicapped by the economic policies of the Kruger government.

A new era in Anglo-Boer relations began in June 1895 when the Unionist (Conservative) government of Lord Salisbury took office in Britain and Joseph Chamberlain, the most vigorous member of Salisbury's Cabinet, was appointed to the Colonial Office. Chamberlain, a Birmingham industrialist who had resigned from the Liberal Party in 1886 over Gladstone's policy of Irish Home Rule, was an avowed imperialist who hoped soon to press ahead once more with Carnarvon's policy of federating South Africa under the British Crown. The new Colonial Secretary was a man of positive action, but before he could plan an initiative of his own Chamberlain was overtaken by events in South Africa itself. Within weeks of taking office the new government was left with little alternative but to intervene in the tariff war that had flared up over railway rates between the Transvaal and the Cape Colony, Lord Salisbury threatening force if Kruger did not reopen the Drifts across the Vaal River. Kruger complied and the crisis subsided.

Relations between Britain and the South African Republic further deteriorated following the Jameson Raid in December 1895, a foolish, desperate and thoroughly mismanaged conspiracy organized by Rhodes and a group of close associates, many of whom had links with deep-level mining, to engineer an Uitlander coup and the overthrow of the Kruger regime. The political consequences of the Raid were disastrous. Boer mistrust of the British government's intentions, and of Chamberlain's intentions in particular, was heightened, for it soon became evident that British officials in South Africa, and even the Colonial Secretary himself, must have been implicated in the conspiracy, however indirectly (it later required all Chamberlain's political ingenuity to clear his name officially). Chamberlain felt obliged to deflect some of the suspicion and criticism of British policy in South Africa by taking up the issue of Uitlander grievances, which previously had been regarded as the domestic concern of the republic. In the aftermath of the Raid the South African Republic tightened its alliance with the Orange Free State and began importing substantial quantities of arms from Europe. In the 1898 presidential election Afrikaners closed ranks and rallied behind Kruger (on the basis of the votes gained in the 1893 election by Kruger's principal opponent, General P. J. Joubert, there had earlier seemed a possibility that he might be defeated). In the Cape Colony Rhodes resigned the premiership, his machinations having destroyed the political cooperation between English- and Dutch-speaking colonists that he had assiduously built up during his career in Cape politics. In the general election of October 1898 the *Afrikaner Bond*, and its English-speaking allies who were opposed to Rhodes, won a narrow victory in a bitterly fought contest and W. P. Schreiner, a moderate independent who favoured Anglo-Boer conciliation, became Prime Minister.

J. C. Smuts, who at the age of only twenty-eight was appointed State Attorney in the South African Republic in May 1898, wrote some years later that he believed the Jameson Raid had made war between Britain and the republic unavoidable. Historians have tended recently to regard Chamberlain's appointment of Sir Alfred Milner as High Commissioner in May 1897 as perhaps a more important turning point in Anglo-Boer relations.[6] Milner was a distinguished administrator and an ardent imperialist, but he was also an authoritarian and a man of inflexible views. Although he believed initially that reform in the Transvaal, instituted by those members of the Afrikaner oligarchy opposed to Kruger and more amenable to mining and Uitlander interests, promised a way of achieving a settlement of South African affairs consistent with British interests, he became profoundly pessimistic following Kruger's overwhelming re-election as President in February 1898. 'There is no way out of the troubles of S. Africa except reform in the Transvaal or war', he wrote to Chamberlain on 23 February, and made it clear that he had given up any hope of spontaneous reform.[7] The effective rejection by Kruger's government of the recommendations of the Industrial Commission of Enquiry of 1897, set up to investigate the depression in the mining industry, and Kruger's dismissal of Chief Justice Kotze, a vigorous opponent of the President whose removal from office Milner interpreted as an assault on judicial independence, served further to reinforce the High Commissioner's appraisal of Transvaal affairs. Milner in particular became committed to the partisan interpretation of the issues at stake put forward by the South African League, a British South African organization founded in 1896, which soon urged that the British government intervene directly in the affairs of the republic. Through widespread coverage of its activities carried in the British and South African press, and through the medium of the High Commissioner, who in turn encouraged and directed much of its propaganda, the League was able to bring its point of view to bear upon ministers and officials in Britain and upon the British public. Milner and the League exaggerated the disabilities and desire for reform of ordinary Uitlanders, introduced into the debate the red herring of a possible pan-Afrikaner conspiracy to take over the whole of South Africa and eliminate British influence in the region, and minimized the steps being taken by progressive members of Kruger's Cabinet to achieve genuine political and economic reforms within the republic.

For J. A. Hobson, the economist and Radical Liberal MP whose book *The War in South Africa: its causes and effects* was first published in 1900, the South African League represented the real villain of the peace, the instrument of 'a small confederacy of international financiers working through a kept press'. In Hobson's view Britain ultimately went to war 'to place a small international oligarchy of mine-owners and speculators in power at Pretoria' (p. 197), and his account of the origins of the war, later refined within a general analysis of the relationship between capitalism and imperialism, *Imperialism: A Study* (1902), deeply influenced Lenin's treatise *Imperialism: The Highest Stage of Capitalism* (1917). Recent scholarship has tended to play down the importance of the League, indicating that its links with leading mining finance houses were much less direct than Hobson believed, and showing that the League's activity was skilfully manipulated by Milner. Nonetheless there can be little doubt that some of its members in turn exercised an important influence over the High Commissioner, and that the atmosphere of crisis generated by the League in Johannesburg made any chance of a negotiated settlement of the dispute between the British and Transvaal governments much more difficult to achieve. Marxist writers have also pointed out that some historians, following Hobson's obsession in *The War in South Africa*, have paid too much attention to examining the intrigues of individual capitalists and too little attention to analysing capitalism as a set of productive relationships.

Milner's diplomatic strategy from the middle of 1898 onwards was directed towards strengthening the loyalty and political cohesion of English-speaking South Africans, manipulating and channeling Uitlander discontent and opposition to Kruger's government, maintaining the franchise at the centre of the diplomatic stage, and, together with Chamberlain, educating the British press and public opinion to the seriousness of the grievances of British subjects in the Transvaal and to the possibility of war if a satisfactory settlement of affairs was not achieved. Throughout, Milner and Chamberlain looked upon British 'suzerainty' over the Transvaal, embodied in the 1881 Pretoria Convention, as the instrument by which reform in the republic could be insisted upon. Although Chamberlain and Milner often disagreed over the details of British policy and over the pace at which diplomatic pressure should be brought to bear on the republic, from late 1898 onwards, following Milner's return to South Africa after consultations with his superior in London, the locus of British diplomatic initiative undisputably came to rest with the High Commissioner, and Chamberlain and his colleagues were left to respond to events rather than exercise control over them. Early in 1899 the South African League produced an Uitlander petition with over 21 000 signatures calling for British intervention on their behalf. In June Milner abruptly broke off direct talks with Kruger at Bloemfontein when the President refused to agree to the enfranchisement of all Uitlanders who had lived in the republic for five years. By the middle of 1899 it was apparent that the British public was prepared to accept and support military intervention in South Africa and that no European power would attempt to help the South African Republic should war be declared. Chamberlain nonetheless still hoped vainly that war might ultimately be avoided. However, when further offers of franchise reform by the Pretoria government were rejected, and when in September British military reinforcements were dispatched to South Africa, Kruger, President Steyn of the Orange Free State and their advisors became convinced that Britain was intent upon using force to destroy the independence of the South African Republic, and, wishing to seize the military initiative before British reinforcements arrived, Kruger's government issued an ultimatum calling for the removal of imperial troops from the republic's borders. The ultimatum expired on 11 October; on the following day the first shots of the South African War were fired at Kraaipan, a small settlement in the northern Cape situated close to the frontier of the South African Republic.

References

1. The suzerainty question is discussed by G. H. L. Le May, *British Supremacy in South Africa 1899–1907*, Oxford, 1965, 1, and by Leonard Thompson, 'Great Britain and the Afrikaner Republics, 1870–1899' in Monica Wilson and Leonard Thompson eds., *The Oxford History of South Africa*, II, Oxford, 1971, 322.
2. J. S. Marais, *The Fall of Kruger's Republic*, Oxford, 1961, 3.
3. Johannes Meintjes, *President Paul Kruger*, London, 1974, 176.
4. Social formation in the republic before the war is discussed by Stanley Trapido, 'Landlord and Tenant in a Colonial Economy: the Transvaal 1880–1910', *Journal of Southern African Studies*, 5, 1 (1978), 26–58. For an earlier study of the origins of the 'poor white' problem see Laurence Salomon, 'The Economic Background to the Revival of Afrikaner Nationalism', in J. Butler ed., *Boston University Papers in African History*, I, Boston, 1964, 217–42.
5. A. Jeeves, 'The Control of Migratory Labour on the South African Gold Mines in the Era of Kruger and Milner', *Journal of Southern African Studies*, 2, 1 (1975), 3–29.
6. The first chapter of Le May's *British Supremacy in South Africa* is entitled 'Sir Alfred Milner's War'.
7. Le May, 12.

CHAPTER 1
The Gold Mining Industry in the Transvaal 1886-99

Peter Richardson and Jean Jacques Van-Helten

Gold mining in the Transvaal before 1886

The gold mining industry of the Transvaal in the early years of the South African Republic (SAR) was scattered over a wide area of the country. Mainly alluvial gold production had developed consistently throughout the 1870s and early 1880s, as a result of discoveries in the Murchison Range in the Zoutpansberg district in 1870, at Pilgrim's Rest in the Lydenburg district in 1873, and at De Kaap, also in Lydenburg, in 1882. Within the De Kaap field was also discovered the first significant reef deposit at the Sheba Mine, Barberton, in 1884. In 1892 there were no less than thirteen separate goldfields in operation in the Transvaal outside the Witwatersrand district, producing 114 527 ounces of fine gold.[1]

Despite the proliferation of goldfields, the scale of early production remained very limited. Operations requiring only small amounts of fixed capital worked by 'diggers' were the norm in the Transvaal prior to the development of the Witwatersrand. As a result, the significance of the South African Republic as a gold producer remained strictly limited. In 1885 the Transvaal only accounted for 0·03 per cent of the world's output of gold, Australia and the United States being much larger producers at this time. Furthermore, with the development of the Witwatersrand, the importance of these so-called

African and European miners at the Republic Gold Mining Co., De Kaap, Lydenburg District, Transvaal, in 1888. As this photo suggests, not all mining in these early fields was alluvial, although the majority of hard rock mining was on outcrops using unsophisticated equipment such as the small skip on the left and gold pan and hand crusher in the right foreground. Also typical was the employment of small groups of African labourers by individuals or groups of 'diggers'.

'outside districts' steadily declined. In 1892 they still contributed 8·6 per cent of total Transvaal production – by 1899, only 4·5 per cent, while the volume of output of these areas had risen only very slightly.[2]

The successful exploitation of the Witwatersrand gold deposits revolutionized metalliferous mining in the Transvaal. In 1886, when the fields were first declared a public digging, the Transvaal still produced only 0·16 per cent of the world's gold. By 1898 the SAR was the largest single source of supply of the metal, accounting for no less than 27·55 per cent of the world's output. Such a large and expanding production from one source inevitably tended to give an increasingly centralized

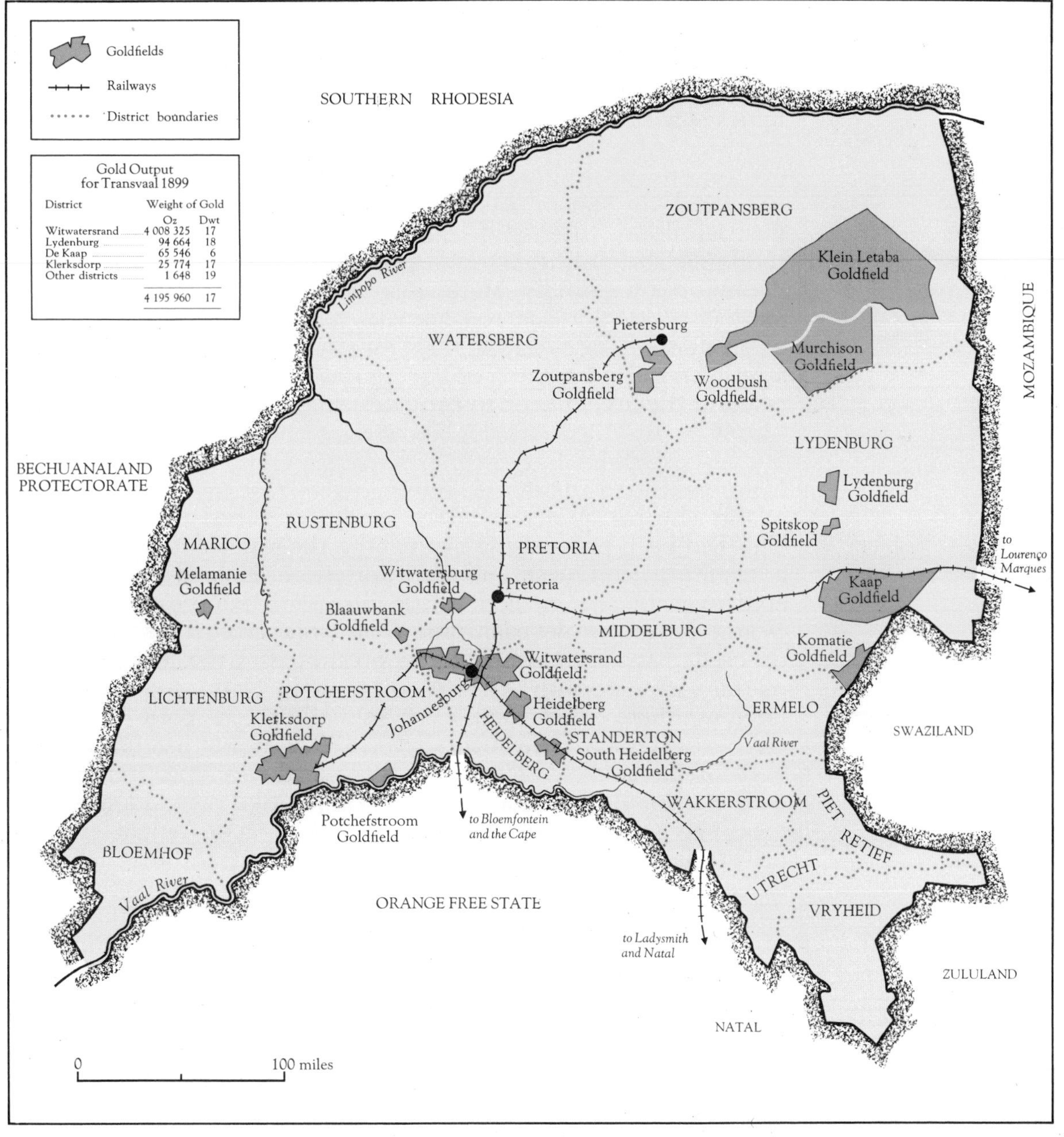

Gold Output for Transvaal 1899

District	Weight of Gold Oz	Dwt
Witwatersrand	4 008 325	17
Lydenburg	94 664	18
De Kaap	65 546	6
Klerksdorp	25 774	17
Other districts	1 648	19
	4 195 960	17

The goldfields of the Transvaal in 1899.

pattern to the geographical location of the industry. Thus as the ill-fated Selati railway scheme, designed to facilitate the exploitation of the northern goldfields, languished between 1890 and 1899, between 1892 and 1895 no less than three trunk railway routes were constructed, connecting Cape, Natal and Portuguese ports with the Witwatersrand. At the same time that gold production was becoming more centralized as a result of the Witwatersrand discoveries, the organization of production also underwent a fundamental change. Increasingly, large companies operating with substantial amounts of capital, and very sophisticated technology, replaced small, undercapitalized diggers and their syndicates. The transformation of the Diggers Committee of 1887 into the Chamber of Mines in 1889 illustrated this trend.[3]

The mineral revolution

A change of this magnitude could not be confined to the mining industry alone. The massive development of the gold mines effectively ensured that the Transvaal, and later the southern African regional economy, underwent an economic revolution, creating a society dominated by the demands of industrial capitalism. As the power-house of successful industrialization, the gold mining industry transformed the economic and political complexion of the subcontinent.

Most profoundly, the demands of the industry created a marked acceleration in the changing pattern of social relations of production, not only in the Transvaal but in most of British South Africa and in parts of Portuguese East Africa as well. As a result of the urgent need to provide a sufficiently large and cheap supply of unskilled African labour, not only for the gold mines but also for the burgeoning demands from agriculture and from coal and diamond mining, the restructuring of the relationship of Africans to the land intensified in the 1890s. This had been progressing throughout the nineteenth century as a result of conquest and expropriation. Helped by serious epidemics of the virulent cattle disease Rinderpest and Red Water Fever, proletarianization of large groups of Africans proceeded apace and was actively promoted by the governments of the various South African colonies. In Natal, for example, large numbers of Africans went annually to the gold mines of the Witwatersrand throughout the 1890s, notwithstanding the growing demands for labour from the coal and sugar industries of the colony. The result of the competitive demand was increasingly harsh restrictions on African rent tenancies on private lands in Natal, a growing movement towards labour tenancy agreements and an increased incidence of taxation on Africans. This process had parallels among the white population of the Transvaal as well. Since the 1790s, socio-economic pressures among the settler population had tended to generate a stratified society. After the Great Trek and the subsequent closure of the frontiers of the Boer republics beyond the Orange River, these pressures were accelerated by the extensive subdivision of farms and the policies of land speculators. In effect they generated an enforced pressure of population on available land, giving rise to what was known as the 'poor white' problem. As with the African population of the subcontinent, the difficulties of this class within settler society were intensified by the mineral revolution of the period from 1867 to 1886, which put a premium on the holding of large tracts of speculative property for prospecting purposes.[4]

A further consequence of this change was a pronounced northward shift in the balance of economic power in southern Africa, from the Cape to the Transvaal. Throughout the nineteenth century the Cape Colony had been the economic centre of the subcontinent, wool and, latterly, diamonds providing the source of its economic power. However, as the full extent and potential of the Witwatersrand goldfields became apparent, it was evident that the Cape's earlier supremacy could not long be retained. In 1890 Cape customs receipts were still greater than those of the inland republic, but by 1896 the SAR was earning greater revenue from this source than either of her maritime rivals. This passing of economic hegemony, which is the key to so much of the politics of the pre-war decade, was also reflected in the rivalries of railway building, receipts, and customs policies, which did so much to embitter the relations between the British colonies, and between each of these and their Boer neighbours.[5]

The effects of the development of a mining industry of the magnitude of the Witwatersrand were by no means confined to the southern African subcontinent, sizable and portentious as these were in this region. The restructuring of relations of production between Africans and the settler communities, and the concomitant northward shift of economic power, was paralleled by a rapid development of European immigration into South Africa generally, and into the Transvaal in particular. Between 1886 and 1899 there was a net outward migration from the United Kingdom of British subjects to British South African ports of 75 500, many of whom found their way to the South African Republic. Between 1895 and 1898 only the United States attracted more emigrants from the United Kingdom than did South Africa. So great was the demand for employment along the Witwatersrand that in 1890 the Emigrants Information Office in London, a department of the Colonial Office, enlarged its usual brief of issuing information only on British colonies of settlement, and printed a pamphlet on the SAR.[6]

Furthermore, the size and regularity of the gold deposits of the Witwatersrand were such as to require and attract large amounts of foreign capital throughout the 1890s. The scale of capital invested in the Witwatersrand mines, particularly by British investors, was sufficiently large to make an appreciable difference to the pattern of new overseas portfolio investment. In three major investing booms, in 1889, 1895–6 and 1899, and more modestly in-between, British and other foreign capitalists provided the overwhelming bulk of funds required to float and to operate the gold mines, and thereby tied the development of the mining industry ever more closely to the vicissitudes of the international economy as a whole. Although the majority of pre-war capital invested in the mining industry was British, estimates vary about the precise proportions of foreign participation. Experts estimate that between 60 and 80 per cent of foreign capital on the Rand was British at the outbreak of the war. These figures relate to a total capital investment of £74 million, including vendor's interests, cash and premiums. France and Germany were also sizeably represented in the purchase of Witwatersrand gold mining shares. Wernher, Beit and Company, the premier mining finance house, had institutionalized links with the Banque Française de l'Afrique du Sud in Paris, while another house, Albu and Company (later General Mining) was a protégé of the Dresdener Bank in Germany.[7]

Influence upon world trade

The output of the Witwatersrand goldfields was also significant in its effects upon world trade. This occurred in two ways. Directly, it created in the interior of the subcontinent a large and expansive market heavily dependent upon imported stores and foodstuffs, as well as capital goods for its development. The low level of the transport infrastructure and the high level of demand also meant that the market had an appreciable influence upon capital goods markets not directly related to mining. This was seen in the development of railways, and the expansion of harbour facilities in the Cape and Natal to cope with the new capacity generated by the Witwatersrand development. The value of stores consumed directly by the mining industry rose from £410 367 in 1890 to £4 737 049 in 1898, while imports rose from £493 991 in 1886 to £10 632 895 in 1898 for the SAR as a whole. Railway construction in South Africa totalled 3 111 miles between 1880 and 1899, of which 2 046 miles were constructed between 1890 and 1899.[8]

Indirectly, the expansion of gold output facilitated the development of world trade by promoting the expansion of the world's gold stock at a time of rising demand for gold for currency purposes. The rapid demonetarization of silver after 1873, and the consequent increase in the number of countries operating on a gold basis for their currency for the purposes of international trade, posed problems for the expansion of world trade as a whole, in a time of relatively static output of gold. The inelastic supply of gold posed a constant threat to trade expansion that was not solved until the discovery of the Witwatersrand fields. The substantial additions to the world's stock of gold eased problems of international liquidity by facilitating an expansion of money supplies without dangers of inflation. This development was particularly important for Britain, which by the 1890s had become the financial centre of world trade. Between 1850 and 1913 the volume of world trade increased ten times over, while an increasingly large share of that overall trade was financed by British sterling credits. Britain's ability to finance upwards of one half of all foreign lending was based upon the strength of the country's balance of payments, which made sterling a currency of unquestioned strength, and upon the international gold standard and the concomitant convertability of sterling, by means of which the outstanding balances in the fluctuations of the movements of capital and commodities were adjusted through the flow of the money commodity, gold, from debtor nations to creditor ones. Between 1890 and 1896 the volume of gold reserves held by the Bank of England doubled to reach an all time high of £49 million. This was a direct reflection of the role of British financial institutions in the conduct of increased world trade, and also of the quantitative impact of the South African discoveries on the available stock of gold currency. This strengthening of the Bank's reserves at a time of increased demand for gold currency was achieved by astute use of the Bank rate, open market operations and the gold devices.[9]

The nature of the Rand deposits

The previous history of gold mining, in southern Africa and elsewhere, had made such a massive development as took place in the Transvaal during the last decades of the nineteenth century seem highly unlikely. Prior to the discovery of the Witwatersrand fields, gold mining had either been alluvial or based upon the mining of rich veins of gold ore that had intruded into the surrounding quartz. Neither system of mining was capable on its own of sustaining production on a sufficiently large scale to initiate an industrial revolution or to affect the pattern of world trade and commodity movements. The former system of production was, especially in southern Africa, small in scale, while the latter was notorious for the patchiness of its deposits, which tended to make deep-level mining under these circumstances an almost wholly speculative operation. The enormous size of the Witwatersrand deposits, and above all the regularity of the gold-bearing reefs, led to an important transformation in geological knowledge and expertise.[10]

The Witwatersrand goldfields lay on a plateau of the southern African high veld, approximately 6 000 feet above sea-level, which formed the watershed of rivers feeding the Indian and Atlantic Oceans – the headwaters of the eastward-flowing Limpopo draining to the north, and the headwaters of the westward-flowing Vaal River draining to the south. As they were worked initially, the gold deposits of the field were exploited along an outcrop of gold-bearing ore about 40 miles

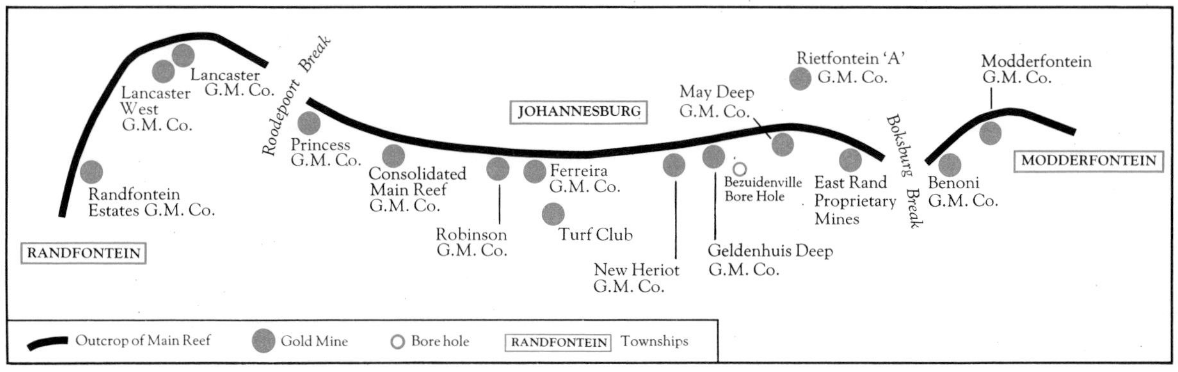

Diagram of the Witwatersrand, 1899. This shows the principal mines and townships of the Witwatersrand.

in length, in a direction from east to west of the present-day city of Johannesburg. With the exception of two big breaks in the formation, one at Boksburg in the east and the other at Roodepoort in the west, gold bearing ore was found to be present right along the strike of the outcrop, and in regular amounts sufficient to make it payable along a greater part of its length. However, the reputation for regularity and size that the Witwatersrand enjoyed was subject to four qualifications that had important influences upon the structure of the industry.[11]

Firstly, the full extent of the deposits and their precise nature was only gradually appreciated. The novelty of the Witwatersrand deposits in contemporary geological experience was such that the likelihood of the deposits being intersected at depth, in quantities sufficiently regular to justify extensive deep mining operations, was only realized slowly. Four years after the opening of the Witwatersrand fields as a public digging, the great majority of mining claims were still held on ground within 3 000 feet of the outcrop. However, the regularity of yields on the southward slope of the reef down to 800-900 feet below the surface suggested that payable ore could be intersected at greater depths by sinking vertical shafts at extensive distances south of the outcrop. Borehole operations, for example at the May Deep Level Mine in 1890 and at Bezuidenville in 1895, confirmed these prognostications. On the strength of these and other findings whole areas of mining claims on the dip of the reef were pegged, so that between 1890 and 1895 mining ground south of the outcrop was claimed for distances of up to 8 600 feet, although actual deep-level production did not begin until the end of 1895, when the Geldenhuis Deep started crushing.

Outcrop workings on the Main Reef, Witwatersrand goldfields. This picture of the fields, taken before 1890, shows clearly the technically simple nature of the workings prior to the proving of the deep-levels. The similarity of the operations with those shown on p. 18 is noticeable.

By 1899, 30 per cent of all Witwatersrand gold mining companies were deep-level concerns. This development of deep-level operations made the industry markedly more dependent on imported skilled labour from Europe and Australia and North America. In 1895 the State Mining Engineer estimated that 34·3 per cent of all working costs went on white labour. By 1897 there were 11 642 white men employed in the Transvaal mines, the great majority of whom worked on gold mines.[12]

Secondly, although six series of gold bearing reefs, or beds, were present on the Witwatersrand fields, only one, the Main Reef series, was consistently payable. Thus, in 1899 there were 156 outcrop and deep-level mines in existence on the Rand, and 124 of these – and all the deep-levels – were on the Main Reef series. Of the remaining 32, only three were payable, the Lancaster and the Lancaster West on the Battery Reef series, and the Rietfontein 'A' on the Du Preez reef. The Main Reef series, like the other adjacent five reefs, was a conglomerate of white quartz pebbles cemented together by a mixture of silica and sand, thickly sprinkled with pyrites, in which the gold was found in very fine specks, rarely visible to the naked eye. Moreover, in the Main Reef series itself, several gold bearing reefs were often identifiable. These were of varying width and separated from each other by surrounding 'country' rock of varying thickness and hardness. The special composition of the reefs was known locally as *banket*, after a layered sweet-cake eaten by the Boers that resembled the geological formation of the Witwatersrand.[13]

Thirdly, although the Main Reef series, in relation to other adjacent formations, was uniformly payable, the basis of payability in each area of the reef varied quite substantially. In most mines, whether outcrop or deep-level, exploration, development and actual operations were concentrated on only the richer deposits of ore in the Main Reef series, at least in the period prior to the war. The prevalent level of working costs before 1899 meant that as a rule only two of the available reefs were worked in any one property, known generally as the South Reef and the Main Reef Leader. Of these two, the South Reef was generally the thinner and the richer, although it ceased to be payable east of the Heriot Gold Mine.[14]

Lastly, despite the size and regularity of the deposits, even the Main Reef series was, by international standards of mining, of low grade. Thus while the average grade of gold ore mined in Canada at the time was in excess of 10 penny weights (dwts) to the ton, and in Western Australia, 12 dwts, on the Rand the average grade of all reefs in the Main Reef series was no more than 6½ dwts. This low average grade was a general feature of Rand properties and was not synonymous with deep-level mining. Nor was a low average grade of ore on all mines inconsistent with individually rich reefs that could be worked at the expense of poorer deposits in times of high working costs.[15]

The increasing depth and consequent cost of gold mining throughout the period 1886–99, the difficulties of working on a

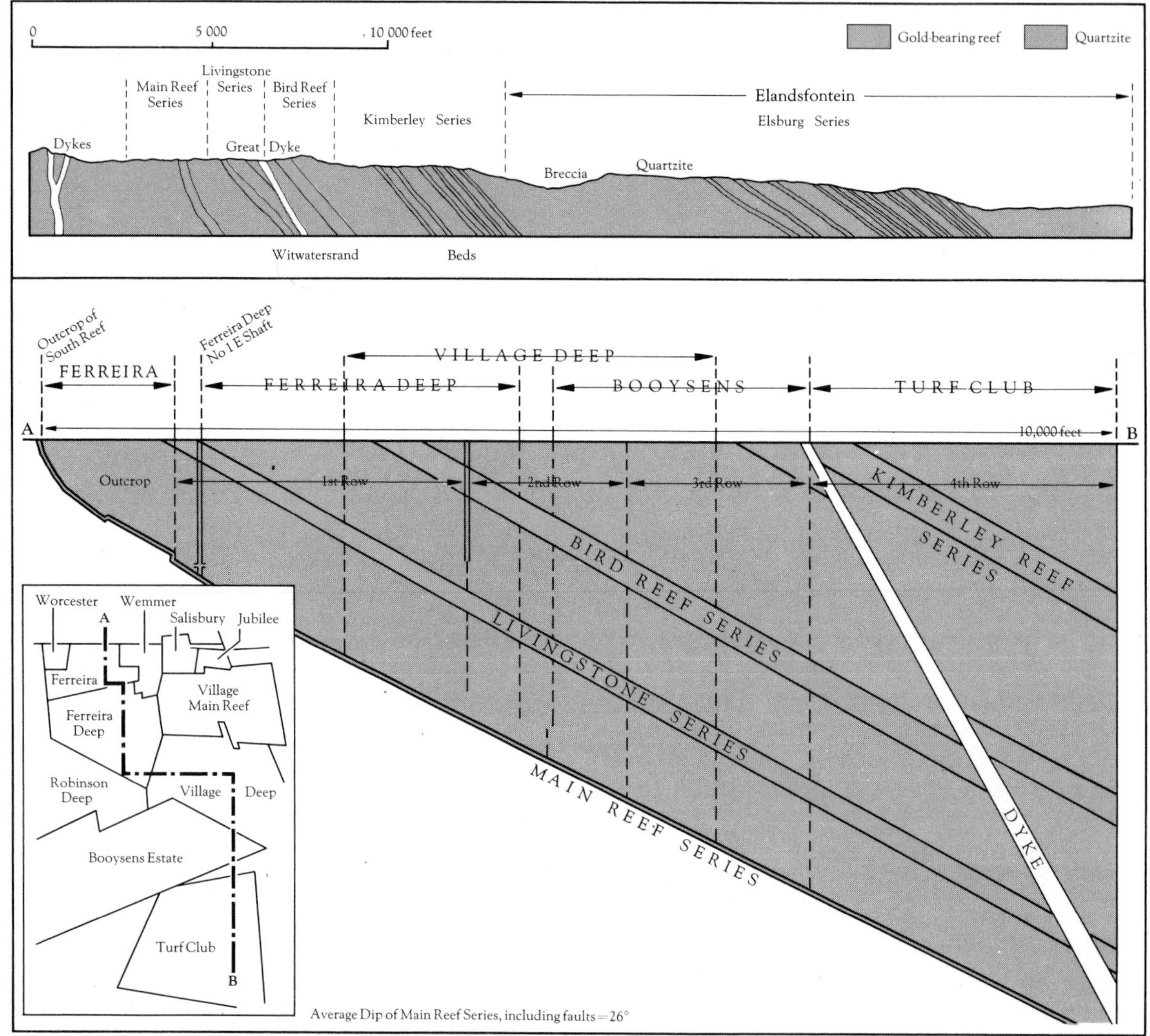

Above: cross-section of the central Witwatersrand.

Below: geological cross-section of the Witwatersrand. This shows five of the most important series of gold-bearing reefs on the Witwatersrand. The position of mines on subsidiary reefs is shown in the accompanying diagram.

relatively restricted number of reefs, and the low average grade of ore, had a decisive effect upon the character of the mining industry. Throughout the period under review, and continually thereafter, the industry was forced to consider the prevalent level of costs as the *decisive* factor in mining operations. This problem was accentuated still further by the fact that as producers, the mines generally received, at least in England, a ceiling price for gold, which was fixed by the Bank of England at 77 shillings and 6 pence a 'standard bar' of 22 carats. London was, of course, the world's main bullion market. This forced the industry to absorb cost inflation either through reductions in aggregate working costs, by substituting high cost factors for lower ones, or by taking a reduction in its profit rate. To deal with these problems the industry increasingly became more monopolistic in the pre-war years. Whereas there were 44 separate mining companies in 1888, in 1899 there were only nine major mining finance houses, controlling the destinies of 114 out of the 124 Main Reef outcrop and deep-level companies.[16]

Monopoly capitalism in the South African gold mining industry was not something that arrived fully fledged at the opening of the goldfields, but emerged as a direct response to both the immediate environment of the industry, and the vicissitudes of the international economy of which it became increasingly a part.

A major causal factor in this development was the geological structure of the Witwatersrand reefs. The large amounts of pyritic or refractory ores, which increased as mining moved to depths of over 200 feet, posed a serious technological problem of ore recovery. The enormous costs of providing equipment and technological expertise capable of overcoming this problem necessitated financial resources on a large scale. The group system of mining finance houses was the direct result of, and coincided with, a fundamental change in the system of ore recovery. This was a two stage process, moving from a single amalgamation system in 1887, through the Plattner cyanide concentration method, to the MacArthur-Forrest process by 1893. By the latter date, too, all the mining groups were participating in the highly specialized technology of the Rand Central Ore Reduction works.[17]

A second major factor was the relative shortage of domestic capital formation. Although the initial development of the outcrop companies after 1886 was undertaken with capital accumulated on the Kimberley diamondfields, the volume of investment was, by later standards, rather small. None of the mines were particularly deep and the oxidized ore at the surface was easy and cheap to treat, even though the amalgamation process was inefficient. The small scale of this investment was therefore totally inadequate to fund the development of deep-level companies whose floating became a real possibility after 1890, when H. Eckstein and Company purchased a large number of claims south of the outcrop mines. This potential difficulty was turned into a crisis by the consequences of the 1889–90 boom and

Below left: African miners hand drilling in a stope in a Witwatersrand deep-level gold mine, 1897. The development of the deep-levels required a substantial and continuing division of labour as well as increasing concentrations of capital. This process is shown here at the point of production. Holes of approximately 3 feet in length would be drilled by these specialist miners using hammers and steel drills, or jumpers. On completion of the requisite number of holes in a body of ore-bearing ground, or stope, the holes would be filled with explosive and fired to release rock. After firing, the loose rock would be shovelled into trucks by 'trammers', concentrated at the bottom of the mine and then brought to the surface by mechanical haulage for crushing.

Below right: ore being brought to the surface by a system of continuous rope haulage on an inclined shaft at the Crown Deep Gold Mine, Witwatersrand, c. 1898. Ore was usually deposited automatically into the ore-bins in the crusher stations by a mechanical tipping process, and the skips returned to the mine to repeat the operation.

collapse in mining shares. The large losses sustained by investors damaged stock market confidence generally, but had a particular impact upon South African 'Kaffirs', or mining shares. Thus, at a crucial time of moving into deep-level operations, the main source of funds for mining development began to dry up. In order to stabilize the market for future investment, attract outside funds, particularly from Europe, and to pool technological and administrative resources for deep-level mining, the group system of control was born. The nine main gold mining groups in the 1890s all owed their origin, therefore, as much to the financial crisis associated with the collapse of the first great investment boom as to the financial exigencies of deep-level mining. The importance of this association between the development of monopoly within the industry and financial boom and collapse, was demonstrated again following the 1895–6 boom.[18]

In the pre-war period the groups maintained a predominantly mining orientation in their investments. Diversification, such an important feature of later investment patterns among the mining finance houses, was very limited at this stage. Only Lewis and Marks, which had relatively small interests in the gold mining industry, and was not part of the inner sanctum of the Chamber of Mines, had different interests, which anticipated future trends in mining investment. Furthermore, the majority of groups at this stage were simple partnerships rather than multinational companies. Unquestionably the most important was Wernher, Beit and Company, whose interests after 1890 included the H. Eckstein Group of companies and the extremely profitable Rand Mines Ltd. Even the premier mining finance *company*, the Consolidated Gold Fields Group, had originated in the partnership of Rhodes and Rudd on the Kimberley diamond fields. However, the key to the success of the Group system was to be found, primarily, in the ready access that they had to both the money markets of London, Paris and Berlin and to large European banking consortia, such as Rothschilds. The subsequent access to vast and readily available funds provided the deep-level companies with the necessary amounts of pre-profit outlays in a manner that the earlier outcrop companies with their limited, largely domestic, capital formation could not match. Moreover, by providing a system of 'endorsement' or underwriting for investors, the mining finance houses attracted speculative funds on a scale that individual companies, however good their prospects, could not hope to match, and in addition enabled such funds to be channelled to the separate mines within the Group in need of development finance. Lastly, by creating an altogether new type of mining company, the finance houses represented a spreading of risk for less speculative investment, which nevertheless wished to participate in the development of the Rand. Not that this stopped the groups from participating in forms of speculative activity, particularly in land deals and mining claims, which earned them the justifiable criticism of discerning financial correspondents in Europe. The growing disillusionment of the

Above left: circular sorting table, Angelo-Driefontein Gold Mines, Witwatersrand, 1899. Rock sent up from the mines often contained a large amount of waste sandstone. To eliminate this, the rock was taken from the ore-bins through a revolving screen where it was sprayed with water and thence onto the sorting table for the waste to be extracted.

Above right: stamping battery on the New Primrose Gold Mine, Witwatersrand, 1899. From the sorting table the ore was fed into the jaws of gyrating crushers and the rock fed from there into a bin which already contained small particles of rock, or 'fines', suitable for milling. The ore was then taken to the mill and fed into mortar boxes. In these boxes the ore was broken by the stamps to a consistency of fine sand and slimes and then taken by water through screens over copper amalgamating plates. Most of the free gold was caught at this stage. The pyritic portion of the ore, in sands, and the fine gold, in the slimes were carried over the plates into the base of the tailings wheel.

investing public with these practices, especially after 1895–6, is an important theme in the financial history of the Rand in the pre-war years. The decline in the possibilities for these so-called 'windfall profits' as a result meant that increasingly the source of profit and capital accumulation on the Rand became associated with actual productive operations of mining rather than speculative operations of 'the scrip industry' [share market].[19]

However, it would be wrong to suggest that monopoly capitalism originated solely from the demands of mining finance or technological innovation. The legal and institutional environment of the developing industry also played a crucial part. Central to this aspect of the problem was the Transvaal Gold Law, first formulated in 1885 by the Volksraad of the SAR on the lines of Kimberley mineral legislation, but subsequently amended to a greater or lesser degree nearly every year between 1886 and 1899. Two principles of the law gave particular encouragement to the elimination of small groups of diggers or independent miners. Firstly, unlike the original Kimberley legislation, the Gold Law permitted the amalgamation of large numbers of gold mining claims in proclaimed areas, without imposing the necessity of working them. By simply allowing the payment of a license fee on any number of gold mining claims, these provisions permitted the engrossment of large tracts of mining ground by rich groups whose access to funds enabled them to resist working the ground until the most appropriate time. Such a provision had the opposite effect upon small diggers and syndicates. By demanding a license fee on unused or developing ground, the state taxed the small diggers to a disproportionate degree and forced them into operations that might have been better delayed, or forced many such claim holders to give up their land to the larger groups for fear of incurring further losses. The poor bargaining position of the sellers in this situation created a process that was known locally

Tailings wheel and cyanide vats on the New Kleinfontein Gold Mine, Witwatersrand, 1900. The tailings wheel was used to elevate the sands and slimes to a point whereby the force of gravity could be used to aid the process of extraction. By a complicated series of hydraulic classifications, the sands and slimes were seperated into different vats and treated with cyanide solution. From these vats the solutions were pumped to an extractor house, where the gold bearing solution would be treated by some form of zinc precipitation method, an acid solution and finally a smelting furnace to produce molten gold. The use of tailings increased the rate of recovery by as much as 20 per cent.

as 'freezing out' – the deliberate immobilization of mining ground by large groups to create an almost total monopoly in the holding of claims.[20]

Secondly, by giving disproportionate advantages to the owners of freehold property in the prospecting and working of gold mining claims, the Gold Law gave substantial encouragement to land speculation and to the elimination of small producers. These advantages operated in various ways.[21] The origin of the provisions, which were so very favourable to property owners, was a desire to secure the maximum benefit for the original occupants of the land, the Boer farmers. However, the immediate value that such provisions gave to the land encouraged a large market in farms along the Witwatersrand, which naturally favoured those with access to the sufficient funds, such as the mining groups, to pay inflated prices. These companies, therefore, secured benefits both as owners under the Gold Law, and as property speculators. With such a valuable captive market a massive proportion of capital invested in the Rand became tied up as vendor's capital. This was money raised by the mining companies, among other things, to buy land for mining purposes. As the owners were often the parent mining finance house, this resulted in the profits on such sales being redirected back to the company that had originally guaranteed the floating of the mine on the Stock Exchange. Thus, in 1895, £16 174 499-worth of new equity capital was invested in the Rand Mines of which £10 565 678 was in vendors' interests. The existence of large amounts of vendors' capital created a highly leveraged financial structure whereby the holders of ordinary shares received disproportionately low returns compared to the vendors. In addition, vendors were able to release selectively their shares as the market moved 'upwards', thus making further speculative profits.[22]

Monopoly, as a form of defensive protection, also received substantial encouragement from the prevalent difficulties faced by the mining industry as a direct result of policies imposed by

The mining industry and the state

the Boer government. Some of these policies stemmed from the simple inability of a relatively small society to provide the necessary administrative support and expertise required by a process of industrialization of the size of that associated with the development of the Witwatersrand. This can be seen in the dependence of the state on the administrative expertise of the joint resources of the industry in drawing up the draft for the 1895 Pass Law and in the policing measures taken by the industry as a result of the persistent inability of the state to enforce the gold theft clauses of the Gold Law.[23]

Many more of these policies, however, emanated from deliberate decisions taken by Kruger's government. At times it showed a systematic unwillingness to meet demands made on it by the mining industry, especially if they ran counter to interests, such as agriculture, that provided the government with its source of political power. A serious grievance, that emanated from the 'obstructiveness' of Kruger's government, was the failure to determine the mining rights under the *Bewaarsplatzen*, or reserved places, used for machinery and water rights. More importantly, between 1890 and 1899, despite persistent requests, the state failed to provide any effective mechanism that would have facilitated the employment of a cheap and reliable unskilled African labour force by the mines, because of the impact this would have had upon the agricultural labour market. No attempt was made to facilitate or control recruiting either by direct methods within the Transvaal or by agreements with other governments outside the SAR. No legislation was introduced before 1895 that made desertion and/or breach of contract effectively a punishable offence. Furthermore, at no time before the war did the Boer government seriously come to grips with the problem of the liquor traffic, which undermined the efficiency of the available labour by as much as 30 per cent.

Labour supply

The adoption of monopolistic practices by the industry in the labour market to cope with this situation was fitful, but the underlying trend was clear. The pre-war period is often seen as the classic period of competition among the mines for unskilled African labour. It is true that the 'tout' or commission system and the plethora of independent recruiters succeeded in constantly expanding the size of the unskilled labour force throughout this period. There were, on average, 75 788 Africans at work throughout 1897, and this number rose substantially thereafter. Nevertheless, the system of free recruiting was very inefficient and extremely wasteful and accentuated the tendency for African wage rates to rise above levels acceptable to the industry. Furthermore, the system was dependent on the ability of the mining groups to cushion the impact of the shortages and wage rises that were integral to its operation. In addition, after 1893, independent recruiters were substantially aided by the Native Labour Department of the Chamber of Mines. This was formed specifically to offset the double disadvantage of free recruiting and the lack of state support. Moreover, the premier labour market for the mines in this period, southern Mozam-

African recruits for the Transvaal mines being brought to the Witwatersrand by train. The development of the transport infrastructure not only facilitated the development of an internal market for agricultural produce and commercial goods, but also greatly facilitated recruiting by the mining companies, as this picture shows most strikingly.

bique, was chosen because it offered the advantage of being both marginally less competitive than other areas of southern Africa and was capable of supplying large amounts of relatively cheap labour for longer periods than anywhere else. This feature cheapened the overall cost of labour for the industry as a whole and reduced the rate of turnover.[24]

Even when competition for the available labour was at its fiercest, therefore, this only served to reinforce the realization that for the industry the best policy was to work towards a general system of wage agreements and reductions. This was attempted in 1890 and again in 1897, but on both occasions inter-group competition seriously undermined it. It can be seen most clearly in 1896 when, presented with sufficient labour supply for the first time, and the possibility of state cooperation through the Pass Law, the Chamber of Mines promoted the Rand Native Labour Association. This was based on the necessity for both wage reductions, which followed in 1897, and tight laws against desertion and a system of quotas for the available labour. However, administrative difficulties, official obstruction and continuing fluctuations in the African supply undermined this first substantial attempt at monopsony[25] in the labour market, but it was a sign of the drift of events in this as in so many other areas of the mining industry.[26]

Kruger's government also adopted a policy of industrialization that directly raised the cost of mining production. Naturally, this tended to make it even more difficult for independent small-scale producers to survive in the economic environment of the SAR. The essence of this policy was the granting of monopolistic concessions to various individuals or syndicates for the production, manufacture or transport of various items of consumption. Three of these concessions, those concerned with the railways, dynamite, and liquor, particularly affected the mining industry and further severely damaged an already strained relationship between the industry and the state.

Dynamite monopoly

The manufacture of explosives in the Transvaal was a monopoly that as early as 1887 had been granted to a group of enterprising businessmen. By 1894, this exceedingly lucrative enterprise had been taken over by the Hamburg-based Anglo-German Nobel Trust. High duties were charged on any imported explosives and the enviable position occupied by the Nobel Trust and its local Modderfontein factory was fully exploited by the Trust continually raising the price of explosives. By 1895–6 the average price for No. 1 dynamite was 85 shillings per case of 50 lbs, which was about 40 shillings above the relatively free market prices prevailing in Kimberley. Under the terms of the monopoly the Trust was allowed to raise prices up to a fixed maximum of £4 15 shillings a case and while the Trust and its local subsidiary chose not to exercise this right, it created continued uncertainty about future price levels. With respect to the deep-level mines, this uncertainty was exacerbated by the fact that overall consumption of cheap dynamite relative to the more expensive blasting gelatine was declining rapidly after 1893. In 1896, 22 204 cases of dynamite and 81 109 cases of blasting gelatine were consumed on the Rand. By 1898 only 15 005 cases of dynamite were being used but 166 194 cases of blasting gelatine. Repeated requests by the Chamber of Mines and the British government to open the explosives market to foreign, mainly British, competition, and thereby cheapen the price, was studiously ignored by the Boer government. The importance of this will be appreciated when it is realized that in 1895 explosives accounted for 8·6 per cent of all working costs on the Rand.[27]

Railway concession

The activities of the Netherlands South African Railway Company were scarcely less detrimental to the interests of the gold mines. The company possessed a monopoly of all railway traffic linking the SAR with the sea. The company created an additional burden for the industry by imposing exceptionally high rates for coal, imported mining machinery and foodstuffs. These high rates, which were primarily charged by the company in order to repay old loans and provide large dividends for investors, even provoked an exasperated Chamber of Mines, in 1897, to demand that the SAR nationalize the railway. The Chamber's demand, however, was not just the result of the company's refusal to lower its rates substantially, but also stemmed from its shunting charges for coal and from its refusal to deliver coal in bulk. In fact, prior to the war, the only dent that the industry secured in the company's armour was in 1898 when a 10 per cent reduction in charges was introduced following the findings of the Industrial Commission of Enquiry. This Commission, which was set up in 1897, represented a watershed in relations between the industry and the state. It originated in the government's concern over the continued depression in the mining industry and the consequent fall in state revenues in the aftermath of the 1895–6 boom. The resultant report, which was largely the work of the industry's representatives on the Commission, was particularly favourable to the mines. Its failure to confront some of the more unsavoury speculative aspects of mining development, and its deliberate confrontation of Boer and concessionaire interests, meant that only a minimal number of its recommendations were implemented.[28]

Liquor concession

The oldest concession in the Transvaal was that granted to the Proprietors of Hatherley Distillery near Pretoria for the manufacture of liquor. Throughout the 1890s the majority of liquor trading was conducted, legally or illegally, with the growing army of African labourers along the Witwatersrand. As the traffic developed the Chamber of Mines became increasingly vociferous in their opposition to it and by 1895 were claiming that it was one of the 'greatest difficulties with which local employers have to deal'. It described the consequences of this monopoly in the following terms:

> 'In very many cases the liquor supplied to the natives is of the vilest quality, quickly inflaming those who take it to madness, and causing the faction fights which sometimes have fatal results, and always lead to the, at any rate, temporary disablement of some of the combatants, and the damaging of property. Accidents, too, are often attributable to the effects of drink, and altogether, as stated in the resolutions, a large percentage of the deaths among the natives here is directly due to drink. In its bearing on the labour question, drink also plays an important part. The shortness in the supply, as compared with the demand for labour has been accentuated by it. Where possible more natives are kept in the compounds than are actually required for the work to be done, to make allowance for those who are disabled by drink.'[29]

The economic implications of drink, rather than any humanitarian concern about alcoholism, had by 1895 turned the members of the Chamber of Mines into prohibitionists. They maintained this position up until the war.[30]

Conclusion

The impact of these policies of neglect and obstruction was a double one for the industry. On the one hand they raised directly and indirectly the costs of production and kept large amounts of low-grade ore out of production. On the other, they created a climate of insecurity that was detrimental to the further development of the industry. The proving and working of the deep-levels accentuated their impact as a result of the dependence of this type of mining on a continued flow of investment and a generally low and controllable level of costs. After 1895 the industry was forced into a more overtly hostile position against the government as the growing volume of deep-level production pinpointed these grievances more sharply than ever. The first indication of this shift was the clear involvement of some of the leading 'Randlords' in the Jameson

Raid. Again in 1897–8 the climate deteriorated further when Kruger, strengthened by the demise of Boer opposition, effectively rejected the findings of the Industrial Commission of Enquiry of 1897. By only tinkering with the railway rates and the Gold Law, the government did nothing to head off the growing opposition to the monopolies and concessions. Neither did it attempt to reduce the cost of production by lowering the cost of living for the white working class, of fuel, or of African labour. By then the major mining houses were prepared to contemplate the actual replacement of the Boer government by the British. Thus in June 1897 Samuel Evans of Wernher, Beit and Company was claiming that the relations of production were not being modified rapidly enough and that an additional burden of £8 175 000 per annum was being imposed on the mining industry by Kruger's regime. The amelioration of this situation was one that, in his opinion, could be 'obtained by good government really favourable to the industry'.[31]

References

1. *4th Annual Report of the Witwatersrand Chamber of Mines, 1892*, 108; 'A Descriptive and Statistical Statement of the Gold Mining Industry of the Witwatersrand', Annexure to *13th Annual Report of the Transvaal Chamber of Mines, 1902*, 2.
2. *4th Annual Report of the Witwatersrand Chamber of Mines, 1892*, 108; *11th Annual Report of the South African Republic Chamber of Mines, 1899*, 298; *Annual Report of the Transvaal Government Mining Engineer for year ending 30 June 1910*, Table of Output of Transvaal Gold Mines as Proportion of World Output, 1884–1909.
3. *Annual Report of the Transvaal Government Mining Engineer for the year ending 30 June 1910*, *loc. cit.*; J. Van Der Poel, *Railway and Customs Policies in South Africa, 1885–1910*, London, 1933, *passim*.
4. See for example H. Slater, 'Land, Labour and Capital in Natal: The Natal Land and Colonization Company, 1860–1948', *Journal of African History*, 16, 2 (1975), 257–83; C. Bundy, 'The Emergence and Decline of a South African Peasantry', *African Affairs*, 71, 1972, 369–88; S. Trapido, 'Landlord and Tenant in a Colonial Economy: the Transvaal 1880–1910', *Journal of Southern African Studies*, 5, 1 (1978), 26–58; C. Van Onselen, 'Reactions to Rinderpest in Southern Africa, 1896–7'. *Journal of African History*, 13, 3 (1972), 473–88.
5. C. De Kiewiet, *A History of Southern Africa, Social and Economic*, London, 1941, 122–6.
6. B. R. Mitchell and P. Deane, *Abstract of British Historical Statistics*, London, 1972, Table 19, 50; *Annual Report on the Emigrants Information Office for the year ending 31 December 1890*, Cd. 6277, 1891.
7. S. H. Frankel, *Capital Investment in Africa*, London, 1938, Table 14, 95; R. V. Kubicek, 'Finance Capital and South African Gold Mining, 1886–1914', *Journal of Imperial and Commonwealth History*, 3, 3 (May 1975), 386–95; Banque Francaise de l'Afrique du Sud, *Annuaire Francaise des Mines d'Or*, I, Paris, 1896, 1–5, 83; Paul H. Emden, *Randlords*, London, 1935, 205–9.
8. *2nd Annual Report of the Witwatersrand Chamber of Mines, 1890*, Return of Stores Consumed; *11th Annual Report of the South African Republic Chamber of Mines, 1899*, Return of Stores Consumed; *Rapport van den Inspecteur Generaal van Invoerrechten van de Zuid-Afrikaansche Republiek voor het jaar 1893*, No. 6 1894, Pretoria, 1894, 3; *ibid., voor het jaar 1898*, No. 7 (1899), Pretoria, 1899, 3, quoted in D. Hobart Houghton and J. Dagut, *Source Material on the South African Economy: Volume 1, 1860–1899*, London, 1972, 323; M. H. De Kock, *The Economic Development of South Africa*, London, 1936, 351; J. J. Van-Helten, 'British Capital, the British State and Economic Investment in South Africa, 1886–1914', Institute of Commonwealth Studies (University of London), Collected Seminar Papers, SSA/77/13.
9. R. S. Sayers, *Bank of England Operations, 1890–1914*, London, 1936, 71–91; Marcello de Cecco, *Money and Empire. The International Gold Standard, 1890–1914*, Oxford, 1974, 104. For details of the gold standard and sterling convertability see R. Tiffin, *The Evolution of the International Monetary System. Historical Reappraisal and Future Perspectives*, Princeton, 1964; D. Williams, 'The Evolution of the Sterling System', in C. Whittlesey and J. S. G. Wilson eds., *Essays in Money and Banking in Honour of R. S. Sayers*, Oxford, 1968.
10. J. H. Curle, *The Gold Mines of the World*, London, 1899, 73–81.

11. Frederick H. Hatch and J. A. Chalmers, *The Gold Mines of the Rand: Being a Description of the Mining Industry of the Witwatersrand, South African Republic*, London, 1895, Chapter 2.
12. Curle, 73–5; Annexure to *13th Annual Report of the Transvaal Chamber of Mines*, 2; G. A. Denny, *The Deep-Level Mines of the Rand*, London, 1902, *passim*; Witwatersrand Chamber of Mines, *The Mining Industry. Evidence and Report of the Industrial Commission of Enquiry*, Johannesburg, 1897, 200; South African Republic, *Annual Report of the State Mining Engineer, 1898*, Pretoria, 1899, 5 (in Houghton and Dagut, *op. cit*; 316–17).
13. Curle, 24–5, 37–8.
14. Hatch and Chalmers, *loc. cit.*
15. Transvaal Chamber of Mines, *The Gold of the Rand: A Great National Industry, 1887–1923*, Johannesburg, 1924, 14–15.
16. M. H. De Kock, *Selected Subjects in the Economic History of South Africa*, Cape Town, 1924, 50; Great Britain, *Report Received From Mr. Henry Birchenough, Special Commissioner Appointed by the Board of Trade to Inquire Into and Report Upon the Present Position and Future Prospects of British Trade in South Africa*, Cd. 1844, 1904, 17.
17. Hatch and Chalmers, *passim*; E. P. Rathbone, 'Some Economic Features in Connection with Mining on the Witwatersrand Goldfields', *Transactions of the Institute of Mining and Metallurgy*, V, 1896–7, 56 *et seq.*; J. B. Taylor, *Recollections of the Discovery of Gold on the Witwatersrand*, Cape Town, 1936, 11–16.
18. Hatch and Chalmers, 88; F. Pollak, *Witwatersrand Outcrop and Deep Level Companies*, London, 1897, 11–23; F. A. Johnstone, *Class, Race and Gold: A Study of Class Relations and Racial Discrimination in South Africa*, London, 1976, 14–15.
19. Emden, *loc. cit.*; Kubicek, *op. cit.*; M. Fraser and A. Jeeves (eds.) *All That Glittered: Selected Correspondence of Lionel Phillips, 1890–1924*, Cape Town, 1977, 6–8; J. J. Van-Helten, 'Milner and the Mind of Imperialism', Institute of Commonwealth Studies (University of London), Collected Seminar Papers, SSA/78/5.
20. W. Bleloch, *The New South Africa*, London, 1901, 59–61.
21. Law No. 8, 1885, on Digging For, and Dealing in Precious Metals and Precious Stones in the South African Republic, in South African Republic, *The Gold Law of the South African Republic as Amended by Volksraad, and Passed 28 July 1886*, Pretoria, 1886.
22. Frankel, *loc. cit.*; Transvaal, *Report of the Mining Industry Commission, 1907–8*, Pretoria, 1908, 8–11.
23. J. P. Fitzpatrick, *The Transvaal From Within: A Private Record of Public Affairs*, London, 1899, 102–4, 295–6.
24. Great Britain, *Mines and Quarries: General Report and Statistics, Part IV, Colonial and Foreign Statistics, 1897*, Cd. 112, 1899, Table of Persons Employed at All Transvaal Gold Mines, 1897; S. T. Van Der Horst, *Native Labour in South Africa*, London, 1971, Chapter VII.
25. Monopsony is strictly speaking a situation in which there is only a single buyer in a given market, whose bargaining position is such that the purchaser alone determines the price of sale. In practice, monopsony is often used, as with the case of monopoly, to indicate an advance state of concentration of purchasing power rather than a complete monopoly.
26. A. Jeeves, 'The Control of Migratory Labour on the South African Gold Mines in the Era of Kruger and Milner', *Journal of Southern African Studies*, 2, 1 (1975), 11–12.
27. *5th Annual Report of the Witwatersrand Chamber of Mines, 1893*, 79; *8th Annual Report of the Witwatersrand Chamber of Mines, 1896*, Return of Stores Consumed; *9th and 10th Annual Reports of the South African Republic Chamber of Mines, 1897 and 1898*, Returns of Stores Consumed; Witwatersrand Chamber of Mines, *The Mining Industry etc.*, 200; J. J. Van-Helten, 'A Bunch of Hamburger Shylocks – The Case of the South African Explosives Industry, 1886–1914', Paper Presented to African Studies Association of the UK Annual Conference, 1978.
28. J. J. Van-Helten, 'German Capital, The Netherlands Railways Company and the Political Economy of the Transvaal, 1886–1900', *Journal of African History*, 19, 3 (1978), 369–90; Conyngham-Greene to Milner, 22 January 1898, encl. 1 in Milner to Chamberlain, 9 February 1898, C.9345, 1899.
29. *7th Annual Report of the Witwatersrand Chamber of Mines, 1895*, Presidents Report.
30. C. Van Onselen, 'Randlords and Rotgut, 1886–1903', *History Workshop Journal*, 2, 1976, 33–89.
31. G. Blainey, 'Lost Causes of the Jameson Raid', *Economic History Review*, 2nd Series, 15, 1965, 350–66; for a dissenting view see R. V. Kubicek, 'The Randlords in 1895: A Reassessment', *Journal of British Studies*, 2, 1972, 84–103; R. Mendelsohn, 'Blainey and the Jameson Raid: The Debate Renewed', Institute of Commonwealth Studies (University of London), Collected Seminar Papers, SSA/76/10; Fitzpatrick, 302–32; Milner Mss. 325/2 f.10, Evans Memo, 1 June 1897.

CHAPTER 2
British Imperial Policy and South Africa 1895-9

Andrew N. Porter

South Africa: an imperial problem

Beginning with the conquest of the Cape in 1806, and initially with the intention of protecting her sea-route to the east, Britain extended her claim to supreme authority over much of southern Africa during the nineteenth century. At such a distance from London, however, this claim was always both difficult to realize and open to challenge; Britain's determination to enforce her supremacy wavered as often as ideas about the best methods of securing her political influence altered. To imperial statesmen in the 1890s this South African 'problem' seemed as intractable as it had ever done. The reasons for this lay with the discovery of gold and the phenomenal growth of the Rand after 1886, by which the Transvaal replaced Cape Colony as the economic centre of South Africa. This change, which for the first time made it economically desirable that the Transvaal should be drawn permanently into the British empire, also reduced the likelihood of such an occurrence. Instead, by 1894–5, other developments inimical to imperial interests were in progress. The new wealth of the Transvaal gave impetus to the longstanding Boer search for their own outlet to the sea and complete emancipation from British domination. The establishment of the mines' future at last made possible completion of a railway from the Rand to the port of Lourenço Marques (Maputo), both the Transvaal's shortest route to the sea and one that avoided British territory. The railway was finished late in 1894. Still more disquieting for imperial rulers were the likely effects of the South African Republic's separatist ambitions on the British colonies of Natal and the Cape. These colonies had always competed vigorously for the trade with the interior. Now they no longer controlled all the ports or railways on which the Transvaal depended; they could only maintain or increase their share in the wealth of the Rand by drawing closer to the Transvaal. This was likely to be encouraged by the large numbers of Englishmen now flocking to the Rand, and the day was foreseen when the

> 'English South African colonies will have no fear of the South African Republic, but on the contrary their self-interest will be very strongly attracted to it. . . . In a generation the South African Republic will by its wealth and population dominate South Africa. . . .The commercial attraction of the Transvaal will be so great that a Union of the South African states with it will be absolutely necessary for their prosperous existence.'[1]

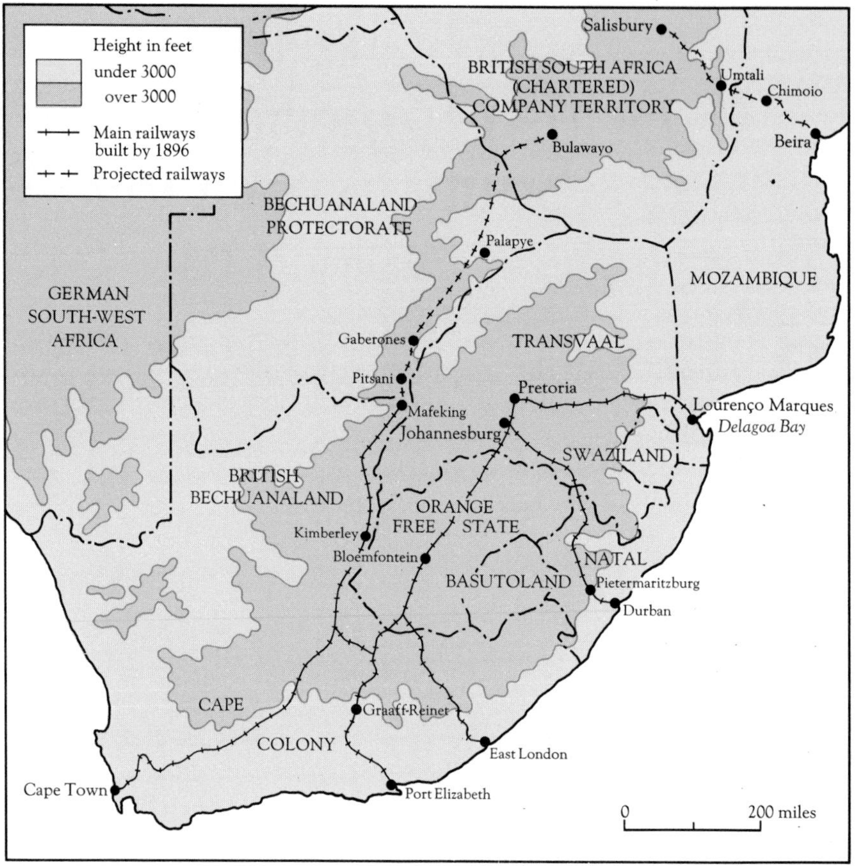

South Africa 1896, showing the boundaries of political units, major towns, principal rivers, and main railways.

A union under Transvaal auspices – be it English- or Boer-controlled – it was feared would not remain part of the British empire.

International interest in the subcontinent

Such developments were regretted not simply for the loss to Britain of direct political and economic links. In a decade when the tightening of ties between Britain and her colonies of white settlement was widely favoured as one way of ensuring Britain's survival as a great power, an independent English-speaking South Africa would be intolerable. It would bring economic weakness, grave strategic vulnerability, and encouragement for colonial separatist movements elsewhere. Moreover, Britain's loss would certainly be her rivals' gain. International competition and the partition of Africa into European colonies and spheres of influence had not passed southern Africa by. Germany and France had their territorial footholds in South-West Africa (Namibia) and Madagascar, and, with other powers, were anxious to profit from both the economic boom in the republic and Portugal's wish to develop her colony of Mozambique. Foreign statesmen welcomed advances in southern Africa not just for their own sake but for the opportunity they might furnish for putting pressure on Britain elsewhere. In order to protect her supremacy in South Africa, Britain might be prepared to make diplomatic concessions in other areas disputed among the great powers, such as the Far East. Transvaal ambition and the interest of Britain's competitors thus neatly dovetailed: the Boer government welcomed foreign presence and support as strengthening its own independence. From 1894 onwards, imperial officials were deluged with information about foreign concessions, discriminatory railway rates, and the growing volume of non-British trade and shipping. Mounting foreign investment in the republic was viewed with alarm, and overt German diplomatic support for the Transvaal was interpreted as further evidence of a concerted attempt to undermine Britain's supremacy in South Africa.

Domestic political constraints on imperial policy

Difficulties there were enhanced not only by their relevance to wider African or global power conflicts, but by the domestic political constraints under which imperial statesmen felt they had to operate. To be successful, especially in such threatening times, foreign and imperial policy was thought to require decisiveness and consistency of aim. Yet many felt that Britain's system of democratic politics shaped by the nineteenth-century reform acts made this very difficult. They were troubled by the pronounced swing of the electoral pendulum, popular lethargy and indifference towards foreign affairs broken only by unpredictable bursts of wild enthusiasm, and widespread ignorance of the importance of imperial questions to Britain's prosperity. Politicians were often denounced for failing to educate and lead the country in these matters.

In Britain, although imperial questions were often considered by the Foreign Office and Cabinet, the Secretary of State for the Colonies was formally responsible for South African affairs. Information reached him especially from the Governor of Cape Colony, who, as Imperial High Commissioner for South Africa, also sent on much correspondence from British officials in other places, such as the Agent in Pretoria. In June 1895 Lord Salisbury's Unionist ministry was formed and Joseph Chamberlain took over the Colonial Office. An ardent imperialist, his day-to-day administration was guided by three principal aims – economic development of the empire, the education of its peoples as to its value, and the promotion of political unity. Chamberlain's new Under-Secretary later described how Chamberlain 'told me at once that . . . England had not yet realized what the British Empire really stood for or what a part it might play in the world or of what development it was capable and that he meant to try and make England understand.'[2] A policy designed to strengthen the empire as a whole in the face of a hostile world was thus intended to proceed apace with a programme of popular education in the virtues and necessities of empire. Chamberlain shared the widespread disquiet concerning the effects of democratic politics on imperial affairs, and, with his unique combination of radical political experience and imperialist convictions, set out to remedy English democracy's shortcomings.

The new Colonial Secretary.

The third Marquis of Salisbury, whose Unionist government took office in June 1895. In Chamberlain's absence on holiday, Salisbury acted decisively in the Drifts crisis of October by threatening force if Kruger did not re-open the Vaal River crossings.

Chamberlain's interest in South Africa dated back at least to 1880 when he became Liberal government spokesman on these questions in the House of Commons. Originally sympathetic to Boer requests for the restoration of their independence, like many people he became increasingly critical of them, as – with independence largely restored by the Anglo-Transvaal Conventions of 1881 and 1884 – they sought under President Kruger's leadership to avoid their remaining obligations, to expand their borders at Britain's expense, and encourage Britain's foreign rivals. However, Chamberlain was hardly much warmer in his attitude towards the Cape. Cecil Rhodes, its Prime Minister since 1890, not only stood for that same white-settler attitude towards black Africans that offended Chamberlain's humanitarianism, but was also ambitious to forge a colonial-dominated South African federation at odds with Chamberlain's imperial design. Chamberlain liked and trusted Rhodes little more than he did Kruger.

In 1895 South Africa was at first simply one area among many where Chamberlain sought in minor ways to indicate that, after Liberal neglect, the empire was now in safe hands. In accord with his general principles, he was willing to listen and provide information to those with South African interests, but his early major initiatives in policy and publicity were directed elsewhere. Although Chamberlain shared the common vision of a federated South Africa within the empire, there were few signs that he had immediate plans of his own. His hand was forced by events in South Africa itself.

Relations between the Transvaal and the Cape reached breaking-point in summer 1895 over railway policy. With the opening of the Delagoa Bay railway, the Cape attempted to corner as much as possible of the Rand's traffic rather than agree to a division between competing lines. The Transvaal then obstructed first the railway and then the road route from the Cape ports, finally closing the Vaal River crossings (known as the Drifts) on 1 October. Rhodes's ministry appealed for British intervention, and, with Chamberlain absent on holiday, Lord Salisbury authorized a virtual ultimatum to the republic with the comment,

> 'I am convinced Chamberlain will agree with me. The Transvaal government is unfriendly to us and it is a great mistake to run away from them [*sic*]. The Cape Government must be supported to the end in this matter.'[3]

This paralleled Salisbury's firm stand against German claims to a voice in matters affecting the Transvaal, and Portugal's attempts to encourage Britain's rivals in Mozambique. Kruger gave way, and reopened the Drifts.

Rhodes's conspiracy

The combination of Transvaal unfriendliness and European pretensions hardened British hearts against the Boers to the benefit of Rhodes. It re-emphasized what had long been obvious, that Rhodes was too powerful a man to be ignored or crossed

Cecil Rhodes. By 1895 Rhodes had become convinced of the necessity to intervene directly in the affairs of the Transvaal to secure the overthrow of Kruger's govenment.

by an imperial government aware of its own weakness in South Africa and conscious of the need for allies. Since 1888, Rhodes, with his wealth and the British South Africa Company, had played a vital role in imperial attempts to pin down the Transvaal and limit European 'interference' by encircling the Boer heartland with British-held territory. Imperial statesmen too hoped with Rhodes that economic development of the north would counterbalance the Transvaal's riches. By 1895, however, the policy of encirclement and economic development had been weakened by Portuguese intransigence, the breakthrough of the Delagoa Bay railway, and Rhodes's discovery that his expectations of a Rhodesian 'second Rand' were baseless. If his dream of federation and desire for more sympathetic government in the Transvaal were to be realized, pressure had to be put on Kruger in some other way. Rhodes's own success in winning support from the Cape Dutch, and their criticisms of Kruger's government, doubtless encouraged his decision to intervene directly in Transvaal politics to secure Kruger's downfall.

Rhodes's plans involved no merely conventional support for the reform movement in the republic. He aimed to exploit existing discontent and to organize a rebellion in Johannesburg; this would be assisted by a force, under his lieutenant, L. S. Jameson, entering the Transvaal from neighbouring – perhaps company – territory; the finale would involve imperial intervention to annex the territory, and the installation of a Rhodes-dominated government. Such reckless scheming was characteristic of Rhodes, but how far the imperial government would follow him this time depended largely on Chamberlain, and on the discussions initiated by Rhodes in August 1895 concerning the future of Bechuanaland.

The Bechuanaland Protectorate was very important to Rhodes. Through it ran the proposed railway route to the Chartered Company's territories, and Rhodes had long expected

Dr Leander Starr Jameson.

that it would be given to the company. Its transfer would not only swell the company's resources, but would be a major step towards Rhodes's federal ideal. There was now the additional fact that a Bechuanaland base would be convenient for Jameson's force. The Liberal government in 1892 had promised financial assistance with the railway, and later land grants as well in order to keep the company solvent. Chamberlain had then approved this policy. When he took office, his own penchant for railway building and economic expansion, the difficulty of financing it from imperial government sources, and Boer hostility to economic cooperation, all favoured a substantial Chartered Company presence in the Protectorate. Rhodes sensed his opportunity. With his Johannesburg plans moving forward, with Cape–Transvaal relations deteriorating, and therefore the importance of a rapid transfer of territory increasing, Rhodes's representatives in London broached the subject with Chamberlain. In doing so, they not only argued the general case for transfer, but hinted at the Johannesburg schemes which made it still more pressing.

Colonial Office involvement in Rhodes's scheme

The Colonial Office had kept half an eye on the troubled situation in Johannesburg for some years. Although Chamberlain immediately refused to receive information that might be said to make him party to Rhodes's plans, he had inadvertently heard enough to confirm the Colonial Office's general fear that upheaval in Johannesburg was inevitable and that it would have substantial repercussions outside the Transvaal. For the imperial government this was a very difficult situation; it had done nothing to provoke trouble in the Transvaal, and was in no position to avoid or prevent the trouble that was brewing. There was no reason to suppose that imperial aloofness would either deter Rhodes or end the unrest. Such a course only raised the prospect of a successful revolution, wholly independent of the imperial government, which would bring an alienated Rhodes and his allies to power in the Transvaal and finally destroy imperial influence. Chamberlain realized that the only possibility of containing Rhodes lay in maintaining some imperial contact and control, strong enough to give a hold over him if the revolution proved successful, yet sufficiently fragile to avoid any embarrassment if it failed. Above all, it was important that nothing should upset construction of the railway or the economic development of Bechuanaland and the north.

The agreement with Rhodes by which Chamberlain attempted to secure this was reached early in November 1895, both men fearing further delay lest revolution in Johannesburg overtake them. Chamberlain knew that land for the Bechuanaland railway had to be handed over before any storm, because if Rhodes failed, to transfer it and restart the railway later might be very difficult. If, however, the scheme had already received official blessing and the railway strip been handed over, then even if Rhodes or the British South Africa Company suffered, Chamberlain would be able to argue effectively for the imperial government continuing both the railway and the development of the north. Rhodes, on the other hand, wanted to complete his arrangements for Jameson's force and knew time was short. By skilful negotiation, Chamberlain avoided alienating Rhodes while forcing him to drop his claim to the whole Protectorate. Rhodes accepted a very limited grant of land for the railway, and agreed to begin building at once; he gave up the imperial subsidy for its construction, and accepted the establishment of extensive African reserves under imperial control even within the railway strip. Chamberlain thus satisfied the Tswana chiefs and humanitarians who dreaded Chartered Company administration, and secured both his railway and the territory's future development at a great financial saving to the imperial government. By retaining most of the Protectorate, he left Rhodes with a major interest in continuing to court the favour of the imperial authorities. The strip of land transferred favoured Rhodes's plans for Jameson's invasion by running close to the Transvaal border, but this was unavoidable. Not only had this most economical route for the line long been notionally settled, but to support it Rhodes negotiated land agreements with some local African chiefs which Chamberlain was unable to dispute.

Chamberlain's involvement in these transactions was not that of an aggressor preparing to assault the Transvaal: it squared perfectly with the defensive character of British policy in the 1890s. Foreseeing certain trouble, believing Rhodes and the Uitlander organizers far more likely to succeed than fail, conscious of imperial weakness yet anxious to defend imperial interests, Chamberlain acted so that 'If the rising is successful it ought to turn to our advantage.'[4] Identical motives, the same distrust of Rhodes and his allies, prompted Chamberlain – unwisely, as it later transpired – to require reassurance that Rhodes intended raising the British flag in the Transvaal after the uprising, and, just before Christmas, to suggest that an early rising would avoid other threatening international disputes.

The Jameson Raid, December 1895

There was no early rising; indeed, there was no rising at all. The Uitlanders' toothless bite was less ferocious than their bark, whatever impressions had been created in London. Rhodes had great difficulty in persuading Uitlander political leaders to join in his plans; little support came from the mining houses unconnected with Rhodes; and the plotters' military preparations were at best inept. It is hardly surprising that while Jameson in Pitsani mustered less than half the 1 500 men he had counted upon, the Reform Committee in Johannesburg lost heart and cohesion, and decided over Christmas to postpone the whole exercise. This was rapidly made known to all involved, but Jameson, with a fake appeal from the Uitlanders in his pocket and ignoring all orders to sit tight, invaded the Transvaal on 29 December 1895. Rhodes did not try to stop him. He and Jameson hoped wildly at the last moment to provoke the revolution they had originally expected to assist. It was a vain hope; instead, Jameson's troops were as easily rounded up by Boer commandos as were the Uitlander Reform Committee members by the police.

The repercussions of the Raid

The Jameson Raid changed the face of South African politics. Kruger's position was greatly strengthened, partly by the evidence of extensive foreign support, but above all by the sympathetic banding together of Afrikaners throughout South Africa. The Transvaal's internal squabbles were momentarily forgotten and memories of the Raid contributed much to Kruger's overwhelming victory in the presidential election of February 1898. In the Cape the hard-won cooperation of English and Dutch fostered by Rhodes was destroyed by the Afrikaner Bond Party's sense of outrage and deception. Within a fortnight Rhodes himself resigned as Prime Minister, his constructive contribution to South African politics finished.

Imperial stock too began to fall as it became clear that Chamberlain could hardly escape public association with Rhodes's machinations. At the start of 1896, however, Chamberlain, aware of the imperial government's conflict of interests with Rhodes, was confident that he had circumvented any possibility of guilt by association. Convinced of the probity of his policy, he naturally and immediately condemned the Raid. No longer content merely that the imperial government should not be harmed by Rhodes's failure, Chamberlain responded to events in ways designed to substantiate imperial claims to supremacy. His first opportunity arose from the German Kaiser's telegram congratulating Kruger on defeating Jameson and preserving the Transvaal's independence. The British Cabinet heartily endorsed a forceful diplomatic protest and dispatched a naval squadron to Delagoa Bay. More important, Chamberlain proclaimed an imperial interest in Uitlander grievances. Urging the High Commissioner, Sir Hercules Robinson, to go up and confer with Kruger, Chamberlain proceeded in three dispatches to argue that the existence of these grievances, which had provided the basis for Rhodes's plans,

Jameson and other participants in the Raid photographed on board ship on their return to Britain.

Chamberlain presses for domestic reform in the Transvaal

clearly created unrest and threatened South African stability. He suggested reforms including a municipality for Johannesburg under the Uitlanders' own control, which would give them a measure of efficient self-government and make both Boer and Uitlander look to the imperial government.

This marked a crucial change in British policy. Before the Raid no one had wanted, or felt able under the Convention of 1884, to make an issue of grievances. These were regarded as the Transvaal's domestic responsibility; the Uitlanders were not much esteemed, and the Colonial Office had not collected evidence about their condition. Chamberlain now felt otherwise. Recognition of the reality of grievances shifted responsibility for the present uproar on to the republic. Imperial pressure for reforms might create a new body of popular support inside South Africa; this would be welcome to the imperial government conscious of the limitations of its influence, and free it from dependence on unreliable individuals like Rhodes. The many grievances requiring attention would produce occasions in plenty for imperial intervention and so destroy any idea that Britain intended abandoning South Africa. Finally, South African responsibilities were reinforced by domestic necessity, for this issue provided Chamberlain with a perfect focus for his campaign to educate the British public as to the importance of empire. Trained in the shadow of Gladstone, Chamberlain appreciated the potency of an appeal to principles of civil and political liberty. From now on, he used the South African question to illustrate the value and importance of empire by stressing publicly and as frequently as possible the connection between British imperialism and, in a twentieth-century phrase, 'human rights'. If this image could be fixed in people's minds, anti-imperialism or indifference to empire might become a thing of the past. Politicians would be able to rely on consistent support and be the stronger in facing foreign rivals.

Rhodes and companions in the Matopo Hills, Rhodesia. Following the Raid and his resignation of the Cape premiership, Rhodes travelled north to deal with the Shona and Ndebele rebellion which began in March 1896 and was subsequently brutally suppressed.

An extremely attractive course, it nevertheless had one fatal flaw: it ignored the interests and opinions of the Transvaalers. Chamberlain never asked himself what he would do if reforms he felt necessary were refused. Publicity made this dangerous, for if reforms constantly demanded were persistently refused only two courses lay open – ignominious retreat or a resort to force. Grievances and their remedy used as propaganda required frequent simple reiteration, but as a diplomatic problem – involving the Transvaal government with its distinct style of negotiation and suspicion of Britain – the remedying of grievances required much greater secrecy and subtlety. In 1899 it was the propaganda that was to triumph; diplomacy collapsed and the two sides fell into war. The tale of British policy from the Raid to the war is also the story of how the dangers implicit in Chamberlain's approach were realized.

Suspicions of imperial complicity in the Raid

The shadow of the Raid was a long one. Chamberlain and his colleagues understood neither how powerful was the belief in his personal complicity in Rhodes's plans nor that time only intensified these suspicions. Rumours abounded and the transfer of the Bechuanaland Protectorate territory seemed with hindsight strangely fortuitous. The various investigations into the Raid – the trial of the Reform Committee in Johannesburg and of Jameson in London, the Cape Parliament's enquiry, and the British Parliament's Select Committee of 1897 – only made the role of the imperial government appear more equivocal. With Chamberlain as one of its members and after a highly unsatisfactory public exmination of witnesses, the 1897 Select Committee formally cleared the imperial authorities in London of all involvement. Many onlookers however remained sceptical of proceedings dubbed 'The Lying in State at Westminster'.

At the heart of this committee's failure to convince was its handling of a series of telegrams describing Colonial Office attitudes and the Bechuanaland negotiations, which had passed between Chartered Company representatives in London and Rhodes between August and December 1895. Composed by men who had reason to exaggerate imperial involvement, ambiguously phrased, and imperfectly preserved, these telegrams were superficially damning, as Chamberlain realized when he was first allowed to examine them in June 1896. That they also seriously misrepresented Chamberlain's involvement was recognized by one of Rhodes's principal negotiators, who observed that

> 'if our [telegraphic] code ever gives up its secrets . . . everyone will believe that he [Chamberlain] was a much more inward conspirator than he really was.'[5]

Chamberlain was prevented from publishing all the telegrams with a full explanation of imperial policy because it touched on 'too many thorny questions of foreign and colonial politics'.[6] He therefore had to try to combine suppression of the most seemingly incriminating telegrams with setting the public record straight at the enquiry. It was an unfortunate choice of tactics, inevitably producing obvious evasions and distortion. Contemporaries naturally misunderstood this situation, and, followed by many subsequent historians, saw in it evidence that Chamberlain was simply trying to cover up his hostile designs on the Transvaal.[7]

However mistaken their understanding of the situation, critics in Britain and South Africa ceased to trust Chamberlain and the imperial policy which he continued to conduct. Boer hearts hardened steadily. Chamberlain's suggestions for reform in Johannesburg were resented, and Kruger refused Chamberlain's invitation to Britain to discuss Uitlander grievances. The Transvaal embarked on an extensive armament programme, and concluded a defensive alliance with the Orange Free State. Then, Chamberlain, still hedging his bets and seeing Rhodes as necessary to the economic development of the north, scandalized the Boers by his refusal to revoke the British South Africa Company's Charter and his defence of Rhodes's 'honour'.

A French caricaturist's interpretation of the Jameson Raid. Chamberlain's complicity in the Raid was widely suspected, and the Colonial Secretary's subsequent actions did little to allay suspicion.

Chamberlain and the 'cover-up'

This episode merits some comment, for it led to suggestions then and later that Chamberlain was blackmailed, that he had whitewashed Rhodes to avoid exposure of his own 'guilty' role in the Raid. In fact, Chamberlain, believing himself innocent in this respect, did not fear the exposure of any 'guilt'; what did worry him was that publication of the suppressed telegrams *now* would ruin the strategy he had been forced to adopt at the enquiry into the Raid. Explaining the telegrams in May 1897 would have raised difficulties that had not existed when he had originally proposed publication to Lord Salisbury. His fear that they might be revealed arose from the knowledge that some of Rhodes's subordinates believed in rehabilitating their leader by trying to damn Chamberlain; the Colonial Secretary could not be sure that they would not follow Jameson's example and go it alone, and even Rhodes himself might be persuaded by their desire to publish. In these circumstances, Chamberlain's defence of Rhodes, unfortunate and tactless as it was, seemed necessary in order to avoid reopening the enquiry and to calm the more extreme of Rhodes's supporters; it was also perhaps one step towards restoring popular confidence in a chartered company that still had an important place in the imperial government's plans.

Of course, all this only worsened relations with the Dutch everywhere. Reform in the Transvaal and opposition to Kruger made little headway, and Kruger's re-election as President seemed to confirm the resistance to change. Boer intransigence and suspicion were also reflected in their continuing search for international allies and diplomatic recognition. Extradition or commercial treaties with European states, adherence to international conventions, and the establishment of diplomatic representatives abroad were regarded as routes to emancipation. The Boers joined Germans, French and others in attempts to control Delagoa Bay or the operations of its port in order to give their claims to independence greater weight.

British statesmen continued to fear this combination of Transvaal and European intrigues, and tried persistently to restrict the Transvaal's activity. They insisted first that, in accordance with the 1884 Convention, Pretoria should submit for Britain's approval all agreements made with foreign states. At Lisbon, meanwhile, the Portuguese government was urged not to make arrangements in Mozambique that would weaken Britain's right under their treaty of 1891 to purchase the territory should Portugal wish to sell. These matters were quietly dealt with by the Foreign Office, but in Chamberlain's view were not the stuff of which propaganda was made. He therefore kept the remedying of Uitlander grievances to the fore, setting out details and establishing the Transvaal's poor record in his press releases, speeches, official publications for Parliament, and even his evidence at the Raid enquiry in 1897. Occasionally, he relaxed this direct pressure on the Boers, but never allowed the public equation of imperial activity and Uitlander liberties to disappear completely. Not only was this central to his wish to instruct the British public in the values of empire, but at times he hoped that a vociferous public opinion would give added weight to his diplomatic representations.

All these strands came together early in 1897. The republic had enacted legislation on immigration and the expulsion of aliens that the British government regarded as breaching the 1884 Convention. Kruger's rejection of this view just when foreign 'interference' in southern Africa was increasing, prompted a full-scale protest. In mid-April very stiff dispatches were sent to Pretoria, a naval demonstration was mounted at Delagoa Bay, and Chamberlain published the whole correspondence in advance of any Boer reaction in order to inform and get public opinion behind him. Early in May the Boers retreated, agreeing to repeal the offending legislation. The passage of the legislation confirmed yet again beliefs that the Boers could not be trusted; its repeal reinforced the conclusion, drawn most recently from the Drifts crisis, that the Boers understood only uncompromising language, and that if the use of force was threatened they would back down. Chamberlain's publication and definition of the British position at the earliest opportunity reinforced the impression of decisiveness. It also increased Boer distrust of him by making him appear far more precipitate and intemperate than he was, and abolished the delay that more discreet diplomacy might have provided for reflection and reconsideration of alternatives. A momentary British victory thus pushed the sides apart and boded ill for future exchanges.

Sir Alfred Milner

Those exchanges were now vitally affected by the retirement of Lord Rosmead (as Sir Hercules Robinson had become), and the appointment of Sir Alfred Milner as the new High Commissioner and Governor of Cape Colony. A brilliant administrative career in Egypt and Whitehall had proved Milner the perfect civil servant. In addition, he detested democratic politics and politicians, and was a single-minded imperialist. He later labelled himself a 'British Race Patriot', anxious to prevent the loss to the empire of English-speaking settler communities lest the state be 'irreparably weakened'. None of these qualities fitted him to deal patiently with self-governing colonists or Boers. What mattered was his acceptability at home. In London his intellectual distinction, Balliol education, and wide circle of friends brought him admirers and contacts in every political quarter. A man so widely approved was of inestimable value to a Colonial Secretary who never wanted for critics of his South African policy. The job itself mattered little, the innate versatility of Britain's ruling classes being taken for granted. Most agreed that in Milner

> 'we have the best man in the British Empire
> for the toughest job in the British Empire.'[8]

At first Milner was sanguine that patience and personal exchanges would improve relations with the Transvaal. After the April crisis, he welcomed diversion of attention from South Africa by the royal Jubilee, and looked to the growing industrial recession and revival of opposition to Kruger to produce

Sir Alfred Milner, who arrived in South Africa on 5 May 1897 to take up the post of High Commissioner and Governor of the Cape Colony in succession to Lord Rosmead.

President S. J. P. Kruger, whose overwhelming victory in the 1898 presidential election and subsequent dismissal of Chief Justice Kotze convinced Milner that there was 'no way out of the troubles of S. Africa except reform in the Transvaal or war'.

change. Early in 1898 the government's failure to introduce industrial reforms and Kruger's re-election helped dispel his optimism. He became convinced that either reform had to be forced upon the Transvaal, or a war would be inevitable; sometimes he seemed calmly to accept war as the only possible outcome. His handling of Kruger's dismissal of Chief Justice Kotze showed how his tactics also changed. Choosing to interpret it as an attack on judicial independence, an erosion of civil liberties, Milner worked for 'a strong expression of local opinion'[9] in favour of Kotze, and established contacts with Uitlander politicians. He made a provocative speech at Graaff Reinet to encourage 'loyalists' to put pressure on Kruger, and carefully arranged timing of its publication in London to inform British opinion. Hoping for public demonstrations in South Africa and new interest at home, Milner then sent a dispatch urging Chamberlain to work up to a crisis – intending thereby to push the British government into intensifying its intervention on behalf of the Uitlanders, and promote the confrontation that would ultimately end in reform or war.

Milner's moves failed and he was sharply reminded that the international situation made any South African complications undesirable. The popular agitation had therefore to be reined in. However, the episode illustrates vital aspects of Milner's approach, his readiness to act secretly and independently of Colonial Office instructions to get his own way, and his realization that publicity and popular opinion in both Britain and South Africa were important. Milner appreciated the importance Chamberlain attached to public opinion, and turned this to his own advantage. Chamberlain's methods were appropriated by Milner and increasingly used to bind the imperial government to a course of Milner's own devising.

Although Chamberlain remained anxious to tackle the Transvaal over Uitlander grievances and breaches of the 1884 Convention, and publicize his dealings to his audience at home, events during 1898 showed how difficult this could be. While he felt that in the Kotze case 'all . . . has been satisfactorily reported in this country' by the press,[10] among the other material gathered by the Colonial Office there was nothing of particular public interest and no satisfactory occasion for publishing it. In response to Boer requests for international arbitration in disputes with Britain, Chamberlain had spelt out the Cabinet's view that Britain had a legal authority – 'suzerainty' – over the republic. While technically important and the subject of much debate, this lacked popular appeal, and in any case events at Omdurman and Fashoda were far more exciting. The Transvaal gave no open provocation, and the Colonial Office felt its campaign flagging. Foreign Office officials, too, reluctantly concluded that several years' diplomacy had checked neither Transvaal activities in Europe nor rival powers' scramble for concessions in Mozambique and around Delagoa Bay which might be turned to the republic's advantage. Even the Anglo–German Agreement of 1898 affecting Mozambique, which implied that Germany would no longer regard Delagoa Bay as a port of international interest, was soon seen to offer no real safeguard for Britain. Delagoa Bay remained her weak spot; one official expressed the common view when he minuted that 'the question never will be settled till the place is actually English.'[11]

After his reprimand Milner bided his time. He no longer looked for a sudden outburst of agitation, but, with weakening faith in Dutch support for imperial intervention in the Transvaal, turned to the problem of generating imperial loyalty and political cohesion among English-speaking South Africans, especially Uitlanders. He kept up contacts with men such as J. P. Fitzpatrick in the Transvaal and Edmund Garrett, editor of the *Cape Times*, and felt encouraged by the Cape Progressive Party's revival. However, he knew that the Uitlander awaited signs of determination from the imperial government, and it was to provoke this that he visited England late in 1898. He went, he said, to interview '*all* the leading politicians and pressmen . . . and to stamp on rose-coloured illusions about S. Africa'.[12]

At this time Milner and Chamberlain differed on two related points. Milner wanted steady pressure designed to culminate in a showdown with the Boers. Chamberlain, while sympathetic, saw difficulties arising from the need to consider wider international questions, and from the limited nature of the grievances that he felt he could act upon under the 1884 Convention. Here again Milner went further, rejecting the Convention as worthless, and wanting to make a stand not on grievances but on the franchise for the Uitlanders. With first-hand knowledge, and perhaps greater realism, Milner was prepared to trust the Uitlanders with the franchise, arguing that anything less than full political power would awaken no enthusiasm for Britain while delay in pressing for it would alienate them altogether. All British officials believed that the Uitlanders were, or soon would be, a majority of the adult male population, and Milner had long thought 'there will be no ultimate peace without extension of the Franchise.'[13] However, Chamberlain, as in 1895–6, distrusted the Uitlanders' imperial sympathies should they control the Transvaal's government, and stuck to his idea of a municipality for the Rand.

The Edgar case

Nevertheless, failure to draw the Transvaal into the imperial network meant that Milner's arguments found ready listeners and had some effect. When in December 1898 unrest spread among Uitlanders on the Rand following the shooting of one of their number, a certain Edgar, by a Boer policeman after a brawl, Chamberlain showed greater willingness to intervene and adopt a less legalistic approach. Edgar's death, he noted, 'may be very important and may give us the right of remonstrance and action – outside the Convention – which we have not hitherto had.'[14] He was, however, unable to take any steps himself. In Milner's absence the acting High Commissioner, General Sir William Butler, refused to intervene, thinking the matter best left alone. Chamberlain therefore had to await Milner's return to Cape Town for the situation to be clarified.

Milner assumes the initiative

British dependence on officials on the spot now increased dramatically. Not only had Chamberlain to rely on Milner because of the regard in which he was held in England, but the rapidity of events in 1899 and Milner's determination to control them left London officials little scope for initiative. On his return Milner used his opportunities skilfully. First, he and his subordinates strove to create the appearance of Uitlander support both for the franchise as the solution to their difficulties and for imperial intervention to secure it. The complex divisions within the Uitlander community made this tricky, but through careful timing and publicity Milner achieved much success.

While in London he had fixed the appointment of W. F. Monypenny as *The Times* correspondent in Johannesburg and editor of the widely-read newspaper *The Star*, with the intention of moulding British opinion while uniting the Uitlanders. Arriving in February 1899, Monypenny under the local British officials' guidance immediately backed the mounting agitation and the franchise as the solution to Uitlander grievances. The agitation was organized by the South African League, whose leaders were determined to petition the Queen about grievances and were in touch with Milner about tactics through the British Agent in Pretoria, Conyngham Greene. As protest grew, the Boer government, wanting to calm the Rand, tried to secure the support of the leading mining companies by putting forward proposals for settling major questions in dispute with the industry. These included an offer to support enfranchisement of the Uitlander after five years if the mining houses dissociated themselves from the political unrest and press criticism. J. P. Fitzpatrick played an important role in these 'Great Deal' discussions, and with Milner's encouragement worked to make the franchise central to a settlement. Late in March, against the background of Monypenny's campaign, Milner engineered the public revelation in *The Times* and *The Star* of both the petition and the secret Great Deal negotiations, at the crucial point when the mining houses appeared temporarily united in demanding both the franchise and a settlement acceptable not just to themselves but to the Uitlander community as a whole. A press campaign was begun for public meetings of Uitlanders to endorse the franchise solution.

The Colonial Office, ignorant of Milner's intrigues, was impressed by the spontaneity of developments – the growing agitation, the clear demand for the franchise, the apparent solidarity of mining capitalist and ordinary Uitlander. Now Milner succeeded where in 1898 he had failed, and Chamberlain was pushed into action. Early in March, Chamberlain had told the capitalists that the government's goal was a municipality and urged them to demand the same. Suspicious of the Uitlander community, he also believed 'that the British public is . . . more likely to be stirred by concrete cases of oppression than by the general injustice of non-representation of the Uitlanders in the Legislature',[15] and made municipal self-government the focus of his public speeches. Now he had to change ground and accept the franchise, for Milner's manipulations had exposed the irrelevance to both Boer and Uitlander of a municipality and shifted the centre of public discussion.

Chamberlain's and Milner's concern with publicity now interlocked. In his speeches and publications for the British public, Chamberlain had to explain the significance of the franchise. Milner had to ensure that each step or commitment was made known, to sustain Uitlander confidence in Britain and to prevent imperial and Boer politicians agreeing to a weak compromise. Such publicity necessitated the simplification of the issues involved, so that they should be easily understood and contrary interpretations ruled out. For Milner, speed and decisiveness also became all-important. Together these preoccupations again led Milner to compromise the British government's position, and progressively destroyed the basis for constructive Anglo–Boer diplomacy.

This became evident in May 1899 when Chamberlain sought from Milner an analysis of Transvaal affairs for publication alongside the Uitlander petition to the Queen, which contained 21 000 signatures, and the government's reply to it. Milner wrote passionately of 'thousands of British subjects kept permanently in the position of helots' on whose behalf 'the case for intervention is overwhelming'. Chamberlain realized that such language required either an ultimatum or Milner's recall, but for the moment publication was avoided. Although British government opinion was hardening, although the grievances question was seen as the last opportunity of making the Boers toe the imperial line, and Milner's assertion that British South Africa's loyalty would not survive a failure was accepted, no one wanted conflict. Even though the international situation had eased and Britain could afford to be intransigent, it was still felt – as Chamberlain had once remarked – that a

> 'war in South Africa would be one of the most serious wars that could possibly be waged.'[16]

The Bloemfontein Conference, 31 May-5 June 1899

A proposal by President Steyn of the Orange Free State for a conference between Milner and Kruger at Bloemfontein was therefore guardedly welcomed, both for the chance it offered of a settlement and for the information it would give the public. Chamberlain, while anxious to avoid provocative issues like 'suzerainty' and widen the field for negotiation, had to give Milner plenty of leeway. The High Commissioner, however, saw the conference proposal as a delaying tactic. He therefore used his freedom of initiative rather to restrict its scope. While his subordinates tried to organize Uitlander activity in Johannesburg to coincide with the conference, Milner refused to go with any but his own wholehearted supporters, confined discussion to the franchise, and cut the conference short on 5 June when Kruger insisted on the naturalization of the Uitlanders well before their receiving the vote.

Chamberlain was furious with Milner, but the Bloemfontein conference marked an important stage on the road to war. It destroyed any remaining Boer confidence in Britain's

MORAL SUASION.

Sir Alfr-d M-ln-r *sings*:—
THERE WAS A "HIGH COMM." WHO SAID, "HOW
SHALL I TACKLE THIS WILY OLD COW,
I WILL SIT ON THIS STILE
AND CONTINUE TO SMILE,
WHICH *MAY* SOFTEN THE HEART OF THIS COW!"

THE SMILE THAT FAILED.

Sir Alfr-d M-ln-r *again sings*:—
THERE WAS A "HIGH COMM." WHO SAID, "NOW
I'VE CONFERRED WITH THIS WILY OLD COW!
I *HAVE* SAT ON THIS STILE,
AND CONTINUED TO SMILE,
BUT IT'S HAD NO EFFECT ON THE COW!" [*Exit.*

These two cartoons from Punch *appeared on 31 May and 14 June, ie. immediately before and after the Bloemfontein Conference. They present a wholly unconvincing picture of the attitude of the High Commissioner, though one that was widely accepted in Britain. Milner regarded the conference, sponsored by President Steyn of the Orange Free State, as 'a good stroke of business on the part of the enemy', refused to allow the moderate-minded Cape Prime Minister, W. P. Schreiner, to attend the meeting, restricted discussion to the franchise issue, and prematurely broke off negotiations on 5 June against Chamberlain's wishes.*

sincerity in negotiation. Unaware of the tension between Milner and the imperial government, the Boers saw in Milner's intransigence the mirror image of Chamberlain's 'untrustworthiness' and 'aggressiveness'. Discussion was of no further use to them. The imperial government was also thrown back on its last resort, that of making demands on the Boers, which ultimately, if not met, would have to be enforced. The alternative – Milner's recall – was impossible unless the grievances policy and with it British claims to supremacy were to be abandoned. Since 1896, however, too much publicity had been given to the issues involved for retreat to be possible without complete loss of credibility in both 'the power and authority of the British Empire . . . [and] the position of Great Britain in South Africa'.[17] Lord Salisbury deplored Milner's handling of affairs, but maintained:

> 'the real point to be made good to South Africa
> is that we not the Dutch are Boss.'[18]

His colleagues agreed; while many would have preferred another ground for dispute, they recognized that none was available.

The final collapse of negotiations

Milner's actions left the British government in its reluctance to face war with no other hope than that the Boers might yield in the face of a serious threat, as in 1895 and 1897. So from mid-June 1899 onwards, pressure was applied. A stream of official material, including Milner's 'helots' despatch, was published to substantiate Uitlander claims and justify their demand for the franchise. Ministerial speeches stressed British determination; words were supported by military preparations. On three occasions, twice in July and again in August, the Boers made offers involving the franchise. Twice Chamberlain felt sure the crisis was over. But in Britain there remained always a residual distrust, a desire for clarification or investigation of proposals, a fear lest any loophole allow the Boers to go back on their apparent words. Milner, afraid lest Britain's grip on the Boers slacken and the Uitlanders give up in despair, shared and encouraged these suspicions. Boer insistence that Britain should make concessions in return – perhaps abandon the controversy over 'suzerainty' – irritated British statesmen by its assumption that here was a bargain between equals. On each occasion therefore Britain requested safeguards or modifications, and the Boers, no longer prepared to negotiate, withdrew their offers, the last early in September.

Cartoon from Punch, *14 June 1899.*

The declaration of war

For the remainder of that month the imperial government considered its final demands, confident now that most of the British people were behind them but uncertain how to compose a satisfactory ultimatum. Their difficulties were resolved when the Transvaal, after delivering its own ultimatum for the removal of imperial troops from its frontiers, declared war on 11 October 1899. When Parliament met to consider the conflict, Chamberlain, in defending the government's policy, appealed to 'the man in the street'. 'He knows perfectly well that we are going to war in defence of principles – principles upon which this Empire has been founded and upon which alone it can exist',[19] – namely peace, good government, and what another called 'the ordinary rights of Englishmen the world over' in an area of Britain's particular responsibility. Chamberlain did not, however, mention the need to preserve British authority in an area containing one of the principal life-lines of the empire in the Cape sea route to India, the government's desire to stop foreign infiltration into that region, and its wish to see that if the Transvaal continued the strongest province in southern Africa it should do so under British auspices. These were of vital importance but incapable of awakening at home or in South Africa the popular support felt necessary to secure them. To do that Chamberlain seized upon 'grievances'. These were then handled by Milner in a way that made inevitable a war that British statesmen no less than Boer had wished to avoid.

References

1. Chamberlain Papers JC 10/1/71, University of Birmingham Library, Lord Selborne to J. Chamberlain 18 October 1897.
2. Selborne Papers 191, 76–7, Bodleian Library Oxford, 'Some memories and reflections in my old age'.
3. *Ibid.* 15, f3–5, Lord Selborne, Memorandum on the Drifts Question, 15 October 1895.
4. Chamberlain to Lord Salisbury 26 December 1895, cited in J. L. Garvin, *The Life of Joseph Chamberlain*, III, London, 1934, 78.
5. Grey Papers, University of Durham, Earl Grey to B. Hawksley, 12 June 1896.
6. Salisbury to Chamberlain 12 June 1896, cited in E. Drus 'A Report on the Papers of Joseph Chamberlain relating to the Jameson Raid and the Inquiry', *Bulletin of the Institute of Historical Research*, 25, 1952, 51.
7. For other views of the Raid and its effects, see J. Van der Poel, *The Jameson Raid*, London, 1951; E. Pakenham, *Jameson's Raid*, London, 1960; J. S. Marais, *The Fall of Kruger's Republic*, London, 1961; R. E. Robinson and J. Gallagher, *Africa and the Victorians. The Official Mind of Imperialism*, London, 1961, chapter 14.
8. Selborne Papers 15, f102–4, Selborne to Grey (copy) 5 April 1897. On Milner, see J. E. Wrench, *Alfred Lord Milner. The Man of no Illusions 1854–1925*, London, 1958; A. M. Gollin, *Proconsul in Politics. A Study of Lord Milner in Opposition and in Power*, London, 1964; V. Halperin, *Lord Milner and the Empire*, London, 1952; G. H. L. Le May, *British Supremacy in South Africa 1899–1907*, London, 1965.
9. Milner Papers 6, f244, Bodleian Library Oxford, Milner to C. Greene (British Agent, Pretoria), 18 February 1898.
10. CO 417/243, f40, Public Record Office London, minute by Chamberlain 29 March 1898.
11. CO 417/271, f407, *ibid.*, 26 January 1899.
12. C. Headlam ed., *The Milner Papers*, I, London, 1931, 299.
13. *Ibid.*, 65.
14. Milner Papers 5, f145, Chamberlain to Milner, 30 December 1898.
15. CO 417/299, f264, minute by E. Wingfield, 24 April 1899.
16. House of Commons, *Parliamentary Debates*, 4th series, vol. 15 column 914, 8 May 1896.
17. *Ibid.*, 75, c. 702, Chamberlain, 28 July 1899.
18. Milner Papers 16(1), f87–96, Selborne to Milner, 27 July 1899.
19. *Parliamentary Debates*, 4th series, 77, c. 266, 19 October 1899.

PART TWO

WAR

Both sides entered upon war with confidence. The Boer ultimatum had been issued in the knowledge that it would be at least six weeks before the British army corps arrived in South Africa, and that until then the imperial forces would be outnumbered and on the defensive. In October 1899 the Boers brought between 32 000 and 35 000 men immediately into the field against a British garrison in the Cape Colony and Natal numbering only about 20 000. Their forces were familiar with the country and well-armed with the most modern and sophisticated weaponry. The republics were expectant too of a large-scale uprising by Afrikaner sympathizers in the Cape, and optimistic of overseas support. Some Boer leaders also apparently hoped that the serious famine in the Indian subcontinent would generate sufficient unrest to compel Britain to divert valuable military resources there to restore order. Bearing all these considerations in mind, J. C. Smuts, Kruger's young State Attorney, urged a bold strategy of penetrating swiftly and deeply into the British colonies to inspire widespread rebellion in the Cape and seize the colony's main ports, and to capture Durban on the Natal coast, and thereby disrupt the landing in South Africa of the main body of the British army.

British public opinion, diligently nurtured by Chamberlain and Milner during the preceding months, responded with open enthusiasm to the coming of war. Large cheering crowds lined the streets as soldiers marched from barracks to embark for South Africa, and when on 22 October the Guards set out for war there was a crowd assembled of such proportions they could scarcely make their way through it. The *Daily Mail* noted

> 'even total strangers, carried away by the enthusiasm, broke into the ranks and insisted on carrying rifles, kit bags . . . and at Waterloo all semblance of military order had disappeared. The police were swept aside and men were borne, in many cases, shoulder high to the entraining platform, while others struggled through in single file.'[1]

The British empire and Afrikaner republics seemed so unevenly matched it was widely believed that once the troops dispatched from Britain arrived in South Africa the recalcitrant Boer states would be overrun without difficulty and the war draw rapidly to a successful conclusion, certainly within six months and possibly even before Christmas (the war was in fact to last over two and a half years). The prices of Rand gold shares on the London stock exchange soared. In Parliament, which assembled in special session on 17 October, the government easily obtained a supplementary vote of £10 million (by June 1902 the war had cost more than twenty times as much), and the War Office remained confident that 75 000 soldiers would be enough to ensure victory (almost 450 000 troops were eventually needed).

The opposition urged caution against over-optimism and Sir Henry Campbell-Bannerman, the Liberal leader, reminded the government that his party took no responsibility for the course being pursued in South Africa. The onset of war, however, split the Liberals into three groups: a small radical wing led by John Morley and C. P. Scott considered the war immoral and wholly unjustified; a larger Liberal Imperialist wing, headed by H. H. Asquith, Sir Edward Grey and Lord Rosebery, regarded it as just and necessary; and between these two extremes a centre grouping, led by Campbell-Bannerman himself, expressed serious reservations about the wisdom of the diplomacy that had preceded the call to arms, but promised qualified support for the government while the Boers remained on British soil. The Liberals were in a difficult position because of the apparent widespread popularity of the war and the public's confidence in the British army's ability to gain a long-awaited victory over the Boers. Very few people shared the sentiments of the virulent anti-imperialist Wilfred Scawen Blunt, who believed the war would soon become 'the first nail driven into the coffin of the British Empire'.[2]

In South Africa the anticipated Boer offensive was launched on three fronts. The republics' main force crossed from the Transvaal and Orange Free State into the northern districts of Natal, compelling the advanced detachments of the British garrison to retire to Ladysmith, where the main body of imperial troops in the colony was stationed. Between 29 October and 2 November General Piet Joubert, the veteran Boer military leader, succeeded in laying siege to the town. On the western front commandos moved into the northern Cape and the Bechuanaland Protectorate to sever British communications along the railway from Cape Town to Bulawayo in Rhodesia, and to besiege the garrisons in Kimberley and Mafeking. A third force, composed of Free Staters, invaded the Cape midlands, where commandos rapidly gained recruits from among the colony's Afrikaner population.

It had been expected that the British garrison in South Africa would be on the defensive during the first weeks of the war until reinforcements arrived. Nonetheless the ease with which the Boers were able to invade the Cape and Natal and establish their positions caused some alarm. Worse was to follow, for when the army corps landed in South

Africa British troops were unable to make any significant headway in driving back the Boers and relieving the beleaguered forces in Ladysmith, Kimberley and Mafeking. On all three major war fronts the Boers inflicted startling defeats on the British forces: at the Stormberg in the Cape midlands on 10 December; at Magersfontein on the western front on the following day; and at Colenso in Natal on 15 December. 'The week which extended from 10 December to 17 December, 1899, was the blackest one known during our generation, and the most disastrous for British arms during the century', wrote Sir Arthur Conan Doyle afterwards.[3] More alarming than the 'black week' reverses themselves was the manner of the British defeats. At Colenso General Sir Redvers Buller, the Commander-in-Chief in South Africa, lost 1 200 men and ten guns. Thoroughly dispirited he recommended surrender to Sir George White, the commander of Ladysmith, though the message was not acted upon. The Cabinet was deeply dismayed. It was clear that Buller had lost his nerve, and that British strategy, tactics and leadership demanded close scrutiny, especially since in some war zones – on the Tugela in Natal, for example – the Boer forces were greatly outnumbered by British troops. 'Our generals seem neither able to win victories nor to give convincing reasons for their defeats', remarked Asquith from the Liberal ranks.[4] The defence committee of the Cabinet met urgently to take stock of the situation and decided to appoint Lord Roberts of Kandahar as Commander-in-Chief to supersede Buller, and to send Lord Kitchener of Khartoum to South Africa as Roberts's Chief-of-Staff. In response to the black week defeats further reinforcements were ordered, and volunteering gathered pace especially among the middle and upper classes.

In retrospect some of the initial gloom in Britain during the previous month was somewhat misplaced, for in spite of their handsome victories the Boers failed to press home their military advantage by driving more deeply into the British colonies. Joubert's advanced patrols in Natal reached Mooi River, only fifty miles from Pietermaritzburg, but the General cautiously chose to concentrate his forces around Ladysmith rather than press on to Durban and the sea. In the Cape a large proportion of the invading commandos entrenched themselves around Kimberley and Mafeking. The bold strategy advocated by Smuts and others of the younger generation of Boer commanders, Louis Botha and J. H. de la Rey prominent among them, was not followed through by the Boers' conservative military leadership, and the republics' best opportunity of avoiding ultimate defeat was lost.

Roberts and Kitchener arrived in South Africa with substantial further reinforcements early in the new year. Upon his arrival Roberts announced a new plan of campaign: to advance along the railway northwards from Cape Town to Kimberley, and from there to dispatch his main force eastwards towards Bloemfontein in the Free State in a bid to isolate the Boer forces in the south. Buller was maintained in his command of the army in Natal, provided with reinforcements, and instructed to press on with the relief of Ladysmith and the reconquest of the colony. Buller's force suffered two more serious defeats at Spion Kop (24 January) and Vaalkrantz (5-7 February) before White's garrison in Ladysmith was eventually relieved on 28 February. Roberts's main army advanced steadily through the Cape towards the republics. The siege of Kimberley ended on 15 February, and on 27 February – the anniversary of the Boer victory at Majuba in 1881 – General P. A. Cronjé and 4 000 burghers surrendered to Roberts at Paardeberg, the Boers' most humiliating defeat of the war. The route was now open to Bloemfontein, which was captured on 13 March. Moving northwards across the Vaal River Roberts's force entered Johannesburg on 31 May and Pretoria on 5 June. In a separate operation British relief columns on 17 May linked up with Major R. S. S. Baden-Powell's garrison in Mafeking, and the last of the three major sieges of the war came to an end. In Britain news of the relief of Mafeking was enthusiastically received, 'Mafeking Night' witnessing unprecedented scenes of crowd celebration and the birth of a new word in the English language (maffick, v.i., exult riotously, according to the Oxford English Dictionary, though there was little riotous behaviour compared to the occasions during the war when anti-war meetings were violently disrupted and the property of opponents of the war attacked by vengeful jingo crowds).

Meanwhile in South Africa, the Cape Colony had been beset by political crisis since the onset of war. W. P. Schreiner, the Prime Minister, headed a cabinet composed of three Englishmen and three Afrikaners; his government depended for its majority in the Cape House of Assembly upon the support of the *Afrikaner Bond*. During the months immediately preceding the outbreak of war Schreiner desperately urged moderation and conciliation, he refused to permit the transport of war materials through the Cape to the republics, nor would he allow the colony's frontier towns to be fortified. When war came he hoped operations would be conducted exclusively by British rather than colonial troops, that President Steyn of the

Orange Free State would refrain from ordering his commandos to cross over into the Cape, and that the colony could thereby maintain a neutral role, albeit uneasily. Steyn in fact temporarily held back the invasion of the Cape in response to an urgent plea from Schreiner to give conciliation a last chance, but it was obvious that Anglo-Boer relations had broken down irreparably and that the Cape could not maintain a non-combatant role in the war. Young Cape Afrikaners welcomed the invading Free Staters, and in the predominantly Afrikaner rural areas there was little support for the British cause. The Cape Mounted Riflemen and the Cape Police were placed under imperial military control, additional colonists called to arms, and martial law proclaimed. Measures such as these were intensely disliked by Schreiner and his colleagues, but looked upon in the circumstances as unavoidable. The operation of martial law regulations, especially the disarming of many Afrikaners and the detention of men on grounds of suspected disloyalty, served only to estrange further Cape Afrikaner opinion in the country districts. Free State commandos, with local support, annexed the frontier districts of Colesberg, Aliwal North, Albert, Barkly East and Dordrecht during November 1899, while to the west Transvaal commandos captured Vryburg and later advanced through Prieska, Kenhardt and Gordonia.

Following the retreat of the Boer commandos early in 1900 several hundred Cape rebels were captured or surrendered. In the interests of justice to those colonists who had remained loyal during the invasion, Chamberlain and Milner pressed for the trial of rebel leaders and the disfranchisement of their rank and file supporters. Schreiner's cabinet was divided on the issue, the *Bond* refused to support the proposal, and on 13 June 1900 Schreiner resigned, his role as mediator between Afrikaner and British interests in the Cape having finally proved untenable. Sir Gordon Sprigg, a veteran former Prime Minister, formed a new government. At their annual congress at the Paarl, two days after Schreiner's resignation, the *Bond* passed a resolution condemning the war as 'bloody and unrighteous'.[5]

Having occupied Johannesburg and Pretoria, Roberts's army struck eastwards, driving the republican government and the main body of the Transvaal commandos along the railway towards the Mozambican frontier. By September 1900 British troops had gained tenuous control of the entire railway network of the Transvaal including the line from Pretoria to the Mozambique frontier, thereby denying the commandos their last direct link with the outside world. Turning over his authority to Schalk Burger as Acting President, Kruger sailed from Lourenço Marques on 20 October abroad the Dutch man-of-war *Gelderland* bound for Holland, which he intended to use as a base for seeking European aid for the republics' cause. Kruger was destined never to see his country again, for he died in exile in Switzerland in 1904. On 30 July 1900, 4 500 Free Staters surrendered to General Sir Archibald Hunter, having been trapped by British forces in the Brandwater Basin. Republican morale was at a low ebb, and between March and July 1900 almost 14 000 burghers drifted back to their farms to avail themselves of Roberts's proclamations promising protection of person and property to those burghers who gave up their arms and signed a pledge to take no further part in the fighting. The war in South Africa seemed rapidly to be drawing towards its conclusion.

Following the occupation of the Boer capitals both republics were annexed to the British Crown, the Orange Free State on 24 May (to be known afterwards as the Orange River Colony), and the Transvaal on 1 September, though in view of the continuation of the war the validity of the annexations in international law was questionable. It was decided that military rule should prevail in the annexed colonies so long as the exigencies of war demanded, and Lord Roberts was given plenary powers for the military administration of the former republics with the condition that he should consult the High Commissioner on all matters of political significance. In May it was agreed that once circumstances permitted Milner would assume administrative responsibility for the new colonies and would retain the office of High Commissioner, which in future would be based in the Transvaal rather than the Cape. In the meantime George Fiddes, Milner's imperial secretary, was appointed as civilian advisor to Roberts at Milner's insistence. Relations between the civil and military authorities were never easy, largely because the period of military administration was destined to last far longer than anyone on the British side originally expected; contrary to earlier forecasts, the occupation of the Boer capitals did not signal the imminent capitulation of the republican forces.

Indeed, it was soon evident that the Boer forces had been scattered not broken, and that the resolve of the republican leadership to continue the struggle remained undampened. With the capture of Cronjé at Paardeberg in February and the death through illness of Joubert on 27 March, the military leadership of the republics had passed into the hands of Louis Botha and Christiaan de Wet, respectively elected Commandant-Generals of the Transvaal and Orange Free State. Botha's principal advisers were Smuts and De la Rey, De Wet's, President Steyn and General J. B. M. Hertzog, all men of vision, boldness and determination. In the same way that the serious reverses of black week compelled the British to reappraise their strategy and tactics, so the occupation of their capitals and the subsequent annexations of the republics forced the Boer leaders to analyse the mistakes of the past and to formulate a fresh plan of campaign for the future. Experience had shown that it was senseless to permit manpower losses in set-piece defensive engagements. Furthermore, it was imperative for the Boers to regain the military initiative lost at the beginning of the year, to raise republican morale, and to inject a new sense of purpose into the commandos. The Boer leaders concluded that the emphasis of their campaign in future should be on a war of movement; authority would be decentralized and vested in local commanders operating in areas familiar to them, though overall strategy would be coordinated centrally. It was agreed, too, that as soon as practicable small groups of commandos should return to the Cape to extend further the British army's area of operations and to inspire a second Afrikaner rebellion in the colony. Botha took charge of the eastern Transvaal, De la Rey returned to the west. De Wet began preparations for a fresh invasion of the Cape by Free State commandos. A new stage of the conflict had begun, the guerrilla war, a protracted phase of operations, more ruthless and brutal than the phase of conventional warfare preceding it.

By regrouping their forces in small, mobile guerrilla units operating in familiar country and living off the land, the Boers were able to achieve remarkable success in evading capture, seizing British supplies, disrupting railway communications (135 train-wrecking incidents were recorded between December 1900 and September 1901), and inflicting sometimes quite startling casualties on the British army of occupation. The British high command was totally unprepared for this type of warfare, the army's intelligence gathering and scouting was weak, and far too few mounted men were available to combat the new Boer tactics effectively. The difficulties that confronted the British army were vividly described by Captain March Phillips in his book *With Rimington* (London, 1901, 123).

> 'As for our wandering columns, they have about as much chance of catching the Boers on the veldt as a Lord Mayor's procession would have of catching a highwayman on Hounslow Heath . . . [the Boers] are all around and about us like water round a ship, parting before our bows and reuniting round our stern. Our passage makes no impression and leaves no visible trace.'

It was largely under the direction of Lord Kitchener, who succeeded Roberts as Commander-in-Chief at the end of November 1900, that a coherent response to the Boers' methods was devised. Already before Roberts's departure, however, farm-burnings and the destruction of crops and livestock had been instituted in some districts, initially as reprisals against Boer attacks on communications, but soon used as a means of denying the commandos access to shelter, food, draught animals and fresh horses. In this way the British army sought to restrict the areas in which the guerrillas could operate. The suffering heaped upon the dependants of commando fighters by these brutal methods was also intended as an inducement to encourage men to surrender.

Under Kitchener's leadership during 1901 the British forces were divided into smaller, more mobile columns, each relying on accurate intelligence, often provided by African scouts, to track down the elusive commandos. A vast network of blockhouses connected by barbed-wire barricades was built, at first intended simply to defend the railways, but extended to divide the republics into large squares to be systematically cleared of supplies and the guerrilla groups within them. By the end of the war 8 000 blockhouses and 3 700 miles of barbed-wire barricades had been constructed. About 30 000 farmsteads were destroyed during the course of operations. Civilians, both white and black, were removed from the devastated countryside and interned in concentration camps, where a dreadful loss of life occurred. As many as 26 000 Boer women and children and 14 000 Africans perished in the over-crowded, insanitary and ill-organized camps (in November 1901 the white camps were transferred from military to civilian administration, and a remarkable decrease in the mortality rate afterwards took place). The idea of restricting the movements of guerrilla fighters by constructing fortified lines and sweeping the civilian inhabitants of entire districts into concentration camps had been tried earlier, with little success, by the Spanish in Cuba (similar tactics had been used by colonists against African opponents in South Africa as well). Moreover, in the guarded camps set up by Don Valeriana Weyler y Nicolau, the Spanish Captain General of Cuba, an appalling death rate had also occurred.

Kitchener's tactics were complemented by other measures. Captured burghers were deported to prisoner of war camps overseas, in St Helena, Bermuda, Ceylon and India. Severe penalties were introduced for those found guilty of assisting the commandos. Auxiliary forces, such as the National Scouts in the Transvaal and the Orange River Colony Volunteers, were raised from among surrendered burghers in order to improve British intelligence and to attempt to drive a wedge between those Afrikaners who believed further resistance was useless, the handsuppers (*hensoppers*), and those who remained in the field, the bitterenders (*bittereinders*).

Kitchener's methods were ruthless and draining on British manpower. He was unable – evidently sometimes unwilling – to curb the zeal of some of his units which indulged in excessive brutality and looting. The activities in the north-eastern Transvaal and Swaziland of one group of irregulars, Steinaecker's Horse, led by a flamboyant German mercenary, Colonel Steinaecker, drew protests from British officials who requested the corps's disbandment. Kitchener refused to entertain the suggestion, one of his officers remarking, 'No-one thinks S[teinaecker] an angel but he has his uses.'[6] More and more Kitchener relied on Africans to close their neighbourhoods to Boer activity, to provide intelligence of guerrilla movements, to participate in the destruction of farmsteads and crops, to round up the livestock of Afrikaner families and bring civilians into the concentration camps, and to guard the lines of blockhouses and wire barricades. Possibly as many as 30 000 armed Africans were engaged in duties with the British forces by the end of the war, though attempts were made to conceal the extent of African involvement in view of the tacit agreement by both sides at the beginning of the war that black people would be excluded from the fighting.

Patience and tact were qualities singularly lacking in Kitchener's make-up. His methods, and the resultant hardships suffered by Boer civilians, engendered a profound bitterness towards Britain among members of the Afrikaner community. The large-scale devastation of property in the republics made the imperial objective of achieving rapid reconstruction much more difficult. Kitchener's insistence on subordinating all other considerations to those of military expediency strained almost to breaking point his relationship with the High Commissioner. Milner first moved to Johannesburg in February 1901, and following a visit to Britain to consult with Chamberlain (during which he was raised to the peerage), he returned to the Transvaal in August to begin arrangements for the reconstruction of the annexed colonies once peace had been achieved. Milner had described as 'barbarous' the army's methods of dealing with the guerrillas as early as October 1900. He became deeply concerned about the extensive devastation wrought in the republics, angered by the Commander-in-Chief's unwillingness to allow the railways to be used for transporting supplies and materials to the Transvaal that would be needed when the war was over, and exasperated by Kitchener's reluctance to permit sufficient civilian personnel to return to Johannesburg to resume gold mining operations on a meaningful scale. By September 1901 Milner was pressing Chamberlain for Kitchener's replacement: 'I am sure we shall get on better without him, not because anyone else will conduct the war better, but because someone else *may*, if put in on that distinct understanding, obstruct the work of reconstruction less.'[7]

Kitchener's methods caused considerable embarrassment to the Unionist government in Britain, which had won a resounding victory at the polls in the 'khaki election' of October 1900. The appalling conditions in the concentration camps, first drawn attention to by Emily Hobhouse, who visited South Africa in January 1901 on behalf of a voluntary organization, the South African Women and Children Distress Fund, brought adverse publicity both at home and abroad. The tedious prolongation of operations dampened the enthusiasm for the war that had been evident during the first year of military activity. There were few victories to celebrate yet still heavy casualties to mourn (in all Britain lost 22 000 men, of whom two-thirds died from disease). Members of the pro-Boer movement in Britain, who had found little support during the early months of the war, grew in confidence and were generally able to hold orderly anti-war meetings without fear of these being broken up by crowd violence. The Liberal Opposition too became more confident and strident in its criticism of government policy, being able to take the Unionists to task over the excessive ruthlessness and unnecessary prolongation of the South African campaign. Though still deeply divided over the merits of the war, the rifts in the Liberal Party became less obvious once the conduct of the campaign became the main target of criticism by Members of Parliament. The pro-Boer and Campbell-Bannerman factions of the party came together to condemn Kitchener's scorched earth tactics, which Campbell-Bannerman described in a famous speech in the House of Commons as amounting to 'methods of barbarism' (unwittingly echoing Milner's privately-expressed description of army policy eight months before[8]). Lloyd George, a vigorous opponent of the war, accused ministers of pursuing 'a policy of extermination against children in South Africa', and, continuing in characteristically emotive fashion, he likened the government's policy to that of Herod, who had also 'attempted to crush a little race by killing its young sons and daughters'.[9]

Added to the problems of the government and the army was the irritation of renewed Boer guerrilla activity in the Cape Colony. On 16 December 1900 – Dingane's Day, the date commemorating the Voortrekkers' victory over Dingane's Zulu at the Battle of Blood River in 1838 – 1 700 Boer commandos led by Hertzog and P. H. Kritzinger entered the Cape. Fourteen districts were almost immediately placed under martial law once again, and by the end of January 1901 martial law had been extended to the whole of the colony with the exceptions of the seaports and the Transkei. The Cape remained a theatre of Boer operations until the end of the war. Subsequent invasions of the colony were launched by De Wet, briefly, in February, by Van Reenen in April, and by Smuts in September; smaller groups of burghers and rebels operated independently in the Cape throughout almost the whole of 1901 and the early months of 1902. Already by the middle of 1901 much of the north-west Cape had fallen into republican hands, and later Boer operations extended throughout almost all the colony's most westerly districts. Though the scale of Boer activity was never allowed to get too much out of hand, the sporadic warfare, and the incitement to rebellion caused by the presence of republican guerrilla groups in the colony, remained to the last a thorn in the side of the British army, and led to strained relations between the military and the Sprigg government.

In the interests of maintaining cordial relations with the Afrikaner community in the Cape, the Sprigg administration persistently urged that martial law restriction be relaxed and that the government be given greater control over the activities of the armed forces in the colony. In particular a long-running quarrel developed over cases of excessive zeal on the part of military officers between Major-General A. S. Wynne, commanding the western Cape, and James Rose Innes, Sprigg's Attorney-General. Disputes arose over the arbitrary internment of suspected republican sympathizers and numerous other instances of injustice towards individuals. The military were especially hostile towards those who remained vociferous in their opposition to the war. John X. Merriman, the South African Party politician, former member of Schreiner's cabinet and a leading proponent of Anglo-Boer conciliation, was confined to his home in Stellenbosch by military orders. The editors of the newspapers *Ons Land* and *South African News* were imprisoned, accused of publishing seditious libel, and the publication of the African newspaper *Imvo Zabantsundu* was suspended by the army on account of the pro-Boer sympathies of its editor, John Tengo Jabavu. The military generally, and Kitchener in particular, remained insensitive to the difficulties faced by those with responsibility for civilian government. Kitchener pressed for the extension of martial law to the seaports, suspecting arms were reaching the commandos through them; the Sprigg government was eventually persuaded to agree to this on condition that civilians were given a greater role in its enforcement. The Commander-in-Chief later ordered the prohibition of cereal farming over a wide area of the colony on the grounds that crops sooner or later found their way to the invading forces and their rebel allies, an order that deeply dismayed the government because of the hardships it generated.

Kitchener's action placed considerable stress on the Sprigg government. On the one hand ministers were liable to lose whatever support they retained among Cape Afrikaners by agreeing to stern and oppressive measures at the behest of the army; on the other hand, by wishing to moderate the policies of the military and thereby appearing to obstruct the effective prosecution of the war, ministers were in danger of further estranging themselves from the loyalists, represented politically by Jameson's Progressive Party. The Progressives were soon campaigning for the suspension of the Cape constitution and the restoration of direct imperial rule to ensure that no further difficulties were placed in the way of dealing effectively with the guerrilla war and rebellion in the colony.

In June 1900 the Boer leadership had been informed that the British government was prepared to accept nothing less than 'unconditional surrender' as a means of ending the war. The formula was first suggested by Milner, and approved by Chamberlain and Lord Salisbury. Nonetheless, on his own initiative, Kitchener opened peace negotiations with Botha in February 1901, using Botha's wife, Annie, as an intermediary. The two men met at the end of the month in Middelburg in the eastern Transvaal, Kitchener presenting for the consideration of the republican governments draft peace terms approved by Milner and ministers in London. In return for the surrender of the Boers' independence, the British government was prepared to give financial assistance to rebuild and restock farms, guarantee private property, the property of the churches and the funds of public trusts, and to postpone any moves towards the enfranchisement of black people until after the introduction of representative government in the annexed colonies (to be achieved 'as soon as possible' after the peace). Kitchener, anxious to end the war at almost any cost, was disappointed by the terms and pressed for improvements. In particular he wanted representative government to be introduced almost at once, and a full amnesty granted to all rebels (with disfranchisement as the only form of punishment). Milner and Chamberlain were unwilling to agree to Kitchener's suggestions, and the British terms were subsequently rejected. Kitchener blamed Milner's intransigence on the amnesty question for the breakdown of talks.

> 'Milner's views may be strictly just, but to my mind they are vindictive, and I do not know of any case in history where, under similar circumstances, an amnesty has not been granted.
>
> 'We are now carrying on a war to be able to put 2–3 000 Dutchmen in prison at the end of it. It seems to me absurd, and I wonder the Chancellor of the Exchequer did not have a fit.'[10]

In reality the negotiations never stood any chance of success. The British government would under no circumstances agree to the republics retaining their independence, and the Boers were not yet prepared to accept anything less. Indeed, President Steyn and many Free Staters were angered by Botha's willingness to meet Kitchener in the first place. In June 1901 the governments of the two republics met at Waterval, and after consulting President Kruger in Europe with Kitchener's consent, they resolved that 'No peace conditions will be accepted by which our independence and national existence or the interests of our Colonial brothers shall be the price paid.'

During the first half of 1901 Kitchener's counter-insurgency tactics met with only limited military success. Some of the areas of 'reconstruction under arms', the heavily defended districts set up to provide security for surrendered burghers, were so seriously denuded of British troops that the commandos were able to move back into them and seize supplies almost with impunity. No major guerrilla leader was apprehended in the republics during 1901, the Boer forces simply scattering more widely to evade the British columns. Acting President Schalk Burger and President Steyn remained in the field until the end of the war. By the close of the South African summer of 1901–2, however, the effective area of Boer operations had become dangerously restricted, supplies were becoming difficult to obtain without these being seized from African peasants (relations between the guerrilla fighters and many African communities were already strained in a number of districts), and the commando leaders, even the skilful De Wet, were finding great difficulty in crossing the heavily defended British lines. In January 1902 General Ben Viljoen was captured. Because of a scarcity of horses it was impossible to extend intensive Boer operations in the Cape beyond the far western districts of the colony. On 7 March 1902, in a spectacular manoeuvre, De la Rey succeeded in capturing Lord Methuen and 600 men at Tweebosch, but the victory was of little consequence; indeed, it only served to underline the problems that beset the remaining guerrilla fighters, for it was impossible for them to take prisoners, and though some burghers pressed for Methuen to be taken hostage for the release of a Boer prisoner of similar rank, De la Rey arranged for his captives and their seriously wounded commander to be returned to the nearest British base. In the following month the republican governments met at Klerksdorp and agreed to open peace talks with Kitchener and Milner, talks that ultimately led to the surrender of Boer independence and the signing of peace on 31 May 1902.

References

1. *Daily Mail*, 23 October 1899, quoted by Byron Farwell, *The Great Boer War*, London, 1977, 55.
2. W. S. Blunt, *My Diaries*, quoted by Farwell, 54.
3. Sir Arthur Conan Doyle, *The Great Boer War*, London, 1900, 197.
4. Quoted by G. H. L. Le May, *British Supremacy in South Africa, 1899–1907*, Oxford, 1965, 45.
5. See T. R. H. Davenport, *The Afrikaner Bond, The History of a South African Political Party, 1880–1911*, Cape Town, 1966, 210–35.
6. Public Record Office, London, CO 291/27/4357 sub in encl. 1, Major W. Congreve to Johannes Smuts, 1 January 1901.
7. Quoted by Le May, 122.
8. *Ibid.*, 90.
9. Quoted by P. Magnus, *Kitchener, Portrait of an Imperialist*, London, 1968, 219.
10. *Ibid.*, 225.

CHAPTER 3

Military Aspects of The War

Howard Bailes

When news reached Britain on 30 October 1899 of Sir George White's defeat at Lombard's Kop and the imminent investment of Ladysmith, there was a sense of *déjà vu* among military commentators. The conflict was following the pattern so often seen in Britain's nineteenth-century wars; an initial reverse succeeded by retribution (as during the Indian Mutiny in 1857 and the Zulu War in 1879) or, less frequently, defeat followed by a settlement humiliating to the imperial power (such as at Majuba and the subsequent peace with the Boers in 1881). This time, however, the expeditionary force itself suffered a series of defeats unparalleled in Victorian campaigning, reverses 'which made the blood run cold in the veins of every patriotic Englishman'.[1] The era of Gladstonian liberalism had passed, and the national shock and indignation aroused by the military disasters of 'black week' in December 1899 helped to ensure the prosecution of the war on a scale to which the imperial policing of Victoria's reign appeared almost insignificant. This shift in scale was the crucial military problem faced by the British army throughout the South African War.

Victorian army reform

Army reform in Victorian Britain had been a long and complex process. Its origins lay in the pre-Crimean period, decades before the profound changes of Edward Cardwell's era (1868–74) – the abolition of purchase, the introduction of short-service, and the reconstitution of the War Office. Reforms during the 1880s and 1890s had been of lesser scope but equally pervasive, a leaven working at every level from the War Office to the rank and file. While some reforms were ill-considered, and many were inadequate, it makes little sense to call the British army in 1899 unreformed. Training had been undergoing significant alterations. Army services had been rationalized and lines of responsibility clearly drawn, as the creation of the Pay, Service, Ordnance and Medical Corps indicated. By 1886, for the first time, Britain possessed a standing mobilization scheme that worked superbly when put to the test. Military efficiency, however, has meaning only within a particular historical context. Almost every organizational reform of the late Victorian period had been geared to the policy summarized in a memorandum of 1888 written by the then Secretary of State for War, Edward Stanhope. This statement laid down that the army should be capable of dispatching only two corps for overseas service, after the calling out of the Reserve.[2] The

Stanhope Memorandum has often been criticized for putting economy before efficiency, and this stricture is certainly valid. Nonetheless, such a policy was true to the nature of Britain's nineteenth-century military experience, which comprised chiefly punitive expeditions within her own empire. Moreover, in the political circumstances of the time, it is difficult to conceive of any War Secretary winning parliamentary consent for a major increase in the establishments. Almost unavoidably, every section of Britain's military infrastructure underwent the strain of expansion to a degree for which there was no existing machinery or preparation.

Staff training and organization

The requirements of small wars also had implications for staff training and organization. Victorian military theorists had paid some attention to the 'higher combinations of war', but their approach tended to be abstract and academic. Lord Wolseley had always attempted to form an orderly system of staff delegation in his wars, and by the 1890s it had become normal to appoint, for active service, directors of railways and transport and commanding generals of communications. But campaigns were limited in size and duration, and large-scale manoeuvres occurred only four times in the late nineteenth century (1871, 1872, 1873, 1898). The handling of large bodies of troops was foreign to the practical experience of most British generals, and no uniform system existed for the transmission of information between a commander and his subordinates. Moreover, Lord Kitchener's Sudanese campaigns of 1896–8 had revealed and nourished his constitutional propensity to dispense with such staff organization as had been developed over the preceding years. At War Office level, the absence of a General Staff for contingency planning, a body possessed by every other European Great Power, meant that the information gathered by the Intelligence Department before the war could not be usefully deployed. Within the confines of their resources, Sir John Ardagh, Director of Military Intelligence, and his colleagues at Queen Anne's Gate had performed their duties impeccably.[3] But the gleaners of vital information were an unimportant adjunct to regular administration, and planning for the future was impaired accordingly. As Spenser Wilkinson, first Chichele Professor of War in the University of Oxford, sardonically remarked after Britain's defeats in South Africa:

> 'It is as though a man kept a small brain for occasional consultation in his waistcoat pocket, and ran his head by clockwork.'[4]

For the inadequacy of maps available at the outbreak of war there were only contemporary circumstances to blame. It was estimated that to have provided a large-scale map of the theatre of war at all suitable for military purposes would have required a grant of £100 000 and several years of survey work. As Major E. H. Hills, in charge of mapping in 1902, pointed out to the Royal Commission headed by Lord Elgin that conducted a general enquiry into the war, not only was the money unavailable but, in the explosive situation of the late 1890s, it would have been a political impossibility to essay such a task.[5] That no individuals had been culpably negligent, however, was small solace to commanders obliged to commence operations with scanty or misleading cartographical guidance. By October 1899 the only maps available of any military worth were a dozen of South Africa, hastily compiled by the Intelligence Department earlier in the year, and a few available copies of a survey of the Transvaal produced by the government of the South African Republic.

Including available reservists, the British army in October 1899 numbered some 320 000. Of these, including reinforcements hesitantly dispatched in September, only 20 000 were stationed in South Africa. By the end of 1900 nearly 250 000 troops had been sent there, and by the close of the war the grand total of British forces used in South Africa exceeded 400 000. The inadequacy of the Stanhope policy, from the purely numerical point of view, was patently obvious. Even by providing about 60 000 more troops for overseas service than it had been officially required to do, the Regular army made up only three-fifths of the forces employed in South Africa.[6] Nevertheless, this achievement itself was a final vindication of short-service. On 7 October 1899 only 1·63 per cent of the Reserve failed to answer the order for general mobilization.[7]

New technology

In some respects the South African War was one of marked contrasts. Its earlier engagements adumbrated the prolonged battles and massive casualties of the First World War, while the later stages were those of a purely imperial war of pacification (though with similarities to modern guerrilla warfare). Alfred Mahan, the American naval theorist, could regard it as an interesting anomaly in the development of military science. To Jean de Bloch, prophet of the Western Front, the conflict embodied the essence of modern warfare.[8] Technologically, the war was a combination of disparate elements. Oxen, horses and mules remained a substantial and vital part of the lines of communication. But the railway network guided strategy to an extent unknown in Victorian campaigning, while steam traction engines, hitherto used only experimentally, made a novel and significant addition to military transport. By the end of the century the tactical use of telegraphy was a practised art, but telephony in active operations was untried. Towards the close of the war every second or third blockhouse had been provided with a telephone, while throughout the campaign telegraphs were used on a vast scale; over thirteen million transactions were recorded on 27 000 miles of main line and cable.[9] Searchlights dramatically symbolized the new technology. Electrical illumination was used to protect depots and hospitals, and the Kimberley garrison used five great lights, belonging to the De Beers Company, to protect the perimeters of the town's defences. In weaponry, the British were on a par with other European powers. The artillery's chief arms were the 12- and 15-pounder breech-loaders; only a handful of quick-firers and

Ox-drawn carts and waggons remained an essential component of the military transport system in South Africa, though the railway network guided strategy to an extent hitherto unknown in campaigns during the Victorian period.

Steam traction engines were used for purposes of military transport for the first time during the war.

New technology extended to the use of steam ploughs for digging entrenchments, though most earthworks were still dug by manual labour.

heavy ordnance were used. Although the infantry's training had recently undergone a myriad of small improvements, it was still far from commensurate with the power of the weapons they carried, .303 inch magazine Lee-Metfords. Cavalry took the field with carbines, sabres and, if in the lancer regiments, with lances as well. Later in the war they often abandoned the arme blanche and replaced the carbine with the rifle.

Boer military system

Boer styles of warfare exercised a peculiar fascination over British military commentators. Many, especially civilians not forced to grapple with it, wrote rhapsodically of their enemy's prowess. The mounted rifleman, his resource and native sagacity untrammelled by a complex organization, had the universal appeal of the partisan:

> 'What men they were, these Boers! . . . . thousands of independent riflemen, thinking for themselves, possessed of beautiful weapons, led with skill, living as they rode without commissariat or transport or ammunition column, moving like the wind. . . .'[10]

The Afrikaner states formed the purest kind of the nation-in-arms. Regular forces consisted solely of about 600 Staats Artillerie and 1 400 state police (Zuid-Afrikaansche Republiek Politie: ZARP) in the Transvaal, and less than 400 artillery troops in the Orange Free State. Between them, the two governments possessed seventy-five guns. All other military resources were drawn from the civilian population. Each district, subdivided into two to four field-cornetcies, elected a Commandant upon the declaration of war, popularity and family connections weighing more heavily than military ability in gaining votes. Central food depots were established for durable items such as sugar and coffee, and maize flour and cattle on the hoof were the main sources of provisions.[11]

A nation-in-arms. Boer fighters in the Transvaal assemble at the beginning of the war.

The defects of the Boer military system were the complement of its virtues. Personal initiative and the paramountcy of the small group were admirably suited to scattered forces fighting in their native terrain, but strategy suffered accordingly. That military authority should rest upon persuasion befitted an army whose leaders and led were of similar (though by no means identical) social standing, but it often caused paralysis when resolute action was needed. Lack of coordination among their leaders were one reason for the Boers' failure to exploit their first successes, despite their initial superiority in numbers. Recent research has shown that the republics had about 55 000 men available for military service in October 1899, of whom between 32 000 and 35 000 were mobilized at the outbreak of war.[12] In quality of armament the Boers yielded to none. Gunnery counted for little in their tactics, but their artillery was of the latest design, and the Mauser .276 was the finest infantry arm in existence. Quantities of rifles and ammunition were not only ample but excessive for Boer requirements; the surplus was intended for use by Afrikaner rebels in the Cape Colony.

Boer strategy

For it was the great Afrikaner hope, at the onset of war, to overwhelm White's garrison in north-western Natal and simultaneously to advance into the Cape Colony, rousing it to rebellion. If successful, this grand dual sweep would secure the ports of Durban and Cape Town and the nerve centres of the railway network – Vryburg, Kimberley and Ladysmith. The Boer governments could then expect a negotiated peace.

The Free State artillery assembled at Kroonstad in preparation for war. The Boers' armaments were of the latest design, and in some categories their weapons were of superior quality to those possessed by the British army.

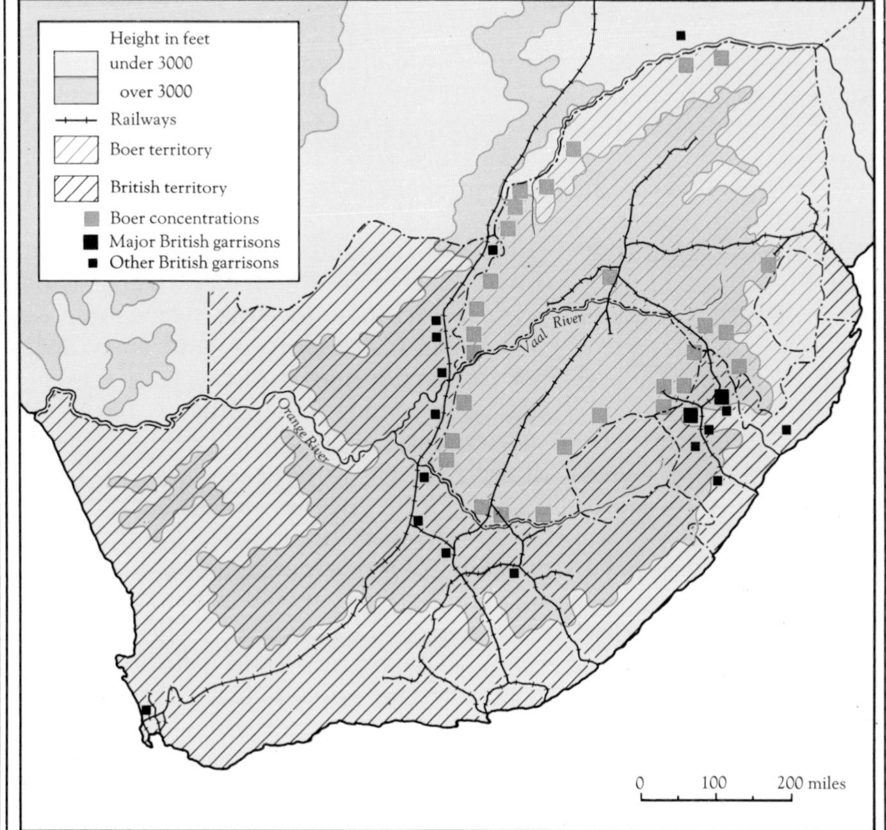

Strategic dispositions 11 October 1899

The republican forces were optimistic:

> 'There was not a man who did not believe that we were heading straight for the coast, and it was as well that the future was hidden from us, and that we did not know how strength and enthusiasm were to be frittered away in a meaningless siege. . . .'[13]

By coalescing around Mafeking, Kimberley and Ladysmith, the Boers lost their best opportunity of avoiding ultimate defeat.

Outbreak of war

When Kruger's ultimatum expired on 11 October the only major British concentration in South Africa was under White's command at Ladysmith. He was widely criticized at the time, by his countrymen as well as by foreigners, for not drawing his forces south of the Tugela River and abandoning the town altogether. There were, however, sound reasons for his stand. It was as impracticable to contemplate stemming the invasion along the Tugela as it was at the defenceless borders of the vast salient thrust into enemy territory that formed the apex of Natal. At that season the river was sufficiently low for it to be passable on foot, and it was impossible for White to distribute his forces along the entire 80 miles between the Drakensberg heights and the Buffalo River so as to prevent a crossing. Moreover, not only was Ladysmith a significant railway junction, but it possessed psychological importance as the chief town of northern Natal. As such, it was a magnet to Commandant-General Joubert's forces. Less intelligent was White's retention of an advanced detachment at Dundee, but in this matter he was constrained by the urgent appeals of Sir Walter Hely-Hutchinson, the Governor of Natal, whose natural wish was to have the reassuring presence of British troops as far north as possible. In this he was supported by Major-General Sir William Penn-Symons, in command at Dundee.

Talana Hill, 20 October 1899

By the time that White had decided his course of action, the Boer lines of invasion had clearly emerged. Westwards they moved into Bechuanaland and Griqualand, southwards across the Orange River towards central Cape Colony, and eastwards into the apex of Natal. Piet Joubert, a man 'unfit to lead armies' according to Deneys Reitz,[14] commanded the bulk of the Natal invasion. Encamped in a depression crowned by the Talana heights, Penn-Symons' little force of some 4 000 was an ideal target. Fully aware of Joubert's converging movements, Penn-Symons made no attempt to entrench his troops, confident in their inherent superiority over Boer riflemen. At the cold hour before dawn on 20 October the British camp was roused by the sight of Boers lining the eminence 500 feet above the plain. A hasty rally, and deployment of every gun and rifle available, enabled the British to hold off the enemy and to retreat to Ladysmith, carrying with them their dying general, shot through the stomach. This encounter bore in miniature some of the features of the early British disasters; an unwise and even reckless choice of positions, scanty defensive preparations, and over-reliance upon the stolid bravery of the British infantry. Though Talana was technically a victory for the defenders, the casualty figures told the truth; while Boer losses were about 140, British casualties were 500, 12 per cent of the force engaged.[15]

Almost simultaneously, the model battle of Elandslaagte, fought to the north-east of Ladysmith, momentarily removed the second threat to White's force. J. H. Kock was hovering in the vicinity of the town, and White dispatched Major-General John French to stall the projected offensive. The battle's execution, however, was in the hands of one of the army's most advanced tacticians, Colonel Ian Hamilton. Against a chiaroscuro of storm-clouds, lightning and the haze of the setting sun, his Devonshires moved in a vastly extended formation across

Below: General P. J. Joubert and his staff photographed at Newcastle in northern Natal, 17 October 1899. Joubert was 68 years old at the outbreak of war, and his cautious and unimaginative conduct of the war was criticized by younger commanders and led Deneys Reitz to describe him as a man 'unfit to lead armies'.

Bottom: the arrival of Boer transport at Elandslaagte.

Elandslaagte, 21 October 1899

the level veld towards the Boer position, entrenched among the ridges and kopjes south of Elandslaagte Station. Once within 1 200 yards, the Devonshires held the enemy by rifle fire while the remainder of the brigade crept around their left flank. At dusk and in pouring rain the supporting infantry closed on the kopjes, the Devonshires charged as the Boers began to vacate their trenches, and the cavalry closed the engagement in dramatic style by galloping from the station and riding down the fleeing burghers with sabre and lance. Undoubtedly, Elandslaagte was a tactical masterpiece. It did, however, encourage the supposition that entrenchments could always be carried by skilful tactics and good artillery preparation. Moreover, losses were not inconsiderable – about 8 per cent of the British force engaged, in three hours of fighting.[16] Strategically, the effect of the battle was nullified by the withdrawal to Ladysmith.

Lombard's Kop, 30 October 1899

The humiliating battle of Lombard's Kop formed the last episode leading to the final investment of the town. In a grand attempt to shatter the cordon closing around him, White conceived a plan, extraordinarily ambitious against an enemy as numerous as his own force, of outflanking the Boers' left and capturing them within a crescent potentially some eight miles in extent. Misjudging the Boer dispositions, White sent his troops turning within, instead of around, the curve of the enemy position. Furthermore, a detachment of some 1 000 men, dispatched to Nicholson's Nek in order to guard the British left, was itself surprised into precipitate surrender in the afternoon of 30 October, 'Mournful Monday'. Sir George White's cup of bitterness was filled to the brim, and his name became equated with 'an unsullied ignorance of the conditions of South African warfare'.[17] Unjust this may have been, but Lombard's Kop exemplified both the inexperience of British commanders in strategic coordination and their faith in the single decisive battle. The failure to establish the extent of the Boer left was illustrative of the poverty of British reconnaissance and intelligence, which was to last well into the following year.

Buller's strategy

Towards the end of November the tide of invasion slackened, and in Natal and the Cape Colony the Boers were turning on the defensive. Hopes of a large-scale rising in the Cape had proved illusory. Before the war the British Cabinet had endorsed a vague plan of a direct advance to be mounted by the expeditionary force through the Free State to Bloemfontein, White's intended role being to stem the Natal invasion until the western movements should relieve him of its pressure. His manifest inability to protect Natal changed the whole complexion of affairs. General Sir Redvers Buller, commanding the forces in South Africa, arrived at Cape Town on 31 October, and during the next ten days resolved upon an alternative strategy. Lieutenant-General Lord Methuen was to advance along the western railway, relieve Kimberley, and return immediately to clear the northern districts of the Free State. French and Lieutenant-General Sir William Gatacre were to hamper the Boer invasion of the Cape Colony, the former to

Opposite: British prisoners of war captured during the early engagements in Natal, October 1899.

operate in the Colesberg district and the latter to cover the route to East London. Buller took upon himself the onerous task of clearing Natal.[18] The offensive powers of Methuen's force of 20 000 men were grossly over-estimated, but otherwise little was intrinsically misguided in Buller's strategy.

In the execution of his scheme, however, Buller was completely out of his depth, a brave tactician and capable administrator placed in a command far beyond his abilities. The mainsprings of his erratic behaviour and apparent paralysis during the Natal campaign have prompted some remarkable speculations.[19] Perhaps, however, the explanation lies simply in what Buller himself freely admitted and indeed pleaded when his appointment was discussed; that he would make a capable chief subordinate but not a 'good first man'.[20] At all events, he approached his task in a profoundly unimaginative spirit.[21]

The outcome in the Cape Colony of Buller's tripartite strategy was the least complicated and may be considered first. French strove to limit the Boer incursions into the Colesberg district for three exhausting months. Rarely endangering his troops (two cavalry brigades and divisional attachments) he conducted reconnaissances in force rather than direct engagements.

Members of General French's force in the Colesberg district sleeping beside their weapons.

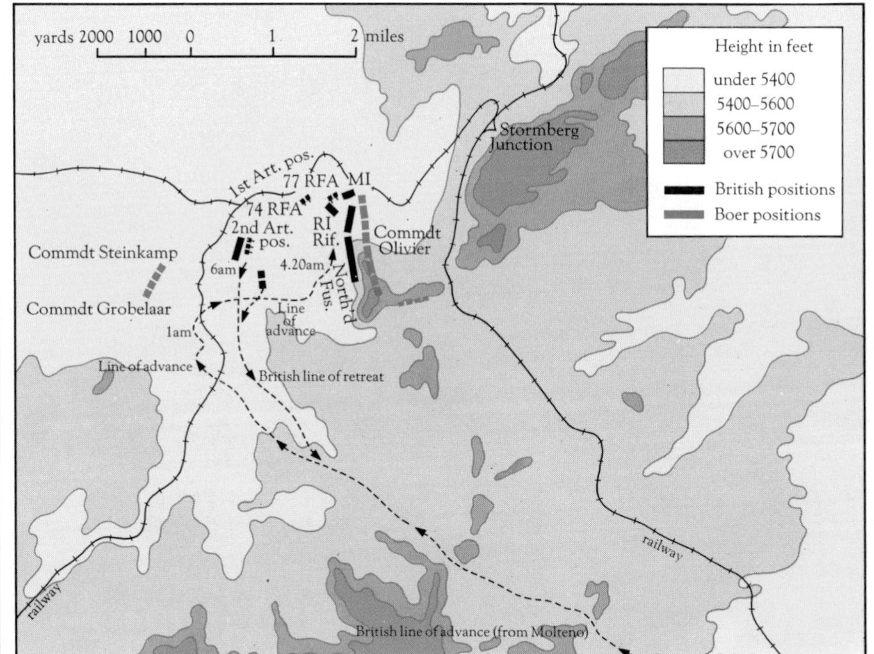

STORMBERG
10 DECEMBER 1899

Key to abbreviations

North'd Fus
Northumberland Fusiliers

RI Rif
Royal Irish Rifles

RFA
Royal Field Artillery

Stormberg, 10 December 1899

By contrast, Gatacre's operations opened with the first of the three black week disasters. Anxious to draw small detachments out of danger, White had ordered the evacuation of Stormberg junction in October. Free Staters occupied the little town on 22 November, six days after Gatacre had established headquarters at East London. Fearful of widespread disaffection in the Cape, he had every reason for striking an immediate blow to establish British prestige in his area. Within this, Stormberg was the only significant enemy position. Gatacre planned an attack in the classic manner employed by Wolseley with such success at Tel-el-Kebir in 1882: a night march followed by a dawn assault. Even with immaculate preparations Wolseley's strategem had almost miscarried, and Gatacre's was marked by confusion at every stage. At the last moment he decided to move in a westerly direction, rather than to march directly upon the town. In a typical instance of the lack of coordination in British strategy, the officer commanding the Molteno garrison was not aware of this change of direction. After a delayed and exhausting train journey from Putter's Kraal to Molteno, the troops began their eight-mile march to Stormberg. Day was dawning as the footsore men reached Stormberg valley, yet not a scout was sent ahead. Defeat was almost certain. The British walked directly into Boer rifle-fire, were caught against the central kopje of the enemy position, and within minutes were scattering back to the plain. In brief, Stormberg was a simple advance and recoil, but one so confused that nearly 600 men were left behind to be taken prisoner. Thereafter, until he joined the main army after Roberts's occupation of Bloemfontein, Gatacre held his own around Queenstown, his task rendered much easier than it might have been by the Boers' passive stance in the environs of Stormberg.

Methuen's forces storming a kopje at Graspan, 25 November 1899. Although technically a British victory, little was achieved by the engagement, De la Rey merely removing his forces further up the railway towards Magersfontein.

Belmont and Graspan 23, 25 November 1899

The beginning of Methuen's advance on the western flank was heralded with two victories, similar in nature: the retreat of the Boers from Belmont on 23 November, and from Graspan two days later. Little was achieved by these victories, however, except to shift dispositions further up the railway. Casualties were not severe, but were alarmingly concentrated in certain units. Half the losses of Belmont were borne by the Grenadier Guards when they were caught in cross-fire for a few minutes. Nonetheless, these engagements seemed to demonstrate the efficacy of the traditional one-day battle. Methuen, therefore, attempted no course other than to hold closely to the railway, moving straight into the Boers gathered at their strongest points. But for the next encounter, his chief opponent, General de la Rey, resolved upon an ingenious shift in tactics. Rather than concentrating upon outstanding kopjes, which gave cover to assaulting troops in the 'dead' ground at their base and were exposed to artillery fire, he entrenched his 3 000 burghers along the banks of the Riet, east and west of Modder River bridge.

Modder River, 28 November 1899

Like so many of such ruses – often no more than an application of mother-wit and familiarity with the local terrain – this strategy was an eminent success. Willows and mimosa bushes fringing the lower bank provided useful cover, while the gentle rise of the exposed veld southwards formed a potential death-trap to those approaching. It was saved from being so only by the Boers' slightly premature release of grazing fire as the British walked into their ambush. A few infantry on the left managed to cross the shallow river; otherwise, throughout the day and night of 28 November, the British simply clung to such cover as was available and attempted to return the fire. Their position on the Riet was of no strategical significance to the Boers, and they abandoned it in the grey light of morning.

De la Rey had sought only to damage the advancing army, and this aim had been achieved; 500 of the 10 000 British engaged were killed or wounded.[22]

Magersfontein, 11 December 1899

After Modder River the Boers were heavily reinforced, chiefly by General Piet Cronjé's burghers from Fauresmith, and they entrenched themselves afresh around Magersfontein Mountain. The ensuing battle was a grimmer version of Modder River. Considering no strategic diversions, Methuen adhered strictly to the railway. Rather than holding the heights, the Boers lay along their base in deep, narrow trenches. Again Methuen relied upon a night march and a dawn assault to carry the enemy position. The battle was distinguished, however, by the dispersal of the attackers into uncoordinated groups, each of which stalled or advanced according to local circumstances and initiatives. This aspect of the modern battlefield, remarked upon by military writers since the Austro-Prussian War of 1866, was a phenomenon of which the British in 1899 had little direct knowledge. Magersfontein was their first major introduction to conditions hitherto discussed rather than experienced, and its chief shock fell upon the Highland Brigade. Entrusted with the task of storming the mountain, the Highlanders began their march in the early hours of 10 December. Just as they were about to change their serried ranks to fighting formation, an explosion of magazine fire from the mountain foot revealed that yet another trap had been sprung.

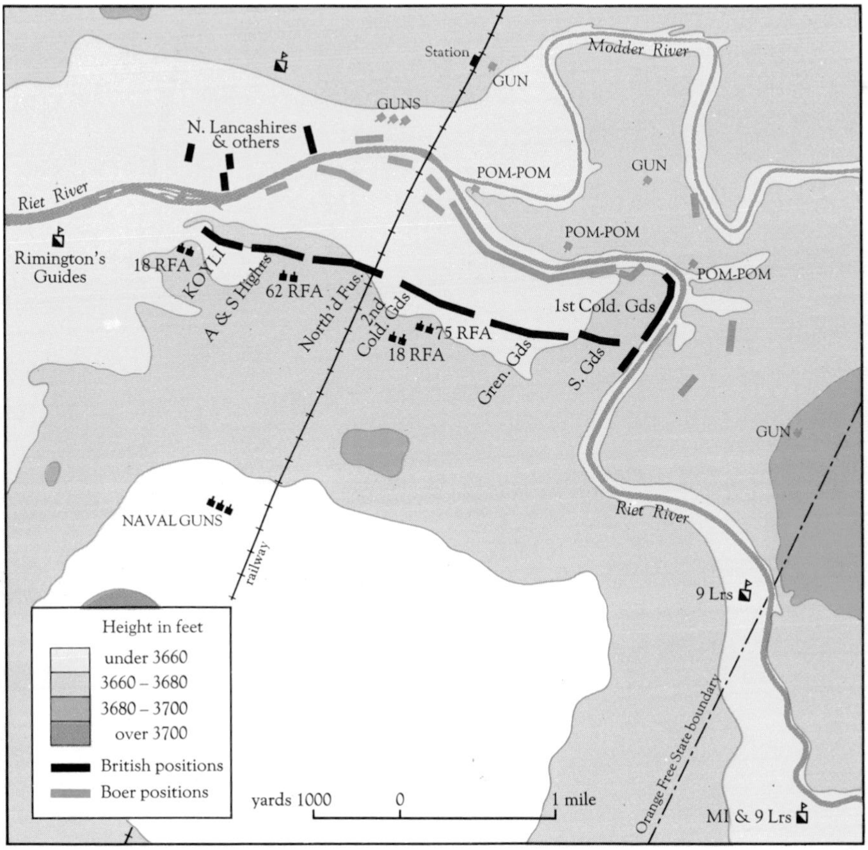

MODDER RIVER
28 NOVEMBER 1899

Key to abbreviations

N. Lancashires
North Lancashires

A & S Highrs
Argyll and Sutherland Highlanders

North'd Fus
Northumberland Fusiliers

Cold. Gds
Coldstream Guards

KOYLI
King's Own Yorkshire Light Infantry

RFA
Royal Field Artillery

Lrs
Lancers

MI
Mounted Infantry

Gren Gds
Grenadier Guards

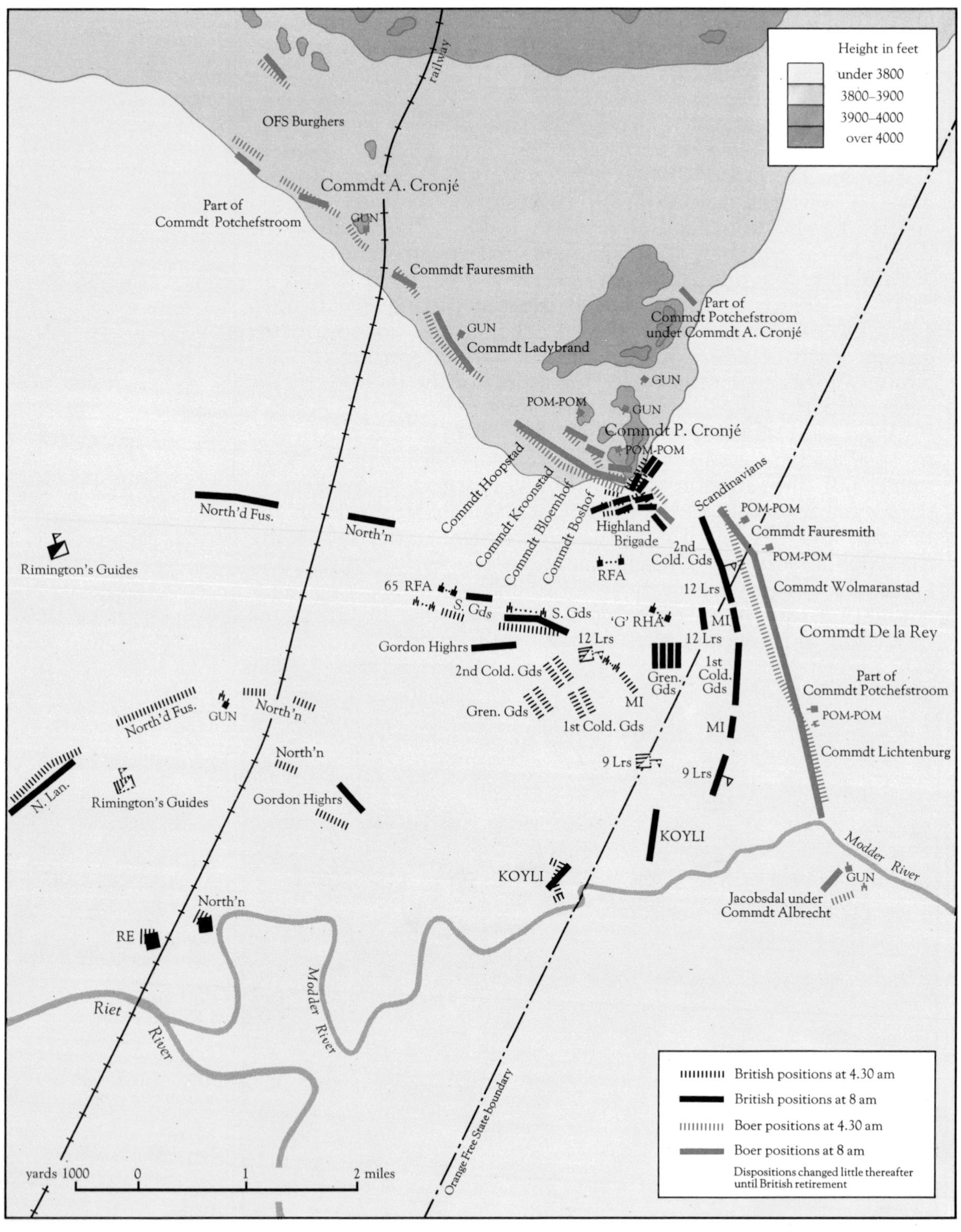
Height in feet
under 3800
3800–3900
3900–4000
over 4000
railway
OFS Burghers
Commdt A. Cronjé
Part of
Commdt Potchefstroom
GUN
Commdt Fauresmith
GUN
Commdt Ladybrand
Part of
Commdt Potchefstroom
under Commdt A. Cronjé
GUN
POM-POM
GUN
Commdt P. Cronjé
POM-POM
Commdt Hoopstad
Commdt Kroonstad
Commdt Bloemhof
Commdt Boshof
Scandinavians
POM-POM
Commdt Fauresmith
POM-POM
Commdt Wolmaranstad
Commdt De la Rey
Part of
Commdt Potchefstroom
POM-POM
Commdt Lichtenburg
North'd Fus.
North'n
Rimington's Guides
Highland
Brigade
2nd
Cold. Gds
RFA
65 RFA
S. Gds
S. Gds
12 Lrs
'G' RHA
MI
12 Lrs
12 Lrs
Gordon Highrs
2nd Cold. Gds
Gren. Gds
1st Cold. Gds
Gren. Gds
MI
1st Cold. Gds
MI
North'd Fus.
GUN
North'n
North'n
N. Lan.
Rimington's Guides
Gordon Highrs
9 Lrs
9 Lrs
KOYLI
KOYLI
Modder River
GUN
Jacobsdal under
Commdt Albrecht
North'n
RE
Riet River
Modder River
Orange Free State boundary
yards 1000 0 1 2 miles
British positions at 4.30 am
British positions at 8 am
Boer positions at 4.30 am
Boer positions at 8 am
Dispositions changed little thereafter
until British retirement

An eighteen-centimetre gun, nicknamed 'Joe Chamberlain', in action with Methuen's force at Magersfontein. The British assault on the Boer position was executed with considerable misunderstanding, the artillery in the rear shelling not only the Boer entrenchments but also British troops at the base of Magersfontein Mountain. The British forces suffered almost a thousand casualties.

The Highlanders had not intended to attack in quarter column; contrary to what many popular historians have written, close formations for assault had been officially forbidden in the British army since the 1880s, and extended formations had become normal in training. Caught by surprise in the act of deployment, however, the brigade lost all semblance of direction. The majority huddled at the base of Magersfontein; a few struggled up its shoulders. Believing that the entire brigade lay at the mountain foot, the gunners in the rear showered the heights and their own troops with shrapnel, thus grimly demonstrating the problems of communication posed by the range of the modern battlefield. All day they lay prostrate in the sandy veld, under fire, soon waterless, tormented by the blazing sun, flies and sunburn on their bare legs below their kilts. As concealed riflemen began to work around the right wing of the brigade, they broke in fragmented sections towards the rear, and towards evening, by tacit consent, the fire on both sides died down. On this occasion, however, the Boers did not vacate their positions, and during the following day Methuen withdrew to the Modder. The distribution of losses testified to the potentially annihilating effect of modern weaponry; of the 968 British casualties, nearly 80 per cent were

MAGERSFONTEIN
11 DECEMBER 1899

Key to abbreviations

RE
Royal Engineers

North'n
Northamptonshire Regiment

KOYLI
King's Own Yorkshire Light Infantry

RHA
Royal Horse Artillery

RFA
Royal Field Artillery

Cold. Gds
Coldstream Guards

Gren Gds
Grenadier Guards

Lrs
Lancers

MI
Mounted Infantry

North'd Fus
Northumberland Fusiliers

N. Lan
North Lancashires

borne by the Highlanders. Subsequently, by his own inclination and at Buller's wish, Methuen remained on the defensive until Cronjé's evacuation of Magersfontein three months later, as part of the general recoil accompanying Lord Roberts's march on Kimberley.

The chief threat to the garrison and populace of Kimberley was disease; protected by barbed-wire, earthworks and searchlights, they suffered only 31 direct casualties during the four-month siege and bombardment. But the insanitary conditions they endured are suggested by the fact that deaths from other causes amounted to nearly 1 600.[23]

Colenso, 15 December 1899

As he arrived at Frere Camp on 5 December, Buller was burdened with a sense of depression. Amazingly, he believed that he was confronting Boers numbering 120 000, and he gloomily observed in correspondence with the Secretary of State for War, Lord Lansdowne:

> 'the enemy have had the whip hand of us ever since the war began, and we have had to attack with inferior forces their superior forces in selected positions.'[24]

This fatalistic acceptance of pitched battles at his opponents' strongest points marked Buller's entire conduct of the Natal campaign. Initially he contemplated holding the Boers at Colenso, forcing Potgieter Drift five miles upstream, and marching to Ladysmith by the Acton Homes road running in from the west. Alarmed by the news of Magersfontein, however, he decided to avoid elaborate manoeuvres and to rely simply upon direct assault of the main Boer position around Colenso. The immense difficulties facing Buller should be emphasized. For several miles east and west of the little town

Boer riflemen. At Colenso Buller resolved upon taking the Boer position by direct assault in broad daylight, an unimaginitive decision with disastrous consequences.

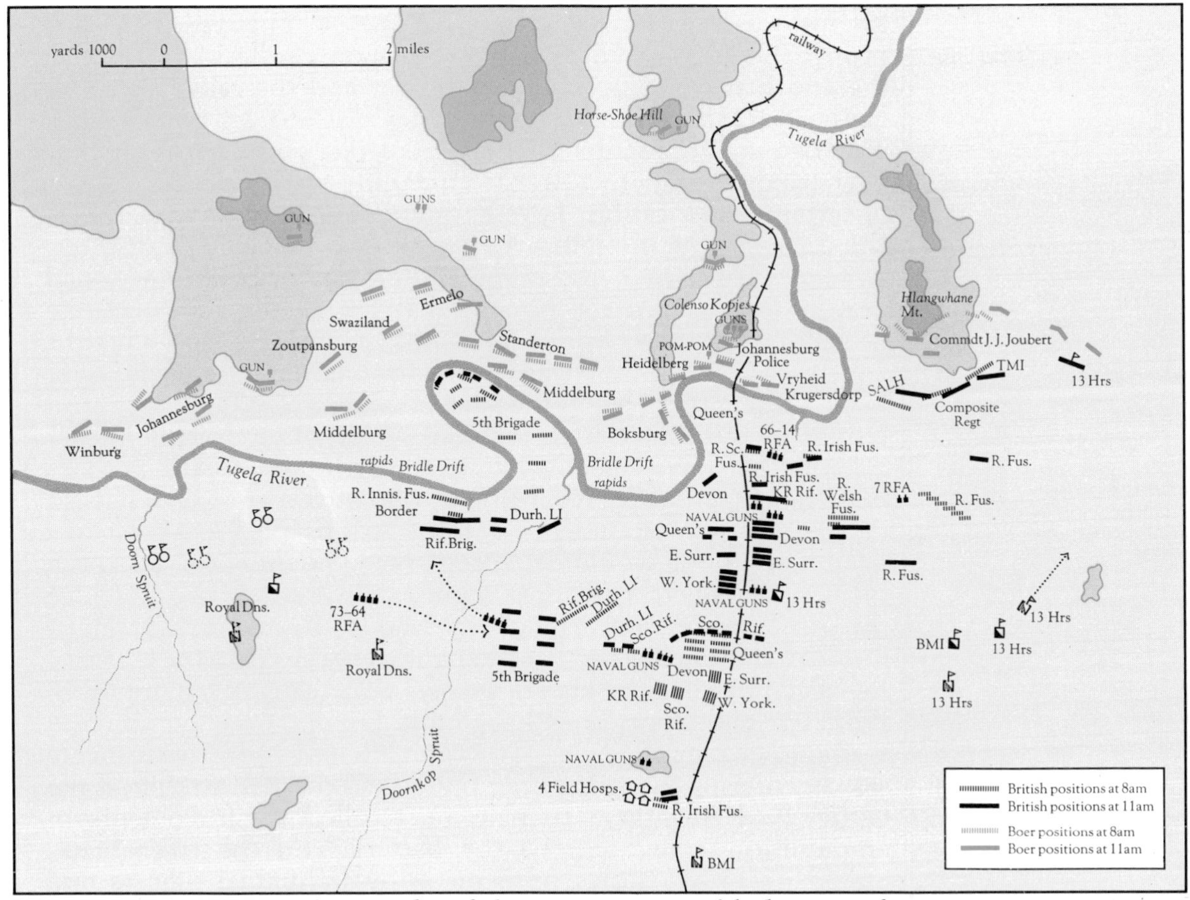

COLENSO
15 DECEMBER 1899

Key to abbreviations

Commando units

Border
Border Regiment

R. Irish Fus
Royal Irish Fusiliers

R. Innis Fus
Royal Inniskilling Fusiliers

R. Fus
Royal Fusiliers

Sco Rif
Scots Rifles

W. York
West Yorkshire Regiment

E. Surr
East Surrey Regiment

Hrs
Hussars

cont'd overleaf

of Colenso, the northern side of the river is a tumbled mass of forbidding heights, commanding the gentle slopes of the south bank. Fordable drifts were numerous, but they had the advantages, for the defenders, of channelling offensives towards predictable areas. Behind Colenso lay range upon range of kopjes and outcrops, providing a hardening line of retreat should the first position be forced. Nevertheless, Buller's appreciation of the strength of such topography, when defended by magazine fire, was so limited as to lead him to consider that a direct advance upon it was safer than taking advantage of any one of the several outflanking routes available. Counting upon unimaginative British generalship – a blow to the Boers' railway could have shaken their entire position – Joubert put his trust in entrenchments and natural landforms, 'the golden texts of Boer strategy'.[25]

Secrecy was out of the question. For two days before 15 December the great amphitheatre around Colenso echoed to the boom of naval guns and to the explosion of lyddite shell. Except, perhaps, for those who had studied the effect of artillery upon earthworks during the Russo-Turkish War, the British assumed that the bombardment would shatter the Boer defences and demoralize their occupants. In fact, the artillery preparation served only to apprise them, superfluously, of their enemy's intentions. In the circumstances Buller's plan of

SALH
South African Light Horse

Queen's
Queen's Regiment

BMI
Bethune's Mounted Infantry

Royal Dns
Royal Dragoons

Rif Brig
Rifle Brigade

Devon
Devonshire Regiment

Durh LI
Durham Light Infantry

TMI
Thorneycroft's Mounted Infantry

assault was foolhardy in the extreme. He proposed a two-pronged attack; by the 5th Brigade upon Bridle Drift, and by the 2nd Brigade upon Colenso proper and the railway bridge. In the rear, the 4th and 6th Brigades were to act as supports. The two main assaults were to take place in broad daylight over exposed terrain, towards an enemy whose numbers were uncertain and locations known only in vague outline.

Like Magersfontein, the battle began with a disaster. Colonel C. J. Long, the commanding officer of artillery, had been ordered to protect the central attack. On his own initiative he galloped his two batteries ahead of Major-General Hildyard's 2nd Brigade, until they were well within half a mile of the river bank. At length, at 6 am, the silent Boers released their fire, and grounded the batteries in a storm of bullets and shell. Long's quixotic gallantry usually has been attributed to his faith in close-range gunnery. According to one of the most widely read of the war correspondents – John Atkins of the *Manchester Guardian* – Long would often remark: 'The only way to smash those beggars is to rush in at them'.[26] On the left, the attack of the 5th Brigade, commanded by Major-General Arthur Hart, foundered immediately. Fanning out westward into the curve of the river's meander, Hart's troops were caught by fire from right, left and front. They halted and began to disintegrate into scattered groups. By 8 am, when the 6th and 2nd Brigades were slowly entering the firing line, Buller had decided to call off the battle. Ordering them to halt, he recalled reinforcements of ammunition being sent to the batteries on the river bank. Suicidally brave efforts were made by individual officers and men to rescue the guns, but Buller was determined upon their abandonment and immediate cessation of the entire engagement.

After the event he telegrammed to Lansdowne, 'I am frightened by the utter collapse of my infantry on Friday [15 December]'.[27] In truth, his rank and file had borne marvellously

The collapsed ironwork of the Colenso bridge.

the traumas of their first encounter with the Boers; the collapse was that of their commander. On 16 December Buller flashed to White a message that soon became world-famous. If he could not hold out for a month, Buller advised: 'firing away as much ammunition you can and making best terms you can.' When news of this heliogram reached the Cabinet they were deeply perturbed. Lansdowne immediately replied with asperity that the government would regard the abandonment and surrender of White's force as a 'national disaster of the greatest magnitude'. Buller therefore resigned himself to another phase of what he termed 'pegging away'.[28]

The appointment of Roberts and Kitchener

Colenso marked the high tide of Boer success. On every front the British had been defeated disastrously or were barely managing to stave off the invaders. Half of Natal was overrun, the Cape Colony lay exposed to a general offensive, and south-eastwards the Free Staters held a great salient of territory to within 120 miles of the coast.

The actual danger to Ladysmith, Kimberley and Mafeking was much less than its potential since the Boers were content merely to encircle the towns and shell them regularly. But this did not lessen the affront of the sieges to national pride. Public excitement and bitterness in Britain were intense, and Buller's supersession was a foregone conclusion. Predictably, the choice of a successor fell upon Lord Frederick Roberts of Kandahar, whose reputation rivalled that of Wolseley. Two days after Colenso, Roberts accepted the post of Commander-in-Chief in South Africa, Lord Kitchener of Khartoum to accompany him as Chief-of-Staff. Sensitive to his predecessor's feelings, however, Roberts allowed Buller a free hand in Natal. This, as subsequent events showed, was a misplaced courtesy. The Natal forces, however, did share in the flow of reinforcements, which were placing an almost intolerable strain upon the supply and transport machinery of the War Office. By the end of December the entire Field Force of 47 000 men had arrived in South Africa. Before the close of the year two more divisions were mobilized, one reaching the Natal theatre of war in early January. On the eve of his next engagement, Buller's available troops numbered some 30 000.

Thus reinforced, he returned to his original plan of holding the Boers at Colenso and appraching Ladysmith from the west. Laboriously, he shifted the main army 15 miles upstream. The Boer front moved accordingly. Buller planned to hold the enemy at Potgieter's Drift, to send the bulk of his force across Trichardt's Drift, and to swing around Spion Kop and the Twin Peaks. The execution of this movement was entrusted to Lieutenant-General Sir Charles Warren. In his obscure, contradictory, and sometimes nonsensical evidence before the Elgin Commission, Buller spoke bitterly of Warren's apparently wilful refusal to advance his left and hold back his right.[29] Neither then nor afterwards did Buller seem to realize that he had charged Warren with an impossible task. For the plan rested upon the assumption, unwarrantable in view of the inadequacy of reconnaissance, that upon Bastion Hill lay the extreme right of the Boer position. Not only did this extend several miles further west, but the Boers had been given ample opportunity to reinforce the hilltops from the Rangeworthy Heights to the Twin Peaks. The deliberate movements of Sir Redvers' supply columns were visible to the naked eye from the eminences he planned to by-pass, and the founder of the Army Service Corps never jeopardized his troops' provisions and medical comforts.

Spion Kop, 24 January 1900

By 21 January a foothold on the far bank of the Tugela had been secured, and the Rangeworthy Heights taken, but it had become plain that the outflanking attempts were futile. On that day Warren and Buller consulted. The former returned with the impression that his commander was happy for him to retire, assault either side of Bastion Hill, or take Spion Kop and thence enfilade the trenches of the surrounding kopjes. Warren's choice of the last course was probably the most unhappy he could have taken. For Spion Kop was a salient jutting into the enemy position, so indefensible and exposed to fire from Green Hill, Conical Hill and the Twin Peaks that the Boers themselves had avoided holding it in strength. Thus, aided by a dense mist, Colonel A. W. Thorneycroft had little difficulty in occupying the summit on the night of 23 January. As the warmth of the rising sun cleared the miasma, the realization dawned that Spion Kop, so commanding a position when surveyed from a distance, was militarily a death-trap. A few inches below the surface, spades and picks struck a bed of igneous rock. All the efforts of the defenders secured them only shallow depressions less than two feet deep. Below the crest of the hill the terrain dropped away precipitously, so that where the slopes spread out an area of 'dead' ground was formed, that is, ground inaccessible to the fire from the natural summit. Adroit skirmishers would be able to creep to within a few hundred yards of the closely huddled infantry. Spion Kop

SPION KOP

Key to abbreviations

RFA
Royal Field Artillery

R. Lanc
Royal Lancashires

Lan Fus
Lancashire Fusiliers

S. Lan
South Lancashires

TMI
Thorneycroft's Mounted Infantry

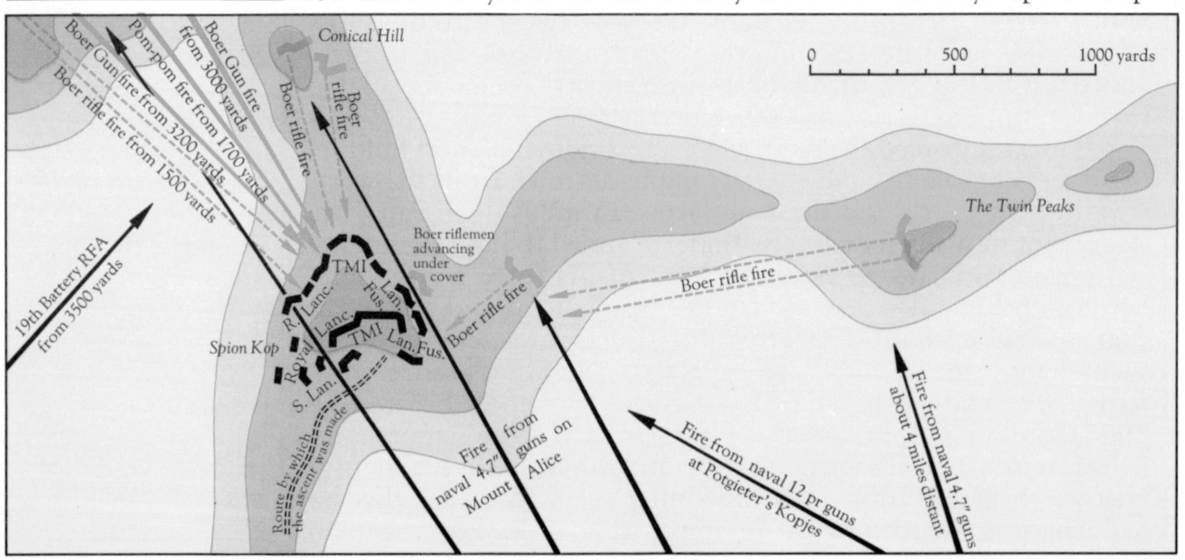

should never have been occupied at all, as intelligent scouting might have shown. By 8.30 am the mist had cleared completely, the Boer guns began to find their range, and rifle fire from the adjacent heights began to rake the elevated plateau. Warren neither devised a means to protect the British position nor permitted retirement (hardly practicable) or surrender.

More troops, under Major-General Talbot Coke, were packed on to the summit during the morning. Hitherto, Buller had remained passive in the rear, but while the reinforcements were clambering up the mountain he indulged in a momentary and erratic interference. Stirred by accounts of Thorneycroft's cool-headedness during the night march, Buller ordered Warren to place him in command on Spion Kop. In an extraordinary instance of the fragmentation of command so common in this war, Warren omitted to inform Coke of his decision. By late evening, with dead and wounded lying in serried ranks, the ordeal had gone beyond human bearing. Talbot Coke scrambled

A still picture taken from an early film showing British troops at Spion Kop.

Above: members of the Carolina commando photographed two hours before they became involved in the fighting at Spion Kop. Forty-six of their number were killed in the action that followed.

Opposite above and below: 'Men were staggering along, or supported by comrades, or crawling on hands and knees, or carried by stretcher. Corpses lay here and there. Many of the wounds were of a horrible nature. The splinters and fragments of the shells had torn and mutilated in the most ghastly manner. I passed about two hundred while I was climbing up.' Winston Churchill's description of the aftermath of Spion Kop.

down the mountain to confer with Buller, and in his absence, Thorneycroft, of his own volition, ordered retirement. With a bitter irony, the Boers were simultaneously evacuating the flanks of Spion Kop and the Twin Peaks, seized by the King's Royal Rifles in the only diversionary action of the day. To the British, the suffering seemed to have been all on one side, but the Boers too were near breaking point, and according to Deneys Reitz:

> 'it was only Louis Botha's presence of mind which averted a general panic and retreat from the Tugela.'[30]

Nearly 1 100 British were killed, wounded or made prisoner on this futile day.[31]

Relief of Ladysmith 28 February 1900

A further effort to break the Boer defences, the battle of Vaalkrantz between 5 and 7 February, was a signal failure. Yet another poor estimation of the extent of the Boer position rendered the offensive a disaster. On 11 February the entire force withdrew to Chieveley, carrying with them a further 2 000 casualties. It was something of a surprise, therefore, when the London press learned of the success of Buller's fourth attempt to reach Ladysmith. Several extraneous factors accounted for the eventual change in Buller's fortunes. Officers and men were learning to apply effectively those techniques that progressive tacticians had long been advocating. Scores of witnesses testified to the Elgin Commission about how rapidly the men grew adept at constructing, and subordinate officers at devising, their field defences. The breakthrough to Ladysmith was not a single battle, but a series of careful assaults on particular positions, each consolidated before the next was essayed. Cingolo, Monte Cristo, Hlangwane, Hart's Hill and finally Pieter's Hill were taken in a gradual succession, with almost a ratchet technique. Artillery and infantry were learning to coordinate; at the taking of Hart's and Kitchener's Hills, the Boer defences were shelled

virtually until the second before the infantry sprang from their trenches. This stage of the relief of Ladysmith lasted almost a fortnight, and during that time the rumble of the guns never ceased. To soldiers who had endured campaigning such as this, the early trench warfare in Flanders was not an entirely novel experience. According to the official estimate the relief of Ladysmith cost the army in Natal 5 500 casualties. Sir Redvers Buller published a Special Army Order on 3 March, announcing that these operations had 'added a glorious page to the History of the British Empire'. It was hollow rhetoric.

Roberts's strategy

Save for the master-stroke of his flank march to Bloemfontein, Roberts's command was less one of remarkable strategy than one of a grand logistical achievement. While Roberts was immensely praised in his day, many contemporaries were still inclined to feel that his cautious, painstaking approach prolonged the conflict unduly and indeed paved the way for guerrilla warfare. E. M. de Vogüé's remark was typical:

> 'the citizen-soldiers and improvised generals of the veld would not have withstood a few well-disciplined seasoned regiments, vigorously led. An army ever so poorly drilled would have overthrown them at the first shock.'[32]

Historians today, influenced by twentieth-century experience of guerrilla warfare, are less inclined to suggest that an attenuated period of pacification could have been avoided. Lord Roberts's careful unfolding of a unified strategy, and his concern to secure the basic network of communications before crushing the enemy in detail, were admirably devised.

On board the *Dunottar Castle* Roberts devised his grand scheme, simple but comprehensive. He intended to consolidate his forces, move directly up the western railway to Kimberley, loose his main army from the railway in an eastward drive to Bloemfontein, advance to Pretoria, and finally to complete his communications by securing the easterly branch lines to Durban and Lourenço Marques in Mozambique. His first aim was to construct a field force suitable to the task before it. A few sentences can scarcely suggest the range and precision of the preparations. A new cavalry division was organized under French and the proportion of mounted infantry greatly increased. The Director of Military Intelligence, Colonel G. F. R. Henderson, began to compile a comprehensive map of the theatre of war. In an admittedly controversial move, regimental transport was drawn into one central department. For the general instruction of his troops, Roberts issued 'Notes for Guidance in South African Warfare'.[33] Hardly new to advanced thinkers, they provided a useful summary of the lessons of the veld – the need for concealment, marksmanship, mobility and individual initiative. Colonel Percy Girouard, the experienced Director of Railways, devoted his attention to the minutia of timetables. By the end of January nearly 60 000 troops had been drawn into the area between the Modder and Orange Rivers. Impeccable secrecy veiled the Commander-in-Chief's intentions. Piet Cronjé was convinced that Roberts planned only a direct assault towards Kimberley. His deception was partly due to the indefatigable Henderson who, even more adept than Wolseley in spreading false rumours, 'revelled in the deceits he practised'.[34] Cronjé remained entrenched behind Magersfontein, confident that 'The English do not make turning movements. They never leave the railway, because they cannot march.'[35]

Relief of Kimberley, 15 February 1900

In the relief of Kimberley the cavalry played a crucial role. Their aim was to outflank both Cronjé's position, and the town's defences, by swinging in a great arc eastward from Ramdam to Dronfield. Primarily, their march of 11 to 15 February was a test of endurance, relieved only by French's brilliant stroke at Klip Drift. With a trail of dead and dying horses disfiguring their route, the cavalry pushed on to within six miles of Cronjé's headquarters. Still sure that these movements were a feint, he ordered a shallow defensive crescent to be formed south of the Modder River, around Klip Drift. Approaching the enclosed wings of the Boer position, French threw his 5 000 horsemen in an exhilarating gallop through the undefended centre. He then forced his exhausted troops around and above Kimberley. This, with word of the army moving northward in his wake, dissolved the investment on 15 February. The Boer forces thereupon divided like waves before a

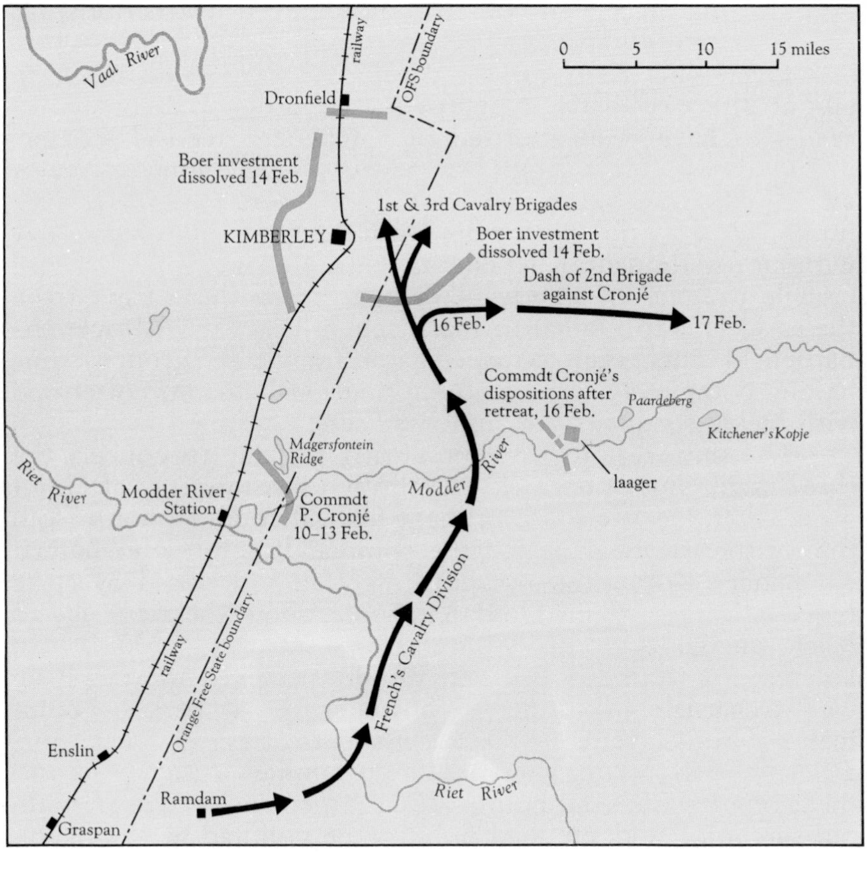

Relief of Kimberley 11–15 February 1900

liner, J. S. Ferreira northward and Cronjé eastward. Cavalry enthusiasts the world over were thrilled by French's dash.[36] In fact, no shock had been used at all; French had executed a lightning manoeuvre rather than a genuine charge.

On route to Bloemfontein Roberts contracted influenza, and during the brief period when his direct authority was suspended occurred what many regarded as the only major disaster of his command. After sparing a few hours to celebrate in Kimberley, French had headed off Cronjé and his enormous waggon-train near Paardeberg Drift. That he could do so with a force only a quarter of the size of that of Cronjé clearly revealed the Boers' temporary demoralization. The events that followed resembled a Plevna in miniature, an initial costly and uncoordinated assault followed by a patient siege and bombardment. After the event Roberts disclaimed certain knowledge about who gave the orders on 18 February, and asserted: 'I never intended Lord Kitchener to take command. He went to the 6th Division as my representative.'

Paardeberg, 17-27 February 1900

This was less than ingenuous. On 17 February Roberts wrote to the senior officer at Paardeberg, Lieutenant-General Thomas Kelly-Kenny:

> 'please consider that Lord Kitchener is with you for the purpose of communicating to you my orders, so that there may be no delay such as reference to and fro may entail.'[37]

As Kitchener had been bound by no detailed instructions, his decisions naturally prevailed.

Overriding Kelly-Kenny's protests, he resolved upon an all-out direct offensive. None of the subordinate commanders seems to have been apprised of Kitchener's tactical scheme, such as it was. At 6.30 am on 18 February he launched major attacks from the south and west. Two hours later these were immobilized by the grazing fire from the river bed. Apparently without forethought, Kitchener then ordered General Sir Henry Colvile to conduct an advance along the southern bank from the east. This too failed to make much headway. All over the battlefield units began to disperse into fragmented groups, some halting completely, others attempting local assaults, often led with reckless gallantry by junior officers.

The only serious attempt during the day to concert the three major lines of attack was thrown into disarray at about 5 pm when De Wet, in a brilliant tactical coup, stole up from the south-east and stormed the commanding hill later named Kitchener's Kopje. But not until nightfall had closed over the bloodstained battlefield did Kitchener allow the struggles to reach the laager to cease. By that time over 1 200 British lay dead or wounded.[38] When Roberts received the news, he was at Paardeberg in a matter of hours to take personal command. Cronjé, refusing De Wet's entreaties to break out, remained with his burghers and their families to suffer the torment of a lyddite shell bombardment in an enclosed area, without sanitation and supplied only by the polluted waters of the

Opposite
PAARDEBERG
18 FEBRUARY 1900

Key to abbreviations

DCLI
Duke of Cornwall's Light Infantry

Glo'cester
Gloucestershire Regiment

Shrops LI
Shropshire Light Infantry

Oxf LI
Oxford Light Infantry

W. Rid
West Riding Regiment

Essex
Essex Regiment

RFA
Royal Field Artillery

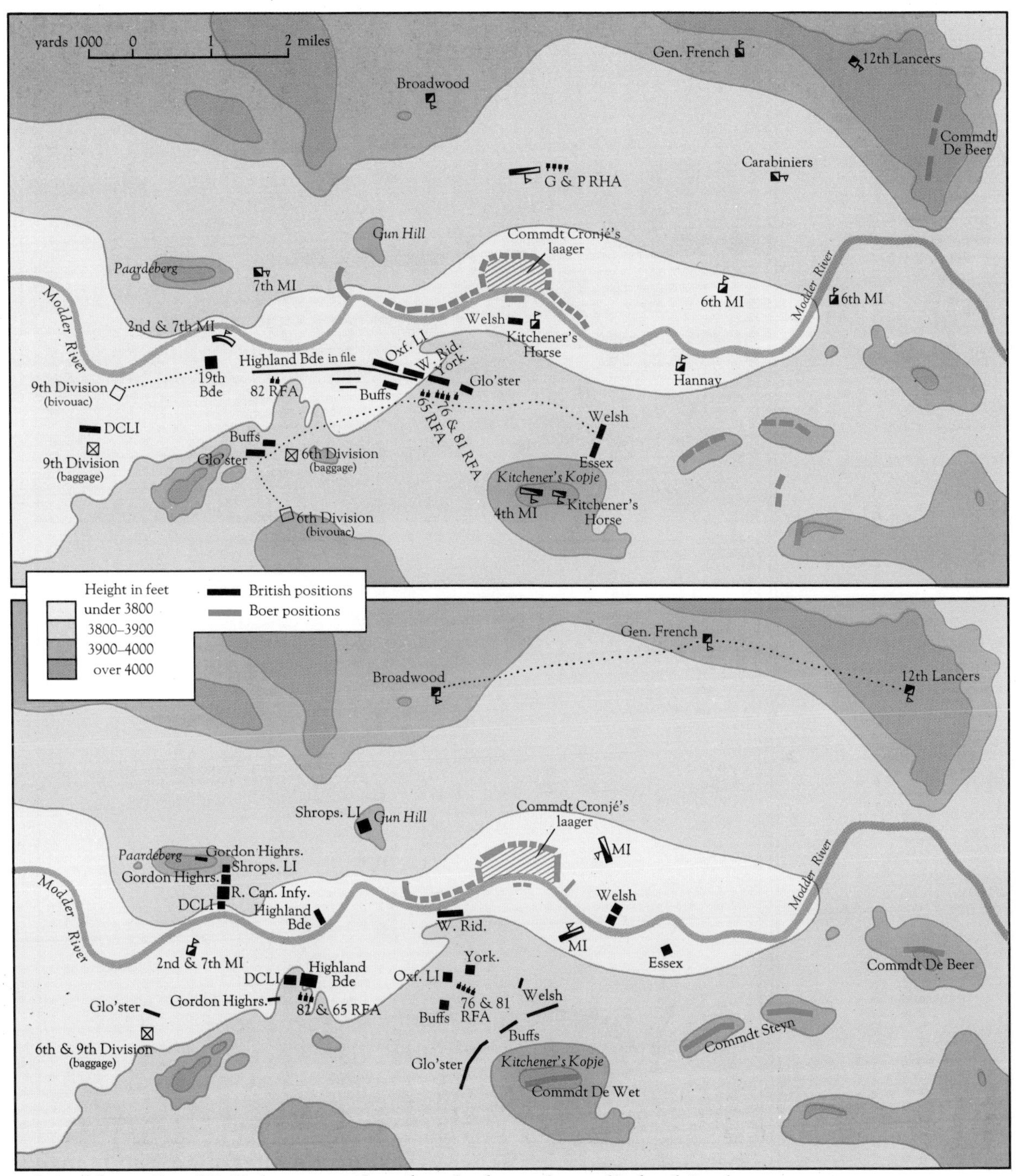

Modder. On 27 February, the day before the relief of Ladysmith, Cronjé surrendered with nearly 4 000 fighting men. It was the greatest catastrophe to Boer arms in the war. Thereafter ends and means tended to combine, the only real aim of the Boers was to prolong the struggle. Joubert died on 27 March, but younger leaders were becoming prominent; the new Commandant-General of the Transvaal, Louis Botha, J. H. de la Rey, Christiaan de Wet, the new Orange Free State Commandant-General, and from January 1901, Jan Smuts. In De Wet the

The site of the Boer laager at Paardeberg following the surrender of Cronjé and almost 4 000 men. The burghers in the encampment, some of whom were accompanied by their wives and children, had been exposed earlier to the terrifying ordeal of an intense lyditte shell bombardment by Roberts's artillery.

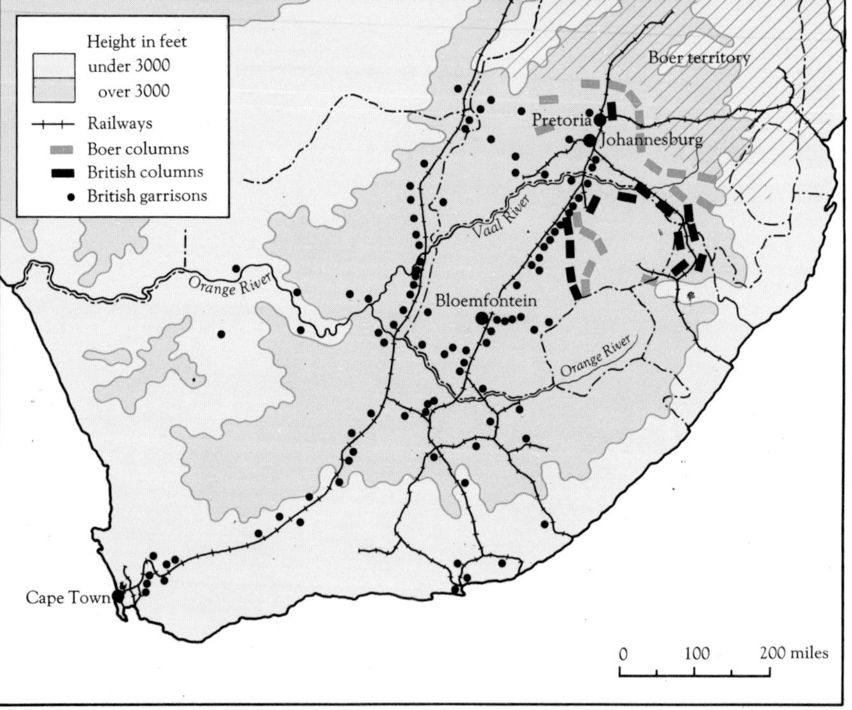

Boers possessed a leader whose extraordinary cunning and tenacity made him a born partisan. At a *krijgsraad* (war council) on 20 March it was resolved to continue the war and, at De Wet's insistence, to abolish the burdensome waggon-laagers.[39]

The fall of the Boer capitals

Certain that the fall of their capitals would strike a final blow to the Boers' resistance, Roberts concentrated upon reaching Bloemfontein and Pretoria. On 4 April the British flag was raised in the Free State capital, but simultaneously De Wet launched an offensive that heralded the Boer revival. While commandos north of Bloemfontein occupied British attention, he attacked south-eastwards in the style for which he was to become ledgendary. Striking successively at Sannah's Post, Dewetsdorp and Reddersburg, he paused to besiege Wepener, having taken over 1 000 prisoners in five days. Ian Hamilton freed Wepener, with some ease towards the end of April, but De Wet's achievement was psychologically uplifting to the Boers. Yet though the British might be delayed, they could not be halted. While Mafeking was relieved in the far west and Buller moved deliberately through Natal, the main army resumed its march to Pretoria. Peace was expectantly awaited by the British public, and books and articles in the vein of Sir Edward May's *A Retrospect on the South African War*, published in 1901, began to appear.

The guerrilla war

Yet what Kitchener termed the 'insensate resistance'[40] of the third and final phase of the war was to persist for nearly two years. It is not easy to imagine any European army of the period subduing the Boer guerrilla forces in a substantially shorter time. So long as the mounted riflemen could avoid capture and secure – usually from their foes – ammunition and basic commodities, they could exist indefinitely as the 'gadfly of regular armies'.[41] For the partisans, this stage of the war was a feat of endurance; for the British, frustration and tedium were its hallmarks. All semblance of conventional military activity disappeared during the last year, presenting problems for military historians as well as for commanders. As the compiler of the Official History of the War wrote ruefully in his preface: 'Now, as then, only the size of the campaign can be truly stated, for shape it had none.'

Nevertheless, some general trends are distinguishable. Accompanying the more distinct movements of the chief leaders was a host of local and disparate offensives; railways, depots and bridges were continually liable to destruction and glancing assault. De Wet's next campaign typified on a large scale what occurred hundreds of times during the latter half of the war. After a brief rest at Frankfort with the now peripatetic Free State government, on 7 June he cut the railway between Pretoria and Kroonstad, overwhelmed the Vredefort Road and Rodewal garrisons, and captured stores worth over £100 000. Such a feat could hardly be bettered. Yet, in the nature of guerrilla warfare, its effect was short-lived. Within a week communications were restored, and the loss in stores made only a dent upon the resources now at Lord Roberts's disposal.

British commanders as yet hardly realized that they were fighting a guerrilla war. By the end of June Buller had reached the northern borders of Natal. De la Rey had retreated to the western Transvaal, Louis Botha was withdrawing from the environs of Pretoria, and subsequent events in the Free State seemed to confirm that peace was near. Hunter from the north and Lieutenant-General Sir Leslie Rundle from the east drove some 9 000 Boers into the triangle of land between the Wilge and Caledon Rivers, known as the Brandwater Basin. Rent by internal schisms and quarrels over leadership, the Boers failed to concert their resistance, and by the end of July over 4 000 had surrendered. The British commanders, moving with justifiable caution (which earned Rundle the inimitable soubriquet of 'Sir Leisurely Trundle') failed to capture President Steyn and De Wet, who stole away northwards. With them went the pick of the Free State army. Throughout the guerrilla war the relative significance of captures was diminished by the fact that it was the old, the sick and the disheartened who were usually taken first. A fruitless chase, known as the first hunt of De Wet, followed his escape.

With Roberts's advance to Komatipoort completed by the end of September, the Boers lost the Delagoa Bay line entirely and were severed from the outside world. Ironically, however, a widespread recrudescence of hostilities marked the close of Roberts's command. Resistance erupted afresh in the north-east Free State during November, and on the 16th of the month De Wet marched south to begin preparations for the invasion of the Cape Colony. Roberts immediately dispatched a column in pursuit, but the rest of the second hunt of De Wet was left to the sledgehammer techniques of Lord Kitchener, who assumed the post of Commander-in-Chief on 29 November. Although headed off and forced to race north once more, De Wet preoccupied British attention sufficiently long to allow Pieter Kritzinger and J. B. M. Hertzog with 1 700 commandos to cross the Orange River into the Cape shortly before Christmas. Moreoever, heartened by De Wet's virtuoso display of mobility, the Transvaal forces revived under Ben Viljoen in the north-east and Botha on the high veld south of the Delagoa Bay line.

The Free State leaders then concerted a scheme with Botha, the vast scope of which was equalled by its unreality. Hertzog was to march to Lambert Bay and meet there a ship supposedly coming from Europe with arms and mercenaries.

De Wet's commando crossing the Orange River, February 1901.

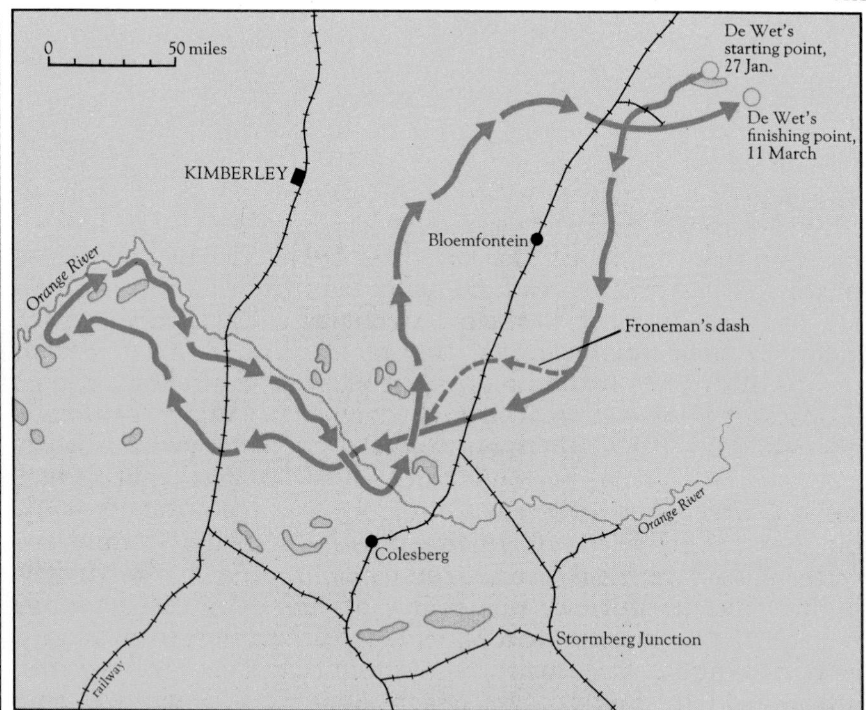

Third, or Great, Hunt of De Wet January – March 1901

Meanwhile, Kritzinger would agitate the Cape Colony midlands to rebellion, Botha would march to Durban, and De Wet would cross the Orange, join with Hertzog, and advance on Cape Town. Lambert Bay was reached by Hertzog in January 1901, but hopes of external assistance proved chimerical. He and Kritzinger were driven westwards during February, drawing after them most available British forces. By 10 February De Wet was across the Orange. Kitchener immediately ordered a great net of columns, covering 160 miles, to be thrown out from Kroonstad to Naauwpoort. The extraordinary agility of De Wet's flight is easily appreciated by a glance at the map, especially when it is considered that some of the fifteen pursuing columns executed convolutions as intricate as his own. Superior horsemanship, knowledge of the country and scouting skills enabled him to dodge his pursuers for six weeks and eventually to escape from the Cape. The British columns seemed to be incapable of effective cooperation. In part, this was attributable to the inadequacies of higher staff training and structure. There was also a technical aspect to the problem. While cable lines could easily accompany a force moving along a predictable route, it was impossible for telegraphers to keep pace with the roving columns during the guerrilla war. Difficulties of communication worsened accordingly.[42]

Kitchener's methods

Under Kitchener's guidance, British operations grew increasingly massive and mechanical in nature, while the Boer forces became ever more fissiparous, disintegrating like mercury at the touch of his ponderous columns. Kitchener's methods were twofold; first, netting and driving the enemy precisely like game, and second, striking at their means of subsistence. Thus, he adopted the blockhouse system and a scorched-earth policy.

Initially, blockhouses were expensive masonry structures, built for railway protection. Soon, however, Kitchener envisaged fencing the entire theatre of war with lines of cheaper, galvanized-iron constructions. As a military engineer, he found this task his *métier*, and pursued with unflagging diligence the building of a vast pattern of blockhouses, joined by barbed-wire, equipped with telegraphs, telephones and a variety of traps and alarms. Until the last days of the war, the antennae of this great system spread gradually over the veld. Kitchener's warfare aimed at the bases of Afrikaner society. Apart from guarding their fortifications, the occupation of most British troops during the second half of the war was the destruction of crops and homes (this activity in fact began under Roberts's command). Most of the men captured were shipped to prison camps in St Helena, Bermuda, Ceylon and India; Roberts had set the precedent after Paardeberg by incarcerating Cronjé's burghers in St Helena. Civilians, mostly women and children, were massed in local concentration camps. From the strictly military point of view, this policy at first rebounded to the benefit of the guerrilla forces, as it released them from family responsibilities. Eventually, the mounting death-toll of the disease-ridden camps – in which over 20 000 women and children died – helped to sap the Boer will to resist.

From the early months of 1901 military operations lack any narrative development. The significance of Kitchener's succession of drives lies in their qualitative aspects rather than in what they added to the course of events. Whether there was any viable alternative to blockhouses and drives as a means of grappling with the Boers' art of evasion may be doubted.

A feature universal to the drives was the disparity between their damage to property and their effect upon enemy personnel. At first, when the Boers retained some cohesion during De Wet's attempt to raise the Cape Colony in January and February 1901, the difference was not so marked. Kitchener's first great sweep, conducted by French between the Delagoa Bay and Natal railway lines, yielded 732 prisoners, 1 000 rifles and uncomputed amounts of grain and forage.[43] The proportions soon changed. In July Kitchener planned a drive on an unprecedented scale. The intention was to form nearly all mobile columns into a contracting circle between the Vaal and Modder Rivers, enclosing the enemy against the blockhouse line between Bloemfontein and Jacobsdal. Directed by Major-General E. Elliott, this great movement, lasting from 29 July to 7 August, secured nearly 750 vehicles, 2 600 horses and 20 000 head of cattle. Only 326 prisoners were taken, however, and 17 Boers killed or wounded. Elliott's next drive, in which he swung north-eastwards, hoping to enclose the Boers against the Wittebergen at the foot of the Drakensberg range, was still more frustrating. A comparable quantity of livestock and waggons was taken, but only 21 surrenders were secured and 24 casualties inflicted upon the enemy.[44]

Opposite above: blockhouses were initially stone-built structures designed to protect railway communications. Once the system was extended, blockhouses were constructed more quickly and cheaply by using wood and corrugated iron.

Opposite below: the rotting carcases of 1 500 horses slaughtered by the British at Winburg in the Orange Free State to prevent them falling into the possession of the Boer forces.

Incendiarism was practised on a large scale in both republics. Here British troops destroy a Boer farm and its outbuildings in the Orange Free State.

These results typified the last year of attrition. The mobility of the British forces increased, drives became better organized, blockhouse lines filled in, and the Boers' scope for manoeuvre steadily decreased; but dramatic results continued to elude the British forces. Yet Kitchener took his methods to their logical conclusion. At the beginning of 1902 he ordered drives to be conducted with the aim of forming, literally, a continuous barrier. The driven area was to be swept by an unbroken line of men, wire or blockhouses; the whole system was to form a wall rather than a net. With this ideal in view the final operations were carried out. Of these, the very last drive of the war is illustrative. From 6 to 11 May 1902 Ian Hamilton advanced slowly across the western Transvaal, relying upon a dense picket-line to maintain his living fence, forcing the enemy against the railway line with its many blockhouses north and south of Vryburg. During the night of 11 May a few hundred riflemen were caught between 17 000 advancing troops and the roving searchlights of the trains stationed along the line. Silhouetted against the glare, their tiny numbers curiously

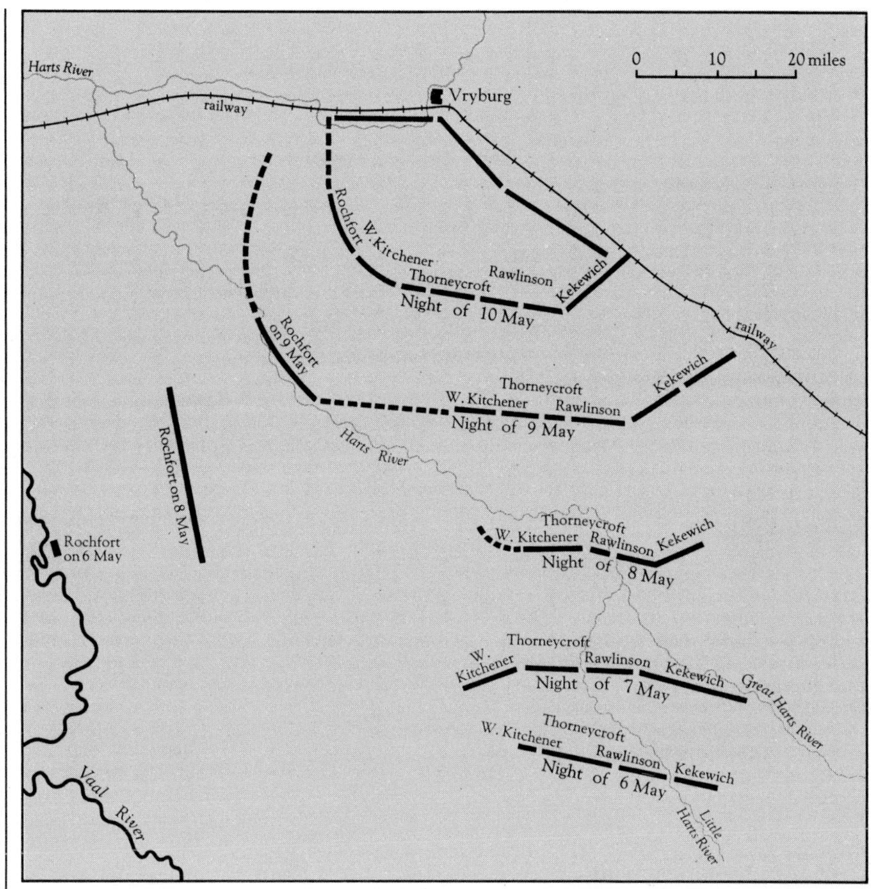

General Hamilton's Drive 6–11 May 1902

evocative of the entire conflict, this handful of troops wisely surrendered. By then, peace negotiations had been seriously in progress for a month, the physical endurance of the guerrillas was reaching its limit, and the war was faltering to a close.

Lessons of the war

The war left military theorists, and soldiers concerned with their profession, with a sense of perplexity. Its lessons were least controversial in the sphere of high organization. The next few years witnessed a radical restructuring of the British War Office and the establishment of a General Staff devoted to staff training and contingency planning. At other levels confusion tended to prevail. Conventional strategists regarded the attenuated struggle as a consequence of the initial failure of generalship, and therefore dismissed the war as irrelevant. Enthusiasts for mounted riflemen tended to advocate their claims to the denigration of infantry and artillery alike. Most progressive thinkers felt that the trench battles of the first stage of the conflict indicated that earthworks should be avoided rather than attacked; forthcoming wars, therefore, would be mobile, swift and decisive. Ultimately, the South African War gave ambiguous guidance for the future. With hindsight, it is not difficult to point out where misinterpretations of the evidence led to erroneous assumptions. Military planners, however, have the obligation to predict from past events, a constraint from which military historians are exempt.

References

1. Jean de Bloch, 'Some Lessons of the Transvaal War', *Contemporary Review*, 77, April 1900, 461.
2. Public Record Office (PRO), London, WO 33/56, 'Further Paper from the Secretary of State laying down the requirements from our Army . . .'.
3. British Parliamentary Papers, *Report of Her Majesty's Commissioners Appointed to enquire into . . . the War in South Africa*, Cd.1789, 1904, *40*, 10–13, 154–8 (report henceforth cited as *Elgin Report*, and British Parliamentary Papers as PP); PRO, 30/40/13, Ardagh Papers, memoir of Ardagh.
4. S. Wilkinson, 'Surprise in War', *Cornhill Magazine*, NS 8, January–June 1900, 328.
5. *Elgin Report*, Cd.1789, *40*, 37, 20–36.
6. *Ibid.*, Cd.1792, 1904, *42*, 48–80 (statement from the Adjutant General's Department).
7. *Ibid.*, Cd.1789, 1904, *40*, 277.
8. Captain A. J. Mahan, *The Story of the War in South Africa*, London, 1900 preface; Jean de Bloch, 457–71, and (among his many publications) 'Militarism in Politics', *Contemporary Review*, 80, 1900, 773–90, and 'Reply to Some Criticism'. *National Review*, 37, 1900, 381.
9. *Elgin Report*, Cd.1790, 1904, *41*, 371.
10. F. Woods ed., *Young Winston's Wars. The Original Despatches of Winston S. Churchill, War Correspondent 1897–1900*, Newton Abbot, 1975, 177.
11. J. F. Maurice and M. H. Grant eds., *History of the War in South Africa, 1899–1902*, London, 1906–8, I, 81–4 (henceforth cited as *British Official History*); Deneys Reitz, *Commando*, London, 1929, 22; Christiaan de Wet, *Three Years War*, London, 1903, 9–10.
12. According to the *British Official History*, the republics had 87 000 men available for military service (I, 85), though the British Intelligence Department calculated that only 53 643 men were available (PP, Cd.1789, 157–8), a figure more in keeping with that provided by J. H. Breytenbach, the South African state historian, of 54 667 (*Die Geskiedenis van die Tweede Vryheidsoorlog in Suid-Afrika, 1899–1902*, I, Pretoria, 1969). Breytenbach estimates that between 32 000 and 35 000 men were mobilized in October 1899 (153), while some other historians put the figure at 38 000 men.
13. Reitz, 26.
14. *Ibid.*, 17.
15. *British Official History*, I, 462.
16. *Ibid.*, I, 464.
17. John B. Atkins, *The Relief of Ladysmith*, London, 1900, 83.
18. *Elgin Report*, Cd.1792, 1904, *41*, 172.
19. E. G. Norman Dixon, *The Psychology of Military Incompetence*, London, 1977, 52–68.
20. Buller Papers, PRO, WO 132/5, Sir Henry Campbell-Bannerman to Buller, 29 June 1899.
21. *Elgin Report*, Cd.1792, 1904, *41*, 170.
22. *British Official History*, I, 467.
23. *Ibid.*, I, 329, 469 (casualties at Magersfontein); II, 68–9 (casualties at Kimberley).
24. *Elgin Report*, Cd.1790, 1904, *41*, 626, 623, Buller to Lansdowne, 9 January 1900 and 13 December 1899.
25. Atkins, 139.
26. *Ibid.*, 163.
27. *Elgin Report*, Cd.1790, 1904, *41*, 625, Buller to Lansdowne, 18 December 1899.
28. *Ibid.*, 175, heliogram to White; 624, Lansdowne to Buller, 16 December 1899; 179, statement by Buller.
29. *Elgin Report*, Cd.1790, 1904, *41*, 178.
30. Reitz, 78–9.
31. L. S. Amery ed., *The Times History of the War in South Africa*, III, 1905, 295.
32. *Warnotes. The Diary of Colonel de Villebois-Mareuil*, translated by F. Lees, London, 1902, xviii.
33. *Elgin Report*, Cd.1789, 1904, *40*, 531–2.
34. F. M. Sir W. Robertson, *From Private to Field-Marshal*, London, 1921, 107.
35. Count A. W. Sternberg, *My Experiences of the Boer War*, London, 1901, 114.
36. 'Concerning Our Cavalry', *Blackwoods Edinburgh Magazine*, 167, January 1900, 774.
37. *Elgin Report*, Cd.1790, 1904, *41*, 62 (evidence of Roberts), and 281, Roberts to Kelly-Kenny, 17 February 1900.
38. *British Official History*, II, 590.
39. De Wet, 79.
40. PP, Cd.695, 1901, *47*, 17, dispatch by Kitchener, 8 July 1901.
41. *British Official History*, II, 93.
42. *Elgin Report*, Cd.1790, 1904, *41*, 371.
43. PP, Cd.522, 1901, *47*, 6, dispatch by Kitchener, 8 March, 1901.
44. PP, Cd.820, 1902, 69, 7, 25–6, dispatches by Kitchener, 8 August 1901 and 8 October 1902.

CHAPTER 4

Life on Commando

Fransjohan Pretorius

The well-proven commando system formed the basis of the military organization of both the South African Republic (Transvaal) and the Orange Free State. This system had been developed during the eighteenth- and nineteenth-century wars against black people, and during the first struggle for the Transvaal's independence in the war of 1880–1. The essence of the system was that the armies of the republics consisted mainly of unpaid non-professional burgher forces. Apart from the artillery corps and other specialized units, neither republic possessed a standing army.

Mobilization

A fortnight before the outbreak of war General Piet Joubert, Commander-in-Chief of the combined republican forces, ordered the commandant of each district in the South African Republic to call up his burghers for active service by means of the field-cornets (*veldkornets*) of each ward and lead them to pre-arranged locations on the borders. Five days after Joubert's mobilization, President Steyn also ordered his Free Staters to proceed to the borders. With a view to the continuation of the essential services in the republics and the retention of a general reserve, the governments decided initially to mobilize not more than 60 per cent of the burghers liable for military service. All white male citizens of the republics between the ages of sixteen and sixty years, who could provide no lawful excuse for their exemption, were liable for military service. After the various setbacks between February and July 1900 the governments of the republics were obliged to call up all burghers available for military service. Although there are no statistics available, it seems that there were some eligible burghers who never went on commando. Nonetheless, events such as the removal of women, children and old men to the concentration camps, and the transition of the struggle from the conventional phase of military operations to the guerrilla war created circumstances in which many boys under 16 and elderly men above 60 years of age chose to take up arms rather than go to the camps. It was not an uncommon sight at the front to come across old men of seventy or more and boys of eleven or twelve fighting with the commandos. Even some of those burghers who voluntarily surrendered their arms to the British authorities later rejoined the commandos either by choice or compulsion. For the Afrikaner people the war was a national cause fought by a people's army.

Opposite page.
Above: Transvaal burghers photographed with their families and accompanying African servants immediately before setting off for war. A waggon commandeered from a local tea merchant stands on the railway truck.

Below left: perhaps the best known photograph of the war. Three generations prepare for combat: P. J. Lemmer, 65; J. D. L. Botha, 15; and G. J. Pretorius, 43.

Below right: members of the Hollander Corps leaving Pretoria, 6 October 1899.

Preparations for war had been made well in advance and with much enthusiasm. The commandos' Mauser rifles, bought in large quantities by the government after the Jameson Raid, were inspected and oiled, and their shoulder bandoliers filled with ammunition. Horses to be used on campaign had been stabled for some time. The commando law laid down that each burgher liable for military service had to be equipped with a riding horse, saddle and bridle, a rifle and thirty rounds of ammunition, and provision for eight days. Impecunious burghers were provided for by the government.[1]

Apart from the uniformed artillery corps and a handful of other units, no special measures were taken for the burgher's clothing on commando. The same corduroy trousers, dark coat, wide-brimmed hat, and home-made leather shoes that he was accustomed to wearing in everyday life on the farm were considered suitable for his military venture. Officers could not be easily distinguished from the rank and file, as they wore the same ordinary clothes as their men.

Everything the burgher would require on commando was packed in saddle bags or tied to the saddle: a blanket, a tarpaulin in case of rain (some men possessed raincoats), a three-legged pot for cooking, a kettle for boiling water, and bags of flour, meat and salt. Winter, the *biltong*-making season, had just passed and the *biltong* was hanging in long rows in the larder. *Biltong* consisted of strips of beef or venison cut about a foot long, salted and air-dried to a nourishing and tasty food. It was inconceivable that a burgher would depart without his *biltong* and *beskuit* – hard oven-baked rusks made by Boer women. The preparations completed, often three generations, father, son and grandson, departed for the front together, as the photograph on the opposite page shows most strikingly.

'When once the Boer left his home', remarked Howard Hillegas, the American journalist who accompanied the republican forces, 'he became an army unto himself'.[2] He needed no one to care for himself and his horse, no orders were necessary for his guidance. At the arranged meeting-place where the individual burghers assembled to form a commando, some had already turned up with big white-tented ox-waggons stacked with ammunition, commissariat stores, and such extra luggage as some might wish to carry – even iron bedsteads were brought, though these had to be abandoned of course once the war developed into its irregular phase towards the middle of 1900. The commando having been formed, the procession to the front began. There was no obvious order or discipline, merely a group of mounted burghers proceeding with rifles and bandoliers slung over their shoulders.[3] If the commando came from a district a long way from the front, the men embarked at the nearest railway station.

The Boers, with their Calvinist background, looked upon the war as inherently just. A manifesto issued by the republican governments at the outbreak of the war reflects this very clearly. It concludes,

P. AMM & SONS.
Amms "Java" & "Yemecca" Coffees
ARE THE BEST.
P. AMM & SONS
TEA MERCHANTS

P.J. LEMMER
J.D.L. BOTHA
15 JAAR
C.J. PRETORIUS
43 JAAR

Religious ideals

> 'To the God of our Fathers we humbly entrust the justness of our cause. He protects justice; He blesses our arms; under His banner we march to battle for Freedom and for Fatherland!'[4]

For the Boer, politics and religion were cut from the same cloth. Singing the national anthem or patriotic songs in church services in the field or elsewhere was not uncommon. Moreover, the absolute sovereignty of God was acknowledged. As a follower of Christ, the Boer accepted that nothing could happen to him that was contrary to the will of God, and it is not uncommon to find statements to this effect in Boer diaries and memoirs. To General Smuts this perfect trust in God was something for which 'the modern world has no parallel'.[5]

The Boers saw a direct analogy between the destiny of the Afrikaner people and that of the Old Testament Israel. In a sermon in the field on 15 July 1900, the Reverend P. A. Roux took Isaiah 66:8 as his text:

> 'Shall a country be born after one day's labour, shall a nation be brought to birth all in a moment? But Zion, at the onset of her pangs bore her sons.'[6]

Services were conducted with scriptural readings mostly from the Old Testament. For most of the Boers religion was not a habit but an attitude towards life. Military failure or success, or a safe crossing of a river amidst great peril, offered the opportunity of a prayer to God or the singing of a hymn of praise. Thanksgiving services and prayer meetings were held regularly in the laager, even during the war's guerrilla phase.

The Bible was for many the main source of inspiration, and was read constantly. There are persistent references to Biblical texts (especially of the Old Testament) in Boer war diaries and in telegrams sent by officers, most often attributing victory to God. The Boers were constantly visited on commando by ministers of the three Afrikaans churches, men who made no distinction between their own members and those of other churches. About fifty ministers assisted the commandos on a full time basis. The most well-known was the Reverend J. D. Kestell, chaplain to President Steyn. At the beginning of the war Sunday was considered a day of rest and no duties such as preparation for battle were to be performed on this day. However, circumstances often made this impossible, and it proved impractical to regard Sunday as a rest day during the war's guerrilla phase. Most foreigners in the Boer laagers were deeply moved by the spiritual life the Boers led. To them the evening services in small groups were noteworthy, although they seem to have had little appreciation for the quality of the Boers' singing. 'To a connoisseur of music it must be a torment', a German volunteer concluded. 'The sound was unharmonious,' wrote a Russian nursing sister, 'for the Boers are in general not a musical people, but they sang with great inspiration and the effect at night and in such circumstances was a powerful one.'[7]

'God protects justice' ('God bescherme het Recht'), the words on the white panel of the republican flag hanging upside down in the tree behind the assembled burghers.

In these difficult and trying years the burghers relied heavily on their religion, which represented the bulwark of their national spirit. And when the end came and their independence was lost many burghers believed, 'We had sinned – but not against England!'[8] The role of religion in the life of the Boer at the turn of the century is crucial to understanding life on commando.[9]

Nevertheless, there were some who strayed from their religious ideals. On 1 December 1901 the Reverend J. P. Liebenberg wrote in his dairy:

> 'And should the dear Lord not be sorrowful over us! There is with all our anxiety and affliction still so much sin: disobedience and misbelief, vanity and apostasy from God.'

The Reverend A. P. Burger regarded such offenders as a minority who 'only formed the plaster-work of the solid building of the Afrikaner people'. Whereas Liebenberg regarded apostasy in a strictly theological sense, many Boers, even General De Wet and President Steyn, considered the actions of those Afrikaners who collaborated with the British army as tantamount to apostasy.[10] Once again the close ties between politics and religion are evident.

Looting and the destruction of property

Although strictly forbidden by officers, the destruction of property and the looting of shops, houses and farms by commandos did take place, especially during the initial Natal campaign. It was a spontaneous action by some men, but to what extent it was representative of the burghers as a whole is difficult to assess. The British authorities maintained that the looting in Natal was fairly widespread, and the Reverend J. M. Louw preached against the misconduct of 'many' in Natal. A large number of burghers, however, disapproved of such actions, and there were cases later in the war when punishments were inflicted by officers for these kinds of offences. In this regard S. B. Spies concludes:

> 'While it cannot be said that the exhortations of Steyn and Joubert [to respect all private property and individuals] were implicitly obeyed, the destruction of property by the Boers on commando was not sanctioned by their leaders.'

It seems that orderly proceedings depended on officers who could enforce discipline on their men. Generally, shopkeepers who were willing to supply burghers in occupied territory received cash for their goods.[11]

Drunkenness on commando did occur, but only on a small scale. Once when General Piet Fourie came upon 'one sad spectacle of drunkenness' (in the words of the Reverend Kestell), he there and then poured all the liquor on the ground. Rompel, war correspondent of *De Volksstem*, regarded the Boers as 'moderate in drinking', and the occasional bottle of brandy, whisky or champagne was looked upon by the rank and file as a welcome gift. De Wet maintained that the Boers were no drunkards; 'on the contrary,' he stated, 'when compared with other nations, they are remarkable for their sobriety, and it is considered by them a disgrace for a man to be drunk.' Drunkenness was also highly dangerous, of course; an inebriate soldier became an easy target.[12]

Military discipline

According to General De Wet, real discipline did not exist among the burghers. Although as the war progressed discipline improved, throughout it was always far from perfect. 'I do not intend to imply that the burghers were unwilling or unruly,' De Wet wrote later, 'it was only that they were quite unaccustomed to being under orders.'[13] Other observers remarked upon the same themes.[14] The Boer commando fighter was a self-reliant individualist on his farm, accustomed to acting on his own initiative and unwilling to take orders from anyone. Every burgher was his own general. He knew the veld and in this way acquired the natural ability to provide for himself in the most desperate circumstances. At least during the early stages of the war the Boer force was also a democratic military institution. The system of election of officers effaced almost all traces of authority between officers and men. The burgher regarded his elected officer as a public servant and often obeyed or disobeyed his orders as he chose. The burgher had elected his officer for social and political reasons and as such did not regard him as his superior in the military sphere. The field-cornets were supposed to have authority over their men, the commandants over the field-cornets, and the generals over the commandants, but this authority could only be applied with the approval of those in the lower ranks. It is surprising to observe how sometimes the will of a single field-cornet or the collective determination of a group of burghers could influence a war council or even determine policy or strategy. The following argument advanced by an ordinary commando fighter is typical of the outlook of many burghers:

General Christiaan de Wet (arm raised) addresses a meeting at Potchefstroom, 27 August 1900. De Wet was one of the Boer generals most concerned about discipline on commando. A rigorous disciplinarian himself, he regularly ordered the use of the sjambok *even for minor cases of disobedience. However, because burghers were unaccustomed to being under orders, even De Wet had to acknowledge that there were limits beyond which he dare not go in the enforcement of unpopular decisions.*

> 'I am fighting for the country and not for the field-cornet, I shall shoot the Englishman when he enters the country, but I won't be dictated to. Kruger asked whether we wanted to fight, and when we said "yes" we knew that it was the will of God. Kruger might be the president, but the people are king. I won't allow . . . [myself] to be dictated to by a field-cornet.'[15]

Discipline improved when after a few months it was laid down that the Commander-in-Chief was to *nominate* field-cornets and commandants. The new leaders were men not only of social, political and religious standing, but also men of authority who as such had a positive influence on discipline. Their task was also made easier by the gravity of the Boers' military predicament; by the middle of 1900 it was clear to all that the war would not follow the pattern of that of 1880–1, and that defeat could only be avoided by tight discipline.

A serious problem at the beginning of the war was that many burghers refused to go to battle, preferring to remain in the laager during the fighting. Whether these men were predominantly *bywoners*, poor Afrikaners, many of whom later joined the British, still needs to be examined. In the later irregular phase of the war the problem was largely overcome by the fact that the commandos were 'purified' of unwilling burghers who had gone home or had joined the enemy, although there were at the later stage those who had been commandeered against their will or those who did not regard the Boer cause with the same patriotic fervour as the die-hards. It is also true that idleness leading to apathy sometimes jeopardized attempts to maintain discipline on commando.

Absenteeism

Leave and absenteeism were factors with which the Boer leaders had constantly to contend, especially during the early stages of the war. According to the Reverend Kestell, in the majority of cases there was no sound excuse to justify a request for leave: 'It was simply because they could not stand the confinement of the life in a laager', he concluded. Perhaps more realistically, men on commando were naturally anxious about the security of their farms and families and the maintenance in their absence of their livelihoods. At home, however, female relations and friends sometimes made life difficult for the burgher on leave from the front, arguing that they 'thought more of a man who fights for his country than of one who is constantly at home'.[16] Initially there was no system of awarding leave, and burghers were granted absence on an *ad hoc* basis by their commandant. The problem soon arose that some commandants granted permission for leave more easily than others, so that the generals had to take over the function. The phenomenon of absenteeism became known as 'leave pest'. Later, when many women and children were interned in concentration camps, and when harvests were destroyed by the British, the need for leave diminished, and visits home were made mainly when a commando fighter was in his own neighbourhood. Interestingly, during the war's early stages, there seems to be a clear correlation between low morale and absenteeism, such as during the first few weeks in Natal, in February 1900 on all fronts, and in May 1900 in the northern Free State.

The problem of the waggon laager

One of the best examples of lack of real discipline among the Boer forces concerns the cumbersome waggon laager. In the initial stages of the war many burghers brought luxuries on their waggons, such as beds and mattresses and stoves, luxuries which in due course had to be given up as the war moved into its irregular phase. The lack of mobility caused by an overburdening waggon laager was partly responsible for General Cronjé's surrender with 4 000 men to Lord Roberts at Paardeberg on 27 February 1900. At a war council on 17 March 1900 at Kroonstad it was therefore decided to abandon all waggons, only a small number to be retained for food and ammunition. However, in June 1900 it was found that waggons were again accumulating dangerously, especially among the Free State forces, since men on commando wished to keep their waggons and oxen out of the hands of the British troops, who were confiscating all transport and livestock. De Wet became convinced that waggons had to be dispensed with, but he knew he could not get rid of them by force: 'The great fault of the burghers', he wrote later, 'was disobedience, and this came especially to the fore when their possessions were in jeopardy.'[17] The First De Wet Hunt between July and August 1900, when more than 50 000 British troops attempted to catch De Wet and his 2 000 men, who were accompanied by a baggage train of 460 waggons, represents a watershed in this respect. Thereafter the waggon laagers were mostly abandoned, though they remained a problem right to the end of the war.[18]

Waggon laager at Paardeberg, February 1900. The lack of mobility caused by having so many waggons accompanying his force was one of the factors that contributed to Cronjé's surrender.

Methods of punishment

Difficulties over discipline among the Boer forces should not be construed to mean that disciplinary measures were not frequently enforced. There were many cases of serious and less serious attempts to punish offenders who shot at game in the field contrary to commando orders, or, especially during the irregular phase of the war, of punishments meted out to burghers whose horses were found on inspection to be in a weak or sore condition because of neglect. The nature of the punishments enforced were often humiliating. A petty form of punishment was *paksaal* (pack-saddle). The offender's rifle, ammunition and bridle were fastened to his saddle, and he was then compelled to walk around camp for hours with his saddle on his head, while he was teased and ridiculed by the rest of the commando. Another method of dealing with offenders was *beesvelry* (tossing). The victim was thrust into a bloody hide, freshly stripped from a slaughtered bullock. Holes were cut into the hide to provide a good grip for a few pairs of hands. Thereupon the victim was tossed in the air. The moment he hit the blood-smeared surface he was tossed again and again until at last he was considered to have suffered enough for his offence and had satisfied the mocking onlookers. Striking a match during a dangerous operation at night was punished by a few *sjambok* cuts, a treatment which De Wet enjoyed meting out even for minor cases of disobedience.[19]

Social distinction

When considering the extent to which social distinction was evident on commando something of a paradox emerges. On the one hand political equality among the Boers was a striking feature of the period. Furthermore, the idea of equality accorded with the Boers' religious belief that every (white) person was equal before God.[20] The social differences that existed were not enforced or drawn sharply. *Bywoners* (sub-farmers or squatters) and other poorer Afrikaners were not especially looked down upon while on commando. On the other hand, a Boer aristocracy of wealthy families existed, and it was from this group that the leading Boer officers were almost exclusively drawn. In the field the Boer leaders did not obviously set themselves apart from their men. Of General De Wet a foreign volunteer testified:

> 'We enjoy his simple meal, because he does not live better than any other burgher, he desires no better accommodation, no better food, no better clothing; he does not want to be more than any other.'[21]

Although the Boer aristocrat, the ordinary burgher and the *bywoner* were all compelled to share the hardships generated by commando life, the wealthier burgher was in a much more favourable position. At critical moments he was able to obtain enough food either by purchasing supplies from the local population or by using his influence with members of the commissariat. As the war progressed one clear distinction became apparent between the wealthy and poor burghers, namely the possession of horses, of which the ordinary commando fighters usually had two, the wealthy burghers more. In Cronjé's laager in February 1900, as well as during the general retreat in May of the same year and especially during the guerrilla phase of the war, many burghers were left without any horses. Since the Boer fighter depended almost entirely on his horse, these men were placed in a very difficult position, and a foreign volunteer who also had lost his horse remarked:

> 'As infantryman one cannot achieve anything of significance, one does not belong to the Boer army and is ever in the company of an Afrikaner of lesser sort.'[22]

African participation on commando

Although from a political and military point of view this was a white man's war, coloureds and blacks whose chiefs had been brought under Boer control and were loyal to the governments were also to be found in the service of the Boers. The constitutions of both republics provided for this. The blacks did not, however, form part of the armed forces, and were officially forbidden to take up arms against the British. Indeed, the laws of the republics forbade the possession of firearms by Africans and coloureds within their borders. The Boers found the thought of full-scale black participation in the war completely alien to them. S. B. Spies has concluded:

> 'There may have been instances where Africans fought on the side of the Boers during the war of 1899–1902

> [e.g. at Mafeking], but these were rare and isolated occurrences, and did not have the approval of the Boer higher commands or governments.'

The blacks were therefore used either as labourers on the farms of commandeered burghers (in other words, ordered to remain on the farms of their employers), or as servants (commonly called *agterryers*) for many of the burghers on commando. Here they had to attend to the livestock of the Boers, guard the horses during a fight or skirmish, drive carts, ride spare horses, fetch wood, kindle fires and make coffee and prepare food.[23] Although an ancestor of this author was murdered on commando by his *agterryer*,[24] the relationship generally seems to have been very cordial. 'We remained with our masters in the field', recalled an old *agterryer* in 1967, 'and wherever they trod we followed.' This loyalty arose from the fact that each Boer child on the farm usually had a black child of the same age attached to him as a playmate. As they grew up together the black became a constant companion in hunting and war. Therefore, in spite of differences of race and education, a strong attachment arose on both sides.[25]

Since the *agterryers* did not form part of the armed forces of the republics, no exact statistics are available of the numbers involved. If St Leger is correct in his view that the majority of the Boers had *agterryers*, as many as 40 000 blacks may have accompanied the Boers, though this figure is almost certainly an overestimation. References to numbers are not found in diaries or memoirs, probably because the Boers regarded the *agterryers* as mere servants, inferior to the white race and having nothing to do with the white man's war. In fact, the Boer did not regard the black man as his equal. This is evident from the disgust among the burghers when foreign volunteers associated with black women. These foreigners were subsequently excluded from Boer society.[26]

African drivers crossing a swollen river. Large numbers of African servants (agterryers) *accompanied the Boer forces, and played a vital supportive role in the military system of the republics.*

Sentry duty and scouting

The physical experience of life on commando can best be illustrated by describing some of the outstanding daily events. There was sentry duty, of course, a time-honoured task in the Boer experience. This took two forms. First there was group picket duty, where thirty men under a corporal, who was appointed as a liaison officer between the field-cornet and the burghers, went out to picket about half an hour's walking distance from the laager. There, the burghers with their Mausers and blankets would await dusk; someone would read from the Bible and say a prayer, followed by the singing of a psalm. Then they were ready for their watch duty. The picket usually consisted of an entrenchment of rocks, corrugated iron and sandbags. While two men were on guard duty the rest wrapped themselves in their blankets on beds of hay inside the picket. This kind of sentry duty occurred during the first months of the war on all fronts. The second type was that of single guards posted around the laager, or, later, during the irregular phase of the war, around the commando. As one of the burghers put it, one soon learnt to view sentry duty as one of the toughest, most tedious and nerve-racking jobs, without which no well organized commando dared to pass the night. Changing of the guard occurred just before sunset and just after sunrise. The fact that one group released the other only when the first group returned to the laager sometimes cleared the way for a surprise attack. This was also made possible when the Boer intelligence system failed.

Burghers, with Mausers and blankets, ready to leave camp for sentry duty.

Burghers on sentry duty at Spion Kop, January 1900.

However, the superiority of Boer scouting was one of the outstanding features of the war. Organized scouting corps served as the most important intelligence service of the Boer forces. Initially there was a Cycling Corps under Captain Danie Theron, used mainly for transmitting dispatches and scouting. In March 1900 Theron's Scouting Corps was formed with the specific purpose of gaining information about the enemy and assessing the Boers' own position. The corps became the eyes and ears of the rest of the Boer forces, and some adventurous foreign volunteers became members of the unit. After Theron's death in September 1900 other scouting corps were formed which did useful work all over South Africa, especially in the Cape Colony. Ordinary burghers were also used for scouting. The finest tribute to the Boers' scouting system came from Sir George White, the British Commander of Ladysmith, who complained,

> 'I could not move a gun, even if I did not give the order till midnight, but they knew it by daylight next morning.'

The Boers' successes in this field can be attributed above all to their familiarity with the country and its terrain.[27]

Dispatch riding

Coupled with sentry duty and scouting was the system of dispatch riding. Because of the nature of their military operations during the irregular phase of the war, the Boers did not require the same effective communication system as the British, who needed a sound system to track down the scattered commandos. However, through their dispatch riders, who easily passed through the British lines at night, the Boers maintained regular contact between the furthest post in the Cape Colony and the remote north-east corner of the Transvaal. Journeys could take a long time, however, as a ride of sixteen days (that is, fifteen nights) in October 1900 from Lydenburg in the eastern Transvaal to Bethlehem in the eastern Free State reveals.[28]

Foodstuff and munition supplies

The Boers coming from sentry duty after sunrise received their first cup of coffee and *beskuit* of the day. As the war progressed coffee became an extremely scarce commodity, and was supplemented by some ingeniously prepared beverages, such as that made from the roots of a wild tree that were cut up and roasted, or other drinks concocted from corn, barley, maize, dried peaches and sweet potatoes. Water was abundant, especially after heavy rain, but some commandos did experience difficulties operating in the arid north-western Cape during the war's irregular phase. Sugar became extremely scarce even before July 1900.

After coffee the man appointed as cook for the day for his close group of five or six men began work. The eight days for which the burghers had to provide for themselves when called to the front were soon over, and it became the responsibility of the governments to provide for them by means of commissariats, which were located on all fronts. The commissariats were mostly improperly administered. The system was frequently abused, and shortages were common. In the last two years of the war much smaller commissariats equipped with meat, corn and flour often accompanied the scattered commandos. Field-cornets, commandants or even individual burghers bought additional provisions when these were available from farms through which they were passing. Hideouts in mountainous areas were used to store food, and crops were sometimes secretly cultivated. The commandos' staple diet consisted of meat, roasted, boiled or dried, and bread and porridge (made from maize). *Biltong* was an invaluable source of food when going out on a sortie lasting a few days or more. *Stormjagers*, cakes baked in boiling fat, were also made from flour.[29]

Slaughtering cattle in a Boer laager.

Members of General de Wet's force dining on the veld. As the war continued food supplies became increasingly scarce, and burghers were often obliged to ambush British convoys or seize cattle and grain from African settlements.

Foodstuff and munition supplies generally became more difficult once the war entered its irregular phase. Even at the beginning of the war Lourenço Marques in Mozambique, described as a 'hotbed of intrigue' by a British newspaper, was the only connection the two republics had with the outside world, and the British government did everything in its power to prevent imports through this harbour. Through the skilled diplomacy of their minister plenipotentiary in Europe, Dr W. J. Leyds, the government of the South African Republic managed to receive a consignment of three million cartridges and two hundred Mausers (worth £3 million) immediately before the declaration of war. But three days after the fighting began the British government signed a secret agreement with Portugal whereby she undertook to protect Portugal and her possessions in exchange for a promise not to allow munitions to pass through Mozambique to the Boers. Portuguese officials in Lourenço Marques not only prevented munitions officially passing through the port to the republics, but also supplies of foodstuffs such as coffee and sugar. Despite this, and despite the alertness of British agents in Europe and Lourenço Marques, Leyds succeeded by means of bribery and misleading consignment notes to smuggle through contraband throughout the war, and he was still busy with this when the war ended. This was also made possible by making use of other harbours in Mozambique, such as Inhambane, Quelimane and Beira. Until his *exequatur* as Consul-General of the South African Republic in Lourenço Marques was withdrawn in November 1900, Gerard Pott also found the most ingenious ways of smuggling through contraband.[30] The extent to which these imports aided the Boers in the field, or prolonged the war, can only be guessed. Their influence has probably been over-estimated because the distribution of supplies to the scattered commandos during the last two years presented difficulties of its own.

The Boers found many ways through which they lightened their burden. A common remark according to Kestell was that 'everything was scarce; but nothing completely lacking'.[31] Men were appointed to tan hides and make boots to replace worn-out footwear; soap was manufactured by boiling the ashes of maize-cobs and various weeds; corn mills were mounted on waggons and hidden when the British troops approached; salt was dug up in dry pans, although this source was eventually exhausted. The problem of clothing, a serious one by the middle of 1901, was also solved. Overcoats were made of sheepskin and trousers and jackets were mended with leather or made from enemy blankets. At this stage the custom of *uitschudden* (stripping) came into force. This meant that when British soldiers were captured their clothes were stripped from them and worn by those burghers who needed them. Throughout the irregular phase of the war captured British convoys also supplied the commandos with provisions. Indeed, a German volunteer on the Boer side believed that munition and foodstuffs would never be lacking so long as there were British troops in South Africa. This was true, especially of munitions, and many a burgher laid down a British Lee Metford following the conclusion of peace. No burgher, it was said, dared complain to his commandant that his ammunition supply was exhausted, for he would simply receive the reply that a diligent burgher acquired his own ammunition from enemy sources. Nonetheless, in spite of all these improvisations, the lack of foodstuff and other supplies undoubtedly became a serious problem during the last two years of the war.

'with horse, saddle and bridle'

The Boer was pre-eminently a mounted rifleman. He was called upon to appear on commando 'with horse, saddle and bridle . . .'. Although the number of infantrymen increased as the war progressed because of the shortage of horses, the mounted men were the important group that kept the war going during the last two years of the struggle. Life on commando turned the ordinary farm horse into a commando horse and gradually hardened the animal into a war horse. Compared to the imported English, Australian or Argentinian horses of the British mounted troopers, the Boer horse was tough and accustomed to South African conditions. With good reason Major General J. P. Brabazon declared in a report on the Imperial Yeomanry that 'the horse of the country is the horse for the country', something that the Imperial Yeomanry learned to their regret. For the burgher on commando his horse was his first love. The care expended on his horse was one of the reasons why the Boer was an excellent fighter. His first concern was for his animal, sparing him whenever he could, but taking everything out of him when necessary, which partly explains the irregular pace of a commando on trek, in contrast to the precise regularity of the British mounted columns. The condition of the Boers' horses does not appear to have deteriorated significantly as the war dragged on. The winter of 1901 did take its toll, but most animals recovered after strenuous treks.

At night the horses were tied next to their masters with ample forage, but a lack of forage ensured that they were brought into an enclosure and knee-haltered. This meant that a rope was run through the halter near the horse's muzzle and tied close above the knee-joint of the near fore-leg. In this way the horse could not move away at any pace beyond a slow walk. To catch and saddle it in a hurry after the 'saddle-up' whistle had sounded therefore only took a matter of a few seconds. If the commando did not depart on the following morning the horses would be allowed to graze during the day in the same way. During the guerrilla phase of the war it sometimes happened that the order was given at midnight or even later to saddle up and be ready to move off at a moment's notice. The Boers' dexterity in the harnessing and unharnessing of waggons and carts enabled them to gain valuable time on the enemy, which was no small advantage during the guerrilla war when the Boers still retained some waggons in the field.[32]

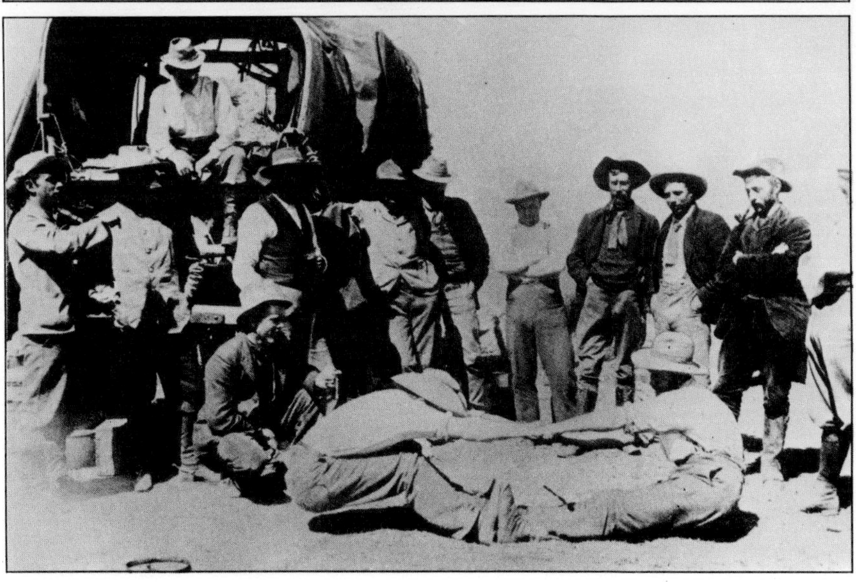

Recreation in the Boer laager: above, leg wrestling; below, a test of strength.

Health and medical services

There remains for discussion the question of general health and the medical services available to the Boers. The 'Transvaalsche Roode Kruis' (Red Cross) in the South African Republic, was organized on a voluntary basis and subsidized by the state in the purchase of medicine, bandages and other necessary provisions. It was established in 1896 and was bound by the Geneva Convention. At the beginning of the war the twenty-odd sections of the TRK operated on all fronts as field hospitals, as well as in some towns. There were even four ambulance trains fitted out to carry wounded and sick men from the front to Pretoria. This system of moving patients by rail generally worked well before the fall of Pretoria in June 1900, though many of the Boers who were wounded or fell ill close to their own farms preferred to return home as soon as the opportunity arose. The TRK as a whole, however, did not function properly and already in January 1900 the government was obliged to appoint a Medical Commission, which assumed most of its responsibilities. In the Orange Free State Dr A. E. W. Ramsbottom of Bloemfontein established an ambulance immediately preceding the outbreak of the war, which was assisted by the TRK and the foreign ambulances that were organized to assist the republics. These came from countries where the Boers enjoyed considerable support. There was an Irish-American ambulance, a Russo-Dutch ambulance, a Belgian ambulance, and three German and three Dutch ambulances. The medical services of the Boers were further extended by a number of medical doctors, both from South Africa and overseas, who chose to work independently of these organizations.

During the war there was a remarkable success in the healing of wounds and a low incidence of infection. Interestingly, it seems that the Boers suffered much less seriously from typhoid than British soldiers. This was the view of a Russian doctor, Kukharenko, who served on both sides, and his opinion

A Boer ambulance. On the right of the photograph a bullet is being removed from a wounded man lying on a make-shift bed.

was supported by another doctor from the Russo-Dutch ambulance, Von Rennenkampf, who reckoned that the Boers might well have picked up the disease from staying on British camp sites. Despite claims in Boer reminiscences that the burghers never even suffered from colds while on commando, the ambulance personnel, according to Sister Izedinova, always had a few cases of men weakened by chill. The men who suffered most in this way were the youths of between fifteen and twenty, the main causes being inadequate food and frosty nights spent in the open air at sentry posts. Many a young Boer had not yet outgrown childrens' diseases, while rheumatism and lumbago also occurred widely among the older men.

The Europeans coming to the support of the Boers were shocked by the suspicion and prejudice with which the local people regarded them. At the beginning of the war this attitude was an obstacle, particularly to those foreign ambulances that immediately went into the field. A report by Dr Muller, who went to the field with his Dutch ambulance in August 1900, shows that this attitude had hardly changed by the later stages of the war. As early as the middle of 1900 the Boers experienced great difficulties in obtaining supplies, especially imported medicine and other medical requirements. Up to that stage the ambulances had managed somehow or other with the aid of the Medical Commission to overcome difficulties in obtaining foodstuffs, medical supplies and bed linen. However, after the fall of Pretoria the foreign ambulances mostly left the country, Dr Muller's being the only medical team of the period that was fitted out and left for the front. During the next month (September 1900) President Steyn advised a foreign volunteer returning to Germany that the Boers did not need ambulances but rather individual doctors from Europe. During the irregular phase of the war it often happened that wounded or sick men had to be content with only very rudimentary medical treatment, and many fell into the hands of the enemy.[33]

References

1. J. H. Breytenbach, *Die Geskiedenis van die Tweede Vryheidsoorlog in Suid-Afrika, 1899–1902*, I, Pretoria, 1969, 31–3, 38–9, 132–3; C. R. de Wet, *Three Years War*, London, 1902, 9; W. H. Ackermann, *Opsaal. Herinneringe aan die Tweede Vryheidsoorlog*, Johannesburg, 1969, 193 *et passim*.
2. H. C. Hillegas, *With the Boer Forces*, London, 1901, 53.
3. *Ibid.*, 60.
4. Breytenbach, 139–40 (translation). See also speeches by General De Wet on p. 69 of O. Hintrager, *Met Steijn en de Wet op Kommando*, Rotterdam, 1902; N. Hofmeyr, *Zes Maanden bij de Commando's*, 's-Gravenhage, 1903, 30–1; H. Ver Loren van Themaat, *Twee Jaren in den Boerenoorlog*, Haarlem, 1903, 35.
5. Ver Loren van Themaat, 320; S. Izedinova, *A Few Months with the Boers. The War Reminiscences of a Russian Nursing Sister*, Johannesburg, 1977, 67; A. Barry, *Ons Japie. Dagboek gehou gedurende die Driejarige Oorlog*, Johannesburg, 1960, 3; De Wet, 38, 63, 173, 193, 237, 264, 276, 355; C. Plokhooy, *Met den Mauser. Persoonlijke Ervaringen in den Zuid-Afrikaanschen Oorlog*, Gorinchem, 1902, 62; J. D. Kestell, *Through Shot and Flame*, London, 1903, 190–2, 195; T. van Rensburg ed., *Oorlogsjoernaal van S. J. Burger 1899–1902*, Pretoria, 1977, 1–2, 64, 98; R. de Kersauson de Pennendreff, *Ek en die Vierkleur*, Johannesburg, 1960, 121; Zuster Hellemans, *Met het Roode Kruis mee in den Boeren-Vrijheidsoorlog*, Amsterdam, 1901, 17; J. D. Kriel, Die Verhouding tussen Kerk en Staat in die Republiek van die Oranje-Vrystaat, 1854–1902, *Archives Yearbook of South African History*, 16, 1 (1953), 207; G. D. Scholtz, *Die Geskiedenis van die Nederduitse Hervormde of Gereformeerde Kerk van*

Suid-Afrika, II, Cape Town, 1960, 91–2; Smuts to W. T. Stead, 4 January 1902, cited in W. K. Hancock and J. van der Poel eds., *Selections from the Smuts Papers*, I, Cambridge, 1966, 436.

6. Private Collection, diary of Jacob de Villiers, 15 July 1900; Hintrager, 48.
7. Izedinova, 67; Hintrager, 32, 67, 117–18; Kestell, 5, 44, 55, 129, 164, 166, 169, 200, 227, 231; Kersauson, 11, 128–9, 133; Ver Loren van Themaat, 57, 59, 235, 247, 252, 265–6, 279, 308, 326; A. J. V. Burger, *Worsteljare*, Cape Town, 1936, 10, 15, 41, 65, 82–3, 84; P. J. du Plessis, *Oomblikke van Spanning*, Cape Town, 1938, 98, 179; Plokhooy, 56, 90; Hofmeyr, 62, 67, 143, 156; Hillegas, 57, 83–4, 112, 224–6; Breytenbach, 74–5; O. J. O. Ferreira ed., *Krijgsgevangenschap van L. C. Ruijssenaers, 1899–1902*, Pretoria, 1977, 170; S. E. St. Leger, *War Sketches in Colour*, London, 1903, 195–6; C. J. Barnard, *Generaal Louis Botha op die Natalse Front, 1899–1900*, Cape Town, 1970, 68.
8. De Wet, 361.
9. See the lectures delivered in 1898 by Abraham Kuyper at Princeton University subsequently published under the title *Lectures on Calvinism* by Wm. B. Eerdman, 1961 and earlier.
10. Ackermann, 290 (trans.); Burger, 84 (trans.); Hintrager, 124–5; Ver Loren van Themaat, 317.
11. Plokhooy, 6, 9–12; Kestell, 12–13, 114, 130; Ruijssenaers, 59; Ver Loren van Themaat, 59; S. B. Spies, *Methods of Barbarism? Roberts and Kitchener and the Boer Republics, January 1900–May 1902*, Cape Town, 1977, 30.
12. Kestell, 111; F. Rompel, *Heroes of the Boer War*, London, 1903, 18–19; De Wet, 81; Jacob de Villiers, 15 July 1900; Ver Loren van Themaat, 158; D. Mostert, *Slegtkamp van Spioenkop*, Cape Town, 1938, 106; H. J. C. Pieterse, *Oorlogsavonture van Genl. Wynand Malan*, Cape Town, 1941, 86.
13. De Wet, 13–14, 80.
14. Cf. Hillegas, 103; Jacob de Villiers, 17 August 1900; Hintrager, 7; Kestell, 17–18.
15. Hillegas, 91; Ver Loren van Themaat, 18 (trans.).
16. Kestell, 31; Ver Loren van Themaat, 61 (trans.). See A. G. Hales, *Campaign Pictures of the War in South Africa (1899–1900)*, London, 1901, 122–123.
17. De Wet, 156. See F. Pretorius, *Die Eerste Dryfjag op Hoofkmdt. C. R. de Wet* (Published as no. 4 of *Christiaan De Wet-Annale*), Bloemfontein, 1976, 59–60.
18. Hintrager, 104.
19. Ver Loren van Themaat, 101, 174; Kestell, 100–1, 116; Ackermann, 169, 172–3; Plokhooy, 35–6; Kersauson, 130, 133; Jacob de Villiers, 16 July 1900; De Wet, 359; Hales, 123–4; P. Pienaar, *With Steyn and De Wet*, London, 1902, 139–40.
20. Cf. P. W. Grobbelaar ed., *Die Afrikaner en sy Kultuur. Mens en Land*, I, Cape Town, 1974, 148–9.
21. Ver Loren van Themaat, 325 (trans.), cf. 245, 252; Plokhooy, 63–4; Hillegas, 81–2.
22. Ver Loren van Themaat, 87 (trans.), cf. 193, 231; Plokhooy, 52.
23. Breytenbach, 32, 36–7; Spies, 345n, 156; Ackermann, 360, 365, 367, 370; Ver Loren van Themaat, 180, 269; D. J. N. Denoon, 'Participation in the Boer War; People's War, People's Non-War, or Non-People's War?' in B. A. Ogot ed., *War and Society in Africa*, London, 1972, 110.
24. T. H. Lewis ed., *Women of South Africa*, Cape Town, 1913, 276; oral evidence of Mmes. H. J. W. Pretorius, A. van Rooyen and W. Mandy, 4 December 1978.
25. Ackermann, 369 (trans.); Izedinova, 88; cf. Kestell, 259–60.
26. St. Leger, 187; Ver Loren van Themaat, 159, 177.
27. Hales, 99; Plokhooy, 65–9, 72; Ver Loren van Themaat, 52, 210; De Wet, 26; Burger, 100; Du Plessis, 18; Breytenbach, 68–71; Hillegas, 107–8.
28. Kersauson, 12; Breytenbach, 106; Rompel, 32, 34.
29. Plokhooy, 42–6, 53, 55, 57; St. Leger, 187; Hintrager, 26, 34, 41; O. T. de Villiers, 44; De Wet, 10–11, 253, 288; Ver Loren van Themaat, 53–4, 96, 138, 146, 228, 238; Burger, 98.
30. For Leyds' secret war activities see L. E. van Niekerk, 'Dr W. J. Leyds se Geheime Oorlogsbedrywighede' in *Historia*, 23, 1 (1978), 15–31 (shortened and published as 'Master spy was Boer lifeline' in *The Star* (Johannesburg), 9 September 1978, 14).
31. Kestell, 207.
32. Public Record Office, London, WO 108/263, Report on the Imperial Yeomanry, 16 October 1900, 6; Hillegas, 76–8; Hales, 98; De Wet, 219; Ackermann, 144, 374–7; Kersauson, 59; Ver Loren van Themaat, 105, 252, 286–7; Rompel, 32; Plokhooy, 59; C. M. Bakkes, 'Die Boer as Berede Skutter gedurende die Tweede Vryheidsoorlog' in *Infantry in South Africa, 1652–1976*, 5, Documentary Service, Pretoria, 1977, 29.
33. Izedinova, 16, 18, 30, 53, 94, 137, 142, 146, 237, 241; Hintrager, 88, 91, 123; Breytenbach, 71–4; Plokhooy, 68; Ver Loren van Themaat, 21; Ackermann, 144, 271; Hellemans, *passim*; J. C. Roos, 'Het Transvaalsche Roode Kruis gedurende die Tweede Vryheidsoorlog, 1899–1902', MA thesis, University of South Africa, 1943, 155, 156, 158 *et passim*; *De Vereeniging Het Nederlandsche Roode Kruis in den Transvaalsch-Engelschen Oorlog, 1899–1901*, 's-Gravenhage, 1901, *passim*.

CHAPTER 5

Tommy Atkins in South Africa

William Nasson

Working class experience in South Africa

Many ordinary British soldiers in South Africa found life tedious, dreary and boring. The more articulate representatives of the military rank and file had time to write (sometimes copiously) about their wartime experiences, and the substance of this body of writing reflects the unglamorous life of Tommy Atkins in South Africa. Some of the reactions of the ordinary soldier have in this way filtered through, and these letters, while not equalling in scope the mass of correspondence, diaries and personal reminiscences bequeathed by the officer class, do serve to illuminate areas of common experience shared by British working class soldiers during the years 1899–1902.

A hard-headed view of the war, often coloured by bitterness and cynicism, emerges from the letters written by ordinary troopers. A sense of injustice and resentment at shabby treatment is a notable recurring theme in working class writing, the feeling that, as one trooper phrased it, 'Tommy was anything but treated fair . . . they put us down to the lowest of the low'. Regular soldiers discovered that far from being welcomed as rescuing heroes by the English-speaking white community in South Africa, the settler 'swells' of Natal and the Cape Colony were often less than generous towards common soldiers. Angered by the attitude of white civilians in Ladysmith, a regimental drummer, writing in the aftermath of the relief of the town (and without recourse to punctuation), complained:

> 'When Ladysmith was first Besieged the Civilians stowed all their food away and Poor Tommy Atkins that is the Soldiers name starved with them but what was the result when Ladysmith ran short they did not share with Tommy the Poor Absent Minded Beggar as they called him in England if anyone saw Ladysmith they would want to know what we are fighting for it is a miserable looking place and don't Forget it has a fat graveyard with our poor Lads but I hope they are better off out of the misery of a life such as this.'[1]

Recruitment

What prompted working class men to join the ranks and service the imperial cause when, even as late as 1900, conditions of army service were still brutally severe? Before turning to the reality of Tommy Atkins' South African experiences, a brief look at recruitment and the motives of recruits is necessary. The pioneering study by Richard Price, *An Imperial War and the British Working Class* (1972), has suggested that the British working class did not respond to the patriotic call in the large numbers and with the jingoistic zeal that had once been supposed. Working class responses to the recruitment drive were in the main determined by fairly unromantic factors such as the desire to alleviate unemployment; soldiering for its own sake, it has been argued, provided little glamour for working class Victorians. Incidents such as Mafeking night, formerly thought to have been symbolic of working class enthusiasm for the war, have been interpreted recently as representing little more than spontaneous mass expressions of relief at the saving of British lives.[2] Yet, as M. D. Blanch argues in Chapter Nine, it remains unreasonable to assume that some feelings of popular patriotism and militarism did not play a part in encouraging working men to enlist. It is incorrect to suggest that unemployment directly propelled men into the ranks of the army. Clearly other factors were at work in popular society, and the role of imperialist and militarist ideas in encouraging working men to enlist cannot easily be discounted as salient factors.[3]

Life aboard ship

Militarist and imperialist ideologies were reinforced during the journey to South Africa. Presented with an ideal, immobile audience, officers on ships lectured Tommies on Boer 'attributes' and South African conditions. Information transmitted ranged from rudimentary political analysis ('Now the facts about the Cape. Rebels and Disloyals abound not excepting Judges and Magistrates to say nothing of Parsons. . . . Subjects of His Majesty turn rebel and shoot Poor Tommy'[4]) to more bizarre anthropomorphic topics, such as the 'animal' nature of Boer eyesight (ie. his 'savage' gift of optical superiority). Throughout the voyage, however, soldiers were reassured about 'Johnny Boer's' general genetic inferiority in comparison with Anglo-Saxon stock.

Dull lectures were undoubtedly the least unpleasant feature of life at sea. Cocooned within the iron walls of steamers, soldiers found that the mode of life aboard troopships was harsh. Living space and toilet facilities were minimal; personal hygiene for more than six hundred troops crammed aboard the SS *Gaul* in February 1901 became an intensely competitive activity: 'water is only turned on for an hour each morning and there are 680 troops scrambling wildly for it', remarked one soldier.[5] The shipboard environment with its poor sanitation and inadequate ventilation, coupled with the fact that large numbers of recruits had never been to sea before, resulted in a not insignificant incidence of illnesses and accidents. Matters were not improved by the provision of poor food. 'Bad Pork and High Fish', in the words of one victim, had a disastrous effect upon men in his contingent aboard a ship in January 1900, resulting in acute food poisoning, dysentery and several deaths at sea attributed to diarrhoea.

Once soldiers arrived in South Africa, any illusion that the constant assurances of officers beforehand that the Boers would prove to be inferior opponents was speedily dispelled. An anonymous correspondent wrote in December 1899:

> 'War is no blooming joke . . . there is no doubt it is a much harder business than people expected . . . to all intents and purposes Boers are just as well-armed and a good many of us think their Art [ie. artillery] is better. . . .'[6]

Another man, pinned down along with his regiment by Boer firepower, reflected:

> 'We were forced to lay there for hours, the Boers 'pinking' away at us every time we moved or exposed ourselves . . . it was awful.'[7]

'The motivation to combat'

The limits of army leadership and obedience were regularly tested during campaigns and on a number of occasions the latter element was found gravely wanting. Officers were acutely conscious of the need to maintain a stiff upper lip even in the most desperate of situations. Harried by a Boer force near Ladysmith in November 1899, one officer wrote:

> 'Really some days it is hard to be cheerful: things seem to go wrong and fellows get hit with shells but one must remain cheerful for the sake of the men.'[8]

Ordinary Tommies were less obsessed with the need to preserve 'the motivation to combat', and in the face of what they collectively considered to be impossible odds, they broke ranks and ran, voting with their feet in the most emphatic manner possible. The primary code was, not unnaturally, that of self-preservation. The abandoning of a position in the vicinity of Spion Kop by panic-stricken troops was described by one observer as 'just too absolutely sickening to think of . . . some filthy funking regiment gets the blue panic and runs away'. When officers resorted to crude physical coercion to restore order among the troops they ran the risk of precipitating a complete breakdown of discipline. At Colenso, in January 1900, Tommies refused to advance, their nerve broken by the potentially lethal effects of Boer shelling; when officers attempted to manhandle them, their action provoked outright violence. Writing privately, Colonel H. F. N. Jourdain noted:

> 'There were instances of general officers hitting, kicking and praying the men to go on, and in some instances, threatening them with death, but to no avail. Brigadier Woodgate was shot at while attempting to keep his brigade steady. . . .This is not for publication.'[9]

The conclusion of the officer who declared that 'Tommy is the best chap going and there is a jolly . . . esprit de corps among us all'[10] was echoed from below by a member of the City of London Imperial Volunteers (CIV) who similarly perceived the existence of a corporate harmony within the military: 'We are men in all sorts of conditions, eating, sleeping and drilling shoulder to shoulder, indeed for there is no room between. Our

Above left: British Tommies aboard the SS St Andrew, bound for South Africa. Troopships were often overcrowded and insanitary, resulting in many illnesses and even death.

Above right: 'Are you a Boah?' A cartoon that formed the central feature of a mock coat of arms for the distinctly middle-class City Imperial Volunteers.

accents are various but our dress the same and our duties the same.'[11] However, statements extolling *esprit de corps* emanating from the ranks of volunteer contingents like the CIV and Imperial Yeomanry should be treated with caution. These formations were not predominantly working class in social composition and the attitudes of lower middle class clerks[12] in the CIV were very different from Tommy Atkins' attitudes towards his military superiors. The preoccupations of working class soldiers in the Regular army on the one hand and the middle class Volunteers on the other diverged sharply. Tommies were acutely aware of the limits of their social mobility and held no hopes of joining the exclusive commissioned ranks to become 'nobs'. By contrast, an ingratiating attitude towards professional officers marked the behaviour of many Volunteers, who were often anxious to move upwards into 'vacancies'.[13] It was these men, rather than Tommies, who seemed so enthusiastic about consensus and social unity in the army. The typical lower middle class Volunteer became frustrated with the officer elite only in so far as social obstacles blocked his own entry into the professional military caste. Officers in South Africa were not unaware of the pretensions of status-obsessed Volunteers, and J. F. C. Fuller, while expressing a preference for pale-skinned 'savages' from Bethnal Green, reserved his scorn for the 'respectability' introduced into his Oxfordshire regiment by the enlisting of those whom he disparagingly dubbed 'simpering shopkeepers' sons'.

The relationship between officers and men

When considering Tommy Atkins' relationship with his officers one has to bear in mind the specific nature of military tactics in South Africa as they developed after 1900–1. During sieges and set-piece engagements officers were more apt to be physically and socially remote from the rank and file, finding kinship in their mess and solitude in their personal quarters. The involvement of officers with ordinary soldiers was generally confined to periods of action. But with the onset of guerrilla warfare and the increasing deployment of small, mobile patrols, the officer did not necessarily have available to him the material prerequisites of rank. In short, bereft of the usual distinguishing symbols of army hierarchy, officers were obliged to live much more on the level of the men they commanded, often being as vulnerable as they were to food shortages and the effects of inclement weather. Of course, the agencies of social separation were never wholly absent, soldiers, for instance, being crammed into open cattle trucks while officers rode in half-empty railway carriages. But increasingly the emphasis swung away from formal social demarcation. After 1900 the Royal Fusiliers relieved officers of their swords and provided them with rifles and bayonets 'so as not to distinguish them from the men'. Such measures to make officers 'look like the men' did not, of course, constitute a sudden desire by the army to democratize its relationships. The motive was the more pragmatic one of attempting to reduce the high mortality rate among officers, who were becoming the favoured targets of Boer sharpshooters. With officers becoming increasingly enmeshed with ordinary Tommies, the quality of 'leadership' revolved less around the formal dictates of rank,

Soldiers of the 1st Welsh Regiment relax in camp.

and more on the informal, personal qualities of individual officers. Regular officers were indeed judged by Tommies on such personal attributes. Popular officers were invariably those who paid extra attention to canteen and accommodation arrangements, and expressly concerned themselves with the wounded. Hostility directed against officers was nearly always motivated by the specific actions of particular men. Officers who ordered soldiers to dig trenches for them before their own were dug and who enforced army regulations to the letter, such as by docking pay from Tommies to recoup the cost of water-bottles lost in action, earned for themselves an unenviable reputation among the rank and file.

Drunkenness

Courts Martial and *ad hoc* disciplinary measures against drunkenness and associated disorderly behaviour became increasingly numerous as the war dragged on. The scale of drinking indulged in by troops was not typified by the officially regulated tot system, whereby measured quantities of rum were sometimes imbibed before combat in order to fortify the martial spirit of soldiers. Indeed, evidence suggests that the army in South Africa was somewhat loath to issue official quantities of alcohol, as football teams competing for regimental sports shields found to their dismay when the regular rum ration was withdrawn and replaced by soda water. Probably increasingly heedful of the effects of alcohol on fighting efficiency, the British army was reluctant to add its own issue to the vast pool of South African liquor that Tommies seemed able to tap everywhere. Near Wepener in April 1901 it was reported that '36 cases of whisky were taken off a truck and over 40 men found drunk, of whom one has died of alcohol poisoning. Kitchener's Fighting Scouts were apparently the chief offenders, but many men just out from England were also implicated.'[14] An officer at Rusten-

A quiet game of cards at a water-hole on the veld.

'Pillow-fighting' was one way of relieving the boredom of long periods of military inactivity.

burg reported that he was unable to bring picket lines up to full strength because among his already tipsy men 'the proportion of the hopelessly drunk and incapable had risen to fifty per cent'. In view of the causal relationship between alcohol consumption and insubordination, drunkenness posed an additional problem to army discipline over and above its detrimental effects upon fighting efficiency. Punishment of drunken soldiers who clashed with officers did not err on the side of leniency. Two privates who were found guilty of insubordination after drinking 'a native brew' were given 112 days' hard labour, and at Boksburg on 27 December 1900 two men found guilty in similar circumstances were spread-eagled and lashed to the wheels of a moving waggon. The absence of statistics make it impossible to estimate whether troops in South Africa were perhaps more drunk more frequently than in other wars. It may safely be assumed, however, that in view of a particularly abundant local supply and the fact that Tommies were being deployed in increasingly mobile, smaller formations, the military found great difficulty in the rigid imposition of temperance.

Looting

Tommy Atkins was not inappropriately dubbed the 'loot-loving' soldier by British observers of the South African War. His acquisitive propensities were given free rein in a war that saw lengthy periods of relative inactivity for many soldiers, a high degree of freedom when moving about the countryside in small groupings, and the systematic destruction of property under official orders. Looting by individual soldiers from the corpses of the enemy did not become part of the ritualized function of battle in South Africa. The capture of such personal booty was strongly disapproved of, and in any case few Boer fighters carried items of gold and silver worth removing from

Loot seized from the farms of Afrikaners is auctioned by British troops at Belmont in the northern Cape.

bodies. Looting by Tommies was a collective activity, far removed from battlefields, in which groups of men plundered Boer and, frequently, black property. (The property of British subjects, especially in the Cape Colony, also suffered at the hands of British forces.) On one occasion between sixty and seventy men of the Lincolnshire Regiment (whose traditional marching song, appropriately, was 'The Lincolnshire Poacher') joined forces with local blacks near Kimberley in a systematic plunder of farmhouses, an exercise that culminated in an extended drinking session.[15] The acquisition of loot was more often than not directly related to the material needs of ordinary soldiers and looked upon by participants as a solution to common deprivation. Captured cattle and sheep were communally cooked and shared out. Dairy produce and items of clothing were also much favoured. While Tommies were relatively unconcerned with curios and trophies, they were, however, avid collectors of Kruger rands, sometimes found in farmhouses. Again, this was prompted not so much by a desire for gold in its own right, but by the dictates of acceptable wartime currency. Black civilians often refused payment for private items supplied to Tommies other than in gold coins.

Relationships with African workers

The relationship between ordinary soldiers and black labourers employed by the British army was frequently one of mutual antagonism. It is clear that many soldiers accepted the South African class and racial structure as the basis of their behaviour towards Africans. And it is equally apparent that many blacks, who may have expected that white troops from overseas would not have been influenced by settler attitudes, received a rude surprise. Reports suggest that a substantial proportion of assaults upon blacks in the army, and attacks upon, and robberies of, civilian Indian and Chinese traders, can be attributed to members of white colonial contingents, notably Australians.[16] But Tommies also made a sizeable contribution to the level of casual violence that sometimes characterized encounters between blacks and soldiers. It was inevitable that British troopers would seize opportunities to assert their muscle over those even lower in the army pecking order, and the actions of Tommies at camps ranged from beatings and stabbings of labourers to the forcible drowning of an African mule-driver in a pig trough at Green Point Camp in October 1901. Black mule-drivers resorted to indirect verbal retaliation, yelling 'Englishman' at their animals when whipping them. Troops also rapidly absorbed colonist's ideas about what constituted 'native work': in December 1900 a fatigue party from the Manchester Regiment addressed a formal complaint to their platoon commander in protest at having been made to undertake heavy manual work of a kind they considered to be more suited to 'a gang of niggers'. Sometimes such sentiments were accompanied by a resentful belief that blacks were better off than they were. Drummer Goodwin of the West Yorkshire Regiment, faced with the sight of 300 soldiers digging along a railway line, wrote angrily, 'instead of getting the Kaffrars to do it they make Tommy do it as they have him on the cheap'.[17] Yet the specific substance of Tommies' attitudes towards black South Africans must be distinguished from the more overtly racist ideology of middle class officers, who favoured the use of racial stereotypes and fanciful biological notions when discussing blacks. While plebeian 'Alf' or 'Bert' may have enjoyed his newly-acquired dominance, he rarely indulged in genetic explanations for the inferior position occupied by local blacks.

A young soldier performing fatigues at Standerton. Many ancillary duties during the campaign were performed by Africans, and when Tommies were expected to do heavy manual work there were frequently complaints.

Indeed, as the war progressed, Tommies and blacks became increasingly involved in close personal relationships. A private stationed in King William's Town, for instance, wrote to the local magistrate about his anxiety that the wages of a black labourer employed in his section of the Remounts Department should safely reach the relative to whom it was being sent. While aware of a possible flaunting of local convention, a human concern was uppermost:

> 'I hope I am not taking an undue liberty in troubling you on behalf of a Native, but [I] know of no other way . . . to ensure [the money's] safety.'[18]

Tommies were far more inclined than the officer elite to view blacks as fellow *men*, hostile and devious perhaps, but nonetheless inhabitants of a recognizable world. More than one soldier saw analogies between black labourers and Irish navvies, and between malnourished black children and Glaswegian urchins. A popular complaint among soldiers was that 'the natives look upon us as gold mines' and it is undoubtedly true that blacks, however young, grasped every opportunity to benefit from the Tommies' presence in South Africa. 'Whenever we pass a native village crowds of little niggers run along by the train and the Tommies throw them coins and bits of biscuit . . .',[19] wrote Lieutenant Corlebar Rowlandson in October 1900. Blacks supplied troops with alcohol, clothing, food and trinkets, rode with them officially in railway cattle trucks, and accompanied them unofficially on looting expeditions. Newspapers, sometimes a week old, were sold to soldiers by black children at twice their original price. One trooper, after being charged 3 pence for two eggs at a kraal, noted ruefully 'they are keen enough about money and the days of glass beads are gone'. But the financial traffic was not all one way – new soldiers arriving in Cape Town were delighted to be greeted by young blacks offering to buy old campaign badges at prices from four shillings and sixpence to seven shillings and sixpence.[20]

Right from the outset, Tommies readily took to the arms of compliant black women. One correspondent from Port Elizabeth noted in June 1900 the enthusiasm of 'appreciative Tommies' at the sight of 'philanthropic damsels' among a group of Africans at the harbour entrance.[21] Prostitutes operating in the vicinity of camps were invariably black and supplied merchandise other than sexual favours to nearby troops; in September 1901, for instance, Martha Daga and Liza Machadoeka were each fined £5 for supplying illicit liquor.[22] Many soldiers discovered to their chagrin that prostitutes drove hard bargains. After a liaison with a girl, one Tommy had great difficulty in procuring change and reported that 'at last she opened her mouth and let me take out two sixpences . . . now I dare not touch them!' Whether half-naked or well-dressed, African women were relatively welcoming, and a frequent diversion from the drudgery of army duties. Private Fred Bly privately recorded having deserted picket duty in favour of spending 'most of the day flirting with a nice Kaffir girl who also gave me eggs, milk and cakes'.

As Tommies seemed to pay scant regard to South African social mores governing public consorting between white men and black women, methods of separation had to be found. Patrols were accordingly used to enforce army displeasure not merely at troops consorting with prostitutes *per se*, but at the apparent lack of circumspection shown by Tommies in their choice of partner. In April 1900 one Scottish trooper stationed at Stellenbosch reported, 'There is a patrol sent out every night in Stellenbosch to keep the soldiers from speaking to the black ladies for fear it should lower the dignity of the British soldier in the eyes of the Dutch.'[23]

Attitudes towards the Boers

While the periodic outcries against alleged assaults by British soldiers upon Boer women in concentration camps could not have been wholly without foundation, it is apparent that many Tommies regarded Boer women with some physical distaste. The most significant factor when considering relationships between Tommies and Boer women is the degree of general animosity that existed between members of the Boer community and invading soldiers. Troops not unnaturally encountered greater hostility and less receptivity to their attentions among Boer women than was the case with blacks; one index of this is the fact that the majority of 'rescue homes' established by the Salvation Army during the war years for women 'given up to a life of shame' were for African and Coloured women.[24] This contrast was noted by an officer of the Ayrshire Yeomanry:

> 'The young Dutch ladies gave Tommies looks which would have turned milk sour. The black ones however are very friendly . . . and grin at a great rate.'

Nonetheless, it is probable that the ladies of Worcester referred to here would have been of rather more substantial means than many Boer girls of the poor, landless *bywoner* class. Like their black counterparts, poverty would have driven at least some *bywoner* women to take advantage of the financial rewards to be gained by placing themselves at the disposal of Tommies. A soldier stationed at Beaufort West remarked in January 1901,

> 'Some of these poor Boer girls here are quite friendly and pretty as well, and I notice they don't wear drawers.'

Apart from instances of compassion towards individuals, rank and file attitudes towards the Boers were, not surprisingly, ones of conventional hostility towards an enemy. Tommies, for example, often refused to buy 'blarstid Dutch skoff' for fear of being poisoned, and jeered at Boer complaints of ill-treatment when soldiers took charge of gangs of conscripted Boer labourers. Many, perhaps already insulated against the shock of inflicting death in close combat by their participation in the systematic violence practised by gangs in British ghettoes, be-

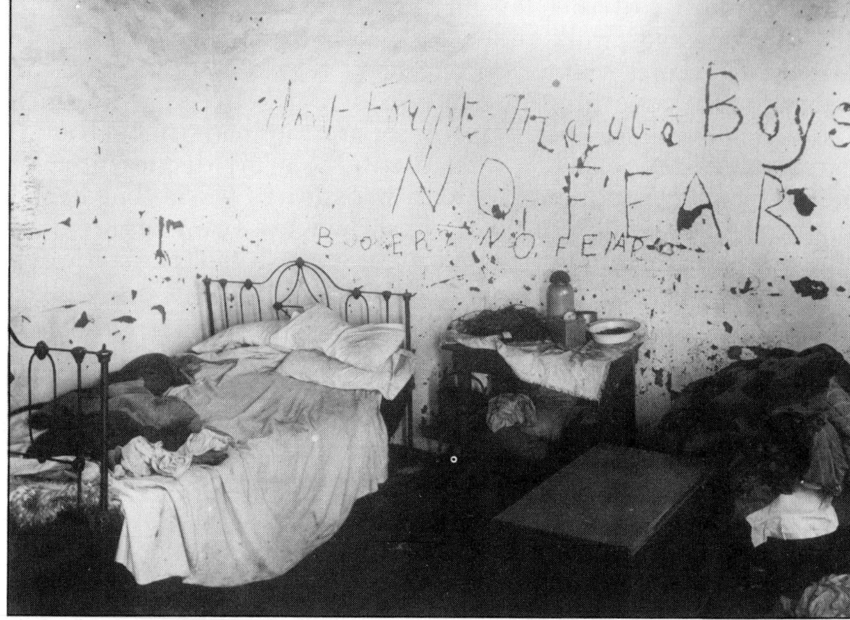

The interior of a Boer homestead with graffiti scratched on the wall by British soldiers—'dont Forget Majuba Boys. Boers no fear'.

came enthusiastic killers of Boers: 'The Boys were all High Spirited telling one another how they Bayonetted and Shot the Boers.' Private Henry Rooke wrote to his parents,

> 'so I said to my comrades do your duty boys as you know we do so we crawled back a bit and stuck every one in the sanger [stomach] with our bayonets and it was full of blood.'[25]

Tommies' diet

A persistent source of complaint by ordinary soldiers during the South African campaign was the provision of food. Tommy Atkins' diet revolved around tinned meat, bloater paste and occasionally jam. For the majority of troops even these spartan provisions became unheard-of luxuries. A private in the Border Regiment complained of having had to march a full day in 'Awfull Heat' on two biscuits,[26] while another tried in vain to exchange his 'miserable dog biscuits' for eggs from civilians. Others were occasionally more successful at such transactions, sometimes pooling their financial resources and purchasing chickens and turkeys from Africans accompanying columns. At times of particular adversity, and dependent on local conditions, food supplies deteriorated rapidly, Tommy Atkins finding that his concern for nutrition placed him on a par with the most deprived of local blacks. A squadron of the 10th Royal Hussars was on one occasion reduced to producing cakes made out of insect powder, with dire results: 'Some of C Squadron's farriers made cakes out of insect powder and were ill. They threw them away and hungry niggers got hold of them, ate them, and were ill too', reported one soldier. But perhaps the most persistent privation was not the occasion when rations became totally unavailable; far worse, overall, was the regular and widespread recourse by the military to the issuing of half-rations. We have already seen how much looting and trading

A field bakery. On the march Tommies had to forsake such luxuries as freshly-baked bread and accustom themselves to tinned beef (when available) and 'dog biscuits', rusks that were so hard and dry they had to be softened with saliva or gnawed at impatiently.

A scratch meal shared by the rank and file. All too often half-rations had to be issued because of supply difficulties, and the looting and trading activities of Tommies were often directly related to the need to maintain an adequate level of nutrition.

activities during the war were related to Tommy Atkins' desire to supplement his food supply in order to maintain an adequate level of nutrition. Thus half-rations could sometimes be supplemented with local mealies and fruit. But when such additional resources were absent, the inadequacies of army biscuits became all too apparent.[27] After being assured by officers of the imminent arrival of a supply convoy, one private wrote gloomily,

> 'I . . . suppose the convoy will generally turn up all right, but not before the two dog biscuits have to be spun out for three or four days.'

Service conditions

Men waiting for treatment at a field hospital near Paardeberg drift. In all, the British army lost 22 000 men during the war, of whom 13 250 died from disease rather than wounds sustained in action. Enteric fever accounted for most of these deaths, and in addition 31 000 men had to be invalided home because of it.

The British army in South Africa paid, fed and provided accommodation for its soldier employees. In practice, the service conditions it provided for its working class recruits were wretched. Tommies on campaign activities were badly housed, their flimsy tents offering little protection against torrential rains, and army blankets (often one between two men) provided little warmth. Occasionally soldiers were enterprising enough to construct more hardy portable makeshift shelters out of scraps of wood and iron and even biscuit tins, but scavenging for these items was not an activity many of them relished. It was inevitable that pneumonia and exposure would be added to the cases of fatigue, enteric and dysentery that took their toll of the ranks. Pay remained low and moreover came at irregular intervals. The strict enforcing of army economies, whereby soldiers were made to pay for the replacement of damaged or lost equipment, added to the strains that Tommies were compelled to endure.

The South African sojourn proved to be a singularly unglamorous one. One soldier, while cursing the activities of pro-Boers in Britain, remarked that he would have liked to have

been able to force 'the bastards to toil week in and week out, up and down this dusty road'. When it came to relieving the actual drudgery of campaign marching, soldiers did not take to the spontaneous singing of patriotic songs with marked enthusiasm. 'Soldiers of the Queen' and 'Sons of the Empire' certainly featured in their repertoire, but in the main Tommies preferred the strains of domestic songs, so central to Victorian popular culture. What troops craved were sketches and songs that entertained, diverted and helped to defuse frustrations. Working class soldiers accordingly regaled one another with 'Goodbye Mother Annie', 'The Lodger in our Yard' and the 'Burglar and the Judge'. Their re-creations of a familiar world helped, temporarily at least, to block out the more depressing features of military life in an alien colonial environment.

Increasingly frustrated, the great majority of working class soldiers were unflagging in their wish for a speedy return home. Relatively few considered settlement in 'the white man's country'. The few that stayed after the war did not find eldorado. One Highland Fusilier was moved to write derisively of South Africa, 'the country of promises some are stupid enough to call it'. Another, after making enquiries about local police work, estimated that the wage offered was equivalent in real terms to no more than the £55 a year he could earn as a driver in Britain. Few working class soldiers had the capital available to set themselves up in farming. Those Tommies who became involved in duties such as regulating the pass-control system under military administration might have expected that their experience could have been put to practical use in post-war South Africa. But here, too, there appear to have been few vacancies for ex-soldiers, despite the increasingly important role played by a white labour aristocracy in controlling and policing a black labour force. White settlerdom offered surprisingly few opportunities and incentives to Tommies to prolong their stay in South Africa.

OVERHEARD NEAR TABANCHU, DURING THE LATE CAMPAIGN.

Boer Lady :—" Well, how do you like South Africa ? "
T. A. :—" It ain't no place for a white man."
Boer Lady :—" Well, nobody asked you to come here."
T. A. :—" It ain't the likes of you, dear, that will keep me here when the war's over."

A cartoon that perhaps sums up the reluctance of most troopers to remain in South Africa once the war had ended, and which also hints at the mutual hostility that often existed between British soldiers and Afrikaner women (from St George's Gazette, *30 September 1902).*

References

1. National Army Museum (NAM) 7403–29–27, Drummer H. Goodwin, South African War Diary 1899–1901, entry for 2 March 1900.
2. Gareth Stedman Jones, 'Working Class Culture and Working Class Politics in London 1870–1900', *Journal of Social History*, 7, (1974), 482; Richard Price, *An Imperial War and the British Working Class*, London, 1972, 135.
3. See Chapter 10; Anne Summers, 'Militarism in Britain before the Great War', *History Workshop Journal*, 2, 1976, 104–23; John Gooch, 'Attitudes to War in Late Victorian and Edwardian England', in Brian Bond and Ian Roy eds., *War and Society*, London, 1975, 88.
4. NAM 6610–8, *The Orient*, 1 December 1901, MS troops' journal, *SS Orient*.
5. NAM 6901/1–1–4, Harold Hardy, Boer War Letters, Hardy to his mother, 26 February 1901.
6. West Yorkshire Regiment Historical Records No. 78, anonymous correspondent to his brother Walter, 1 December 1899.
7. NAM 7310–85, Fred H. Bly, Boer War Diary, entry for 10 February 1900.
8. NAM 6903/6–2, R. G. Jelf, Letters 1899–1901. Jelf to his parents, 3 November 1899.
9. NAM 5603/10, H. F. N. Jourdain, Boer War Journal No. 2, entry for 29 January 1900.
10. Greater London Council Record Office, P/FEY 237A(4) Peachey Records, H. G. Peachey to his mother, 28 June 1900.
11. J. B. Lloyd, *1 000 Miles with the CIV*, London, 1901, 10, cited by M. van Wyk Smith, 'Poetry of the Anglo-Boer War' *Humanitas*, 3, 2 (1975), 213.
12. Price, 199. More generally, see Price's 'Society, Status and Jingoism: The Social Roots of Lower Middle Class Patriotism 1870–1900', in Geoffrey Crossick ed., *The Lower Middle Class in Britain 1870–1914*, London, 1977, 89–112.
13. Rhodes University, Cory Library, MS 6738, Trooper W. S. Royle, 'In the Boer War 1900, Letters', letter to unknown recipient, 19 May 1900.
14. Liddell Hart Centre for Military Archives (LHCMA), Clive Papers, Capt. Percy A. Clive, MS Diary, South Africa 1899–1900, entry for 18 May 1900.
15. I owe the reference to 'The Lincolnshire Poacher' to Dr J. M. Lonsdale. Generally, see Lewis Golding, 'Looting a Boer Camp', *Chambers's Journal*, 4, 161 (1900), 95.
16. NAM 6807–425, Jack Dauty, Boer War Letters, Dauty to his mother 21 September 1901; NAM 5603/10–4, H. F. N. Jourdain, Boer War Diary No. 4, entry for 7 November 1900; Stanley Trapido, 'The Origin and Development of the African Political Organization', *Collected Seminar Papers on the Societies of Southern Africa in the 19th and 20th Centuries*, I, Institute of Commonwealth Studies, University of London, 1971, 93.
17. NAM, Goodwin Diary, entry for 5 July 1900; South African Library, Cape Town, MS 366, J. P. Hess, Journal, entry for 18 March 1902.
18. Cape Archives (CA), Archive of the Special Magistrate, King William's Town, I/TAM 7/27, Private W. Melbourne to Special Magistrate, 9 October 1900.
19. NAM, Corlebar Rowlandson, Boer War Letters, NAM 7708–42–91, Rowlandson to his mother, 5 October 1900. See also NAM 7611–17, Nurse D. L. Harris, Diary 1900–1, entry for 5 May 1900.
20. For probable resale on the lucrative local market in war paraphernalia, one soldier in Pretoria was offered the signature of Leyds for £5 by an African, see NAM 7207–52, J. Haigh, Letters 1900–02, Haigh to his parents, 28 June 1900.
21. NAM 7201–41–1, R. S. Waters, South African Diary 1900–1, entry for 28 June 1900.
22. CA, Archive of the Chief Magistrate, Graaff-Reinet, I/GR 14/90, Police Station Register, entry for 2 September 1901.
23. NAM 7208–8, John Paterson, Boer War Letters 1899–1901, Paterson to his parents, 20 April 1900.
24. *All the World*, January 1902, 113–14.
25. NAM 7805–65, Henry Rooke, letter to his parents, 9 March 1900.
26. J. B. Morrell Library, University of York, Leonard Bowe, MS Dairy of the Boer War, entry for 16 April 1900; Frederick William Unger, *With Bobs and Kruger*, Struik reprint, Cape Town, 1977, 175.
27. NAM 7510–30–2, Lt.Col. Allen Perry, Boer War Diary, entry for 1 June 1900; NAM Goodwin Diary, entry for 23 February 1901; NAM Hardy Letters, Hardy to his parents, 15 May 1901; CA, Archive of the Chief Magistrates of the Transkei I/CMT 3/9, R. I. Gunter to O. C. Remounts, 17 May 1900.

I am indebted to Dr J. M. Lonsdale of Trinity College, Cambridge, for useful insights into the subject, and for his constructive criticism of an earlier version of this chapter.

CHAPTER 6

The Siege of Mafeking

Brian Willan

The Mafeking myth

More than any other episode of the South African War the siege of Mafeking captured the imagination of the British public. From the start of the siege in the middle of October 1899 until its eventual relief seven months later, Mafeking was rarely out of the newspaper headlines. During a period when at times (particularly during November and December 1899) the war was going very badly for Britain, Mafeking's seemingly heroic resistance provided one of the few bright spots of the campaign, a useful distraction from military reverses suffered elsewhere. When the town was relieved on 17 May 1900 – the military authorities not considering it expedient to arrange this any earlier – the news was greeted with an unprecedented orgy of rejoicing and hysteria, unrivalled even by the later victory celebrations of 1918 and 1945. The siege of Mafeking swiftly attained the characteristics of a legend. Colonel R. S. S. Baden-Powell, the commander of the garrison, became one of the most popular heroes the country had ever seen, and the defence of the town was accepted almost without question as one of the most gallant feats of arms in the history of the British empire. One newspaper account expressed the almost universal view that the gallantry of Mafeking's defenders 'places the name of this small border town in the list of memorable sieges of the world.' Even John Morley, the Radical politician, talked of the 'spectacle of British heroism' and of every Englishman's admiration for the 'physical and moral pluck' displayed in the defence of the town. *The Times*, trying to make some sense of the continuing scenes of jubilation several days after Mafeking had been relieved, thought that Mafeking symbolized 'the common man of the Empire, the fundamental stuff of which it is made . . . .'

In the years after the siege Mafeking passed further into the mythology of the British empire. No one was more active in perpetuating the legend than Baden-Powell himself. In a stream of publications and interviews in the forty years after the siege he firmly imprinted his version of the episode upon the imagination of the English-speaking world. His accounts of the siege were by no means always consistent with one another. His assessment of the number of Boers surrounding Mafeking, for example, rose over the years from 5 000 to 12 000. But for Baden-Powell and his many admirers even the word Mafeking came to symbolize and to embody the highest moral qualities of the British national character. Almost necessarily, this has had the effect of obscuring the reality and the memory of the experiences and perceptions of those people who actually lived in Mafeking at the time of the siege. Virtually all the accounts of the siege that were published at the time or soon afterwards came from outsiders – from war correspondents or army officers, who under normal circumstances would never have gone near Mafeking. For over seventy years the only book about the siege written by a resident of Mafeking was the privately printed and largely unread diary of Charles Weir, a clerk in the Mafeking branch of the Standard Bank. Between the appearance of this journal and the publication in 1973 of the diary of Sol Plaatje, an African court interpreter, there was nothing. Mafeking's own view of its siege has been neglected. It is with this that the present account is primarily concerned.

'Marvellous defence . . . Pluck and devotion . . . Continuous bombardment . . . Spirited sorties . . . Gallant repulse of Boer attack', so ran the caption to this contemporary illustration, which portrays the myth rather than the reality of the siege.

On the eve of war

Mafeking, on the eve of the siege, was a prosperous and neatly laid out town of some 1 500 whites and 5 000 blacks, the latter mostly Barolong living in the adjacent settlement of Mafikeng. Baden-Powell described the town as 'a very ordinary-looking place . . . . Just a small tin-roofed town of small houses plumped down upon the open veldt.' So it might have seemed to an outsider. In fact, Mafeking was important as the administrative capital of the Bechuanaland Protectorate (although it lay within the Cape Colony), as a railway junction on the line to Bulawayo in Rhodesia, and as a trading and market centre for the surrounding districts. For the Cape government, however, Mafeking was regarded – as relations between the imperial government and the Transvaal deteriorated further in 1899 – as an embarrassment and a liability. When several of Mafeking's leading white citizens requested military protection against the possibility of invasion from across the Transvaal border, just a few miles away, the Cape authorities – anxious not to precipitate war – refused. Mafeking turned instead to Baden-Powell and his Protectorate Regiment, then based at Ramatlabama in the Bechuanaland Protectorate. Initially he, too, was unwilling to commit any part of his force to the defence of Mafeking. But by September he had changed his mind and began to prepare – secretly, in view of the opposition of the Cape government – for the town's defence. Shortly afterwards he moved in the whole of his regiment to protect the mountain of supplies that by now were arriving. Mafeking, of no great military significance hitherto, was thereby turned into an important and attractive military objective for the Boer forces.

The siege begins

When war broke out the Boers duly crossed the border and surrounded the town. The siege began. There were several initial skirmishes, but thereafter relatively little real fighting took place for the remainder of the siege. Unwilling to risk heavy casualties, the Boers made no serious attempt to take the town until relief was on its way seven months later. Instead, they shelled and 'mausered' the town from a safe distance in the hope that this would lead to its surrender. The first bout of shelling – followed by a request to surrender – was wholly ineffective and was greeted with derision. With the subsequent arrival of a large siege gun (affectionately known as 'Big Ben' by those in Mafeking) matters did become rather more serious, but even this caused surprisingly little damage, and casualties were light – only four white civilians were killed from shelling during the entire siege. Normal means of communication between Mafeking and the outside world were cut off, but the town was never completely invested. On occasions both blacks and whites travelled through the Boer lines with little apparent difficulty. Early in November, for example, a bank official from Vryburg bicycled to within ten miles of Mafeking and then walked the rest of the way. At the beginning of the siege there were – according to an English doctor serving with the Boer forces – some 6 000 Boers in the vicinity of Mafeking, but this number was reduced after

The Creusot gun, popularly known in Mafeking as 'Big Ben', which was used by the Boers to bombard the town. It was one of four guns of its type possessed by the republics, and could fire a 43 kilogram shell a distance of about ten kilometres. This photograph was found in the Boer laager after Mafeking's relief.

a few weeks to some 2 000 when many of them returned to their farms or went to other theatres of war. Their lines – consisting of sentries every hundred yards – certainly did not constitute an impenetrable barrier.

Life during the siege

For those inside Mafeking daily life during the siege was an often incongruous mixture of disruption and normality. In the early months of the siege, when the Boers were serious if inept in their attempt to bombard the town into submission, shelling was their main preoccupation. A large number of shelters were hastily constructed and long periods of time were spent underground. Some of the shelters were quite elaborate affairs. Vere Stent, the Reuters correspondent, was attracted to the shelter belonging to Ben Weil, the government contractor, because he thought it was 'quite the most comfortable and safest bomb-shelter in town'. Not all of the townspeople were able to take shelter in such comfort. Charles Weir, for example, complained that the one he shared with several other people 'was very small and narrow'. Shelling was a nuisance more for the inconvenience than the damage and danger it caused. The aiming of the Boer gunners seems to have been highly erratic, and many of the shells failed to explode. Casualties were in fact more often caused by tampering with unexploded shells (highly valued as souvenirs), and Baden-Powell had to issue several warnings about the dangers of this practice. Shelling was usually for very limited periods, and in the latter stages of the siege would cease for days – even weeks – on end. After a while the townspeople became so little concerned about it that the shelters were largely abandoned and they returned to their houses; diseases likely to be contracted in unhealthy underground shelters were more of a hazard than the shelling itself.

Defence duties

Apart from the shelling, for the majority of Mafeking's able-bodied white male population by far the greatest disruption to their lives was caused by duty in the Town Guard. This unit served throughout the siege and made up an important part of the town's defensive ring that Baden-Powell set up. It had a strength of three hundred men, and manned the forts on the eastern side of the town and the trenches of the inner perimeter. A separate contingent of over one hundred men was also formed from employees of the railway, the largest single employer of labour in town. Not everybody was anxious to participate in Mafeking's defence. The town had a heterogenous population that had strong trading links with the Transvaal, and pro-British feeling was far from universal. Two of the town's traders, for example, had refused to cooperate until threatened by Baden-Powell with what amounted to an open invitation to the other townspeople to loot their stores. A good many of those who served in the Town Guard felt rather strongly that they were being obliged to do a job that was the proper responsibility of either the colonial or imperial government. By and large the townspeople were not, according to Angus Hamilton, one of the war correspondents, 'appreciative of the honour and glory which falls to them by playing so prominent a role in the defence of the town'.

> 'Those who were local merchants,' he went on, 'men of peace, for the most part, with no very keen enthusiasm for martial glory, have seen the industry of a lifetime completely wrecked by the diffidence of the general staff and the unwillingness of the Government to take such precautions as would have placed the town beyond the probability of attack.'

Lady Sarah Wilson, daughter of the seventh Duke of Marlborough, emerges from her bomb-proof shelter, '. . . 18 feet by 15 feet and . . . 8 feet high, boarded with matting and pannelled wood walls painted white. With three large port-holes for windows it much resembles the cabin of a yacht . . .' (Daily Mail, *4 January 1900*).

Dissatisfaction within the ranks

As relief failed to materialize, even the most staunchly loyal of citizens came to grow bitter about their apparent neglect by the imperial military authorities. Mafeking's inhabitants had been 'doing Tommy Atkins' work for six solid months', wrote Charles Weir towards the end of the siege. 'I suppose there is a reason for it,' he went on, 'but it is pretty hard on us all the same. I have stuck up for the Government all through, but at the same time I do feel we are receiving little consideration.'

Continuous sentry duty in the Town Guard soon lost its novelty. Hamilton thought that 'by far the greatest proportion of hardships of the siege has fallen to the share of the Town Guard'. The life they led was 'one of the roughest description', the work they did was the 'most laborious, the least interesting, and totally without compensation'. Those whom Baden-Powell dismissed as 'grousers' often had real and justifiable complaints. The only rewards the Town Guard received from the military authorities for its hard and boring work, according to one townsman (Edward Ross, an auctioneer), were 'plenty of kicks, sneers, arrogance, and very little thanks'. Discontent became particularly acute during the second month of the siege, when it was realized that relief was unlikely to be imminent. Ross described the state of feeling:

> 'Many of the Town Guard . . . are complaining at the very scant courtesy shown them by the imperial officers in charge here. These are men who hold very high positions in the town, and who are now living in the trenches and doing Tommy Atkins' work for no pay and less thanks. It is the beginning of callousness and much grumbling in the camp. One certain corner is in a very disaffected state; most of the men in one of the redoubts talk of getting up a petition and working for the removal of their commander. It is to be hoped that not much of this is going to happen, or there is no knowing what the end would be.'

Among the Bechuanaland Rifles, another contingent consisting almost wholly of Mafeking men, the unfair dismissal of one of the NCOs and the arrogant behaviour of the commanding officer, Captain Cowan, produced what Ross described as a 'sort of small rebellion'.

Dissatisfaction within the ranks of both the Town Guard and the Bechuanaland Rifles was intensified by the easy life that the staff officers were seen to enjoy. While the Town Guard were confined 'day and night' in their 'damp and muddy trenches', Ross complained, Baden-Powell and most of his staff were 'filling themselves with fiz, brandies and sodas, etc.', in the ample comfort of their bomb-proof shelter and getting all 'the kudos, Awards of Merit, DSOs, CMGs, etc.' It was an understandable enough feeling and Baden-Powell seems to have displayed little sensitivity towards it. The rigours of martial law were a further cause for complaint, and several prominent townspeople found themselves summarily thrown into gaol for various misdemeanours. G. H. Whales, the editor of the

Members of the Town Guard on sentry duty on the outskirts of Mafeking. For most of the townspeople, life during the siege was an unglamorous, tedious and distressing experience.

Mafeking Mail, was one; another was J. W. de Kock, a prominent lawyer and future Member of Parliament and Mayor of Mafeking, who, according to his friend, Charles Weir, was 'rather free with his criticism of the Imperial Government'. Baden-Powell also came in for a good deal of criticism from the townspeople for the way he handled information – in siege conditions one of the most sought after commodities. One such incident occurred in January 1900 when an issue of the *Mafeking Mail* (which continued to appear throughout the siege) was suppressed because it contained an article that called upon the military authorities to deny a rumour that news had recently come into the town via the road to the south, which was reported to be clear of the enemy; by attempting to suppress a rumour of which everybody seems to have been aware, the effect was only to give to it further credibility. As time went on there were accusations that Baden-Powell was deliberately prolonging the siege for the sake of his reputation, while bringing upon the town unnecessary damage from Boer shelling. He responded with several sharp proclamations and threats about 'grumblers'. One of these notices, he requested, should be destroyed afterwards since he would be very ashamed

> 'if the fame of Mafeking and its heroic defence should be marred by any whisper amongst envious outsiders that there was any want of harmony and unity of purpose amongst us.'

THE MAFEKING MAIL

SPECIAL SIEGE SLIP.

ISSUED DAILY, SHELLS PERMITTING. TERMS: ONE SHILLING PER WEEK, PAYABLE IN ADVANCE.

No. 83 Thursday, March 1st, 1900. 140th Day of Siege

The Mafeking Mail.

THURSDAY, 1st MARCH, 1900.

SECOND AFTERNOON CONCERT AT THE MASONIC HALL.

The Concert of Sunday last was a grand success. We had prepared an exhaustive report for insertion in Monday's issue but more anxiously looked for news from the outer world coming to hand, even though a month old, the Concert naturally gave it the floor. By the same cause it was crowded out of yesterday's slip and this morning another of those rudely hasty shells came into the printing office and—God knows where that "copy" is. We don't. Trying to write new copy we find, that the shell report when it burst in the editorial sanctum entirely knocked the concert report out of the editorial cranium, but we can recollect the crowded Hall although the seats were four shillings each, at which everybody grumbled—but paid, the sweet singing of Mrs. Lees, and the uproarious laughter at the recitation of Sherlock Holmes, and the sketch of Corney Grain, an oh! the facial expression, that, we shall never forget, nor the worried physiognomy of the Sergt.-Major, as time passed and supplementary turns were put up and still the celebrated scientific detective had not appeared, and how the said face relaxed and resumed its usual placidity when he finally did appear. This is all we can remember about the concert except the programme, which was as follows:—A capital opener, "The Irish Jubilee," by Mr. Adams, put every one in good humonr, although it was twenty minutes after the published time before a start was made. The popular Sergeant-Major Layton sang "The Lads in Red." Mrs. Lees next gave "Alone on the Raft" and the lady got an ovation that shewed the audience appreciated good music. The Rev. W. H. Weekes sang "The Gallant Salamander" with his usual ability. Mr. Wedderburn next sang "It's comin' on again," and when, referring to the chorus, he told the audience to "let it go," they just did. Mr. Taylor at the piano sang two comic pieces, which were much appeciated, then the Ker—no, Sherlock Holmes come on and made everybody's sides ache, The second part went through with the proper swing. It was "The Holy City," by Mr. Hall; "The Coster's Sister," by Mr. King; "Mona," by Mr. Crittenden; 'The Song for Me," by Mrs. Lees; Sketch, by Mr. Corney Grain; while Ventriloquism, by Mr. Lees concluded a first-class entertainment. Messrs. Grayson and Taylor, at the piano, were excellent. The result of the bookings was, as before mentioned, Ten Pounds Fifteen Shillings handed over to the Sports and Prizes Funds.

NARROW ESCAPES.

When the shell just mentioned came into our office Mr. S. Hall, of the Railway, and Paymaster to the Bechuanaland Rifles, with Mr. Hampson, Produce Merchant, were within a few feet of the explosion. Beyond scratched heads—and on the part of Mr. Hall, a bruised arm—they fortunately escaped injury, a fact on which we offer them our cordial congratulations. May they be safely underground the next time a ninety-four pounder bursts near them, is our ambiguous but sincere wish.

NOTICE.

A letter has been sent to General Snyman by the Colonel Commanding to the following effect:—

That as General Snyman has used armed Natives for the invasion of our territory, and is employing them directly against us, the Colonel proposes to act in a similar manner.

If, therefore, the armed Natives are not withdrawn across the Border by the 3rd proximo, and the Chief Saani restored to his people, steps will be taken for carrying into effect an invasion of the Marico and Rustenburg Districts by Linchwe, Khama, Bathoen, etc.

Mafeking Garrison.

GENERAL ORDERS

By Colonel R. S. S. BadenPowell, Commanding Frontier Force.

Mafeking, 28th February, 1900.

The Colonel Commanding has much pleasure in placing on record a clever and plucky piece of scouting performed on Monday night by Sergt. Major Taylor and Private Oliphant in the Brickfields. These men made their way close to one of the Boer outposts and listened to the conversation of the men; then got in the Boer communication trench and inspected the rear of their work and returned through their outposts, having gained useful information as to their disposition, etc.

It is regretted that two men were wounded in the Brickfields on Monday night mainly through their own carelessness in exposing themselves above the parapet, and in lighting pipes in view of the enemy.

The enemy having kept their Krupp and one-pounder Maxim hidden away the past week or more, we rigged up a Dummy Armoured Truck with a stove-pipe gun to the South of the Stadt in order to tempt out and to see if they were still here. The trick was a complete success, both these guns and the big gun have, in the course of the day, wasted a large amount of ammunition on the Dummy. For a time the quick-firing guns turned on our horses and cattle, but these were very quickly driven in out of danger. The cattle and horse-guards are highly to be complimented on their coolness and good work under the heavy fire, notably Troopers White and Ekstein, Cape Police, and it is thanks to their efficient work that we had not a heavy list of casualties among the animals.

Field General Court Martial.—A Field General Court Martial, composed as under, will assemble on Friday, the 2nd prox., at such place and time as the President may appoint, for the trial of the prisoner named in the margin,* and of such other prisoners as may be brought before it.

* No. 261, Trooper W. A. Fauldsin, Protectorate Regiment.

President: Captain Marsh, Protectorate Regiment.

Members: A Subaltern, Protectorate Regiment; a Subaltern, Bechuanaland Rifles.

The prisoner will be warned and all witnesses directed to attend. Proceedings to be forwarded to the Chief Staff Officer.

Countersign.—A Countersign will be used nightly in future and will be duly notified. As Sentries are very confused, apparently, as to the proper form of challenge, great care should be taken to make the following clear to them on posting:—

On seeing any person approaching they should challenge: "Halt, who goes there," after receiving the reply they should call out: "Advance one and give the Countersign"; if this is correct they will say as usual: "Pass Friend" (or "Grand" or "Visiting Rounds" as the case may be) and "All's Well."

Mafeking, 1st March, 1900.

Court of Summary Jurisdiction.—The Court of Summary Jurisdiction will meet to-morrow, Friday, the 2nd March, at the Court House, at 10-15 a.m., for the examination of such prisoners as may be brought before it. President: Major Lord Edward Cecil, D.S.O.; Member: C. G. H. Bell Esq., C.C. & R.M.

By order,
E. H. CECIL, Major,
Chief Staff Officer.

Correspondence

Hold over till to-morrow for want of space.

NOTICE.

Situation Required.

WHEREAS MARY, a Massarwa, 16 years, believed a good household servant, is at present confined in the Mafeking Gaol, and there being no suitable women's accommodation for the same, the Court of Summary Jurisdiction are prepared to indenture, for a definite period, the said Mary according to law, to any suitabe person willing to take her as a servant. Application should be made to Mr. Heale, the Gaoler.

ASSESSMENT OF PROPERTY.

List of names of owners whose property will be assessed on Sunday next, 4th March:—

Erf No.		
Erf No.	45	J. A. Hill
,,	45	Bechuanaland Rifles
,,	31	St. John's Rectory
,,	12	N. D. Farquharson
,,	17	J. L. Reid. (Agent: J. Winter)
,,	12	W. C. Bland
,,	7	E. Isaacs
,,	64	S. Cohen & Son
,,	63	I. Amod
,,	64	C. Williams
,,	63	Abdul Gaffor
		D. Webster
,,	92	H. H. Bradley
,,	110	J. G. Stenson
,,	?124	R. Spiers.

Given the boredom and frustrations of the siege it is hardly surprising that problems and feelings of this kind should have arisen, or that Baden-Powell should have become one of the main targets of criticism. For many townspeople the question of compensation was coming to assume rather more importance to them than 'the fame of Mafeking and its heroic defence'. Another group of outsiders, the war correspondents, also came in for criticism. They were regarded with a mixture of curiosity and hostility. Edward Ross thought they were 'a funny crowd' who had 'nothing better to do than kick their heels and row with one another'. Vere Stent, however, complained that he was forced to leave Dixon's Hotel because of the 'gross incivility' he met there. William Hayes, the doctor, was not enamoured of the war correspondents either. Furious at Vere Stent's accusation that he had operated on Africans in the hospital without using anaesthetics, he banned all the correspondents from the hospital premises. Both accuser and accused appealed to Baden-Powell for support. Nor was Hayes impressed by the antics of Lady Sarah Wilson, who became a correspondent for the *Daily Mail* after arriving in Mafeking in dramatic circumstances during the course of the siege: 'We have one more lady to look after, that is all.' Tensions developed among the townspeople themselves. Most commanders in the Town Guard made themselves unpopular with their fellow citizens over whom they had temporary control. 'I suppose they forget that they have to afterwards live amongst those to whom they are making themselves thoroughly obnoxious. Residents will know very well to whom I am referring,' Ross commented. There were also fierce disputes among the town's doctors. Conditions in the hospital wards deteriorated, and a board of enquiry had to be appointed. Ross thought that the hospital was

Attitudes to the war correspondents

Opposite: an edition of the Mafeking Mail Special Siege Slip, *issued daily 'shells permitting'. The broadsheet was used by Baden-Powell to communicate general orders, encourage confidence in his conduct of the town's defence, and maintain morale among the besieged.*

Below: a sketch plan of Mafeking during the siege drawn by Baden-Powell (from Sketches in Mafeking and East Africa, *1907).*

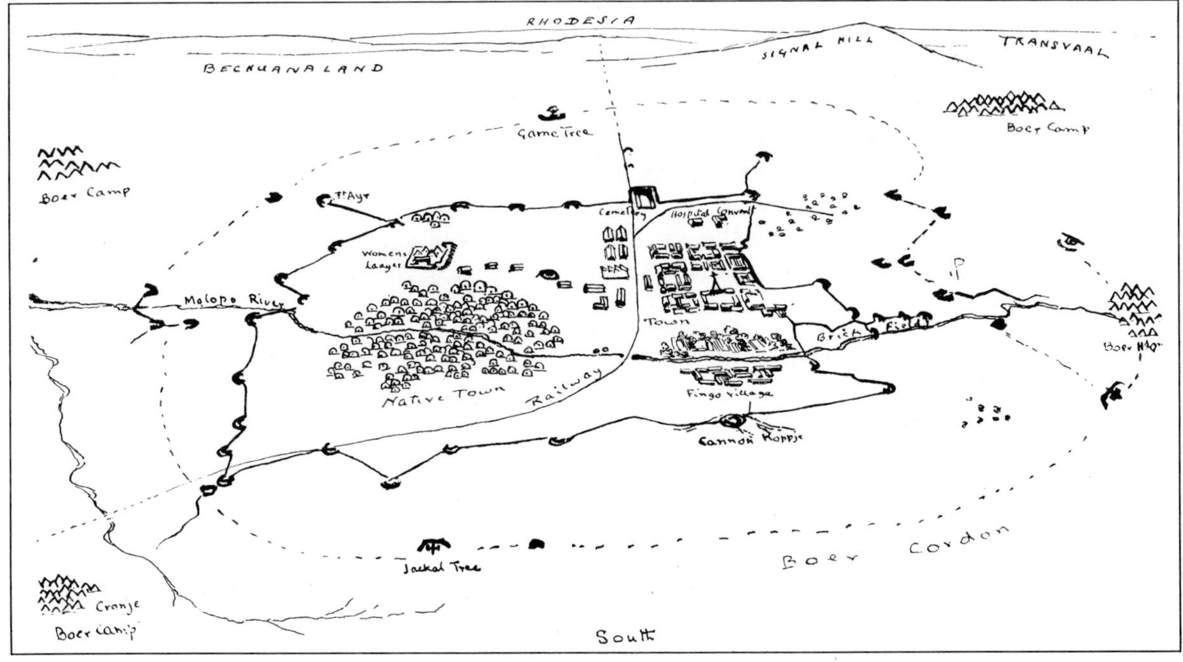

'about the last place to go if one is seedy', adding that 'all that go there seem to die without anybody knowing the matter'. Charles Weir wrote in shocked terms of the dance held by the nurses 'in a room adjoining the ward in which were men groaning with pain'. One of the patients complained that the place was 'more like a music hall than a hospital'.

Drunkenness was also quite a serious problem during the siege. For most of the siege liquor seems to have been in plentiful supply. Charles Weir wrote that a great deal of liquor was consumed 'to keep up pluck when the shell fire was heavy' during the early part of the siege, but thought that 'in most cases it had the opposite effect'. It did not stop there. On two occasions Baden-Powell ordered all bars to close for a week because of excessive drinking. It was after one such session that E. G. Parslow, one of the war correspondents, was murdered by Lieutenant Murchison, an officer in the Protectorate Regiment: the latter's subsequent imprisonment deprived the garrison of its best artillery officer. One of the clerks working in HQ had to be got rid of, as Baden-Powell put it, 'owing to his fondness for the bottle'. Other individuals were notorious for being frequently drunk. In January 1900 Baden-Powell issued special instructions to all bar-keepers informing them that if they were found supplying Major Baillie, formerly an officer in the Queen's Own Hussars, and one Lieutenant Brady, with any liquor – directly or indirectly – they would be 'liable to summary penalties': in the event of 'any further instances of drunkenness being reported' against the two men they would both be 'lodged in the jail for their own safety and for defence reasons'.

Entertainment and recreation

Drink was one form of relief from the monotony and inconvenience of the siege. Sundays provided another form of relief, and one that was much more acceptable to the commanding officer. At the beginning of the siege it was agreed – after a polite exchange of correspondence between Baden-Powell and Cronjé, the Boer commander – that all hostilities would cease during the sabbath. With several exceptions this weekly truce was respected on both sides throughout the siege. Mother Stanislaus, a sister in the Convent of Mercy, considered Sunday to be a 'heaven-sent day of mental relaxation' which 'preserved the sanity of the whole garrison, at least the civilian part of it'. She welcomed the rest from the nursing work that the nuns – despite their lack of training – carried out. Sundays were also especially appreciated by the other female inhabitants of Mafeking, confined for most of the time – in the early stages of the siege anyway – to the so-called Women's Laager where conditions seem to have been far from pleasant. But on Sundays there was no shortage of entertainment. Concerned to maintain morale, Baden-Powell was in his element in organizing a wide variety of theatrical, musical, and sporting events. Elaborate programmes were produced to accompany them, and Baden-Powell himself frequently took a leading role in these events. Albert Shimwell, his chief staff clerk, was among those who were impressed: 'What a wonderful man our Colonel is,' he

Drawing water rations in the Women's Laager.

wrote, 'he can sing, recite, mimic, in fact do almost anything under the sun.' Edward Ross was also amused: if Baden-Powell 'ever got broke in the Army', he thought, 'there is always a future waiting for him in the Music Hall.' But after a while even the antics of the commanding officer lost their appeal. Patience began to wear thin. Angus Hamilton commented that Baden-Powell's efforts to keep the townspeople amused soon

> 'developed into a Sabbatarian charade in which we all assume an active cooperation, and try to think that we are having a giddy and even gushing time.'

Others disapproved of such merrymaking for religious reasons. Charles Weir was a serious, church-going man who preferred to spend his spare time reading books such as Samuel Smiles' *Self Help*. 'It really grieves me very much', he said, 'to see how much Sunday is made a great day of amusement here.' He thought it was 'unnatural' to see 'the whole town in a business bustle and at sport on Sunday'.

If Sundays in Mafeking seemed to highlight the unreality and absurdities of the siege, the weekly cessation of hostilities was at the same time very much a product of contemporary notions of 'civilized warfare'. There was some argument – and lengthy correspondence – between the rival commanders about exactly how this should be defined, and there was a great deal of hypocrisy on both sides. Baden-Powell, for example, claimed immunity from shell fire for the convent on the grounds that it was being used as a hospital (which it was), but continued to use the building as a machine gun and observation post.

African participation in the siege

By far the greatest contravention of the supposed conventions of 'civilized warfare', however, was in the use by both sides of Africans as combatants. This occurred frequently elsewhere during the war, but there was no greater contrast between myth and reality than during the siege of Mafeking. The contribution that Africans made to the defence of the town has formed no part of the legend. In fact, there were probably four times as many blacks as whites in Mafeking for much of the siege, and many more of them than their white fellow citizens took part in offensive and defensive operations. Baden-Powell had never been in any doubt that the local Barolong settlement should be included within his lines of defence; the town otherwise would have been much more difficult to defend. Fortunately for him, there existed among the Barolong a long tradition of supporting the British against the Boers, and throughout the siege he was able to count upon their willingness to defend their section of the town. But, like many of the whites in Mafeking, they too were far from enthusiastic about the predicament in which they were placed. Most prominent among these was Wessels, the Barolong chief. Beyond defending his people against the Boers, he was reluctant to render further assistance to the British military authorities. He was reported to believe that 'the English wish to make slaves of his people'; that they would 'not be paid for any services rendered'; and that they would not be given any food 'but left to starve when the critical moment came'. Wessels was, however, soon deposed and replaced by a council of chiefs and headmen who were more favourably disposed towards the British cause.

Throughout the siege a force of some five hundred armed Barolongs defended the *stad* and the south-western section of the town's defences, on one occasion attacking and overrunning

Chief Wessels of the Barolong (seated, centre) with his principal counsellors, among whom were Silas Molema (seated left) and Lekoko (seated right). Wessels was suspended from his duties in January 1900 because of his opposition to Baden-Powell's conduct of operations.

a Boer fort opposite them. Contingents were also raised from the small local Mfengu community; from the miscellaneous group of black refugees who had sought refuge in Mafeking on the outbreak of hostilities (the 'Black Watch'); and from the local coloured community. Despite Baden-Powell's claim that he only armed Africans to enable them to defend themselves, they were, in fact, engaged in a wide range of officially-sanctioned offensive operations. Many so-called cattle raiding expeditions had the equally important objective of attacking and killing the enemy. Mathakgong, one of the Barolong military leaders, was one of the true heroes of the siege, constantly engaged in sorties behind the Boer lines and responsible for bringing large numbers of cattle into Mafeking. Had he been white he might have been awarded a Victoria Cross for his exploits. Along with the coloured contingent, the Mfengu contingent was primarily involved in the skirmishing that went on – particularly in the

MAFEKING,

23rd January 1900.

To General Sneyman,

near Mafeking.

Sir,

I have to thank you for your courteous reply to my letter of the 21st instant.

I am glad to learn with reference to the firing on the white flag that Your Honour's opinion coincides with mine on the subject. I would, however, point out that it was not merely one Burgher who fired on my White Flag, as you appear to think, but at least 20 or 30 Burghers stationed in your advanced trench near the Brickfields.

I am also glad to learn that it is not your intention to use Armed Natives against the white troops here, as such course of action (apart from its undesirability, in this country, where whites of all Nationalities have to stand together against Natives), would justify the English in allowing the Basutos to join in the war, in bringing Ghoorka troops from India, in using our "Dum Dum" bullets, and other such acts as would be much to be deplored.

As regards my so called employment of Armed Natives I can only refer you to my previous letters in which I warned your predecessor and yourself that the result of your action in attacking the Natives and looting their Cattle only led them to take up arms in self defence and to take retributory measures. I may add that the Barolongs have asked me to take them on as troops but I have declined to do so, and have refused to allow any Natives to go out after Cattle except the Barolongs who have had their Cattle stolen by your people.

Referring to Your Honour's remarks regarding work going on on Sunday, we had no working parties employed that day, as it was being observed as a general holiday in honour of the 100th day of the siege; I cannot find that any work was done except that the wires of some of the defence mines were overhauled by one or two men. At the same time I was myself much interested in watching your Burghers completing work on the fort opposite to our Western Defences on Sunday afternoon.

I have the honour to be,

Sir,

Your obedient Servant,

R. S. S. Baden-Powell Colonel.

Commdg. H.M.Troops, Mafeking.

A letter written by Baden-Powell to General Snyman dealing with the question of African participation in the siege – '. . . the Barolongs have asked me to take them on as troops but I have declined to do so'.

Above left: armed African levies with a white officer guarding an entrenchment close to the Boer lines.

Above right: seated from left to right, F. Whiteley, Mayor of Mafeking; C. G. H. Bell, Magistrate and Civil Commissioner; and Captain H. Greener, Chief Paymaster. Standing between Bell and Greener is Sol Plaatje, the court interpreter, secretary to three war correspondents, and diarist.

second half of the siege – in the 'brickfields' in the south-eastern part of the town. On another occasion, only one survivor of a thirty-three strong Mfengu raiding party returned after being trapped by the Boers behind their lines.

Africans contributed to the defence of Mafeking in numerous other ways. African labour constructed all the trenches, dug-outs, shelters, and other defensive works – on several occasions under heavy fire from the Boers. At great risk to themselves, Africans acted as spies for the military authorities, and it was upon their reports that Baden-Powell's local military intelligence was almost wholly based. They were severely reprimanded, however, if they produced information that turned out to be false, and the penalty for suspected spying for the enemy was death by firing squad. Africans were also responsible for carrying nearly all the dispatches through the Boer lines that enabled news of the siege to reach the outside world with such regularity. In the early months of the siege this was a risky business and a number of them were killed or captured. Towards the end of the siege, however, the risks seem to have been much less: when it was not possible to sneak through the lines without being seen, the payment of two shillings and sixpence was generally sufficient, according to Edward Ross, to secure a safe passage through.

Disenchantment in the *stad*

At one stage the Boers were believed to be making a particular point of shelling the *stad* in the hope that this would cause its inhabitants to rise against the British. They did not, in the event, react as drastically as this, but their treatment at the hands of the British military authorities during the siege certainly gave rise to a considerable amount of dissatisfaction. On several occasions trench diggers and dispatch runners went on strike over conditions and rates of pay. As the siege wore on, though, it was the question of the supply and distribution of food that caused the most trouble. The Barolong were very unhappy, for example, about the methods used in the commandeering and redistribution of grain supplies – worsened according to Sol Plaatje, the court interpreter, by the fact that 'the arrangement is in the hands of young officers who know as little about Natives and their mode of living as they know about the man on the moon and his mode of living.' On other occasions it seems only to have been the restraining influence of C. G. H. Bell, the Magistrate and Civil Commissioner, that prevented Baden-Powell from taking steps (such as the commandeering of all Barolong cattle) that could well have proved disastrous.

Some of the Barolong shared the same feelings of boredom and annoyance towards the siege as Mafeking's white residents. Others were similarly irritated by what they saw as the unnecessarily close supervision of their lives by the military authorities. When he was carrying out a census in the *stad* in March 1900 Sol Plaatje reported meeting one woman who told him that what made the siege – 'unlike all previous sieges of Mafeking' – so intolerable was the fact that 'the unfortunate people are counted like sheep'. For the white population of Mafeking, and the annals of imperial history, there was only ever one siege of Mafeking: for some of the Barolong this was their sixth. Twenty years earlier they had held out for two years against surrounding Boer forces. Sieges were nothing new to them.

An African spy is sentenced to death at a Court of Summary Jurisdiction during the siege. Presiding are Lord Edward Cecil, Baden-Powell's Chief of Staff, and C. G. H. Bell (both seated). Immediately behind Cecil, Sol Plaatje props himself up against the wall.

Ben Weil, the government contractor, who was largely responsible for the vast expenditure on supplies before the siege began.

Food for the whites in Mafeking was never really in short supply. There were, not surprisingly, complaints about the quality of food towards the end of the siege (nobody liked horse meat very much) but, thanks largely to Ben Weil, the government contractor, and Lord Edward Cecil, Baden-Powell's Chief of Staff, who assumed personal responsibility for the vast expenditure on supplies before the siege started, there was always enough to go round. For many of the Africans matters were different. The worst sufferers were the 2 000 or so non-Barolong refugees. They met with little sympathy from either the military authorities or the Barolong. By the time Riesle's Hotel was putting on its famous nine course Christmas luncheon some of them had already died of starvation. On the same day, Bell noted in his diary that he was 'considerably worried during all hours of the day by hungry Natives, who lean against the garden wall and stare at me', complaining of their hunger. Over the next few months many more of them died. The diarists give harrowing accounts of the scenes that followed. Ina Cowan, a nurse at the hospital, wrote that she saw 'as many dreadful things as I ever wish to see'. J. E. Neilly considered that

African starvation

> 'probably hundreds died from starvation or the diseases that always accompany famine . . . many more were found dead on the veldt, and others succumbed to hunger in the hospital.'

Plaatje – well-fed himself throughout the siege – wrote in March 1900 that it was

> 'a miserable scene to be surrounded by about 50 hungry beings, agitating the engagement of your pity and to see one of them succumb to his agonies and fall backwards with a dead thud'.

Some of the black refugees tried to steal food from white households. Baden-Powell responded by putting on extra patrols. Some of those who were caught were shot. At least one case of cannibalism was reported.

Measures to combat starvation

Baden-Powell provided some relief in the form of soup kitchens (which operated at a healthy profit), but these barely represented a serious attempt to deal with the problem. In fact, his objective was to drive as many Africans as possible out of the town – those not useful in its defence, that is – in order to reduce pressure upon food supplies. His policy, as he told Bell, was 'to induce them to go and stay in the country till the bad times are over'. The first group thus obliged to try to make their way through the Boer lines in January 1900 were unsuccessful. Several were shot by the Boers, and the rest were forced to return. Edward Ross considered it all to be

> 'very hard luck on them, having no choice but that of two deaths, one being shot by Dutchmen, or that of staying here to slowly starve to death.'

In the ensuing weeks and months many more died in the attempt to get through the Boer lines. A number of white residents of Mafeking – not normally noted for negrophile tendencies – thought Baden-Powell's treatment of Africans unduly harsh. Charles Weir, for example, thought that he 'might have done more to save the lives of the natives'. Eventually, though, the Boers seem to have relented and let many of them pass through their lines unmolested. A month before the end of the siege Bell estimated that fully three-quarters of the normal population of the *stad* had left.

Issuing rations in the Barolong stad.

An African soup kitchen during the latter stages of the siege. The soup was rendered from the carcases of dead horses; white starch was added to the concoction to thicken it and give the impression that a substantial meal had been consumed.

The relief of Mafeking when it came was, like much of the rest of the siege, an incongruous affair. Members of the relieving column were amazed by what they found. One of them expected 'to see nothing but shattered and roofless buildings with the inhabitants living like rabbits in dugouts among the ruins.' Instead, he found that the town 'appeared outwardly very little changed from the tidy little village that I had last seen a year before.' Amazement soon turned to bitterness and resentment. Another trooper in Colonel Plumer's relief column thought that the contrast between 'the clean, plump, pink-and-white faces of the besieged with those of the relieving force, haggard, gaunt, and dust-grimed' struck a 'jarring note', which was 'as it were, incongruous and incorrect'. They were not impressed with the reception they received, and they were far from pleased about having to march on again two days later. 'Ragged, travel-stained and thin,' another of the relief force recalled, 'they were not happy'. For the whites in Mafeking there remained, after seven months, adequate supplies of food. It was they who supplied the relieving force, not the other way round.

The legacy of the siege

Some people did very well out of the siege. Mafeking owed a great deal to Ben Weil for his foresight in laying in such large stocks of food and other supplies, but he did not do so badly out of this either. Perhaps upset by the allegations of profiteering that were made against him, he retired to London after the war, and celebrated his experiences each year with a 'Mafeking Dinner' on each anniversary of the relief. He died in 1945 at the ripe old age of 96. Africans had in general suffered much more than the white population, but some of them did well too. Several of the chiefs and headmen acquired a reputation for being able to handle the military authorities and turned this to their advantage after the siege. Sol Plaatje, the court interpreter, also owed a lot to the siege. He suffered little real physical hardship, and thrived on the additional range of duties that came his way. The extensive practice he gained in typewriting (he typed out, among other things, three siege diaries as well as writing his own) undoubtedly helped him to pass the Cape Civil Service typewriting examination five months after the end of the siege, the first African to do so. The work he did for the war correspondents – Stent, Parslow ('This murder has not only deprived me of a good friend but has wrecked me financially'), and Hamilton – was an important step along the road to his becoming one of South Africa's leading journalists himself. His weekly reports on the 'Native situation' also brought their reward – for Bell, the Magistrate and Civil Commissioner for whom they were written. This arrangement, Plaatje wrote subsequently, was 'so satisfactory that Mr Bell was created a CMG at the end of the siege'.

A shield and address presented to Ben Weil by the Barolong people 'in appreciation both of your personal qualities, and of the valuable services which you rendered to us during the Siege of Mafeking'. Many more Barolong would have died but for the large stocks of food Weil obtained before the siege began.

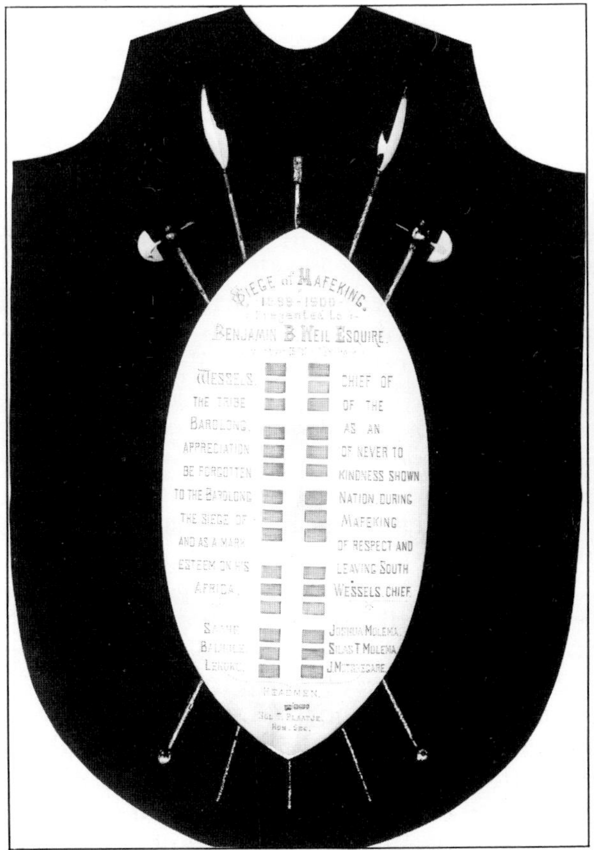

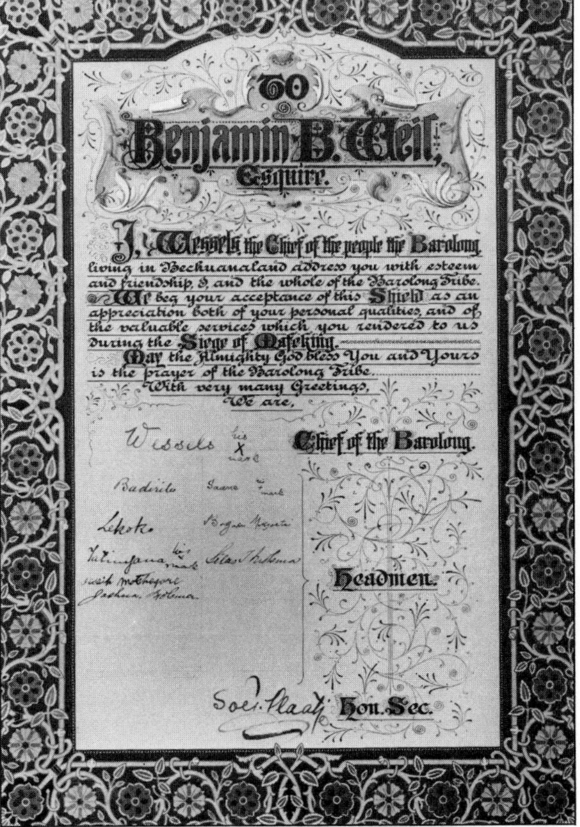

To
Benjamin B. Weil,
Esquire.

I, Wessels, the Chief of the people the Barolong living in Bechuanaland address you with esteem and friendship, I, and the whole of the Barolong Tribe. We beg your acceptance of this Shield as an appreciation both of your personal qualities, and of the valuable services which you rendered to us during the Siege of Mafeking.

May the Almighty God bless You and Yours is the prayer of the Barolong Tribe.

With very many Greetings,
We are,

Wessels his X mark Chief of the Barolong.

Headmen.

Sol. Plaatje Hon. Sec.

R. S. S. Baden-Powell, fêted as the hero of Mafeking, though British officials soon found that his military abilities scarcely matched his soaring reputation. In December 1901 Milner minuted privately to Chamberlain, '. . . he is not a good organizer. He has too many "happy thoughts", he is too constantly changing his plans, and in doing so he worries and fails to gain the confidence of the men under him' (Milner Papers, 43).

Nobody, however, did better out of the siege of Mafeking than Baden-Powell. His appointment to the command of the Rhodesian and Protectorate Regiments in 1899 was not his first appointment in Africa. In the late 1880s he had been in Natal, in 1895 he had been a member of the Asante expedition in West Africa, and in 1897 (by this time a Lieutenant-Colonel) he had participated in the suppression of the Ndebele rebellion in Rhodesia, narrowly escaping a court martial for his over-enthusiastic interpretation of his duties. It was Mafeking, however, that provided Baden-Powell with his great opportunity, and he made the most of it. Within days of the end of the siege he was promoted to the rank of Major-General, thus becoming the youngest General officer – an elderly looking forty-three – in the British army. From a purely military point of view, though, it is difficult to resist the conclusion that his reputation was built on somewhat shaky foundations. Certainly he displayed a good deal of ingenuity in securing the defence of Mafeking. Some of the ruses he devised to deceive the Boers, if they did not always achieve their object, were undoubtedly good for morale. But on the few occasions that he took the offensive the results were, to say the least, unfortunate. The greatest disaster was the Game Tree fiasco of 26 December 1899, a foolhardy, ill-prepared and largely pointless attack on a well-defended Boer fort that resulted in twenty-six British killed and over fifty wounded. In keeping with the British tradition of presenting defeat and disaster as triumph, attempts were made both at the time and subsequently to give this episode some lustre. But for those in Mafeking at the time Baden-Powell was clearly at fault. Edward Ross thought that 'the whole affair has been a very sad mistake from start to finish', while Bell confided to his diary that Baden-Powell had made 'the mistake of the siege', and one that 'it is to be hoped he will not repeat.'

Others who played important parts in the siege received rather less than their fair share of the credit. When Charles Peachey, an officer in the Imperial Yeomanry, arrived in Mafeking several months after the end of the siege he wrote home that 'they give Colonel Vyvian the credit and not Baden-Powell in the town here'. Few questions, though, were raised publicly about Baden-Powell's command of the siege or the wisdom of his decision – quite against the orders he took out with him to South Africa – to risk committing half of his original force to months of harmless inactivity. The officer commanding the other half of his original force – Colonel Herbert Plumer – contributed substantially more to the military campaign in South Africa than did Baden-Powell himself. It would have been more still had he not had to worry about relieving Baden-Powell in Mafeking. Yet he too received little recognition for his achievements compared to that heaped upon Baden-Powell.

Propaganda and censorship

Baden-Powell's reputation was not wholly a matter of the British public's need for a hero. He himself was a man with a keen sense of the importance of public opinion and of the possibilities provided by the siege for the advancement of his career and reputation. From the beginning, news that came out of Mafeking was formulated with more than a passing concern for the audience to which it was directed. Baden-Powell's own dispatches struck precisely the right note of casual bravery, making light of all difficulties, that so excited the admiration of the British people. The war correspondents, the other main source of news, were kept firmly in line. At the start of the siege they were informed by Baden-Powell that criticism of the conduct of the siege would not be permitted, and that all their dispatches would be censored. Most of the correspondents, however, shared Baden-Powell's strongly imperialist sentiments and his appreciation of what the British public would like to hear about the siege. They were also well aware that in their grasp they had the story of a lifetime. One of the correspondents, though, Angus Hamilton of *The Times*, was not prepared to go along with this cosy consensus, and took a rather more critical line. As a result he soon became *persona non grata* with Baden-Powell and the military authorities, and most of his dispatches ended up – according to one of the other correspondents – in the censor's wastepaper basket. Those of his dispatches that did get through were ignored by his newspaper. And when Baden-Powell eventually wrote to *The Times* with a request that Hamilton should be dismissed, the newspaper's manager not only agreed with alacrity but told Baden-Powell that he should have taken this step himself without consulting him about it. A dissenting voice about Mafeking could clearly be tolerated neither by Baden-Powell nor by the leading opinion-formers in England.

For the people of Mafeking their main reward – as Edward Ross had predicted during the course of the siege – was to be the privilege of 'making history for the British Empire'. This in itself was not without some more immediate material advantage. In the months and years after the siege local traders and hoteliers profited from the trail of visiting dignitaries, and others, who made their way to the town to offer their congratulations or simply to satisfy their curiosity. Compensation for loss and damage was paid by the imperial government, but it was not generally considered to be anything like just or sufficient. A lot of money was made from the sale of souvenirs of the siege. But Mafeking was unsuccessful in its claim to the 'Wolf', a gun constructed in the railway workshops during the siege and used successfully against the Boers. Baden-Powell considered this to be his personal property and took it back to England with him. It stands today in the Royal Artillery Museum in Woolwich, London.

African disillusionment

Mafeking's African population had even greater reason to feel that the hardships they endured had not been sufficiently rewarded. The Barolong people were presented with several memorials in recognition of their loyalty and assistance, but the promises of land made to them were never fulfilled. They took up this matter with Joseph Chamberlain when he visited Mafeking at the beginning of 1903, but to no avail. Moreover, they had to fight hard for the compensation due to them. A deputation travelled to Cape Town in 1903 to see the Cape Prime Minister and managed to obtain from him a promise that their claims would be re-investigated. Mafeking's small Mfengu community, which had suffered such heavy losses in life during the siege, was also made to feel that its sacrifices were not appreciated. The Mfengu, too, were promised a piece of land that they never received.

The siege was not the only occasion during the war when Africans in Mafeking suffered heavy losses. Despite their strong protests, the Barolong were disarmed immediately after the siege. As a result they could only watch as a Boer commando carried off hundreds of their cattle in a raid on their *stad* early in 1902. But for some the bitterest blow was the attempt by Baden-Powell to distort the record of their contribution during the siege. Even at the time few of the actions in which they were engaged were mentioned in the General Orders. At the end of the siege Baden-Powell repeatedly prohibited the *Mafeking Mail* from giving a true account of the part played by the Barolong in defeating the final Boer assault upon the town – which came through the *stad* – on 12 May 1900. Worst of all, in Sol Plaatje's opinion, was the evidence that Baden-Powell gave before the *Royal Commission on the War in South Africa* in 1903. Asked whether the Barolong had been employed in military operations, he replied: 'No, we tried to make them defend their own town, but on the first attack they all ran away, so we did not rely on them at all.' 'Here we have a man', Plaatje wrote, 'than whom few white men, dead or alive, have ever had greater reason to thank black men for honours received', who was now 'coolly and deliberately lying' about what had actually happened. It was not the first time, nor was it to be the last, that such misrepresentations were made about the events that took place during the siege of Mafeking.

References

Because I have tried to let the townspeople speak for themselves wherever possible in this chapter, it would have been distracting to footnote every quotation. The manuscript sources used were as follows.

Letter from Baden-Powell, September 1917 (Dorset County Archives)
Diary of C. G. H. Bell and the Bell Papers (Cory Library, Rhodes University, Grahamstown)
Diary of William Hayes (Cape Archives, Cape Town)
Letter from Charles Peachey, September 1900 (Greater London Records Office)
Diary of Edward Ross (Cory Library)
Diary of Mother Mary Stanislaus (Mafeking Museum)
Diary of Albert Shimwell (Cory Library)
Despatches of Vere Stent (Witwatersrand University Archives, Johannesburg)
The Times Archives (Printing House Square, London)
Weil Papers (British Museum)

The following newspapers and magazine articles were also consulted.

Glasgow Weekly Herald
Koranta ea Becoana/The Bechuana Gazette
Mafeking Mail
The Times
B. May, 'To Mafeking in 1900', *The Critic*, 2, 1934–5
'The Relief of Mafeking. A Personal Narrative', *Army Quarterly*, 11, 1925–6
'With Plumer to the Relief of Mafeking, by one of his Troopers', *Blackwoods Magazine*, December 1900
'With the Boers around Mafeking 1899–1900', *Blackwoods Magazine*, January 1902

CHAPTER 7

Women and the War

S. B. Spies

The role of women in South African society

The feminist contention that women's role in the past has been minimized by historians is probably at least as applicable to the historiography of South Africa as it is to that of other countries. Yet women have by no means been 'written out' of the South African War of 1899–1902. The contemporary furore surrounding the implementation of the British scorched earth and concentration camp policies and the emergence after the Peace of Vereeniging of a considerable body of literature, mostly first-hand accounts by women, who, so it was claimed, had borne the brunt of the war, ensured that from a feminine point of view the war became one of the best recorded episodes of South African history. This made it difficult for historians to ignore the impact of the conflict on women. Not surprisingly, women's sufferings in general, and their experiences in concentration camps in particular, were most heavily emphasized, perhaps at the cost of other facets. Recent research, by revealing new nuances and perspectives – the most significant of which will, it is hoped, be reflected in this synthesis – may have produced a more balanced picture. But it should be recognized that the full implications of the war for women both in South Africa and in Britain still await delineation, let alone detailed study.

At the close of the nineteenth century neither in Britain nor in South Africa did women have a direct share in the decision-making process. Shortly before the outbreak of the South African War women had been enfranchised in two parts of the British empire – New Zealand (1893) and South Australia (1894) – but women in Britain and in the South African colonies and republics still did not have the vote in parliamentary elections. By 1899 more than three decades of organized, but as yet non-militant, agitation in Britain had kept the question of women's suffrage before the public. Apart from the ardent protests of the Cape author Olive Schreiner against the subordinate position of women in society, the feminist cause in South Africa received only mild support, in the main confined to the British colonies. In April 1914 Louis Botha, then Prime Minister of the Union of South Africa, was referring primarily to the Anglo-Boer War when he asked:

> 'If woman had had a vote, would all this trouble have occurred? Would woman not have secured that at any rate there should have been less misery . . . ?'

But Botha was not advocating women's suffrage. Earlier, throughout the existence of the republics, Boers of both sexes were opposed to women officially being accorded a role in the political arena, and often used scriptural arguments as a basis for their views.

Nevertheless, as the Cape politician J. X. Merriman informed a Canadian friend in 1900:

> 'Oddly enough in South Africa the women have always exercised a great influence. I say "oddly", because they are so utterly and entirely opposed to the modern view of "women's rights".'

In fact, Boer women from the time of the Great Trek (during which in particular they had at times exercised a decisive influence) had not only shared many of the vicissitudes of the establishment and early history of the republics, but had on occasion actually been in the forefront of events. Olive Schreiner, writing shortly before the outbreak of the 1899 war, maintained not only that the Transvaal War of 1881 had been largely a woman's war – 'it was from the armchair beside the coffee-table that the voice went out for conflict and no surrender' – but that it was still largely the woman's voice that urged the Boer nations forward or held them back. She emphasized that apart from woman's traditional role

> 'in producing and rearing, at a risk to life almost as great and at the cost of suffering immeasurably greater, the warriors of the nation . . . the Boer woman's share in the defence of the state is more direct, more conscious and unmistakeable.'

Olive Schreiner's feminist bias needs to be taken into account. But there nevertheless was a strong Afrikaner tradition of women's involvement in communal life and political affairs, although they were not accorded formal rights. Women ameliorated the harshness of pioneering conditions, played a leading role in educating their children, and their support or incitement of their men during times of political crisis was often decisive. Their influence was grounded in their position as the focal points of tightly-knit, often large, family units.[1]

The role of Boer women in the war effort

The outbreak of war in October 1899 immediately disrupted most of these family units. Boer women, as they had in past campaigns, assumed control of the farms as the men were called up for commando duty. They despised cowards and shirkers, induced their men to join the fighting forces and often compelled burghers on furlough to return to the front. They assisted the Boer commissariat, nursed the wounded, and later the sick, in concentration camps, and organized relief for indigents. But even before the British invasion of the republics there were women who abandoned their farms and flocked to the towns because they lacked food and clothing or because they felt imperilled by neighbouring Africans. Frequent complaints about the provision made for these destitutes by the republican authorities culminated in some burghers threatening to stop fighting unless their families received better treatment. Transvaal women volunteered to take over the duties of republican officials to free as many men as possible to join the commandos, but by then the enemy was at the gates, and within a month of the offer having been made, British forces occupied Pretoria.

Despite the pleas of some Boer women to be armed and to be allowed to fight, and despite fanciful tales of corps of Amazons being recruited, there was no widespread active female participation in the conflict, although there were isolated instances of women who were caught up in hostilities. An American newspaper correspondent who was in South Africa during the first phase of the war cited the examples of Mrs Otto Krantz, who remained in the field during the Natal campaign, and Helena Wagner of Zeerust, who spent five months fighting in the laagers and trenches without her identity being revealed. There were probably other cases of active feminine participation in the war, but the Boer authorities were opposed to women fighting and even to their traditional presence in laagers except if they were nurses. Nevertheless, instructions forbidding women to be at the front were often ignored during the early months of the war. The stern, be-

Below left: Helena Wagner of Zeerust, who is reputed to have fought on the side of the Boers during the Natal campaign without her identity being revealed.

Below right: Hendrina Joubert, wife of the Commandant-General of the South African Republic, who was rumoured to have been her husband's chief military counsellor.

Hester, the wife of General P. A. Cronjé. She was in the laager at Paardeberg when her husband surrendered on 27 February 1900, and later accompanied him to St Helena.

spectacled Hendrina Joubert – called by some 'the general in petticoats' and rumoured to be her husband's chief military counsellor – accompanied the Commandant-General to the front, as she had done in the past. General P. A. Cronjé's wife, Hester, together with some fifty other women, was in the laager at Paardeberg when he surrendered on 27 February 1900; she accompanied him into exile to St Helena, but the other female camp-followers were sent to their homes when their men were dispatched to prisoner-of-war camps.

As the commandos started retreating, both Boer governments had no option but to leave families behind in areas of their republics that were occupied by the enemy. The Transvaalers' initial scheme to evacuate these families before British forces overran their districts proved impossible to implement. Once the phase of regular warfare came to an end, certain women living in British-controlled towns smuggled messages to the commandos in the field. The belief, held by some British officers, that the bitterness of these women strengthened the resolution of the fighting Boers, was probably correct, and women also harboured and protected spies in the towns. On the other hand, Susanna de Wet appears to have played a role in persuading her husband, General Piet de Wet, to surrender in July 1900.[2]

The destruction of property in the first months of the war by Boer commandos in Natal and Cape Colony, and by British raiding columns in the Orange Free State, can be attributed to lack of discipline and not to the authorization of the respective high commands. From March 1900 Roberts ordered houses to be burnt. This scorched earth policy originated as a punishment for resistance to the British occupation of republican territory. In some cases the houses that were burnt or blown up had actually been occupied by the families of the men on commando

Below left: British troops destroy a farmhouse and its adjacent buildings. Incendiarism was instituted in the republics as early as March 1900.

Below right: General Louis Botha's ruined farmhouse.

who had attacked the lines of communication or British columns, but in most instances there were no direct links between the men who had committed these legitimate acts of war and the non-combatants whose homes were destroyed. Moreover, once incendiarism, for whatever reason, had been sanctioned by the Commander-in-Chief, houses on farms and in *dorps* began to be destroyed with a casual ruthlessness. Roberts, and subsequently Kitchener too, came to accept these tactics, together with the destruction of supplies, as a means of preventing the commandos operating in certain districts, but there can be little doubt that they were also calculated measures that used the sufferings of women and children as a lever to induce men to surrender. Roberts, in September 1900, declared:

> 'Unless the people generally are made to suffer for misdeeds of those in arms against us the war will never end.'

In October 1902 Milner admitted that it was likely that as many as 30 000 farmhouses had been destroyed during the war; in addition, a number of villages had virtually been razed to the ground.

An officer who served with Brigadier M. F. Rimington's column has described a typical scene as women

> 'huddle together in their cotton frocks and big cotton sun-bonnets while our men set fire to the house. . . . The fire bursts out of windows and doors with a loud roaring and black volumes of smoke roll overhead. . . . The women . . . cling together, comforting each other or hiding their faces in each other's laps.'

During Roberts's command in South Africa no general orders were issued to provide for these families rendered destitute as a result of the farm-burnings. Some officers sent them to nearby British towns, but often the women and children were left to

The implications of incendiarism

Devastated farm buildings. Milner calculated that as many as 30 000 farmhouses were destroyed during the war.

fend for themselves. They fled to neighbouring farms or even to the Cape Colony or sought refuge in African kraals. On occasion commandos erected scanty shelters or put families in waggon-laagers, which were in turn attacked by British columns or hostile Africans.

Black women too experienced the horror of incendiarism; Roberts had ordered that, beyond confiscating their stock, columns should not harm Africans, and Kitchener subsequently stipulated that while Africans on Boer farms should be brought in, their property should be respected. But by the first quarter of 1901 African refugees, whose huts and villages had been burnt by British troops, started streaming into Basutoland. Despite warnings that serious repercussions would ensue, zealous officers persisted in burning African huts, maintaining that they were being used by commandos. Nor, assuredly, was the burning of Qulusi villages late in the war, on Botha's orders, the only example of the destruction of the property of Africans by Boer forces.[3]

Gezina Kruger, the wife of the Transvaal President.

Roberts's policy towards civilians

From July 1900 Roberts dispatched train-loads of destitute Boer families living in Pretoria and Johannesburg to the commandos as they retreated along the Delagoa Bay railway line. By the beginning of September when some 2 500 women and children had been handed over to the fighting Boers, who had accommodated them at Barberton, Roberts announced his intention of sending out not only indigents but all families of fighting burghers living in districts occupied by British forces: it was stressed that not even Annie Botha, the wife of the new Commandant-General, nor the aged Gezina Kruger, the wife of the Transvaal President, would be exempt from the measure. The Free State President, M. T. Steyn, suggested that if Roberts implemented his threat, two ships would be chartered at Delagoa Bay to take the families to Europe. However, after those families who had been sent out earlier once again came under British control as the commandos retreated from Barberton, it became apparent to Roberts that the hard-pressed fighting Boers were in no position to receive further dependants.

Roberts had cited considerations of supply (aggravated by continual Boer attacks on the railway lines from the Cape and Natal ports) and security (the transmission of intelligence to the commandos) as justification for the expulsion of families from Pretoria and Johannesburg. But Botha interpreted these measures as

> 'an attempt to revenge the determination of myself and my burghers to persevere in the struggle upon our wives and children.'

Indeed, when the expulsion of women had first been suggested by Colonel J. C. Mackenzie, the Military Governor of Johannesburg, he had stressed that 'it will not be without its effect on diminishing the strength of the enemy's commandos', and Major-General G. T. Pretyman, his counterpart in the Orange River Colony, believed that it would be beneficial to the British cause if the inhabitants were in that way made to feel the hardships of war, while Roberts had commented: 'Botha no doubt thinks . . . [the women] a nuisance, but for that I am not sorry.' Although the expulsion of these families did initially dent the morale of the Transvaal leaders, on the other hand, the arrival of irreconcilable women waving *vierkleurs* and singing the *volkslied* may actually have encouraged the men to persist in their struggle.[4]

Concentration camp system

As early as May 1900 Brigadier-General E. Y. Brabant had suggested the establishment of protected camps for surrendered burghers. In August and September 1900, as the impracticability of forcing the burghers in the field to take care of their families had become apparent, and as the scorched earth policy became more draconic, members of the military establishment and certain civilians revived the idea. A camp for the families of fighting Boers had actually arisen at Mafeking in July, and in the last week of September 1900 the formation of what the British authorities called 'refugee camps' received official sanction. However, the term 'concentration camp' was a more appropriate description, for these camps, from their inception, housed not only, or even mainly, refugees who had voluntarily placed themselves under British protection, but also families of fighting burghers who had been driven into the camps, and in Cape Colony and Natal so-called 'undesirable' women who had been expelled from the republics. By the time Roberts left South Africa at least nine such camps were in existence. Kitchener, in December 1900, extended the system by emphasizing that all people should be removed from certain districts persistently occupied by commandos. He ordered the inmates to be divided into two categories:

Boer women, wearing distinctive white bonnets, attempt to prevent a calf from falling into the hands of a detachment of British troops raiding their farm.

> '1st Refugees, and the families of neutrals, non-combatants and surrendered burghers. 2nd. Those whose husbands, fathers or sons are on commando. The preference in accommodation, etc. should, of course, be given to the first class.'

Chamberlain's statement in the Commons in August 1901 that the concentration camp system was the only humane alternative to leaving the women and children on the veld requires, at the very least, some qualification, as for some months the families had indeed simply been left on the veld. The differences in the ration scales for 'refugees' and 'undesirables' were of no great consequence and they were subsequently abandoned, but Kitchener's initial insistence on them and that preferential accommodation should be provided for the first-mentioned category, would also appear to militate against the acceptance of a purely humanitarian motive.

In fact, the concentration camp system inaugurated by Roberts and developed by Kitchener owes it origin, as Milner recognized, to military considerations, and formed part of the strategy to end Boer resistance. Only five days after he had assumed command, Kitchener wrote to Roberts:

> 'The women question is always cropping up and is . . . difficult. There is no doubt the women are keeping up the war and are far more bitter than the men. . . . I really think the only solution that will bring them to their senses is to remove the worst class to Kaapmuiden and form a camp there.'

In addition, Kitchener believed that if he confined women to camps under British control it would be possible 'to work on the feelings of the men to get back to their farms'. After the war, a British intelligence officer elaborated on the latter point:

Boer women on board an open railway truck about to be transported to a British concentration camp.

Boer families after their arrival at a concentration camp with the limited possessions they had been allowed to bring with them.

> 'It was thought that pressure might be brought to bear on the commandos through their womenfolk and that they would not be able to bear separation from their families. All is fair in love and war; it was apparently expected that the Boers would be prepared to abandon war for the sake of love.'

The camps accommodated indigent families and those civilians whose presence on the farms was considered to hamper military operations. They were also established to provide surrendered burghers with a guarantee that they would be safe from being compelled to fight again by their compatriots in the field. It was further believed that men on commando would come to realize that the only means of seeing their families in the camps would be by surrendering.[5]

Civilians had been taken from their homes before 21 December 1900, but it was after the promulgation of Kitchener's notice of that date, and particularly after the commencement of the military drives the following month, that thousands of women with their families were swept from the farms into the concentration camps. The vast majority of these women remained loyal to the republican cause, but there were some who curried favour with the authorities by acting as informers. By the end of the war there were more than forty camps for whites, including three to house the families of National Scouts, with altogether more than 116 000 inmates, situated on the railway lines in the Transvaal and Orange River Colony, and in the Cape and Natal. Conditions, which varied considerably from camp to camp, were determined largely by the personality and ability of the superintendent, by the site, and by the facilities available. Many camps had not been properly prepared to receive the inmates when the women and children were driven in; tents were the most common type of accommodation, but sod or reed huts, sheds, stables, and in one instance the grandstand of a racecourse, were used when tents were in short supply; beds and mattresses were not always available; rations were usually inadequate or unsuitable for women and children; sanitary arrangements were often unhygienic; in some camps the water supply was insufficient, and initially no soap was issued to the inmates; in certain camps fuel was scanty.

Deaths in the camps

From their inception deaths occurred in the camps, but the mortality rate reached a crescendo in the South African winter and spring of 1901: 2 666 deaths in August (a mortality rate of 311 per 1 000 per annum), 2 752 in September (287 per 1 000 per annum) and 3 205 in October (344 per 1 000 per annum). Conditions in the camps were greatly improved during the last seven months of hostilities, but 27 927 Boers died in the concentration camps, which is certainly many more than, and possibly double, the number of men on both sides who were killed in action. More than 22 000 of those who died in the camps were children under the age of sixteen years, and more than 4 000 adult women died. These deaths were particularly damaging to the Boers because, according to Smuts, the total white population of the two republics was not much more than 200 000: if Smuts's estimate was correct, more than 10 per cent of the white inhabitants of the two Boer states perished in the concentration camps. Admittedly, according to the British official history of the war, more than 16 000 British soldiers also died of disease, and mortality rates in many Cape towns at the close of the nineteenth century were high (comparative statistics for the republics are not available), but it still cannot be disputed that the deaths in the concentration camps reached extraordinary proportions.

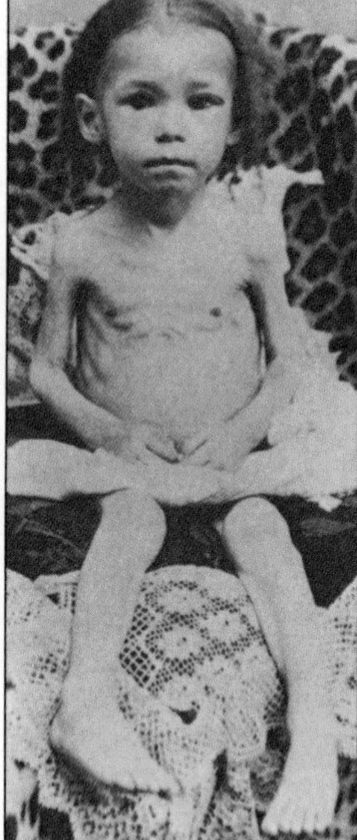

Below left: a tent family in a concentration camp. In many camps rations were unsuitable and inadequate, sanitary arrangements unhygienic and fuel scanty, leading to an appalling loss of life. It seems likely that more than 10 per cent of the white inhabitants of the Boer states perished in the camps.

Below right: an emaciated Boer child from the Bloemfontein camp. Of the 27 987 civilians who perished in the camps, more than 22 000 were children under the age of sixteen.

The general insanitary condition of the country that resulted from the devastating nature of the war, together with exceptionally severe epidemics of measles, pneumonia and dysentery, were no doubt contributory causes of many of the deaths. Whether there would have been as many (or as Milner claimed more) deaths if civilians had been left on the farms is questionable. Chamberlain argued that it was hardly an answer

> 'to say that the aggregation of people who are specially liable to infectious disease has produced a state of things which is inevitable. The natural remark is: "Why then did you bring them together?" If we say that it was because they would have starved on the veld, we enter into a hypothetical consideration and cannot of course prove that in the alternative the mortality rate would have been as large.'

Kitchener, who with others connected with the administration of the camps believed that the high death rate could be attributed to the insanitary habits of the inmates, maintained that

> 'it is impossible to fight against the criminal neglect of the mothers – I do not like the idea of using force . . . but I am considering whether some of the worst cases could not be tried for manslaughter.'

While it is likely that the habits, ignorance and superstitions of many women made them unsuitable members of a camp community, there surely must also have been other contributory causes, for how else can the lower mortality rates in certain camps and the marked reduction in the number of deaths in the latter stages of the war be explained?

Numerous observers – not all of them sympathetic to the Boers – pointed out serious shortcomings in the organization and administration of the camps. Roberts and Kitchener may be indicted for having exercised inadequate control over the camps, but the neglect and carelessness of certain officials certainly did not have official sanction. Even less can it be substantiated that the concentration camps policy was a deliberate attempt to exterminate the Afrikaner nation by killing the women and children. Nevertheless, as Milner stated,

> 'while a hundred explanations may be offered and a hundred excuses made, they do not really amount to an adequate defence [of the concentration camp system].'

He admitted that 'the abuse so freely heaped upon us for everything we have done and not done is not without some foundation.'

Desertions from the camps

Although the concentration camps were guarded and some were fenced in, forty-three women and forty-eight children escaped. The general superintendent of the Transvaal camps believed that the taunts and gibes of women in the camps had been largely responsible for the desertion too of more than three hundred men from the camps who rejoined the commandos. Not only were the camp authorities unable to prevent these escapes but they were not always able to provide protection, as they were supposed to, to surrendered burghers and their families. Boer forces raided more than one camp to release the men for fighting and to obtain supplies, and when a commando was repulsed from the Belfast camp in the eastern Transvaal in September 1901, one woman was killed and two children wounded in the crossfire.

It was not only the *sufferings* of the women in the camps that concerned the Boer peace delegates at Vereeniging in May 1902. General J. B. M. Hertzog stated that the inmates were being exposed to destructive moral influences and the assistant state attorney of the South African Republic, who also decried the immorality in the camps, asserted that, 'Our female sex stands under the influence of the enemy and is beginning to . . . deviate from the morals of our forefathers.' After the Transvaal authorities had protested to Salisbury in November 1901 about the treatment of women and children in the camps, Kitchener informed the Boers in the field that as they had complained about the way the British authorities were dealing with their families, it was assumed that they were in a position to provide for them on their own behalf, and that all women who were willing to leave would be sent with their families to the commandos. The Transvaalers did not react, but the Free Staters angrily retorted that owing to the devastated condition of the country it was impossible for the fighting Boers to receive their families. In fact, women were not sent out of the camps – Kitchener informed Brodrick that the point of the message was to 'make them drop the subject and beg us to continue keeping their women and children' – but no more families were brought into the camps. There were thus a few thousand women and children deprived of shelter and supplies who struggled to survive on the bare veld, and, according to Botha, at the end of the war there were 2 540 such families in the Transvaal alone.[6]

African women in concentration camps

The privations of Boer women in the concentration camps received much publicity during and after the war. It is less well known that African women, too, endured hardships in British concentration camps. As early as July 1900 blacks started leaving their tribal areas to seek protection within the British lines. When Kitchener issued orders concerning the clearing of the country, he instructed his officers to bring in only those Africans living on Boer farms, and Emily Hobhouse found black maid servants in concentration camps for whites, sometimes sharing the same tents as their white mistresses. During the drives, however, Africans were cleared not only from white farms, but also from their own *stads* and from mission stations. The men were employed by the military and civil establishments while their families, together with the families of men in Boer service, were accommodated in separate concentration camps that were established along the railways in the Transvaal and Orange River Colony. By the end of the war there were more than sixty such camps, containing more than 115 000 inmates, which were controlled by a separate Native Refugee Department. Self-sufficiency was the aim for these camps – inmates were required to erect their own huts and crops were cultivated, largely by women and children, for their own maintenance and for military use. Until the crops were reaped, the inmates received rations that were not as varied nor as nutritious as the rations provided in the camps for whites. Some women from the black camps were sent as servants to private employers. Dissatisfaction with conditions led to more than four hundred desertions and there were a number of attempts on the part of commandos to infiltrate the camps. Whereas October 1901 had been in the white camps the month with the highest mortality rate, in the black camps the death rate reached its peak in December 1901 – 372 per 1 000 per annum – which was more severe than the highest mortality rate in all the white camps in any one month. Altogether it would appear that at least 14 000 Africans, mostly children, died in these camps during the war, although the recorded statistics of deaths in the black camps are even more incomplete than those in the white camps. Humanitarian considerations cannot be regarded as the prime motive for the establishment of camps for Africans, who were, in fact, cleared from the country to prevent the commandos obtaining assistance and supplies and also to provide labour.[7]

'a bad and dangerous lot'

In addition to the tens of thousands of Boer women who were driven into concentration camps, both Roberts and Kitchener singled out for special treatment certain women living in the towns who were considered to be particularly irreconcilable and bitter. In August 1900 Roberts had contemplated sending a number of prominent Pretoria ladies, including the wife of General Lukas Meyer, and Mrs A. H. Malan, the daughter of General P. J. Joubert, to the Cape or Natal because their presence in the Transvaal was considered to be undesirable for military reasons. Milner's objections contributed to Roberts's decision to abandon these expulsions. But in January 1901 Kitchener ordered Isie Smuts (wife of General J. C. Smuts) and Ella de Wet (wife of Botha's secretary, N. J. de Wet, who was to become Chief Justice of the Union of South Africa) out of the Transvaal to live in a house in Pietermaritzburg. Smuts himself in February 1901 expected Kitchener to go further and to enforce large-scale transportation of Boer families overseas. In fact, four months later Kitchener, becoming aware that the concentration camp policy was not having the desired effect of ending the war, pressed a scheme upon the British government whereby all present prisoners of war, and Boers who should subsequently surrender, would be permanently settled with their families in Madagascar, Fiji or Java. He pointed out that the scheme would clear the concentration camps (thereby relieving the government of the embarrassment that had resulted from the unfavourable publicity regarding the policy) and free the British of 'a bad and dangerous lot'.

Annie, the English-speaking wife of General Louis Botha. Both Roberts and Kitchener used her as an intermediary in their efforts to persuade the Boer leaders to lay down their arms.

> 'The Boers [he informed Brodrick] are uncivilized Africander [*sic*] savages with only a thin white veneer. . . . The Boer woman in the refugee camp who slaps her protruding belly at you and shouts "When all our men are gone, these little Khakis will fight you" is a type of savage produced by generations of wild lonely life. Back on their farms and their life on the veldt, they will be just as uncivilized as ever and a constant danger. Change their country and they may become civilized people fit to live with.'

The British Cabinet regarded the scheme as absurd and was not prepared to sanction it. Having being thwarted in transporting Boer families wholesale, Kitchener in November 1901 suggested sending the wives of certain Boer leaders who were still in the field to Europe. The six women, selected as some of the most irreconcilable – the wives of President Steyn, Generals P. H. Roux, Schalk Burger, Tobias Smuts and C. R. de Wet – were, he maintained, suspected of transmitting information to the commandos and stirring up unrest in the concentration camps. Once again the Commander-in-Chief's scheme was vetoed, and it is apparent that the likelihood of the women fomenting pro-Boer propaganda in Europe, as well as the consideration that the proceedings would be condemned and ridiculed as waging war on women and children, swayed the scales against the proposal.[8]

Boer women as peace emissaries

Both Roberts and Kitchener made use of Boer women as peace emissaries – by sending them from time to time to the commandos to persuade them to lay down their arms. Annie Botha, the English-speaking wife of the Commandant-General of the Transvaal forces, whose father, John Cheere Emmett, claimed to be a near-relation of the Irish patriot, Robert Emmet, had remained in Pretoria after the occupation of the capital and remained on good terms with the British establishment. Roberts allowed her to visit her husband in the field at the beginning of June 1900. No meeting between the rival military commanders resulted, as had been hoped, and Smuts subsequently commented that

> 'probably the mind of Lord Roberts was not capable of seeing the insult he was offering his opponent by trying to seduce him from his plain duty through the influence of his wife, but as a man of honour Botha would, and I know did, feel this most keenly of all.'

In February 1901 she was once again used as an intermediary, this time by Kitchener, between the British Commander-in-Chief and her husband, and on this occasion her influence seems to have been, at least in part, responsible for Botha meeting Kitchener at Middelburg on 28 February 1901. Subsequently, Annie Botha was permitted to go to Europe, and in Holland she probably informed Kruger and Leyds of the situation in South Africa. Kruger's private secretary appears to have been disappointed by her despondency and noted in his diary that he was beginning to doubt whether the female sex was worthy of receiving men's confidences. In November 1900 Hendrina Joubert's mission to Botha, bearing a message urging peace from the Transvaal industrialist Sammy Marks, was sanctioned by Roberts, but it merely caused resentment in Boer ranks. Earlier, in July, Lieutenant-General Archibald Hunter had failed to persuade Rachel Isabella Steyn to exert influence on her husband, the President of the Orange Free State, to end the war. In the same month Major-General H. L. Smith-Dorrien burnt farms in the eastern Transvaal and then sent the former occupants to their husbands to persuade them to surrender. Women dispatched from the concentration camps to induce surrenders had limited success, but from a British point of view this practice also had its drawbacks: some desertions from concentration camps were precipitated by a woman who, after her return from the commandos, informed the male inmates that if they were prepared to take up arms again their earlier surrender would be forgiven by the Boers in the field.[9]

Rachel Isabella Steyn, wife of the President of the Orange Free State. In July 1901 unsuccessful attempts were made by the British to persuade her to exert influence on her husband to end the war.

On October 1900 Major-General J. C. C. Barker replied to General P. R. Viljoen's protests about the treatment of Boer women by stating:

> 'Hardships must necessarily occur in war time even to ladies but let General Viljoen ask himself . . . whether English women in this country did not suffer as great or greater hardship at the beginning of the war, losing husband, homestead, . . . and every prospect in life.'

The plight of Uitlander women

Uitlander women who were resident in the Transvaal experienced their greatest upheaval immediately before or after the outbreak of hostilities when their families left their homes either voluntarily or under compulsion. Most of them went to live in Natal or Cape Colony. Lionel Curtis reported that Uitlander refugees in Durban were living

> 'like Kaffirs in huts made of tins and boxes. The contrast with the trim rows of tents in the Boer refugee camps with free rations, hospitals, etc. is rather too painful. One cannot help feeling that there has been a grave oversight on the part of the British Government to support the Boers and do nothing for our own people.'

Curtis's idealized picture of a Boer concentration camp does not bear scrutiny, but undoubtedly there was distress among the Uitlander refugees in Durban and Cape Town. All the Uitlanders who left the Transvaal must have suffered discomfort, but according to a contemporary report only about 3 000 out of a total of some 60 000 refugees were so destitute that they had to receive relief. Many of these women, who had never worked for wages before, went into domestic service or became employees in factories or supported themselves by needlework or other means, while their husbands often joined the irregular colonial forces. Some men were allowed to return to the Witwatersrand following the British occupation of Johannesburg, but their families were only permitted to go back to their homes after the end of the war. In Cape Colony a committee of ladies under the presidency of Dr Jane Waterson, whom Milner regarded as being 'worth a dozen men' organized relief for these refugees.[10]

Colonial women were forced to endure the privations of siege warfare in Ladysmith, Kimberley and Mafeking. In Cape Colony a number of families had relatives serving with the Boers and women organized meetings of protest against British military measures in the republics. Merriman sympathized with their views, but considered that the speeches appealed to feeling rather than to reason, and that they demonstrated 'the unfitness of women for public life'. Olive Schreiner, who was prominent in decrying the war itself and the methods employed, published a warning that 'the hour of external success [for Britain] may be the hour of irrevocable failure.' She also stressed the irreconcilable nature of Boer women:

> 'If there were left but five thousand pregnant South African born women and all the rest of their people destroyed, those women would breed up again a race like to the first.'

Kitchener's pleas, which have been quoted for the resettlement of Boer families overseas, were expressed – probably unconsciously – in similar terms.

Of course, there were also many Cape women, including some of Dutch descent, who were fervent supporters of the British war effort. Dorothea Fairbridge, who was to write numerous novels and historical works in later years, helped establish the Guild of Loyal Women. As Lady Edward Cecil (later Viscountess Milner) noted during her stay in Cape Town:

> '. . . all the movement for the Victoria League, for the Ladies Empire Club in far away Grosvenor Street and for much else started over the tea cups at Rondesbosch and Claremont.'[11]

Women from neutral countries

Women who were subjects of neutral countries did not escape the blast of war. Roberts's decision in June 1900 that all employees of the Netherlands South African Railway Company who were not republican burghers would be deported to Europe led to over 1 700 women and children, the majority of whom were Hollanders, being sent from the Cape port of East London to Flushing. Nurses from various European countries served in South Africa. The initial reluctance of the republican authorities to allow women to accompany the ambulances provided by continental organizations was only overcome when these organizations declared that their trained female nurses were essential to them. Boer women obtained valuable training from these nurses from Europe, which enabled them to continue caring for their wounded countrymen when the republican Red Cross medical service collapsed during the second phase of the war. In July 1900 nurses attached to the 2nd Netherlands Ambulance

Detachment were arrested and returned to their country when uncensored letters from Pretoria civilians to men on commando were found in their possession. Neutral women residents of the republics were also swept into the concentration camps. Some of them were sent overseas after Kitchener had advised that it was cheaper to deport indigent foreigners than to feed them in South Africa at government expense, but there were still neutral subjects in the camps in 1902. Finally, regarding neutral women and the war, it may be noted that it was the young Queen Wilhelmina of the Netherlands who sent the Dutch man-of-war the *Gelderland* to Delagoa Bay in October 1900 to convey the Transvaal President to Europe, an act, according to Kruger, 'which was appreciated in the highest degree by the Boer nation'.[12]

British women

In a recent assessment, in which the masculine nature of the imperial enterprise has been emphasized, it has been noted that in the Anglo-Boer War period many of the leading imperialists, including Rhodes, Milner (who married only at the age of 67), Baden-Powell (who married at the age of 55), Jameson and Kitchener, were bachelors – 'the empire was not acquired in a fit of absence of mind, so much as in a fit of absence of wives' – and it has been speculated whether the history of South Africa would have been different had it been otherwise. At the heart of the empire, however, there was a formidable queen. Victoria was no warmonger, but she considered the Boers to be merciless and cruel, just like the southern slave-owners in *Uncle Tom's Cabin*, and she approved of the war as 'a struggle to avoid national humiliation and as an expression of high tone'. She was deeply concerned about army matters and avidly followed the fortunes of the 'soldiers of the queen' in South Africa, who in turn appear

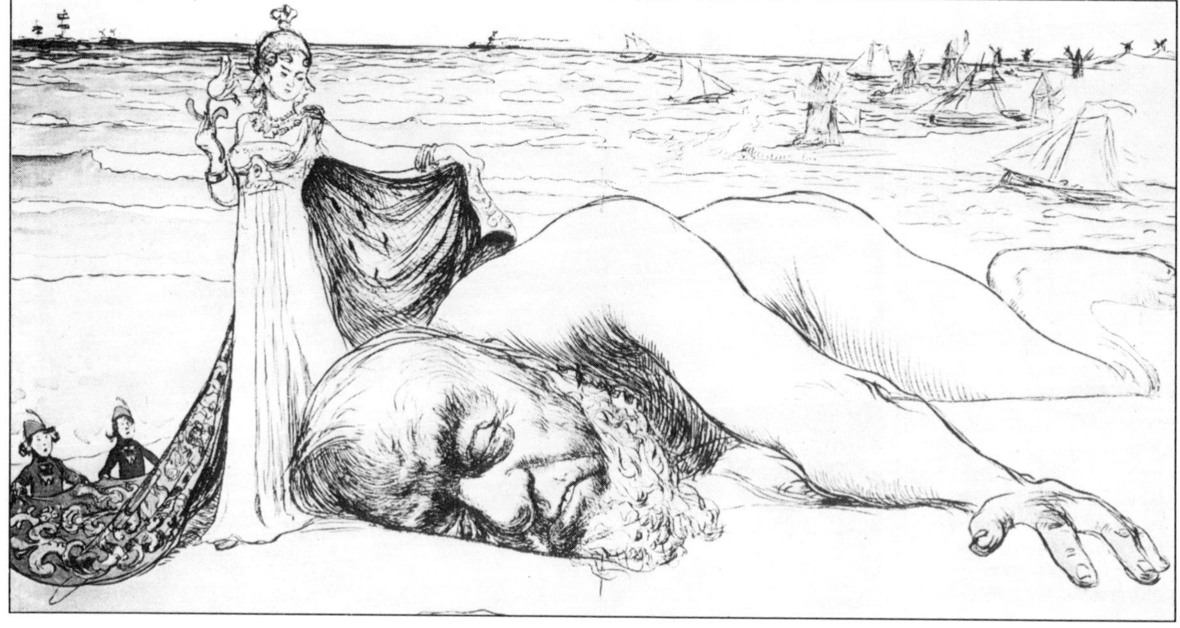

The abandoned ex-President Kruger, an embarrassment to the European powers, here sheltered by Queen Wilhelmina of the Netherlands (from Jean Veber, Les Camps de reconcentration au Transvaal, *special number of* L'Assiette au beurre, *28 September 1901).*

to have been inspired by her interest. Many Boers too were impressed by the Queen, although Smuts put it too strongly when he averred that the Boers' 'admiration for the venerable figure of the aged Sovereign-Mother is as keen as that of the truest Englishman.'[13]

Merriman, when he was in England halfway through the war, was struck 'by the difference between the life and death feeling in South Africa and the incident of Empire here'. Nevertheless, large numbers of British women of all classes were drawn into the currents of the conflict owing to their relationship with men engaged in the struggle. Two upper class ladies whose husbands were initially on Baden-Powell's staff experienced life in the theatre of war. Lady Sarah Wilson, youngest daughter of the 7th Duke of Marlborough, was arrested by Boer forces outside Mafeking on account of her amateur spying activities, but was allowed to return to the besieged town in exchange for a horse-thief. Her subsequent nursing and journalistic activities in Mafeking during its investment earned her the sobriquet of the 'heroine of Mafeking'. Lady Violet Cecil, daughter-in-law of the Marquess of Salisbury, left Cape Town to join her husband, who was district commissioner at Zeerust, when he informed her that her presence 'would steady the district more than anything'.[14]

A considerable number of other upper and middle class British women came to South Africa to render valuable service in hospitals, with nursing units or in relief organizations. Before the war started there were very few female nurses used in the British medical corps, despite the valuable services rendered by

Lady Sarah Wilson, her husband Captain Gordon Wilson (seated left), and party. The Wilsons were typical of those for whom South Africa at the turn of the century represented an upper class adventure playground.

Members of the Russian ambulance that served with the Boer forces, pictured at Newcastle Convent, Natal.

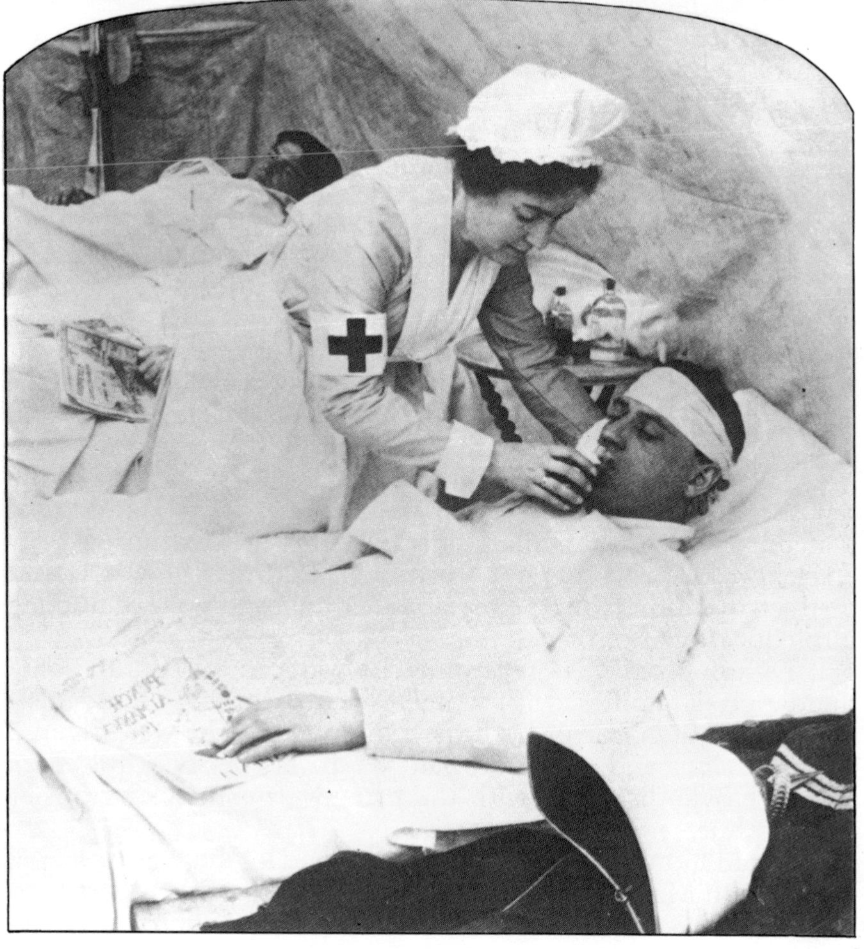

A British nurse attends to a wounded soldier in a field hospital close to the Tugela River in Natal. The Army Medical Corps was at first very reluctant to send women as nurses to South Africa.

Florence Nightingale in the Crimea four decades earlier. Despite the urgent representations of British medical officers in the field in the early months of the war that more women nurses be secured, the Army Medical Department was at first reluctant to send women to South Africa in that capacity on the grounds that that country was not a proper place for women under wartime conditions; that soldiers preferred to be nursed by male orderlies; that women would interfere with the wounded soldiers' freedom; and that flirtations would occur. Before the war ended, however, the War Office sanctioned the establishment of a permanent Army Nursing Service with far more members than the previous organization had had. The historian of nursing in South Africa has expressed the opinion that during the war the British Army Nursing Service sorely needed a vigorous leader of the calibre of Florence Nightingale 'who could have championed the cause of the sick against the prejudice and ineptitude of the controlling authorities'.[15]

Apart from the nurses and relief workers, Cape Town was also swarming with women camp followers who were less useful. Merriman likened this 'smart horde' to

> 'the crew who used to follow Louis XIV to his fights or like the crowd at Brussels depicted in *Vanity Fair*.'

Their disturbing presence attracted the attention of Queen Victoria, who informed Milner, through Chamberlain, that she 'strongly disapproves of the hysterical spirit which seems to have influenced some of them'. Milner also hated these

> 'frivollings of fashionable females . . . and their mutual jealousies, feuds, backbitings and the total unsuitableness of a sort of quasi-Monte Carlo background to that grim tragedy . . . in the veld.'[16]

Social reformers and humanitarians

Prominent British social reformers interpreted the war in different ways. Josephine Butler saw Britain as the instrument of Divine Justice inflicting punishment on wrongdoers whose deeds could be likened to those of Arab slave-dealers. Emmeline Pankhurst was one of the few socialists who believed that the Fabian Society should take a stand on the war, while Beatrice Webb, who admired Boer efficiency, but who was not a pro-Boer, felt that the war would distract attention from the research her husband was conducting into educational reform.

Differing attitudes regarding the war caused rifts in some middle class families, with women often adopting an independent line. Dutch-born Mrs Lecky, in opposing the war, differed from her husband, the historian W. E. H. Lecky, while Mrs Conan Doyle disagreed with the pro-government views of her son, Arthur.

Maud Gonne, the actress from Ireland – who was to marry Major John MacBride, who fought on the side of the Boers with the 'Irish Brigade' – believed that 'England's difficulty is Ireland's opportunity.' She was an extreme example of passionate feminine opposition to the British government's South African policy. Maud Gonne together with Irish women distributed leaflets to dissuade their countrymen from joining the British army – it was postulated that soldiers killing people in an unjust war were guilty of murder – and attempts were made to shame Irish girls from 'consorting with the soldiers of the enemy of their country'. Maud Gonne also travelled to Brussels to propose to the Transvaal envoy, Dr W. J. Leyds, (without gaining his approval) that Irishmen should be used to plant bombs disguised as lumps of coal in the bunkers of South Africa-bound troopships.

'England's difficulty is Ireland's opportunity.' Maud Gonne, the actress and fervent Irish nationalist.

A number of well-connected middle class British women were driven by sympathy for the Boers or humanitarian impulses – or both – to become actively involved in alleviating Boer distress. Margot Asquith and the wives of Alfred and Neville Lyttelton did not wish to be associated with more partisan groups and organized relief for Boer women and children under the aegis of the Victoria League. Mary Kingsley, the niece of the author Charles Kingsley, who had herself become renowned as an explorer and reformer in West Africa, died of enteric while nursing Boer prisoners of war at Simonstown. Her work inspired her friend, Alice Green, the wife of the historian J. R. Green, to visit and report on the conditions of Boer prisoners of war on St Helena. The Quaker Helen Harris, who was married to Professor Rendel Harris of Cambridge, visited the concentration camps, but she was only permitted to do so on condition she 'took some help with her beyond good words'. Jane Cobden Unwin, the daughter of the free-trader Richard Cobden, and wife of the well-known publisher, played a leading role in W. T. Stead's Stop-the-War Movement. The daughter and grand-daughter of John Bright – members of the Clark family of Street, Somerset – provided relief for the inmates of the concentration camps and subsequently became life-long friends of Jan Smuts. The South African Conciliation Committee, the Society of Friends and the South African Women and Children Distress Fund all had women's sections, which collected funds and sent some of their members to South Africa to alleviate the distress of Boer families.

Mary Kingsley, who died of enteric fever while nursing Boer prisoners of war in South Africa.

Emily Hobhouse was undoubtedly pre-eminent among these humanitarian British women whose sensitive concern for Boer women during the war contributed towards Anglo-Boer reconciliation after 1902. She had become concerned about the plight of Boer families in 1900, and from January to April 1901 she visited concentration camps in the Orange River Colony. Apart from the material aid she brought to the camps, her warm sympathy helped lighten the burden of hardship of those interned – although some British officials cynically believed that her advent coincided with the inmates' realization that they were being cruelly treated. Her disclosures focused attention on the harshness of military actions against civilians, and although

Above left: Emily Hobhouse, pre-eminent among British humanitarian women from the middle and upper classes who helped Boer families during and after the war. Her book The Brunt of the War and Where It Fell *(1902) is a testimony to the inhuman treatment of Boer civilians by the British authorities.*

Above right: Millicent Garrett Fawcett, who led a Ladies' Committee appointed by the War Office to investigate conditions in the concentration camps following Emily Hobhouse's disclosures about their maladministration.

Campbell-Bannerman's 'methods of barbarism' speech was probably not solely attributable to her revelations, her proddings not only led to reforms being instituted while she was in South Africa, but also stirred the War Office into dispatching a committee of ladies under Millicent Garrett Fawcett to investigate conditions in the camps. Emily Hobhouse, who was not herself made a member of the commission, believed that both Mrs Fawcett and another member, Dr Jane Waterson, were markedly biased against the Boers, and Labouchere observed that all the members of the commission belonged to high Conservative families. Nevertheless, the commission did effect significant reforms in the administration of the camps. As for Emily Hobhouse, upon her attempt to return to South Africa – according to her to investigate the condition of British refugees at the coast, though it is doubtful whether she would have confined her activities to that sphere – she was placed under arrest on her arrival in Cape Town in October 1901 and was promptly returned to England, drawing from Chamberlain the sardonic comment that 'the military are terribly afraid of women'. After the Peace of Vereeniging she was able to go to South Africa to continue aiding distressed families, and she came to occupy a special place of honour as a friend of Boer women. During the war she maintained that she had been unable to investigate the camps for blacks, although she did raise the matter with the Aborigine Protection Society. Earlier, as a result of Harriete Colenso's requests for help, the Aborigines Protection Society did launch a Zulu Relief Fund.[17]

Women and the war

Women during the South African War have been most clearly discernible to historians as victims, and the hardships endured by women have continued to be the most searing memories of the war. These memories were perpetuated by the erection in 1913 of Anton van Wouw's Women's Monument, south of Bloemfontein. The poorer class of women probably suffered most during hostilities, but even those who were self-supporting and who belonged to the most prominent families were severely hit by the war. The wives of the presidents of both republics, Rachel Isabella Steyn and Gezina Kruger (who died in Pretoria in 1901 while her husband was in exile), and the wives of all the Boer generals, including Annie Botha, Isie Smuts and Mynie Hertzog, who were married to the men destined to be the first three premiers of a united South Africa, experienced the misery and humiliation of existing in a war-torn, enemy-occupied country.

In May 1902, and subsequently, the Boer leaders gave precedence, as reasons for their surrender, to the sufferings of women and children caused by the destruction of shelter and supplies on the veld and the concentration camp policy. Their statements, stressing that the republics were defeated not on the field of battle but by barbaric methods of attrition, may have been primarily intended for posterity, but the state of the country and the condition of the civilian population undoubtedly weighed heavily with the Boer delegates at Vereeniging. Whether the methods employed against the civilian population and the emphasis placed on these tactics were the most effective means of ending Boer resistance is a more difficult question to answer and one that cannot, of course, be finally resolved. The compilers of the *Times History of the War* believed that 'the work of destruction distracted the troops from their primary aim of crushing the Boers in the field', and it is furthermore not unlikely that the harsh treatment of their property

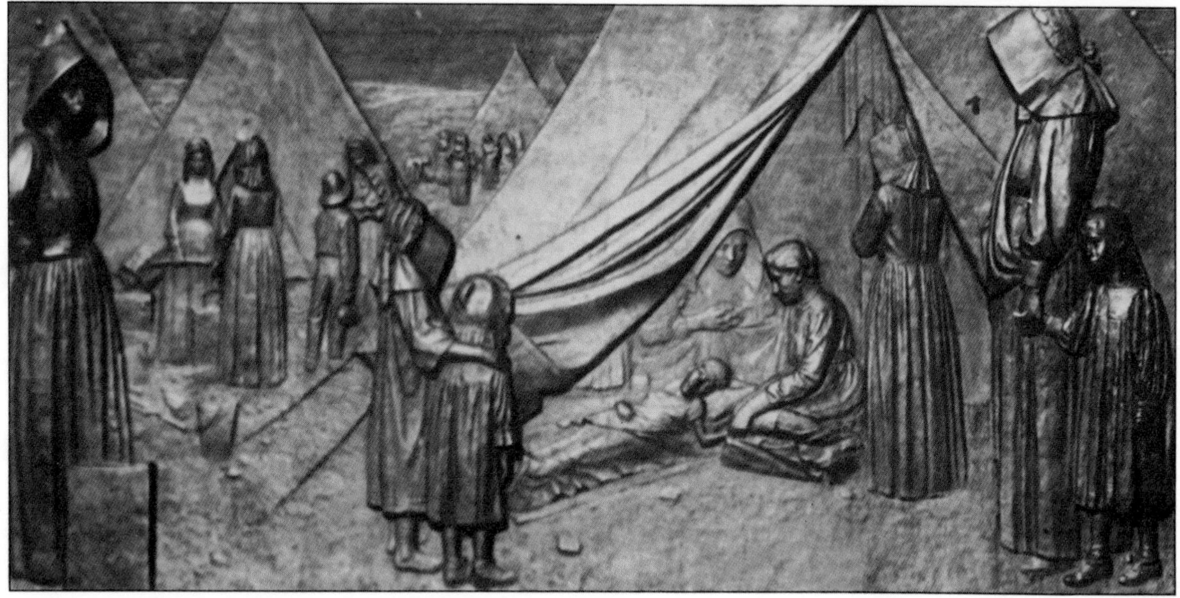

A panel depicting a concentration camp scene from Anton van Wouw's Women's Monument near Bloemfontein, erected in 1913.

and their families incensed the fighting Boers and made them more determined to persevere in the struggle. But whatever view is taken of the military efficacy of these measures, it is evident that the treatment of women, far from being a peripheral consideration of the British high command, occupied a remarkably central position in the overall strategy of the war.

Women's role in the conflict was not, however, confined to passive subjection to male military and political power, even though the war did not provide the opportunities that were offered by the First World War for altering women's status and position in society. The South African War temporarily jostled the feminists in Britain off the stage before the curtain rose on suffragette violence. Nevertheless, suffragists tried to capitalize on the war: Millicent Garrett Fawcett considered that the government's presentation of Uitlander representation in the Transvaal as an issue in the Anglo-Boer conflict made the denial of political rights to women in Britain more difficult to defend, and it was also argued that British women who died in childbirth during the South African War had 'lost their lives in service to the state'. In South Africa the homage that Boer women received from their countrymen for their heroism during the war had no practical repercussions on their post-war status, and the enfranchisement of white women in South Africa in 1930 clearly had no connection with women's role in the war of 1899–1902.[18]

References

1. For feminist views of women in history see Mary Beard, *Women as Force in History*, New York, 1946 and Berenice A. Carrol ed., *Liberating Women's History. Theoretical and Critical Essays*, Urbana etc., 1976. On the role of women in South African history and their position in Boer society, see E. Stockenström, *Die Vrou in die Geskiedenis van die Hollands-Afrikaanse Volk*, Stellenbosch, 1921, and *Geskiedenis van die Vrouebeweging en die Vrouestemreg in Suid-Afrika tot 1930*, D Phil thesis, Stellenbosch, 1944, as well as W. K. Hancock and Jean van der Poel, *Selections from the Smuts Papers*, III, Cambridge, 1966, 139–40. Botha's statement in 1914 is in *Union of South Africa. House of Assembly Debates*, Fourth Session, First Parliament 1914, cc. 1693–4. Merriman's observation is in P. Lewsen ed., *Selections from the Correspondence of John X. Merriman 1899–1905*, V.R.S. 47, Cape Town, 1966, 222. Olive Schreiner's views are in *Thoughts on South Africa*, London, 1923, 201.
2. On the initial impact of war on Boer women, their participation in the war and the women left behind in British occupied territory see S. B. Spies, *Methods of Barbarism? Roberts and Kitchener and Civilians in the Boer Republics January 1900–May 1902*, Cape Town etc., 1977, 18, 21–2, 32–3, 37–40, 42–6, 54, 128, 136, 312; L. S. Amery ed., *The Times History of the War in South Africa*, III, London, 1905, 80; H. C. Hillegas, *With the Boer Forces*, London, 1900, 275–94; J. D. Kestell, *Through Shot and Flame*, London, 1903, 67–8. On Susanna de Wet see A. M. Grundlingh, *Die Vrystaatse en Transvaalse Burgers wat die Republikeinse Oorlogspoging vanaf 1900 versaak het: Hulle Rol en Posisie gedurende die Tydperk 1900 tot 1907*, MA thesis, University of South Africa, 322.
3. On the scorched earth policy and its effect on women see Spies, 29–30, 41–6, 111–2, 120–7, 175–9, 186, 227, 291–2; E. Hobhouse, *The Brunt of the War and where it Fell*, London, 1902, 1–89, 95–113, 286–95 and *War Without Glamour*, Bloemfontein, 1924, 23–5, 89–90; Roberts's declaration in September 1900 is in *Telegrams and Letters sent by Field Marshal Lord Roberts, April 1900–December 1900*, V, 12; the description by Rimington's officer is in L. M. Phillipps, *With Rimington*, London, 1902, 202.
4. On Boer women being sent to the commandos see Spies, 128–43. Botha's interpretation is in Roberts Papers, WO 105/27. Confidential Papers, No. 52, 670/4a. The comments of Mackenzie, Pretyman and Roberts are respectively in the Archives of the Political Secretary (Transvaal Archives, Pretoria), PSY.49, J3; the Archives of the Military Governor, Bloemfontein (Orange Free State Archives, Bloemfontein), MGB.14, telegrams dispatched; and *Telegrams and Letters . . . Roberts*, IV, 28.
5. On the origin and intended purpose of the concentration camps for whites see Spies, 47–8, 143–53, 181–90. The quotation regarding the different categories of inmates is in the

Archives of the Military Governor, Pretoria (Transvaal Archives, Pretoria), MGP.258, Circular Memorandum, No. 29. Kitchener's comments are in Roberts Papers (National Army Museum, London), R33/4 and Kitchener Papers, PRO 30/57/22, Y/9. The intelligence officer's elaboration on the point is in G. B. Beak, *The Aftermath of the War. An Account of Repatriation of the Boers and Natives in Orange River Colony 1902–1904*, London, 1906, 22.

6. On conditions in the concentration camps and the development of this policy see Spies, 191–201, 214–26, 252–62; Hobhouse, *The Brunt of the War* and *War Without Glamour*, *passim*; J. L. Hattingh, 'Die Irenekonsentrasiekamp', *Archives Year Book for South African History*, 30, 1 (1967), 94–182; J. C. Otto, *Die Konsentrasiekampe*, Cape Town, 1954, 57–168. Smuts's estimate is in Hancock and Van der Poel, III, 140 and the statistics of British deaths are in F. Maurice and M. H. Grant, *History of the War in South Africa 1899–1902. Compiled by the Directions of His Majesty's Government*, IV, London, 1910, Appendix 17, 681–97. Chamberlain's remarks are in Milner Papers (Bodleian Library, Oxford), 41 and Milner's statements are in C. Headlam ed., *The Milner Papers*, II, 229, 231. The Boer views on immorality in the camps are in J. D. Kestell and D. E. van Velden, *The Peace Negotiations between the Governments of the South African Republic and the Representatives of the British Government which terminated in the Peace concluded at Vereeniging on the 31st May 1902*, London, 1912, 175, 199; See *ibid.*, 55 for Botha's estimate of the number of families on the veld.
7. Spies, pp. 157, 181–3, 200, 227–31, 262–9; Peter Warwick, 'The African Refugee Problem in the Transvaal and Orange River Colony, 1900–1902', *Southern African Research in Progress, Collected Papers 2*, University of York, 1977, 61–81. See chapter 8 for further details.
8. Spies, 153, 234–7, 273–5. Kitchener's views are in Roberts Papers (National Army Museum), R33/32 and Kitchener Papers PRO 30/57/22, Y/62.
9. Spies, 92–3, 95, 98–101, 208–9, 219, 226, 366; Smuts's comments are in Hancock and Van der Poel, I, 552.
10. A. A. Mawby, *The Political Behaviour of the British Population of the Transvaal 1902–1907*, Ph D thesis, University of the Witwatersrand, 1969, 36–7; Violet Brooke-Hunt, *A Woman's Memories of the War*, London, 1901, 30–1. Barker's comment is in Roberts Papers, WO 105/26; Curtis's description is in Lionel Curtis *With Milner in South Africa*, Oxford, 1951, 244–5; for the estimate of the number of refugees who received relief, and details of women working in the colonies see *The Star* (Johannesburg), 30 April 1902; Milner's opinion of Dr Waterson is in Headlam, II, 231.
11. Merriman's views are in Lewsen, 213. Olive Schreiner's statements are in Olive Schreiner, *An English South African's View of the Situation. Words in Season*, 2nd ed., London, 1899, 82, 87, Lady Edward Cecil's observation is in Viscountess Milner, *My Picture Gallery, 1886–1901*, London, 1951, 153.
12. Spies, 136, 158–60, 217. On nursing see C. Searle, *The History of the Development of Nursing in South Africa 1652–1960 (A Socio-Historical Survey)*, Pretoria, 1965, 209. Kruger's comment is in *The Memoirs of Paul Kruger*, London, 1902, II, 362.
13. The masculine nature of imperialism has recently been emphasized in Ronald Hyam, *Britain's Imperial Century 1815–1914. A Study of Empire and Expansion*, London, 1976, 138–41. Victoria's views of the Boers and the war are in Elizabeth Longford, *Victoria R.I.*, London, 1964, 439–40, 552–3 and the Boers' views of Victoria are in Hancock and Van der Poel, I, 168.
14. Merriman's views are quoted in A. M. Davey, *The British Pro-Boers, 1877–1902*, D Litt et Phil thesis, University of South Africa, 1976, 187. For Lady Sarah Wilson's exploits see Brian Roberts, *Churchills in Africa*, London, 1970, 143–61, 181–96, 216–34, 292–308. The quotation concerning Lady Violet Cecil comes from Viscountess Milner, 205.
15. Searle, 191, 202.
16. Merriman's comments are in Lewsen, 181–2, while the views of Victoria and of Milner are in Headlam, II, 73–4.
17. On British women and the war see Davey, 88–92, 96, 105, 135, 204–5, 228–30, 277, 280–2, 285–7; Spies, 195–8, 216, 221–2, 224, 254–5, 264–5; Maud Gonne MacBride, *A Servant of the Queen. Reminiscences*, London, 1974, 291–2, 302–5; Cecil Howard, *Mary Kingsley*, London, 1957, 221–4; A. R. Fry, *Emily Hobhouse. A Memoir*, London, 1929, *passim*; J. Fisher, *That Miss Hobhouse*, London, 1971, *passim*. Chamberlain's sardonic comment is in CO 417/340, 36213. On Harriete Colenso see Colenso Collection (Natal Archives, Pietermaritzburg), H. E. Colenso, Letters Received 1900 (reference provided by Dr Ruth Edgecombe).
18. See Spies, 284–93 on the military efficacy of the measures employed by Roberts and Kitchener. See Arthur Marwick *Women at War 1914–1918*, London, 1977, 163 for the argument regarding women and childbirth and *passim* for the effect of the Great War on women's rights. See Ray Strachey, *The Cause. A Short History of the Women's Movement in Great Britain*, Trowbridge, 1974, 287–8 for the observation regarding Uitlander representation and the suffragists.

CHAPTER 8

Black People and the War

Peter Warwick

The South African War was fought in a region where white people made up only a fifth of the total population. At the beginning of the war there were approximately one million whites in South Africa compared to four million Africans (including those living in Basutoland, the Bechuanaland Protectorate and Swaziland). Whites in the Cape Colony were outnumbered by Africans 3:1, in Natal the ratio was almost 10:1, and in the Boer republics the ratios were 4:1 in the Transvaal and 2:1 in the Orange Free State. In addition, South Africa had a coloured population of almost 500 000, most of whom lived in the Cape, and an Asian community of 100 000, most of whose members lived in Natal.

Loss of political independence

During the nineteenth century the indigenous peoples of southern Africa had gradually come under white settler control. The Xhosa and other neighbouring Nguni communities of the eastern Cape were defeated in a series of nine frontier wars beginning in the late eighteenth century and ending in 1877. The land to the east of the Kei River, known as the Transkei, was afterwards progressively annexed by the Cape government between 1879 and 1894. The Zulu, the most successful and well-organized African military power in the subcontinent, were first defeated by the Voortrekkers at the battle of Blood River in December 1838, but it was not until a little over forty years later that the Zulu kingdom of Cetshwayo was finally overthrown by General Wolseley's forces at Ulundi in July 1879. Thereafter the Zulu army was broken up, the state truncated and partitioned into thirteen separate political units, and the traditional chiefs supplanted by white officials as the most powerful men in their districts. In 1897 Zululand was incorporated into Natal. The Sotho of Basutoland (modern Lesotho) first accepted British protection in 1869. There followed a short period during which Basutoland was administered by the Cape Colony, and during which too, in 1880–1, the Sotho defied an order by the government in Cape Town to disarm them. Following a bitter struggle the Sotho were permitted to retain their firearms, and in 1884 direct imperial rule was established in the colony. The territory of the Tswana chiefdoms along the margins of the Kalahari Desert was annexed by Britain in 1885, becoming the Bechuanaland Protectorate (modern Botswana), and Swazi political independence was terminated by the Swaziland Conventions of 1890 and 1894, according to which the Transvaal assumed responsibility for the administration of the

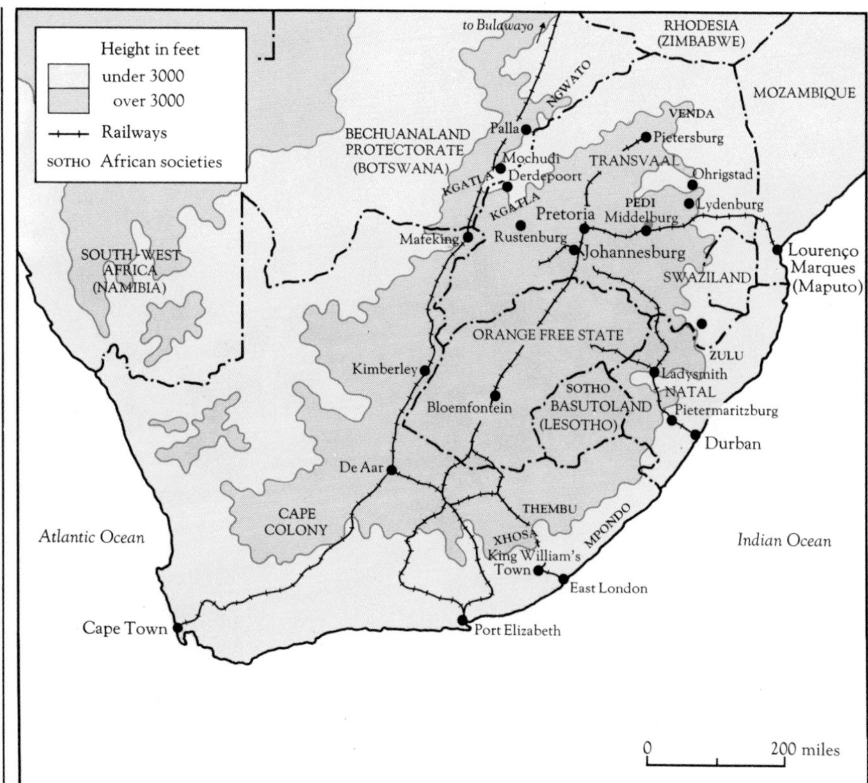

South Africa at the time of the war, showing the main African groups of the area and some of the settlements mentioned in the chapter.

country. In the Transvaal itself the Pedi chief, Sekhukhune, was finally defeated in 1879, and the Venda peoples and their allies in the Zoutpansberg were subjugated by a series of military expeditions mounted by the Pretoria government during the 1890s. Mphephu, the Venda leader, was ultimately defeated by General Joubert in 1898, just a year before the outbreak of war between the two white communities.

Loss of economic independence

The ending of the political independence of the traditional African societies of southern Africa was accompanied by a gradual but inexorable process of undermining their economic self-sufficiency. Thousands of square miles of land were alienated for white settlement, and regular taxation was introduced to encourage Africans to seek work on the white man's farms and in the white man's industries. The mineral revolution, in particular, led to a tremendous growth in the demand for cheap African labour. Because of land scarcity and increasing population pressure on the cultivable land available, and because of the fiscal pressures placed on black people to acquire cash for taxes and rents, a large-scale system of African labour migration from the rural areas to the towns came into being. Already by the end of the nineteenth century many thousands of African men travelled long distances to the gold mines, to the diamondfields or to the seaports to work for six months, returning home to their wives and families to eke out a living for the rest of the year. Thousands of other Africans worked regularly for white farmers in return for a plot of land to cultivate on their own behalf.

The mineral revolution in southern Africa created an enormous increase in the demand for cheap African labour. Here African employees of De Beers are engaged in sorting and washing stones on the diamondfields at Kimberley while their white overseers look on.

Two African migrant workers on their way to the Witwatersrand gold mines. Because of rural poverty and the need for cash to pay European-imposed taxes and rents, Africans were prepared to travel long distances to work in the urban centres.

The black elite

In spite of all these pressures a small section of the African population prospered. In the rural areas most districts had a small number of African families (usually including chiefs and their most important officials) with access to sufficient land to enable them to earn a comfortable – in some cases, affluent – living from the sale of surplus agricultural produce and livestock. In some districts of the Boer republics absentee landlordism enabled peasant communities to thrive independently of the labour system. There existed, too, especially in the Cape Colony and Natal, a small class of relatively prosperous African traders, craftsmen and teachers. Similar groups could be found as well among the coloured and Asian communities. Many of the coloured and African members of the modernizing middle class were Christians, they were literate and articulate, and in the Cape Colony they were able to bring their point of view to the attention of the white colonial government through letters and petitions to white officials, and through the columns of their own two newspapers *Imvo Zabantsundu* and *Izwi Labantu* (both printed in English as well as in the vernacular). At election times, in particular, politicians could be approached more directly, for a 'colour-blind' franchise operated in the Cape whereby any adult male, irrespective of the colour of his skin, was entitled to register as a voter provided he could pass a simple literacy test and either owned property to the value of £75 or had an annual income exceeding £50. Though the number of African voters was never large and the proportion of the total black population enfranchised was small, in about seventeen constituencies candidates were obliged to make at least some gesture towards African voters to stand any chance of electoral success.

The elite and the coming of war

The coming of war between Britain and the Boer republics in 1899 elicited considerable interest among the most westernized and politically-conscious African, coloured and Asian groups in South Africa. It was widely believed that the defeat of the Boers would be accomplished without undue difficulty, and that once the republics had been overthrown, the political, educational and commercial opportunities afforded to black people in the Cape would be extended to those resident in the Transvaal and Orange Free State. In particular, the hope was generated that once these territories were administered directly by Britain, the Cape's relatively liberal – though not, of course, democratic – franchise would be extended throughout South Africa.

Such optimism on the part of members of the black elite was encouraged by statements made by prominent British spokesmen during the early months of the war. Chamberlain told the House of Commons in October 1899 that

> 'The treatment of the natives [in the Transvaal] has been disgraceful; it has been brutal; it has been unworthy of a civilized Power.'[1]

John Tengo Jabavu, editor of Imvo Zabantsundu, *whose 'pro-Boer' views during the war were unpopular among many Africans as well as among British settlers in the Cape. The publication of* Imvo *was suspended by military orders in August 1901.*

The Colonial Secretary implied that affairs there would be run very differently under British administration. No less a person than the Prime Minister, Lord Salisbury, informed Parliament that following victory in the South African campaign,

> 'There must be no doubt . . . that due precaution will be taken for the kindly and improving treatment of those countless indigenous races of whose destiny I fear we have been too forgetful.'[2]

Later, Milner told a deputation of coloured people in Cape Town that he 'thoroughly agreed . . . it was not race or colour, but civilization which was the test of a man's capacity for political rights'[3], a statement widely interpreted as an assurance that once the war was over the political rights enjoyed by black people in the Cape would be extended to those living in the Boer republics. In these circumstances most members of the black educated elite endorsed Britain's military intervention.

The support of the African intelligentsia for the British side in the war was not universal, however. Most significantly, John Tengo Jabavu, the influential Mfengu editor of the African newspaper *Imvo Zabantsundu*, which was published in King Williams Town in the eastern Cape, remained critical of British policy in South Africa throughout the war. Jabavu, who was never afraid to speak out against the views of the majority of his people, argued in a long editorial in *Imvo* during the first week of the war that the British government had succumbed to the influence of an irresponsible war lobby, and that the Boers had been called upon 'at a moment's notice to make their conservative state as liberal as any Utopia'. In Jabavu's estimation the war represented 'the very quintessence of unfairness'.[4]

Jabavu's reaction to events largely stemmed from his political loyalty to the white South African Party in the Cape, and in particular to two of its leading members, John X. Merriman and J. W. Sauer, both of whom strongly supported Anglo-Boer conciliation. The uncomfortable position of these men, who on the one hand preached a more enlightened management of African affairs and on the other hand criticized Britain for going to war against the Boer republics, whose harsh treatment of Africans they were unable to defend, was a position that Jabavu took upon himself to share – and shared all the more uncomfortably because of his own black skin. The *Eastern Province Herald* accused Jabavu of having 'embraced Krugerism with both arms': 'To find the docile *Imvo* now turning to lick the hand that wielded the sjambok is more amazing than amusing,' the newspaper concluded.[5] Jabavu persistently argued that condemnation of the war did not imply approval of the system of race relations practised in the republics, but many people, both black and white, were unsympathetic to the finer points of the 'pro-Boer' case. The military eventually brought the publication of *Imvo* to a halt in August 1901, and it did not reappear until four months after the conclusion of peace, its financial position much weakened.

During the early engagements in Natal an Indian Ambulance Corps was established composed of 300 'free' and ex-indentured Indians and 800 indentured workers from the sugar estates who were dispatched to the front by their employers. M.K. Gandhi played a prominent role in recruiting free Indians and joined the corps himself. He is pictured here (seated fifth from the left in the centre row) with other members of the ambulance.

Asian opinion in South Africa was overwhelmingly pro-British. The most influential of the Asian leaders at this time was Mohandas K. Gandhi, later to achieve world-wide renown as a nationalist leader in his home country, India. Gandhi had arrived in South Africa on a legal assignment in 1893, and he stayed on to help Asians in Natal defend their legal and political rights. He founded the Indian National Congress and became editor of the newspaper *Indian Opinion*, and it was in South Africa that he began to develop the techniques of passive protest known as *satyagraha* (soul force), based on the teachings of the pacifist Jain sect of Hinduism. At the beginning of the South African War Gandhi persuaded his fellow Asians that while justice was undoubtedly on the side of the Boers, if they wished to achieve their freedom as members of the British empire here was a golden opportunity to demonstrate their loyalty and worthiness by assisting the British with every means at their disposal.[6] Accordingly, Gandhi played a prominent part in organizing an ambulance corps composed of members of the Asian community that was active on the British side in a number of the most important engagements on the Natal front during the early months of the war.

White fears of an African rebellion

Whereas the opinions on the war of the most westernized and articulate black people in South Africa were reasonably well-known, there was much greater uncertainty about the possible reaction of traditional African rulers and the many thousands of blacks in the rural areas who looked to them for leadership and protection. There was a genuine fear among many whites that, once they embarked upon a civil war, disaffected African groups would seize the opportunity to advance their own interests and possibly even attempt to overthrow white rule altogether.

Military precautions

Because of fears about the response of African people to the war, neither the British nor the Boers at the outset committed all their resources to do battle with one another. Both sides took precautions to ensure that troops were held in reserve to be prepared to counter African disturbances. In Natal a military contingent was dispatched to watch over the African communities on the colony's border with the Transkei, and less than one in five white males of military age in Natal was called out for active service against the Boers. White troops were maintained in the eastern Cape and 4 000 African levies assembled in the Transkei to be prepared not only to defend the area against a possible Afrikaner insurrection or republican invasion, but also to be on hand to deal quickly with any sign of African unrest. It has been calculated that at the beginning of the war only between 56 and 65 per cent of the Boer republics' fighting strength was placed in the field. A large force under Commandant Klaas Prinsloo was garrisoned between the Steelpoort and Olifants Rivers in the eastern Transvaal to discourage Pedi resistance against white control. Between 800 and 1 000 burghers were posted to the Transvaal's border with Swaziland, and the frontier between the Orange Free State and Basutoland was guarded by over 1 000 commandos.

However, settler fears of large-scale African resistance during the war proved illusory. By the end of the nineteenth century most African societies had become reconciled to the military superiority of the white settlers, and had become accustomed to seeking the redress of grievances through political action within the framework of the colonial system. In any case, it was hardly the most auspicious moment to launch a last-ditch effort to rid South Africa of the white man with the additional presence in the country of almost half a million soldiers. Rather than plot rebellion, most traditional African rulers sought to increase their power by other methods. Lerothodi of the Sotho, Kgama of the Ngwato, Lentshwe of the Kgatla, and Dinuzulu, the son of the defeated Zulu king, Cetshwayo, all succeeded in consolidating their influence among their own people during the war, when white control over their internal affairs was much less rigorous than in peace time.[7] Many chiefs also appreciated that considerable political benefit might be derived from supporting the winning side in the war. From the outset most Africans believed Britain would emerge victorious, and once the Boer capitals had fallen almost all the traditional rulers of the region gave the British army their enthusiastic support. Some chiefs, too, sought to profit from the war by hiring out waggons and teams of oxen to the military, and by supplying the army with horses, cattle, animal products, grain and tobacco, for which they received highly inflated prices because of the increased wartime demand for food and the dislocation of white commercial farming.

African resistance

African resistance to white authority nonetheless occurred in some regions – especially in the Transvaal, where a number of black groups took advantage of wartime circumstances to revenge themselves upon individual officials and liberate themselves from irksome obligations. Africans in some areas reoccupied land that had been expropriated by white settlers during the previous century; throughout the war cattle-thieving from white farms took place regularly; and in both the republics, as well as in parts of Natal, black tenants frequently refused to provide labour to their landlords. 'From the farms that I have visited, I hear almost without exception the same story, viz., that the Kaffirs will not work', remarked one British official in 1902.[8] Similar comments were made by returning Boer farmers in the Transvaal and Orange River Colony.

Kgatla and Pedi

Violence also erupted from time to time, sometimes with serious repercussions. In the western Transvaal three Kgatla regiments, acting in consort with a British force under Colonel G. S. Holdsworth, led an assault on a Boer encampment at Derdepoort in November 1899, during which the local Volksraad member, J. H. Barnard, was shot dead. (Once the Kgatla attack commenced, Holdsworth's force beat a hasty retreat into Bechuanaland, leaving the Kgatla to extricate themselves from a difficult situation.) Because of Kgatla hostility large numbers of Afrikaner families from the region hastily moved into laagers or fled to Rustenburg, and when Smuts entered the western Transvaal in the middle of 1900 he found that almost all the farms in the area had been abandoned by their white occupants. Following the withdrawal from the Pedi heartland of Commandant Prinsloo's force in June 1900, the local Boer official, J. Van der Wal, had to flee for his life from Schoonoord, and during the course of the year the Pedi, led by the young chief Sekhukhune II, wrested themselves completely from Boer control. In the neighbourhood of nearby Ohrigstad, Pedi farm servants conducted a ruthless campaign of resistance against their white employers and landlords. 'The domestics, knowing the locality well, come forth at night to plunder and murder, and many comparatively innocent people have been the victims', lamented Roland Schikkerling, a young Boer diarist serving on commando.[9]

Zulu

In the south-eastern Transvaal a number of Zulu communities whose lands had been alienated to white settlers conducted a campaign of their own against the Boer commando units operating in the region. When the Boers in reprisal destroyed the village of one Zulu group involved, the Qulusi, the victims – possibly with the connivance of the local British magistrate, A. J. Shepstone – organized an impi (regiment) and assaulted the Vryheid commando at Holkrans, killing fifty-six commandos, including the ruthless and unpopular veldkornet, J. Potgieter, whose body it was said afterwards had received forty-five assegai wounds. General Botha referred to the incident at Holkrans as 'the foulest deed of the war',[10] and an account of the episode published over thirty years later described it as 'one of the darkest tragedies ever enacted on South African soil . . . the whole incident has points of similarity with the murder of Retief and his men by Dingaan.'[11]

'white man's war'

The South African War has been popularly portrayed as a 'white man's war', a phrase commonly used by contemporaries, and one that derives from the tacit agreement between the protagonists that black people should not be armed to take part in military operations. Britain was confident that her regular army and white volunteers would easily be capable of defeating the Boer republics. It was believed, too, that there was no group of indigenous collaborators whose military assistance might be decisive in winning the war. 'I need hardly say, there is no resemblance or analogy between the native tribes of South Africa and the native princes of India and their troops', A. J. Balfour told the House of Commons.[12] Above all, the British government had to take account of the convention that had grown up in South Africa during the nineteenth century that black soldiers were not to be employed in armed struggles between the two white communities. The South African point of view on this issue, to which, generally speaking, almost all colonists (both Dutch- and English-speaking) subscribed, was summed up by J. C. Smuts:

> 'The peculiar position of the small white community in the midst of the very large and rapidly increasing coloured races and the danger which in consequence threatens this small white community and with it civilization itself in South Africa, have led to . . . a special tacit understanding which forbids the white races to appeal for assistance to the coloured races in their mutual disputes . . . otherwise the coloured races must become the arbiters in disputes between the whites and in the long run the predominating political factor or "casting vote" in South Africa. That this would soon cause South Africa to relapse into barbarism must be evident to everybody.'[13]

It was commonly believed, too, that the military methods of black people were unacceptably brutal, and that white women and children would not be shown mercy by black soldiers. The unwillingness of settlers to arm African auxiliaries in 1899 was also based on an awareness that to provide blacks with large numbers of modern firearms, and instruct them in their use, would increase the possibility of African resistance to white control. Under no circumstances did the British government wish to bring about, however unwittingly, a social revolution of this kind in South Africa, nor did the Cabinet wish to offend unnecessarily settler opinion on the race question. Accordingly, Chamberlain told the Commons late in the war:

> 'The reason we have not employed natives is not because we do not think they . . . might fairly be placed in the field even against civilized nations, but because, in the peculiar circumstances of South Africa, we believe it would be bad policy.'[14]

It was for this reason, too, that the government was opposed to non-white troops from elsewhere in the empire entering South Africa to fight against the Boers on Britain's behalf.

It soon becomes evident, however, once one begins to question seriously the popular image of the war as one confined to white participants, that black people played an indispensable part in military operations. From the beginning of the war both sides depended on non-whites for the performance of ancillary duties. Transport-riding, for example, was an almost exclusively coloured and African pursuit. Over 5 000 Africans, most of them transport drivers and leaders, were employed by Lord Roberts's columns during the long haul to Bloemfontein in February–March 1900, and 7 000 Africans took part in General French's march to Machadodorp in the Transvaal later in the same year. The British army also depended on black workers for carrying dispatches, proclamations and messages, for constructing fortifications, for supervising horses in the remount and veterinary departments, and for sanitary work and other labour duties in the military camps. The Boers also conscripted Africans and coloureds to dig trenches, drive wagons, collect firewood, attend to horses and to perform other duties related to their

Below: although the British government was opposed to non-white troops from elsewhere in the empire entering South Africa to take part in the fighting, some Indian soldiers were brought to South Africa to perform ancillary duties. Here Indian doolie bearers transport wounded soldiers to a field hospital.

Bottom left: the British forces depended heavily on African and coloured transport drivers. A number of drivers attached to the Kaffrarian Rifles are shown here with their waggons at a bivouac after crossing the Orange River on 27 August 1900.

Bottom right: African dispatch runners were an essential part of the system of field communications. Many Africans were also used to pass surreptitiously through the Boer lines surrounding the besieged towns of Ladysmith, Kimberley and Mafeking. Here three British soldiers conceal messages in the garments of a runner bound for Ladysmith.

campaign. Many commandos were accompanied by coloured or African after-riders (*agterryers*), by custom the personal servants of Boer settlers, whose task it was to assist their employer in combat by supervising his horse, cleaning and loading his rifle, and generally serving him while in the field. Tasks such as these were unglamorous, largely taken for granted by soldiers, and their significance has rarely been drawn attention to by historians. Yet their successful completion was essential to the effective performance of both armies. African and coloured ancillary workers performed tasks to which white participants were either unsuited or unaccustomed, and African cooperation enabled a larger number of white personnel to serve actively in operations. Although precise statistics are unavailable, it seems likely that as many as 100 000 black people were employed in various capacities on the British side during the war; on the Boer side at least 10 000 Africans and coloureds accompanied the commandos, and possibly many more.

African ancillary workers

The ancillary duties performed by black people could be defined without too much difficulty by contemporaries as non-combatant categories of military employment, and therefore permissable for Africans to become involved in. Other forms of work in which black people became involved were not so easily defined, and throughout the war allegations were persistently made that the opposing army was employing substantial numbers of Africans as combatants. In February 1900 General Buller was informed by one of his officers in Natal that 'most men at the front are aware that there are armed natives fighting with the Boers.'[15] Later in the war the Boer general, J. Kemp, protested to Kitchener that in many instances the war was being fought 'contrary to civilized warfare on account of it being carried on in a great measure with Kaffirs'.[16]

Stemming the Boer invasion

For purposes of defence the British army enlisted the active support of a number of Africans and coloureds during the difficult first months of the war. To guard the frontier of the Bechuanaland Protectorate, and parallel to it the railway line from Mafeking to Bulawayo in Rhodesia, the Kgatla chief, Lentshwe, and Kgama of the Ngwato were provided with 6 000 and 3 000 rounds of ammunition respectively. Kgama mobilized between 800 and 1 000 men to defend the border between his reserve and the Transvaal. In the Transkei, as we have seen, 4 000 Mfengu and Thembu levies were assembled to defend the region. In the Cape Colony itself Africans and coloureds were occasionally mobilized to participate in the operations designed to halt the Boer advances beyond their frontiers. Alfred Harmsworth defended the magistrate's building at Klipdam with armed groups of coloureds and Africans, and the Boer occupation of Kuruman was initially resisted by a small force of local coloureds and white policemen. At Mafeking Baden-Powell permitted over 500 Africans to take part in the town's defence system during the siege. Another 200 Africans were enrolled as special constables in Herschel to discourage incursions into the district by Free State commandos.

Many Boer commandos were accompanied to the front by one or more of their coloured or African servants. These men were known as after-riders (agterryers). *After-riders formed an integral component of the Boer military system, as this scene from the veld suggests.*

Captured Boer shells and rifles in the charge of a British Magazine Officer and his African staff. Though Africans were permitted to handle weapons, ostensibly they were not allowed to use them.

From the beginning of the war both sides depended heavily on non-whites for scouting and intelligence work. In October 1899 magistrates in the Cape and Natal were requested to provide reliable men for scouting purposes. The number of scouts employed by the British army rose as the value of their intelligence work became recognized more widely. A circular was issued informing officers that 'For purposes of obtaining information, natives can be frequently employed with more success than patrols.'[17] African scouts were used with particular success during the guerrilla stage of the war when, to counter the tactics of the Boer commandos, the army divided its men into smaller and more mobile columns, each of which depended upon reliable information about the enemy's movements for its success. Groups of African scouts, up to fifty in number, came to be attached to all the British columns. The Boers soon began to appreciate the value of African intelligence to the British army, and any African suspected by the guerrillas of working for the military, or of supplying information about them to the British, was likely to be executed. Because of the alarming casualty rate among unarmed African scouts, it was agreed in December 1900 that any African who already possessed a rifle when he entered military employment should not be disarmed. By the end of 1901 almost all the scouts attached to British columns bore firearms. Even the *Times History of the War in South Africa* acknowledged that these men could hardly be classified as 'non-combatants'.

> 'As time went on most columns came to be accompanied by parties of armed native scouts, who did most valuable service; so valuable, indeed, that under exceptionally able direction, something like a tactical revolution was carried into effect, with not unimportant results. It would be an abuse of terms to describe these men as non-combatants. . . . The only justification was sheer military necessity.'[18]

A group of armed African scouts attached to the 4th Battalion of the Scottish Rifles Mounted Infantry at Boshof. By the end of 1901 almost all African scouts assisting the British columns bore firearms.

The Boers, too, employed large numbers of black scouts, though usually they were not armed. According to the official German account of the war, the information conveyed to the commandos by African scouts was 'remarkably accurate and . . . transmitted with extraordinary rapidity.'[19]

Throughout the war the British army relied on chiefs in Basutoland, Bechuanaland, Swaziland and the Transkei to protect these regions from Boer penetration, while at the same time allowing the British forces to draw supplies and labourers from them. Parts of Zululand were occupied by Boer forces between January and May 1900, and during this period local chiefs kept the Natal government constantly informed of events there. Later Dinuzulu mobilized a regiment to patrol Zululand's border with the Transvaal, organized an extremely efficient intelligence network in the neighbouring areas of the republic, sent some of his most trustworthy men to act as scouts with the British army, and in 1901 dispatched groups of armed Zulu across the Transvaal border to assist the British forces capture Boer livestock.

During the guerrilla stage of the war, in particular, the British army became dependent on the active involvement of Africans in a variety of ways. Blacks were employed throughout the republics to round up the cattle of Afrikaner families and bring these into the garrison towns in return for a share of the livestock apprehended; Africans participated in the destruction of farmsteads and crops, and in bringing into the concentration

A kit inspection by an officer of the Zululand Native Police, whose members were engaged in duties along the border. Dinuzulu also mobilized a regiment to patrol Zululand's frontier with the Transvaal, and he assisted the British forces in a variety of other ways during the war.

African participation in the guerrilla war

camps civilians removed from the countryside; and armed black sentries were enrolled to guard the lines of blockhouses and barbed-wire barricades that were erected to restrict the mobility of the Boer guerrilla units. As a further measure to button up the movements of the commandos and deny them access to food supplies and fresh horses, various African chiefs in the republics were encouraged to resist the encroachment of guerrillas into their localities. In the eastern Transvaal, for example, the region north of the Blood River in Middelburg district was defended by Malekutu, who on military orders concentrated his people into closely guarded settlements and organized intensive patrols, thereby preventing any Boer incursions into his territory. Micha Dnikoanyani, a close adherent of the Pedi chief Sekhukhune II, completely closed the strategically important Waterval valley to guerrilla penetration. By his action he blocked all the waggon routes that the Boers could have used to transport grain from the Ohrigstad valley to Dullstroom and Roos Senekal, and from there to the commandos on the high veld. 'Chief Michal [*sic*] . . . has been quite invaluable to us, worth a whole column really', Captain A. W. Baird at Middelburg wrote.

> 'The importance of holding Waterval valley cannot be overrated. Two attempts have already been made to turn him out . . . and both unsuccessfully.'[20]

No commando dared to move westwards beyond the Steelpoort River into the Pedi heartland controlled by Sekhukhune II. The far western region of the Transvaal was largely controlled by regiments of the Kgatla chief, Lentshwe, whose principal settlement was at Mochudi, just across the Crocodile River in Bechuanaland. After the war F. Edmeston, a British official in the Pilansbergen, noted that the army had been

'Paying off old scores', the title of a sketch by a British war artist, W. T. Maud (1865–1903), in which he portrays one of the many skirmishes during the war between the Pedi and Boer guerrilla fighters. The Pedi controlled a large area of the eastern Transvaal and on occasions inflicted heavy casualties on the Boers.

'relieved of all anxiety as to this district, which was held by these people as far north as Palla.'[21] In September 1901 Lentshwe's regiments along the banks of the Crocodile River repulsed a Boer force of four hundred commandos.

Of those Africans and coloureds in more regular military employment, Kitchener finally admitted in April 1902 – with some reluctance and only after considerable pressure had been brought to bear on him by the War Office – that arms had been issued to 10 053 men. This figure, of course, does not represent the total number armed since, as Kitchener himself admitted, he did not have complete day-to-day control over all the actions of his subordinate officers. 'The temptation on the spot to relieve our men of hard work is no doubt very great', the Commander-in-Chief confessed.[22] Furthermore, this figure does not include those Africans in military employment who after December 1900 had been permitted by the army to retain firearms that were already in their possession. In March 1902 Lloyd George suggested there were as many as 30 000 armed blacks in British employment, and though it is unclear on what basis he arrived at this calculation, the total may not be unduly inaccurate. The employment of armed Africans by the British army, both on a regular and irregular basis, and the hostility shown towards the guerrilla fighters by some of the African communities in the Transvaal and Orange Free State, seriously alarmed the commandos during the latter part of the war. The Boers' third reason for making peace in May 1902 was:

> '. . . the Kaffir tribes, within and without the frontiers of the territory of the two Republics, are mostly armed and are taking part in the war against us, and through the committing of murders and all sorts of cruelties have caused an unbearable condition of affairs in many districts of both Republics.'

Armed Africans with the Boer forces

Africans and coloureds, however, also fought on the Boer side, though in much smaller numbers. Cronjé conscripted local Tswana people to help his force maintain the siege of Mafeking, and during the siege of Ladysmith, too, the Boers regularly employed armed Africans and coloureds in their outposts at night. African workers who defected from the Boers to the British military camps in Natal frequently reported that armed blacks accompanied the republican forces, and their reports corroborate British eyewitness accounts. Of course, after-riders may often have been mistaken for Boer commandos – an understandable error, for in combat an after-rider loaded his employer's rifle, wore an ammunition belt, and was usually dressed in similar garments. However, it seems inconceivable that in exigent circumstances after-riders would be prevented from engaging the enemy on their own account. Certainly this appears to have happened at the battle of Vaalkrans in Natal in February 1900. 'Prisoners say that Kaffirs were only used as after-riders,' General Buller told the Natal Governor, Sir Walter Hely-Hutchinson, 'but several officers saw Kaffirs, on more than one occasion, firing on our men.'[23]

Conditions of military employment

Africans and coloureds became involved in military employment for a variety of reasons. Labour enlisted by the Boers was largely conscripted and unpaid. The *krijgswette* (martial law regulations) of the two Boer republics held all inhabitants between the ages of 16 and 60 liable for military service during the war. Nowhere is it stated that only whites could be mobilized, and indeed the *krijgswette* specifically state that coloureds (*kleurlingen*) were liable to be called up. To refuse to serve with the republican forces was punishable by a fine of £5, by imprisonment, or by twenty-five lashes.

On the British side, some categories of work performed by Africans were well-paid. Those men who enrolled at the De Aar labour depot in the northern Cape were paid 60 shillings a month, about 10 shillings more than the comparable rate on the gold mines before the outbreak of war. Drivers and leaders could earn up to 90 shillings a month, and some scouts were equally well-paid. Other African workers, however, received as little as 30 shillings, and the usual rate of pay for an ancillary worker seems to have been between 40 and 50 shillings a month. Military contracts with the British army were usually for three months, shorter than the period customary for industrial labour at this time (invariably six months), and this was generally popular among workers. Clothing and blankets were sometimes supplied by the army, and regular rations were also available. Some workers were fortunate enough to have meat issued to them daily, a practice that J. W. Weir, the chairman of the Indwe Mining Company, blamed above all for the movement of some of his workers into military employment.[24] There existed, too, the possibility of acquiring loot. Although conditions of work varied a good deal between departments, and

African farm labourers. At the outbreak of war Africans in the Boer republics were conscripted to work on farms in an effort to maintain agricultural production in the absence of farmers, their sons and some of their regular servants at the theatre of war.

A group of African workers engaged by the British army during Roberts's march through the Free State, pictured with their white overseer. The total number of African labourers employed by the British army during the war probably exceeded 100 000.

working for the army certainly could be dangerous, the impression became current among Africans in some districts that military employment involved duties that were less onerous than those on the mines.

African poverty during the war

Poverty, however, was perhaps the most important factor that propelled Africans to accept work with the army. For many African families the war had disastrous material consequences. The disruption of the migrant labour system at the outbreak of war temporarily deprived many Africans of an income upon which they depended to buy grain and pay their taxes and rent. The return to the rural areas of thousands of men normally absent at work increased the pressure on food resources, and in the already overpopulated districts of Natal, Zululand and the Transkei, where the war was accompanied by especially meagre harvest yields, famine rapidly spread. In order to alleviate the destitute circumstances of their families, many men enrolled as ancillary workers with the British army. In the Bathurst district of the Cape, where crop yields in 1900 were especially poor, 72 per cent of the adult male population enlisted with the military. The initial recruitment to the De Aar labour depot was concentrated largely in the King William's Town district, one of those worst affected by harvest difficulties, and from where over 3 000 Africans left to join the army. In 1901 it was reported in Peddie that the local food supply was 'practically nil, and many families have been put in dire straits'. So many men left the district to work for the military that apparently few able-bodied men remained.[25]

The outbreak of war disrupted the migrant labour system, depriving many Africans of an income upon which their families in the impoverished areas of the countryside depended. Here 3 000 migrant African workers are photographed leaving Johannesburg at the beginning of October 1899. The British army recruited thousands of labourers from among those thrown out of work at the onset of war.

The African concentration camps

In the Transvaal and Orange River Colony the livelihood of many thousands of Africans was destroyed by Kitchener's scorched earth campaign. During the first half of 1901 separate African concentration camps were established to accommodate those blacks uprooted from the land. Most of the refugees came from Boer farms where they had resided as labour tenants, cash tenants or sharecroppers, but as the guerrilla war dragged on Africans from locations and even from mission stations were also compelled to seek refuge in the camps. By the end of the war over 115 000 Africans had been interned. In June 1901 a Native Refugee Department was set up, its 'first consideration . . . the supply of native labour to the Army'. Since most of those who entered the camps possessed little or no food, and since only in exceptional circumstances were rations provided free of charge, most African men had little choice but to accept work at the uncompetitive wage of 30 shillings a month. By April 1902 over 13 000 refugees from the camps were to be found working for the military. Most of those who remained were women and children, the elderly and the infirm.

The herding together of refugees in hastily organized and frequently insanitary camps unavoidably produced many deaths. In all, 14 154 deaths were recorded, one in ten of those concentrated, and many other deaths must have gone unrecorded. The overwhelming number of fatalities occurred among children (81 per cent). Half of the deaths took place during the three months of November and December 1901 and January 1902; in December, the worst month, the annual death rate reached 436 per 1 000 per annum in the Orange River Colony camps and 320 per 1 000 per annum in the camps in the Transvaal (the combined figure, 372 per 1 000 per annum). Conditions of life were appalling. Huts and tents were placed too close together and did not afford sufficient protection against the weather. Some refugees had only a few grain bags tied together for shelter. Water supplies were often contaminated, and the diet of the refugees lacked fresh vegetables and milk. The situation was not helped by deplorable medical facilities. In the Orange River Colony doctors usually visited the refugees only twice a week, and at Rodevaal it was reported in February 1902 that the camp had not been visited by a doctor for over a month.[26]

Conditions in the camps

The reports made by staff of the Native Refugee Department present a picture of undismayed refugees, grateful for the protection afforded in the settlements against starvation and Boer depradations. 'The natives seem generally contented', remarked one senior official.[27] The letters of missionaries who visited the camps paint a very different scene. The Methodist Hugh Morgan wrote that he had heard stories of suffering, personal injury and oppression that had astounded him. The Reverend W. H. R. Brown, who visited the camp at Dry Harts, was alarmed by the dreadful physical condition and low spirits of those whom he found there. 'They are in great poverty and misery, and our visit was a comfort to them. Many are dying from day to day – what is to become of the survivors I cannot think.'[28] Refugees understandably complained bitterly of the treatment they received. Two inmates of the Honingspruit settlement, Daniel Marome and G. J. Oliphant, lodged their protest with the Deputy Administrator of the Orange River Colony, Major H. J. Goold-Adams.

> 'We have to work hard all day long but the only food we can get is mealies and mealie meal, and this is not supplied to us free, but we have to purchase same with our own money.
>
> Meat we are still not able to get at any price, nor are we allowed to buy anything at the shops in Honingspruit . . .
>
> We humbly request Your Honour to do something for us otherwise we will all perish of hunger for we have no more money to keep on buying food.'[29]

Conditions gradually improved during the final months of the war. The largest camps were broken up and refugee settlements dispersed over a wider area. Greater attention was also paid to improving the refugees' diet. The system of free rationing was extended, fresh milk was supplied regularly, and stores were opened to supply so-called 'luxuries', such as flour, sugar, coffee, tea, syrup, clothing and blankets. By April 1902 the alarming death rate had been brought under control.

African refugees after the war

Unfortunately, the cessation of military operations did not alleviate the plight of many refugees. Although the run-down of the camps took place with great haste, a large number of Africans missed the opportunity to cultivate enough land for their needs during the season ahead. The shortage of seeds, draught animals and even the most rudimentary implements, such as picks and hoes, added to the difficulties of those leaving the camps. Refugees whose livestock and grain had been confiscated by the army received only minimal compensation since military receipts had been carelessly and haphazardly issued. The rehabilitation of white agriculture was given first priority in the programme of rural reconstruction. In the Transvaal £1 183 594 was spent by the Repatriation Department to supply seeds, implements, livestock and transport to white farmers; only £16 194 was expended on African resettlement by the Native Refugee Department.

In the regions of the former republics where the activities of the British army had been concentrated, evidence of African impoverishment after the war is overwhelming. In the neighbourhood of Amsterdam in the Transvaal it was reported that African communities everywhere were close to starvation: 'They are now living principally on roots; rats also form a large part of their diet.'[30] Sheep stealing from white farms in the district occurred on a large scale and was attributed almost

Matros, an African peasant farmer from the southern Free State who supplied food to British troops operating in the area, photographed with two of his grandchildren.

entirely to famine. The Reverend C. Paulsen wrote from Volksrust that 'the people are starving, yea dying, from hunger.'[31] Even Colonel G. F. de Lotbiniere, the Superintendent of Native Refugees, conceded that the Piet Retief, Wakkerstroom, Standerton, Ermelo, Bethal, Carolina and Heidelberg districts were all bordering on famine six months after the end of the war.[32] Because of the droughts of 1902 and 1903 conditions did not rapidly improve, and large numbers of Africans who had been interned in the camps had little alternative but to continue to sell their labour in order to raise money to buy food. Many became bitter about their experiences.

Post-war disillusionment

Following the conclusions of peace, disillusionment also set in among other groups of black people. Many Africans in the Transvaal hoped that the defeat of the Boers would signal the return to them of much of the land colonized by white settlers since the Great Trek, and accordingly some families moved on to deserted farms during the war, planting crops and grazing livestock and building new homes for themselves. Once the war ended, however, Boer farmers were assisted to reoccupy their land by British soldiers and members of the South African Constabulary, and African families were evicted and their crops left standing in the fields. The disappointment of Africans in the rural areas was voiced by an African contributor to the magazine *South African Outlook*.

> 'One strong incentive reason that impelled the Natives of the New Colonies to put themselves at the disposal of His Majesty's troops in the late war was that the British Government, led by their known and proverbial sense of justice and equity, would, in the act of general settlement, have the position of the black races upon the land fully considered, and at the conclusion of the war the whole land would revert to the British Nation, when it would be a timely moment, they thought, for the English to show an act of sympathy towards those who have been despoiled of their land and liberties. Alas! This was not the case. The black races in these colonies feel today that their last state is worst than their first.'[33]

African workers in the industrial region of the Transvaal hoped that the overthrow of the Pretoria regime would bring about a substantial improvement in their conditions of work. When Roberts's troops had arrived on the Rand in 1900 crowds of workers had jubilantly burned their passes, expecting they would not be needed under an enlightened and progressive British administration. But labour conditions worsened rather than improved. African wages in the gold mining industry were reduced; a much more sophisticated network of control over the black work force was devised; prosecutions for desertion and breach of contract increased; and conditions in the labour compounds deteriorated. Workers responded by refusing to migrate to the goldfields, and in May and June 1902 a spate of strikes and mass walk-outs occurred on the gold reef.

Gandhi in 1906, the year in which he informed Lord Elgin on behalf of the Indian community in the Transvaal that their plight was worse under British administration than it had been before the war under Boer rule.

Although the war provided opportunities for chiefs to enhance their positions within traditional politics, few rulers were able to extend their influence within South African society at large. Those chiefs who rendered valuable assistance to the British forces received few favours in return. Sekhukhune II, who ousted the Boers from the neighbourhood of his principal settlements and collaborated with the British columns operating in the eastern Transvaal, aspired to have restored to him a meaningful measure of domestic autonomy in Pedi affairs. He hoped, too, that the Pedi's locations would be substantially extended because of serious overcrowding. After the war, however, both these wishes remained unfulfilled. Lentshwe, the Kgatla chief, who had driven the Boers from large areas of the western Transvaal, was unable to persuade the British government to create an enlarged Kgatla reserve that would unite those of his people living in the former republic with those residing in the Bechuanaland Protectorate. And in spite of the considerable assistance provided by the Zulu to the British army, the Natal government was permitted after the war to alienate large parts of Zululand for white settlement.

Disappointment of the black elite

Perhaps the greatest disappointment of all was experienced by those members of the black middle class who had hoped throughout the war that Britain's ultimate victory would usher in a new period of liberty and enlightenment in South African affairs. Their hopes were first dashed by clause eight of the peace agreement, which stated: 'The question of granting the franchise to natives [in the Transvaal and Orange River Colony] will not be decided until after the introduction of self-government.' Africans appreciated that, left to their own devices, neither the British nor the Boers in the former republics would ever agree to political rights being extended to black people. On the first day of the reappearance of *Imvo* in October 1902 John Tengo Jabavu condemned the terms of the peace agreement, and wrote that because the British, the Boers and the African population were all entitled to live in the country, 'each should be accorded by the others the common rights of citizenship.' In a document sent to Edward VII the Orange River Colony Native Congress pointed out that

> 'it seemed to them deplorable that before bloodshed ceased the avowed cause of Justice, Freedom and Equal Rights, for which the war had been undertaken, should have been so easily abandoned.'[34]

African criticism of British policy intensified after the war when it became more apparent than ever that the government had no intention of attempting to reshape race relations in the Transvaal and Orange River Colony. Coloured and Asian leaders also became deeply critical of imperial policy in South Africa. In 1905 Dr Abdullah Abdurahman, the Cape Malay member of the Cape Town City Council, President of the African People's Organization, and a devoted admirer of the British constitution and the British way of life, refused to sign a farewell address to

Lord Milner from the City Council in Cape Town, and he condemned the High Commissioner for leaving the rights of coloureds at a lower ebb than when he arrived. 'Our lot today is infinitely worse than under the Boer regime', Gandhi informed Lord Elgin, the Colonial Secretary, in the following year on behalf of the Asian community in the Transvaal.[35] By this time the optimism generated among leading members of the African, Asian and coloured communities at the outbreak of war had evaporated.

References

1. *Parliamentary Debates*, 4th series, Commons, vol. 77, c. 271, 19 October 1899.
2. *Ibid.*, Lords, 78, c. 257, 1 February 1900.
3. *Further Correspondence Relating to Affairs in South Africa*, Cd.547, 1901, 34.
4. *Imvo Zabantsundu*, 16 October 1899.
5. Reprinted in *Imvo Zabantsundu*, 13 November 1899.
6. M. K. Gandhi, *Satyagraha in South Africa*, Madras, 1928.
7. Peter Warwick, 'African Societies and the South African War, 1899–1902', D Phil thesis, University of York, 1978, *passim*.
8. Public Record Office, London (PRO), CO 179/224/39318 encl. 1(f), Colonel Roch, Vryheid, to Chief Staff Officer, Natal, 16 August 1902.
9. R. W. Schikkerling, *Commando Courageous (A Boer's Diary)*, Johannesburg, 1964, 326–7.
10. PRO, CO 179/229/3538 sub. in encl. 1, Botha to Sir Arthur Lawley, 10 November 1903.
11. *Natal Mercury*, 21 December 1935.
12. *Parliamentary Debates*, 4th series, Commons, 79, c. 57, 15 February 1900.
13. W. K. Hancock and Jean van der Poel eds., *Selections from the Smuts Papers*, I, Cambridge, 1966, 484, Smuts to W. T. Stead, 4 January 1902.
14. *Parliamentary Debates*, 4th series, Commons, 98, cc. 1123–4, 2 August 1901.
15. PRO, CO 179/210/8629 encl. statement by Lieutenant Lambton, 12 February 1900.
16. PRO, WO 32/8048 encl. J. Kemp to Kitchener, 15 July 1901.
17. Adjutant-General's circular memorandum No. 37, 17 May 1901.
18. V, 250.
19. *The War in South Africa, October 1899–February 1900, Prepared in the Historical Section of the Great General Staff, Berlin*, trans. Colonel W. H. H. Waters, London, 1904, 137.
20. Transvaal Archives, Pretoria, SNA 3, 210/01, Capt. A. W. Baird to David Henderson, Director of Military Intelligence South Africa, n.d.
21. *Ibid.*, Lt G 122, 110/7, F. Edmeston to C. Griffith, Rustenburg, 27 April 1902.
22. PRO, Kitchener Papers, 30/57/22, Kitchener to Brodrick, War Office, 13 April 1902.
23. PRO, CO 179/210/8629 encl. Buller to Hely-Hutchinson, 13 February 1900.
24. Speech reported in *Izwi Labantu*, 9 July 1901.
25. *Cape Colony Blue Book on Native Affairs*, 1901, 2, 16, 17, 21.
26. Peter Warwick, 'The African Refugee Problem in the Transvaal and Orange River Colony, 1900–2', *Southern African Research in Progress, Collected Papers 2*, University of York, 1977, 61–81. See chapter 7 for further information and comparative material on the white concentration camps.
27. Orange Free State Archives, Bloemfontein, CSO 82, 71/02, Captain F. Wilson Fox to H. F. Wilson, 6 January 1902.
28. Archive of the Methodist Missionary Society, Incoming Correspondence Transvaal 1901–03, Rev. Hugh Morgan to Rev. Hartley, 3 September 1901; Archive of the United Society for the Propagation of the Gospel, Reports Africa 1901, 1 (27347), Rev. Brown to Rev. Tucker, 3 September 1901.
29. Orange Free State Archives, CSO 74, 4282/01, 23 November 1901.
30. Transvaal Archives, SNA 16, 2369/02, monthly report of Captain Vignoles, South African Constabulary, 13 October 1902.
31. *Ibid.*, SNA 16, 2217/02, Rev. Paulsen to Assistant Resident Magistrate Wakkerstroom District, 1 October 1902.
32. *Ibid.*, SNA 17, 2500/02, De Lotbiniere to Sir Godfrey Lagden, Secretary for Native Affairs, 7 November 1902.
33. Francis Wilson and Dominique Perrot eds., *Outlook on a Century, South Africa 1870–1970*, Lovedale SA, 1973, 271.
34. T. Karis and G. M. Carter eds., *From Protest to Challenge*, I, Stanford, 1972, 48–9.
35. See H. J. and R. E. Simons, *Class and Colour in South Africa, 1850–1950*, London, 1969, 69–71.

CHAPTER 9

British Society and the War

M. D. Blanch

Four-fifths of British society at the time of the South African War can be classified as working class. In assessing the reaction of British society to the war particular attention must be given to the attitudes of working people and to the nature of the propaganda directed towards them. But the working class was itself split into several subgroups; between the grades of foremen, skilled, semi-skilled and unskilled workers existed profound differences in wages, housing and lifestyles. Research has indicated, too, that the social and political attitudes of working men varied with status,[1] in particular between the skilled and unskilled, where, Gareth Stedman Jones has concluded, 'a gulf is fixed'.[2] One needs to be sensitive to such differences in outlook, yet the great problem in researching working class attitudes is that working people leave behind few records of their opinions.

The debate

From Hobson through to Schumpeter,[3] there has developed a general notion that working class people supported the South African War, being in some sense psychologically stimulated by empire. More recently, scepticism of this view has been voiced by, among others, Henry Pelling and Richard Price.[4] Focusing on those aspects of the war that have traditionally been taken as evidence of working class support, they claim that the increase in army recruitment was an essentially middle class phenomenon, that the 1900 general election did not demonstrate any massive pro-government swing, and that close analysis of crowd celebration and mass protests casts doubt on their political significance. They argue that the war was an irrelevancy for most working people, and that when working men were called upon to give an opinion on the conflict it was as likely to have been one of condemnation as of support. Price's work in particular is one of originality and refreshing methodology; however, different conclusions will be suggested here.

This analysis of middle and working class reactions to the war concentrates on four separate themes. First, the South African War is placed within the wider context of late Victorian popular imperialism. Attitudes of adults in 1900 were to some extent conditioned by their experiences over the previous twenty or more years. Therefore we will begin with a very brief analysis of some of the ways in which nationalism and imperialism were presented in the schools between 1880 and 1899 and, critical to later argument, summarize society's involvement with militarism in this period in the Regular and Auxiliary armies. Second, the war's military phases were directly linked to shifts in attitudes at home. What is needed then, is a chronology of change in political attitudes. Again, one important measure of reaction to the war is in recruitment to the army, but this has never yet been satisfactorily discussed; new evidence on this is presented here. Finally, we will examine crowd demonstrations and music hall patriotism during the war, and their relationship to the place of nationalism among working people.

Nationalism and militarism in the schools

Popular society, on the eve of war, was already imbued with a degree of nationalism and militarism. The roots of this are to be found in the style and content of teaching in the schools, and in popular involvement at all levels with militarist organizations in the period between 1880 and 1899.

In this period all children attended school from five to eleven or twelve years of age; most went to the Board or Church schools, where discipline was severe. Over and above the overt causes of strict discipline – large classes, poor teachers, rebellious children – it was cardinal for the late Victorian school, whether for the middle or working classes, to see itself as a disciplining institution *per se*. Discipline was repressive, almost military – compulsory sitting, standing still, taking up pens 'by number'; 'too much the practice of the drill sergeant',[5] complained one teacher, and another, 'The military ideal of automatic action to a given response is largely the ideal of much school discipline.'[6] Indeed 'we give [the pupil] a little knowledge it is true, but we rob him of his personality.'[7]

This early acquaintance with militaristic authoritarianism was reinforced by the increasing use in schools of military drill as physical training (popularly known as PT).[8] Some teachers, indeed, enjoyed this so much that they had to be checked – one school inspector found an infants' school doing 45 minutes marching drill 'including the babies', which, he concluded, was too long.[9] Drill was more than mere PT. It taught total obedience; as one headmaster wrote, 'The class at drill should be a mere machine'.[10] It taught the submission of all individuals to one common aim, that of the squad, of particular value (wrote one popular teacher-trainer) to 'youths . . . who feel already the stirring of the blood towards the days of active service which lie before them'.[11] For drill was profoundly militaristic; it copied and helped popularize army practices and could lead to a closer involvement with youth and adult paramilitary movements. Thus in one Clerkenwell school, it was reported, the boy regiments sang military songs as they marched from assembly.[12]

In the middle class Public schools there were 110 army cadet corps. Paramilitary cadet movements outside the school were also born and flourished – the army cadet battalions (with active working class units in London, Manchester and Surrey), the Church Lads' Brigade, which was formed in 1891, and the Nonconformist Boys' Brigade, established in 1884.

Bugler Dunne, who went to South Africa in 1899 aged only fourteen. In the late nineteenth century military ideals were imparted with enthusiasm in both the Public schools and Board schools.

Proposals to introduce compulsory cadet corps in Board schools, though discussed in Parliament, never succeeded. Denied cadet corps of their own, many teachers in elementary schools clearly enjoyed their second best. Not that this drill met with universal approval; it was attacked in the *Journal of Education*, for instance, as being responsible for 'mafficking' in the poorer parts of London.[13]

Fired by Seeley's *Expansion of England* in the 1880s, many teacher-trainers and writers of schoolbooks went further and imbued history and geography teaching with all manner of nationalistic moralizing. Thus a major concern of geography teaching was, according to the Codes of the Board of Education, the acquisition of empire; this was unquestionably regarded as a 'good thing'. Indeed, one book published in 1901 still talked of the empire's countries 'all living peacefully and prospering' with the British flag defending 'the precious gift of freedom' for them.[14]

History readers inevitably portray the British as brave and honest, and in describing battles hint at racial ascendancy. Other races are not nearly as glorious – especially the Irish, Africans and Asians.[15] Military stories were very popular, claiming 24 out of the 40 stories in the popular Cambridge Readers for instance. These 'good and valiant'[16] heroes, paradigmatic of 'English' honesty, courage, loyalty, duty, self-discipline and patriotism, provided examples for the children to model themselves on. Sometimes a certain sleight of hand might be necessary though; 'it must be *our* victory over *our* enemies'.[17]

It should also be added that some Boards (Birmingham, Huddersfield and Burton-on-Trent, for example) provided formal moral instruction as well, including lessons on patriotism, courage, duty and loyalty.[18] And for the rest, of course, a whole fund of late Victorian (often blood-soaked) popular imperialistic literature, by Henty, Ballantyne, Kipling and Rider Haggard, was available.[19]

The evidence, then, suggests that a significant part of school time in the period 1880–99 was spent in transmitting nationalistic and imperialistic values to children. Linked to the drill and discipline, it would seem that the ethos of the teaching was often militaristic and emotive.

Sons of the Blood, a magazine illustration, typical of the late nineteenth century, celebrating British militarism. Regimental uniforms from all over the empire are carefully depicted in the scene.

The Regular army

Militarism in British society by 1899 was not uncommon, since there existed for all members of society military and paramilitary organizations that men might join. There were a quarter of a million men in the Regular army in 1898, with a Reserve of nearly 79 500 recent ex-soldiers who were mobilized on the outbreak of war. Between 1881 and 1898 nearly 600 000 men enlisted, principally recruited from the unskilled and semiskilled working class.[20] Because it recruited in competition with the civil labour market, and its pay was low, the Regular army fared better in times of unemployment. It is untrue to say, however, that unemployment *drove* men in.[21] Hungry, workless men could join the Militia instead (see below). The introduction of short service (six years) made the army an attractive short term proposition for young men to experience adventure, excitement and travel in the very many 'little wars' that were emblazoned on every recruiting poster.[22] The excitement of conflict has always provided a powerful recruiter; other men joined because they liked the pomp, the show and the uniform.[23]

Irrespective of their reasons for joining, these 600 000 working men were subject to both formal and informal ideological training, which was itself an education in nationalism. Thus besides drill and discipline, great stress was laid on *esprit de corps*, loyalty to the regiment, which was a form of transferred patriotism.[24] The army cultivated, too, a deference among its soldiers to the innate leadership of the aristocracy and the upper middle class gentlemen, who formed its officer corps.[25] Service in the army abroad encouraged racist and authoritarian attitudes towards foreigners, especially black ones.[26]

The Militia

The Militia, a part-time army raised for home defence, was a very similar body to the Regular army. In 1898 it stood at about 144 000, and from 1881 it had recruited some 656 000 men. It, too, principally drew on unskilled labour;[27] a recruit underwent three months' continuous training with the Regular army, and would subsequently have to take one month off work each year for continuation training. One reason for joining the Militia was to survive unemployment; it was also a good source of income for strikers in Wales![28] Over one-third of the recruits enlisted because they wished eventually to enter the Regular army; three months' Militia training and regular food built them up sufficiently to enable them to scrape through the Regular army's not too exacting medical standards.

Both the Regular and the closely connected Militia armies may be seen as powerful tools for the education of the working class into nationalism. Over the period 1881–98 in excess of one million working men joined these armies. These men were principally drawn from the unskilled working class, in which, we may therefore suggest, there existed a very large number of families whose links with the army were traditional and continuous. A major reason for joining the Regular army, then, was that working men were stimulated by the experiences retold by their fathers and uncles and brothers. Thus was militarism recycled, as it assumed a place in popular culture.

Another organization linked to the transmission of militaristic nationalism was the Volunteer army. The Volunteers were quite different. They were also part-time; but they were unpaid, and drew their support in general from skilled workers, and even from the lower middle class.[29] In 1898 there were nearly 230 000 Volunteers, and from 1881 they had recruited a total of about 797 000 men. Men joined because they liked the ceremonial and the drill;[30] many were encouraged to join by employers forming units based in their factories. Of course, the Volunteers were also a social club, but a very specific, notably militarist, club. They, too, cultivated *esprit de corps* and patriotism; and they went from strength to strength!

The Volunteer army

(1883) 'One Englishman is worth two or three of any other country.'[31]

(1888) 'It was generally said that one Englishman was equal to six foreigners.'[32]

Employers were happy to sponsor such units; as one Sheffield employer attested, Volunteer training 'graft[ed] in the people discipline . . . every Volunteer is worth five per cent more to an employer of labour than an ordinary man.'[33]

The Yeomanry

Finally, there was the Yeomanry. A small body, some 10 200 men in 1898, it was officially the cavalry of the Militia. The Yeomanry was almost exclusively a rural middle class and aristocratic formation; it is of more importance, and will be studied in greater depth in the later section on wartime recruiting.

Table 1 is a summary of the total number of men recruited to military organizations in the United Kingdom and Ireland between 1881 and 1898. To be more precise, it is limited only to those men who would by 1899 be less than forty years old. The numbers joining the Regular army from the Militia and the Volunteers have been subtracted to avoid double counting.

Table 1. Adult males who would be aged 40 years and under by 1898, and who joined one of the military forces of the Crown, 1881–1898.

Regular Army	594 215
Militia	432 801
Volunteers	730 154
Yeomanry (1898 only)	10 207
TOTAL	1 767 377

If we discount the number dying on active service, or from sickness, and ignore those who joined the army before 1881, then we may conclude that on the eve of war 22·42 per cent of the entire male population of the United Kingdom and Ireland aged 17–40 years had previous military experience.

Viewed in these terms, and in conjunction with the education of children over the same period, we may conclude that powerful pre-war influences helped shape popular response to the war itself.

Popular imperialism

In the years immediately preceding the war, middle class opinion, in as much as it was reflected by the press and politicians, was becoming increasingly caught up in the heady whirl of imperialistic politics. The Jameson Raid of December 1895 produced a fund of anti-Boer (and anti-German) jingoism. Even the radical *Reynolds News* spoke of the 'ignorant, grasping and superstitious Boers';[34] and for the first time an anti-Jameson public meeting was mobbed and broken up. This was indeed new – none of the meetings held between 1882 and 1885 calling on Britain to evacuate the Sudan had ever been broken up. In this same year Lord Northcliffe's *Daily Mail* was born; guided by the simple order to 'explain, simplify, clarify', this imperialistic newspaper achieved a meteoric growth. By 1898 it had a circulation of 430 000, by 1900 almost a million,[35] achieving for the first time outside London a circulation equal to many of the provincial dailies.[36]

Celebrations of the 1897 Diamond Jubilee were followed by the Battle of Omdurman (September 1898) and the 'avenging' of the murder of General Gordon in the Sudan. The *Labour Leader* complained bitterly at the time that workers were more interested in celebrating the victory at Omdurman than supporting the Welsh coal strike.[37] Then came Fashoda, and near war with France. Again *Reynolds News*, which at first criticized Fashoda as 'disgraceful and idiotic', quickly changed its view to anticipate a war 'with perfect confidence in our cause and might'.[38]

Attitudes to the war in South Africa

That war was brewing in South Africa was clear for many years. But not everyone awaited the war with perfect equanimity. Indeed, there was a very strong and growing anti-war feeling. An anti-war meeting in Trafalgar Square was called by the Social Democratic Federation as early as 9 July 1899, and by the outbreak of war twenty-five working class bodies had sent protests to the Colonial Office.[39] The Social Democratic Federation, led by H. M. Hyndman, at first opposed the war, although more from a dislike of the 'Jew capitalists and Christian financiers' than as any expression of support for the 'criminal' Boers who, Hyndman felt, had originally stolen the country from black people. The Independent Labour Party and the Trades Union Congress were also against the war, but splits soon developed in the fragmented groups of the Left. Both the Fabians and Robert Blatchford (founder and editor of the socialist *Clarion*) declared support for the war, and even the SDF apparently had 'jingo socialists' within its ranks, for in the later stages of the war its executive resolved that anti-war agitation was a 'waste of time and money'.

The only independent working class organizations that seem to have supported the government *prior to* the war were those already committed to Tory policies – the Conservative Working Men's Clubs, the National Free Labour Association, and its stooge, the London United Workmen's Committee.

The Liberal Party, already split over Home Rule, was once again divided. Some Liberals supported the government, taking ostrich-like refuge in the myth that the war was all about the democratic enfranchisement of Uitlanders, and against a 'Prime old Tory oligarchy'.[40] The Boer ultimatum, and the subsequent Boer invasion of Natal, swung many Liberals and Liberal newspapers firmly behind the government. Thus provincial Liberal daily newspapers spoke of the 'freak' victory of Majuba (27 February 1881) and prophesied the rapid overpowering of the Boer armies,[41] or they turned to criticize Liberals in their own ranks 'for not having the honesty and courage to say openly, "Our rulers are upright men." '[42] The Tory press, of course, was more vehement, and the 'yellow press' like the *Daily Mail*, wildly so. Just a handful of newspapers were left to lead the opposition to the war, including the *Morning Leader*, *Manchester Guardian*, *Speaker*, *Edinburgh Evening News* and, from 1901, the *Daily News*.

The early checks received by the army, culminating in 'black week' in mid-December 1899, further silenced opposition to the war. It was to many inconceivable that Britain could withdraw while being beaten; thus in one pro-Boer MP's constituency, Holmfirth, the Liberal Council advised that attempts should be made to stop the war only 'after the Boers have been driven back into their own territory'.[43] Even if the war was wrong, it could not be *lost*, as Bernard Porter says in the next chapter.

To help crystallize support for the war, all the newspapers gave a very fulsome coverage, and the yellow press, in particular, fomented outrage stories and reported massive victories when none occurred.[44] Criticism of Britain's conduct of the war by foreigners was useful in generating jingoism. The normally sober *Birmingham Daily Mail*, for instance, urged 'stalwart Englishmen, armed with good horsewhips' to go over to France and 'administer a severe castigation to the vulgar cowards . . . the Parisian, like a dog, barks loudest in his own kennel!'[45]

The jingo crowd

Then came the 'victories', each one greeted with greater crowd enthusiasm than the last. At the relief of Ladysmith, khaki-clad troopers in the cities were carried 'shoulder high up and down the streets in a pandemonium of cheers and songs'.[46] Some children in schools burned effigies of Kruger, while others merrily lined up to cheer and sing.[47] Out of some factories issued workmen, parading likenesses of Kruger through the streets;[48] in the music halls the audiences whipped themselves into a paroxysm of patriotic eulogy.

The occupation of Pretoria also called forth scenes of 'unrestrained joy', as did the departure of Volunteers to the Colours (discussed below), speeded by crowds singing 'Soldiers of the Queen' and gifts of khaki bibles from their chaplains.[49] Then came the relief of Mafeking, so eagerly awaited that in the Lozells area of Birmingham it was celebrated two days before the official dispatch giving news of the end of the siege arrived.[50] To use the word that was later coined to describe the phenomenon, the streets in the cities were filled with 'mafficking' crowds.

Above left: the vast jubilant crowd that assembled outside the Mansion House, London, after news was received of the relief of Ladysmith.

Above right: a hero of the hour mobbed by an enthusiastic jingo crowd. Sir George White, VC, who failed to break out of Ladysmith, encounters similar difficulties outside the London Hippodrome, 9 April 1900.

'Staid citizens, whose severe respectability and decorum were usually beyond question or reproach were to be seen parading the streets, shouting patriotic songs with the full force of their lungs, dancing, jumping, screaming in a delirium of unrestrained joy.'[51]

In this climate it is no surprise that anti-war meetings were increasingly broken up. At the beginning of the war such meetings were possible, but with the succession of defeats, these meetings came to be regarded as treachery. On 26 January 1900 S. C. Cronwright-Schreiner arrived in Britain from South Africa to put the Boers' case. He was the husband of the writer Olive Schreiner, and he and his wife had lived in Johannesburg since 1898. Cronwright-Schreiner was heard in relative peace in London and Hastings (18 and 19 February) but then began a long series of what pro-Boer Liberals termed 'mob rule'.[52] In Leicester (20 February), Edinburgh (7 March and 18 May) and Scarborough (12 March) meetings were mobbed and broken up – in Scarborough, order was restored only after the army had intervened. In Leeds (14 March), Liverpool (15 March), Gateshead (9 March), Sheffield (10 March), York (11 March) and Attercliffe (29 May) meetings had to be abandoned. Elsewhere – Dundee, Huddersfield, Leicester, and later Leeds and Sheffield – meetings were cancelled in advance. Occasionally a meeting might succeed in being held, either in secret (Manchester, 7 May) or with the help of the army (Aberdeen, 20 May). On 20 July Cronwright-Schreiner returned to South Africa, having held only two good open meetings.

The relief of Mafeking as it was celebrated in an English country town.

The apparent victory over the Boers, shown by the occupation of their capitals (May, June 1900) and the flight of Kruger to Europe (11 September 1900), seems to mark a basic turning point in popular interest. From then on, opponents of the war felt able to begin to voice their objections, and leaflet campaigns started. The protracted counter-insurgency operations, the tedious division of South Africa by barbed wire, and the barbaric resettlement of Boer women and children in concentration camps lacked the news value of a Paardeberg or a Mafeking. In short, the war became more than boring, it became embarrassing. The *Daily News*, acquired by Lloyd George and R. C. Lehman in 1901, added its voice to the protests; the protests were swelled by letters written home by soldiers, complaining about the conduct of the war. And there were, after all, other wars to give attention to – rebellious Sudanese soldiers in Uganda, small essays forth against indigenous peoples in Nigeria and Somalia, continual problems on the North-West frontier from Afghans and Pathans, and above all the illustrious China War against the Boxer rebels. Of course, Boer atrocity stories continued; one newspaper even tried to recapture interest by announcing that there were Boer spies in the Midlands.[53] Nobody could ignore a war that still employed nearly 300 000 British soldiers; but the climax had passed. So in 1901 and 1902 peaceful anti-war demonstrations were held throughout the country,[54] and with a few exceptions that prove the rule these generally took place without the mob interference that characterized such gatherings earlier in the war.

'Members gave ten rousing cheers, and then, at a signal, uncovered and sang "God Save the Queen".' A cartoon of how the Stock Exchange greeted the news of Cronjé's surrender at Paardeberg, which appeared in the Illustrated London News, *3 March 1900.*

The exceptions included the infamous Lloyd George riot at the Birmingham Town Hall on 18 December 1901.[55] A crowd of between 40 000 and 100 000 gathered. The meeting was broken up, all of the windows of the Town Hall smashed, its doors rammed in by telegraph poles, and in the subsequent baton charge by the police twenty-seven people were injured and one man died. Lloyd George escaped, disguised as a policeman. But here one must pause, for while it is generally accepted that nearly everyone participated in rejoicings such as Mafeking, it is difficult to suggest that everyone took an *active* part in the organic vengeful crowds that broke up peace meetings. Certainly, large numbers of people gathered; incited to do so by the newspapers, many came out of curiosity.

Thus in Birmingham the local Unionist press made the self-fulfilling prophecy that there would be trouble. 'This most virulent anti-Briton' (Lloyd George) had 'made out our soldiers . . . to be wholesale inhuman butchers'.[56] 'Many men who have lost sons or brothers or friends [and] . . . the returned soldiers and militiamen [want] . . . to see the man who lauds our country's enemies and accuses our troops of barbarism.' The press then started a rumour that 'two hundred Irish toughs have been engaged to eject intruders . . . it seems incredible that Birmingham people should be challenged.'[57]

The retributory crowd needs leadership. The leadership of vengeful elements was usually Tory and/or middle class. Thus large numbers of students were implicated in the Cronwright-Schreiner riots in Scotland,[58] and in London clerks and the 'Stock Exchange gang' were blamed for inciting violent behaviour.[59] In Birmingham the honour of having first seen the non-existent Irish toughs and later leading the 100 000-strong crowd was claimed by mob orator and Conservative 'working man' Councillor J. G. Pentland. He and another Tory councillor, William Lovesey, had sent out sandwich-boardmen throughout the city, urging men to come and demonstrate 'For King! For Country! For Birmingham wants no traitors!'[60]

LETTERS TO THE EDITOR.

THE PROJECTED PRO-BOER MEETING.

Sir,—At the meeting which Mr. Lloyd-George, M.P., will address in Birmingham on December 18th, no doubt a few discharged soldiers from South Africa will be present. Perhaps Mr. Lloyd-George will repeat to our faces the accusations he made against us in our absence.—Yours, etc., ONE OF THEM.

To the EDITOR *of the* DAILY POST.

Sir,—Going about town to-day, I observed some "strange" faces; this led to enquiry, and I found out they were "imports" for "chucking out" purposes. I don't charge the Birmingham Liberals with these dirty tactics, but surely they are not so low as to patronise such below-the-belt work. If the money is being found by wily emissaries, then I publicly say by all means let us show what loyal Birmingham men can do. The promoters can have no other object than to insult Mr. Chamberlain, and if this is tolerated it will have an influence for evil few can see the end of.

A staunch Liberal called on me and gave me his tickets, saying, "I have done with them now. My son has gone to the front. I detest such traitors as Lloyd-George and Co." A man against his country is a rebel. Mr. Chamberlain will not be insulted in our Town Hall; nor will the people stand it.

17, Moat Row. J. G. PENTLAND.

respect to his advancing years and useful municipal services in the years that are past. That any material number of Birmingham Liberals desire to ally themselves with the pernicious anti-British principles associated with Mr. Lloyd-George we cannot believe, and it is thoroughly discreditable that any handful of pro-Boer politicians should bring into the city and give a platform at the Town Hall to a firebrand like Mr. Lloyd-George, whose violent attacks on the Colonial Secretary, Lord Milner, and all who are most instrumental in prosecuting to a finish a just and necessary war against the enemies of this country have made his name to stink in the nostrils of every loyalist in Birmingham and every true patriot throughout the Empire. In his speech at Derby a fortnight

Newspaper cuttings prior to the infamous Lloyd George riot in Birmingham, 18 December 1901. The newspapers here, the Birmingham Post *and* Mail*, played an important part in inciting the riot, which resulted in one man dead and 28 injured.*

A recent study of the Birmingham riot also blames local gunworkers, who had been told by a foreign arms dealer that Lloyd George's peace policy would close the factory.[61] As the disturbance grew, many who had come as spectators got caught up in the excitement. Then the police arrived. Those arrested were nearly always working class – in Birmingham their occupations were given as basket maker, painter, joiner, machinist, shunter, silversmith, brass polisher, art metal worker, and one non-working class man arrested, a bank clerk.[62] There were two others, 'strips of boys', and this is important, for youth was a common feature of all the riots. Thus a further factor in the riots was the sport of 'police-baiting' by youths. It is clear, therefore, that these vengeful riots are not a good indicator of general working class attitudes.

Conservative and Unionist performance in elections

Another, and more precise indicator of popular attitudes is the Conservative and Unionist performance in elections. The war figured in Unionist propaganda in many of the annual November municipal elections, and crucially in the October 1900 'khaki election'. In Birmingham, for instance, eight out of thirteen municipal contests between 1899 and 1902 became, however inappropriately, embroiled in the issue of the government's conduct of the war, this influence becoming progressively weaker as the war continued. Unionist propaganda stressed Liberal treachery, a treachery comprehensible to working men. In Sheffield Park ward in 1899 the voting miners were told to remember 'the murdered soldiers'. In Sheffield Brightside ward there was a 'Vote for Grafton and no Little Englanders! War! War! War!' campaign.[63] And it does seem that in these municipal elections there was at first some positive response to this essentially irrelevant propaganda; against all expectations, the Conservatives captured Sheffield Park ward in 1899.

Graph 1(A) (p. 224) shows the Unionist percentage of total votes in municipal elections in Birmingham between 1899 and 1902, and 1(B) the same for the two wards of Sheffield where imperial politics played a part. The 1900 dotted figure on 1(B) represents the general election result (a defeat of the sitting pro-Boer MP) in the Brightside constituency, since there were no municipal contests in that year in the Brightside or Park wards.

The graphs do suggest that, however apparently irrelevant to municipal politics, the imperial question helped produce increasing Unionist votes until 1900 in these two cities. Then, with disillusion in Unionism, voters turned instead to those parties with more positive and realistic social policies. It should be indicated that voters in these elections would be men *and women* drawn in part from the semi-skilled, but mostly from the skilled workers and others higher on the social ladder.

The 'khaki election' of 1900 is a popular touchstone for historians analysing social attitudes. Fought by the government on its conduct of the war, it resulted in a government majority of 134 seats; this is especially notable, since it defied the 'swing of the pendulum' theory – it was the second successive victory for the Unionist cause.

The Unionists, in fact, stood little chance of losing, for the Liberals, disorganized and demoralized, failed to contest 143 'safe' Unionist seats. In contested seats, Unionists invariably called into question their opponent's loyalty, irrespective of whether or not he was a pro-Boer.[64] Indeed, there were sixteen Liberals, active supporters of the government over South Africa, who lost their seats. In many constituencies Liberals tried to show that, while they admired the soldiers' tenacity and reviewed British victories with pride, they disagreed with the government's organization of the war. No matter: 'Don't vote for Pro-Boers, Little Englanders, Krugerites'[65] ran one election poster in such a constituency, for the election, said Joseph Chamberlain, was to be not a vote of confidence in the government, but in the 'honour and courage of our troops'.[66] Of the pro-Boer MPs, fourteen lost their seats and only two pro-Boers recaptured Tory seats (in Camborne and Grantham).

The 'khaki election', October 1900. A card issued by the Tories in the Holmfirth constituency near Sheffield, where the sitting MP was a 'pro-Boer' Liberal, H. J. Wilson.

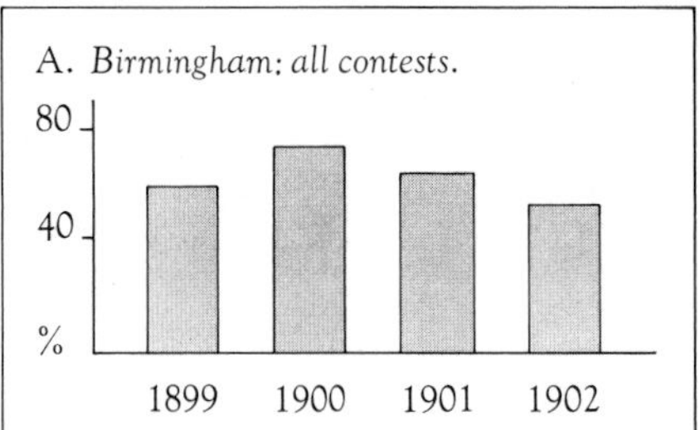

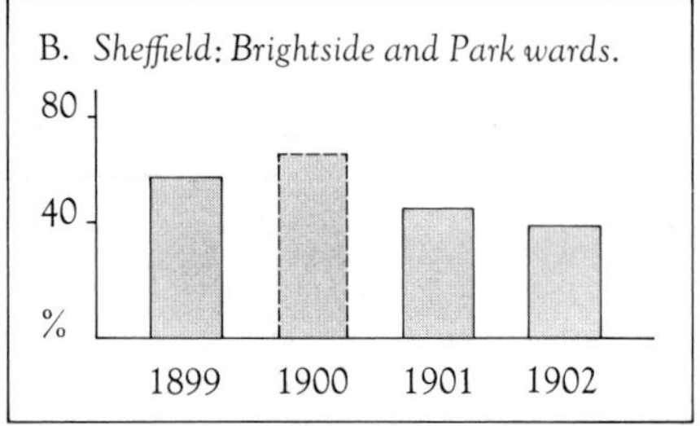

Graph 1. Percentage share of votes for the Conservative and Unionist parties in municipal elections, 1899–1902.

The average turnout of voters in the election in England was 76·1 per cent, but in urban areas just 73·4 per cent,[67] which compared, say, to the 1906 general election was quite low. Richard Price suggests that because it seemed so prejudged a result interest in the election did not run high. But equally it should be noted that the 'khaki election' was held on a stale register, fifteen months old. This would particularly have affected urban areas, for these had high removal rates; in Paddington North, for instance, 18 per cent of the electorate had moved,[68] and in Birmingham East it was claimed that 30 per cent had left the constituency.[69] Low urban polls are therefore deceptive – interest in many urban working class areas was higher than the figures indicate. Thus in Birmingham East, although the poll was only 59·9 per cent, if none of those who had removed returned to vote, then the hypothetical turnout of available voters rises to 86·3 per cent.

The swing to the Unionists was an urban phenomenon; total votes in London swung by 2·2 per cent, whereas the rest of England swung by only 0·4 per cent. Table 2 shows that the strength of the Unionist Party was rooted in the urban working class vote. It should be added, however, that recent research

Table 2. Urban and non-urban voting, general election 1900

	Percentage turnout	*Percentage Unionist vote*
England: Major urban areas	73·4	54·5
Other	77·9	51·6

indicates that Unionist candidates in working class constituencies also had to advocate policies of social reform to gain popular support; the imperialist issue was not the only one propounded by Unionists.[70]

The position of skilled working men in this respect is important. In so far as research allows, it can be suggested that skilled workers were less prone to being swayed by Unionist nationalistic propaganda. First, continuing the study of Birmingham wards right down to 1914, it is clear that while 'lower working class' wards fluctuated wildly towards Unionism over nationalistic issues, the solid Labour and Liberal vote was rooted in the skilled workers' wards. Second, recent research also suggests that the 'lower working class' in the past had a greater propensity to support the Conservatives than the 'higher working class', this being essentially due to deference.[71] Finally, in so far as working people were prepared to consider the ethics of the war, thinking skilled workers in working men's clubs were happy to listen to pro-Boer speakers, and in some cases to give them their support.[72] This is particularly true of the period of increasing disillusionment with the war that followed the 'victories' of early 1900 and Mafeking night. To many of these skilled workers the war was irrelevant; how could they be expected to fight for votes for Uitlanders when there were still many disenfranchised workers in England? Further research is needed, however, before anything more than a tentative conclusion can be put forward that unskilled and semi-skilled workers were more likely to support the Unionists on the traditional patriotic platform.

Military recruitment

Another positive and relatively precise indicator of society's reaction to the war is the recruitment of men to serve in the army in South Africa. Table 3 calculates the recruitment to the Regular army between 1899 and 1902.

Table 3. Recruitment to the Regular army 1899–1902

	1 Recruits with no previous military experience	2 Recruits from the Militia	3 Recruits from the Volunteers	4 Imperial Yeomanry	Total
1899	23 259	16 396	3 045	—	42 700
1900	43 992	23 165	*20 962	10 242	98 361
1901	28 516	15 662	†14 221	17 252	75 651
1902	30 507	18 994	8 300	7 239	65 040
Total	126 274	74 217	46 528	34 733	281 752

Source: *General Annual Return of the British Army*, 1902 (Cd. 1496, 1903), and 1903 (Cd. 1904, 1904)
* of which 14 559 on one-year engagements, including 1 664 CIV.
† of which 6 776 on one-year engagements.

It will be seen immediately that, in columns 1 and 2, there was a massive rise in enlistment in 1900 from those groups that had traditionally filled the ranks in peacetime. The defeats of 'black week' reached the public in the week ending 17 December 1899 and produced no immediate rise in recruiting. But, of course, men had to give notice at work and make their personal arrangements; many would want Christmas – perhaps their last – at home, before enlisting. Consequently, the reaction to defeat hit the recruiting offices at the very beginning of the new year. The Sheffield office was 'besieged' by men wishing to join up, with Regular recruiting up by half and (said the recruiting officer) 90 per cent of the recruits were 'men in full employment . . . of excellent physique . . . who are joining because they want to become soldiers'.[73] In Birmingham a hundred men turned up on New Year's Day alone.[74]

Response to the call. The Gordon Highlanders march through Edinburgh accompanied by an enthusiastic working class crowd, with small boys to the fore.

The numbers joining the army without previous military experience (column 1) must be taken as almost entirely working class. The army was not a respectable institution for the middle class to join; their avenue to the front was through the Volunteer Force and the Imperial Yeomanry. Given the greater sacrifice that would be needed for skilled workers to join up, and bearing in mind a parallel study of recruitment in the opening weeks of the First World War,[75] it is also strongly suggested that the bulk of these recruits, as well as the ex-Militia recruits, were unskilled and semi-skilled workers.

A crucial question is, how much greater are the numbers in columns 1 and 2 than would have been the case in peacetime? If we accept that unemployment was a major conditioner[76] of recruiting for these groups in peacetime, we may estimate by regression on the pattern for 1881–98 that, without the war, the numbers recruited for 1899–1902 might have totalled 128 015. In other words, the war produced an estimated extra working class recruitment in the above groups of about 72 476.

Large numbers of Volunteers also joined the army. As a response to 'black week' the government agreed that 110 unmarried rank and file and four officers from each Volunteer battalion could join their Line battalion as a composite unit. The response was quite overwhelming – several times that number volunteered,[77] so the government allowed further drafts at regular intervals. It also agreed to the raising of two independent formations, the City Imperial Volunteers (CIV), and the Imperial Yeomanry (IY).

Price, in a detailed study of CIV recruiting, discovered that it contained 51·6 per cent of non-working class recruits.[78] This is not surprising, and it would be dangerous to assume that this atypical unit was representative of Volunteer recruiting to the Regular army generally. For the CIV were drawn from the London battalions, the 'class battalions'[79] of the City, including the Honourable Artillery Company, London Scottish (7 Middlesex), Queens Westminster (13 Middlesex), Inns of Court (14 Middlesex), Civil Service Rifles (12 Middlesex)[80] and the special corps of the Bank of England, Lloyds and the insurance companies.[81] Considerable pressure was placed on the legal profession to enlist,[82] insurance companies encouraged volunteering and gave free life and dependants' insurance policies to their soldiers.[83] The CIV, said the Lord Mayor of London, was carefully selected from among marksmen of high physique, aged 20–30 years.[84] The normal Volunteer recruiting, by composite companies, was most probably drawn from a cross-section of the Volunteer battalions, which, as we have seen, were composed of some 74·5 per cent working class with a distinct bias towards the skilled worker.[85] Since peacetime recruitment to the Regular army from the Volunteer regiments averaged 2 239 from 1881 to 1898, we may conclude that there were about 37 570 extra Volunteer recruits to the Regular army during the war, of which about 27 990 (74·5 per cent) were working class.

The Imperial Yeomanry provided another outlet for middle class militarism. According to Price, 41·6 per cent of these recruits were 'non working class'.[86] Not that working class men were averse to joining the Yeomanry; a trooper's pay of five shillings per day was five times the regular rate for a private of infantry (and for that matter, well in excess of pay rates for unskilled and most semi-skilled workers). Consequently, recruiting offices were put under considerable pressure. In Birmingham 3 000 men applied to join the IY in 1900 alone, but recruiting officers would always take the 'higher class':

> 'You see, they are a very good class of men that are going out, and I want to see at least two "characters" for each applicant.'[87]

Many working men were also rejected on medical grounds – a number, for instance, failing because one tooth was missing![88] There was therefore this double bias against working class candidates, compounded by a distinct preference for men who could ride and shoot.

The return from war on 29 October 1900 of the City Imperial Volunteers, a distinctly middle class outfit whose membership included nine barristers, seven architects, two bankers, thirty civil servants, four schoolmasters and a ship owner.

Much like the 'Pals' battalions of the First World War, the CIV and IY were structured for and by the middle class. The CIV and IY provided respectable, even genteel, soldiering. They helped carry over the camaraderie of the large business firms and the public schools. The spirit of patriotic adventure was inextricably woven together with the sport of the rugby club and the old school tie. But there were also very many lower middle class men, particularly clerks, in the ranks. This may be ascribed to the peculiar social position of the lower middle class. Desperately trying to maintain a middle class appearance on a pitifully inadequate salary, even more desperately fighting to keep above the mass of the labouring population, volunteering for war was a token and a proof of their commitment to the system.

But what stimulated working class recruitment? Soldier autobiographies suggest that the excitement of adventure and conflict was a powerful draw; it stimulated and responded to that tradition of militarism among unskilled and semi-skilled working people identified earlier. Unskilled workers came from the tough and hard ghettos of the city; many would have participated in the 'scuttler' and 'peaky' gangs that 'terrorized whole districts'. In the army they could participate in a different, institutionalized form of violence.

Table 4, then, summarizes the estimates of middle class and working class recruiting to the Regular army between 1899 and 1902. Column 1 represents the estimate of peacetime recruitment based on the unemployment index; if this is correct, then 120 764 additional working class men and 24 016 middle class recruits sailed forth to war.

Table 4. Recruitment to the Regular army 1899–1902

	Estimated peacetime recruitment 1899–1902	Additional wartime recruitment Working class	Additional wartime recruitment Middle class	Total
Recruits from the Militia, or without previous experience	128 015	72 476	—	200 491
Ex-Volunteers	8 957	27 990	9 581	46 528
Imperial Yeomanry	—	20 298	14 435	34 733
Total	136 972	120 764	24 016	281 752

It should also be noted that by 1901 sixty-eight of the Militia battalions had volunteered for service abroad. This, of course, was quite outside their normal role;[88] to the above figures then should be added 45 566 extra working class recruits. These, with the total above and the number in the Regular army when war began, add up to over 657 000, which means that the Regular commitment (including other theatres of war and home defence) was 8·3 per cent of the entire male population of Great Britain and Ireland aged between 18 and 40 years.

Finally, recruiting to the Volunteers during wartime soared, some 242 808 new recruits joining. This was partly due to the infection of militarism, to the extra duty of periodic mobilization for home defence, and to pay being provided at annual camp for the first time. Militia recruiting, once the battalions departed abroad, fell to just 157 606 over the course of the war.

We may conclude that for some time at least during the South African War 14·2 per cent[90] of the entire male population aged 18 to 40 years was in uniform; that there was a strong middle class and aristocratic commitment to the war, and particularly from members of the lower middle class; and that the great bulk of Regular recruits probably still came from those groups which had always provided soldiers – unskilled and semi-skilled workers.

War propaganda

The propaganda of the Boer War was everywhere, and some examples of it are reproduced in this chapter. There was patriotic china, patriotic children's games, and patriotic advertisements that hung on awkward puns like 'Don't Botha about De Wet, Buy a Smither's Superfine Umbrella'.[91]

Children learnt of the war at school, and from their books and comics; in 1900 Lord Northcliffe's *Boys' Friend*, already anti-Boer, went one step further and showed the British at war with the Russians and the French, and sinking their navies.[92] The paramilitary boys' movements gained ground, and drew into closer association with the Regular and Volunteer armies. The Heyrod Street Lads' Club in Manchester, for instance, was able to parade 1 408 members of their Boys' Brigade Company under Regular army instructors in 1900.[93] The Church Lads' Brigade, with half of its governing body in the Regular army by 1900, published in its magazine war prayers and stirring stories of the conflict, including one of a boy trumpeter who bravely shot three Boers.[94] The Jewish Lads' Brigade practised the tactics of attack and defence as well as bayonet drill at its camps.[95] In ordinary and non-military boys' clubs military drill with dummy rifles began to be offered, and lectures were given on the war, too.[96] New military groups began to be formed, such as the Lads' Drill Association and the Boys Empire League.

Below and opposite: advertisers were quick to grasp the value of popular imperialism, as these examples show.

THE RELIEF OF LADYSMITH

TWO YEARS AGO TO-DAY

is commemorated in the celebrated "Bovril War Picture," of which this is a rough copy.

THE RELIEF OF INFLUENZA SUFFERERS BY

BOVRIL

is an event that is happening TO-DAY.

Above: imperialism for toddlers, an extract from the Active Army Alphabet *by J. Hassall, published in 1900.*

Outside the clubs, children invented their own game, 'Boer versus Briton', attacking and defending kops, spruits and veld, and which we only learn about when the occasional fatality was reported in the newspapers of the day.[97]

Adults learnt of the war from the newspapers and the cinema. The cinema was on its way to becoming a thriving industry by 1900; few music halls were without their 'bioscope' or 'viagraph', showing all the 'Latest Pictures, Recent Events in the Transvaal, Leading Generals at the Front'. But early cameras were too cumbersome to be on hand when the Boers attacked. Consequently, soldiers sometimes staged mock attacks for the benefit of the camera,[98] or the cameraman recruited actors to fight the battle for him. These latter masterpieces, filmed in locations as diverse as London's Hampstead Heath and a garden on the outskirts of Bolton, show scruffy unwashed Boers sometimes attacking a hospital tent, or shooting in the back a British soldier who has just given a wounded Boer some water.[99] There is no indication given in the surviving music hall programmes of the period that these were reconstructions! There were also light-hearted pieces, such as that showing President Kruger engaged in a boxing match with John Bull; Kruger at first wins by cheating and pretending to surrender with a white flag – John Bull finally triumphs, and his second (Uncle Sam) kicks Kruger's second (France) off the stage.[100]

Working class perspectives on the war were reflected through the music hall and popular theatre. Some music halls included short dramatic pieces in their repertoires; they, and

Propaganda film, shot on London's Hampstead Heath, though music hall patrons were not told this was entirely fictional. In this frame, the unwashed Boer shoots a well-spruced Englishman in the back, having just been given a drink of water. The film ends with the Boer being soundly thrashed by another soldier, who is at present lying dead on the left of the picture.

the theatres, showed plays and playlets based on the war in South Africa like 'A Soldier and a Man', 'One of the Best', 'On Her Majesty's Service' and 'The Absent Minded Beggar or, for Queen and Country'. One of the most popular, returning many times after the war, was 'Soldiers of the Queen', an anti-semitic drama depicting events from 'Majuba Hill Disaster to the Present Day', and including in Act 3 a new 'Patriotic Song – Revenge is Sweet'.[101] Music halls also focused on the soldiers' life in playlets like 'The Scapegrace' or 'Drummed Out'.[102] Nor was the South African War the only war to be represented; in Birmingham a hundred children helped re-enact the storming of the Taku Forts in China by the Naval Brigade.[103] There were also patriotic songs, comedians appearing in military costume, and even an unrideable donkey named Kruger![104]

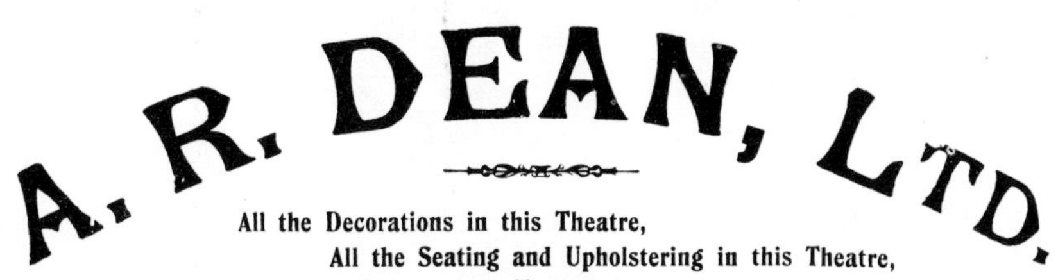

A. R. DEAN, LTD.

All the Decorations in this Theatre,
All the Seating and Upholstering in this Theatre,
All the Carpets and Linoleum in this Theatre,
All the Furnishing throughout,

HAVE BEEN EXECUTED BY

A. R. DEAN, LIMITED, The LARGEST HOUSE FURNISHERS In the MIDLANDS.

MONDAY, APRIL 30, 1900, for Six Nights, JOHN F. PRESTON'S Powerful Dramatic Co. (under the direction of HERBERT HOLLISTER and ERNEST R. ALLEN), in the Celebrated South African Military Drama—

'Soldiers of the Queen;' or, 'Briton and Boer,'

Founded on Actual Facts and Incidents that have occurred in South Africa from Majuba Hill Disaster to the Present Day.

Jack Willoughby, of the 94th Regiment, afterwards Captain of Cape Mounted Rifles	Mr. LEWIS LESLIE
Hans Muller, a wealthy Boer	Mr. HERBERT HOLLISTER
Reuben Brown, of Manatoppo Farm	Mr. THOMAS BOWMAN
Captain Richard Forrester, of the 95th; Ralph Forrester, alias Forsyth, his Half-brother	Mr. E. R. ALLEN
Tom Pinch, Soldier, Ostrich-Feather Dresser, &c.	Mr. HERBERT WOODIN
Bugler Baxter, late of the 50th West Kent Regiment	Mr. R. C. SMITH
Solomon Levi, a Jew Financier, Agent, &c.	Mr. HARRY RIGNOLD
Umgilligazi, a Matabele Chief	Mr. HORACE BUTLER
Sekukina, a Matabele Chief	Mr. ALFRED WADE
Karoei, a Matabele Madman	Mr. WILSON LOWTHER
Piet Uys (Boers)	Mr. F ERNSTONE
Hendriek Hoosten (Boers)	Mr. J. WALL
Susie Brown, Reuben's Daughter	Miss JENNY FDGAR
Mary Ann, her Maid	Miss WINIFRED PREECE
Tant Tannie, a Boer Woman	Miss L. JOHNSON
Milmo, the Witch of the Matabele	Miss LILLIE WOODS
Bertha (African Farm Servants)	Miss JENNY SMITH
Gretchen (African Farm Servants)	Miss G CABLE
Liza (African Farm Servants)	Miss GLENVILLE
Madchen (African Farm Servants)	Miss GLADYS MAUDE
Grace Forrester, Captain Forrester's Wife AND Dick Forrester	Miss JEANNIE BURGOYNE

Boers, Soldiers, Natives, &c.

ACT 1—THE MASSACRE AT MAJUBA. Scene—Plateau, near the Summit of Majuba, February 26th, 1881. Britons and Boers in Conflict—The Red Cross Nurse—The Soldiers, Comrades in Arms—The Attack by the Boers—Stand Shoulder to Shoulder like Sons of Britain and Soldiers of the Queen—Tableau 1.

ACT 2—THE LION WAGS HIS TAIL—The Transvaal. Scene—Exterior of an African Farm, May, 1896. After Jameson s Raid—The Plot of the Boers to Arm the Matabele against the British—Tableau 2. NOTE—Specialities will be introduced in this Act by **Miss Winifred Preece** and **Mr. Herbert Woodin.**

ACT 3—THE LION SHOWS HIS TEETH—Life in Johannesburg. Scene 1—Exterior of the Reform Club, Pritchard Street—The Murder—Tableau Scene 2—Corridor of the Saloon. Scene 3—The Empire Gambling Saloon. NOTE—In Act 3 will be introduced a new and original Patriotic Song, written and composed by SAM RICHARDS, ESQ., entitled, "**Revenge is Sweet.**" This Song is the Sole Property of JOHN F. PRESTON.

ACT 4—THE LION'S CLAWS PLOUGH DEEP. Scene 1—Pretoria—Commencement of the War. Scene 2—Boer Laager near Ladysmith—The War—Triumph of the Soldiers of the Queen—Grand Tableau, illustrating **The Relief of Ladysmith, Meeting of the Victorious Generals.**

Entirely New and Elaborate Scenery, specially painted for this production by C. F. Markham. Correct and Costly Military Uniforms, Weapons, &c., by John Hyman & Co. Costumes of the Country by Mrs. Sam May. The extensive Properties and Mechanical Effects by J. J. Glover and J. Webster. New and Original Music by J. Akid, Esq., M.D., R.A.M. Special Overture arranged by J. Hudson, Esq. The Supernumeraries drilled by Sergt.-Major Bowman, late 11th Hussars.

Popular theatre soon grasped and fed the interest in the war. This provincial theatre bill from April 1900 shows a play 'Founded on the Actual Facts and Incidents that have occurred in South Africa from the Majuba Hill Disaster to the Present Day'. In Act 3 'a new and patriotic song' is promised, 'Revenge is Sweet'.

Some of the most popular material in the working class music halls and theatre was that set in working class communities. The drama 'The Great World of London' advertised a caste of 'thieves, gangs, Salvation Army shelters, A Flower Girl, A Detective from Scotland Yard, Discharged Prisoners, Male and Female Tramps, Outcasts, Vagrants, Ex-Convicts, Waifs and Strays, Station Loafers, Newsboys and numerous

'Good-bye, my Blue Bell' was a favourite music hall song during the war. Here the song's second verse, a mixture of bravado and pathos, is reproduced and illustrated on a popular postcard of the day.

other characters'.[105] The plots invariably show a fall from grace, with hope then sparking anew; eventually, the scales of justice are brought to balance and the hero surfaces resplendent. It is almost as if these playlets project aspirations of perfection on an imperfect world; they translate the boredom of working class society into excitement by selecting colourful characters, and by depicting events like suicide, robbery and murder. They impose a gratifyingly happy solution on an unhappy reality.

Patriotic material, too, was emotive and stirring. But perhaps its popularity went deeper, for it offered the working class an opportunity to reflect upon themselves not as a class but as a national community. It was perhaps an alternative vision, but in stressing racial and imperial qualities it too generated feelings of enhanced status and position. It too glossed over the great cracks in society and provided individuals with a fleeting vision of corporate unity and community. This surely is what the 'mafficking' crowds were all about – an extension of the music hall stage onto the streets. In bursts of emotive frenzy the working class experienced the entertainment of victory woven into national solidarity and impressive status.

In what ways can working class people be said to have 'believed' in this patriotic material? As Hoggart says, the working class took all sentimental songs 'seriously . . . [but this] is not an unqualified matter. It subsists with an awareness that songs like this . . . are "very sentimental", and that strain of awareness expresses itself in the strain of debunking songs about sentimentality.'[106] Thus Dan Leno's parody of the famous 'jingo' song: 'I don't want to go to war/I'll be slaughtered if I do/I ain't a Briton true/And I'll let the Russians have Constantinople.' But, Hoggart suggests, sentimentality 'touches old chords . . . suggests values which people still like to cherish'. Debunking songs laugh affectionately at emotions; they do not destroy them.

Conclusion

The propaganda and presence of the South African War in British society was ubiquitous, focused as it was through popular leisure, the newspapers, political parties, military and paramilitary organizations and the schools. Many among the middle class who might have opposed the war accepted it as one forced upon Britain by the Boers' initial acts of aggression. Others, taught in imperialistic Public schools, led by their churches, or perhaps guided by anthropomorphic attitudes towards the Boers as uncivilized beings, supported the war with intellectual fervour. The place of the lower middle class in this is crucial, whether in leading crowd riot or volunteering for war; they were above all the real 'jingoes'. The propaganda of the Unionists and Liberal Imperialists, of newspaper editors and of military men, and of those who led the anti-Boer riots, was essentially generated from outside the working class.

There appears to have existed among working people a level of innate and inchoate nationalism upon which this propaganda was designed to act, and into which it was assimilated and modified. This innate nationalism was fed in the schools, and through the high level of involvement with the military in the late Victorian period. It was at its strongest among those most involved with the military, and least intellectually disposed to challenge it – unskilled and semi-skilled workers. Fleeting expressions of this nationalism may be glimpsed in popular leisure and in crowd celebration; the nationalist myth helped impart to the working class community a sense of belonging and of status. The mobilization of such a myth helped form, for instance, the anti-semitic and militarist British Brothers' League in London's East End in 1901. This movement locked into war nationalism, and helped whip up an hysterical paranoia of virulent anti-Jew racism.[107]

But working class nationalist expression was highly volatile, being rooted in what Hoggart calls a 'moment by moment approach to life'.[108] Nor can this nationalism be seen as comparable to middle class patriotism since it had few 'intellectual' roots. For this reason working people could hold what appeared to 'educated' people to be two entirely contradictory opinions at the same time, or at different times about the same event, as Hoggart, Price and Roberts, among others, have noted.[109] This apparent ambivalence of attitudes could arise between values expressed about things outside direct working class experience (like patriotism and the Boers) and their relationship to values concerning areas of life that people knew and understood. As Roberts has claimed:

> 'Whatever their arguments with the local employers, the ultrapatriotic mass remained intensely loyal to the nation, and the system as a whole. One week, a striking docker might hurl stones at the police and the next, assured of his daily bread, applaud the marching Territorials or cheer a prince to the skies.'[110]

Of course, as Hoggart says, there was a consistency in working class culture, but it was not one forged from an enduring or systematized ideological value system.

The mobilization of this nationalist myth, then, is seen in the early political contests, in crowd display and in the massive recruitment to the Regular army. But after the victories of mid-1900 enthusiasm waned; the displays of frenetic patriotism all but ceased. Middle class protest against the war gained ground, and skilled artisans in working men's clubs were prepared to listen to, and consider, the Boers' position. In municipal elections skilled workers turned increasingly away from imperial and towards social politics. Thus one worker commented that while a returning Volunteer was carried home shoulder-high

> 'crowds of people jostled and cheered him along in a mad frenzy of delight. . . . Soon after the celebrations, the hero became an ordinary man again who received only ordinary notice from the same people who had cheered him, which made me wonder whether he was a hero after all.'[111]

References

1. Noticed by Mayhew and many since, see E. P. Thompson and F. Yeo, *Unknown Mayhew*, London, 1973, 95–7. More recently, see R. Q. Gray, 'Styles of Life. The Labour Aristocracy and class relations in later nineteenth century Edinburgh', *International Review of Social History*, 18, 1973.
2. G. Stedman Jones, *Outcast London*, Oxford, 1971, 338.
3. J. A. Hobson, *The Psychology of Jingoism*, London, 1901, 3; J. A. Schumpeter, *Imperialism and Social Classes*, London, 1957, 17.
4. H. Pelling, *Popular Politics and Society in late Victorian Britain*, London, 1968, 87; R. Price, *An Imperial War and the British Working Class*, London, 1972.
5. A. L. Jenkyn-Brown, *Experiences in Birmingham Board Schools*, Birmingham, 1899, 17.
6. M. E. Sadler ed., *Moral Instruction and Training in Schools*, I, London, 1908, 323–4.
7. R. E. Hughes, *School Training*, 1905, 87; see also P. E. Barnett, *Common Sense in Education and Teaching*, 1902, 43.
8. P. C. McIntosh, *Physical Education in England since 1800*, London, 1952.
9. *Mr. Broscombe's Reports*, 2 March–8 September 1896, Birmingham Education Offices.
10. F. W. Hackwood, *Practical Methods of Class Management*, 1897, 20–1.
11. J. J. Findlay, *Principles of Class Teaching*, 1902, 88–9.
12. Charles Morley, *Studies in Board Schools*, 1897, 292.
13. 'Military Drill in Schools', *Journal of Education*, December, 1900, 748.
14. *King Edward Readers*, Standard V, 1901, 5–6.
15. V. E. Chancellor, *History for their Masters*, Oxford, 1970.
16. *Pitman's Readers*, 1901, 6.
17. E. E. Kellett, 'Teaching of Patriotism' in *Journal of Education*, March 1900, 18.
18. F. W. Hackwood, *Notes for Lessons on Moral Subjects. A Handbook for Teachers in Elementary Schools*, 1888 (etc).
19. See J. O. Springhall, 'Youth and Empire. A Study of the Propagation of Imperialism to the Young in Edwardian Britain', DPhil thesis, University of Sussex, 1968.
20. Statistics are drawn for this and for the following sections from *General Annual Return of the British Army*, and *Annual Return of the Volunteer Corps*, 1881–1904.
21. This is an important argument but impossible to develop here. See my PhD thesis, 'Nation, Empire and the Birmingham Working Class, 1899–1914', University of Birmingham, 1975, chapter 11.
22. Eg. posters in the National Army Museum, Accession Numbers 6412/151/1 and 6.
23. A. F. Corbett, *Service through Six Reigns, 1891–1958* (privately printed), Norwich, 1953.
24. Anon., *Experiences of a Soldier*, c1896, National Army Museum, Acc. No. 17008–13.
25. A British Officer, *Social Life in the British Army*, 1900, x.
26. See, for example, F. Richards, *Old Soldier Sahib*, London, 1966, 21.
27. *Royal Commission on the Militia and Volunteers*, Appendix, Cd. 2064, 1904, 210, question 2, referred to hereafter as *Norfolk Commission*.
28. *Norfolk Commission*, q. 18568.
29. 73·8 per cent skilled and labour 'aristocracy'; 12.8 per cent unskilled: *Norfolk Commission*, Appendix VIII, 253, q. 2.
30. *Norfolk Commission*, q. 7695, q. 11907.
31. Annual Dinner of the Handsworth Rifle Corps, *Birmingham Daily Gazette*, 27 February 1883.
32. South Staffordshire Regiment, *Handsworth News*, 10 March 1888.
33. *Norfolk Commission*, q. 9151.
34. *Reynolds News*, 12 January 1896.
35. A. P. Wadsworth, 'Newspaper Circulations, 1800–1954', *Transactions of the Manchester Statistical Society*, 1954–5, 25.
36. Sir J. A. Hammerton, *With Northcliffe in Fleet Street*, 1932, 118.
37. *Labour Leader*, 10 September 1898.
38. *Reynolds News*, 16 October and 30 October 1898.
39. Patricia Knight, 'British Public Opinion and the Rise of Imperialist Sentiment in Relation to Expansion in Africa, 1880–1900', PhD thesis, University of Warwick, 1968, 437–9.
40. *Contemporary Review*, January 1900.
41. *Daily Argus*, 5 September 1899.
42. *Sheffield and Rotherham Independent*, 12 October 1899.
43. H. J. Wilson Papers, Sheffield Library, MD2506, MS diary of events, 20 January 1900.
44. Criticized by the 'respectable' press, *Sheffield and Rotherham Independent*, 16 Oct. 1899.
45. *Birmingham Daily Mail*, 28 November 1899.
46. *Birmingham Daily Post*, 2 March 1900.
47. *Sheffield and Rotherham Independent*, 2 March 1900.
48. *Ibid.*
49. *Handsworth Herald*, 17 February 1900.
50. *Ibid.*, 26 May 1900.
51. *Ibid.*
52. H. J. Wilson Papers, Sheffield Library, MD2506.
53. *Midland Express*, 22 October 1901.

54. Eg. Clerkenwell, 25 July 1901, and Sheffield, 17 February 1902. In Battersea the pro-Boers took over a pro-war meeting, echoing their Borough Council's anti-war resolution of March 1901.
55. Other exceptions, Queens Hall, 19 June; Brighton, 22 Nov.; Derby, 9 Jan. 1902.
56. *Birmingham Daily Mail*, 11 December 1901.
57. *Birmingham Daily Post*, 17 December 1901.
58. S. C. Cronwright Schreiner, *Land of Free Speech*, 1906.
59. Price, chapter 4.
60. *Midland Express*, 19 December 1901.
61. D. McCormick, *Pedlar of Death. Life of Sir Basil Zaharoff*, London, 1965.
62. *Midland Express*, 20 December 1901–2 January 1902.
63. *Sheffield and Rotherham Independent*, 2 November 1899.
64. A traditional device, see R. McKenzie and A. Silver, *Angels in Marble. Working Class Conservatives in Urban England*, London, 1968, 51ff.
65. *Daily Argus*, 4 October 1900.
66. *Ibid.*, 19 September 1900.
67. Calculated from election returns in *The Times*.
68. *The Times*, 1 October 1900.
69. *Daily Argus*, 1 October 1900.
70. Price, chapter 3.
71. McKenzie and Silver, 89, 182–3.
72. Price, chapter 2.
73. *Sheffield and Rotherham Independent*, 17 February 1900.
74. *Birmingham Daily Post*, 2 January 1900.
75. Blanch, 363–6.
76. Correllation between recruitment and the unemployment index published in the *Labour Gazette* 1881–98 is +0.4766, which at the 5 per cent level is significant.
77. *Volunteer Service Gazette*, 5 January 1900; local newspapers 24 December–5 January.
78. Price, 256.
79. *Norfolk Commission*, q. 16486.
80. *Volunteer Service Gazette*, 22 December 1899.
81. *Norfolk Commission*, 253.
82. *Volunteer Service Gazette*, 29 December 1899.
83. *Norfolk Commission*, q. 5336 and q. 5331.
84. *Volunteer Service Gazette*, 22 December 1899.
85. See also *Norfolk Commission*, q. 6085, for a sample of those volunteering from the LNW Railway – 81 per cent working class.
86. Price, 258.
87. *Midland Express*, 2 January 1901, quoting a Birmingham recruiting sergeant.
88. *Ibid.*, 22 January 1901.
89. Unless Militia Reserve. At least 75 per cent of the unit had to volunteer, and this decision was not binding on those who wished to stay behind.
90. 1 122 692. Totally discounts the Militia Reserve, and the Militia who did not go abroad eg. the young soldiers and the men who voted against going. Thus it is an underestimate because we cannot tell how many eventually joined the Regular army.
91. F. Willis, *Peace and Dripping Toast*, London, 1950, 133.
92. E. S. Turner, *Boys will be Boys*, London, 1948, 173.
93. F. P. Gibbon, *A History of the Heyrod Street Lads' Club and of the 5th Manchester Company, the Boys Brigade 1899–1910*, Manchester, 1911, 43.
94. *Brigade*, December 1899.
95. Jewish Lads' Brigade, Manchester Battalion, *Annual Reports 1899–1903*, 1903, 22–3.
96. Knott Mill Institute, *Inauguration Ceremony*, Manchester, 8 March 1900, 5; Hulme Lads' Club, *Annual Report*, 1900, 7.
97. *Sheffield and Rotherham Independent*, 25 January 1900.
98. National Film Archive (NFA), 'A Skirmish with the Boers near Kimberley', c1900.
99. NFA, 'Boers attack a Red Cross Hospital' and 'The Despatch Bearer', c1900.
100. NFA, 'A Prize Fight between John Bull and President Kruger', c1900.
101. *Caste*, 5 March–26 March 1900.
102. Tivoli Theatre of Varieties (Birmingham), *Programmes*, 2 December 1901, 3 March 1902.
103. *Ibid.*, 5 May 1902.
104. *Ibid.*, 21 July 1902.
105. Metropole Theatre (Birmingham), *Programmes*, 12 October 1908.
106. Richard Hoggart, *Uses of Literacy*, London, 1971, 165–6.
107. G. Gainer, *Alien Invasion*, London, 1972, 67–73.
108. Hoggart, 135.
109. Robert Roberts, *The Classic Slum*, London, 1971, 69; Hoggart, 134–5; Price, 4.
110. Roberts, 69.
111. V. W. Garratt, *Man in the Street*, London, 1939, 63–4.

CHAPTER 10

The Pro-Boers in Britain

Bernard Porter

Introduction

Whether or not the South African War really was a 'popular' war in Britain, it was widely assumed to be so at the time, even by those who opposed it. The assumption was natural: the press was predominantly for the war; so was the majority in Parliament; and as for the wider public, so far as its real opinion could be guessed at, the fact that anti-war meetings were invariably howled down, and pro-war demonstrations never, indicated a very pronounced bias in favour of the war. The tiny eccentric minority which seemed to comprise the anti-war section of the population for the most part accepted the appearance of things, and took its comfort mainly from the hope that the majority would recover its wits soon. 'I have great faith in the good sense of my countrymen', said the radical MP Henry Labouchere shortly after the beginning of the war; 'they may be fooled for a short time, but not for long.'[1] During the first year of the hostilities at least, the war's opponents were certainly outshouted, and by most politicians it was accepted that they were greatly outnumbered too.[2]

Yet there can be little doubt that really it was more a matter of noise than of numbers. Before the war had begun government ministers had been very far from confident that a war in South Africa would find general favour with the public, which seemed more critical than otherwise of their diplomacy with the Boers.[3] When the war finally broke out that criticism was to a large extent muted, but not converted. Throughout the war there were far more critics of Chamberlain's South African policy than expressed their criticism openly. They restrained themselves for a number of reasons: out of a sense of group loyalty – the nation was at war, there was an enemy on British soil, consequently criticism had to be suspended and the nation act as one until the war had been won; out of a feeling of impotence – 'the public,' wrote the Liberal leader Campbell-Bannerman wearily to one of his flock, 'are not in the humour for party speeches';[4] out of concern for Liberal party unity, which was very much under threat over the issue of the war; or out of simple cowardice. For if there may have been some doubt as to the extent of pro-war feeling, there could be no doubt at all of its passion. Outspoken critics of the war had windows and property smashed, noses bloodied, and meetings broken up by drunken mobs, while the police merely looked on, and the government, when it was appealed to, regretted it but hinted that really the critics had only themselves to blame, if they would persist in expressing such treacherous and offensive opinions.[5] It was an unsympathetic time for lovers of peace. Not everyone who was unsure about the morality of the war was prepared to venture his hand into this furnace. Those who were so prepared were the 'pro-Boers'. It was this willingness to persist in their opposition to the war in spite of the circumstances – occasionally, one suspects, *because* of them, by those who relished (and may have exaggerated) the persecution – which to a great extent distinguished them from the rest.

The name 'pro-Boer' was not otherwise an exact political category. It was given to them – and to many others who deserved it very much less – by their political opponents, to emphasize the sense of betrayal which was associated with the stand they took. In strict terms, however, it was a misnomer, and was generally indignantly rejected by those to whom it was applied. Their opponents charged them with effectively aiding the Boer cause by their attitude, which it was claimed encouraged the Boers to hope for a crumbling of the British resolve against them. But very few of them – apart from the Irish Nationalists, for their own reasons – wanted the Boers to win. If they had they would have voted in Parliament against supplies for the war. In the event only two or three very peripheral Liberals ever did during its first (and most difficult) fifteen months: though the war was wrong and should be stopped it could not be *lost*, and consequently, said Labouchere, 'we cannot refuse to give them arms, and ammunition, and pay for the soldiers.'[6] Neither did they sympathize very greatly with the Boers' cause. Of course there was a measure of support for them, some of it going back many years to the time of the earlier Transvaal War, or before. They were, after all, white, and Protestant, and underdogs: in any other situation – if their foes, for example, had been France or Germany, or a Zulu impi – it might have come naturally to Britons to be on their side. And most of the pro-Boers made a point of vigorously rebutting the grosser calumnies against the Boers' character. Some of them even admitted to a certain admiration for their courage, for their 'high and splendid faith',[7] and for the political virtues of the Orange Free State. But this was not usual. By far more of the pro-Boers that 'splendid faith' was regarded as mere bigotry, and the politics of the Transvaal itself seen as reactionary and corrupt. In part this attitude may have been dictated by the pressures of the time. The popular image of the Boer was already firmly set, and was a highly unflattering one. It may have been too pervasive to hope to dispel. The more opportune course, therefore, was to concede at least some of his imperfections, which anyway were not germane to the pro-Boers' case. 'Nobody', declared the young Liberal pro-Boer G. P. Gooch, 'maintains that the government of the Transvaal is satisfactory';[8] not even Labouchere, to whom it appeared to be 'a thorough Conservative government' – so much so that 'if he had been there he would in all probability have been an opponent of Mr Kruger.'[9] 'It is undeniable', wrote one anti-war journalist,

> 'that many of the [Uitlanders'] grievances were vexatious, and that a wise government would have removed them. But the Transvaal government was not a wise one. It was obstinate, narrow, and to a certain extent corrupt.'[10]

But that did not matter. To become a pro-Boer did not require one to support in any way at all any aspect of the life and politics of the Boer republics. What it did require was a conviction that the faults of the republics did not justify war with them, and that consequently the war should be stopped.

Opposition to the war was frequently portrayed as an act of national betrayal. In this cartoon from Punch, *11 December 1901, the anti-war faction is accused of prolonging the war by encouraging the Boers to hold out.*

A war of aggression

The pro-Boers shared with the other, more numerous but less conspicuous, critics of the war the belief that the war had been forced on the Boer republics by the British government. This was in spite of certain inconvenient facts: that for example it was the Boers, and not Britain, who had issued the ultimatum which had set the match to the fire; and that the Boers when the war started revealed themselves to be well prepared for it – all of which, in Campbell-Bannerman's experience, made the pro-Boer case a difficult one to put over.[11] But they did have a case: which was, essentially, that Britain had harassed the Boers into issuing their ultimatum by an aggressive diplomacy which fully justified their arming in their own defence. Consequently the responsibility for the war was Britain's, and not the Boer republics'. From Britain's standpoint it was not a defensive war but an offensive one. As well as this, it was unnecessary. It was being fought ostensibly because the republics refused to redress certain grievances. But those grievances (said the pro-Boers) were exaggerated, anyway had been nine-tenths conceded by the Boer governments, and even if they had not been were not worth going to war over. The question could have been settled amicably. That it had not been was the fault of Chamberlain's and Milner's abrasive styles of diplomacy. Either they had been incompetent; or they had been bluffing and their bluff had been called; or the Uitlander grievances were really a cloak to cover their real designs, which all along had been secretly set against the independence of the republics. This last explanation was the one which was generally favoured. Milner certainly, and Chamberlain probably, had purposely caused the pre-war negotiations to fail, because they had wanted more than they professed to demand. What they had wanted was to annex the Boer republics. If the negotiations had succeeded they would have been left without a pretext to do this. Only war gave them the opportunity.

The capitalist conspiracy theory

Some of the pro-Boers stopped there: but many went further. Although Chamberlain and Milner were greatly to blame in this affair, they were not necessarily at the bottom of it. Behind them were the capitalists. That capitalists loomed so very large in pro-Boer propaganda was not surprising. It did not require a particular grievance against the capitalist system, or any unusual proclivity to conspiracy theories of politics, for a pro-Boer to see a capitalist conspiracy at work here. The Jameson Raid had been a capitalist conspiracy. South Africa's most active imperialist, Cecil Rhodes, was a notorious capitalist conspirator. The whole of the Transvaal problem was to do with gold mining, and gold mining companies, on the Rand. 'If the Rand had been a potato field instead of a goldfield,' said one MP in 1899 – and the assertion was incontestible – 'there would have been no war.'[12] In fact scarcely anybody at all pretended that capitalists were not involved in some way. What the pro-Boers contended was that they were involved to the extent of pushing the British government into a war which was

The pro-Boers had to contend with a public image of the Afrikaner that was, to say the least, unflattering. This picture of the capture of Cronjé and his wife at Paardeberg appeared in the Illustrated London News, *28 April 1900.*

not justified in the national interest, in order to line their own pockets. The mining magnates and the financiers who funded them wished to free themselves from what they regarded as oppressive Boer taxation, and also to free themselves to recruit cheap African labour, in order to reduce the costs of gold mining and hence increase their profits. They were powerful men: they directly owned most of the South African press, could influence much of the British press, and had the sympathetic ear of the High Commissioner and the Colonial Secretary. By these men, with their methods of 'bribery, blackmailing, organized espionage, political and social coercion', and their 'disregard of every kind of moral principle',[13] the *Manchester Guardian* claimed that 'from the time of the Jameson Raid until today British policy in South Africa has been more or less successfully "rigged" '.[14] The war was their doing; it was in fact 'a war for the meanest and most mercenary of ends and aims which ever prompted conquest or aggression';[15] an unjust war, 'waged on behalf of capitalists',[16] and to the detriment of the real interest of the nation as a whole.

'New Imperialism'

This anti-capitalist line against the war, like most of the other arguments used against it, did not originate in the war itself, but went back a little before it. By both its supporters and its opponents the war was seen not as an isolated event, but as the culmination of a succession of events in South Africa and elsewhere, under which there lay a broad movement of politics which was known at the time as the 'New Imperialism'. The New Imperialism was already the subject of a lively debate before the war came along. In this debate were forged most of the attitudes and arguments of the war years. The anti-capitalist argument was one. A controversy had been going on for some time over whether colonial annexations benefited Britain economically: whether 'trade followed the flag'. Old-fashioned Liberals maintained that it did not. It was this conviction that the New Imperialism was 'uneconomic' which led the rather less old-fashioned Liberal economist J. A. Hobson to speculate why, in that case, it was persisted in; and in 1898 to come up with an answer: that it was because certain special sections of the capitalist community were able to manipulate policy away from the national economic interest, to further – at the expense of it – their own profits.[17] To this theory the South African War appeared to come as a dramatic confirmation, the more telling because it had been, in a way, predicted.

For nearly everybody who opposed the war – even those who did not share the view that its capitalist aspect was central – a great deal of their distaste for it derived from this association of it with what they (and many others) regarded as one of capitalism's less acceptable faces. Likewise, it was from those sections of informed public opinion which found this kind of thing most distasteful that by and large the leading opponents of the war were likely to be drawn. They included of course the bulk of the Labour movement. The Labour movement has been accused of being tardy and half-hearted in its opposition to the war at this time, restrained by the fear that its rank and file might be prey to baser emotions than its leadership felt were respectable. In fact the Labour press (with one exception) was consistently against the war from the beginning, as were nearly all Labour MPs, who could be the most scathing and savage of all the critics in Parliament of this 'capitalist war'. What is true, however, is that Labour was not in the forefront of the organized pro-Boer agitation: partly because it felt it had no real common cause with the middle class Liberals who led it (or they with it); partly also because Labour leaders tended to regard their primary concern as lying elsewhere, in social questions which they suspected the war was to a great extent intended to distract them from. Labour spoke against the war, but neither took any great part in the *movement* against the war, nor organized one of its own.

Those who objected to the 'capitalist' nature of the war also included a large section of the Liberal Party, by whom the character of the pro-Boer movement was really set. Nineteenth-century Liberals of course could hardly be expected to be as

The socialist case against the war was that it was the fruit of a capitalist conspiracy, designed merely to line the pockets of unscrupulous millionaires like Rhodes, or faceless foreign (or Jewish) speculators, at the cost of working class lives. These cartoons are from the Labour Leader, *16 December 1899 and 17 March 1900.*

THE ALCHEMY OF COMMERCIALISM.

THE SOLDIERS OF THE ——?

Liberals also distrusted the financial agencies they saw making profit from the war. This caricature of 'The Throgmorton-street Patriot' appeared in the Westminster Gazette, *23 December 1899.*

II.—The Throgmorton-street Patriot.

"Buy 'em, my vrend, buy 'em till you're black in the face. Vy, it'll be all over in a veck ven ve get out there."

full-bloodedly 'anti-capitalist' as socialists; but some of the more radical ones were far from happy with certain contemporary flowerings of the capitalist plant, which appeared to them to be grotesque mutations of it. There was among them for example a considerable prejudice, almost medieval in its nature, against certain types of capitalists: the types who instead of manufacturing or selling things made their money by financial speculation, the more so when they were, or could be presented as being, foreigners or Jews. To a great extent Liberal (and socialist) opposition to the war in South Africa may have been coloured, as some of its propaganda was, by anti-semitism: though it was not a very virulent strain of anti-semitism, and was probably not at the root of the pro-Boers' disapproval of the capitalists who were claimed to have fomented the war, which arose from their activities, rather than from their supposed race or religion.[18] This distrust of their activities was very deep-rooted. In a way they appeared to negate the whole of the Liberals' capitalist ethic. For decades international capitalism had been fondly regarded by Liberals as fundamentally inimical both to colonial expansion and to war. One of the basic premises of classical political economy was that the needs of everyone in the world were best served by the free operation of the laws of supply, demand and the division of labour among nations. From this it followed that anything that interrupted trade, like war, or attempted to 'corner' it, like colonialism, was incompatible with it. This South African kind of capitalism, therefore, which was the ally both of colonialism and of war, was a perversion of the true spirit. It was hostile to the real interests of the economic system, and to morality, with which the system was supposed to be entirely consistent.

'the heathen Deity Mars'

The moral element was very prominent in the anti-war case. What was supposed to mark off most clearly the capitalists who had brought on the war from the general run of capitalists – as it also marked off the 'New Imperalists' from older kinds of imperalist – was their complete and cynical amorality. For those who believed, as one Liberal professed in 1901, 'that there is a moral law for nations as well as for individuals', the war appeared quite simply as 'absolutely wrong and a crime'.[19] The most intransigent of the pro-Boer MPs, the old prohibitionist Sir Wilfrid Lawson, saw in it a turn away from his God, the Prince of Peace, towards 'the heathen Deity Mars'; 'from what is going on,' he told the House of Commons in October 1899, 'I think the religious world is rapidly losing all power over the people of this country.'[20] It also indicated a turn away from another of the Liberals' deities: from the late and very much lamented William Ewart Gladstone, and the 'grand old Liberal cause' which he had embodied.[21] Liberal pro-Boers tended to be the reactionaries within the Liberal Party. The new, vigorous, progressive shoot of the Liberal tree was the 'Liberal Imperialist' one, which Lord Rosebery (from a distance) was tending and watering and prophesying would in the future 'control the destinies of this country'.[22] The section from which the pro-Boers were mainly recruited was generally older, in years[23] and also in its fashions. For many years now it had been struggling to keep the Liberal Party unsullied by illiberal sirens who had already (in 1886) carried one large section of the party away, and were now threatening to seduce the whole. Their task they saw as a restorative one: to revive the old values, 'to keep touch with the great and ennobling ideas of the past',[24] and to help 'the principles of Gladstone and Bright' to 'triumph once more'.[25] Since Gladstone's departure they had no one of even remotely comparable stature to lead them. They were a routed army left with a few lieutenants but no general; defiant still, but demoralized. Their stand on the question of the war was an expression of their dissatisfaction, not only with the war, but also with the contemporary tendency of politics as a whole. To outsiders however they appeared as survivals from the past, elderly fundamentalists, naive and even cranky idealists who were essentially out of touch with the times. Sometimes they appeared like this even to themselves.

"SO PERPLEXING!"

OLD LIBERAL PARTY. "OH, DEARY ME! WHICH PLATFORM SHALL I TAKE?"

AN ALMOST EXTINCT SPECIES!

["The remains of a prehistoric animal were dug up close to the City Liberal Club a few days ago." *Daily Paper.*]

WAS IT THE OSAPLESADÕNT (PHILANTHROPOD MAJUBATHERIUM) OR SHELL-LESS DISARMADILLO!?

Above left: the divisions in the Liberal Party are illustrated by this cartoon from Punch, *1 August 1900. Rosebery and Harcourt were regarded as the heads of the 'Liberal Imperialist' and 'pro-Boer' sections of the party; Campbell-Bannerman was trying to steer a middle reconciliatory course.*

Above right: government supporters liked the pro-Boers to be seen as a small minority of old-fashioned eccentrics. This caricature appeared in Punch, *19 September 1900.*

It was a curious collaboration, this: between old-fashioned Liberalism looking for guidance to a golden age in the past, and the newer socialist fashion, whose golden age was yet to come. Both however shared common attitudes: Liberals sharing with the socialists their anti-capitalism, and Labour sharing with the Liberals their Christian moralism. Although it drew such strength from Christianity, however, the pro-Boer movement was given no institutional backing at all by any significant sect or section of the Christian Church. There were many Christian ministers who gave their support to the pro-Boer cause, including some bishops: but there were more who took the 'patriotic' side. ('Nowhere', said Keir Hardie at this time, 'is Mammon more firmly seated than in the church.'[26]) Neither were the humanitarian societies much more helpful: except in significantly refusing their sanction to the government's claim, which was quite frequently made in justification of the war, that the British were better in their treatment of Africans than were the Boers. In fact (the Aborigines Protection Society ruled in 1901), there was not much to choose between them, and indeed it might be that the Boers' way of dealing with them was preferable in many ways to the 'wage slavery' that was contemplated for them by the 'Randlords'.[27] This provided useful ammunition for the pro-Boers; but otherwise the humanitarian societies took no part in the anti-war agitation: which, of course, it was no part of their function to do. The organization of the pro-Boer movement, therefore – in so far as it was 'organized' – was entirely *ad hoc*, and political. It was centred chiefly around two 'committees': a 'Transvaal Committee', which was superseded (but not replaced) by the 'South African Conciliation Committee' after the war had begun, and a 'Stop the War Committee'. The membership of these committees included some clergymen, businessmen and academics, but was predominately made up of backbench MPs and political journalists. They arranged meetings, sent out lecturers, and published many hundreds of anti-war pamphlets, mostly reiterating the same arguments.[28] The cause had some help too from other political organizations with wider briefs, such as the National Reform Union and the new (in February 1900) League of Liberals against Aggression and Militarism. It was supported by a few newspapers: most of the Labour weeklies, a few London dailies (the *Chronicle* early on, the *Morning Leader* and, from 1901, the *Daily News*), and among the provincial dailies the *Manchester Guardian*. These carried the weight of the offensive against the government, and also drew the main brunt (reflected for the newspapers in declining circulation figures)[29] of the jingo fire.

Below left: stop-the-war meetings often encountered violence, especially during the spring of 1900. From Punch, *4 April 1900.*

Below right: pro-Boers were also depicted as cowards, and in some circles the disruption of their meetings was positively relished. From Punch, *20 July 1900.*

"Whatever have you been doing with yourself, Murphy? You look all broken up!"
"Well, yer 'Anner, I wint to wan iv thim 'Shtop-the-War' Meetings lasht noight!"

Scene.—*A Pro-Boer Meeting. Riotous Opposition making itself felt.*
Orator. "Gentlemen, we do not disguise from Ourselves the Fact that Ours is not a Popular Cause. But that does not discourage Us. We shall continue to stand up fearlessly to the Last, to battle for the Thing we believe to be right." (*Uproar*) * * * (*hastily to his Neighbour*) "Quick—tell me, which is the Back Door to this Hall?"

The differences between the anti-war committees were less ideological than stylistic. The Stop the War Committee was dominated by the famous investigative journalist of the day W. T. Stead, who had never been known to pull his punches – in the past more often in the cause of militarism than against it – and whose brashness rubbed off on the Committee too. Members of the other committees felt that the Stop the War Committee's 'extremism' did more harm than good to their common cause. The South African Conciliation Committee, which included a number of renegade Unionists among its members (including its president, Leonard Courtney), strove for a more moderate, reasonable tone. The Conciliation Committee favoured a negotiated settlement of the war; the Stop the War Committee wanted it stopped immediately and unilaterally. Both assumed that there would be no difficulty about stopping the war, and no damage to Britain's interests in doing so. After all it was Britain who had started the war, Britain alone who wished to prolong it, and Britain who was the only combatant whose ambitions went beyond the *status quo ante*. Consequently it would only require Britain to 'show willing' for the whole war to come to an end almost at once.

'methods of barbarism'

As the war went on, without any sign of coming to an end, the pro-Boers added another string to their bow: which was criticism of the methods by which it was being prosecuted. In February 1901 a motion was put to the House of Commons (and overwhelmingly defeated) condemning

> '. . . the wholesale burning of farmhouses, the wanton destruction and looting of private property, the driving of women and children out of their homes without shelter or the provision of food, and the confinement of women and children in prison camps',

all of which was stigmatized as 'in the highest degree disgraceful and dishonouring to a nation professing to be Christian'.[30] By the Liberal leader four months later it was called 'methods of barbarism'[31], in a famous phrase which was taken at the time to mark Campbell-Bannerman's final adhesion to the pro-Boer wing of his party. From the winter of 1900–1 onwards, in fact, more and more Liberals who previously had refrained from committing themselves began to poke their heads up over the tops of their trenches, and to commit themselves on the pro-Boer side: provoked into that action, perhaps, by their resentment at the tactics which had been used against them in the 'khaki election' of the previous autumn, and especially at the Unionists' rather indiscriminate use of the epithet 'pro-Boer' against even the most meticulously 'loyal' of them. If they were to be tarred with that brush anyway, they might as well deserve it. As well as this, the further the war was prolonged, the more distant became the original fount of difference between the

pro-Boers and others; and the more weary people became of the war. There was a great deal here on which pro-Boers could unite once again with all those sections of political opinion which were not ineluctably shackled to the government. They could unite, for example, in criticizing the conduct of the war for its ineptness (although some pro-Boers refused to be drawn into this on the grounds that it would imply that they wanted the war to be prosecuted harder).[32] And they could unite in their criticisms of 'methods of barbarism', on the grounds that those methods would merely alienate their enemy, and consequently prolong the war and then put at risk all chances of a lasting peace, which, as pro- and anti-Boer Liberals now came together to point out, could only really be founded on the Boers' goodwill.[33]

A villainous French caricature of British treatment of Boer women and children, published in September 1901. As the prosecution of the war became progressively more ruthless and drew increasing criticism both at home and abroad, the pro-Boers could unite to condemn British 'methods of barbarism' and the 'unnecessary' prolongation of the war.

Consequently, towards the end of the war the pro-Boer strain in British politics became less defensive, more confident, and probably more significant – but also less distinctive; transmuted and mingled with other strains, so that it lost its original purity. Pro-Boers became the advocates of generous peace terms for the Boers: which Rosebery too was now recommending.[34] When the war ended they led the cry for responsible government in the newly-annexed colonies: again with the support of the Liberal Imperialists with whom now they appeared to be perfectly in tune. Apart from Rosebery, who for reasons that were not altogether clear to anybody at the time decided to cut himself off from it, the Liberal Party came together again on the basis of a version of imperialism which they could all share and agree on. For very few of the Liberal pro-Boers had ever been 'anti-imperialists' in an absolute sense. Campbell-Bannerman had not been able to see what the war had to do with 'imperialism' anyway: those who opposed it opposed it on its merits; those who supported it 'have all along repudiated the notion of our wanting to grab anything'.[35] He strongly denied that he was hostile to the British empire, as did most of the leading Liberal pro-Boers. 'If Imperialism', said one of them in January 1900,

> 'means sober pride in the great Empire we control, a most earnest desire to knit together in the bonds of friendship the various populations that belong to it, a firm determination to preserve the integrity of our Empire at all costs, and the using of the means of advancing civilization among all kinds and conditions of men – then there is no one more of an Imperialist than I am.'[36]

What they had objected to was the 'new' imperialism, which was something different, and something which, in the often reiterated opinion of many of them, was more likely to weaken the empire than to strengthen it. James Bryce in February 1900 claimed that by provoking the war the government had struck a heavy blow against Britain's imperial interests: for the 'best and surest foundation' for imperial strength and unity was 'the affection of our fellow-subjects'.[37] 'I want us', said Labouchere a year later, 'to have a colony which will be a strength, and not a weakness, to the Empire.'[38] The Labour MP Keir Hardie took the same line: 'You cannot build up an Empire of free peoples by force.'[39] And as the war went on, and Chamberlain's flower faded, many of the self-styled imperialists within the Liberal party found themselves basically in sympathy with this position too. To one of them, for example, who regarded his Liberal Imperialism as 'inherent', and the British empire as 'infinitely the most important impersonal consideration on earth', it had come to appear by January 1902 that the government had done 'great disservices to the best kind of imperialism'.[40] This 'best kind of imperialism' came to be the formula for reconciliation, the common ground on which both sections of the party could meet. The Liberal pro-Boers had only ever really objected to one particular element in Chamberlain's imperialism, which was the force implicit in it. Consequently when, later, that element of force appeared to be removed, by the Boers' voluntary acceptance of a position within the new British South African Union whereby they could govern themselves (and their blacks), the rest was easy. The Liberal pro-Boers' 'anti-imperialism' proved to be wholly compatible with the 'imperialism' of their old foes within the party: who also preferred, in this instance, imperialism by consent if they could get it, rather than at the point of the sword. So the problem that had divided them receded, and the voice of pro-Boerism became lost in a kind of Liberal imperialist consensus.

The pro-Boers' influence

For this reason it is not easy to isolate and assess the effect that the pro-Boers may have had on policy. While they were still pro-Boers and most on the defensive, during the first few months of the war, they can have had very little. Government ministers and the pro-government press regarded them (or affected to regard them) as unimportant, unrepresentative of opinion as a whole: a very light breeze indeed, and consequently not needing to be trimmed to. The most that could be said at this time was that they required to be *answered*, and so at least forced the government into justifying its policies, especially against the 'capitalist conspiracy' charge, which it clearly regarded as dangerously plausible. They were also vilified a great deal: which may have indicated on the part of their opponents a less than complete confidence in their impotence. After the first flush of the war passed, the pro-Boers' power to irritate appears to have increased. As the war became more and more protracted, so were their propositions given time to sink in, and maybe to strike home among the uncommitted. The *Annual Register*, which had tended before to play them down a great deal, reported that from about the spring of 1900 popular resentment against them cooled, so that 'by degrees' they now 'came to be regarded with good humoured indifference', and their arguments were 'listened to with more attention'.[41] As this happened the tone of confident contempt with which government ministers had felt able to address them in the past wavered a little. A bitterness crept into debates in Parliament which had not been there before. The khaki election of October 1900 was fought with considerable acrimony on both sides, which may have been born partly of the government's feeling that things were no longer going all its own way in the propaganda war. Chamberlain was more liable to become ruffled in exchanges with pro-Boers in Parliament.[42] At the end of the autumn session of 1900 Labouchere felt that at least they had 'singed the government's wing'.[43] And yet the army went on fighting, and fighting 'hard', if not to the point of unconditional surrender, then to a point very close to it. The government was not deflected from its purpose by the pro-Boers, however keenly it may, towards the end, have felt the pin-pricks which assailed it from their direction.

A Lilliputian Keir Hardie measures up to Chamberlain. Newspapers commonly derided the feebleness of the government's critics, but this cartoon, from the Evening News *in 1900, does no great injustice to Hardie.*

If the pro-Boers were materially effective at all, then it was after the war had come to an end, when the constraints on criticism of 'the nation under arms' were lifted, and it was revealed how shallow was the reservoir of real support in the country for 'imperialism' of the Chamberlain type. If the South African War was allowed to carry on to its bitter end, there was never another war like it. The Unionist government continued in power for another three and a half years, but only on the parliamentary majority it had won in the khaki election of 1900. The climate quite suddenly had become colder for it. When the next clear chance of an imperial annexation came up in 1904 (in Tibet) the government forwent it, on the grounds that this kind of thing was no longer in keeping with the public mood. In 1906 it was quite spectacularly defeated at the polls by a Liberal Party still led by the 'pro-Boer' Campbell-Bannerman; and very soon afterwards its solution for the continuing South African problem was rejected too, in favour of a policy strongly tinged with the 'reconciliatory' philosophy of the pro-Boers. And the pro-Boers themselves, as individuals, did not do so badly afterwards. During the war it had not been comfortable to be one of them, but in the long run it turned out to be worth it. For most of the leading pro-Boers these were the last battle-scars they would be able to boast, at the end of long Liberal careers. For a few others, however, this was where they won their spurs. They included two future prime ministers, in David Lloyd George and James Ramsay MacDonald. Their 'treachery' in 1900 (like MacDonald's again in 1914) did them no lasting harm at all.

Pro-Boerism therefore came very much into its own after the end of the war. But it was not by its own, unaided efforts. It was not as if the pro-Boers had in any way 'converted' the country, or even the Liberal Party. In the first place the country may not have needed converting to any very great extent. During the war it had appeared more 'imperialistic' and militaristic than it was now: but that was very largely because, as we have seen, it *was* wartime, which had the effect of obscuring the real degree of opposition and apathy there was in the country towards the 'New' Imperialism. In the second place, to the extent that the country was converted, it was likely to have been the war itself which did it, and especially its long wearisome perpetuation: which cooled popular ardour much more effectively, by bringing home to people the perils of an aggressive policy, than could any mere argument at all. Thirdly: it was not in the end pro-Boerism which triumphed, but a kind of Liberal imperialism which may have been leavened by pro-Boerism (and also by the circumstances of the time), but was also very greatly affected by the other, imperialist strain in Liberal thinking at the time, to which therefore was due at least as much of the credit. Only those aspects of pro-Boer thinking became effective which could be reconciled with Liberal imperialism: which most aspects of pro-Boer thinking could be, once the war, which was the only question over which there was a fundamental difference between them, was out of the way.

If this was the extent of the pro-Boers' influence on the dominant, establishment politics of the day, however, there were other areas of politics where its impact may have been greater. If Liberals by and large returned to type after the war, the Labour movement did not to quite the same extent. Forced by the magnitude of the South African War to give close attention to the phenomenon of imperialism almost for the first time, those sections of the Labour movement which were represented in Parliament never entirely abandoned this interest: Ramsay MacDonald in particular maintained it for many years afterwards. Like the Liberals, Labour MPs very rarely translated their pro-Boerism into an out-and-out anti-imperialism. Nevertheless their attitude was more fundamentally critical of imperialism than was the Liberals', partly because of the greater attraction for them of the 'capitalist conspiracy' theory, which some Liberals shared, but not quite so monolithically as Labour. We have seen that the 'economic theory' of imperialism did not originate in the South African War, or even as a *critical* explanation of imperialism: originally, it was a theory advanced by capitalists themselves, in support of colonial expansion. What the South African War did was not to reveal 'capitalist imperialism', but to give a bad name to it, and to provide the 'economic theory' of imperialism with its most convincing practical corroboration. For J. A. Hobson, the pro-Boer who pointed this lesson most clearly in the pages of the *Manchester Guardian* and then in a series of books and articles he wrote about the war and its context at this time, the war provided 'an illumination to my understanding of the real relations between economics and politics . . . the simplest and plainest example of the interplay of political and economic motives in Imperialism'.[44] Hobson's explanation of imperialism, born out so clearly as it seemed to be by this affair, was widely influential at the time among Liberals who learnt from it to try to cleanse *their* imperialism of its corrupt, exploitative aspects if they could; and among socialists who took it to place imperialism in its proper economic and historical perspective. After the war 'economic imperialism' could never again appear the same. Its supporters were pushed on to the ideological defensive: a defence which was very successfully maintained for a long time, but a defence all the same. This the war had done, helped in a small measure by those who during it had opposed it, and made the anti-capitalist point then: the pro-Boers.

The pro-Boers, however, were less effective than they were right. They were not right in everything. Whether their analysis of the causes of the war was correct or not is still a matter of controversy, though much of it has become generally accepted since their time. Whether their judgment of its *morality* was justified or not is also still essentially debatable, though it would not probably be debated very long today. On some things they were almost certainly wrong: such as their attitude towards the 'native question', which they believed would not essentially be affected by the war, and tended at the time (though less afterwards) to underestimate the importance of. About one thing, however, they were right: this was the long-term effect of the war on Britain's position in South Africa. Shortly after the beginning of the war F. C. Selous, a well-known big-game hunter who was also a pro-Boer, wrote to *The Times* a letter which quite accurately predicted what would happen if the war were persisted with. 'In that case', he wrote,

> 'we shall have entered upon a course which, though it may give us the goldfields of the Transvaal for the present and the immediate future, will infallibly lose us the whole of South Africa as a British possession within the lifetime of many men who are now living.'[45]

That was the kernel of the pro-Boers' case during the war; and it turned out to be true.

References

1. *Parliamentary Debates*, 4th Series (4PD), vol. 77, c. 637, 25 October 1899.
2. But not by most Labour MPs, see for example Henry Broadhurst in the same debate: 4PD, 77, c. 672.
3. See R. E. Robinson and J. A. Gallagher, *Africa and the Victorians*, London, 1961, 444.
4. Campbell-Bannerman Papers, British Museum (BM), Add. Ms. 41214, f.62, Campbell-Bannerman to J. E. Ellis, 1 November 1899.
5. See 4PD, 80, cc. 926–9, Balfour, 15 March 1900.
6. 4PD, 88, c. 587, 11 December 1900.
7. A. M. S. Methuen, *Peace or War in South Africa*, London, 1901, 144.
8. G. P. Gooch, *The War and its Causes*, London, 1900, 26.
9. 4PD, 88, c. 224, 7 December 1900.
10. Methuen, 66.
11. H. Gladstone Papers, BM, Add. Ms. 45987 f.37, Campbell-Bannerman to Herbert Gladstone, 10 November 1899.
12. 4PD, 77, c. 534, Duckworth, 23 October 1899.
13. F. R. Statham, *South Africa and the Transvaal; the story of a conspiracy*, London, 1900, 7.
14. *Manchester Guardian*, 20 March 1901, 5.
15. 4PD, 77, c. 620, Davitt, 25 October 1899.
16. 4PD, 78, c. 529, Bryn Roberts, 2 February 1900.
17. J. A. Hobson, 'Free Trade and Foreign Policy', *Contemporary Review*, August 1898.
18. For a discussion of the role of anti-semitism in the thought of J. A. Hobson, see Colin Holmes, 'J. A. Hobson and the Jews', in *Immigrants and Minorities in British Society*, London, 1978.
19. 4PD, 89, cc. 190–1, Pirie, 15 February 1901.
20. 4PD, 77, c. 767, 27 October 1899.
21. *The Times*, 28 March 1900, 8, reporting Spence-Watson's speech to a meeting of the National Liberal Federation.
22. *Annual Register*, 1899, 220, reporting Rosebery's speech at Bath on 27 October.
23. See I. Sellars, 'The Pro-Boer Movement in Liverpool', *Transactions of the Unitarian Historical Society*, 12, 2 (1960), 81.
24. Campbell-Bannerman Papers, BM, Add. Ms. 41213, f.22, F. A. Channing to Campbell-Bannerman, 11 November 1899.
25. *Ibid.*, f.12, F. A. Channing to Campbell-Bannerman, 8 November 1899.
26. *Keir Hardie's Speeches and Writings*, London, 1928, 101.
27. See *The Aborigines' Friend*, 6, 1 (1901), report of Annual General Meeting.
28. See J. S. Galbraith, 'The Pamphlet Campaign on the Boer War', *Journal of Modern History*, 24, 2 (1952).
29. See Stephen Koss, *The Pro-Boers*, London, 1973, xxxi.
30. 4PD, 89, c. 1265, 26 February 1901.
31. In a speech at a dinner at the National Reform Union, 14 June 1901: see J. A. Spender, *The Life of the Right Hon. Sir Henry Campbell-Bannerman*, I, London, 1923, 336.
32. For example, 4PD, 78, c. 654, Dillon, 5 February 1900.
33. For example, Asquith's speech in the Commons, 19 February 1901: 4PD, 89, cc. 503–10.
34. For example, Rosebery's speech at Chesterfield, 16 December 1901: The Marquess of Crewe, *Lord Rosebery*, II, London, 1931, 571–2.
35. Campbell-Bannerman to Sydney Buxton, 31 October 1899, in Spender, I, 254.
36. 4PD, 78, c. 218, Sir R. T. Reid, 31 January 1900.
37. *Ibid.*, c. 474, 2 February 1900.
38. 4PD, 92, c. 154, 28 March 1901.
39. 4PD, 88, c. 298, 7 December 1900.
40. 4PD, 101, cc. 504, 507, Norman, 21 January 1902.
41. *Annual Register*, 1900, 130.
42. For example, 4PD, 88, cc. 177–98, 6 December 1900.
43. *Ibid.*, c. 776, 13 December 1900.
44. J. A. Hobson, *Confessions of an Economic Heretic*, London, 1938, 59, 60.
45. *The Times*, 24 October 1899, 15.

CHAPTER 11

Collaborators in Boer Society

Albert Grundlingh

An important aspect of the impact of war upon society is the reaction and behaviour of the inhabitants of a seemingly conquered territory under enemy occupation. Apart from the rank opportunist or coward, one man may regard cooperation with the apparent victors as his highest duty in order to ensure the survival of his own people, while another may believe just as sincerely, and for the same reason, in continued and dogged resistance. The vexed question of collaboration is inherent in protracted warfare, and in this respect the South African War was no exception.

Oath of neutrality

After the demoralizing Boer defeat at Paardeberg (27 February 1900) and the British occupation of Bloemfontein (13 March 1900) many Free State burghers voluntarily surrendered their arms to the British forces. This was in response to a proclamation issued by Roberts on 15 March in which he assured the burghers that they would be allowed to return to their farms and that their property would be respected by the British forces, provided they signed an oath of neutrality and thereby agreed to abstain from taking any further part in the war. Roberts pursued a similar policy in the South African Republic following the occupation of Johannesburg (31 May) and Pretoria (5 June).[1]

From a legal point of view, Roberts's proclamations accorded with prevailing customs of warfare, but it is equally pertinent to note that by his action the Commander-in-Chief hoped to make the moral force of the oath of neutrality supply his army's manpower deficiency as an occupying force.[2] The British forces soon discovered that the occupation of the Boer capitals and the subsequent annexation of the republics (the Free State on 24 May 1900 and the South African Republic on 1 September 1900) did not mean the end of Boer resistance; consequently, Roberts was unable to exert effective authority over these territories, nor could he meet his obligations towards the burghers who had taken the oath of neutrality. He nevertheless expected them to honour their side of the agreement.

Meanwhile, those Boers who continued the armed struggle in the Free State and in the Transvaal were compelled to endure damaging losses of manpower. No fewer than 5 940 Free State burghers voluntarily surrendered their arms between March and July 1900, while nearly 7 960 Transvalers availed themselves of Roberts's offer before the end of June. The combined figure of 13 900 men represents almost 26 per cent of those

Lord Roberts, whose proclamations promising protection of person and property to those burghers who agreed to take no further part in the war led to 13 900 men laying down their arms following the occupation of the Boer capitals.

liable for military service in the two republics, or approximately 40 per cent of the number initially mobilized.[3] These figures indicate that Boer society was unable to bear all the strains of war. Immediately prior to the conflict few – if any – burghers had openly challenged President Kruger's policy, but between March and July 1900 this seemingly monolithic front collapsed and a definite process of polarization set in. After the war General Christiaan de Wet significantly described Roberts's proclamations as the 'deadly lyddite bombs which . . . shattered Afrikanerdom'.[4] Admittedly, a large number of those who surrendered their arms were subsequently re-commandeered or rejoined voluntarily, but the period shortly after the fall of the Boer capitals nonetheless represents the formative phase in the history of Boer collaboration. The surrendered burghers, as they were called by the British, or the 'handsuppers' (*hen-*

soppers), as the fighting Boers labelled them, without any doubt compromised the military interests of the Boers by deserting from the commandos. From the nucleus of these burghers emerged those who first acted as peace envoys to their fighting compatriots and later in various ways were to aid the British cause.

The 'handsuppers'

To understand why a considerable number of burghers voluntarily surrendered their arms it is necessary to refer briefly to the initial mobilization of the Boers, to the lack of formal discipline in the republican forces, and to the morale of the Boer commandos after their military setbacks in the first half of 1900.

Not all the burghers liable to do military service responded to the initial call-up. In certain districts up to 13 per cent of the burghers ignored the mobilization orders. This indifference is significant, as it can readily be assumed that these men, even if they were later forced to join a commando, would not have hesitated to surrender their arms at the earliest opportunity. At the beginning of the war the Boer officers – elected by the rank and file upon whom they were dependent for their position – were unable to exercise rigid discipline. It was often left to the discretion of the individual whether he would adhere to the Boer cause or not. To the burgher unaccustomed to lengthy campaigns and concerned about his property and family, there was very little formal restraint that prevented him from leaving the commando of his own free will. In fact, the initial lack of discipline in the Boer forces created a hotbed in which apostasy was later to flower. Defeatism swept through the Boer ranks after General P. A. Cronjé surrendered with nearly 4 000 men to Roberts at Paardeberg in February 1900. General Christiaan de Wet was an eyewitness to the profound effect this had on the commandos:

> 'No words can describe my feelings. . . . Depression and discouragement were written on every face. The effects of this blow, it is not too much to say, made themselves apparent to the very end of the war.'[5]

The Boers were still further demoralized by the British occupation of Bloemfontein on 13 March 1900, and when Roberts invaded the Transvaal and occupied Pretoria morale reached a low ebb. In June 1900 Lieutenant-Colonel V. I. Gurko, the Russian military attaché with the Boer forces, made these pertinent observations on the spirit of the burghers:

> 'Seeing the demoralization of the Transvaal army, daily watching men, who positively do not want to go on exposing themselves to danger . . . one could come to the conclusion that the cause has been finally and irrevocably lost – and that the struggle cannot go on for the lack of those prepared to go on fighting.'[6]

Viewed against this background it is not surprising that numerous burghers succumbed to Roberts's offer to surrender.

General P. A. Cronjé surrendering to Lord Roberts at Paardeberg on 27 February 1900, a profoundly demoralizing defeat.

More specifically the motives of the surrendered burghers can be classified into three categories. (These categories are, of course, not mutually exclusive, and more than one factor often affected the decision to abstain from further participation in the war.) In the first place there were those who regarded the continuation of the unequal struggle as unrealistic and detrimental to the country. To them an early end to the war was imperative and in the interests of the whole Boer nation. Secondly, some surrendered burghers were so exhausted and war-weary that they became completely indifferent to the ultimate result of the conflict. They were only interested in dissociating themselves from further participation in the war. In the third category were those who were primarily concerned about their personal and material welfare; self-interest was their chief motive.[7]

After they had taken the oath of neutrality, the surrendered burghers found themselves in an invidious position. The British expected them to honour the oath of neutrality, but were unable to protect them and their property; simultaneously the Boer commanders made a determined attempt to re-commandeer as many surrendered burghers as possible. Many an ex-combatant was faced with the grim alternative of being treated by the British as an oath-breaker or by his own people as a renegade. The surrendered burghers reacted in various ways to this predicament. Some voluntarily rejoined the commandos; others resisted and were eventually obliged to seek protection in the concentration camps established by the British. These options did not appeal to a number of surrendered burghers. They decided to leave the theatre of war completely, and with their families and cattle took refuge in the neighbouring territories – Basutoland, Bechuanaland, Mozambique and Rhodesia. Generally, they were well received. In Bechuanaland, the paramount chief of the Ngwato, Kgama, even sent fifty armed Africans to protect them from being commandeered by their compatriots across the border.[8]

The Burgher Peace Committees

As the war progressed some of the surrendered burghers who had remained in the republics tried to convince their fighting countrymen that a continuation of the struggle would be futile. Before the end of December 1900 there were sporadic attempts of this nature to persuade the men on commando to lay down their arms. These efforts made little impact on the men in the field, but they paved the way for a more organized peace movement, namely, the Burgher Peace Committees.

The initiative for a large-scale peace movement emanating from the surrendered burghers had the full cooperation and encouragement of the British authorities. In late November 1900 two surrendered burghers, J. B. Wolmarans and J. W. Erasmus, who had left the Transvaal and had made their way to London, managed to secure an interview with Chamberlain. Wolmarans, a prominent Pretoria citizen, and Erasmus, an ex-member of the second Volksraad, impressed upon Chamberlain the desirability of sending peace emissaries to the fighting Boers. Chamberlain duly responded and asked Milner and Kitchener to investigate the possibility. The Commander-in-Chief was prepared to entertain this idea, especially when similar opinions were being voiced by certain surrendered burghers in the Transvaal. On 15 December – the same day that Kitchener received Chamberlain's telegram – he had an interview with Meyer de Kock, a surrendered burgher from Belfast, who also declared himself in favour of such a policy. Kitchener granted permission for a central peace committee to be formed in Pretoria, and this was followed by the establishment of seven other local committees in the Transvaal. A number of peace committees also sprang into existence in the Free State. These committees were not intended to discuss questions of policy: their main object was to inform the fighting burghers that Britain was determined to win the war and that further resistance would thus be futile; that there was no possibility of foreign intervention on behalf of the republics; and that those burghers who voluntarily laid down their arms would be assured of better treatment in future.

A determined effort was made during the first quarter of 1901 to communicate with the Boers in the field. In the Transvaal twenty-four men were sent out to various commandos, and the British printed 28 000 propaganda leaflets for distribution among the fighting Boers, giving the views of leading surrendered burghers. The peace envoys met with stiff opposition. They were regarded as deserters and a number of them were fined or imprisoned. Meyer de Kock was less fortunate. After a military trial he was condemned to death for the leading role he had played in the peace movement, and on 12 February 1901 executed by Boer firing squad. In the Free State a peace envoy, J. J. Morgendaal, was captured. While some controversy still surrounds his death, it appears that on 9 January 1901 the Boer commando that had captured him was preparing for an expected attack from a British column. Morgendaal was thought to be deliberately procrastinating and on the spur of the moment

General C. C. Froneman flogged him. Morgendaal retaliated with a cutting remark, whereupon General Christiaan de Wet, who had been watching the proceedings impatiently, lost his temper and ordered Froneman to shoot Morgendaal. He was not killed outright, but died ten days later. Morgendaal had no proper military trial and Kitchener initially regarded his death as cold-blooded murder, but later considered it to be a case of manslaughter. There was no premeditated plan to shoot Morgendaal, and the confusion and excitement at the time apparently caused De Wet to over-react. The circumstances of Morgendaal's death, in fact, exonerate the Boers from charges that in this particular case they violated the prevailing practices of international law.

The peace movement was not only confined to the Transvaal and the Free State. A deputation led by General Piet de Wet, Christiaan's brother, also visited the Cape Colony in an effort to enlist the support of influential Afrikaner politicians and churchmen; but the leading Afrikaners in the Colony were wary of supporting one Boer faction against another. The De Wet deputation also approached the prisoners of war encamped near Cape Town; the majority showed little enthusiasm for the deputation's cause, but it nevertheless succeeded in establishing a separate camp for those in favour of immediate peace.[9]

As a pressure group to influence the Boer leaders, the peace committees were generally ineffectual. Since their members had

Below left: Piet de Wet. Below right: Christian de Wet. 'General Piet de Wet came to me and asked if I saw any chance of being able to continue the struggle. The question made me very angry, and I did not try to hide the fact. "Are you mad?" I shouted, and with that I turned on my heel and entered the house, quite unaware that Piet de Wet had that very moment mounted his horse, and ridden away to follow his own course.' Christiaan de Wet's remarkably dispassionate account of the final rift with his brother on 19 July 1900, published in Three Years War *(1902). Piet de Wet, who became a prominent member of the burgher peace movement and a leader of the Orange River Colony Volunteers, is never mentioned again in the book.*

voluntarily surrendered their arms they had no *locus standi* in the eyes of the Boer generals. In fact, if one considers the wartime status of the surrendered burghers their attempts at peace appear rather unrealistic. A. Cartwright, editor of *The South African News*, pertinently observed in the edition of 17 January 1901 that for any such attempt to have a chance of success, 'it would be necessary for a peace envoy to be a citizen of a neutral state, . . . a condition which is not fulfilled by a surrendered member of either the Republican armies, whose President or Commandant-General would necessarily treat him as a deserter.' Although the Boer leaders refused to deal with the peace envoys, some of the rank and file were more receptive to the overtures of their former comrades. The number of surrendered burghers increased considerably during February and March 1901, and although this was not exclusively in response to the message of the peace emissaries, it can be claimed that the propaganda campaign definitely had some impact at the grassroot level.[10]

From neutrality to collaboration

The peace movement represents an important phase in the history of the Boer collaborators. The initial intention of the surrendered burghers was to adopt a neutral stance, but by actively campaigning for peace under British auspices they firmly committed themselves to a partisan role. The organized peace movement was also a clear manifestation of the mounting dissatisfaction in the ranks of the surrendered burghers and of their increasing exasperation at the uncompromising policy of their compatriots who wished to continue the war at all costs. Furthermore, the existence of the burgher peace committees accentuated the polarization in Boer society. Two clearly defined factions had developed: those who considered it futile to continue a war that ruined the country, and those who firmly believed in continuing the struggle for independence. Some surrendered burghers did not resign themselves to the fact that they were unable to influence the republican leaders. They responded to the determination of the fighting Boers with equally resolute, though perhaps less justified, action. In September 1901 the central peace committee of the Free State resolved that it was time to implement more drastic measures by raising a well-organized force of surrendered burghers that would assist the British columns in the field.

However, long before September 1901 certain surrendered burghers had already given sporadic military assistance to the British forces. Since June 1900 some surrendered burghers had occasionally acted as guides, and as the war progressed their numbers increased steadily. Statistics to determine the exact rate at which they joined the British ranks are not available, but in April 1902 3 963 Boers were in British service, and by the end of the war this figure had increased to 5 464.[11] This is not an insignificant number when it is taken into account that at the end of the war the number of republican *bittereinders* (bitterenders or die-hards) totalled approximately 17 000 men – only three times more than the Boers in British military service.

The 'joiners'

The employment of surrendered burghers in British ranks was the culmination of the process of polarization that had set in after the occupation of the Boer capitals. With Afrikaner fighting Afrikaner, the breach in republican society was apparently irreparable. Those Boers in British military service obviously went a step further than the ordinary surrendered burgher, and by doing so there can be little doubt that in legal terms they became war-traitors. Although Britain had annexed the South African Republic and the Free State as British colonies while the war was still in progress, it can be argued that the annexations were technically invalid because the British were not in complete control of these territories. Their authority was only recognized at the Peace of Vereeniging and consequently all the Boers still owed their allegiance to the republican and not the British government. In this respect the motives of the war-traitor – whether patriotic and noble or base and mercenary – were also immaterial, and the Boers were thus fully entitled to execute such men when they were captured.

The so-called 'joiners' assisted the British in various capacities. The following groups can be distinguished: the local burgher corps, the guides and scouts who individually joined the British columns, and the National Scouts and the Orange River Colony Volunteers. There were some important differences between the local burgher corps and the guides and scouts on the one hand and the National Scouts and the Orange River Colony Volunteers on the other.

Local burgher corps

The British employed the local burgher corps as well as the guides and scouts on a casual basis. No fixed policy about recruitment, enrolment, remuneration and duration of service was followed. These men were not attested in the imperial army, nor did they receive a British uniform. They were often paid in loot (usually cattle) and only occasionally did they receive pecuniary rewards. Except for one particular body of men, the Farmers' Guard, which operated in the Bloemfontein district, the local burgher corps were also relatively few in number and their participation in the conflict limited. Kitchener was reluctant to admit to the existence of these corps (for fear of adverse criticism from the War Office) and preferred to use them as informally as possible. In contrast to these irregular corps the National Scouts and the Orange River Colony Volunteers were placed on a sound organizational basis and employed as regular military units during the latter phase of the war (October 1901 – May 1902). They were bound by formal conditions of service and instead of loot they received fixed pay. Furthermore, they became attested soldiers in the imperial army and were issued with distinctive uniforms. Their numbers greatly exceeded those of the local burgher corps and, organized on a territorial basis throughout the two republics, they participated to a greater extent in military operations.

In the Free State the first local corps was formed in November 1900 in the Kroonstad district. The district commissioner,

Captain F. R. de Bertodano, and the local intelligence officer, Captain H. M. R. Brett, took the initiative in organizing the corps known as the Kroonstad Burgher Scouts. Before the end of January 1901 seventy men had voluntarily joined their ranks. Their knowledge of the district was put to use by employing them as scouts to inform the British authorities of possible Boer hideouts in the Kroonstad area. More important was the local corps raised in the Bloemfontein district during January 1901. Initially, this was known as the Burgher Police, but in December 1901 the designation was changed to Farmers' Guard. At the end of the war 615 Free State burghers had enrolled in this particular corps. They were used as an auxiliary corps attached to the South African Constabulary for patrolling the so-called 'protected area' surrounding Bloemfontein. Milner was responsible for introducing the idea of protected areas. A cordon of posts was established in an area of twenty miles around the Free State capital and these posts were meant to serve as bases for small operations into the countryside for clearing farms, removing Boer families, destroying crops, capturing stock and expelling bands of Boers. The system was to be extended gradually, and the ultimate goal was to establish a specific area completely protected against Boer incursions in which selected surrendered burghers could farm undisturbed. Milner hoped that the employment of the Farmers' Guard in this way would not only ensure the undisputed authority of the

What we have we hold. A photograph, probably taken for British propaganda purposes, showing members of the Farmers' Guard near Bloemfontein.

British forces in the area around Bloemfontein, but would also give members of the corps who had farming interests in the area a tangible reason to defend their own against invading Boers. The Farmers' Guard met with only moderate success. In the first place they received little assistance from the South African Constabulary, which Kitchener often used as an additional flying column outside the protected area, and, secondly, they were scattered throughout the territory, which made concentrated defence at a specific point virtually impossible. Besides the Farmers' Guard there was another, and quite uniquely composed, corps in the Free State. In the Winburg district a corps consisting of surrendered burghers as well as Africans operated. To at least some of the white inhabitants prevailing racial distinctions had been blurred by the war. This corps, under the leadership of a surrendered burgher, O. M. Bergh, made regular attacks on isolated Boer parties, and apparently also burned farmhouses in the district and molested women and children.[12]

Guides and scouts

In both republics there were also those surrendered burghers who did not belong to a specific corps, but who individually joined the British columns as guides and scouts. In April 1902 Kitchener reported that these men were incorporated into every British column. They were not enrolled for a specific period and their numbers fluctuated according to the exigencies of the military situation. However, at the end of the war 3 042 surrendered burghers were employed in this way. Their services were of particular importance to the British. In contrast to the Boers, who were thoroughly familiar with the terrain on which they operated, the British forces had only the scantiest knowledge of the theatre of war. The British column commanders constantly clamoured for more staff with an intimate knowledge of the operational area. Since the surrendered burghers knew the country and habits of their erstwhile comrades, they were in a position to fulfil this need. The exploits of the guides and scouts were regularly commended by British commanders, and at times their services proved to be of considerable significance. On 11 July 1901 eleven surrendered burghers directly contributed to the capture of President Steyn's bodyguard and several important Free State officials when they guided Brigadier-General R. G. Broadwood's column to Reitz, where the Free State government had spent the night. President Steyn himself just managed to escape in time. The capture of some of their key personnel was a heavy blow to the Free State forces, and it is doubtful whether Broadwood would have been successful without the assistance of men who knew the terrain as well as the whereabouts of the republican government. The guides and scouts were also put to effective use on the Transvaal highveld during the second half of 1901 when they assisted the British columns to carry out harassing night raids on unsuspecting Boer laagers. In addition, the British intelligence service planted

Lord Kitchener, whose decision it was to extend the burgher corps system by forming the National Scouts and Orange River Colony Volunteers.

joiner agents in the Boer commandos. This practice had its obvious dangers and the men employed in this way found it difficult to report back without being detected.[13]

Furthermore, there were several burgher corps that operated in the Transvaal. These corps sprang into existence haphazardly. They had their distinct conditions of service and internal organization, and either acted independently or attached to a column. Often the men had to find their own horses and uniforms, while the British supplied the arms and rations. However, they had one point in common – a claim to loot-money. Six such corps were established during 1901: the Vereeniging Burgher Corps, Morley's Scouts and the Cattle Ranger Corps in the Pretoria area; Beddy's Scouts, which operated in the northern Transvaal; and the Lydenberg Volunteer Burgher Corps and the Lebombo Scouts in the eastern Transvaal. The strength of these corps varied from twenty-five to forty-five men. Their main task was to round up the cattle in their immediate neighbourhood. In this way they aided the British columns in clearing livestock from the countryside. The only remuneration they received from the British was the cattle they captured. A proportion of the cattle was sold by public auction and the money realized divided among the members of the corps. Certain members, however, preferred to keep their share of the cattle. Since these units were somewhat undisciplined, and since their main objective was to enrich themselves by collecting as many cattle as possible, they became known with some justification as looting corps. Occasionally, however, they also acted as guides and scouts for the columns operating in their area. In October 1901 Captain R. W. Morley, the commander of Morley's Scouts, suggested that all the burgher corps in the Transvaal should be merged into one large unit – the National Scouts. He maintained that more men would join a larger corps and that they could be used on a more extensive scale. Kitchener approved the scheme and in the Transvaal the local corps were amalgamated into the National Scouts, while the Kroonstad Burgher Scouts in the Free State were incorporated into the Orange River Colony Volunteers.[14]

Three reasons account for Kitchener's decision to extend the existing system. In the first place he regarded these men as an important military asset to the British columns. Secondly, Kitchener hoped to pursue a policy of divide and rule by exploiting the existing division in Afrikaner ranks. 'There are already two parties amongst them ready to fly at each others throat,' he wrote to the Secretary of State for War, 'and if the Boers could be induced to hate each other more than they hate the British, the British objective would be obtained.' Such a policy, he hoped, would also yield future politicai dividends since, he remarked, 'we shall have a party among the Boers themselves depending entirely on British continuity of rule out here.'[15] Finally, several prominent surrendered burghers, including Piet de Wet, wrote to Kitchener to express the desire to aid the British more actively by forming an organized corps.

National Scouts and ORC Volunteers

A large-scale recruiting campaign was therefore launched in October 1901. British colonial officers and burghers already in British ranks acted as recruiting agents for the National Scouts. The corps was raised chiefly from the surrendered burghers in the concentration camps. Kitchener involved himself directly in the recruiting drive by addressing the surrendered burghers in several concentration camps. At Potchefstroom he tried to convince a gathering of two hundred surrendered burghers that it was in their own interests, as well as in the interest of their country, that they should take an active part in bringing hostilities to a close. In addition to the 'patriotic' appeal, more concrete financial inducements were held out to recruits. Every member received five shillings a day and rations, a corporal seven shillings and sixpence, and a field-cornet and a commandant of the corps ten shillings and fifteen shillings a day respectively. These were fairly substantial amounts for men in possible need. Other, vaguer offers were also made. Unofficially, recruits were given the impression that at the end of the war they would obtain preferential advantages in the settlement of the land; some of the Scouts were even promised farms. These offers never materialized. Both the British high command and Milner were satisfied with the recruiting campaign. In January 1902, 950 belonged to the corps, in April, 1 125 and by the end of the war 1 359 burghers had enrolled. The Orange River Colony Volunteers numbered 448 men at the end of the war.

Only *bona fide* Transvaal burghers who had voluntarily joined were accepted as National Scouts. They were formally enrolled in the British army and had to serve for a minimum period of six months. After attestation, each man was issued with a rifle and ammunition, a horse and saddle, as well as a regular uniform with the letters N.S. (National Scouts) in brass on the tunic. The men were placed under British military law and were subject to the same disciplinary code as the other British troops. After the war they also received 'South African War' medals for their services in the imperial army. At the head of the National Scout organization was Major E. M. H. Leggett, previously of the Imperial Military Railways, who acted as general staff officer for the corps. Captains T. S. Allison and M. C. Jamieson from the Cape colonial forces served as assistant-staff officer and adjutant respectively. The headquarters of the corps was in Pretoria, but six subsidiary depots were also established in the eastern, western and northern areas of the Transvaal. Every unit had its own officers, who were ultimately responsible to the British. Seven units were stationed in the eastern Transvaal, one in the western Transvaal and another in the northern Transvaal. The numerical strength of the units varied considerably. The following are the figures for each unit: 288, 286, 194, 175, 141, 113, 110, 41 and 31 men. Since the men knew their local terrain best, the units were only employed in their own particular districts so that the British were able to use them to the best possible advantage. The

No. 5 wing of the National Scouts taking to the field at Klerksdorp.

Orange River Colony Volunteers consisted of two units organized on similar lines. Particular attention was paid to the families of these men. Some received preferential treatment in the concentration camps, while others were given the privilege of staying in houses in the towns. Separate concentration camps exclusively for the families of National Scouts were also established in Pretoria, Pietersburg and Belfast.[16]

The different units of the National Scouts were attached to various British columns as separate guide and scout sections, and they never acted as a combined force in operations against the Boers. Nor did they fight their compatriots independently without British aid. Some units were involved in a number of conventional battles – at Bosmanskop in the eastern Transvaal (1 April 1902), and at Ystersspruit (25 February 1902), Tweebosch (7 March 1902) and Roodewal (11 April 1902) in the western Transvaal. In the northern Transvaal they were engaged in fairly heavy skirmishes with General C. F. Beyers's commando. The Scouts did not affect the issue in any of these battles. As a rule they were anxious to avoid taking part in intensive fighting. In hard-fought engagements, according to Kitchener, they were only prepared to attack 'when they are convinced of being much stronger and have the best positions; they then show dash and are very good at following up scattered and flying Boers'.[17] It was as guides and scouts that they rendered more valuable service. A British war correspondent, who spent some time with the Scouts in the field, reported in *The Times* of 21 May 1902:

> 'Of the usefulness of these National Scouts there can be no doubt. In operations in their own districts their local knowledge renders them invaluable. It was a knowledge such as can never be acquired by anyone who has not lived all his life on the veld – the instinct that takes them unerringly across a tractless expanse

> of grass on a dark night, that knows the undulations of the ground, imperceptible from a distance, by which a body of men can pass unobserved hard by an enemy's camp. At night one often has occasion to admire the silence and dispatch with which a body of these scouts will fall out from a column on the march, and round up . . . a dozen or more prisoners.'

This account may seem exaggerated, but the gist of it is well supported by other British as well as Boer sources.[18] Indirectly, the Scouts contributed to a substantial number of Boers being captured during the last five months of the war. In the Free State the ORC Volunteers were less active, but nevertheless caused the Boers some concern. Those Scouts and Volunteers who were unfortunate enough to be captured by the Boers were shown no mercy. After a military trial, they were summarily executed. 'What use had humanity for a man having been favoured by destiny with the opportunity of giving his all for an ideal . . . and throws that down and takes service against it because a long purse hires him', an irate Boer commander asked after the execution of a Scout on the highveld.[19]

Boer leaders and the 'unfaithful'

It may be argued that the employment of Scouts and Volunteers was a mistaken policy, embittering the fighting Boers and prolonging their resistance. But the evidence suggests the contrary. During the final peace negotiations in May 1902 several Boer delegates elaborated on the negative influence exerted by these men. General L. Meyer, a representative of the Transvaal government, stated,

> 'We have taught the British how to wage war. Our own people are with them and show them how to trek in the night and where the footpaths are.'

The acting landdrost of Wakkerstroom, H. J. Bosman, strongly deplored the influence of the Scouts: 'If it were not for those unfaithful people in our midst we would never have had such a hard time of it.' General Schalk Burger, Acting President of the Transvaal, concurred. In an effort to convince some of the other delegates that it was imperative to end the war he argued that

> 'Every man we lose makes the enemy stronger . . . and the enemy is being taught by us, and by our people who fight for them, how to carry on war against us. . . . If you do not see these facts it is impossible for me and others to open your eyes to them.'

Of considerable importance are the opinions expressed by the two commanders-in-chief of the republican forces. Botha was particularly concerned about the 'unfaithfulness of our own burghers'. He feared that if conditions did not change there would shortly be more Afrikaners fighting against the republican cause than for it. Emphatically, he declared:

> 'I say we are now so broken up and weakened that if matters go on like this a little longer we shall no more be able to assert ourselves as a party.'[20]

Christiaan de Wet, though he did not mention this during the peace negotiations, was even more convinced that the joiners contributed materially to the Boers' downfall. Shortly after the war he stated unequivocally,

> 'It was through them that we were given the death-blow that forced us to take the ill-fated decision to declare peace.'[21]

Several other Boer officers and men also maintained that the demoralizing effect of the Scouts was instrumental in forcing them to conclude peace.[22] Although it must be taken into consideration that the judgement of the Boers was sometimes impaired by their hatred of the Scouts, in whom they found a convenient scapegoat to blame for the republican defeat, it nevertheless can be claimed on the basis of the evidence cited that the joiners did have a demoralizing effect on the Boer commandos and in this way hastened the end of the conflict. It cannot be argued, however, that the demoralizing effect of these men was the weightiest reason for the Boers to conclude peace. Other considerations – such as the lack of resources, the position of women and children in the concentration camps and on the veld, the arming of Africans and the overwhelming numerical superiority of the British forces – were equally, if not more, important.

The motives of the rank and file

One of the most intriguing aspects of the phenomenon of treason is to determine the true motives of those involved. The historian Donald Denoon has briefly argued that the National Scouts mainly consisted of *bywoners* (poor landless men in the employ of a landed proprietor), while the bitterenders were largely landed men. Accordingly, he is inclined to ascribe the division in Afrikaner ranks to 'economic differentiation'. Although Denoon provides little evidence to substantiate this assertion, and also mistakenly claims that Piet de Wet, one of the leaders of the Orange River Colony Volunteers, owned no land,[23] this hypothesis is tantalizing nevertheless. The available evidence, in fact, seems to indicate that the majority of the rank and file joiners were indeed members of an underprivileged class who shortly before the war had either moved to the towns and cities or had eked out a precarious existence as labour-tenants on the farms. An analysis of the individual land tenure of the National Scout unit for which records are available provides striking proof that 72 per cent of that particular group (consisting of 288 men) were landless.[24] Moreover, J. Wedgwood, a British magistrate in the eastern Transvaal where most of the Scouts hailed from, declared shortly after the war that 'with a few exceptions the joiners are of the *bywoner* class.'[25] Likewise, H. Goold-Adams, the Lieutenant-Governor of the Orange River Colony, maintained after a post-war investigation pertaining to the repatriation of the joiners 'that the majority of these men are persons without property.'[26] The social base of the joiners is significant, as it reflects not only on the structure of Boer society, but also on the way in which the war accentuated the social and economic divisions within Afrikanerdom. Even

National Scouts photographed at Klerksdorp. Most rank and file Scouts appear to have been bywoners, *members of an underprivileged, landless group in Afrikaner society.*

before the South African War some of the *bywoners* had complained about the fact that they were compelled to perform military service without remuneration and were forced to protect the property of others while they had none themselves. They also had to procure some of the commando equipment at their own expense, and during their absence on commando their families had to do without the meagre provisions that they themselves usually provided. Some landlords, in fact, had to force their *bywoners* to take up arms during the war.[27] It is apparent that the *bywoners* in general were members of a disgruntled pre-war class, and it is clear why some fell relatively easy prey to vague British promises that they would be assured of a privileged position in post-war society. In addition, they were being paid to fight for the British, while the Boers offered no remuneration. It would be wrong, however, to assume that the split in Afrikaner ranks can only be explained in economic terms. There were also *bywoners* among the bitterenders who did not become joiners and other motives also influenced the joiners, whether they were *bywoners* or not.

Some National Scouts joined in order to escape the conditions in the concentration camps. The younger men especially were frustrated by the depressing monotony of their existence, and in the midst of despair rashly accepted the invitation to be relieved of their enforced idleness by contributing to the termination of the wartime circumstances that were responsible for their dismal existence. Others were piqued by the way in which the fighting Boers treated them as surrendered burghers, and joined in order to get their own back on their compatriots. There are also indications that ties of kinship may have influenced certain men. Numerous Scouts were either directly or distantly related to one another. Often whole families (father, sons, brothers, cousins, as well as in-laws) were connected with the National Scouts. (The classic exception is of course the Piet and Christiaan de Wet case.)

After the war various National Scouts tried to justify their actions on political and humanitarian grounds. On political grounds they claimed that the British annexations in May and

September 1900 had terminated the existence of the republics and that the Boer governments had no constitutional right to continue the war; therefore the Scouts were obliged to support the new administration in obedience to the will of God that man should honour his rulers. They also argued that the Boer leaders and the republican deputation abroad had deceived them with false hopes of foreign intervention, and consequently they were justified in taking up arms against people who had misled the nation.[28] On humanitarian grounds P. J. du Toit, who acted as a guide to the British columns, stated in his wartime diary that he considered it imperative to do

> 'my share towards bringing this horrible and miserable state of affairs to a speedy termination, for the sake of the country at large, . . . for the sake of women and children in refugee camps and the prisoners of war. . . . This I consider the duty of every true patriot.'[29]

These political and humanitarian arguments, of course, cannot always be accepted at face value since they were often advanced to exonorate the person concerned, but this does not necessarily exclude the possibility that some individual National Scouts were sincere in their belief that they were serving the best interests of their people. Perhaps a disillusioned Milner was the closest to the truth in a statement he made in September 1905 following his departure from South Africa.

> 'I know that a great many of them [joiners] were men of a low type, actuated by base motives, though I do not for a moment admit that this is universally true. I believe that . . . there were some men who were honestly convinced that the war had become criminal from the moment it had become hopeless and that their duty to their own countrymen was to do all they could to bring it to an end.'[30]

The motives of the joiner leadership

It is necessary to separate the motives of the rank and file from those of the leaders. The leading figures were General Piet de Wet and Commandant S. G. Vilonel in the Free State, and Generals A. P. J. Cronjé and J. G. Celliers in the Transvaal. Except for Celliers, their motives seem to have differed qualitatively from those of their followers. Celliers had a pre-war criminal record and had spent two years in gaol for manslaughter. The others were all prominent, influential and prosperous men in pre-war Boer society. Piet de Wet and A. P. J. Cronjé were progressive farmers in the Lindley and Potchefstroom districts respectively. S. G. Vilonel was a capable and respected lawyer in Senekal. It seems likely that these leaders (De Wet, Vilonel and Cronjé) were more genuinely convinced than the rank and file *bywoner* members of the corps of the necessity of taking up arms against their compatriots in order to contribute towards the cessation of hostilities in the general interests of the nation. As for Celliers, a temperamental and unprincipled individual who practised reckless but often effective fighting methods, mercenary aims were apparently the prime consideration.[31]

A. P. J. Cronjé, a prominent leader of the National Scouts, who before the war had been a progressive farmer in the Potchefstroom district. The social background of most members of the joiner leadership differed significantly from that of the rank and file.

The joiners and surrendered burghers had no representation at the final peace negotiations. This omission by the British guaranteed that the bitterenders would become the future representatives of Afrikanerdom. In reality the British had no alternative, for it is extremely doubtful whether the Boers would have agreed to negotiate if the joiners had been represented as a separate faction. This seriously undermined their position and definitely limited their potential as a post-war political pressure group. They were, in fact, a spent force and in a false position the moment the fighting leaders retained their leadership for the future by a negotiated peace.[32]

Repatriation

After the war the civil administration took no particular interest in the repatriation of the joiners. It was only after repeated requests by the Scouts that some of the British officers who had been associated with the corps during the war intervened on their behalf and secured for them some repatriation benefits. Separate repatriation boards were established for the joiners, and those who owned land were provided with the necessary implements to commence farming. The great bulk of them, however, were landless men and the bitterender landlords usually refused to take back *bywoners* who had fought on the British side. For these men the repatriation boards found employment in lowly capacities in the public works department on the railways or in the prison service. Some of the Scouts enrolled in the South African Constabulary, while a certain number also enlisted for the Somaliland campaign (1902–3) to fight Muhammed Abdullah Hasan (the 'Mad Mullah'). Other landless men were accommodated on land settlement farms in the eastern and the western Transvaal.

The settlements were initiated by Major Leggett of the National Scouts and the men were allowed to lease land in return for handing over 50 per cent of the annual yield. The settlements were not a success because of mismanagement and the laxity of the settlers. They were not set up for political reasons; bitter-enders were also accommodated and the idea was simply to provide economic aid on a self-help basis. 'I absolutely put aside all political consideration in this case', Milner declared.[33]

Compensation

The compensation monies granted by the British at Vereeniging proved to be a controversial issue. The bitterender leaders were opposed to the participation of defectors in the £3 million set aside for compensation; the administration was obliged to make special arrangements for compensating the joiners and those Boers who had surrendered under Roberts's proclamation. Once again political considerations did not influence the decision; it was merely an attempt to provide compensation for all sections of the Boer population. The joiners and surrendered burghers were dealt with more generously than the bitterenders, but, like the latter, they were dissatisfied with the amount received. 'Compensation has, on the whole, been rather a curse than a blessing', an exasperated Milner remarked. 'You give a man a pound, and he hates you for it, because he asked for four and expected two, and all his neighbours who have not got anything hate you equally.'[34] The general dissatisfaction of both parties over the compensation issue later proved to be one of the unifying forces contributing to reconciliation in Afrikaner ranks.

Afrikaner disunity after the war

However, in the immediate aftermath of war Boer society was riven with conflict. The bitterenders' dormant hatred of the 'unfaithful' burghers surfaced rapidly and unrestrained after the cessation of hostilities. Defectors were not only ostracized from the Boer community, but their property was also damaged and they themselves physically assaulted on occasions. Eugéne Marais, editor of the Dutch newspaper *Land en Volk*, gave vent to the feelings of the majority of bitterenders when he wrote on 17 October 1902:

> 'The feelings of hate . . . are deep as the ocean and wide as the God's earth. . . . We hate these people from the depth of our hearts because they besmirched our honourable name. It is not possible to forgive and even less to forget.'

This antagonism was keenly felt by some of the collaborators. 'We are branded, distrusted and hated', Piet de Wet complained in January 1903.[35] Some National Scouts found their position so unbearable that they considered emigrating to Rhodesia and British East Africa, but such emigration did not materialize.

Ostracism of the collaborators was not confined to the secular level; the church also turned against them. Ministers who sympathized with the surrendered burghers during the war were forced to resign; bitterender ministers refused to baptize the children of collaborators; collaborators were not allowed to serve on church councils, and eventually were excluded from the sacraments unless they were prepared to confess to their 'guilt'. It may seem strange that the main opposition to the collaborators after the war should come from ministers of the Christian gospel, but the explanation may lie in the fact that the church was the only Afrikaner institution that survived the surrender intact, and for this reason it was the one medium through which Afrikaner society could express its 'official' view on the conduct of the collaborators. A number of Scouts under the leadership of N. J. Breytenbach and S. P. Grobler, both former National Scout officers, protested against the stand taken by the church and argued that a political disagreement was being construed as a moral offence. A church commission was appointed to investigate the matter and protracted negotiations followed, but the two parties were unable (or unwilling) to find common ground. In late 1903 Breytenbach and Grobler decided to establish their own church, the so-called Scout Church. With reluctant British financial aid seven small congregations were founded, but these never showed any viability. The Scout Church was, in fact, doomed to failure. It only received half-hearted support from the colonial administration; it never appealed to the rank and file of the National Scouts who were in any case apathetic towards church matters; and Breytenbach and Grobler were not made of the metal that produces successful church leaders (the latter misspent church money and had to account for it in court). Thus the Scout Church, which had virtually disappeared by 1906, never constituted a major breach in post-war Afrikaner society.[36]

Louis Botha, who after the war urged reconciliation between joiners and bitterenders, and who welcomed former collaborators as committee members of Het Volk.

Reconciliation

The failure of the Scout Church, together with widespread dissatisfaction over post-war compensation, the indifferent attitude of the colonial administration towards the Scouts in general, and the fact that several Scouts made public pleas to be forgiven, made easier Botha's task of uniting Afrikanerdom in the political field. During the post-war revival Botha repeatedly urged the bitterenders to adopt a conciliatory attitude towards their 'weaker brethren'. He regarded such a policy as imperative in order to counter the voting potential of the English-speaking people in the Transvaal. In this he was supported by other Boer leaders, such as J. C. Smuts, C. F. Beyers and J. H. de la Rey. To prove their credibility the Boer leaders even welcomed former collaborators as committee members of the new Boer party formed after the war, *Het Volk*. By 1906 the leaders had largely succeeded in knitting together the torn fabric of Afrikanerdom, and in the election of 1907, which followed Britain's granting of responsible government to the Transvaal, the former defectors supported *Het Volk*. Likewise in the Orange River Colony, where the main reason for reconciliation was the dissatisfaction of both sections on the compensation issue, the overwhelming majority of former dissidents supported the Afrikaner party, *Orangia Unie*, in the 1907 election. The polarization caused by the war therefore had no further repercussions for Afrikaner political development.

References

1. Cd. 426, 3, 7, 23.
2. J. M. Spaight, *War Rights on Land*, London, 1911, 148–9, 373.
3. For the calculations on which these figures are based, see A. M. Grundlingh, 'Die Vrystaatse en Transvaalse Burgers wat die Republikeinse oorlogspoging vanaf 1900 versaak het: Hulle rol en posisie gedurende die tydperk 1900 tot 1907', MA thesis, University of South Africa, 1976, 26–9.
4. *Officieel Verslag van de Verrichten van het Nasionaal Kongres gehouden te Brandfort, 1 en 2 Desember 1904*, 34 (translation).
5. C. R. de Wet, *Three Years War*, London, 1902, 64.
6. E. Williams-Foxcroft, 'The Despatches of the Russian attaché Col. Stakhovitch and Lieut.-Col. Gurko', *Christiaan de Wet Annale*, 3, 1975, 196.
7. For the motives of the surrendered burghers see Grundlingh, 30–3, 168–78.
8. For the treatment of the surrendered burghers by the British and the Boers and their subsequent reaction, see Grundlingh, 34–81.
9. The peace committees and their activities are discussed in S. B. Spies, *Methods of Barbarism? Roberts and Kitchener and civilians in the Boer Republics January 1900–May 1902*, Cape Town 1977, 179–81, 201–9; Grundlingh, 101–60.
10. This is discussed in more detail in Grundlingh, 160–1.
11. CO 417/361/20859, 'Return of Ex-Burghers serving under British', 27 April 1902; CO 417/362/26810, 'Return of Ex-Burghers serving under British', 1 June 1902.
12. For the local burgher corps in the Free State see Grundlingh, 208–12, 219–29; L. S. Amery ed., *The Times History of the War in South Africa*, V, London, 1907, 248–9, 260–2.
13. The individual guides and scouts in British service are dealt with in Grundlingh, 229–42.
14. For the local burgher corps in the Transvaal see Grundlingh, 242–51.
15. Photostat copies in Transvaal Archives, Kitchener Letters, II and IV, Kitchener to Brodrick, 21 June 1901 and 17 January 1902.
16. The recruiting and organization of the National Scouts and Orange River Colony Volunteers are discussed in Grundlingh, 257–62, 266–70; *Times History*, V, 407–8.
17. Kitchener Letters, II, Kitchener to Brodrick, 17 January 1902.
18. WO 32/877/8622, 'Staff Diary Col. Park's Column', 20 February 1902; WO 32/879/8757, 'Staff Diary Pietersburg District', 9 and 10 March 1902; J. Brandt, *Die Kappie kommando of Boerenvrouwen in Geheime Dienst*, Amsterdam, 1913, 159.
19. P. J. le Riche, 'Memoirs of Ben Bouwer', 126. Manuscript in possession of Human Sciences Research Council, Pretoria.
20. These quotations are taken from J. D. Kestell and D. E. van Velden, *The Peace Negotiations*, London 1912, 85, 94, 179, 182, 195–6.
21. C. C. J. Badenhorst, *Uit den Boerenoorlog*, Amsterdam, 1902, 161 (my translation).
22. D. Mostert, *Slegtkamp van Spioenkop. Oorlogsherinneringe van Kapt. Slegtkamp saamgestel uit sy Dagboek*, Cape Town, 1935, 268; P. S. Lombard, *Uit die Dagboek van 'n Wildeboer*, Johannesburg, 1939, 160; F. D. Conradie, *Met Cronjé op die Wesfront*, Cape Town, 1946, 201; R. W. Schikkerling, *Hoe ry die Boere, 'n Kommandodagboek*, Johannesburg, 1964, 378; *Land en Volk*, 27 February 1903 (letter from a bitterender).
23. D. Denoon, *A Grand Illusion*, London, 1973, 17–18; 'Participation in the Boer War: People's War, People's Non-War or Non-People's War?' in B. A. Ogot ed., *War and Society in Africa*, London, 1972, 117–18. For the landed property owned by Piet de Wet see Estate no. 21437, P. D. de Wet, 1929, Master of the Supreme Court, Bloemfontein.
24. Microfilm A462 in Transvaal Archives, Pretoria, WO/unsorted, 'Certificates of Engagement, National Scouts, no. 5 Wing'. On these certificates it is indicated whether the individual owned landed property or not. The following secondary works also refer to joiners as being an 'inferior' pre-war *bywoner* class; J. Visscher, *De Ondergang van een Wereld. Historisch – oeconomische Studie over den Oorzaken van de Anglo-Boer Oorlog*, Amsterdam, 1903, 39–40; E. J. Weber, *Op die Transvaalse Front*, Bloemfontein, 1942, 149.
25. *Transvaal Administration Reports for 1902: Judicial*, (Ermelo-Carolina district), 15.
26. Orange Free State Archives, CSO 139/3001/02, 'Memorandum to Central Repatriation Board', 7 August 1902.
27. Evidence for this is given in Grundlingh, 301–2.
28. These motives and arguments are discussed in Grundlingh, 303–11.
29. J. P. Brits ed., *Diary of a National Scout, P. J. du Toit, 1900–1902*, Pretoria, 1974, 54–5.
30. Milner Papers, 105, Milner to Selborne, 27 September 1905.
31. For the leaders and their motives see Grundlingh, 311–46.
32. L. S. Amery, *Days of Fresh Air. Being Reminiscences of Outdoor Life*, London, 1939, 169; *Times History*, V, 409–10, 571–2; Spies, 282–3.
33. The repatriation of the Scouts and the land settlement scheme are dealt with in Denoon, *A Grand Illusion*, 81–2; Grundlingh, 350–78.
34. For the compensation issue see Denoon, *A Grand Illusion*, 63–4; Grundlingh, 378–93.
35. Transvaal Archives, GOV 615/372, 'Summary of the proceedings of a deputation which met Mr. Chamberlain at Sunnyside', 14 January 1903.
36. Intra-Afrikaner tensions are discussed in Grundlingh, 394–429; V. E. Solomon, 'The Handsuppers', *Military Historical Journal*, 3, 1 (1974), 19–21.

CHAPTER 12
The Anglican Church during the War

Margaret Blunden

The influence of clerical opinion

Joseph Chamberlain, in a speech on the war in Birmingham in May 1900, posed the rhetorical question, 'Who has influenced Her Majesty's Government?'. He answered it, 'In the first rank I put the ministers of religion in South Africa . . . these gentlemen, whose profession inclined them to peace, to whatever denomination they belong, and whether they are British or American . . . all the organizations and almost without exception all their ministers, are heartily on our side.'[1]

It seems likely nonetheless that the Unionist government, rather than being influenced by clerical opinion, regarded it as a welcome endorsement of policies already decided upon. It had been evident, at the time of the first and second Ndebele wars in Rhodesia in 1893 and 1896–7 and at the time of the Jameson Raid too, that British newspapers and public opinion took seriously the political views expressed by South African clergy of the British denominations. In this respect churchmen were not seen as an integral part of colonial society, but as men inclined to peace, and as disinterested observers of events in which they, unlike many others, had no vested interests.

Although Chamberlain found it convenient to conflate all the South African denominations with the British and American, and to ignore, for instance, the Swedish, German and Norwegian missionaries, who mainly supported the Boers, he was correct in claiming the support of most of the English-speaking denominations in South Africa. Anglicans in South Africa were in close accord with most Anglicans in Britain on this question, although a few Church of England clergy criticized their government's action in becoming involved in the war and voiced opposition to the methods employed during the conflict. Four prominent Anglican clergymen signed the National Memorial against the threatened war in South Africa and one of them, Bishop Percival of Hereford, wrote personally to Lord Salisbury, urging that,

> 'In the published dispatches & the known facts of the case we can see nothing that wd justify us in going to war, or wd make a war anything but a hideous blunder and a crime.'[2]

Both Percival, in the House of Lords, and Canon Gore, in a letter to *The Times*, criticized the concentration camp policy. Neither Percival nor Gore were, strictly speaking, pro-Boers, but the children of Anglican rectories did figure prominently among pro-Boer leaders, in the persons of Emily Hobhouse, F. C. Mackarness, Alice Stopforth Green, and the Cape politician J. X. Merriman. Critics of the war were a tiny, unpopular minority of the Anglican clergy in England. The Church of England and its daughter Church of the Province of South Africa substantially agreed on the righteousness of the British cause, whereas some of the nonconformists in Britain were embarrassed by the support for the British cause proclaimed by their associated denominations in South Africa. The Reverend Walter Friend of Port Elizabeth, chairman of the Congregational Union of South Africa, was asked not to speak about the war when he addressed the English Congregational Union in April 1901. Friend could not resist expressing his earnest belief that this was a just war, a remark that provoked a mixed response.[3]

The advent of war

It is not surprising that the Anglicans should have responded patriotically once the war began since they had done so in every earlier nineteenth-century war in which Britain took part, and were to do so again in 1914. More interesting is their position during the summer of 1899, when the gulf between British and South African perceptions of the seriousness of the issues at stake was still wide and government action was, in the view of the Colonial Office, circumscribed by the state of British public opinion. Several bishops of the Province privately expressed concern at the suffering likely to be caused by what would be an internecine war, and Archbishop West Jones of Cape Town in May 1899 had long interviews with the High Commissioner, Sir Alfred Milner, and with W. P. Schreiner, Prime Minister of the Cape Colony, in the hope of promoting a negotiated settlement. Lesser clergy, however, were publicly uncompromising. The most militant expression came in fact from an English clergyman, W. J. Knox Little, Canon of Worcester, who had travelled to South Africa the previous year and had stayed for a time with Cecil Rhodes, himself the son of a Church of England clergyman. Knox Little was not the first visiting Anglican ecclesiastic to be captivated by Rhodes as host, and to give public expression to views taken over from Rhodes on his return. Knox Little's book *Sketches and Studies in South Africa*, published in early July 1899, made a frank appeal for British force against the Transvaal. He urged at this delicate time of deteriorating relations that 'There is something saddening in the notion that English statesmen should waste the courtesies of diplomacy on the Transvaal Government.' Knox Little focused the issue in the simplistic terms that were gaining ground in England; the issue at stake was that of British or Boer supremacy, the one standing for justice and progress, the other for tyranny and retrogression.

The Reverend W. J. Knox Little, Canon of Worcester, an admirer of Rhodes, who believed British politicians should not 'waste the courtesies of diplomacy on the Transvaal Government'.

The clergy of the Province, on the other hand, perceived and projected the issues at stake during the summer months of 1899 in a bewildering variety of ways. The rationale offered for an uncompromising stand, and the view taken of the complicated moral issues raised, were not random. They can broadly be related, among other things, to the South African work experience and to the social and political circumstances of the clergymen concerned. The Anglican Church of the Province was first and foremost a colonial church, in which the white laity had, in regularly-constituted dioceses, an equal voice with the clergy in the management of affairs. The laity also made an important financial contribution since the Church of the Province, unlike the Church of England, had few endowments. Clergy in white parishes naturally tended to reflect the perspectives of their work area. There was no widespread exclusive concentration on the issue of the Uitlander, whose grievances almost monopolized public concern in England. The Archbishop of Canterbury in September refused a request by the president of the International Peace Association to denounce the imminent war from the pulpit of St Paul's on precisely the grounds that the British owed a duty to the Uitlanders and could not treat them as if their grievances did not concern them.[4] Yet the Reverend Charles Baumgarten, writing from the Transvaal to the English Church weekly *The Guardian* (16 August 1899) to endorse Milner's claim that the case for intervention was overwhelming, was unsympathetic to Uitlander claims and placed some emphasis on Boer maltreatment of non-Europeans. Anglican clergy in the Transvaal, whether they had supported the Jameson Raid or not, believed almost unanimously in 1899 that Boer rule should be ended. Baumgarten, an outspoken critic of the Raid who three years earlier had attacked the church's subservience to capitalist interests, had been, like other clergy critical of the Raid, affected nonetheless by the polarization of the two communities that resulted from it. Baumgarten's lack of concern for the Uitlanders was more common in the Cape, where, as Canon Wirgman of Port Elizabeth commented, the Uitlander question was merely a welcome excuse to force a long-standing issue with the Boers.[5] This is certainly the impression given by the correspondence with Lord Salisbury of Canon James Baker of Kenilworth in the Cape Colony, a correspondence that had begun in 1887; Baker's longstanding hostility to the Boers reached a climax in October 1899.[6] Another Cape colonial, the Reverend C. Usher Wilson, Rector of Colesberg, a predominantly Afrikaner area in the north of the Cape, made it clear in an article published in *The Nineteenth Century* in October 1899 that in his eyes the real issue at stake was the threat to British supremacy posed by the *Bond*, the Afrikaner political party in the Cape, not the treatment of the Uitlanders in the Transvaal.

It was colonial clergy, rather than missionaries, who deliberately brought their views to bear on ministers and the public in the summer and autumn of 1899. Colonial clergy were better educated and enjoyed a higher status than most rank and file missionaries, who were generally not graduates and whose position was regarded as equivalent to a curacy 'at home'. There are nevertheless some signs, even before the war began, of a missionary view of the conflict emerging, a view stressing the multiracial issues involved and justifying the British cause in terms of African interests. This view, though rarely deliberately brought to bear on the public or on officials, was taken up by others in the interests of war propaganda.

The missionary interpretation of the war

The chief exponent of a distinctively missionary view of the war was Bishop Bransby Key of St John's Kaffraria in the eastern Cape. Key, a non-graduate missionary who had served long and arduously in an almost exclusively African area on the Cape frontier, was an exceptional figure on the episcopal bench. The other bishops of the Province in 1899 had been educated at Oxford and Cambridge – with one exception from Trinity College, Dublin – and it was rare indeed for a bishop to have served in the missionary ranks. Key's perception of the issues at stake were as distinctive as his position. He put it to his diocesan synod in August 1899 that it was the different way in which the British and the Afrikaners regarded the question of governing Africans that had brought war so near.

> 'The question may have taken a different form for the moment, but the crucial difference between us has always been the way in which we accept this duty. They will learn the lesson too, for they are of our blood – the lesson of the white man's burden. Yes – we may say it with pride – our race has learned at last the lesson of equal rights, and the evil of class or race privilege. On fields of battle our ancestors have bled for this, and it has become part of the nature of us, their descendants.'[7]

Key's speech to his diocesan synod seems not to have been consciously aimed at a wider public. But on 13 October 1899, just after hearing the news of the declaration of war, Key wrote to his diocesan journal in Scotland urging that it should be impressed on friends at home that the real cause of the situation was the 'native question'. The war was a holy war, resting on the broad question, 'Are these natives of South Africa to be looked upon as beasts of burden or human beings?'[8]

The phrase 'holy war' was widely repeated, and Key's arguments were taken up as a justification of the war by men who hitherto had not placed much emphasis on African interests. Canon Wirgman of Port Elizabeth, a colonial clergyman who had in the past been critical of missionary attitudes towards Africans, quoted extensively from Key in an article in *The Nineteenth Century* (April 1900) written to rebut the accusation that this was a capitalists' war. That Wirgman was later, some years after the war, to withdraw his criticism of Afrikaner policies towards Africans suggests that he, like others, used Key's arguments for propaganda purposes. It is significant that no one took up another of Key's arguments that Africans should be allowed to fight alongside British troops.

Bishop Bransby Key of St John's Kaffraria, proponent of a distinctively missionary view of events, who interpreted the conflict as a 'holy war' fought in the interests of the black people of South Africa.

English colonial opinion and liberal African policies

The sharp distinction that Key made between British and Boer policies towards Africans was, of course, an oversimplification that ignored differences in attitudes between the Cape Dutch and the Transvaalers, and between the English in the Cape and the much less liberal English in Natal, with whom Key had little contact. The bishop made a serious misjudgement in identifying the English community in South Africa with liberal African policies in the imperial tradition, and in prophesying their eventual adoption by Afrikaners. Key, who rarely preached to the English community and then only in the Cape, did a disservice to African interests by failing to grasp that those interests would have to be fought for in the teeth of much English colonial opinion. The assumption, so prevalent in England during the war, that a British victory would automatically guarantee just treatment for Africans, was reinforced by the widespread use that was made of Key's views.

A much more accurate assessment of white South African opinion, put by a Natal clergyman in a private letter to Milner in August 1899, was never allowed to reach the public. Dean James Green of Pietermaritzburg had served in the colony for more than fifty years, and like other clergy in Natal, where the Anglicans were the leading denomination among Europeans, he was well embedded in colonial society. His wife was South African-born, and his son Edward Greene, Minister of Railways and Harbours in Natal, was to move at the 1908 Convention on Closer Union the resolution that excluded non-whites from the South African parliament. Green's initial purpose in writing to Milner was to recount an anecdote supporting the idea of a long-standing Afrikaner conspiracy 'to displace the English and convert South Africa into a Dutch settlement', a plan that would have succeeded had not Kruger provoked the English to exert themselves. But already in August 1899 Green was looking beyond the immediate conflict to the great question of relations between white and black. He was not only aware, as Key was not, of the strength of feeling among the English community against liberal African policies, but warned Milner of the grave consequences if the imperial government flouted local sentiment on the question:

> 'How our contest with Kruger will terminate, I will not venture to forecast; but, if we succeed in arranging matters with him, there will still remain the question to be settled by time, which is to be the predominant race, the Dutch or the English? For myself I think it probable that, on the native and Indian question, the English colonist will split with the Home Government, and go over to the Dutch, and in that way we may possibly lose South Africa.'[9]

African interests and war propaganda

Hardly any Anglican clergyman in South Africa or England publicly countenanced the idea voiced by some pro-Boers that the English community fundamentally agreed with Afrikaners over African policies. To accept such a proposition would have undermined much of the moral basis of the war in Church of England eyes. As the Bishop of Stepney acknowledged in a speech in November 1901,

> 'Among the things we said most readily, and which our consciences listened to most eagerly, was that we were to stand in brotherhood with the native races.'[10]

The claim that a British victory would ensure 'justice' for Africans was endlessly reiterated in sermons, addresses and church periodicals, and was even endorsed by those few clergy who had sufficient knowledge to suspect that enthusiasm for this cause among South African clergy was less than their English counterparts might have wished. An English war chaplain, whose account of his experiences were serialized in the *Church Times*, interpreted the war as a righteous one fought for equity and justice between Europeans and Africans even though he recognized, with rare candour, that,

> 'It is within the bounds of possibility that the colonial clergy, as a body, do not take so decided a stand as one might, perhaps, expect . . . because financially they are in the hands of the people and the power of the purse is strong.'[11]

The Church of England officially upheld the justice of the war. The collect recommended by the two Archbishops for use in churches asked for God's protecting care over soldiers fighting for the deliverance of the oppressed, and for the

Holy Communion on the veld, the subject of an illustration by the war artist Frank Craig.

maintenance of justice and equity between man and man. Special services were held for departing regiments, and clergymen volunteered, in excess of requirements, for service as war chaplains. Each division of the army, numbering 10 000–11 000 men, had two Church of England chaplains attached to it with officer rank. One clergyman from the diocese of Worcester went out on active service as trooper chaplain. A special prayer written by the Archbishop of Armagh was distributed by Lord Roberts for the use of soldiers in the field, chaplains were readily forthcoming from other denominations, and it was widely believed that there had never before been such a Christian revival in the army as during the South African War of 1899–1902.

War chaplains

Anglican leaders did not consider their support for the war to be political in the sense in which, it was urged, the Dutch Reformed Church was political. The Archbishop of Cape Town commented that the Dutch church had from the first taken a political line, and an army chaplain writing in the *Church Times* argued that Dutch Reformed ministers were the most powerful and bitter enemies that the British had.

> 'Religion in that Church, as it is in the "Free Churches" in this country, is largely political, and when the two cohabit there is always a tendency for politics to become the dominant partner.'[12]

Dutch Reformed ministers had, during the war as after it, an undeniably potent political influence on Afrikaners in their own areas and, furthermore, attempted to exploit Protestant solidarity with English nonconformists and thus stimulate sympathy for their cause among the British public. Dutch Reformed ministers addressed pro-Boer meetings in England,

A war chaplain stands beside a grave as the body of a soldier is brought to its final resting place.

'Carols for Christmas'. It was widely believed that there was an unprecedented Christian revival in the British army during the war, and services in Anglican churches in the British war zone were generally well-attended because of the number of soldiers present.

and 414 of their number signed a defence of republican policy sent to the Congregational Union in England. The solidarity of Afrikaner civilian support did not encourage such action behind their lines, even had Anglican clergy been prepared to undertake an activist role. Nevertheless, the role of the predikants in reinforcing the military morale of their side, and in justifying and celebrating the righteousness of the cause, was essentially similar to that played for their part by the Anglican clergy and those of other English-speaking denominations.

Clergymen from the Anglican Church of the Province up to the highest levels left their normal work to volunteer as war chaplains, and those who remained at their posts played a prominent part in sustaining morale. Churches in the British-controlled battle zone enjoyed something of a revival brought about by the large number of Anglicans in the British forces. In British-occupied Pretoria, where the civilian element was small and many church people had not returned, the church was reported in 1901 to be enjoying 'unparalleled parochial prosperity' from the large military element and the exemplary churchmanship and generosity of many of its members.[13] There were large congregations in the damaged churches of besieged Ladysmith and Mafeking, and the services held after their relief – like the victory service held in Pretoria in 1902 and attended by Lord Kitchener and 5 000 troops – were a powerful blend of religious, military and patriotic ceremonial.

One or two of the clergy of the Province who wanted to volunteer as chaplains were considered too valuable to leave their own areas, where Anglican clergy played an important part in restraining Africans from attacking the Boers. When William Carter, Bishop of Zululand, approached the Governor of Natal, Sir Walter Hely-Hutchinson, asking him to further his appointment as military chaplain, he was told that he had

The victory service held in Pretoria on 8 June 1902 attended by Lord Kitchener and 5000 troops – a powerful blend of religion, militarism and patriotism.

better stay where he was 'and help people keep their heads'.[14] Bishop Carter recounted in his manuscript notes on the South African War an incident involving his archdeacon – an incident that may have been typical of missionary exertions in many areas of operations:

> 'It was not long after the beginning of the war, when the Boers had occupied the Nqutu district magistracy, and had looted all the stores in the neighbourhood that an impi came to Archdeacon Johnson at 3 a.m. one morning and proposed to him that they should go and wipe out the Boers at the Magistracy. But he held talks and persuaded them to go back to their homes, telling them that it was no affair of theirs.'[15]

African interests after the war

The almost unanimous agreement to keep the war white had many roots – it reflected the view, as Bransby Key recognized, that Africans were not civilized men who could be relied on to follow the canons of accepted military behaviour, and the underlying assumption, apparent in much pre-war comment, that beyond the conflict the interests of the two white races lay in unity in the face of a black population that greatly outnumbered them. It is a convincing general hypothesis that underprivileged groups have benefited from their greater participation than hitherto in modern war.[16] The general agreement during the Anglo-Boer War to restrict African participation to non-combatant support roles – stoutly maintained in public though not always observed in practice – bears some relation to the small gains that the war brought to the African peoples. The war could not, simultaneously, be fought for justice to the African, as so many Anglicans liked to assert at the time, and be 'no affair of theirs' as Archdeacon Johnson urged.

The precise benefits that the war was expected to bring to Africans – apart from increased exposure to missionary endeavour – were rarely discussed. Only two Anglican clergy made any serious attempt to discuss African policies publicly after the war. One of these, Canon Farmer of Pretoria, a missionary whose book *The Transvaal as a Mission Field* was published in London in 1900, was convinced that Africans were not asking for the vote immediately nor did they want to be put on a footing of equality with white men. He suggested a form of separate representation. The Reverend John Bovill from Lourenço Marques in Portuguese Mozambique, where resident white Anglican laymen were few, put forward a detailed list of necessary changes under post-war British administration in his book *Natives under the Transvaal Flag*, also published in London in 1900. Bovill, based in an area that supplied African migrant workers to the Transvaal gold mines, was particularly concerned with labour questions: the pass system should be utterly destroyed, African reserves near the mines should replace the all-male compounds, accredited labour agents should be appointed and workers should be protected in transit to the industrial area. Bovill did not consider the question of political representation, but he advocated assisted voluntary education for Africans, and African freehold land and property purchase.

Such detailed attention to the post-war needs of Africans was extremely rare, and there was, in fact, to be no Anglican pressure on the post-war British administration in the Transvaal to implement any such changes in African policies as those outlined by Bovill. The circumstances of Bovill's work and his point of view were both far removed from those of most Anglican clergy in the diocese of Pretoria, who worked almost entirely among whites and had absorbed some of the racial assumptions prevalent in the locality. The complaints of Anglican clergy in the Transvaal of Boer cruelty to Africans sometimes reflected an objection not to Boer practice but to Boer rule. Although the bishop appointed to Pretoria in 1902 had a liberal record on racial questions in his previous diocese, he was much affected by an establishment belief in supporting constituted authority, and especially British authority, a profound respect for imperial officials such as Milner, and the policy of the Society for the Propagation of the Gospel in London, which was put to him in a letter of 8 May 1903:

> 'We do want to stand up for loyalty at this time and to aid the Government to the utmost of our power, and to stretch every point in the endeavour to do it.'[17]

Before the conclusion of hostilities one attempt was made to bring pressure to bear on the imperial government for the protection of African political rights in the peace settlement. The Reverend William Crisp, formerly a missionary in the diocese of Bloemfontein who in 1901 became secretary of the Cape Town diocese, attempted to organize an address to Chamberlain requesting that the post-war charters establishing civil government in the Orange River Colony and the Transvaal should secure 'full legal rights and equal civic possibilities to Africans'.[18] Crisp's thirty years in the diocese of Bloemfontein, as a member of a celibate brotherhood and as a Setswana expert involved in pioneering missionary work, had been spent at some remove from colonial society. His address, which he invited his fellow clergy to sign, ran into strong opposition from the most senior of the colonial priests, Dean James Green of Pietermaritzburg, who two years earlier had already addressed Milner on the 'native question'. Green attached overriding importance to the continuing good relationship of South African colonists with Britain, and to South Africa's place in the empire. He emphasized to Crisp the opposition to 'equal civic rights' from both Afrikaner and English communities, and the danger to imperial unity if the British government opposed colonial views on this question.

> 'The Dutch are, to a man, opposed to granting the natives civic rights such as they and we enjoy. A large number of Englishmen on your frontier and in Natal are as opposed to it as the Dutch. Why then flaunt as a red rag before them an untried, unproved theory, which, when tried, may prove an utter failure? I can go with Mr Chamberlain in wishing to secure to the native the *right of self-government*, but that, at first, should be through their own tribal organization, which could be modified as they advance in education. Express yourselves in that way, and many amongst the Dutch and English may, to some extent, be satisfied. The native question is a most delicate one. If, twenty-five years hence, the Home Government comes into collision with the Colonists over native matters, the English will join the Dutch, and South Africa may yet be lost to the Empire. I therefore very earnestly pray you in the interests of peace, present and prospective, to express yourselves very differently in regard to *civic possibilities*.'[19]

It is not clear whether Crisp withdrew his projected address altogether, or modified it in the direction suggested by Green. It is clear, however, that there were many Anglican clergy, especially those with white parishes in the former republics, who would not have endorsed 'equal civic possibilities' for Africans. A united Anglican approach to Chamberlain along these lines was impossible.

Green told Crisp that missionaries had in the past done harm by interfering in the politics of Cape Colony; he nevertheless felt moved to write again to Milner warning him of the threat to imperial unity if the British government collided with colonial opinion on the 'native question'. Green proposed a distinction between personal rights and equality before the law, in which all should share, and political rights, which should be reserved for white people in South Africa, who had a special talent in this field.

Dean James Green of Pietermaritzburg, who argued with some force that colonial opinion was not prepared to accept a meaningful extension of civil liberties to black people: 'If, twenty-five years hence, the Home Government comes into collision with the Colonists over native matters, the English will join the Dutch, and South Africa may yet be lost to the Empire.'

> 'I hold therefore, that we do no wrong to others, if the constitution granted to the Colonies gives the franchise to every subject of European descent born in South Africa, or to any other of European descent after so many years' residence, and leaves the Legislature entirely unfettered in regard to granting the franchise to any one not of European descent.'[20]

Milner himself attached great importance to English colonial opinion. Although both Chamberlain and senior Colonial Office officials had grave reservations about handing over decisions on the political future of Africans to an unfettered South African legislature, Milner, in a dispatch to Chamberlain written on 6 December 1901, shortly after his receipt of Green's letter, defended the rectitude and high-mindedness of the best colonial feeling on African questions. Prominent Anglican clergy lent moral authority to the opposition to African political rights while at the same time encouraging Milner to be optimistic about the 'improving tone' of colonial attitudes.

There was, in the event, virtually no protest from either Anglican clergy or those of other denominations to Article Eight of the Peace of Vereeniging, which deferred decision on an African franchise until after the grant of self-government to the annexed Boer states. Those few clergymen who had hoped for a guarantee of African political rights were perhaps deterred by the impossibility of a united front, perhaps affected by the prevailing war weariness. In spite of the precise terms of the peace agreement they very likely placed their trust in the justice that it was so often claimed was the concomitant of British supremacy. Many clergy in the former republics would doubtless have concurred with the Bishop of Natal that 'It was felt on every side that the terms were completely satisfactory.'[21]

The Church of England clergy, little informed for the most part about South African affairs, readily accepted this judgement. Attention was focused on the opportunity created for expanded missionary work; both the Anglicans and the Dutch Reformed Church derived powerful missionary impetus from the ending of the war. As the debate at the Church Congress held in Northampton in October 1902 made clear, the redoubled Anglican missionary effort had a political as well as a religious purpose in reinforcing the imperial loyalty of black South Africans.

The Church of the Province was impelled nonetheless by the justification of the war in African terms, and by the entry of new clergy into the conservative diocese of Pretoria, into a formal consideration of its attitude to African policies. The Provincial Board of Missions privately solicited the opinion of its members in the course of 1902 and 1903 on what should be the church's attitude to African education and to labour, political and social questions. Although the bishops of the Church for the most part privately endorsed the principle established in the Cape Colony of a franchise based on civilization, not colour, the tone of the replies indicated considerable reluctance to adopt 'missionary' attitudes, which were looked upon as offensive to white susceptibilities. The official memorandum, presented in January 1904 to the Provincial Synod of the Church, an organization in which the white laity had a powerful voice, was substantially more negative than the private correspondence that had preceded it. The memorandum, which was accepted without debate, stated that 'The acceptance of Christianity has never involved, of necessity, social equality between individuals in any race, nor does it necessarily involve equality between one race and another.'[22] The 'mere' fact that a man was a Christian did not fit him to take a share in the government of the country unless he understood how to exercise the franchise properly.

Conclusion

The support of the Anglicans and other English-speaking clergy in South Africa was valued by the British government as an apparently independent moral endorsement of the justice of the British cause. In particular, the view expressed by some Anglican missionaries that the war was, in essence, being fought to secure 'justice' for the African, was given wide currency in the interests of war propaganda, and provided a welcome reassurance to the English church-going public. The missionary exponents of this point of view did, however, underestimate the strength of feeling against granting African political rights among the English community in South Africa, and failed to bring pressure to bear to secure guarantees for Africans in the peace settlement. The majority of the Anglican clergy in South Africa shared to some extent the racial attitudes prevalent in the English community, and were reluctant to offend the powerful white Anglican laity. Once the war was over, it was an English colonial, rather than a missionary, point of view that made itself heard in the church's pronouncement on African questions.

References

1. Quoted by Alfred Marks, *The Churches and the South African War*, London, 1905, 2.
2. Salisbury Papers, class H, Bishop of Hereford to Lord Salisbury, 7 September 1899.
3. *The Times*, 27 April 1901, 12.
4. Frederick Temple Papers, 332f.
5. A. T. Wirgman, *Storm and Sunshine in South Africa*, London, 1927, 259.
6. Salisbury Papers, class H, Baker to Salisbury, 24 October 1899.
7. *Foreign Mission Chronicle*, 1, 1 (January 1900), 6.
8. *Ibid.*, 21.
9. Milner Papers, 182, 213f.
10. *Church Times*, 29 November 1901, 654.
11. *Ibid.*, 9 August 1901, 161.
12. *Ibid.*, 26 July 1901, 111.
13. *SPG Annual Report 1901*, SPG, London, 1902, 142.
14. Carter Papers, MSS notes on South African War, 6.
15. *Ibid.*, 3–4.
16. See Arthur Marwick, *War and Social Change in the Twentieth Century*, London, 1974.
17. SPG, Africa Letters Sent, 6, 173f, Bishop Montgomery to Bishop of Pretoria, 8 May 1903.
18. A. T. Wirgman, *Life of James Green* London, 1909, II, 249.
19. *Ibid.*
20. Milner Papers, 178, 125–6f.
21. *Church News from Natal*, 91, July 1902, 65.
22. *SPG Annual Report*, SPG, London, 1904, 149.

CHAPTER 13

The Poetry of the War

Malvern van Wyk Smith

Introduction

I have made for you a song,
And it may be right or wrong,
But only you can tell me if it's true.

With these words of dedication to Tommy Atkins, Kipling opened his *Barrack-Room Ballads* in 1892, a work that had reached its sixteenth edition by the outbreak of the South African War – a war that would prove not only how popular Kipling's image of the common soldier had become, but also how 'true' the soldier regarded this image to be.

Compared to any of its predecessors, the South African War was a remarkably literary war. In most countries of the western world the highly contentious nature of the war, and the neuroses of imperial rivalry, produced two years of violent debate, much of it in the form of polemical verse. At the front, at least on the British side, the Education Act of 1870 and the resultant development of near-universal literacy ensured a mighty crop of soldierly comment, much of it once more in verse. Many contemporaries noticed this new phenomenon: 'Never before has Britain sent forth to the battlefield so large a force of men sufficiently educated to write home. The war, therefore, has been described from day to day, not like all other wars, by professional journalists or by literary officers, but by the rank and file', wrote one observer. A reviewer in the *Bookman* exclaimed on 'our army of a quarter million, each one almost to a man a war correspondent'.[1]

But it was not only at the front that a revolution had taken place since Britain's last major war, in the Crimea, almost half a century earlier. At home complex and far-reaching developments towards universal franchise and education, the growth of socialism and feminism, the quest for an at least relatively humanitarian society, and, not least of all, extensive army reforms in the latter half of the nineteenth century, had by 1899 produced attitudes to war and soldiering among ordinary people that differed radically from those prevalent when Tennyson wrote 'The Charge of the Light Brigade'. George Sturt spoke for much of his generation when he speculated in 1900 whether 'ever before men concerned themselves so much about the abstract morality of a war' and concluded that 'the old excuses for war are dying, if not dead', a sentiment echoed by Thomas Hardy in his most ambitious Boer War poem, 'The

Sick Battle-God'.[2] The soldier had become more attractive, more of an object for compassionate admiration, as war itself had become less acceptable. In this mutation lies the clue to what is most remarkable in Boer War verse and most accurate in Kipling's military portrayals of the 1890s.

Right: literacy at the front. A photograph of a drummer boy writing a letter on his drum, with his sergeant sitting by, reading.

The popular soldier figure of Boer War poetry, Kipling's Tommy Atkins, 'wiping something off a slate', ie. Majuba, 1881 (from H. W. Wilson, With the Flag to Pretoria, *1900, I, frontispiece).*

The poetry of the South African War can be divided both vertically and horizontally. Vertically we may distinguish, firstly, the loyalist verse, sometimes tempered by compassion for the soldier but rarely by misgivings about this particular war or about Britain's imperial cause. In quantity it forms, not surprisingly, the bulk of Boer War verse, though in quality it most frequently collapses into deplorable doggerel. Next comes a substantial body of poetry expressing doubt, protest or pacifism, as much smaller than the previous group as it is more attractive to a modern reader. The third and, once more, extensive group of poems is that produced by the combatants themselves, though here, of course, attitudes from the previous two divisions often emerge too. Afrikaners, both at the time and later, also produced a sizeable collection of verse, and so, finally, did many observers in Europe and in the rest of the English-speaking world.[3]

On a horizontal scale equally extensive strata of verse are revealed. Popular song, broadside ballad, brief lyric or blank verse epic – all were attempted, by labourers and academics, from costermongers to established authors, and their work may be found in penny pamphlet and sumptuous poetry review alike. Indeed, Boer War verse presents a cross-section of the whole contemporary literary scene in England and, to a significant extent, in Europe.

Loyalist verse

Of poems of blood-lust there were many, from music hall and popular press effusions such as

When Tommy joins the 'unt,
With the stabbin' of the baynit,
The baynit, the bloody baynit,
Gawd 'elp the man in front![4]

to the no less brutal exhortations of some establishment poets – Swinburne, W. E. Henley and the Poet Laureate himself, Alfred Austin. The day after receipt of the Boer ultimatum, Swinburne sallied forth in *The Times*:

Speech and song
Lack utterance now for loathing. Scarce we hear
Foul tongues that blacken God's dishonoured name
With prayers turned curses and with praise found shame
Defy the truth whose witness now draws near
To scourge these dogs, agape with jaws afoam,
Down out of life. Strike, England, and strike home.

But it was typical of a new mood in war poetry that even in this early and enthusiastic stage of the war Swinburne was not allowed to get away with these sentiments;

Where are the dogs agape with jaws afoam?
Where are the wolves? Look, England, look at home

suggested W. H. Colby in the *Echo* two days later. Also early in the war, the battle of Elandslaagte on 21 October 1899 offered one of the few classical cavalry charges that the war produced, yet it did not sire a great battle-piece comparable to Tennyson's. The *Illustrated London News* published a magnificent plate in the heroic tradition, but *Reynold's Newspaper* had already undercut it by producing, just before the war, a horrific description of 'a splendid charge' attributed to Dickens:

'There will be the full complement of backs broken in two; of arms twisted wholly off; of men impaled upon their own bayonets; of legs smashed up like bits of firewood; of heads sliced open like apples; of other heads crunched into soft jelly by iron hoofs of horses; of faces trampled out of all likeness to anything human.'

At least one war artist, F. J. Waugh, presented the charge from the traumatic perspective of the man on the ground, and by the time the *Idler* published T. T. Bouve's 'The Last Charge' in April 1901 enthusiasm for it was probably limited:

Trumpeter, blow on, terrific and thunderous,
Blow till thy bugle outrings the wild gales;
Spare not the wounded that writhe and wind under us,
Drown in our ears all their piercing death wails.

Nevertheless, it would be a mistake to suggest that rousing battle-pieces were not written during the war or were not popular. The vogue for public recitation of verse created a steady demand for pieces in the Tennysonian tradition, of which Percy T. Ingram's 'Colenso' serves as a fitting example:

A cavalry charge at Elandslaagte seen from three different perspectives, all illustrative of contemporary attitudes: a heroic plate from the Illustrated London News *(below, left); the war artist F. J. Waugh's version of the man on the ground's view (left) from Wilson,* With the Flag to Pretoria, *I, 357; and a French caricature showing a lancer spearing wounded Boers (below) from* Le Rire, *17 November 1900.*

Over the river, the river of death,
  Over the rush of the river,
Of guns half a score reached the opposite shore,
  The forward assault to deliver;
But caught by the fire of a deep ambuscade,
Like swathes from the sickle the gunners were laid,
Back, back through the river fell Hildyard's brigade,
  Back through the rush of the river.

But the highly derivative nature of such verse has ensured that Ingram's *Songs of the Transvaal War*, and equally popular anthologies such as Edward Tylee's *Trumpet and Flag* (1906) and Frederick Langbridge's *Ballads and Legends* (1903), have been forgotten.

It is, then, not rousing balladry but poetry keenly aware of the ironies and hardships of war that one will find even among poets who did not question England's right to war. Canon H. D. Rawnsley, lampooned by *Punch* for his prolific output

In war, he sings – with gay bravado –
  Each day's excursions and alarms,
The correspondent's escapado,
  Or Bugler Jinks his feats of arms

included much more thoughtful than thoughtless verse in his *Ballads of the War* (1900); for example 'The Last Question':

The curse of battle has its antidote;
  His were brave words, heart-medicine to give,
    Who dumb, because his face was shot away,
Took pencil in his dying hand, and wrote
  Not – "Doctor, have I any time to live?"
    But – "Doctor, did we win the fight to-day?"

Henry Newbolt came perhaps closest to capturing the glowing heroics of an earlier tradition in his *The Sailing of the Long Ships* (1902), but the best poem in the volume, 'Waggon Hill', shows his admiration for the bravery of the Devons outside Ladysmith to be infused with as much sorrow as pride:

Valour of England gaunt and whitening,
    Far in a South land brought to bay,
Locked in a death-grip all day tightening,
    Waited the end in twilight gray.
    Battle and storm and the sea-dog's way!
  Drake from his long rest turned again,
Victory lit thy steel with lightning,
  Devon, O Devon, in wind and rain!

It is possible to point to specific heroic archetypes of the past that were being questioned at this time, notably the dashing but virtually unarmed officer leading his men into assault. Donald Macdonald, war correspondent in Ladysmith, suggested the anomaly of this figure even while still admiring him: 'He has no rifle, no cover. With his useless sword in hand he strides bravely on, pointing the way, a conspicuous target for every sharpshooter on the ridge above him. It is the correct thing to do. It is the caste of the officer as compared with the man – and it is magnificent.'[5] But while most English illustrated papers still presented the officer in this heroic mould, German caricaturists lampooned him mercilessly, and H. C. Macdowall's poem in the *Spectator* (15 December 1900) provides a fair indication of the public debate that surrounded the British officer throughout the war:

Through bitter nights and burning days
  He watched the veldt stretch bare and grim;
At home beside the cheerful blaze
  We wrote our views of him.

We mourned his curious lack of brain;
  We judged him stupid, judged him slow;
How much of what he knew was vain –
  How much he did not know!

Where Duty called, he pressed in haste;
That, too, was wrong, that haste undue;
Why practise with such wanton waste
The only art he knew?

Too well he loved each foolish game;
'Is War a game?' we sternly cried.
And while we talked of England's name
For England's sake he died.

In any gathering of patriotic Boer War poets most readers would expect to find Kipling. Yet Kipling, though he supported the war and expressed the far-sighted belief in 'The Old Issue' that Britain had no choice but to oppose the clear dictatorial and racist tendencies of Krugerism, found it impossible to produce a great battle poem. The contents of *The Five Nations* (1903) presents the war largely as toil and tears, a grim duty of empire in which England has to learn ('The Lesson', 'The Islanders', 'The Dykes') as much as teach. His most moving Boer War poem, 'Bridge-Guard in the Karroo', presents a panorama not of battle but of 'the aching Oudtshoorn ranges', a massive African backdrop against which we watch not the pride of the British army in full operation, but a few soldiers guarding a bridge. They

stumble on refuse of rations,
The beef and the biscuit-tins;

they see themselves as 'forgotten and lonely' and their role as insignificant, but it is the railway line they are guarding, the one sure and visible means of laying down order on a new and hostile land. 'The wonderful north-bound train' brings light into their darkness and 'a mouthful of human speech'. When it has left them, the alien African heaven is still 'monstrous',

The English officer, armed with only sword and revolver, 'a conspicuous target' and a controversial figure in the poetry of the war, here seen heroically in Wilson, With the Flag to Pretoria, *I, 122, and lampooned by a French caricaturist in* Le Rire, *17 November 1900.*

but control of it and progress under it has become just that much surer: the 'solemn firmament' is

> Framed through the iron arches –
>   Banded and barred by the ties.

Thomas Hardy and A. E. Housman, too, did not essentially disagree with Britain's stance in the war, but they responded more powerfully than Kipling to the pathetic case of the ordinary soldier involved in a conflict beyond his understanding and demanding a sacrifice not fully justified by the cause. Several of the 'War Poems' in Hardy's *Poems of the Past and the Present* (1902) express the wistfulness of departure and the ambivalent spell of military glory. The most memorable of Hardy's poems on the war, 'Drummer Hodge', derives much of its power from this unresolved tension between a sense of futile loss and a strong conviction of nameless yet worthy achievement. Once again the alien environment of Africa is redeemed by its intimate union with an unspectacular English soldier who 'never knew . . . the meaning of the broad Karroo':

> Yet portion of that unknown plain
>   Will Hodge for ever be;
> His homely Northern breast and brain
>   Grow to some Southern tree,
> And strange-eyed constellations reign
>   His stars eternally.

While Hardy wrote about the war as a distant and detached observer, Housman was inspired by the personal loss of a brother in the campaign. His 'Illic Jacet'

> Oh hard is the bed they have made him,
>   And common the blanket and cheap

appeared in the *Academy* before the death of Herbert Housman at Bakenlaagte on 30 October 1901, but like the soldier poems in *A Shropshire Lad* (1896) it expresses the gentle melancholy and seductive fatalism that Herbert's death would bring into sharper definition. Housman's Boer War volunteer is no volunteer at all but a spellbound seeker, strangely drawn to a cause that is of uncertain value and certainly without reward. His 'Astronomy', published with the other Boer War poems only many years later in *Last Poems* (1922), joins 'Bridge-Guard in the Karroo' and 'Drummer Hodge' in appealing to alien constellations for judgement, but the verdict here is one of noble folly:

> For pay and medals, name and rank,
>   Things that he has not found,
> He hove the Cross to heaven and sank
>   The pole-star underground.
>
> And now he does not even see
>   Signs of the nadir roll
> At night over the ground where he
>   Is buried with the pole.

Poetry of protest

It is not a far step from Hardy and Housman to the verse of outright protest against the South African War. Hardy's 'Christmas Ghost Story' first appeared on 23 December 1899 in one of the leading Liberal, pro-Boer newspapers, the *Westminster Gazette*, which also regularly published the work of the most substantial poet to give active support to the anti-war campaign, William Watson. Watson was opposed not so much to imperialism (he won a knighthood in the Great War for espousing the cause) as to its total misdirection in a war against a people whom he saw as preserving exactly those virtues that an expanding industrial Britain had lost:

> Unskilled in Letters, and in Arts unversed;
> Ignorant of empire; bounded in their view
> By the lone billowing veldt, where they upgrew
> Amid great silences.

His Boer War poems (*For England*, 1904) all turn on this rural myth, the notion that the Boers upheld a pastoral and patriarchal society of simple Christian verities, with the result that he saw the dead on both sides as lost in a damnable cause:

> Already is your strife become as nought;
> Idle the bullet's flight, the bayonet's thrust,
> The senseless cannon's dull, unmeaning word;
> Idle your feud; and all for which ye fought
> To this arbitrament of loam referred,
> And cold adjudication of the dust.
> ('The Slain')

Much of the pro-Boer movement in Britain and Europe was inspired by the sentiments that Watson articulated, though he left it to G. K. Chesterton to voice in 'Africa' (*Poems*, 1915) the more seamy anti-semitic arguments of a capitalist conspiracy which informed so much of the more radical Liberal and socialist press at the time:

> Leave them the gold that worked and whined for it,
> Let them that have no nation anywhere
> Be native here, and fat and full of bread;
> But we, whose sins were human, we will quit
> The land of blood, and leave these vultures there,
> Noiselessly happy, feeding on the dead.

Pacifists played an important part in extending the range and impact of Boer War verse. The Hague Peace Conference, which ended only a few months before the outbreak of the war, had not only given the growing pacifist movement great encouragement and publicity, but had also made it quite fashionable. Middle-class intellectuals combined in large numbers in the capitals of Europe to form Boer-aid societies and to organize protest meetings and petitions. In Britain pacifist activity was only slightly less feverish. The Ethical Movement and the National Reform Union took the lead, along with

'. . . *leave these vultures there,*
Noiselessly happy, feeding on the dead.'
(G. K. Chesterton)
A French view of Rhodes amidst British casualties, from Le Rire, *17 November 1900.*

several others called forth by the occasion, such as W. T. Stead's Stop the War Committee and the Transvaal Committee. Their publications, such as *Ethical World* and *New Age*, fired off regular salvos of anti-war verse, and socialist papers such as *Labour World*, *Justice* and *Reynold's Newspaper* joined in with numerous satirical sallies of which an attack on Kipling in *Justice* (13 January 1900) may be considered typical:

O God of Battles, by whose fire
Thy Kipling warms his brain;
How blest are they who only pay
While other men are slain!

But often the anti-war press managed to eschew the stridency of versified polemic in favour of more moving expressions of loss. Ella Fuller Maitland's 'Through the Streets', first published in the *Spectator* (2 December 1899) but reprinted in several pacifist papers, is one of the more poignant exercises in this mode:

Through the dim London morning
The soldiers rode away,
The crowd, in sable, round them;
The sky above them grey.

Two strains of music played them –
One mournful and one glad.
It was the mournful music
That sounded the least sad.

At times, however, anti-war verse could verge on the horrific and reveal a sensationalism so close to that of more obviously hawkish poems that the distinction becomes hard to discern. So, for instance, Arthur Stringer's condemnation of war is manifest in the lurid lines of

Men, drunk with drum and trumpet, talked of God,
And reeled down blood-washed roads to Hell.

But what is one to make of Herbert Cadett's 'The Song of Modern Mars'?

Three miles of trench and a mile of men
In a rough-hewn, slop-shop grave;
Spades and a volley for one in ten –
Here's a hip! hurrah! for the brave.
A flash from the front that shames the sun,
The crash of a bursting shell,
And the rat-tat-tat of the Maxim gun –
A machine-made funeral knell.[6]

From the perspective of the First World War, 'Here's a hip! hurrah! for the brave' could be expected to be ironical in the context of 'slop-shop grave', 'shames the sun' and 'machine-made funeral knell', but it is unlikely that the editor of the popular music hall paper where the poem first appeared thought so. Sensibilities about war were changing and are nowhere more ambivalent than in depictions of the horrors of war. Donald Macdonald, writing entirely with admiration of the British resistance around Ladysmith, nevertheless remarked in his book *How We Kept the Flag Flying*:

> 'In Natal war was divested of absolutely everything that once lent it meretricious glamour – no bright uniforms, no inspiring bands playing men into battle, no flags, no glitter or smoke or circumstance of any kind, but just plain primeval killing, without redemption, and with every advantage taken that international law allows.'[7]

'Plain primeval killing' (Donald Macdonald). The new realism of war, potrayed by the war artist, F. J. Waugh (from H. W. Wilson, After Pretoria, *1902, I, 361).*

Poetry from the battle-front

Poems written at the front cannot always readily be told from verses produced at home, but among those known to have been written by soldiers the reader will find everything from ballads inspired by camp song, music hall and Kipling to ambitious attempts at lengthy narratives and complex lyrics. The soldier poet of the Boer War was certainly prolific. 'In the ease with which [he] pumped his muse, and the abundance of the results, we early came to know that the British army is an organized host of poets', observed Julian Ralph after editing the Bloemfontein *Friend* for a month during Roberts's occupation of the town.[8]

In subject and mood these verses articulated every likely and sometimes unlikely response to which fighting men might be given, from the bluntness of Arthur Maquarie's account of finding a comrade sniped in his sleep

At night we bathed our heads
  And laid us down to rest;
The one we lacked was there
  With blood upon his breast.

A little patch of black
  With pink around the rim –
We cursed our sniping foes
  And dug a grave for him

or Private A. Butler's cry of exasperation

War, war! what hast thou done for me,
  And thousands more besides,
Who've had to leave their dear old homes,
  Their children and their wives?

to an anonymous cavalry subaltern's nonsense rhymes on the pursuit of the elusive General de Wet

We have good reason to believe
  Their force is large or small,
And furnished with some fifty guns
  Or else no guns at all;
Commanded by one C. de Wet,
  Which seems a little queer,
As someone else reported him
  Five hundred miles from here

and the remarkably outspoken homosexual poems which Austin Ferrand, killed by a sniper in October 1900, had addressed to Lionel Johnson in England:

The three red flecks on your warm brown skin
  Are three bright gems of Orion's belt:
They stir my blood with fire and wine;
  The slow sky wheels o'er the barren veldt
Till the starlight faints, falls pale and thin.[9]

Two of the more accomplished poets at the front were

'Mome' (G. Murray Johnstone) and 'Coldstreamer' (Harry Graham) who respectively produced *The Off-Wheeler Ballads* (1910) and *Ballads of the Boer War* (1902). Both were imitators of Kipling but turned his vernacular style to sharper satirical use, as in Graham's 'The Army Chaplain':

We're 'miserable worms', says 'e,
An' earth's a blooming 'vale o' tears'.
(I ain't no worm, an' seems to me
This h'earth's no worse nor it appears;
It may be bad, h'or it may not, –
But it's the h'only one we've got.)

Graham was a captain in the Coldstream regiment. Johnstone, a captain in the South African forces during the First World War, could turn out accomplished ballads of action such as 'The Off-Wheeler'

We was racing hard for safety when he crossed his legs and fell,
And he bust the bloomin' traces and we jammed,
And the bullets they was falling – Lord, how them bullets fell! –
So we took the gun across him and be damned!

and poems of a corrosive vividness such as 'The Front':

A bit of a scrap on a bit of a plain,
And somebody shot in the head;
A bit of a row at the front again,
And a bit of the map that's red.
And somebody pulling the wires at home,
Whilst somebody's son lies dead.

Among battle-front poets one may also count the Australian, A. B. Paterson, and Edgar Wallace, both war correspondents. Paterson, author of 'Waltzing Matilda', wrote mainly wry 'bush ballad' narratives, such as (Ambulance) 'Driver Smith'

And he said to the boys that were marching past, as he gave his whip a crack,
"You'll walk yourselves to the fight," says he –
"Lord spare me, I'll drive you back"

'We was racing hard for safety when he crossed his legs and fell'
(Mome, *'The Off-Wheeler'*)
A detail from 'Saving the guns at Farquar's Farm, Ladysmith' (from Wilson, With the Flag to Pretoria, *I, 38).*

Wallace produced some ghoulish pieces that fused a stark journalistic realism to a clipped style, and his poems are all the more striking for the knowledge, gleaned from his notebooks, that some were written *before* the war while Wallace was still a medical orderly in Simonstown:

> A tent that is pitched at the base:
> A wagon that comes from the night:
> A stretcher – and on it a Case:
> A surgeon, who's holding a light.
> The Infantry's bearing the brunt –
> O hark to the wind-carried cheer!
> A mutter of guns at the front:
> A whimper of sobs at the rear.
> And it's *War*! "Orderly, hold the light.
> You can lay him down on the table: so.
> Easily – gently! Thanks – you may go."
> And it's *War*! but the part that is not for show.[10]

Among front-line productions one of the most searing must be 'The Black Watch at Magersfontein', an anonymous ballad that exists in manuscript in Africana collections in Johannesburg and Cape Town and in various bowdlerized printed versions.[11] Based on the disastrous engagement of the Highland Brigade at Magersfontein in which the Black Watch regiment was all but halved

> Nine hundred went to the slaughter, and
> Nearly four hundred fell

the poem gives a crude but vibrant account of the day's action, closing with an excoriating attack on the commanding officer, Lord Methuen, whose reputation in England as the youngest lieutenant-general in the field at the time had become somewhat inflated:

> Such was the day for our regiment,
> Dread the revenge we will take.
> Dearly we paid for the blunder of a
> Drawing room General's mistake.
>
> Where was the gallant General –
> Three miles in rear out of sight.
> No men to issue us orders,
> Men doing what they thought right. . . .
>
> Why wer'nt we told of the trenches?
> Why wer'nt we told of the wire?
> Why were we marched up in column
> May Tommy Atkins enquire. . . .
>
> Do they know this in old England?
> Do they know his incompetence yet?
> Tommy has learnt to his sorrow
> And Tommy will never forget.

Pro-Boer poets

Until the appearance of a powerful body of Afrikaans poetry during the decade after the war, the Boers were not their own best spokesmen. Largely semiliterate and leading a highly mobile existence, they produced (or preserved) only some fairly naïve commando songs and stumbling balladic narratives. One exception was Joubert Reitz, youngest son of ex-President F. W. Reitz of the Orange Free State, himself an accomplished comic rhymster. Most Boer poems were by-products of the enforced inaction of concentration and prisoner of war camps, and Joubert Reitz wrote a number of caustic poems, mostly in English, after being sent to Bermuda at the age of only eighteen. His 'What were your thoughts?' competently dismantles the pious and political rhetoric that permeated Boer as much as British thinking during the war:

No! I think if you'll remember all the things you thought of when
You were fighting like a demon, you will find that your thoughts then
Were not quite so pure and holy as they should be when you stand
At death's door, which might be opened now for you at God's command.
Oh no! You were but as a brute, and thought but that to slay
Was your especial mission, be the chances what they may;
You had but become a savage wishing to avenge the blood
Of your dead and dying comrades lying down there in the mud.[12]

The most able poets in the Boer cause were, surprisingly, English, whether writers such as Perceval Gibbon (*African Items*, 1903) and Kingsley Fairbridge (*Veld Verse*, 1909) who knew the Boers well, or South Africans who were in empathy with the Boers and whose work mostly appeared in the *South African News* and *New Age*, or British poets such as Canon H. D. Rawnsley and Alice Buckton who, though they had no personal experience of South Africa, captured the Boer ambience remarkably well.

During the final year of the war a number of anonymous poems originating from Cape Town were published in *New Age* and soon afterwards collected in *Songs of the Veld* (1902). The authors were three young women, Betty Molteno, Alice Greene and Anna Purcell, all protégées of the South African writer and critic of the war, Olive Schreiner.[13] Betty Molteno wrote rather grandiose defamations of British imperial policy after the manner of Edmund Carpenter

O England, thou old hypocrite, thou sham, thou
Bully of weak nations whom thou wert called to aid

and Anna Purcell wrote one or two moving ballads on the tragic denouement of the war for the Boers, for example 'The Rebel':

Only a youth!
Scarce one and twenty years
Of summer sunshine and of wintry tears
Had o'er him passed! . . .

Only a youth!
His friends in sullen mood
Around him stood, as once before men stood
At Slagtersnek![14]

Alice Greene, however, was a poet of some ability and managed in several powerful ballads to endow Boer resistance in the Cape with the heroic pathos of a stoic struggle. 'The Last March of Lotter's Commando', for instance, presents the rounding up of what many colonists regarded as no more than a marauding band in these terms:

The hollow square. An open-air Cape rebel trial in Graaff-Reinet of the kind referred to in poems by Anna Purcell, Alice Greene and C. Louis Leipoldt. Below: a surviving photograph of the execution by firing squad of Gideon Scheepers, so ill he had to face his executioners tied to a chair.

Then they marched them through the township,
For their friends and foes to see;
They were 'ignorant bywoners',
Rich in neither land nor fee:
But they marched with head uplifted,
Men of upland veld and farm,
With their bearded country faces,
And their air of stately calm.

Even more trenchant is 'The Four Roads', describing four sets of rebel executions, including that of Gideon Scheepers, the most legendary commander of the rebel forces in the Cape, who was so ill that he had to face the firing squad tied to a chair:

Four roads lead out of the town,
And one of them runs to the West,
And there they laid the rebels twain
With the bullets in their breast.
And the English Commandant laughed low,
As he looked at the sleeping town,
'Each road shall bear its vintage soon,
And your feet shall tread it down!' . . .

Four roads lead out of the town,
And one of them runs to the North,
And there they led the dying man
In the Red-Cross wagon forth.
And a bullet has stopped the glorious life,
And stayed the gallant breath.
And Scheepers lies 'neath the road that leads
To the land he loved till death.

Canon Rawnsley was no pro-Boer, but his 'Old Mortality' is one of the most sharply etched vignettes of the enemy produced by any British writer. It is considerably less condescending than Kipling's much better known 'Piet':

With rifle, bible, luncheon-bag, and pipe,
We saw him going forth each day to snipe;
We watched him on the foemen get his bead
Then fire, then turn his Holy Book to read. . . .
We called him "Old Mortality", and came
Almost with love to think upon his name –
This Bible-reading, smoking, sniping Boer,
Whose shots were frequent if his bag was poor;
And tho' his humour was a little grim,
We sighed when Death the Sniper called for him.

But what Rawnsley achieved in one or two poems, Alice Buckton sustained through much of a whole volume, *The Burden of Engela: A Ballad-Epic* (1904). In a series of ballads the work tells the story of a single Boer family's fate during the war, displaying the author's keen insight into proud rural minds and a dramatic ability to capture them in revealing moments. Her range is considerable and can only be suggested here by juxtaposing the brief epigraph on the concentration camp death of the family's youngest son with the end of a poem on Engela's response to a British demand for her horses:

Under the wild moon
A rough stone stands,
Raised too soon,
Marked by alien hands,
Glimmering white afar
In the dead lambs' fold –

"Jaapie – prisoner of war –
Ten years old!"

Four pistol shots rang out in the silence of the night –
The cow-boy started forth from his hut in sudden fright,
And met a reeling woman bearing a stable-light.

Two troopers came at dawn, with a sergeant at their head.
"Yield us the stallions, woman! the brown one and the red!"
She gazed as one that wanders: "Take them," was all she said.

Afrikaans poetry

If Boer poets were relatively little in evidence, the first generation of Afrikaans poets after the war – Eugène Marais, Jan F. E. Celliers, J. D. du Toit ('Totius') and C. Louis Leipoldt – filled the gap with a number of poems probably more remarkable than anything in English. Kitchener's scorched-earth policy, the shipping of prisoners of war to distant shores, the execution of Cape rebels, the deaths of thousands of women and children in concentration camps, and the final trauma of defeat, all ensured a growing rather than diminishing national preoccupation during the next decade with injustice, resentment and self-determination.

Of the four, Du Toit remained the most resolutely concerned with the theme of national sorrow through several anthologies. Eugène Marais, a medical student in London for most of the war, produced least but was responsible for one of the most haunting of these early Afrikaans poems: 'Winter Night'. Published in *Land en Volk* in 1905, it made no explicit mention of the war, but its theme of bleak denudation was readily interpreted as an expression of the post-war mood:

O cold is the slight wind
    and sere.
And gleaming in dim light
    and bare,
as vast as the mercy of God,
lie the plains in starlight and shade.
    And high on the ridges,
    among the burnt patches,
the seed grass is stirring
    like beckoning fingers.

O tune grief-laden
on the east wind's pulse
like the song of a maiden
whose lover proves false.
In each grass blade's fold
a dew drop gleams bold,
but quickly it bleaches
to frost in the cold![15]

Celliers was the only one of the four to serve extensively on commando during the war, but though he wrote several sentimental narratives in the field, it is his later 'Dis Al' ('That's All') that really penetrates the heart of Boer response. Compact, incantatory, it etches into the posture of a single Boer returned from exile the haunting remorse of a nation:

Gold,
blue:
veld,
sky;
and one bird wheeling lonely, high –
that's all.

An exile come back
from over the sea;
a grave in the grass,
a tear breaking free;
that's all.[16]

The greatest achievement among these four poets was, however, Leipoldt's, partly because his identification with the narrower nationalism of the Boer cause was much more ambivalent. Of German parents, he spent the crucial years of Afrikaner reassessment (1902–14) in England and Europe. During the war he edited the *South African News* in Cape Town and attended rebel trials in the eastern Cape, on which he based his powerfully sustained dramatic monologue, 'Oom Gert Vertel' ('Uncle Gert's Tale'). Deceptively underpitched and exploiting an obliquity of narrative that camouflages the speaker's complex motives and self-deceptions, the poem suffers too much in translation and extract to be quoted briefly.[17] In 300-odd lines of colloquial blank verse it dramatizes the large moral and emotional dilemma that Cape Boers faced during the war: the harrowing choice between their legal loyalty to the British crown and their racial affinity with the empire's enemies. Oom Gert, at the time of the events not quite sure of his own position, helps a young Boer who is also his godson and his daughter's wooer to join a rebel commando. When the boy is captured Oom Gert is summoned to witness the execution. The poem is characterized throughout by the narrator's attempts to avoid rather than to tell the story, but Oom Gert's self-knowledge and the extent of his commitment grow till at the end the reader is aware of the full force of the poem's opening line: 'You want to hear the story of our death?'

Poetry from the United States, Europe, and the Empire

Boer poets and their Afrikaner successors were remarkably modest about their prowess on the battlefield, but it was a very different matter in the United States and in Europe. Here Boer admirers became ecstatic at the prospect of two small rural republics, imagined to epitomize all the lost agrarian and edenic virtues of pre-industrial societies, taking on the armies of an opulent and decadent empire. Henry A. Harman of Springfield, Massachusetts, spoke for the majority of American observers when he identified the Boers with the generation of George Washington:

> Brave heroes! They, in that dark hour,
> Their feeble weapons boldly hurled
> Against that mighty, ruthless power,
> Whose morning drumbeat girts the world.

So too did E. van der Meulen and C. S. Hulst when they cast the Boers in a pastoral, Biblical mould:

> And what though the land was his homestead,
> And within its narrow confines
> Himself and his simple kindred
> Beneath its fig trees and vines
> Led harmless lives, and contented?[18]

The popular nature of the Boer cause in America is well attested by the numerous rollicking recitational ballads produced there, two of the best being Bernard Shadwell's 'Rebel of the Veldt' and 'De Wet', both in *Songs of the Veld*.

Unlike their Canadian counterparts, who, possibly because of the challenging proximity of American and French Canadian nationalism, produced the most consistently bad loyalist doggerel anywhere in the empire, Australian poets frequently found themselves in sympathy with the Boers or at least recognized that they might have more in common with these horsemen of veld and farm than with the rulers of the cosmopole. A. B. Paterson, George Essex Evans and J. H. M. Abbott all paid various degrees of southerly tribute to the Boer, but it was Henry Lawson who spelled out the unlikelihood of subduing a race of men so uncomfortably familiar:

> Till your gold has levelled each mountain range where a wounded man can hide,
> Till your gold has lighted the moonless night on the plains where the rebels ride;
> Till the future is proved, and the past is bribed from the son of the land's dead lover –
> You may hold the land – you may hold the land just as far as your rifles cover.[19]

Irish poetry on the war differed from such verse only in its much greater anti-British virulence.

European responses to the war were uniformly and mostly shrilly pro-Boer. Street song, cabaret turn, caricature, magazine poem and the more elevated sonorities of established poets such

The European response to the war was often maliciously anti-British. This is a print from Ludwig Thoma's Der Burenkrieg *(1900), captioned: 'English princesses award the Victoria Cross to the youngest soldier in the British army because, though only thirteen years old, he has already raped eight Boer women'.*

as François Coppée, Edmond Rostand and Sully Prudhomme in France and Willem Kloos and Albert Verwey in Holland were united in hero-worship of the Boer and execration of perfidious Albion. While Dutch poets exploited their racial affinity with the Boers to depict in the Transvaal a kind of lost Holland, French patriotic versifiers used the Boer cause to inflame the spirit of revanchism, which had suffered badly from the Fashoda incident and the Dreyfus affair; for Ernest Daudet the Boers were

> Un symbole vivant et l'immortel exemple
> De ce que peuvent ceux pour qui la Liberté
> Est, après Dieu, l'objet le plus digne d'un temple.

French scurrility reached its worst depths in the political caricatures of Jean Veber (from Les Camps de reconcentration au Transvaal, *special number of* L'Assiette au beurre, *28 September 1901*).

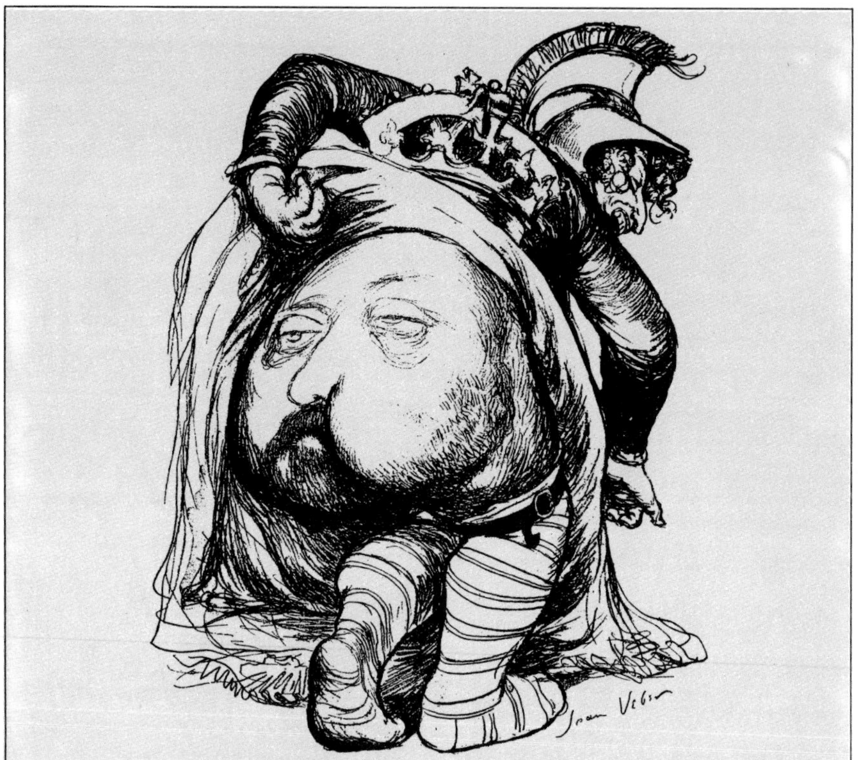

(A living symbol and deathless example of what they can do for whom Liberty is, after God, the cause most worthy of a shrine.)[20]

German writers saw in Boer resistance a struggle of Wagnerian dimensions between Teutonic prototypes – the Boer leaders were persistently cast as 'Heldenbrüder' – and the decadent but numerically overwhelming forces of urban decadence, materialism and just plain British faithlessness.

From this morass of highly polemical continental verse little can be salvaged, except for some German ballads. The outstanding figure here was Friedrich Lienhard, whose *Burenlieder* (1900) presented, like some of Edgar Wallace's poems, a new departure for war poetry into stark realism. His 'Kleingewehrkampf' ('Small arms fire') anticipates Wilfred Owen's 'stuttering rifle's rapid rattle', 'Der gefällte Riese' ('The Fallen Giant') is an account of a Boer shot in the face, and 'Buren-Patrouille' ('Boer Patrol') a sharply drawn glimpse of action:

Ganz tot der Berg! Ein rasches Rieseln nur
Von einem Eidechs, lang und schuppendick,
Der ins Geröll erschreckend fuhr.
Und dann ein Pferdekopf, ein leis Gekeuche –
Ein Hut und Karabiner – Lauerblick
Ins Thal – und wieder fort –
Das war ein Bur.

(Dead-still the mountain! Only the quick rustle of a startled lizard, long and scaly, darting in among the boulders. Then a horse's head, a muffled cough – a hat and rifle – a glance into the valley – and gone. That was a Boer.)

Another accomplished German balladist who turned his attention to the Boer War was Ludwig Thoma, whose *Grobleiten* (1901) and *Neue Grobleiten* (1903) contained several moving pieces on the war, 'Friede' ('Peace') being one of the most poignant:

Uber die Heide geht der Wind;
Es flüstert im Gras, es rauscht in den Bäumen.
Die dort unten erschlagen sind,
Die vielen Toten, sie schweigen und träumen. . . .

Wenn die Herrscher versammelt sind,
Beim festlichen Mahl lasst die Becher schäumen!
Uber die Heide geht der Wind;
Die vielen Toten, sie schweigen und träumen.

(Over the veld blows the wind; it whispers in the grass, it rustles through the trees. Underneath it the slain, the many dead, lie silent and dreaming. . . .

The conquerors gather – let the goblets foam at the festive board! Over the veld blows the wind; the many dead lie silent and dreaming.)

Links with the poetry of 1914–18

To what extent the poetry of the South African War may have influenced that of the First World War is a question that falls outside the scope of this chapter. There was clearly much indirect influence in terms of the changing sensibilities that Boer War verse recorded, but there is at least one poem that suggests more than just a chance anticipation of the poetry of the Great War. It is T. W. H. Crosland's 'Slain', first published in *Outlook*, 11 November 1899, collected in *The Five Notions* (1903) and reprinted in *War Poems by X* (1916) and *Collected Poems* (1917), in any of which it is tempting to think that Wilfred Owen may have read the poem. It uses the language and imagery Owen was to handle so effectively, its epigraph is the Horatian dictum 'Dulce et decorum est pro patria mori' which the later poet was to render notorious, and its final stanza anticipates Owen's ironic deflation of elevated sentiments:

You who are still and white
  And cold like stone;
For whom the unfailing light
  Is spent and done;

For whom no more the breath
  Of dawn, nor evenfall,
  Nor Spring nor love nor death
  Matter at all;

Who were so strong and young,
  And brave and wise,
And on the dark are flung
  With darkened eyes;

Who roystered and caroused
 But yesterday,
And now are dumbly housed
 In stranger clay;

Who valiantly led,
 Who followed valiantly,
Who knew no touch of dread
 Of that which was to be;

Children that were as nought
 Ere ye were tried,
How have ye dared and fought,
 Triumphed and died!

. . . .

Yea, it is very sweet
 And decorous
The omnipotent Shade to meet
 And flatter thus.

Crosland's poem provides thought-provoking evidence that during the South African conflict war poetry came a long way towards poetry of the pity of war.

References

1. Anon., *Pen Pictures of the War by Men at the Front*, London, 1900, Preface; *Bookman*, 22, 1902, 131.
2. Sturt, *Journals 1890–1927*, edited by E. D. Mackerness, Cambridge, 1967, entry for 10 June 1900; Hardy, *Poems of the Past and the Present*, London, 1901.
3. This chapter can cover only some of the major features of Boer War verse. Interested readers are referred to the author's *Drummer Hodge. The Poetry of the Anglo-Boer War 1899–1902*, Oxford, 1978.
4. Quoted in *Literary World*, 6 July 1900.
5. *How We Kept the Flag Flying. The Story of the Siege of Ladysmith*, London, 1900, 64.
6. Stringer, 'The War Spirit', *Bookman* (New York), 14, 1901–2, 416; Cadett in *Success*, 10 February 1900.
7. *How We Kept the Flag Flying*, 149.
8. *At Pretoria*, London, 1901, 189. See also Ralph's *War's Brighter Side*, London 1901.
9. Maquarie, 'Sniped', *The Voice in the Cliff*, London, 1909; Butler, 'Lines on the March of the Oxfordshire Light Infantry across the Orange Free State', typescript in the Royal Green Jackets Museum, Winchester, quoted by permission of Major H. P. Patterson; 'A South African Dream' from Capt. Sir George Arthur, *The Story of the Household Cavalry*, II, London, 1909; Ferrand, 'Guard at Night', *Outlook*, 27 October 1900.
10. Paterson, *Rio Grande's Last Race*, Sydney, 1902; Wallace, 'War', *Writ in Barracks*, London, 1900. Wallace's notebooks for the period are in the South African Library, Cape Town.
11. See *Drummer Hodge*, 194–7.
12. P. R. de Villiers Papers, Transvaal Archives, Pretoria, Acc.284. See also Deneys Reitz, *Commando*, London, 1929, and *Trekking On*, London, 1933.
13. The writers are identified in Anna Purcell's copy of *Songs of the Veld*, described in *Africana Notes and News*, 11, March 1955, 220–1. Their correspondence with Olive Schreiner is in the Murray-Parker Collection, University of Cape Town.
14. A Boer rebellion against British rule in 1815 that led to the execution of five dissidents and was frequently referred to by Olive Schreiner and others as the origin of the Boer–British struggle.
15. Trans. Guy Butler in A. P. Grové and C. J. D. Harvey eds., *Afrikaans Poems with English Translations*, Cape Town, 1962.
16. Trans. Guy Butler, *ibid.*
17. C. J. D. Harvey's translation in *Afrikaans Poems with English Translations* captures the poem's major nuances well.
18. Harman, *Freedom's Footprints* (1899); Van der Meulen and Hulst, *An Epistle to Ahab . . . dedicated to Joseph Chamberlain*, Grand Rapids, n.d.
19. 'As Far as Your Rifles Cover', in Colin Roderick ed., *Collected Verse*, Sydney, 1967.
20. 'Pour le Président Krüger' in Philippe Deschampes ed. *Le Livre d'or du Transvaal*, Paris, 1901.

CHAPTER 14

The United States and the War

Henry S. Wilson

Introduction

The South African war fascinated Americans. After a month's fighting, *The Times* of London observed that Americans displayed almost as much interest in the Boer-British conflict as they did in their own war against Spain, and this curiosity continued unabated until the armistice more than two and a half years later.[1] The spectacle of the farmer militia of the small Transvaal and Orange Free State republics (the latter with a constitution modelled on that of the United States) humiliating the professional soldiery of the world's largest empire inevitably recalled America's own struggle for independence. At the same time, the 'grand rapprochement' at the turn of the century reinforced an increasing Anglo-American diplomatic alignment with a sense of a common cultural heritage as English-speaking peoples and racial identity as Anglo-Saxons. Many Americans managed to combine concern over both the plight of the Boers and the predicament of Britain. Nor could a country whose politics had been wracked for decades by currency conflicts – over whether America, and the world, would fare better with gold, silver, greenbacks or bimetallism – culminating in the Republican administration's adoption of the gold standard in 1900, ignore the future of the world's largest gold supplier.

A number of newspapers and magazines sent their own correspondents to the field, and the fighting and attendant political issues were reported throughout the serious press. While prominent individuals and groups sought to elevate the war and relations with Britain into a pivotal issue in the 1900 election, Americans fought on both sides and supplied the spice of local interest to war reporting. Books were hurriedly published, ranging from Alfred T. Mahan's brief, brilliant analysis of the conventional war and extensive reports from such leading war correspondents as Richard Harding Davis and Howard C. Hillegas, to hasty compilations like Henry Houghton Beck's *History of South Africa and the Boer British War: Blood and Gold in Africa: the Matchless Drama of the Dark Continent from Pharaoh to 'Oom Paul': the Transvaal War and the Final Struggle between Britain and Boer over the Gold of Ophir: a Story of Wild Beasts and Wilder Men in Search of Sport and Guns and Gold*, a book that quite failed to provide the comprehensive enlightenment promised by its amazing title.[2]

Lecturers cashed in on the appetite for personalized reporting. After winning his first election to Parliament, and without taking his seat, Winston Churchill scurried off to North America to entertain audiences with the story of his escape from the Boers. (He, like many another raiding America in search of a fast buck, found the small print in his agent's arrangements disposed of much of the profit.)[3]

Nor did the leader writers and politicians approach the war devoid of ideas as to its causes, however ignorant some of them may have been of the legal niceties of 'suzerainty'. The involvement of prominent Americans, such as John Hays Hammond, Rhodes's undercover agent in Johannesburg, and the American consular agent, Gardner Williams, who smuggled guns in Standard Oil drums equipped with false bottoms, focused attention on the Jameson Raid and the origins of the Anglo-Boer dispute. Some Americans saw the conflict as a straightforward case of British aggression, motivated by greed for territory and gold, against simple pastoral republics. They vehemently endorsed Kruger's appeal that

> 'the great American nation, who had more than 100 years ago to fight the same British nation to secure their liberty, will know how to sympathize with a little sister republic, though faraway, which has now to fight a mighty power in order to maintain its independence.'[4]

For others Britain embodied the progressive spirit of the age that must triumph over the reactionary and isolationist Boers by the same inexorable Social Darwinist processes that had swept American Indians into oblivion.[5] Some Americans were deeply ambivalent, responding intellectually and emotionally to both views of the war, and in this complicated reaction they

'Willing to Learn', a cartoon from Harper's Weekly, *10 March 1900, showing Kruger engrossed in catalogues of the latest available weaponry.*

'Ready for Peace or War', *another cartoon from* Harper's Weekly, *10 March 1900, that also attempts to make some sense of the Boers' ability to resist the might of the British army.*

reflected the widespread feeling at the turn of the century that the United States itself was poised between the rural, isolationist frontier of the nineteenth century and the urban, industrial world power of the twentieth. Editorials in the *New York Times* exemplified the ambiguity, oscillating between sympathy for the Boers as a repository of traditional republican virtues and excoriations of them as pig-headed opponents of progress.

On the more purely political and constitutional issues many Americans also found it difficult to commit themselves unequivocally. On the one hand, the South African Republic sought to preserve or assert (depending on the interpretation of 'suzerainty') its national independence against British imperialism; on the other, the Uitlanders, the mainly British 'Anglo-Saxon' element, were being denied basic civil and political rights enshrined in the American Constitution. With each side grounding its case on hallowed American political principles, Theodore Roosevelt wrote to his sister in 1900 that

> 'the trouble with the war is not that both sides are wrong, but that from their different standpoints both sides are right.'[6]

One way out of the dilemma, frequently resorted to by the *New York Times* when it attacked the Boers, was to argue that because of its treatment of the Uitlanders – occasionally the Africans also were mentioned – the Transvaal was not a true republic along American lines but an oligarchy, compared to which 'Tammany Hall is a magnificent illustration of freedom and majority rule'.[7] With the same standard of comparison in mind, Finley Peter Dunne's fictional bar room philosopher, Mr Dooley, proposed a more pragmatic resolution of the quandary. 'If I was Kruger', he explained to his companion, Mr Hinnissy, 'therre'd've been no war. I'd give them the votes . . . But . . . I'd do the countin'.'[8]

Irish-American response to the war

Many Irish-Americans paid scant heed to the complexities that intrigued Mr Dooley. Maud Gonne, 'the Irish Joan of Arc', imported for the occasion, put the issue squarely to a mass meeting at the New York Academy of Music in February 1900. Quite simply, England was

> 'the robber nation of the world. Hence it matters not what nation England is at war with, right or wrong, it is Ireland's duty to oppose.'

In so far as her speech dealt with specifically South African issues, it accused English officers of deliberately killing every Irishman found in the Transvaal and charged Lord Methuen himself with shooting the Irish stationmaster at Modder River.[9]

Some Irish-Americans moved from verbal violence into direct action against the hated empire that held their kith and kin in subjection. There were plans for a filibustering raid into Canada by 'belated Fenians', which Theodore Roosevelt, then governor of New York, thwarted by threatening to turn out the militia and 'clap them all in jail'.[10] It was put to the United States government that if it did not take legal action to prevent the export of mules and horses for the British army from the port of Chalmette, near New Orleans, then Irish-Americans would have to resort to force.[11] Later, in February 1900, a prominent Irish-American offered to organize an expedition of 5 000 men to fight alongside the Boers, but nothing came of it.[12] Given the laws forbidding recruitment in the United States and the fact that Portugal was bound to have prohibited the overland transit of such combatants through its colonies to the war zone, the Irish societies decided that the most they could manage was an expedition of mercy under the auspices of the Geneva Red Cross. The Ancient Order of Hibernians organized what was ostensibly a Red Cross unit of fifty men under Dr John R. MacNamara, but as soon as they reached Africa they threw away their Red Cross badges and took up arms.[13]

Irish-American politicians tended to dominate the pro-Boer movement. Their natural allies on this occasion among other hyphenated Americans were the German- and Dutch-Americans. Sometimes there were complaints that the rambunctious Irish upstaged the rest, for example when Dutch-Americans greeted the Boer envoys in May 1900 they merely 'desired to emphasize their own ethnic relationship with the far-straying Afrikanders' and were embarrassed by 'an out and out display of hostility to England' from the Irish.[14] Nevertheless, the Irish had the flair and experience to take the lead. Both the German-Americans, who were politically more passive, and the Dutch, accustomed to cooperating and intermarrying with Americans of British stock, were no match for them at this kind of agitation.

Bourke Cockran, Irish-American politician and one of the most prominent supporters of the Boers in the United States, who was nonetheless much admired by Winston Churchill.

Bourke Cockran, the maverick Tammany Democrat, famed as one of the most powerful orators of the period, requested President McKinley before the fighting began to volunteer as a friendly mediator 'to delay, if not prevent, the threatened invasion of the Transvaal'. On 13 September 1899, after receiving the President's acknowledgement, he published his own letter in Pulitzer's *New York World*, thereafter the main pro-Boer newspaper.[15] Yet Cockran, for all his championship of the Boers, did not exhibit the wholesale anglophobia recommended by Maud Gonne. He saw the conflict as a byproduct of Britain's internal class struggle, a plot hatched by aristocrats to block the advance of democracy. And even among the imperialist English aristocracy he was prepared to make individual exceptions. Winston Churchill had fallen under Cockran's spell during his first visit to New York in 1895. Their friendship persisted, with Cockran serving the young Englishman as a political father figure. When Churchill was made a prisoner of war, Cockran anxiously solicited Boer leaders for information on his circumstances, and Churchill stayed with him in New York during his later lecture tour. Nor were ordinary Irish-Americans immune to young Winston's charm. In Chicago he pacified a noisy Irish-American audience with an impromptu passage praising the fighting qualities of the Dublin Fusiliers.[16]

Winston Churchill (on the right) as a prisoner of war in Pretoria in November 1899, looking remarkably detached from the proceedings. Cockran approached the Boers about Churchill's circumstances. Following his escape and subsequent election to Parliament, Churchill stayed with Cockran in New York in December 1900.

Trans-Atlantic accord

Most prominent Republicans in the United States favoured a quick British victory. Theodore Roosevelt, although sympathizing with the Boers and insisting that the Republican administration maintain strict legal neutrality, felt that Britain was undertaking the same role of benevolent international policeman that he sought for the United States in the western hemisphere. Indeed, he expostulated, Britain could no more indefinitely tolerate Boer ill-treatment of the Uitlanders than the United States could 'permanently submit to similar treatment of American citizens in Nicaragua'.[17] He observed further that those who hoped for a Boer victory were generally the same men 'that sympathized with Spain three years ago'. He was sure that 'the interests of the English-speaking peoples and civilization' – to Roosevelt the two were synonymous – 'demand the success of the English army'.[18] Mark Twain was just as forthright:

> 'England must not fail, it would mean an inundation of Russian and German political degradations . . . a sort of Middle Age night and slavery which would last till Christ comes again. Even when wrong – and she is wrong – England must be upheld'.[19]

Secretary of State John Hay was a notorious anglophile, looking the part 'from the tip of his English shoes to the point

Mark Twain: 'Even when wrong – and she is wrong – England must be upheld'.

of his neat gray beard'.[20] While ambassador to Britain he had demonstrated his deeply held convictions when he called for 'A Partnership in Benevolence' in April 1898:

> 'We are joint ministers of the same sacred mission of liberty and progress, charged with duties which we cannot evade by the imposition of irresistible hands.'

But for Hay this mystical partnership was rooted in the reality of capitalistic trade,

> 'for all nations of the world will profit more or less directly by any extension of British commerce and the enterprise and enlightenment that go with it'.

Speaking to a British audience Hay naturally stressed British trade, but as his latest biographer notes, 'he really meant Anglo-Saxon trade'. As he explained later to the American Society in London, Britain and America, through peaceful capitalist competition, would spread the benefits of civilization world-wide. Such rivalry

> 'threatens no one; it injures no one; its ends are altogether peaceful and beneficient . . . all the people of good-will on the face of the earth would profit by it'.[21]

Hay approached the South African conflict briefed by British Blue Books and, more important, by Cecil Rhodes. The

John Hay, Secretary of State and former American ambassador to Britain, a profound anglophile and admirer of Cecil Rhodes, for whom the spread of capitalism and 'civilization' were synonymous.

Englishman, wrote John Hays Hammond, who served as go-between at the ambassador's request,

> 'told Hay the whole story of South Africa as only he could tell it and Hay was won over to Rhodes and his aspirations'.

For Hay, British control over South Africa was as essential to the spread of civilization as the United States occupation was to the 'civilizing' of the Philippines. Without any of the sympathy for the Boers that distinguished Roosevelt, he hoped for a crushing British victory.[22]

The British case was also expounded by a variety of experts on Africa. John Hays Hammond threw himself into the work of explaining Britain's civilizing mission to business audiences, charging the Boers with threatening to disrupt the whole political order in South Africa by simultaneously provoking a massive African uprising and handing the goldfields over to Germany.[23]

Bishop Joseph C. Hartzell, responsible for American Methodist missions in Africa, stumped the country, proclaiming to large and generally enthusiastic audiences that only the British were fit to bear the white man's burden in South Africa. The Boers considered the Africans to be children of Ham and hence treated them as slaves, whereas in the Cape Colony, under British rule, 'blacks have the franchise under the same conditions as their white neighbors'. His perorations preached the pure creed of Anglo-Saxonism:

> 'God has given the unquestioned leadership to the two English-speaking nations, one in Protestant liberty in religion, one in civil justice, and one in freedom of commerce . . . let that unity stand, let it grow naturally as the best interests of humanity require'.[24]

It was all too much for German-American Methodists. The general Methodist conference for 1900 was held in Chicago and representatives of the strong German Methodist church in that city organized separate German-speaking meetings at which they protested that Hartzell had travestied the Boer cause, influenced, it was suggested, by the grant of free land for his missions by Cecil Rhodes.[25]

The black American bishop, Levi Jenkins Coppin, first resident bishop of the African Methodist Episcopal Church in South Africa, fixed on the same racial discrimination by the Boers that Hartzell had denounced. Reaching South Africa in 1900 when the British were already beginning to win the conventional war, he discerned a providential pattern in South African history. The Boers had treated their black neighbours as if they had no souls. 'But how pathetic today' to see the Boers 'by the thousands scattered on islands, in forts, in locations and on transports, with houses destroyed and property confiscated. "Be not deceived. God is not mocked".'[26]

Since it would have been damaging to British prestige to seek outside aid, England's friends were never called on to provide the kind of corporate help sought and given by Irish-, Dutch- and German-Americans to the Boers. The one major voluntary effort on the British side was made by a group of American women married to Englishmen who raised £40 000 to charter, equip and staff a hospital ship, the *SS Maine*. As a committed anti-imperialist Andrew Carnegie refused them help, but his employees gave £500. Winston Churchill's mother, Lady Randolph Churchill, led the group, which also included the Duchess of Marlborough and Mrs Joseph Chamberlain. Lady Randolph, a fervent believer in Anglo-Saxonism, was the founder of the short-lived *Anglo-Saxon Review*, whose motto was 'blood is thicker than water'. She obtained a promise from Queen Victoria to donate a Union Jack and sought an equivalent Stars and Stripes from President McKinley, but the President warily declined. So the ship sailed with a purchased American standard flying alongside the Union Jack and the Red Cross flag. (During the voyage Lady Randolph met a young man Winston's age. Their marriage in July 1900 supplied a splendid occasion for the American colony in London.)[27]

'blood is thicker than water'

Below left: Mrs Joseph Chamberlain, photographed with her husband.

Below right: Lady Randolph Churchill and John ('Jack') Churchill, who was wounded in the leg serving with the South African Light Horse, on board the hospital ship SS Maine *in Durban harbour. Lady Randolph, founder of the short-lived* Anglo-Saxon Review, *had a shrewd eye for publicity and the camera.*

Frederick Russell Burnham, a veteran of the Shona and Ndebele war in Rhodesia in 1896–7, who was called back to Africa from the Klondike to serve as Roberts's Chief of Scouts.

More Americans fought with the British than with the Boers, but they were recruited as individuals not as some anglophile equivalent of MacNamara's band. They were a mixed bunch, including straightforward mercenaries, muleteers stranded in South Africa once they had delivered their charges into British hands – there were accusations that the British impressed them but privation, rather than conscription, seems to have been the operative cause – and some dedicated adventurers, committed to the British side. The most famous of the latter was Frederick Russell Burnham, the archetypal American frontier scout. Burnham used his tracking skills on behalf of Cecil Rhodes against the Shona and Ndebele in the 1890s. While on a prospecting expedition to the Klondike later, he was called back to Africa by Lord Roberts to serve as his Chief of Scouts. After many adventures, which lost nothing in the telling, he was invalided to Britain, where he was entertained by Queen Victoria and the heads of Oxford colleges and was admitted to the Distinguished Service Order.[28]

A more obscure frontiersman, Charles J. Spruce, fled to Africa with a broken heart. Born 'way up in the pure woods' before the coming of the loggers, he was 18 years old when he first encountered urban amenities at Kenosha, Wisconsin. There he fell in love, was jilted, and struck out for the new British frontier in Africa. He took part in the Jameson Raid and was awarded the Victoria Cross for saving the life of a comrade while under fire in the South African War. The citizens of Kenosha expressed little surprise at news of his heroism. Given the hardihood and resourcefulness he would naturally have acquired during those early years, when there were many Indians and more wild animals in the backwoods, he was bound to be an exceptional soldier.[29]

The success of these American frontiersmen on the British side highlights the paradox that Boer military prowess was often credited to 'the very inferiority of Boer civilization'. The *New York Times* dismissed Emile Zola's contention that the victories of the farmer soldiers signalled the obsolescence of professional armies. The Boer population was

> 'not so much agricultural as pastoral . . . virtually the whole South African Republic and the whole of the Orange Free State are inhabited by ignorant and pious "rough riders".'

But no such force could be raised in an advanced country; indeed, the

> 'more remote the ordinary lives of the people from the condition of war, the more necessary it is that soldiering should be made a trade like any other.'[30]

Theodore Roosevelt

Theodore Roosevelt, as organizer and lieutenant-colonel of the original Rough Riders, the first United States volunteer cavalry regiment, naturally had strong views on this subject. It fed his obsession with 'racial degeneracy', the obverse of his conviction that the English-speaking peoples constituted the vanguard of civilization. On the eve of the war he detected in the western world a 'softness of fibre', which, if unchecked, 'might mean the development of a cultured and refined people quite unable to hold its own in conflict'. (Roosevelt, like Rhodes, recommended the tonic of colonial adventure in remote, difficult terrain to keep the racial stock healthy.) Ideas of this kind were strengthened by the early British defeats. The congested cities of Britain and the United States, Roosevelt maintained, had smothered the development of those military qualities that flourished in a 'mounted pastoral population' where men were accustomed to carry guns and to join in make-shift military organizations from their youth onwards. A

> 'brave peasant, and still more a brave man . . . bred in the garret of a tenement house needed years of training before he could be put on a par with a big game hunter accustomed to life in the tropics.'

A regiment composed of men like his own Rough Riders or the Boers was worth any three drawn from the big cities of Britain and America.[31]

Theodore Roosevelt (bespectacled, centre) photographed with the Rough Riders on San Juan Hill, 1898.

Boer envoys in the United States

Cronjé's surrender at Paardeberg on 27 February 1900 and the subsequent imperial advance into the Boer republics marked a partial revival of British military prestige. It also gave added urgency to the Boer search for outside assistance. On 15 May three Boer envoys arrived in the United States to plead their case before the government and people. They disembarked at Hoboken and were greeted by cheering crowds. When someone shouted that ninety per cent of the American people were behind their cause, 'a guttural voice near by called "one hundred per cent of the Germans are with you" and a third voice added "we can take care of the other five per cent between us" '. But this display of solidarity was somewhat spoiled when the accompanying band struck up 'America' and the crowd joined in 'in mighty chorus'. The nearest Boer delegate 'jumped as if he was shot, for he only knew the tune as "God Save the Queen" ', which British South Africans were given to singing aggressively in anti-Boer demonstrations. Eventually, to cover the confusion, the band switched to 'The Star-Spangled Banner', but few of the multitude knew the words or could follow the difficult tune. The whole episode was acidly reported as a typical gaffe by 'hyphenated fellow Americans' ignorant of protocol.[32]

Much subsequent comment took the same tone: the presence of the Boers and even more the tactics of their supporters were considered distinctly embarrassing. Before they landed, Hay had disposed of their request for American mediation by passing it on to the British and receiving a polite negative. What, therefore, did the republics expect the United States government to do? Even so generally a pro-Boer paper as the *Chicago Tribune* observed,

> 'Though the American people sympathize with the Boers, the United States cannot swerve from the strict line of neutrality, without violating its duty.'

There were strong rumours in the press that the envoys had come to seek the establishment of an American protectorate, but talk of annexation and protection was dismissed by the *Tribune* as 'childlike nonsense', while military intervention was even more unthinkable.[33] Nothing must be done that might compromise the Monroe Doctrine, the cornerstone of American foreign policy. Once the United States intervened outside its own hemisphere, then the moral force of the prohibition against European intervention in Latin America would be lost and America would soon be confronted by a European colonial presence, probably German. Even proposals for mediation needed extremely discreet handling. Such an apparently impeccable anglophile as John Hay was chided for what appeared to be a semantic slip – using the term 'intervention' instead of 'mediation' when passing on the Boer request to Britain – which might give the impression to the outside world that the administration was not absolutely committed to that partition of the globe into spheres of influence inherent in Monroeism.[34]

The *New York Times* wryly noted the diplomatically correct and sensible behaviour of the German emperor when earlier he informed the same Boer envoys that he could see no reason why they should visit Berlin, but, unlike McKinley, 'the emperor is not engaged in a campaign for re-election.' Sardonically, the *New York Times* spelled out the constitutional position: 'In their private capacity, even when assembled in a hall, the American people have no foreign relations.' That was the prerogative of the government alone. It was acceptable for newspapers to debate the rights and wrongs of the conflict, but messages of sympathy for belligerent rulers

> 'are a violation of propriety [and] . . . public meetings to express sympathy come very near the line of inadvisable demonstrations'.[35]

The occasion of this rebuke was a mass meeting in Washington, D.C., 'gotten up by Irish Americans and Irish enmity to England', addressed by Webster Davis, who had resigned as Assistant Secretary of the Interior at the outbreak of the South African War. Advised to travel abroad for his health, he decided to visit South Africa. He was generously entertained in the Transvaal, where it was rumoured, quite wrongly, that he had been sent on a personal mission of investigation by President McKinley. Davis became an ardent admirer of the Boers. Back in the United States, a regular speaker at pro-Boer rallies and for the Democrats, he was even mentioned as a possible vice-presidential candidate on the Democratic ticket. Although not selected to run with William Jennings Bryan, his speech pleading the Boer case, alleging that there was a secret alliance between Britain and the United States, and renouncing his allegiance to the Republican Party, was a highlight of the 1900 Democratic convention in Kansas City.[36]

The nub of the Boer representatives' dilemma was this: they had been hustled out of Europe by governments who found their presence and the popular support they aroused diplomatically embarrassing and who hinted that in the United States they would be able to capitalize on the forthcoming election. This ducking of the issue created resentment among some Americans. The Boers and the continental powers seemed to be using America's democratic processes to endanger the national interest. And once in the United States, however much the envoys protested their wish to avoid party politics, they could not escape being embroiled in the campaign. In New York they had been welcomed by the promise of supporters that 'when Bryan is in the White House next year, you'll see that we're for the Boers'. Certain politicians seem to have gravitated to them for political advantage rather than principle. Montagu White, who operated as a discreet lobbyist on behalf of the Boers, described some of their ostentatious well-wishers as 'self seekers, fakers and political charlatans'.[37]

In the Senate, pro-Boer motions were disposed of by powerful Republicans such as Henry Cabot Lodge of Massachusetts and Cushman Davis of Minnesota, chairman of the foreign relations committee. In the House of Representatives, Robert Hitt, Republican from Illinois and chairman of the foreign affairs committee, fulfilled the same function. The offensive motions were referred to the respective committees to be stripped of their anti-British content and reduced to innocuous words.

At the Republican convention in Philadelphia in June 1900 the platform chairman, Senator Joseph Foraker, although deluged with pro-Boer correspondence, produced a platform that dealt with the issue in generalities, except to praise the President for his 'steadfast adherence to the Monroe Doctrine'.

William Jennings Bryan, an anti-imperialist and critic of British policy in South Africa, who was defeated as Democratic candidate in the 1900 presidential election.

More was expected from the Democrats. In addition to Webster Davis's appearance, pro-Boer feeling was catered for by a platform excoriating Britain and praising the courageous Boer defense of their homesteads. But Bryan's opposition to imperialism in South Africa and the Philippines failed to bring victory to the Democrats and indeed aroused so little excitement that he was forced to concentrate his campaign on domestic issues. Of the fourteen men up for re-election who had supported a pro-Boer resolution in the Senate, nine were defeated. On 11 September 1900 *The Times* of London registered its relief that the 'sympathy expressed by American politicians for the Boers was never more than Platonic'. Three months earlier, Mr Dooley had dryly prophesied the failure of the Boer appeals:

> 'Th' wurrld me la–ad, is with the undher dog, on'y as long as he has a good hold an' a chanst to tu–rn over.'

McKinley's death and the succession of Theodore Roosevelt, with his Dutch ancestry, rekindled Boer hopes, but in line with his perception of the United States national interest, Roosevelt brusquely rejected complaints about the unequal effects of American neutrality.[38]

Failure of the pro-Boer movement

Why was the pro-Boer movement so feeble that the administration could maintain its position relatively easily? America, too, was now an imperial power as well as Britain and embarrassed by its own colonial nationalist movement, the Filipino revolt. The acknowledged leader of the anti-imperalist movement, Bryan, indicated the implications of America's loss of innocence when he said, 'Suppose we send our sympathy to the Boers. In an hour England would send back "what about the Filipinos".' The same point applied to the methods as well as the principles of imperialism. Montagu White complained that

> 'The tortures by water cure and pumping sea water into prisoners [in the Philippines] make it very difficult for American Boer sympathizers to protest with anything like consistency against the action of the British in regard to the horrible [concentration] camps.'[39]

That other reference point for comparison, America's civil war, further complicated the response to the prolonged Boer resistance. As soon as Cronjé's surrender was reported, White was faced by the withdrawal of a large subscription because 'it would only be prolonging the agony and encouraging the poor Boers to useless resistance'.[40] In late 1901 Charles Francis Adams published a comparison between the southern Confederacy and the Transvaal in which he called attention to the surrender of Robert E. Lee, whose patriotism deterred him from subjecting the South to the devastation of prolonged guerrilla warfare.[41]

Above all, the Boers were asking the United States government to shift from a position of technical neutrality, which benefited Britain as well as many Americans through its control of the high seas, to one of positive intervention on the Boer side. During the war American exports to Britain and South Africa – chiefly of mules, horses and tins of corned beef – increased dramatically. John Hay insisted that his neutrality policy worked

> 'for the interests of the American farmers, American merchants and American manufacturers . . . we are perfectly free to sell to both belligerents all they are able to pay for'.[42]

A STERILE ATTITUDE OF A PASSIVE NEUTRALITY.

A cartoon that accompanied an article by Montagu White, 'The Policy of Mediation', in Harper's Weekly, *31 March 1900. American mediation was never seriously attempted. John Hay argued that the neutrality of the United States benefited American farmers, manufacturers and traders, and American exports to Britain and South Africa increased dramatically during the war.*

Unfortunately for the Boers, they had no navy and scant cash or credit.

At a deeper level, the political economies of the British empire and the United States were becoming intertwined. *Harper's Weekly* lamented that even New York gas and transit stocks were 'being mysteriously affected' more by British setbacks in South Africa 'than by knowledge of what the companies are earning'.[43] The Republican Party and the bulk of the business community had pinned its faith on gold. The combination of the perfection of the cyanide process of gold extraction, the discoveries of new gold fields in Alaska and, above all, in South Africa

> 'doomed Bryan to political failure far more than any waning in the effectiveness of his oratory or any shortcomings in his political organization'.[44]

The Boers were considered too backward to qualify as stewards of such an important portion of the world's resources as the Rand. Indeed, asserted the *New York Times*, 'the Matabeles would be fighting and loafing in their country a hundred years from today' if Boer not British civilization were responsible for the development of southern Africa as a whole.[45] Desperate Boer attempts to buy congressional and other powerful support by offering Transvaal bonds at a tremendous discount and subsidizing the bondholders to the tune of fifteen to twenty million dollars, along with American trade preferences and shipping subsidies, came too late. The schemes were hurriedly dropped when the Boers learned that no American considered their shares a good investment, and that if their manoeuvres became public knowledge they would be a laughing stock.[46] By contrast, when the British sought to cover part of their war costs by raising loans in the United States, American investors responded eagerly. The solid economic and ideological weight of American capitalism was committed to the notion that British free trade imperialism provided 'a fair field and no favour', an appropriate African equivalent of the Open Door.

References

1. *The Times*, 2 November 1899. John C. Ferguson, *American Diplomacy and the Boer War*, Philadelphia, 1939, within the limits indicated by the title, is a first rate work. Bradford Perkins, *The Great Rapprochement. England and the United States, 1895–1914*. New York, 1968, is the best guide to the general background and has an excellent section on Anglo-American relations during the war.
2. Alfred Thayer Mahan, *The Story of the War in South Africa, 1899–1900*, New York, 1900; Richard H. Davis, *With Both Armies in South Africa*, New York, 1900; Howard C. Hillegas, *The Boer in War*, New York, 1900. Beck's book was put out by the Globe Publishing Co., Philadelphia, 1900.
3. *New York Times*, 29 December 1900 and 31 January 1901.
4. *New York Journal*, 24 December 1899.
5. *New York Times*, 30 August and 5 September 1899.
6. Roosevelt to A. R. Cowles, 2 February 1900 cited in Howard K. Beale, *Theodore Roosevelt and the Rise of America to World Power*, Baltimore, 1950, 99.
7. *New York Times*, 26 December 1899.
8. Finley Peter Dunne, 'Mr. Dooley: His Opinion on the Transvaal', *Harper's Weekly*, 4 November 1899, 1118.
9. *New York Times*, 5 February 1900.
10. Ferguson, 65–6.

11. *Ibid.*, 56.
12. *Ibid.*, 66.
13. *Ibid.*, 66–7.
14. *New York Times*, 17 May 1900.
15. Ferguson, 134–5.
16. Paul Addison, 'Churchill and the United States', *New Edinburgh Review*, 38–9, 1977, 66.
17. Elting E. Morison and John M. Blum eds., *The Letters of Theodore Roosevelt*, 8 vols., Harvard, 1951–4, vol. 2, 1147.
18. *Ibid.*, 1146–7, 1269–70.
19. Twain to William D. Howells, 25 January 1900, cited in Perkins, 93.
20. Perkins, 55.
21. Kenton C. Clymer, *John Hay, The Gentleman as Diplomat*, University of Michigan Press, 1975, 120–1.
22. *Ibid.*, 157.
23. John Hays Hammond, *The Autobiography of John Hays Hammond*, II, New York, 1935, 426–7.
24. *New York Times*, 4 May 1900.
25. *Chicago Tribune*, 1 May 1900.
26. Bishop Levi Jenkins Coppin, *Observations on Persons and Things in South Africa*, Philadelphia, 1905, 72.
27. Mrs George Cornwallis-West, *The Reminiscences of Lady Randolph Churchill*, New York, 1908; *New York Times*, 29 July 1900.
28. Frederick Russell Burnham, *Scouting on Two Continents*, New York, 1926, 271–353.
29. *Chicago Tribune*, 2 May 1900.
30. *New York Times*, 11 February 1900.
31. Roosevelt to C. A. Spring-Rice, 2 December 1899, in Henry Cabot Lodge ed., *Selections from the Correspondence of Theodore Roosevelt and Henry Cabot Lodge*, II, New York, 1923, 1103–4.
32. *New York Times*, 16 and 17 May 1900.
33. *Chicago Tribune*, 16 May 1900.
34. *New York Times*, 22 May 1900.
35. *New York Times*, 12 April and 25 May 1900.
36. *New York Times*, 27 January 1900; Ferguson, 196–7.
37. *New York Times*, 19 and 25 May 1900; White to Leyds, 22 June 1900, *Derde Verzameling (Correspondentie 1900)*, I, Dordrecht, 1931, 172.
38. Ferguson, chapter 5; Finley Peter Dunne, 'Mr. Dooley and the Boer Mission', *Harper's Weekly*, 9 June 1900, 539.
39. For Bryan's response, see Ferguson, 179; White to Leyds, 18 April 1902 in Leyds, I, 717.
40. White to Leyds, 25 April 1900 in Leyds, I, 717.
41. Charles Francis Adams, *The Confederacy and the Transvaal. A People's Obligation to Robert E. Lee*, a paper read to the American Antiquarian Society in Worcester, Massachusetts, 30 October 1901 and subsequently published as a pamphlet.
42. Hay to Senator James McMillan, 3 July 1900, in Tyler Dennett, *John Hay, from Poetry to Politics*, New York, 1933, 246.
43. *Harper's Weekly*, 3 February 1900, 115.
44. Milton J. Friedman and Anne J. Schwartz, *A Monetary History of the United States, 1867–1960*, Princeton, 1963, 8.
45. *New York Times*, 14 September and 6 March 1900.
46. White to Leyds, 31 January and 31 December 1901, 23 January and 12 February 1902, in Leyds, I, 110–14, 532–6, 534–8, 617.

PART THREE

AFTERMATH OF WAR

Following the failure in March 1901 of the Middelburg peace negotiations, the war dragged on for a further thirteen months until in April 1902 the republican governments met again at Klerksdorp and agreed once more to negotiate with Kitchener. The Middelburg talks had broken down, principally, because the Boer leaders had refused to give up their countries' independence. At Klerksdorp the governments again put forward proposals to Kitchener based on this principle. The Boer leaders in return were prepared to demilitarize their states, give the Uitlanders the vote, sign a treaty of friendship with Britain, grant equal rights to the Dutch and English languages, and concur with a general amnesty. Not surprisingly, such terms were quite unacceptable to the British government, which countered with a series of proposals based on those that earlier had been rejected by the Boers at Middelburg. The guerrilla leaders naturally felt unable on their own behalf to enter into detailed negotiations which might ultimately lead to the sacrifice of their countries' independence, and, accordingly, a conference of sixty representatives of the Transvaal and Orange Free State, elected by the commandos, was convened with British approval at Vereeniging to discuss further the British proposals for peace.

The negotiations that began at Vereeniging on 15 May 1902 ended in the signing of peace in Pretoria a little before midnight on 31 May. By 54 votes to 6 the representatives of the republics agreed to surrender their independence and recognize the authority of Edward VII in return for the repatriation of prisoners of war; a general amnesty (with a few exceptions); the limited protection of the Dutch language in the courts; various economic safeguards such as the maintenance of property rights, protection against punitive taxation, the honouring of the republican war debt (to a maximum of £3 million), and generous relief for the victims of war; the promise of eventual self-government; and an agreement that no decision would be taken on the question of extending the franchise to black people until after the introduction of responsible government.

In retrospect it is not surprising that the Vereeniging negotiations should have ended in the signing of peace. Both sides desperately wished to end the fighting. The Boers had been forced to abandon large areas of the Transvaal and Orange River Colony because of the scarcity in many districts of cattle, grain and horses, worsening relations with local African communities, and the pressures placed on guerrilla activity by the extention of the blockhouse network and the growing intensity of the British military drives. The deaths among civilians in the concentration camps during the latter half of 1901 had been profoundly dispiriting; yet when in December of that year the British authorities refused to accept any more women and children into the camps, the commandos were faced with the new difficulty of maintaining and protecting their dependants while they remained in the field. The problem of Boer collaboration had also assumed worrying proportions, and there was little chance of foreign intervention on the Boers' behalf, nor of an Afrikaner rebellion in the Cape of sufficient proportions to place an intolerable strain on the British forces operating in South Africa.

Yet the Boers were not sufficiently beaten to have no alternative but to accept unconditional surrender; the guerrilla war *could* be carried on if necessary, at least for another year, and this meant they were still in a position to achieve a negotiated settlement. It is to the credit of Botha and Smuts, whose eloquence and persuasiveness dominated the Boers' discussions, that they recognized the implications of this keenly. If the war were continued for another twelve months, they argued, the Boers' bargaining position might disappear altogether, and the war end, for them, in ignominious defeat. Their ability to win such wide support among the Boer representatives can also be related to the change that had taken place during the war in the complexion of the republican leadership. Botha and Smuts were themselves representative of the 'new men' who had come to the fore during the fighting – younger and less inflexible in their views than their predecessors, often progressive farmers before the outbreak of war, and men who saw the need to modernize the republics. Though still vigorous supporters of the Afrikaner ideal, they realized that the aspirations of Afrikanerdom might be achieved by methods other than direct military confrontation with Britain.

Britain too desperately wanted peace. The war was becoming increasingly unpopular and embarrassing. The campaign against the guerrillas was tedious, unglamorous, frustrating and draining on manpower. Kitchener himself was anxious to relinquish his responsibilities in South Africa in order to take command of the army in India, a cherished ambition. Milner was keen to see the devastation of the country brought to an end and civilian government restored in order to put into operation his design for the reconstruction of the republics. But Milner was also desirous that the Boers should be thoroughly beaten and dispirited, and that his hands should not be unnecessarily tied by irksome concessions granted in a negotiated peace. Although throughout the discussions at

Vereeniging Milner and Kitchener clashed about the terms to be agreed with the republican representatives, it was Milner's influence that was dominant on the British side, and Donald Denoon has concluded that the terms negotiated at Vereeniging only bound Britain to do those things she was willing to do and refrain from doing those things she did not wish to do.[1]

Milner later spoke with regret that Clause Eight of the settlement had made it impossible for franchise rights to be extended to black people in the annexed colonies before the introduction of responsible government. This, certainly, was the most reprehensible of the terms agreed upon in view of the assurances given to Africans and coloureds at the beginning of the war – by Salisbury, Chamberlain and Milner himself[2] – that their legitimate grievances would not be ignored once the republics had been defeated. Yet during the course of the war Milner consistently urged in private that political rights for black people should not be made a serious issue because insistence on reform would alienate not only the Boers but the English-speaking community as well. And it was the support of the latter group that Milner knew he would have to rely upon to carry through his post-war design.

Having led Britain into war to establish British supremacy throughout South Africa, it was the responsibility of Chamberlain and Milner, once hostilities ceased, to preside over the maintenance and consolidation of British influence. From the outset Milner had successfully pressed to retain control of the formulation and execution of British post-war policy. He enjoyed the full support of Chamberlain until the Colonial Secretary's resignation from the Unionist government over the issue of tariff reform in September 1903. Chamberlain's successor, Alfred Lyttelton, looked upon himself more as Milner's pupil than his superior.[3] In South Africa Milner surrounded himself by a youthful, dynamic and devoted bureaucracy largely composed of recent graduates of New College and Balliol, Oxford. In the Cape parliament J. X. Merriman dubbed them collectively Milner's 'kindergarten'. The kindergarten included among its number Geoffrey Dawson, a future editor of *The Times*; Patrick Duncan, a future Governor-General of South Africa; Basil Williams, the historian and biographer of Rhodes; R. H. Brand, the economist; and Philip Kerr, who was appointed British Ambassador to the United States during the First World War. John Buchan, the novelist and later Governor-General of Canada, was a close associate of the kindergarten.

Milner's reconstruction design was simple enough in conception. On the one hand the Afrikaner population of the Transvaal must be outnumbered by white people of British descent through large-scale immigration. On the other hand the Afrikaners must be denationalized through the introduction of a new educational system in which the medium of instruction would be English, through the creation of an efficient professional bureaucracy, and through rapid and sustained economic growth and modernization. The two objectives of the scheme were closely linked. Economic development and modernization would destroy the basis of Afrikaner nationalism, which Milner interpreted as a function of the Boer people's backwardness and isolation. Prosperity would help to reconcile Afrikaners to British dominance. Economic growth would also create the conditions necessary to promote large-scale British immigration and serve the interests of British capital. Once Milner's aims had been achieved self-government could be safely restored to the Transvaal (and the still Afrikaner-dominated Orange River Colony), and the four settler colonies of South Africa thereafter combined to form a loyal, federal dominion within the British empire capable of assuming responsibility for its own defence.

Milner set about his task with immense energy. Resettlement plans were rapidly put into operation, schemes to promote the scientific development of arable farming and pastoral agriculture were drawn up, and the basis of an efficient, professional administration created. When Chamberlain arrived in South Africa in November 1902 he found the new administration in the Transvaal bursting with vitality and enthusiasm. Already by the time of Chamberlain's visit, however, serious problems were beginning to emerge. Milner had originally bargained upon a short, sharp war with the minimum of economic dislocation and damage to property. By May 1902, however, large areas of the republics had been devastated and it was apparent that considerable capital expenditure was required to set agriculture back on its feet again. Agrarian reconstruction was further hindered by an acute shortage of livestock and by a series of sustained annual droughts.

More worrying were the difficulties encountered by the gold mining industry. Because of the protracted nature of the guerrilla war it had not been possible to resume gold production at the rapid pace Milner keenly desired. Once the war drew to a close, and the mining industry was able to attract the white civilian personnel, equipment and supplies that it needed, the industry was handicapped by a serious shortage of unskilled African workers. In 1903 the gold mines were only able to recruit a black labour force two-thirds the size of that which they had employed at the beginning of 1899, largely because of wage reductions enforced by the Chamber of Mines. The implications of the labour crisis were serious indeed. The mining magnates insisted that labour costs had to be reduced in order to make profitable the extraction of deep-level ore; Milner's entire reconstruction design was based on the revenue that would accrue to government from the taxation of mining profits; and the buoyancy of the Transvaal economy, an essential prerequisite to attract British immigrants, depended upon the stimulus provided by a thriving mining industry. Once the flow of British public money into the Transvaal came to an end in 1903, the economy slumped.

Milner soon encountered difficulties, too, in the political arena. Following the end of the war the executive councils operated by the military authorities in the annexed colonies were retained. In addition Milner created two legislative councils, one in the Transvaal and one in the Orange River Colony, composed of officials and nominees. These held their first sessions in 1903. The defeated Boer leaders, however, refused to serve on the legislative councils; they would only be prepared to cooperate, they told the High Commissioner, on the basis of self-government. Milner cannot have been particularly surprised or perturbed by their decision. More unexpected, and infinitely more worrying, was the opposition he encountered from the British community in the Transvaal. For this Milner himself was largely to blame. His administration was quickly condemned by many English-speakers in the Transvaal as expensive and over-regulating, his imported officials as aloof, inexperienced and ignorant of South African conditions. The lack of an elective element in the Transvaal legislative council was especially disliked, and in 1902, following the publication of his constitutional proposals, a Transvaal Political Association came into being to press for a greater measure of self-government.

Milner's relations with a large section of the British community deteriorated further in the following year when he accepted the proposal that the mining industry's labour deficiency should be overcome by introducing Chinese labourers to the Rand. The importation of workers from China, on short-term contracts ending in compulsory repatriation, began in June 1904, and more than 60 000 Chinese labourers arrived over the course of the next four years. It was a disastrous step, not because it failed to revive the immediate fortunes of the mining industry (by the end of 1905 Chinese workers formed nearly a third of the total mine labour force and the industry was entering a period of rapid growth), but because the political implications of the decision helped to undermine Milner's entire post-war strategy. In Britain the issue of 'Chinese slavery' generated considerable disquiet on humanitarian grounds. The arrival of Chinese labour revealed how closely Milner had come to identify himself with the interests of the deep-level mining companies, since it was they that were experiencing the most acute shortage of labour, and their executives who pressed most vigorously for the importation of Chinese workers. Among the British community most artisans and professional men, and businessmen and industrialists unconnected with deep-level mining, strongly opposed the decision and the autocratic way in which it was taken. Afrikaner opinion was appalled by the prospect of another unnecessary complication to the country's racial problem.

The first post-war Uitlander organization, the Transvaal Political Association, appears to have drawn its membership and support from a wide cross-section of the English-speaking community. But the Uitlanders were not a monolithic group, and it was not long before two main political organizations, quite different in outlook, emerged – the Transvaal Progressive Association, formed in November 1904, and the Transvaal Responsible Government Association, founded in the same year largely from the rump of the Political Association. (English-speaking white labour established its own organizations – the Transvaal Labour Party and the Political Labour League of the Witwatersrand Trades and Labour Council, formed in November 1904 and August 1905 respectively. These groups remained small and were of little immediate political consequence.)

The membership of the Progressive Association had close links with the pre-war Reform Committee and Uitlander Council. The Progressives were reluctant to be drawn into open confrontation with Milner since they believed that full self-government should be granted only when a British majority in a future Transvaal legislature could be guaranteed. In the meantime they favoured an elected representative government without complete control over the executive. Many of the Progressive leaders, including Sir George Farrar and Sir Percy Fitzpatrick (the two principal spokesmen), were connected with deep-level gold mining, the section of the industry that relied most heavily on government support and cooperation. The Responsibles, on the other hand, were led by prosperous professional men such as E. P. Solomon, brother of Milner's Attorney-General,

Sir Richard Solomon, and received financial backing from leading diamond magnates (diamond profits were taxed at 67 per cent, gold profits at only 10 per cent – understandably a source of deep grievance to the diamond interest). The Responsibles were critical of many of Milner's policies, including the introduction of indentured Chinese labour, and wished to see full self-government (ie. responsible government) established at once. In part this was an issue of principle, in part a question of expediency. While they hoped for a British majority in a responsible legislature, they were less concerned than the Progressives about the possibility of Afrikaner political ascendancy since they believed the defeated leaders would be more likely to be loyal to Britain if trusted with political power than if such power were eventually wrung from a reluctant imperial government at some later date.

The Afrikaner leadership did not long remain politically inactive following the conclusion of peace. They refused to participate in Milner's nominee legislative council, as we have seen, and in July 1903 a large protest meeting attended by many of the former commando leaders was held with the High Commissioner's consent at Heidelberg. The decision to import Chinese workers to the mines signalled the return to organized political activity by the Boer community in the Transvaal. During 1904 a series of political meetings was convened throughout the colony to protest against the introduction of Chinese workers. Out of these assemblies a political movement was born in January 1905, *Het Volk* (The People). *Het Volk* demanded full self-government for both the Transvaal and Orange River Colony, the immediate termination of the Chinese labour system, the ending of restrictions on the public use of the Dutch language, and increased relief and more work opportunities for the thousands of impoverished Afrikaners driven from the land by the devastation of the war, by the inadequacy of compensation and the British relief programme, and by the agrarian difficulties of the immediate post-war years. Under the conciliatory leadership of Botha and Smuts, and aided by the influence of the *predikants*, the political differences of the war years were quickly healed, and *Het Volk* rapidly gained the support of the vast majority of Transvaal Afrikaners. In the Orange River Colony a sister political organization was formed in July 1905, *Orangia Unie*. Aside from politics, but never far removed from the political field, Afrikaner culture flourished. A renewed movement in support of the Afrikaans language emerged; nationalist writers like J. F. E. Celliers and Eugène Marais wrote evocatively in Afrikaans verse of the war years and their aftermath; and some two hundred Christian-National Schools were founded, to rival Milner's public schools in which the sole medium of instruction was English.

By the beginning of 1905 it was evident that Milner's reconstruction programme had collapsed. Relatively few British immigrants had been attracted to the Transvaal, the colony was moving but slowly out of economic recession, a large section of the Uitlander population had been alienated by Milner's policies and methods, and the cultural and political identity of the Afrikaner people had been consolidated rather than undermined. Milner recognized failure long before his resignation in March 1905. In May 1904 he suggested to Alfred Lyttelton that elected members might replace the nominees in the Transvaal legislative council. Plans were made for a legislative assembly of thirty-five members, elected by whites only on the basis of single-member constituencies of roughly equal size corresponding approximately to the existing magisterial districts. Such a scheme held out little hope of achieving a British majority. The Lyttelton constitution became operative in theory on Milner's departure on 30 March the following year, but for technical reasons and because of the fall of the Unionist government in Britain in December 1905 it was never implemented.

Twelve months after Campbell-Bannerman's Liberal government took office Letters Patent were issued providing for a new Transvaal constitution based on full self-government, in accordance with the recommendations of the West Ridgeway Committee, which had been appointed by the new government to investigate constitutional development in the Transvaal and Orange River Colony, and whose members had visited South Africa earlier in the year. In the general election that was held in the Transvaal on 20 February 1907 *Het Volk* won a clear majority, and Louis Botha became Prime Minister. A new constitution was introduced in the Orange River Colony in June 1907, and in the general election that was held in November *Orangia Unie* won all but eight seats in the legislative council and Abraham Fischer, the party's leader, formed an Afrikaner government. A remarkable turn-about in Anglo-Boer relations had taken place.

The achievement of self-government in the Transvaal was in part founded upon the ruins of Milner's reconstruction programme, the collapse of which left the Liberal government with little alternative but to plan a fresh approach to Britain's imperial problem in South Africa. A number of prominent Cabinet members, including the Prime Minister himself, had expressed deep concern about Kitchener's methods during the war and the policies pursued by Milner afterwards, and in some respects the South African policy of the Liberals in office can be regarded as a continuation of the approach adopted by pro-Boer members of the party in opposition. The altruism of the Liberals' 'magnanimous gesture' in granting responsible government can be exaggerated. They wished to relinquish their embarrassing responsibility for the administration of Chinese labour as soon as possible. Furthermore, they realized that British interests in South Africa could best be maintained through partnership with the Afrikaner community, and in any case it was still hoped that English-speaking colonists in the Transvaal would dominate affairs. It was these arguments that eventually won over the Liberal Imperialist wing of the party to responsible government. Anglo-Boer cooperation was made easier by the conciliatory approach of Botha and Smuts and other members of the new generation of Afrikaner leaders. When Smuts visited England in February 1906 to press for self-government on behalf of *Het Volk*, his moderation, candour and sharp intellect made a strong impression on Campbell-Bannerman, who in turn was much admired by Smuts for his personal warmth and sincerity, for his practical approach to South African problems, and not least for his reputation as a stern critic during the war of Kitchener's 'methods of barbarism'.

The first concern of the post-war Afrikaner leaders had been to heal the wounds in their society left behind by the struggle with Britain. The second task they had undertaken had been to restore amicable and constructive relations with Britain on the basis of internal self-government for the Transvaal and Orange River Colony. Having achieved both these objectives, *Het Volk* concentrated upon fulfilling its third aim, namely to win greater trust and support among members of the English-speaking community in the Transvaal. Already before the restoration of self-government the party had succeeded in exploiting the division within Uitlander ranks. Alarmed by the close relationship that had built up between the Milner administration and the leaders of the deep-level gold mining interest, some diamond mining and outcrop gold mining executives like J. B. Robinson gave press and financial support to *Het Volk*. Their common desire for self-government and the ending of the Chinese labour system soon brought *Het Volk* and the Responsibles together, and in 1905 agreement was reached on their shared objectives. Following the 1907 general election two members of the National Association (the new name of the Responsibles) were appointed to Botha's cabinet, even though the Nationals had won only six seats in the Transvaal legislature compared to *Het Volk's* 37 and the Progressives' 21. Botha's government maintained a moderate course. A new Education Bill introduced by Smuts stopped short of placing the Dutch language on an equal footing with English in the colony's schools. In 1907 Botha attended the colonial conference in London and spoke warmly of the benefits of membership of the British empire. His visit to England was a remarkable personal triumph, and his enthusiasm for empire not only appeared to vindicate the Liberals' decision to restore self-government to the former republics, but also reassured many Uitlanders that *Het Volk* was likely to remain a loyal and stable party of government.

The final component of *Het Volk's* policy of conciliation was to endeavour to bring the colonies of South Africa into a united political system to overcome the regional disputes of the past, to make possible greater security for South Africa's white population, and to enable more rapid and better planned economic development to take place. *Het Volk's* policy in this respect accorded, at least in general outline, with the aims of British policy. Steps towards closer union after the war had been initiated by Milner through the creation of the South African Customs Union in 1903; the amalgamation of the railway networks of the Transvaal and Orange River Colony; the appointment of the South African Native Affairs Commission in 1903, set up to formulate a common South African policy towards African affairs; and the establishment of the Inter-Colonial Council to administer railways, repatriation, schools and the para-military South African Constabulary in the annexed colonies. However, a major difference in outlook between *Het Volk* on the one hand and Milner, the kindergarten and Milner's successor as High Commissioner, Lord Selborne, on the other was that Botha and Smuts were anxious to achieve a unitary solution whereas the British officials in South Africa envisaged merely a federation of colonies. Afrikaner leaders in the Transvaal also hoped that through unification opportunities for British interference in South African affairs would be lessened, while Selborne and his officials hoped that the stability and prosperity that would result from closer union would at last encourage large-scale British immigration, and that this in turn would weaken Afrikaner political influence.

It was the conflicting interests of the colonies in

the economic field, however, that precipitated a more intense discussion of the closer union issue. For many years customs and railway tariffs had been a source of friction between the landlocked states, the Transvaal and Orange Free State, which wanted low tariffs, and the coastal colonies, the Cape and Natal, which wanted high tariffs. The Transvaal also wished to make greater use of its shortest railway route to the sea, the line to Lourenço Marques in Mozambique. Milner's customs union had done little to resolve these fundamental conflicts of interest. In response to the continuing difficulties in this field a discussion paper, known as the Selborne Memorandum, was issued to the colonial governments in South Africa on 1 January 1907, and published six months later. Written by Lionel Curtis of the kindergarten at the High Commissioner's invitation, the document urged political federation as a means of avoiding a destructive tariff war. The influence of the Selborne Memorandum would have been negligible had it not been for other parallel forces working in the same direction. As we have seen, the leadership of *Het Volk* was committed to achieving a similar objective. For some time, too, Smuts had been in correspondence with ex-President Steyn and with John X. Merriman, leader of the *Bond*-supported South African Party opposition in the Cape parliament, whom Smuts had convinced of the need, if at all feasible, of creating a unified political system in South Africa.

One of the first actions of the *Het Volk* government in the Transvaal was to give notice that the colony would withdraw from the customs union on 1 July 1908 unless agreement was reached on terms more favourable to the Transvaal. When representatives of the four colonies met in Pretoria in May 1908 to endeavour to resolve the customs question, Smuts proposed that a National Convention be convened to seek a political solution to their economic differences. Two factors, other than profound disagreement over tariffs, influenced the acceptance of Smuts's proposal by members of the other delegations. First, in the Cape general election of February 1908 the *Bond*-South African Party alliance won a clear majority and Merriman, now a firm supporter of closer union on a unitary basis, replaced L. S. Jameson as Prime Minister. Secondly, the Zulu rebellion of 1906–8 and the Natal government's difficulty in quickly suppressing the disturbances undermined the confidence of Natal whites in their ability to maintain their own security. For the first time Natalians were now prepared seriously to contemplate closer union. Furthermore, the ruthless and arbitrary way in which the Zulu were suppressed alienated Natal from the British government, and caused politicians elsewhere in South Africa to fear the consequences of Natal being left to its own devices to handle African affairs.

A National Convention composed of thirty delegates from the four South African colonies met *in camera* under the chairmanship of Sir Henry de Villiers, Chief Justice of the Cape Colony, in Durban and Cape Town between October 1908 and February 1909 and again, following consultation with the colonial parliaments, in Bloemfontein in May. A constitution for a united South Africa was finally approved by all four colonies in June, and in September the South Africa Bill, embodying the agreement reached in South Africa with only minor amendments, was enacted by the British Parliament. On 31 May 1910, eight years to the day after the signing of peace in Pretoria, the four settler colonies became constituent provinces of the Union of South Africa, and Louis Botha became Prime Minister and formed the first Union government.

The constitution agreed at the National Convention embodied a unitary political system with a bicameral parliament consisting of a Senate and House of Assembly, a cabinet system of government, and a governor-general as formal head of the executive. The distribution of seats between the constituent provinces was arrived at on the basis of the number of white electors in each colony. In spite of a strong movement led by Smuts in favour of proportional representation, single-member constituencies were eventually decided upon. It was also agreed that the number of voters in constituencies could deviate 15 per cent from the standard quota, and in practice this meant there would be fewer voters in rural constituencies (where Afrikaners predominated) than in urban ones. The constitutional system meant that the Union would be dominated politically by South Africa's Afrikaner population.

For the British government headed by H. H. Asquith, who became Prime Minister following Campbell-Bannerman's resignation through ill-health in April 1908 (he died shortly afterwards), one of the most important considerations to bear in mind was the protection of African political rights in the new arrangement. The non-racial franchise in the Cape was maintained in spite of the opposition of many delegates from the other colonies, but non-whites were excluded from sitting in the new South African parliament (before they had the right to become members of the Cape Assembly, though none had ever done so). Among spokesmen for the African, Asian and coloured communities there was considerable disquiet about the constitutional terms agreed. A 'Native Convention' was held at Bloemfontein in March 1909 at which resolutions were passed calling on the British government to intervene on behalf of the black people of South Africa by insisting on the introduction of a 'colour-blind' franchise throughout South Africa, the removal of the colour bar in the Union parliament, and the inclusion of more rigorous constitutional safeguards for the Cape's non-racial voting system. A deputation led by W. P. Schreiner, the former Cape Prime Minister, and including Dr Abdullah Abdurahman, President of the African People's Organization, John Tengo Jabavu, editor of *Imvo Zabantsundu*, and the Reverend Walter Rubusana, travelled to London to protest against the terms agreed by South Africa's white politicians. They received support from some Liberal and Labour MPs and members of the extra-parliamentary humanitarian lobby, as well as the *Manchester Guardian*. But the government, while sympathetic, remained unmoved, believing union could not be wrecked on these points, not least in the interests of the black population, whom they suggested would be blamed by South African whites if union were thwarted as a result of imperial interference on their behalf. The Liberal government, however, refused to contemplate handing over to South African control the three High Commission Territories of Basutoland, Swaziland and Bechuanaland, in spite of persistent requests from South African politicians, both at the time and later, for these colonies to be incorporated in the Union.

The achievement of union represented a remarkable political triumph for Botha and Smuts. Yet from the time of *Het Volk's* foundation there were Afrikaners in the Transvaal who felt unease about their leaders' enthusiasm for empire and their willingness to compromise Afrikaner ideals for the sake of reconciliation with Britain and English-speaking South Africans. In the Orange Free State ex-President Steyn, De Wet and J. B. M. Hertzog expressed grave reservations about whether Botha and Smuts and other Afrikaner leaders were striving enough to protect Afrikaner cultural and economic interests. Botha appointed Hertzog to his Union cabinet but relations between the two men were never easy, and matters came to a head in December 1912 when in a speech at De Wildt in the Transvaal Hertzog described Sir Thomas Smartt, leader of the opposition in the House of Assembly, as a 'foreign fortune-seeker' and stated bluntly that 'conciliation and loyalty . . . are idle words which deceive no one.' Botha was enraged, asked Hertzog to resign his cabinet post, and, when he refused, resigned himself and formed a new government from which Hertzog was excluded. In November 1913 Hertzog, De Wet and a handful of supporters dramatically walked out of the South African Party congress in Cape Town. Six weeks later in January 1914 the dissidents founded their own National Party, established in the belief that the interests of Afrikanerdom should be pre-eminent, and that 'the interests of the Union come before those of any other country'. At the National Party's first congress in the Transvaal in August 1914 a motion was passed opposing South African participation in the Great War and urging that the planned South African assault on neighbouring German South-West Africa be abandoned.

Some Afrikaners, including a number of the most prominent military leaders of the 1899–1902 war, took their opposition to the invasion of South-West Africa a stage further. General C. F. Beyers, commander of the Active Citizen Force, resigned his commission on 15 September 1914. That night he set out to drive to Potchefstroom with J. H. de la Rey, now a member of the Union Senate and also a vigorous opponent of the planned invasion. While driving through Langlaagte, Beyers' car failed to stop at a road block, troops opened fire, and De la Rey was shot dead. Shortly afterwards Lieutenant-Colonel S. G. Maritz, in command of Union troops on the South-West African border, went over to the Germans to seek their aid. J. C. Kemp, another war veteran and an officer in the Union armed forces, later joined him. Following Maritz's defection a number of well-known Afrikaners, including Beyers and Christiaan de Wet, rebelled in favour of restoring the independence of the former republics. Others joined them, though their motives for doing so varied. The revolt was easily suppressed. Hertzog succeeded in clearing his party from complicity in the insurrection, but the events of 1914 nonetheless served to rally Afrikaner nationalist opinion behind him. In the general election of 1915 the National Party won 16 of the 17 Free State seats in the South African parliament, as well as 7 seats in the Cape and 4 seats in the Transvaal (where the Nationalists gained less than 20 000 fewer votes than Botha's South African Party). In the following year the first Nationalist newspaper, *De Burger*, was founded. Twentieth-century Afrikaner nationalism had been born.

References

1. Quoted by Donald Denoon, *A Grand Illusion*, London, 1973, 26.
2. See pages 189–90.
3. Le May, *British Supremacy in South Africa, 1899–1907*, 162.

CHAPTER 15

Reconstruction in the Transvaal

S. E. Katzenellenbogen

Lord Milner

No other aspect of British imperial policy in southern Africa was more closely associated with the name of one man than the policy that led to the South African War and the subsequent reconstruction of the Transvaal was linked to the name of Sir Alfred (later, Lord) Milner. During the period preceding the war the term 'Milnerism' came into use, and has since been used by historians to refer not only to Milner's general imperial views but also to the reconstruction plans.[1] At least one contemporary critic of Milner's policies blamed 'Milneritis' for South Africa's post-war economic ills.[2] While Milner cannot be held solely responsible for the formulation, execution and failure of reconstruction policies, he was their architect, and an understanding of them requires some understanding at least of his character.

Perhaps because of his father's German ancestry, or perhaps because of his period of study at Tübingen, Milner was a rarity among British politicians and administrators in two important respects: he was both a doctrinaire and a passionate believer in the creative role of political power.

> 'The ideological element in his policy, his concern to frame his actions in accordance with a long-range and comprehensive objective, his opposition to traditional empiricism which he stigmatized as "drift", his hunger for a clear-cut solution and a "clean finish", his belief in "shaping the future", his readiness to use force; all these stem from his early faith in a planned society conceived and ordered by the scientific intelligence.'[3]

This brief description helps explain some aspects of the reconstruction policies framed by Milner, as well as some of the errors of judgment that contributed to their failure.

Reconstruction

The central object of reconstruction was to consolidate the gains supposedly achieved by the war; to ensure British dominance over the Afrikaner in the Transvaal. Milner believed that South Africa would ultimately follow the imperial trend towards self-government under some kind of federal structure. Before that happened he felt it essential that

> 'the British population should be so increased and British interests, British ideas, British education, should gain ground to such an extent that the natural leaning of any federal self-government of the future [would] be towards Great Britain and the Imperial connection. . . .'[4]

Once British control was firmly established in the Transvaal, all the South African colonies; including the Orange Free State, which would join the Transvaal in achieving Crown Colony status, would be drawn into line. In this Milner was recognizing a fundamental reality, the economic and therefore ultimately political dominance of South Africa by the Transvaal. He justifiably expected the Afrikaner majority in the Cape and the even larger one in the Free State would come to accept British/Transvaal dominance if for no other reason than that they would be in no position to resist it. Milner was less justified in believing that by treating Afrikaners fairly, improving administration and promoting agricultural development he would be able to win their acceptance of British control.

Milner's plans depended on the Transvaal's rapid economic recovery and expansion, the key to which was the gold mining industry. The 'overspill' from mining profits was expected to finance the resettlement of the Boers (after initial financial assistance from the imperial government) to create conditions that would attract the number of immigrants from Britain and elsewhere in the empire needed to outnumber and outvote the Afrikaners, promote wider industrialization and provide the revenue needed by the new administration for its expanded services. With little exception, Milner's reconstruction was a complete failure. When the Transvaal achieved responsible self-government in 1907 it did so with an Afrikaner majority firmly entrenched. Afrikaner nationalism, far from withering away, had gained strength by leaps and bounds. The mining industry was only just emerging from the doldrums, and British immigration had fallen very far short of expectation.

While Milner and the administrative staff serving and advising him certainly made mistakes, there are many factors over which they had absolutely no control that contributed to failure. Nothing could be done about the drought years, which were a disincentive to potential immigrants, made it more difficult to resettle Afrikaners on the land, and accelerated the movement of Afrikaners from the land to the towns and cities, where they swelled the ranks of the 'poor whites'. Neither Milner nor anyone else could do anything about the system of agriculture and landholding that had existed prior to the war, nor was there any way of overcoming the difficulties of the mining industry. These last were largely the result of a shortage of unskilled labour as Africans from South Africa and neighbouring Mozambique withheld the labour they had previously provided. In order to understand the role of reconstruction in South African history it is important to look not only at Milner's policies themselves, but also at the context within which they were applied.

Demographic engineering

Basic to the entire scheme was Milner's belief that it would be possible to alter the balance of population in the Transvaal sufficiently to create a British majority in a federal legislature. In November 1901 he estimated the white South African population as shown in Table I.

Table I

	British	Afrikaner	Other white	Total
Cape	200 000	270 000	30 000	500 000
O.R.C.	12 000	75 000	3 000	90 000
Natal	45 000	8 000	2 000	55 000
Transvaal	100 000	140 000	40 000	280 000
Rhodesia	11 000	3 000	1 000	15 000
South Africa	368 000	496 000	76 000	940 000

After five years of British rule following the end of the war he anticipated the population would be as shown in Table II.

Table II

	British	Afrikaner	Other white	Total
Cape	250 000	300 000	40 000	590 000
O.R.C.	25 000	80 000	5 000	110 000
Natal	60 000	9 000	3 000	72 000
Transvaal	250 000	150 000	60 000	460 000
Rhodesia	30 000	5 000	3 000	38 000
South Africa	615 000	544 000	111 000	1 270 000

The Transvaal, together with Natal, were the only settler colonies in South Africa (excluding Rhodesia) in which he expected the British to outnumber the Afrikaners;[5] the other colonies would not be in a position to challenge the Transvaal in any case. The Orange River Colony he considered irretrievably Afrikaner in political complexion, but admitted that there was nothing he could do to alter the population balance there.

Kidger Tucker was a cartoonist whose work appeared on walls around Johannesburg, not in newspapers. In this drawing Tucker captures a view of the Afrikaner common among members of the British community in the Transvaal; imperial officials were somewhat less forthright.

This large increase in British population was expected to be attracted to the Transvaal by the immediate large-scale industrial expansion that it was widely anticipated would result from rapid mining development. But it was not only an increase in the industrial population that Milner sought; he also wanted British people to become involved in agriculture, to be in closer contact with Afrikaners and to help improve farming techniques and agricultural output.

How was this massive shift of the Transvaal's population to be achieved in the short space of five years? Where were 150 000 citizens from Britain and elsewhere in the empire to be found who were willing to migrate to a country in many ways so much less attractive than other parts of the empire? Milner anticipated that some 15 000 soldiers and officers would want to remain in the country after the war. The police force would absorb some 7 100 of them, while the para-military South African Constabulary was expected to start with some 200 officers and 6 000 men. About 400 soldiers would be needed for the British South Africa Police and another 400 for the police forces of Johannesburg and Pretoria. Furthermore, the railways of the Transvaal and Orange River Colony were expected to need an additional 1 500 men. Taking account of the number of soldiers who had been in the country before the war, some 9 000 vacancies were expected in these areas. The remaining 141 000 were to be attracted to the mines and the land.

Land settlement scheme

Although the scheme for settling people on the land was numerically less significant, it bears closer examination because it helps to illustrate some of the errors of judgment made by Milner and his advisors, as well as some of the obstacles to the success of reconstruction generally. In 1900 a commission appointed to investigate the possibilities of land settlement, after taking evidence from army officers and others, reported that a land settlement scheme was feasible under certain conditions. These conditions almost immediately ensured that the scheme would not work, since the provision was included that only people who could invest £300 of their own money should be considered. Furthermore, the military authorities stressed the importance of attracting married men, as they feared that single men would marry Afrikaner women and their children would then 'probably fight against [the British] in the next war'.[6] Here the Commission revealed a lack of awareness shared by many of their contemporaries. Anyone with agricultural skills who had been able to save £300 was unlikely to be prepared to risk his savings by migrating to an unsettled area about which little information was available concerning farming conditions. Men with wives and families were even more unlikely to take such risks. It was not uncommon at the turn of the century for politicians and others to assume that people would be prepared to migrate under such conditions, and indeed some people with families and relatively substantial savings did migrate, but not many. For those who did, prospects in North and South America or Australia were much brighter.

There were a number of rather more specific difficulties in the way of a land settlement scheme, some of which were described in a letter to *The Times* published on 18 August 1900. David M. Wilson, who prior to the war had been appointed by President Kruger to investigate the possibilities of developing the Transvaal's agricultural and mineral resources, pointed out that there was no open or unclaimed land within fifty miles of any town except in the De Kaap valley. That area he estimated could perhaps absorb some 1 000 settlers. There were, he argued, only four major markets for vegetables in the Transvaal, and these were amply supplied by Italian, Portuguese and Asian market gardeners. There was, he thought, some possibility that men with £300 to enable them to survive the first unprofitable year would have some success with maize and forage crops or perhaps with onions and potatoes, or in some new areas with new crops such as oranges and tobacco. Generally, however, the picture he painted was a bleak one.

Wilson also touched on a fundamental weak point in the idea, the difficulty of acquiring land. He was convinced that the Boers would be understandably reluctant to sell their land, and that it would therefore be necessary to purchase it on the open market at prices pushed up by competition. The Commission did in fact have several ideas of providing land for settlement from Crown lands or large tracts held by mining syndicates. The agricultural value of this land was unproven, however, and it was for the most part located in undeveloped areas at considerable distances from means of cheap transport and population centres. The problems were certainly amenable to solution with the introduction of more advanced agricultural technology and the extension of the railway system, but not within the short period of time Milner envisaged.

Underlying the Commission's belief that a settlement scheme could be a success was the assumption that the Boers would accept a substantial rural British presence. On this Wilson also cast doubt, warning that British settlers would have to be grouped together for their own protection. If left isolated, surrounded by Boer farmers, they would find themselves deprived of the friendly help that is so much a part of rural life. He even predicted that they would be cut off from outside support and markets, as the Boers would block roads leading to their farms. As far as Wilson was concerned, the only future for Britons in the Transvaal was in mining. The chances of succeeding in agriculture were small. He advised people to tread warily but that it was better to stay at home, advice that many people seem to have taken.

Wilson's views were not without support. Some members of the Land Commission were convinced themselves that the scheme would not work because settlers would be drawn away from the land by the brighter prospects of gold and diamond mining. The Colonial Office also had reservations, one official minuting that remembering the attitude of the Boers in 1881 after the Transvaal War, they would 'boycott the British out of existence'. In more general terms the minute continued, 'Nearly all colonization schemes fail but they often leave a residue of good colonists.'[7] This minute provides at least an indication of why the Colonial Office gave the land settlement plans only lukewarm support; little in the way of firm support either in policy or finance was forthcoming. But Milner persisted.

Transvaal Land Board

In December 1901 the Transvaal Land Board was set up to advise on the implementation of the scheme. The Board had immediately to face some serious problems. First, no detailed scheme had as yet been drawn up. Second, no land was available for settlement, primarily because the imperial government had not taken Milner's advice to purchase land before the end of the war when speculation pushed prices up. By November 1901 only 531 soldiers had applied to remain in the country after the war, and by the following February the Land Board had acquired only one farm. Milner unsuccessfully pressed the government to give him strong political and financial backing.

In a sense the war ended too soon for the Land Board, leaving it without adequate plans or finance and in no position even to deal with requests for information. Initially these requests came from soldiers considering the possibility of settlement who wanted to know what provisions had been made for land grants, etc. Even the information available was discouraging and the soldiers were, not surprisingly, disappointed to find that they were expected to purchase their farms and to have at least £300 of their own capital; this in view of the fact that the most they would have been likely to save during their war service was as little as £70 and no more than £150.

It soon became apparent that if any part of the settlement scheme were to be salvaged, alternative forms of land tenure would have to be introduced. By July 1902 only three further holdings had been acquired, but by September some 323 men had settled land on squatter's tenure. Half the crop produced was to be turned over to the Land Board, which supplied draught animals, ploughs and other tools, seeds and rations as well as some supervision. This was perhaps a step in the right direction, but the fact that the tools tended to be unsuitable for the soil being tilled was certainly not conducive to the success of squatting arrangements. Furthermore, the series of drought years beginning in 1902–3 brought the number of squatters down to 206. Crown lands, which for military reasons could not be surveyed during the war, were finally offered to the squatters under the Crown Lands Disposal Ordinance and the Settlers Ordinance of 1902, but the continued drought made even these schemes ineffective.

The drought also increased the difficulty of providing cattle. The small number left after the war were not available for settlers, but were handed over by the military authorities to the Repatriation Commission; many of them died within twenty-four hours of reaching their destination. Cattle were imported from Argentina but cost as much as £30 a head at

Cape Town and were susceptible to Red Water Fever. Texas cattle were somewhat more suitable, but succumbed to an outbreak of East Coast Fever that occurred shortly after their introduction, the survivors having to be kept in strict quarantine. It was only at the end of 1903 that plans for irrigation in the Potchefstroom, Christiana and Warm Baths areas were drawn up, and the effects of the drought continued well into 1905 and made new settlement virtually impossible.

Even the Crown Land scheme for settlers was a failure, despite the fact that by the end of June 1903 some 4 640 applications for such settlement had been received. As not enough farms were available, there were only 508 permanent settlers by March 1904, and only another 60 by June 1905. Land settlement was a failure and made virtually no contribution to the swelling of the British population of the Transvaal. Other ideas to promote immigration, such as providing assisted passage for single women and for families, were tried, but these met with an equal lack of success. It might be argued that land settlement would have succeeded had it received firmer financial and political support from the Colonial Office, but this must remain a moot point, and because of the drought and the nature of the land, it seems highly unlikely.

Resettlement and agricultural development

The bulk of the money that was available for agriculture immediately after the war was devoted to the resettlement of Afrikaners on the farms they had occupied before the war, and to attempts to modernize the agricultural system. These efforts were also an essential part of Milner's plan, since his overall strategy depended on the Afrikaner population remaining relatively docile and not making great political demands. This Milner hoped to achieve by satisfying the Afrikaners' material needs, putting off any further demands until such time as he had gained his British majority. Milner was by no means oblivious to the nationalist feelings among Afrikaners, but he does not seem to have fully

British troops loading a waggon with looted possessions from an abandoned farmstead. It is difficult to imagine how Milner could have expected Afrikaners to accept British domination in the light of the devastation and hardships generated by Kitchener's ruthless prosecution of the war.

appreciated the extent to which the bitterness, indeed hatred, of the British had grown during the war. Before hostilities ceased he reversed the policy of confiscating the property of *bittereinders*, which he realized only exacerbated the feelings of resentment towards the British, but this and other similar moves did little to overcome the bitterness growing out of Afrikaners' experiences in the concentration camps, attempts to stifle the Afrikaans language, and the destruction of farms by the British army's burn and destroy tactics.

Quite apart from the psychological effect these tactics had, they added to the difficulty of resettlement and agricultural development. Furthermore, cattle herds, which before the war had only begun to recover from the serious rinderpest outbreak in 1895–6, had been virtually wiped out either by disease or the demands for food from one or other of the armed forces. Attempts to rebuild stocks by importing cattle were unsuccessful, as we have seen. Compensation funds and resettlement assistance tended to be administered in a somewhat chaotic manner, while drought continued to hinder recovery. Underlying all this was the generally poor quality of soil in the Transvaal, which in many areas made it unsuitable for arable agriculture on any commercial scale, the low level of agricultural technology, and the almost medieval system of land tenure and inheritance. The South African Republic had only really begun efforts to promote agricultural development and reform in the mid-1890s, and little progress had been made when war broke out.

Agrarian difficulties

The Transvaal's soil had by the mid-nineteenth century – earlier in some areas – deteriorated even further from its originally poor quality because of the extensive, wasteful methods employed by the primarily pastoral Boer farmers, who left land increasingly prone to erosion and unable to resist the periodic droughts common to the region. Most Boers only cultivated their land to the extent that it was necessary to meet their own immediate needs; the cultivation of forage crops was uncommon, and when markets for vegetables developed on the Rand, it was, as we have seen, Portuguese, Italian and other farmers who met these demands, not Afrikaners. Such an unscientific approach to agriculture was perfectly well suited to the period of the Great Trek, when it was still possible for a man to move on to new territory once the land he lived on became either exhausted or overcrowded. The closing of the frontier and the growing competition for land at the end of the nineteenth century created major problems and challenges for the generally conservative Boers, and their situation was further complicated by the growth of the mining industry in the 1890s. It was primarily in the Orange Free State, where wheat was an important crop, that agriculture was organized on a commercial level. Louis Botha was one outstanding example of the few Boer farmers in the Transvaal who did respond positively to the increased commercial opportunities; though there were others like him, they formed only a small section of the Boer farming community. Their political influence, however, was proportionally much greater than their numbers.

Apart from the essentially conservative nature of the Boer farmer – sharing that characteristic with farmers throughout the world and throughout history – the adoption of more advanced techniques was hindered seriously by custom and law. Roman-Dutch law, which in this respect at least operated in the Transvaal until 1902, although it had not survived as long elsewhere, required a man's heirs to receive a 'legitimate share' of his lands on his death. In the very common cases of intestacy, shares had to be equal. As in pre-industrial France, where Arthur Young reported some extreme cases where a man's holding of land was little more than the area covered by the shadow of a tree, individual shares in land, cattle and water rights tended to become so small as to be totally unviable. Details of land division in the Transvaal are difficult to find, but two examples from the Cape will indicate the nature of the problem. One example is cited of a farm of over 2 000 acres in which one of thirteen people's share amounted to 159 727/1 232 640ths, while another man was entitled to 1/48 141th of an approximately 5 000 acre farm.[8] Cooperation, which would have made it possible for smallholders to work together for their mutual benefit, was conspicuously, though not entirely, lacking, whether because of the Boer's 'rugged individualism', family disputes, greed or simply a lack of will.

By the outbreak of war some changes were being made, but only to a very limited extent. These changes were swamped by the additional problems caused by the devastation of war and the drought years following them. Milner did establish an Agricultural Department, but although this had facilities to assist farmers in many ways, its emphasis tended to be on arable rather than pastoral agriculture, and it had to face opposition from Boers who resented the intrusion of foreigners, however well-meaning, into their affairs. Such animosity became apparent, for example, in the attempts to introduce measures to control and eradicate the diseases that so often destroyed large numbers of cattle. Regulations were introduced, but when it came to enforcing them officials were faced with having to decide whether to stand up to hostile farmers or to follow the path of least resistance. In many cases it was the latter alternative that was followed. Extensive agrarian reform was needed, and Milner did lay the groundwork for it with administrative support and regulations. But as with land settlement, more time was needed to establish new administrative services and to overcome resistance to change. Milner's hopes for rapid resettlement of the Boers, for the satisfaction of their material needs to keep them politically docile, and for the agricultural system of the Transvaal to be put on a modern footing in a short period of time just could not be realized.

'Poor white' problem

One of the most useful reforms Milner introduced was to end, legally at least, the old system of land tenure and inheritance, making it easier for larger farms to remain in the hands of a single person. Tradition was strong, however, and old customs died hard. The old land tenure system also contributed to the further development of another problem that the war and its aftermath exacerbated, namely, the increase in the number of 'poor whites'. This had roots in the period long before the war, some Europeans even in the earliest stages of settlement being unwilling, or for a variety of reasons unable, to gain their livelihood by farming. This made many people turn to transport riding, but this had disappeared with the coming of the railways. Others eked out a bare existence as *bywoners* or sharecroppers who lived on land, often belonging to a relation, to which they had no fixed rights but were forced to share whatever they produced with the landowner. This had been a fairly effective and cheap way for landowners to get at least some benefit from land they did not work themselves, but by the end of the nineteenth century the system had degenerated. *Bywoners* received no benefit from any improvements they might make on the land and had little incentive to work hard. Many landowners found the *bywoners* an increasing burden, and after the war frequently took advantage of any pretext on which they could get rid of them.

With the growth of mining many 'poor whites' were attracted to the towns, though for most the ties to the land apparently remained strong and urban migration was considered temporary. In the towns they found they had to compete with black workers, who worked for lower wages. Most of these urban migrants lacked the qualifications to fill the more skilled or supervisory positions on the mines, which remained the preserve of British workers for some years. Afrikaners gradually moved into these positions, but once again not quickly

Desolation from farm-burning. After the war rural impoverishment drove thousands of poorer Afrikaners off the land.

enough to resolve the problem. As with other aspects of reconstruction, the problems that had to be overcome were not exclusively the result of the war, but had existed before and were made considerably worse by it.

The social problem of the 'poor whites' went largely unrecognized by the British administration. During the reconstruction period there was some attempt made to employ Afrikaners as unskilled workers on the mines. Apart from their reluctance to do manual labour, the supervisory staff of the mines tended to find them less dependable, less productive and less 'tractable'. Attempts to introduce a white labour policy received little support for economic reasons, despite the difficulty mine-owners had in filling their unskilled labour requirements. The 'poor white' problem remained a serious one until the 1930s, when economic expansion enabled the greater part of the unemployed population to find jobs.

Anglicization

For reasons largely beyond his control Milner had been unable to meet the material needs of the rural Afrikaner or to solve the problems of the landless and jobless. He also failed in another aspect of his attempt to contain Afrikaner nationalism, namely, by introducing a new education system, and by making it obligatory for Afrikaners to be able to speak English. The use of Dutch for official purposes was to be allowed only until this process of Anglicization had been completed. In furthering this aim, state-supported schools used English as the medium of instruction. But the impact of this was lessened by provision for parents to request that their children be given fifteen minutes of religious instruction in Dutch each day, and a further three hours per week for the study of the Dutch Bible until the children were confirmed, and thereafter three hours weekly for the study of Dutch literature. Teachers were expected to use their best efforts to promote Afrikaner acceptance of British rule, and imperial history formed a large part of the curriculum. Not surprisingly, this attempt to impose English was resented, and private schools were set up where Dutch or Afrikaans (which was only just beginning to emerge as an accepted language at this time) was the medium of instruction. This policy was really made ineffective, however, by the general apathy of Afrikaner parents, most of whom seemed to feel that there was no need for their children to have more than one year's schooling, if any. Few attended school after the age of five and of those who did, one-third left before the age of ten. This was hardly an effective means of spreading English culture.

Afrikaner nationalism was nourished by these various policies and the circumstances leading to their failure. At the same time the Afrikaners immediately after the war did not form the strongly united body that Milner seems to have assumed they would. Rather they were seriously divided between the *bittereinders*, who had fought on and had only reluctantly – and in the minds of many, only temporarily – given up the struggle against the British, and the *hensoppers* and joiners, who had collaborated with the British. Some National

Another of Kidger Tucker's cartoons. Although drawn in about 1898, it nonetheless depicts accurately the character of white politics in South Africa, which the war and the divisions among Afrikaners immediately afterwards did not change.

Scouts felt themselves sufficiently ostracized from the Afrikaner community to seek permission to establish their own church. This potential schism, which might well have been exploited to advantage, was opposed not only by the Transvaal's Lieutenant Governor but, paradoxically, also by Louis Botha, who thought he was opposing British government policy. If the *hensoppers* had received some strong tangible reward for their collaboration, and had been able to see some real distinction made between them and the *bittereinders*, they might well have formed a separate group within the Afrikaner community. As it was, no special provision for looking after *hensopper* interests was embodied in the Peace of Vereeniging, and they were gradually absorbed back into the Afrikaner community.

The mining industry

While the strength of Afrikaner national sentiment was probably the most important single reason for the demise of Milner's reconstruction policy, the failure to attract the large number of British immigrants that was hoped for, was in some measure due to the failure of the mining industry to achieve the growth expected of it.

Much has been written over the years about the relationship between mining interests and the government in South Africa. The most recent research has revealed that, contrary to what had been widely believed earlier, there was a considerable degree of cooperation between the mining companies and the government of the South African Republic. There has recently been discussion, notably by Donald Denoon, A. A. Mawby and A. H. Duminy, about the nature of the relationship between Milner and the mining magnates. Denoon originally argued that the magnates influenced Milner to frame policies that served their interests, while Mawby, in particular, has argued that Milner manipulated the mining magnates in pursuing his own political objectives. From these discussions it emerges clearly that the magnates did not form a united group that would be able or prepared to press Milner in the same direction at all times. A second point is that both the Milner administration and the mining industry shared a wide field of common interests. The mining companies sought to maximize their profits and looked to government for support. Government on the other hand relied on the mining companies for revenue and for wider economic strength and development, and was therefore prepared, within limits, to assist them. For Milner the 'overspill' from mining was of crucial importance for his entire scheme; he was willing to help the companies resolve some of the problems they faced in resuming and expanding production. That he was not willing simply to give them what they asked for is illustrated by the fact that he increased the taxes they had to pay after the war.

The years prior to the war had seen a large amount of capital being put into deep-level mining as it became clear that the greater part of the Rand's gold lay at considerable depth. General practice in deep-level mining was to sink large shafts on the assumption that a deposit would be profitable, rather than to sink a less costly smaller shaft on the basis that the mine might prove to be of little value. Because ores were of low concentration, profitability depended on raising large quantities of rock to the surface for crushing at a cost as low as possible. For Milner the mines represented a wasting asset; if they were to have the desired impact on the Transvaal's economy, they had to be brought rapidly to a stage of increased productivity. The mining companies' primary concern was to begin showing a profit on their heavy pre-war capitalization, and on the investment in nearly 300 companies floated in the twelve months following the peace, as quickly as possible. This necessitated keeping costs down.

There were two major components of mining costs; labour

and mine stores. The latter became increasingly expensive after the war because of the relative decline in the value of gold compared to other commodities. This was a phenomenon visible from about 1900 to the outbreak of the First World War. As this was outside the control of the companies, or Milner for that matter, the only solution appeared to be to bring the cost of labour down to as low a level as possible. This involved not only paying African unskilled workers less than they had received before the war, but also increasing the number of African workers relative to the number of more expensive white workers. Apart from the attempts to use whites as unskilled labour, which were unsuccessful, the mining companies wanted to try to introduce blacks into the semi-skilled and skilled positions that previously had been reserved for whites. The whites, not surprisingly, resisted.

The idea of limiting the industrial jobs Africans could do, and reserving certain work for whites, was far from new; but neither custom nor the law had made these firmly entrenched policy, except in so far as blasting certificates could not be held by Africans. It might well have been possible for the companies to achieve some changes along the lines desired at this time had they been able to draw on a large supply of African labour. Not only were they not available for skilled work, they were not coming forward in sufficient numbers to meet the demand for unskilled labour.

Labour scarcity

It was clearly in Milner's interest to attempt to ensure the availability of an adequate labour supply. To this end in 1901 he rather hurriedly negotiated a *modus vivendi* agreement with the Portuguese administration in Mozambique whereby recruiting for the Rand mines would be allowed in exchange for preferential rights of entry into the Transvaal for products of the 'soil and industry' of Mozambique, and for a guarantee that at least fifty per cent of the Transvaal's import and export traffic would be channelled through the port and railway of Lourenço Marques. Under the pressure of the immediate need for labour, Milner allowed the Portuguese to gain a very advantageous position, which was to work against some of his basic aims for South African unity, particularly regarding customs and railways. He felt there was no alternative and comforted himself with the view that the *modus vivendi* was but a temporary measure, and that its terms could be modified later. The agreement in fact proved very resilient, remaining for some decades the basis of the economic relationship between the two countries. In the short term it was of little advantage to South Africa since relatively few Mozambicans came forward for work.

Why were Africans so reluctant at this time to work on the mines? The answer to the question can in some ways only be speculative, but some reasons appear obvious. In the first place, mining, particularly at deep levels, could hardly be considered an attractive occupation as long as there were other employment opportunities available. Conditions on the mines and in the mining compounds, where the men were forced to

live, were notoriously bad and the mortality rate high. During the war work became available on the railways and in military employment at higher wages than those paid by the mines. For several years after the war the expansion of the railway networks in the Transvaal and the Orange Free State continued to provide alternative employment. Also, more Africans found they did not have to work at all, as it became easier for them to live off the land. African squatters on Crown lands were relatively well treated; their obligatory period of work was better paid and shorter in duration than that for private landowners, and because of the shortage of administrative staff their rents were often not collected. Also, some of the arbitrary recruiting methods practised before the war were strongly disapproved of by the new administration, and, although they did not cease completely, they were curtailed. Men from Mozambique may well have built up savings that enabled them to postpone seeking wage employment, though it seems unlikely that this factor operated in the Transvaal.

The greatest obstacle to successful recruiting was the decision by the Chamber of Mines to reduce wages from their

Road improvements in Johannesburg were but one feature of the public works programmes initiated by the British immediately after the war. The employment opportunities offered by such schemes contributed towards the gold mining industry's serious shortage of African labour.

1899 level of 50 shillings per month to 35 shillings per month. The Chamber represented the change as an increase on the wartime rate of 20 shillings, imposed by the government of the South African Republic, but this was easily seen as spurious. It was not long before wages began to rise again, though labour supplies remained inadequate. Only farm work was worse paid than employment on the mines.

If labour costs were to be kept low, it was also essential to stop competitive recruiting, whereby individual mines tried to secure labour by offering higher wages. One of the motives behind the formation of the Chamber of Mines in 1889 had indeed been to attempt to stop the 'wages spiral', and several attempts were made to establish centralized recruiting organizations. In 1896 the Rand Native Labour Association was formed. In 1900 this was supplanted by the Witwatersrand Native Labour Association (WNLA). Under the terms of the *modus vivendi* the WNLA was given a monopoly of recruiting there, though the monopoly was broken for a short time some years later. The WNLA also attempted to secure labour in British Central Africa (Nyasaland), German South-West Africa and elsewhere, but with minimal success. One difficulty was that recruits from tropical areas suffered from a higher than normal mortality rate from pneumonia because of the marked change in climate. Recruiting in South Africa and the surrounding areas remained disappointing, and the Chamber of Mines began to look for an entirely new labour source. Ultimately they found it in China.

Chinese labour

The idea of importing Chinese labour was by no means new. During the earliest Dutch occupation of the Cape, Governor van Riebeeck had considered the possibility of bringing in Chinese to solve the labour problem he faced. In the 1870s the Cape government planned to introduce Chinese labourers, but the British government would not permit them to do so. In 1900 the administration in Southern Rhodesia was given permission to recruit Chinese, but under such stringent conditions that the plans were never put into effect. Some mining companies saw Chinese labour as the only solution to their problems, but in July 1902, after a rather stormy meeting held *in camera*, the Chamber rejected the idea and in the following month set up a Committee on White and Coloured Labour. The committee first considered proposals, championed by Frederic Creswell, for the greater use of white labour in order to save 'European civilization' from 'African barbarism'. As manager of the Village Deep Mine, Creswell had shown that with appropriate reorganization, white labour was not as expensive as had been supposed. Similar, though not as carefully organized, experiments on four other mines were rather less successful, and the general feeling continued to be that African labour was cheaper and more profitable than any form of white labour. There was, of course, the underlying feeling that whites should in no circumstances do the same work as blacks, a feeling by no means confined to Afrikaners.

Not surprisingly, the Chamber was less concerned with saving 'European civilization' than with securing labour for its members as cheaply as possible. In December 1902 the special committee came around to the view that the best way of resolving the labour crisis was indeed to import Chinese. Even before securing official approval for the plan, the Chamber began organizing and financing recruitment. A Committee of Agents was formed in October 1903 to be replaced in July 1904 by the Chamber of Mines Labour Importation Agency (CMLIA). Before any formal steps could be taken, however, Milner and the British government had to be persuaded to agree. Milner was at first reluctant, but soon came to the view that Chinese recruiting was the quickest and most efficient way of meeting the mines' labour needs. Convincing Transvaal whites and the British government was more difficult.

Believing that Transvaal whites only needed to be made aware of the facts to be guaranteed of their support, Milner appointed a commission to investigate the country's labour problem. The Chamber, thanks to its unrivalled access to detailed statistics (which it was able to present in the best light for its own purposes) and the influence it could bring to bear on newspaper editors, lawyers, mine managers, etc., not only convinced the majority of the commission of the need for importing Chinese, but was also able to bring about the appearance of widespread support. To secure the acceptance of the scheme by skilled white labour, the Chinese were to be allowed to do only 'such labour as is usually performed in mines in the Witwatersrand district by persons belonging to the aboriginal races or tribes of Africa' and were not to be allowed to do any of more than fifty specified skilled jobs listed in a schedule of the Transvaal Labour Importation Ordinance.[9] Thus the industrial colour bar, previously enforced almost entirely by custom, first became enshrined in statute.

In fact, white support for importation was far from as great as Milner and the Chamber claimed it to be. Even before the Ordinance was debated, a minority of the Labour Commission voiced complaints about the way in which the Chamber of Mines' evidence had been accepted unquestioningly. Four out of thirteen unofficial members of the legislative council voted against the Ordinance, while the Afrikaner members of the legislature who voted in favour of it were not truly representative of Afrikaner opinion, which was never really tested. Their action, however, was repudiated by General Botha. In Britain opinion in and out of Parliament in 1903 was far from convinced that importation should be allowed, but the government was not really made aware of the feelings of dissent in the Transvaal, and in the face of apparently widespread support from the white community the Cabinet reluctantly agreed.

Recruiting in China began in February 1904 and on 19 June the SS *Tweeddale* disembarked the first contingent of

A photograph of the original sign that was displayed at a recruiting office for the South African gold mines in Tientsin in 1905. The sign now hangs in the offices of the Employment Bureau of Africa Ltd, Johannesburg.

Chinese workers at Durban. From then until recruiting ended, a total of 63 296 Chinese were sent to the Rand. These men were not willing to accept uncomplainingly the working conditions imposed on them. It was not without justification that they came to believe they had been deceived, particularly over wages. Disputes with supervisory and management staff were frequent, particularly in the earlier stages of the experiment when language difficulties exacerbated underlying feelings of discontent. The most extreme form of protest was the so-called strike at the North Randfontein Mine in April 1905. This was not typical of the workers' expressions of dissatisfaction, but nonetheless revealed their ability to combine effectively to resist some of the worst aspects of their exploitation. The 'strike' did achieve some small success in changing the wages system for the Chinese, but with government support the mining industry emerged from the dispute assured of a mine wages policy that would always work in their favour, and that gave them an even greater measure of control over their labour force than they had previously enjoyed.

Despite their relative lack of docility, the Chinese were generally considered good workers and from an economic point of view the experiment might well have been extended. There was, however, increasing opposition to recruitment in China itself, while in Britain many people came to view the use of Chinese labour as synonymous with the practice of 'slavery'. This became a major issue in the election of 1906, when the humanitarian lobby launched a popular campaign in favour of terminating the system, a campaign that was strongly supported by the British labour movement and by the Liberal Party. Recruiting ended in November 1906. Under the Botha government systematic repatriation began in 1907. The last Chinese labourers, other than those who had earlier deserted and disappeared, left South Africa in 1910.

Although employed for a relatively short time, Chinese labour helped the mining industry out of a difficult period. At acceptable cost levels, unskilled labour had been made available in sufficient quantity and for a sufficient length of time to enable the industry to recover and profitably exploit new low-grade deposits. By 1906 the post-war boom that had provided alternative employment opportunities for Africans was also at an end, Africans from South Africa itself as well as from Mozambique once again coming forward in sufficient numbers to meet the mines' labour needs.

Well before this time it had become obvious that Milner's reconstruction scheme had failed to attain its basic aim. It was under Afrikaner not British leaders, and with an Afrikaner party, *Het Volk*, in the majority in the legislature, that the Transvaal began its period of responsible self-government in 1907; probably more galling to Milner was the fact that *Het Volk* also had the support of some Uitlanders.

Conclusion

Some aspects of reconstruction produced positive benefits for the Transvaal and South Africa. Municipal governments were set up not only in the major centres, such as Johannesburg and Pretoria, but also in towns throughout the Transvaal and Orange River Colony. This did not have the desired effect of providing sufficient outlet for either Uitlander or Afrikaner political interests, but did mark a significant step in the country's political development. The Inter-Colonial Council was formed in May 1903 to administer the railways in the two former republics, the South African Constabulary, and to distribute the £35 000 000 guaranteed loan put up by the imperial government to finance general development. The Council was heavily criticized for the way in which it spent the money, not entirely without justification. The Council's most lasting contribution to South African development was to amalgamate the railway systems of the two new colonies into the Central South African Railways, the pooled receipts of which went towards meeting the costs of the Constabulary and of servicing the guaranteed loan. The Council's major weakness was that Milner had not been able to secure borrowing powers for it. As a result it could not undertake new railway construction, though an extensive programme of railway development initially promoted by the High Commissioner was carried out and forms one of Milner's more lasting contributions to the country. The Inter-Colonial Council was finally dissolved in June 1908, after having promoted various public works. However, the joint management of the railways survived.

A power station in the Transvaal under construction in 1905. The sponsorship of public works was one of the most beneficial and enduring legacies of the Milner era.

It was also under Milner's aegis that two important steps towards the unification of South Africa were taken. In 1903 a common railway tariff to operate throughout the Cape, Natal, Orange River Colony and the Transvaal was agreed, and in April of the same year a customs union embracing all the British colonies in southern Africa was formed.

For the Transvaal itself Milner's most important contribution was the formation of the Agricultural Department, which encouraged scientific development in both arable and pastoral agriculture. Model farms and agricultural schools were established and extensive research carried out. New strains of many crops were introduced and information made available to farmers. Irrigation and water-boring schemes were put into operation, as were schemes to treat and eradicate pests and animal diseases. The Department's benefits were by no means evenly distributed among Transvaal farmers, but this aspect of reconstruction was the only one to receive virtually universal praise. Louis Botha considered the Agricultural Department to be the only virtue of the Milner administration, and he retained its director, Frank Smith, after he assumed the premiership in 1907. Indeed, Smith was appointed first Director of Agriculture of the Union.

In promoting agriculture, public works and railway building, to say nothing of repatriation immediately following the war, Milner's reconstruction policy did indeed help the Transvaal and all of South Africa to recover from the ravages of the war. Why did he fail to achieve his imperial aims? There were, of course, those factors, such as drought and labour scarcity, that were beyond his control. Likewise he had many responsibilities other than being Governor of the Transvaal, which made it impossible to keep careful watch over his administrative staff, many of whom were inexperienced and unfamiliar with South African problems. Primarily he failed because he set himself an impossible task. His view of empire led him to make assumptions about the unity of Afrikanerdom that prevented him even attempting to take advantage of divisions within the Afrikaner community. His view of Afrikaners also prevented him from seeking meaningful collaboration with their leaders, collaboration that even with the bitter memories of war might well have been forthcoming. In thinking that Afrikaner nationalism could easily be contained Milner helped to stimulate its growth. Similarly, Milner's assumptions about the unity of the British community in the Transvaal were misplaced; he took no account of the different economic interest groups represented, which after the war led to political division within Uitlander ranks. He was therefore unable to enjoy either the constant or unanimous support of the British community. In underestimating the strength of Transvaal British opposition to his policies Milner again showed himself more an idealist than a practical politician. His idealism further led him to set goals for immigration that were totally unrealistic and showed little understanding of the kind of people he hoped to attract.

It may be argued that Milner's aims could have been achieved if he had enjoyed the strong support of the British government. Here again he was unrealistic. Although aware of the growing tide of sentiment in Britain against his imperial views, he continued to think – or hope – that he could carry on virtually on his own. Even before the Liberals' electoral victory in 1906, British public opinion had turned against the idea of British dominance over Afrikanerdom. The war had been expensive and unpopular and the British had lost some of their enthusiasm for dominating other people, particularly if those other people were white. Far from bringing about Afrikaner acceptance of benevolent British rule, Milner was probably more responsible than any other individual for embittering relations between Boer and Briton and for accelerating the dominance of Afrikaners over British, which, as he himself knew, was inevitable once his policies failed.

References

1. See, for example, Eric Stokes, 'Milnerism', *The Historical Journal*, 5, 1 (1962), 47–60, and G. H. Le May, *British Supremacy in South Africa, 1899–1907*, Oxford, 1965, *passim*.
2. Anonymous pamphlet entitled 'Remarks on the Transvaal from an ex-Resident', dated February 1908. I have found no other use of this term in published form.
3. Stokes, 52.
4. Milner to Chamberlain, undated, Milner Papers, 25, cited in Donald Denoon, *A Grand Illusion*, London, 1973, 33–4.
5. These tables are taken from Denoon, 36.
6. Lt. Col. T. Kelly Kenny to Chairman of the Commission, 23 September 1900, Cd 627, 13.
7. Minute by Henry Lambert on Milner's telegram No. 490, 14 August 1900, CO 417/292.
8. W. M. MacMillan, *Complex South Africa*, London, 1930, 82.
9. Transvaal Labour Importation Ordinance, No. 17 of 1904, cited in Sheila T. van der Horst, *Native Labour in South Africa*, Oxford, 1942, 171.

CHAPTER 16
British Imperial Policy and South Africa 1906-10

Ronald Hyam

The Liberal Party and South Africa

The British ministers primarily responsible for formulating imperial policy between 1905 and 1910 were the Colonial Secretaries Lord Elgin (December 1905 to April 1908) and Lord Crewe (April 1908 to November 1910). Crewe took over when H. H. Asquith succeeded Sir Henry Campbell-Bannerman as Liberal Prime Minister. Neither Premier exerted much influence on imperial policy-making, nor even showed any close interest in South Africa after the middle of 1906. More important was the contribution of Winston Churchill, who, in his first ministerial office as Parliamentary Under-Secretary at the Colonial Office (1905–8), gave much help and some hindrance to Elgin.

On becoming Prime Minister, Campbell-Bannerman was anxious about party unity. He had always regarded the South African War as essentially a civil war – but not all his followers agreed with him. The legacy of the internal party split between pro-Boers and Liberal Imperialists was potentially a danger to his new ministry. Elgin seemed an ideal choice as Colonial Secretary since he had never been closely identified with either wing, or indeed with any partisan position. He had held the great non-party office of Viceroy of India (1894–9), and then had chaired the royal commission to inquire into the military preparations for the war and into various logistical questions relating to its conduct, and, with much skill, had produced a unanimous report in July 1903. Furthermore, as a peer, Elgin could stand somewhat aside from the embittered popular arena into which imperial policy in general had been plunged. Elgin had disapproved of the war, but was too patriotic to denounce it; in office he showed – entirely realistically – a marked concern for the principle of continuity of policy. Perhaps partly because of his wide acceptability, both within and without the party, the old split had in practice almost no bearing on the formulation of the imperial policy of the government. There remained a sharp division of opinion about Milner – but he had already left office. In other directions, even in the empire, there was much the Liberals agreed about. Campbell-Bannerman tended to dismiss earlier hostility to his leadership as purely personal and self-interested; and in any case the doubts of Liberal Imperialists about him centred on concern over the soundness of his foreign and defence policies rather than imperial ones. Of the leading Liberal Imperialists only Asquith served on the Cabinet committees set up to deal with South African problems; while Haldane and Grey shared the Prime Minister's confidence in Elgin. In contemplating the awful mess that was South Africa both Elgin and Campbell-Bannerman derived hope from the analogy with Canada. Through the establishment of responsible government Canada had become 'the greatest triumph of British statesmanship', as Campbell-Bannerman declared at the time of the peace negotiations at the end of the war. And it was Elgin's father (the 8th Earl) who had played an integral part in this Canadian achievement, while his maternal grandfather was Lord Durham, whose report in 1839 had recommended the union and granting of responsible government to Canada, and who was increasingly becoming a cult figure. Elgin's family knowledge of Canadian history in the 1840s led him to conclude in January 1906 that 'the feeling between the British and French was more hostile than that between the British and Boer [now]'.[1]

Lord Elgin (as a boy) with his father, the 8th Earl, pictured in 1859. Elgin was encouraged by the example of his father's achievements in Canada in reconciling French settlers to the British flag.

Sir Henry Campbell-Bannerman. He did not play the central part in the formulation of his government's policy towards South Africa, but Smuts admired his role and often spoke warmly of him in after years.

Churchill brought to the Colonial Office knowledge of a more direct kind. He had some on-the-spot experience of South Africa as war correspondent of the *Morning Post*. He had learned to admire much in the Boers, and to realize that they were essential to the development and prosperity of South Africa: the two communities must, he urged from 1900, cooperate in friendly concord, though he would add 'under the supremacy of Britain'. With that caveat, he believed the British should not go on 'fighting the Boers' after the war was over.

In South Africa itself throughout this period the chief British representative was Lord Selborne (High Commissioner from April 1905 to May 1910). His importance in policy-making has been greatly overrated. The Liberals never entirely trusted his Tory views (he had been Balfour's First Lord of the Admiralty). There was wide divergence between them, and although it suited them to avoid an open quarrel, they nearly recalled him in May/June 1906. He had not, in fact, been the Unionists' first choice as successor to Milner: the post had been refused by Arthur Godley. Although regarded as a big improvement on Milner, the Liberals were unimpressed by Selborne. Asquith found him inept at the 'diagnosis and prognosis' of South African affairs, and 'singularly deficient in the larger questions of policy, both in insight and foresight'. Lewis Harcourt (who took over from Crewe at the Colonial Office in November 1910) described Selborne's mind as 'small and not very effective'. Crewe himself regarded him as energetic and loyal but 'rather a dangerous plenipotentiary . . . intensely obstinate, and his ideas run away with him. . . '. Nor was he any better regarded by Colonial Office officials, who found him fussy, fractious, sulky, apt to scold and sermonize, and, because of his shabby appearance, not entirely credible as the king's representative. Tight control was therefore kept over Selborne, and he was retained in office mainly as a channel of communication only.[2]

The abandonment of the Lyttelton Constitution

Selborne's reiterated objections to conceding immediate responsible government to the Transvaal were overruled. By the time they took office in December 1905, most leading Liberal politicians, whether former pro-Boers or not, were agreed that restoration of self-government to the Boer republics was the only hopeful chance of a solution to a very bad situation. It took only a couple of months intensive study of the memoranda and telegrams, and consultation with officials, to confirm their instinct. On Milner's departure from South Africa on 31 March 1905 Lyttelton's representative constitution* had been promulgated, but the constitution had not been implemented immediately, and before any steps in this direction could be taken the Unionist government had fallen. The Liberals quickly concluded that the constitution would prove unworkable. By early February 1906 they were ready at Cabinet

*Under 'responsible government', the executive council is responsible to the elected representatives in the legislative assembly; under a 'representative' system it is not, and is usually nominated by the governor.

level to take this decision in principle, and to consider means of implementing responsible government instead. Procedurally and tactically, there was an alternative: they could either amend the Lyttelton Constitution on the new basis of responsible government, or they could scrap it and write their own constitution afresh. It was undoubtedly Campbell-Bannerman's intervention that led to the adoption of the latter course. His insistence was almost entirely dictated by a determination to put (or keep) the Liberal Imperialists (with their concern for continuity of policy) in their place, and thus to consolidate rank and file support behind himself. Whether or not it was also a gesture deliberately intended to impress the Boers, as, in retrospect at least, it seemed to do, is anybody's guess. (There is, in fact, no evidence, but it is one of those issues upon which a master-historian has said, 'no evidence is as good as any evidence'.) What really mattered, however, was not the formal basis of the constitution but the distribution of electoral power, and it is significant that in the delimitation of the constituencies the Lyttelton proposals were retained. This was done in the face of pressure from Smuts to make the Liberals change their minds, and in the light of the recommendation of the committee of inquiry under Sir Joseph West Ridgeway, which Campbell-Bannerman had initiated (though he would have preferred a full royal commission).

'I think on the whole I am satisfied . . . though at one time I had to show a little fight.' A letter from Lord Elgin to Lady Elgin on 16 February 1906, referring to the Cabinet meeting of that day. At this Cabinet Elgin insisted that the Prime Minister's policy of scrapping the Lyttelton Constitution should be entirely without prejudice to the retention of some of its features.

I said before that Cabinets won't wait — I may now add — they shan't be hurried; if I want my say! I think on the whole I am satisfied with the result of keeping them, though I had at one time to show a little fight.

I must not say more for the Prime Minister solemnly warned us against comparing Cabinet secrets to the members of our families, although he said "those near & dear to us".

I called at 76. and saw Watson — told her of yours having got the horsemaid. She said she had lost the other maid,

It is thus more than clear that the correct way to describe Liberal policy is within the framework of a continuing search for British supremacy: securing British interests was more important to them than conciliating the Boers. Their immediate aim was to produce a British majority at the first election under the new Transvaal constitution. In the event they did not succeed.

As a result, historians have often been tempted to argue that Britain won the war only to lose the peace. If this is so, it certainly was not what the Liberals intended. In fact, it is not so: it reflects a strictly Tory view of matters, in line with criticisms made at the time by Milner ('they have given South Africa back to the Boers') and Balfour ('the most reckless experiment ever tried in the development of a great colonial policy'). It also reflects, perhaps, the crumbling of the purely local position of the South African British community, which by 1907, in electoral defeat and general disillusionment, had to adjust to a permanent minority status.[3] In the wider perspective of empire and Commonwealth, however, what was done in the years 1905 to 1910 was effective enough to secure South Africa's retention in the total structure of British imperial strategic and economic interests. South Africa not only remained a major trading partner in the sterling area, but fought on the British side in two world wars. That this relationship was, broadly, perpetuated so far into the twentieth century owes a great deal to Liberal and pro-Boer insight. As Winston Churchill declared in 1950 on the death of Smuts,

> 'No act of reconciliation after a bitter struggle has ever produced so rich a harvest in goodwill or effects that lasted so long upon affairs.'

The Liberals, of course, had an enormously valuable card up their sleeve, albeit put there by Milner rather than God. They had never regarded it as necessary for British interests to participate directly in the formal government of the Boer republics; to them, wartime conquest of the Transvaal and Orange Free State put into the government's hands territories that it was easy for them to contemplate handing back, since they never particularly wished to possess them, and had always thought that Milner's and Chamberlain's policies were grievously mistaken. They could in office thus play from strength, and by retrocession command a degree of Boer gratitude that might otherwise have been impossible to evoke. The big difference from Unionist policy was that the Liberals saw the need to take the Boers into account, to try to understand their feelings, to listen to them and to work with them – to make South African policy, to quote Churchill's metaphor, 'stand on two legs' (one British, one Boer) and not on one only, which was 'the inherent vice of Milner's policy'. The Liberals were thus carrying on the search for British supremacy, though less overtly and provocatively than their predecessors. There was, however, a complication.

Winston Churchill. Although so young and so recent a convert to the Liberal Party, Churchill played a significant role in the formulation of government imperial policy.

Political implications of Chinese labour

One of the most significant results of the war was the introduction of Chinese labourers into the Witwatersrand mines. In order to make up the short-fall of African mine labourers, 63 000 Chinese were imported. The actual number of Chinese employed by the turn of 1905 and 1906 was some 47 000, but more were already on their way. The incoming Liberal government put an immediate stop to further indenturing: it was almost the first thing the Liberals did. The political effect of Milner's decision to introduce the Chinese was remarkable. The cry that the Chinese were in effect employed in conditions of virtual slavery played a critical part in the unusual size of the Liberal electoral victory in January 1906. In turn this meant that the Liberal government was bound to act to dissociate itself from the whole experiment, if only to fulfil the pledges made by some of their supporters. While crown colony government remained in existence, and while through it they remained responsible even for the day-to-day administration of the indentured system (since immediate repatriation of all the Chinese was out of the question), they were vulnerable to criticism and attack, all of it morally damaging to their position. There was an alarming mortality rate, together with reports of illegal floggings and sexual irregularities; in fact, every kind of embarrassment kept cropping up. Thus it is almost certainly the case that responsible government for the Transvaal was introduced considerably quicker than it would have been if Milner had never brought in the Chinese. The establishment of responsible government got the Liberals off their Chinese labour hook. As Loreburn, the Lord Chancellor, put it in January 1906: 'The one question of Chinese labour makes it necessary that responsible government should be installed in the Transvaal' as soon as possible and preferably within six months. To Sir Edward Grey (the Foreign Secretary) responsible government almost instantly seemed to him to be the 'one way out of the impasse' on Chinese labour.

If, then, we are to identify the four major objectives of the Liberals in making their speedy settlement in the Transvaal, the most important must be the necessity of getting rid of responsibility for Chinese labour, which remained with them as long as a crown colony government system was in force. This is why priority was given to the Transvaal, while the Orange River Colony (with no Chinese) had to wait its turn for responsible government, much to its disgust. Secondly, the Liberals based themselves on an 'absolute determination' (to quote Churchill once again) to maintain the dominance of 'a loyal and English population'. The West Ridgeway Committee pronounced 'British supremacy as vital and essential' and said that it should be demonstrated by working for the outward and visible sign of a British victory at the general election. This was a side of their calculations that ministers played down carefully, and all requests for publication of the report were steadily refused. The report was too honest; Loreburn's opinion was widely shared among ministers: it was

Lord Elgin, an underrated Colonial Secretary who played a major part in the Transvaal settlement and generally showed great concern for the protection and promotion of African interests.

> 'a great mistake to set forth the motive, viz, to secure a British majority . . . so repeatedly and in so marked a way.'

Few, if any, ministers, and Elgin least of all, cared to parade this kind of talk in public, but none of them would be satisfied unless British interests were safely provided for in the constitution. Thirdly, but following West Ridgeway, an actual Boer majority in the new Transvaal parliament was something the Liberals hoped and planned to avoid. Sir Richard Solomon, Milner's moderate-minded Attorney-General (but quite certainly no pro-Boer), was the man they looked to as Prime Minister designate, and not any Boer leader. And so they maintained the Unionist principle of 'one vote, one value' through a system of single-member constituencies roughly comprising the same number of (exclusively white) voters, expecting this arrangement to produce a small British majority. Finally, they were determined not to let their suspicions of the Boers (and notably of Smuts) stand in the way. Churchill identified a danger:

> 'I would do strict justice to the Boers; but when we remember that 20 000 of their women and children perished in our concentration camps in the year 1901–2, is it wise to count too much upon their good offices in 1906?'

But the Gladstonian Liberal principle prevailed against all risk and doubt: Britain did not give responsible government because colonies were loyal and friendly, but because colonies might *become* loyal and friendly if they were given responsible government.

All this amounted to a completely unsentimental policy: a conscious gamble, perhaps, but one meant to consolidate British interests. It is hardly necessary to describe it in terms of conciliation or magnanimity. Only the fact that their electoral arithmetic went astray made the settlement appear more generous than had ever been intended.[4]

Responsible government

The Boer party *Het Volk* won the Transvaal election in 1907, obtaining a clear majority of five seats over all other parties. General Louis Botha became Prime Minister. Although not regarded as an unmitigated disaster, this was not what was meant to happen. What had gone wrong? Essentially, the Liberals made the same mistake as Milner had done in relying too heavily on the British community. Neither saw the vital facts of the situation, which were: (i) that the British community was relatively smaller than they would have liked to believe, (ii) that the British were deeply divided and in no sense a monolithic group, and (iii) that all the Boers and half of the British were opposed to the elite magnate group who had been the favoured collaborators of Milner and Chamberlain. These divisions *were* discerned, and most cleverly exploited, by Smuts.[5]

Unaware of this discrepancy between result and intention, later commentators have widely praised Liberal policy for its magnanimity, and repeatedly appealed to it as a wise precedent

Overleaf: a Punch cartoon, 8 August 1906. The terms of the draft constitution for the Transvaal were announced on 31 July, and it was widely hoped that Briton and Boer would cooperate under it; at any rate this was no occasion for flippancy.

PULLING TOGETHER.

Baby Boer
Baby Briton } "HERE, I SAY, DRINK FAIR!"

for the conciliation of nationalist movements. Professor Mansergh has collected an interesting string of references to it by Irish and Indian leaders as well as by Smuts (especially after the First World War), Attlee (on introducing the Indian Independence Bill in 1947) and Macmillan (after his 'Winds of Change' African tour).[6] In addition, we also find Mountbatten invoking this analogy for Burma in 1945. He wished the Burmese problem

> 'to be treated in a sensible manner as we had done in South Africa after the Boer War, and that we should not use a heavy hand which might result in disaster as it had in Ireland.'

(Churchill disagreed; there was a limit to the applicability of the analogy – a reminder that in politics generosity has to be in line with expediency.)[7]

Neither the Transvaal constitution, nor the one that followed it in 1907 for the Orange River Colony, provided for the enfranchisement of Africans. In this respect the Liberals could plead that their hands were tied by the action of their predecessors. By Article Eight of the Peace of Vereeniging it was impossible to consider the extension of 'native' voting rights until *after* the introduction of responsible government. In South Africa the term 'native' was construed to include the coloured community, and for the British government to have attempted to act even on their behalf would have been open to the charge of a breach of faith.

Whether or not the Liberals in general, and Campbell-Bannerman in particular, deserved the kind of praise they got, their policy undoubtedly brought a striking improvement in the general atmosphere in South Africa. And one result of the war could not be erased: victory had made it certain that the constitutional shape of the union or federation of South Africa would have a British-monarchical complexion and not a Boer-republican one. As the new constitutions were introduced in the Transvaal and Orange River Colony, and a certain constitutional uniformity began to emerge in the future four provinces, so the next step – that of linking them – could immediately be contemplated.

The origins of the Union

The conventional starting point for an analysis of the origins of South African unification is the publication of the Selborne Memorandum in January 1907. In history, as in life, things are seldom what they seem, and this document was neither a memorandum nor by Selborne. Its true author was Lionel Curtis, and it is more properly described as a manifesto. Be that as it may, it initiated the move towards union, which now became rapid. This depended on the fact that the initiative proceeded from the British element. A Boer initiative was impossible, as this would have alarmed the British community, whereas the Boers, with their rising confidence, were happy to accept a British, even a

Copies

While the Imperial troops in South Africa are maintained at their present strength, it is obvious that no large volunteer force artillery equipped as the hon. member suggests with artillery is needed for the maintenance of peace & order; & it is not proposed that any such force should be organised.

In regard to the second part of the question of the hon. member, I must refer him to the answer given by me to the hon. memb. for Preston on June 3. & in regard to the last part of the question I am not yet able to say what reductions will be made in the Constabulary; but substantial reductions are certainly to be expected.

I think it should be [illegible]

WSC 5.6

I do not think it would be fair to the new Govt. to forestall the opinion which they may come to with regard to the Constabulary. E

The Transvaal Govt. have not, so far as I am aware, as yet given any notice of the reduction of the Constabulary.

Minutes by Elgin and Churchill on a draft reply to a parliamentary question relating to the South African Constabulary in the Transvaal, June 1907 (CO 291/121/19519). Although broadly agreed on the main outlines of policy, Elgin and Churchill had several minor disagreements. Elgin, whose minute appears in the right-hand margin, has drawn a line through the most important part of Churchill's suggested reply dealing with the reduction of the Constabulary.

kindergarten, initiative that they knew could not be fully sustained. They believed time and demography were on their side, and by February 1908, with *Het Volk* in power in the Transvaal and *Orangia Unie* in the Free State, and with the South African Party having ousted Jameson's Progressives from office in the Cape, they had good reasons for optimism. Thus while the Boers felt power within reach, the British had not fully understood how far they were losing ground: somehow, it was supposed, the British lion would prevail, and Botha and Smuts would not let them down as collaborators. The political rapprochement that was taking place provided favourable conditions for unification – but it was a suddenly-achieved and short-lived period of perhaps unreal and transient goodwill.

Both sides wanted to see unification. The Boers wanted it in order to assert themselves against the magnates, to be rid of British interference, and to create a firm base for Afrikaner national expansion. To succeed, all colonial closer union movements need just the critical amount of imperial pressure – not too much, but equally not too little, especially if there is a doubtful province to persuade. The South African scheme had full but discreet support from the imperial government, and the doubter, Natal, got no sympathy from Whitehall. For the British government, union was a consummation devoutly to be wished. It would be the fulfilment of a long-term objective: at least from the 1860s Britain would have liked to disengage from South Africa just as soon as strategic necessities and African interests could be reasonably safeguarded. By 1909 the right moment for withdrawal seemed to have arrived. The war had strengthened the weak South African link in the imperial chain: a strong, large, grateful union would improve it yet further. Botha and Smuts once in power quickly commended themselves. Their new Transvaal government soon won almost golden opinions for its frankness, friendliness, reasonableness and helpfulness; it compared more than favourably with troublesome 'British' governments elsewhere, especially white Australia and settler Kenya. Anti-British feeling seemed to be diminishing all round, and there was frequent testimony to improvement in the treatment of Africans. Two *desiderata*, strategic security and African interests, then, it seemed would be safe. On both counts new factors had arisen that conveyed a fresh sense of urgency. One was the appearance of Germany on the international scene as a potential enemy. By the middle of 1906 an Anglo-German war was beginning to be seen as inevitable, and in such a war it was fairly obvious that diehard Boers might attempt to join forces with the enemy in German South-West Africa; Germany would probably make an attack on South Africa one of her primary objectives, and this might provoke a general uprising of the Boers. All this seemed alarming because the Cape route to India would automatically supersede the Suez route in time of war. Ships in the canal would be sitting targets, and insurance rates would in any case be prohibitive: ever since the canal had been opened these were axiomatic principles of British strategic planning. Since the canal would not be used in war, the Cape route retained vital significance. The second precipitating factor was the Zulu disturbances in Natal, starting early in 1906. It had long been part of Liberal theory that a federal government in South Africa would produce a better prospect for African peoples by encouraging larger and more impartial white views and attitudes. Small, weak disunited states in a balkanized South Africa seemed inevitably prone to parochial attitudes and to brutality and panic in the treatment of their African subjects. Self-governing Natal, it was argued, amply demonstrated the truth of this proposition, twice declaring martial law in 1906 and 1907 to cover drastic repression of the Zulu disturbances. It was firmly believed in Whitehall that the Zulu would not have been so harshly treated if Natal had been merely a province of the Union and unable to call on imperial aid to rescue her from the penalty of her mistakes. Campbell-Bannerman wrote: 'These Natal people are tiresome to the last degree. I hope federation will soon squelch them.' Haldane wrote: 'We want federation badly for these native questions.' To Churchill, Natal was 'the hooligan of the British empire', while J. X. Merriman (now Prime Minister of the Cape) regarded it as 'a sort of plague-spot and public danger', and desired union if only because it would put an end to misgovernment there.

Boer prisoners of war marching to camp after being landed in St Helena in 1901. After 1906 Africans trod the same path, for St Helena was used for Zulu prisoners taken during the disturbances in Natal.

For these reasons the Liberal government was anxious to see unification succeed, and so, in the eyes of its critics, it was apparently almost too ready to accept union on South African terms. The South Africa Act (1909) has frequently been judged harshly, and in two main ways. In the first place, white 'liberal' historians (Eric Walker, Leo Marquard, Leonard Thompson and others) denounce the choice of a unitary rather than a federal constitution as misguided. Union, they say, was 'highly unsuitable', perhaps the 'very worst prescription' for a multi-racial society, because the concentration of power at the centre played into the hands of an illiberal elite; as late as 1975 Friedman described union as 'a disastrous choice'. In the second place, Africanist historians complain that African interests were sold out and segregation written in; they take their cue from contemporary African opinion, such as that expressed glumly in the newspaper *Imvo Zabantsundu* (31 August 1909): 'That cow of Great Britain has now gone dry.'

Both these judgments need to be reassessed. Is it really likely that Africans would have been much better off under a federal constitution? Union was certainly more effective than a federal government would have been in eliminating the worst features of Natal native administration, and Africans there were probably better off, at least until 1948, through absorption in the Union. Moreover, it is all too easy to glamorize federation into a panacea. There is wishful thinking here: federations are one of the most difficult forms of government to operate, and most of them have failed. The complexities and costs of a federation were beyond South Africa's means, since her white community was only about a million strong. And in one highly significant way millions of Africans derived actual benefit from the fact that the constitutional form was unitary rather than federal: it deterred the entry of further provinces. We have to remember a central fact about the Act of Union: that it united South Africa but divided southern Africa. It was a provisional union, and it remained so. Yet Botha repeatedly stated his conviction that the Union would never be complete until Rhodesia, Basutoland, the Bechuanaland Protectorate and Swaziland had been included. The British government accepted this vision in principle (and indeed at one time even contemplated adding Nyasaland). Provision was made in the Act to facilitate the incorporation of Southern Rhodesia, and an appended Schedule prescribed the terms on which the three High Commission Territories could at some future date be transferred. In the event none of these territories entered the Union, and what put them all off (white Rhodesians as well as black Sotho) had a good deal to do with the fact that the South African state was a union and not a federation. White Rhodesians in 1922 only narrowly decided against being swallowed up in the Union, but it might have been a very different story if they could have protected their local interests in the looser form of a federation.

African interests

Two main general points need to be made about the view of the South Africa Act as paying inadequate attention to African interests. The Cape 'native' franchise was entrenched when it might have been abolished. Under Section 35 it could only be got rid of by a Bill passed jointly by both Houses of Parliament sitting together, with the final voting representing a two-thirds majority of the total membership of both (ie, not merely of those actually present and voting). This provided better protection than had previously prevailed in the Cape constitution. It was enough to safeguard the African franchise until 1936 and the coloured franchise until 1955; the latter was only undermined with difficulty, through a constitutional circumvention, namely, by an artificial increase in the number of senators. Then again, the Act withheld from the Union the three High Commission Territories, and this ultimately enabled the independent states of Lesotho, Botswana and Swaziland to emerge in the 1960s. They were withheld despite the objections of the Boer leaders. In this significant case Botha and Smuts were thwarted.

Commenting authoritatively upon the passage of the South Africa Act, Professor L. M. Thompson has written in the *Oxford History of South Africa*:

> 'In attaining the primary goal of its South African policy, Britain had sacrificed the secondary goal. . . . The price of [white] unity and conciliation was the institutionalization of white supremacy.'

According to Thompson, the British ministers thus coolly 'washed their hands of responsibility for the political rights of Africans, Asians and Coloured people'.[8] It has indeed often been argued that British ministers in the years leading up to Union were so obsessed with the principle of promoting white self-government that they forgot their obligations to the African majority. The result, it is alleged, was that African interests in general were sacrificed on the altar of Anglo-Afrikaner reconciliation, and in particular betrayed in the South Africa Act. We have, however, already indicated that it is mistaken to see Liberal policy as dictated by magnanimity to the Boers. Granted that conciliation was not their top priority, we are now in a better position to demonstrate how erroneous is the idea that it was also based on unconcern for African interests.

African interests were not overlooked. On the contrary, from the moment the Liberal government came to power there was constant preoccupation with the question of trying to safeguard these interests. The problem was probed exhaustively during the drafting of the new Transvaal constitution in 1906; it became clear, however, that little could usefully be done, beyond resisting Boer demands for the return of Swaziland, which had been a Transvaal protectorate before the war. Effective power to act, it was concluded, had largely disappeared in self-governing colonies; but where imperial control remained, as in the High Commission Territories, the Liberals were determined, as if by compensation, to exert themselves to the full. Tremendous care was taken with the preparation of the Schedule dealing with the High Commission Territories. It still might be thought that, in all, the Liberal government did not do enough for African interests between 1905 and 1910, but what they did actually achieve should not be underestimated, and it cannot legitimately be alleged that they were unconcerned. It may not be unfair to assess some of their reasoning as misguided, but we cannot dub them knaves who cynically ditched the Africans.[9]

Four preliminary observations may be offered upon the earlier currency of the opinion that British action for African interests was inadequate. Firstly, the racial problem in South Africa before 1910 was not as intense as it became subsequently, and it is unrealistic to expect the British government then to have acted as if South Africa were already the world's greatest racial villain – a notoriety that unquestionably belonged to the southern states of the United States of America. In 1899 the future Liberal minister James Bryce could nowhere in South Africa see 'any cause for present apprehension', and in 1902 it was possible for him to list areas of racial tension in the world without including South Africa, which he knew at first hand.

Secondly, much of the argument about apparent unconcern hinges on British failure to promote enfranchisement of Africans. The reasons for this omission were as follows: British Liberals did not consider franchise rights alone to be sufficient to secure adequate attention for African interests, and they decided that for the time being the best way to represent African interests was through the 'development of native institutions' (such as the Basutoland *pitso* or National Council) 'on native lines' under paternalistic guidance, rather than through a 'hasty admission . . . to political rights for which neither they, nor the whites, are as yet prepared'. (The fact that somewhat similar sentiments subsequently became the apologia and smoke-screen for apartheid does not necessarily detract from the well-intentioned sincerity with which they were held by Edwardian Liberals in Britain.) Uninterest in enfranchising Africans does not prove unwillingness to advance their interests, or even to secure some other form of representation for their views.

Thirdly, it is indeed hard to demonstrate that any humanitarian organization (such as the Aborigines Protection Society) or mission society had any direct or decisive influence on framing the government's South African policy. There is another misunderstanding here too: the government tended to give the impression of ignoring attempts from such bodies to bring pressure to bear, but they did so only in the confident belief that Whitehall itself was the true, rational and only effective guardian of the humanitarian tradition, to which outside bodies, with imperfect access to information, could add little or nothing. But they listened, and they continued to respect the power of such bodies to whip up public opinion.[10]

Fourthly, as explained above, although the Union of South Africa was the overriding British Liberal objective, union could be regarded as a way of improving the position of Africans. The British wanted union, and they wanted to protect Africans, but, in fact, they contrived seldom to see any incompatibility between their desire and their duty, between promoting white self-government and securing African improvements. Indeed, the Liberals saw white self-government and union, largely on local terms, as perhaps the only effective means to an improvement in the position of Africans. How, they argued, could Africans hope to be better off while the white overlords were not only divided among themselves, but also apprehensive of a black uprising? They believed the reconciliation of the whites to be the indispensable prerequisite to the elevation of Africans, and they thought that Africans would benefit more from the reduction of white fears than anything else. Experience with Natal suggested that African interests actually required union, because union might steady panicky white opinion, giving more confidence, and thus generosity, to white government. A good governor-general might hold things steady. Much might depend on Britain's showing trust and confidence in South African capacity for liberal development: hence it was necessary to declare at least long-term willingness to transfer the High Commission Territories. Whether, in fact, they genuinely *felt* confidence is another matter.

It may well be the case that in all this there were elements of well-meaning self-delusion. But the government, like most groups of politicians, faced with the embarrassing necessity of balancing imperial strategies and humanitarian sentiments, managed to convince themselves that their main political aim (union) was not inconsistent with their moral obligation (to the African peoples). They even made this conviction seem plausible to their parliamentary opponents, who did not really oppose them.

African rights within the Union

Despite a considerable area of broad agreement, as on franchise rights, and qualified optimism about future improvement, the British government was far from happy with particular South African attitudes and 'native' policies as they stood in 1908. Hence their worry over African interests. There were two distinct problems: the interests of Africans within the Union from the beginning, and the interests of those in the High Commission Territories who could be kept out.

As far as the position of the Africans within the future union was concerned, all hope was placed in the expected good effects of a demonstration of trust in the whites, which might encourage the improvement of attitude that most observers claimed was beginning to take place. The Liberals genuinely believed themselves to be doing the most they could for Africans by establishing a union grounded more upon a demonstration of trust in the new rulers than upon specific safeguards for the protection of Africans. Partly because of their imperfect knowledge of the local situation in detail, which, in any case, had long ago receded beyond effective imperial control, the Liberals knew only too well the impossibility of enforcing paper provisions in the Union against a determined, entrenched, self-governing white community. As Churchill recognized in 1908, they were not the arbiters of the situation: 'We have great influence; but power has passed.' The Liberal government saw no point in hammering the colonials with suggested provisions or contentious declarations, which, while bringing no practical benefit to Africans, would irritate the whites. They concentrated instead on selected priorities.

As a result, although the Cape non-white franchise was constitutionally entrenched, there was no provision for its extension. This was partly because, as already mentioned, the British were sceptical about the Cape franchise on its merits. Selborne had very little faith in it; he thought many had the franchise in the Cape who were quite unfit for it. British ministers at home were more favourable to it than Selborne, but Elgin had doubts about its utility, and, at all events, the Liberals did not regard it as the only possible way of securing African representation. Colonel J. E. B. Seely (Parliamentary Under-Secretary for the Colonies, 1908–11) officially announced in 1908 that they were not committed to this method. In justifying scepticism about the Cape franchise, the southern states of the United States of America were frequently cited as the classic proof of the dangers of prematurely conceding equal citizenship. When one of the civil servants advocated a franchise without a colour bar, Seely replied that unjust decisions by juries on racial grounds and lynchings were in all the world 'most terribly frequent' precisely in the place where a franchise without a colour bar had been imposed upon an unwilling white population, namely in the southern states of the United States.

Close contact was maintained in correspondence between Crewe and Selborne throughout the sittings of the South African National Convention, which opened in Durban on 12 October 1908. Selborne was not allowed to act as an independent negotiator, but he privately suggested to delegates the justice and expediency of giving the vote to such Africans as had 'really raised themselves to the level of the white man's civilization'. When the Convention proved completely unwilling to consider even a franchise with a formidable civilization test, Selborne signified acceptance of a policy of merely continuing the *status quo* in this regard, which would leave Africans everywhere outside the Cape without the franchise. The Colonial Office was satisfied with this and, indeed, even seemed relieved that the draft constitution did not actually restrict future grants of the franchise. Selborne forwarded the draft Bill on 15 February 1909. Officials in the Colonial Office agreed that, as the Bill was the result of compromise achieved only with difficulty between a number of conflicting views, the essential thing was to alter as little as possible, and in practice

Lord Selborne, who remained British High Commissioner in South Africa throughout the years between 1905 and 1910 – despite the fact that the Liberal government did not trust him.

they saw nothing vital to alter.

Some MPs were not quite so accommodating. In answer to a deputation in May 1909 from five of them – Dilke, Alden, Ramsay MacDonald, Keir Hardie and Robertson – Crewe said that while he shared to a considerable extent some of the views they put forward, more particularly a strong feeling against a colour bar excluding Africans from sitting in parliament, and could say this much in private, the practical question was how far the South Africans could be expected to agree to amendment, especially since Australia maintained a colour bar, and in practice no African had ever as yet sat in parliament. The Colonial Secretary also saw a Cape Coloured deputation and an African deputation led by W. P. Schreiner (lawyer and former Prime Minister of the Cape), together with the Reverend Walter Rubusana (Congregationalist minister) and John Tengo Jabavu (the Mfengu newspaper editor), pleading for fuller formal provision for African interests in the constitution. Schreiner described their two interviews with Crewe in July 1909 as not advancing matters 'beyond the facts of great courtesy, real sympathy and earnest attention'. Liberal ministers took much the same line towards the Schreiner mission as Merriman recommended to them. Merriman pointed out that the retention of the Cape franchise had been conceded in the Convention only after a severe struggle and at the price of a colour disqualification for election to parliament; without this bar, he said, union undoubtedly would not have been agreed to; Schreiner's mission, therefore, must not succeed. If it did, bitter feeling, Merriman predicted, would be caused among all white South Africans, perhaps leading even to an attack on existing African rights, which were strongly supported by a minority only; and delicately growing pride in the superior liberty of the Cape system would be destroyed at a stroke. In any case, Merriman added, Schreiner's mission would have an evil effect on the mind of Africans, who would 'be taught to read into the Act of Union an attack on their rights wholly contrary to the spirit in which the Act is conceived'; far worse, it would make the whites more unfriendly, for they would feel 'that their dearest wishes have been imperilled for the sake of some paper guarantee of an equality which they do not believe in. . . . No worse blow could have been struck at the cause of sound relations between the races.' Crewe's comment on Merriman's argument is illuminating – 'Mr Merriman's *apologia* is able and conclusive.' He and his advisers agreed that African interests in the Union were best provided for by not assertively discussing them, and by maintaining the *status quo*.

On the whole British ministers accepted the Union Bill in the form in which it was presented to them. Apart from the Schedule, the only Cabinet discussion appears to have been about possible amendments relating to the better protection of Asian, not African, subjects. Native policy should be mainly settled inside South Africa itself: this was now the fixed conviction of the Liberal government. Asquith, the Prime

Minister, defended this position in Parliament: experience and common sense both showed, he declared, that where difficult racial situations existed, the community must be allowed to adjust itself without outside interference from a distance. British interference was, he said, capricious and spasmodic, often ill-informed and sometimes sentimental, and thus not in the best interests of the Africans themselves. There was no point, he concluded, in wrecking union by attempting to make further changes in favour of Africans.

High Commission Territories

Crewe made an appeal to British willingness to let the South Africans themselves solve problems within their own boundaries as a fact entitling the British government to be allowed to pursue its policy for the High Commission Territories. All Crewe's positive effort was concentrated on this, since this was a situation over which the imperial government had some real control and, being 'the man in possession', could not be charged so easily with interference. Thus Crewe used his Union policy as a lever to extract better conditions for Africans in the High Commission Territories. He could then proceed to use his policy for the latter to deflect British critics of his Union policy. Retention of the Territories was partly designed to sugar the pill of handing over the vast majority of Africans to white rule. The reason for this emphasis was not unrelated to the relative strength of the lobbies in favour of the Union and the Territories' Africans. The protests of Kgama and Letsie, loyal and Christian paramount chiefs, attracted much more sympathy than those of Jabavu and Rubusana, mere journalist and clergyman, who were suspected of being open to manipulation by 'agitators'.

In any case, Crewe felt there was much to be said for deferring the inclusion of the Territories in the Union 'until we see how the new machine works'. Though he was not as mistrustful of the new government as some of those who gave this advice, he recognized that immediate transfer 'would be a leap in the dark'. Once the Territories had gone, 'our power of protest has practically disappeared. . . .' If things did not then go right, 'a terrible responsibility will rest upon us in view of our obligations'. Because it might be difficult to obtain satisfactory terms, he thought that Britain would be in a stronger position and more likely to get them written into the Act if they said in effect: 'Unify, but these are the conditions for transfer' – rather than admit they might be prejudicing unification altogether by insisting on this or that point in favour of African interests. It was no use denying the whole thing was a risk. Current South African attitudes to African rights were not encouraging. He thought the mere terms of a constitution could never permanently check cupidities and mitigate sentiment unfavourable to Africans: constitutions could always be altered. The present South African leaders might keep their word, 'but we are legislating in permanency'.

In October 1908 Crewe defined four general policy con-

Lord Crewe, who was the British minister mainly responsible for the South Africa Act (1909), and especially for withholding the High Commission Territories from the Union.

siderations in the mind of the British government. First, immediate transfer was out of the question; the Territories should be kept in trust, and it would be well to retain control of them as long as was possible without creating friction in South Africa. Second, on the other hand, the Territories must surely be ultimately included in the Union. Third, Britain 'must insist upon insertion in the Constitution of all reasonable specific safeguards for their native inhabitants'; white South Africans must understand that it would be practically impossible to secure the assent of the House of Commons and public opinion to any constitutional act that failed explicitly to provide for the security of Africans in the Territories. Finally, above all, nothing must be done to prejudice the movement for union, which was so desirable in itself. The government must not allow itself to be charged with 'interference', for this might compromise the whole process.

It was proposed, unofficially, that South Africa should administer the Territories, when transferred, by three or four commissioners appointed by the governor-general in council. Legislation would be in the form of proclamations by the governor-general in council on the advice of the commissioners. Further probable conditions of transfer, approved by Crewe, were intimated to the Convention delegates: African land to be inalienable, the sale of intoxicating liquor to be prohibited, the Territories to receive due share of Union customs dues, and the Basutoland National Council to be maintained. Sir Henry de Villiers (Chief Justice of the Cape and chairman of the Convention) agreed to proceed on this basis in drafting the Schedule, which, let it be emphasized, provided for transfer of administration to the Union, not incorporation in the Union.

The Convention discussed the draft Schedule on 17 December. There were frequent divisions. A strong minority did not think the attitude of the British government fair or reasonable. Its conditions, especially the participation of the governor-general in choosing commissioners, were thought to display great mistrust of the future South African government in its dealings with Africans. Merriman was very sensitive on this point, and said the whole movement for union could be wrecked over it. Crewe was somewhat disturbed by this reaction, especially since the proposals did indeed imply mistrust. Once again he repeated that Selborne must be most careful not to give the South African colonial parliaments an opportunity of rejecting the whole scheme of unification on a 'fancied plea' of mistrust and interference, which they might be only too ready to do. It was Selborne's job to elicit workable proposals.

His fears proved groundless almost immediately. By the middle of January all the leading South Africans accepted the informally indicated British position on the Territories. The Natal dissentients, in particular, came quite a long way to meet the British government. Crewe reflected that it had been the saving of the situation that this had been one issue among many, and in the eyes of the South African statesmen not the paramount issue. This was indeed a fortunate circumstance. The British government would have been in a grave difficulty if the South Africans had launched a massive campaign for the inclusion of the Territories. After reading representations from the African leaders, Crewe fully realized that while the Schedule did not make consent of chiefs an essential condition of transfer, there would obviously be difficulty when the time came if their consent, or at least their acquiescence, could not be obtained.

It was felt impossible to insert into the Schedule a detailed code of administrative regulations such as the Basutoland National Council would have liked. Crewe contented himself with trying to attain two ends: securing a continuance of the principles of administration under which Basutoland had prospered, and embodying safeguards in respect of three matters that they regarded as essential in the interest of the population: possession of the land, prohibition of liquor, and maintenance of the National Council. Through the Schedule, he thought, a certain uniform and agreed standard of administration would be obtained; general principles were laid down that might ensure continuity of administration and, above all, avoid uncertainty. The *status quo* would be preserved, but the administration could also take account of the advancing civilization of the inhabitants: for this reason, it was decided not to include specific provision for continuing the jurisdiction of chiefs. The villains to be kept out were the drink-seller, the mineral prospector and the land-speculator; the labour recruiter, however, was not regarded as so harmful. In the government's view there was no point in attempting to prescribe in detail future policy for African development in the Territories: if the South African native policy was sound, they would not listen to absurd or manifestly unjust suggestions; if it was unsound, no safeguards would make it sound.

Thus, although eventual transfer was undoubtedly contemplated and planned, it was not promised, and Britain was wholly uncommitted to a date. Transfer was essentially conditional, and Section 151 of the Act, referring to the Schedule, was purely permissive. Its existence in fact made transfer harder. The British government had no desire to precipitate transfer, especially since Africans themselves were opposed to it. Before transfer could take place, the wishes of Africans would be 'most carefully considered', although the imperial government did not bind itself to obtain their consent – it retained the right of final decision for itself. Parliament, however, would be consulted: notable and important pledges (to be much quoted in the future) to this effect were given in both Houses of Parliament. British policy might seem to have been cunningly devised to conciliate both parties without conceding fully the wishes of either. It was hoped white South Africans would be placated by a clear indication that they had the reversionary interest, Africans by the postponement of transfer. Africans were far from convinced that the Schedule could be 'any permanent safeguard' for their interests, but it was they, as it turned out, who had the better cause to be pleased with the settlement.

In the perspective of imperial history, refusal to relinquish imperial control of the Territories at the time when union was established appears, to some extent, as a departure from the policy that might have been expected, and was indeed expected by the African chiefs, and recommended by Selborne. The normal procedure in the past had been gradually to transfer local Africans to white self-governing regimes, and grants of self-government had invariably been associated with such transfers. The Cape Colony was made to look after Basutoland in 1871, British Bechuanaland (between the Molopo and Orange Rivers) had been transferred to the Cape in 1895, Zululand and Tongaland were transferred to Natal in 1897, and in 1894 Britain had agreed to a Transvaal protectorate over Swaziland. As far as the future was concerned, Africans in Southern Rhodesia were handed over to the new white self-governing regime when it was established in 1923. The case of the Territories in 1909, then, appears exceptional. How did this exception come about? Refusal to hand over the Territories was certainly not the result of white South African indifference or ready acquiescence. As Selborne put it, '*kopjes* of Imperial administration jut[ting] out from the middle of the veld of a self-governing South Africa' were an unwelcome reminder to the Boers that they still were not complete masters of their sub-continent. Botha badly wanted Swaziland: in particular, he had once mentioned possible boycott of the 1906 Transvaal constitution by *Het Volk* if its incorporation was denied, and in the next seven years he repeatedly approached the British government on this question, backed by logical arguments, historical and practical, provided by Smuts.

The British government, however, turned a deaf ear to Boer logic. Was this out of tactical expediency or respect for obligations and vital principles? Since there was nothing positive to be gained for British material interests either by putting the Territories into the Union or by putting them on ice, the decision to take the latter course may reasonably be said to have been based on trusteeship grounds, on concern for African interests. Humanitarian opinions expressed in the House of Commons had some background influence. Parliamentary and public opinion were not simply ignored: as Lewis Harcourt wrote as Colonial Secretary, 'We must recognize the exigencies and prejudices of Parliamentary government' and bow to parliamentary opinion; he acknowledged, moreover, that

> 'so long as Khama is alive, the bare suggestion of handing him over to the Union would bring the whole missionary world and others upon me at once.'

It could even be argued that the retention of the Territories was the course least likely to serve British material interests, partly because these predicated formal withdrawal as quickly as possible from all Africa south of the Zambezi, and partly because the government did not wish to upset white South Africans if they could avoid it. For the 'imperial factor' to remain in the Territories was bound to produce embarrassments and frictions. This was a risk the government felt it had to accept.

Summing up his comments on the passage of the South Africa Act through the House of Commons, Crewe wrote:

> 'We got on quite as well as I expected. . . . In the House of Commons the feeling on one or two of the native questions was very strong, and though I do not think there was any real risk of it being amended, there were one or two critical moments during the progress of the debate. Personally, I think we got as much as was possible in relation to the Protectorate [i.e. the High Commission Territories] and native question generally.'[11]

The government felt that the South Africa Act was a good piece of legislation, and in no sense believed that it neglected African interests. It is, of course, true that the numbers involved in the excluded Territories were relatively small when compared with the black population in the Union. For this African majority, too much hope was perhaps placed on a gamble that the white rulers would respond generously to the confidence shown in them.

In conclusion, we can suggest that the Liberal government in these five years did not give excessive priority to conciliating the Boers. They desired to do them strict justice, and to approach them in a friendly spirit. But any trend towards conciliation was rigorously checked by two other considerations. One was to preserve British interests. The other was to protect the interests of the region's African inhabitants.

References

1. R. Hyam *Elgin and Churchill at the Colonial Office 1905–08*, London, 1968. See especially 36–193 and 278–88.
2. Alfred Lyttelton Papers, Churchill College Archive Centre, Cambridge, CHAN. 2/F.6/2/7, Arthur Godley to Lyttelton, 29 December 1904; Crewe Papers, Univ sity Library, Cambridge, C.40, Asquith to Crewe, 7 July 1908, and C.7/7, Crewe to W. S. Churchill, 29 December 1908 (copy).
3. N. G. Garson 'English-speaking South Africans and the British connection', in A. de Villiers ed., *English-speaking South Africa Today. Proceedings of National Conference, July 1974*, Cape Town, 1976, 29.
4. R. Hyam 'The myth of the "Magnanimous Gesture": the Liberal Government, Smuts and conciliation, 1906', in R. Hyam and G. Martin *Reappraisals in British Imperial History*, London, 1975, chapter 8.
5. D. Denoon ' "Capitalist influence" and Transvaal Crown Colony Government', *Historical Journal*, 11, 1968, and A. A. Mawby 'Political behaviour of the British population of the Transvaal 1902–1907', Ph D thesis, University of the Witwatersrand, 1969, chapter xii.
6. N. Mansergh *South Africa 1906–1961. The Price of Magnanimity*, London, 1962, 89–100.
7. Quoted in C. Thorne *Allies of a kind: The United States, Britain and the War against Japan 1941–45*, London, 1978, 608–10.
8. L. M. Thompson 'The compromise of Union' in M. Wilson and L. M. Thompson eds. *The Oxford History of South Africa*, II, Oxford, 1971, 358, 364.
9. R. Hyam 'African interests and the South Africa Act 1908–10', *Historical Journal*, 13, 1970.
10. D. R. Edgecombe 'The influence of the Aborigines Protection Society on British policy . . . in South Africa 1886–1910', Ph D thesis, University of Cambridge, 1976.
11. Crewe Papers, C.26, Crewe to Sir Matthew Nathan, 18 September 1909 (copy).

CHAPTER 17

Afrikaner Nationalism 1902-14

Irving Hexham

The South African National Party, founded by General J. B. M. Hertzog and his followers in Bloemfontein in January 1914, was the result of forces unleashed by the second Anglo-Boer war of 1899–1902. It gained its distinctive features from a strong sense of national identity felt by many South Africans who, following the war, came to regard themselves as Afrikaners. Some had, indeed, felt this sense of national identity before the war, but for many it was a new and exciting experience. They were, in their own eyes, a nation created by God on the southern tip of the African continent, set apart from other peoples to fulfil a unique destiny.

The development of this awareness of national identity and conviction of divine destiny can best be understood through an examination of four inter-related aspects of the history of post-war South African society. These are the work of the churches in the reconstruction of Boer society, the resistance to British rule manifested through the Christian-National Education Movement, the cultural revival associated with the Second Afrikaans Language Movement, and the growth in popularity of nationalist political theories among Afrikaners. Before any of these developments can be appreciated it is necessary to know something of the abortive attempt to develop an Afrikaner nationalism based upon Calvinism that took place prior to the war. And to understand this, in turn, it is essential to know a little about the Dutch Anti-Revolutionary Movement that inspired Calvinists in South Africa to create a similar movement in their own country.[1]

The Dutch Anti-Revolutionary Movement

The Enlightenment and French Revolution had a profound effect upon Dutch society. Initially, the Dutch middle class welcomed the events in France and in 1793 supported the French armies as they established a revolutionary regime in the Netherlands. But the coming of the French brought ever-increasing domination. Not unexpectedly, this situation led to the development of Dutch nationalism. Among the leaders of the nationalist movement were many Calvinists, whose religion seemed doomed by the liberal reforms of the French period. Even after the restoration of the Dutch state in 1814 nothing was done to restore the fortunes of Calvinism. Indeed, the new Dutch government encouraged a secular spirit, which pervaded social life. Calvinist theologians also found themselves under attack from other

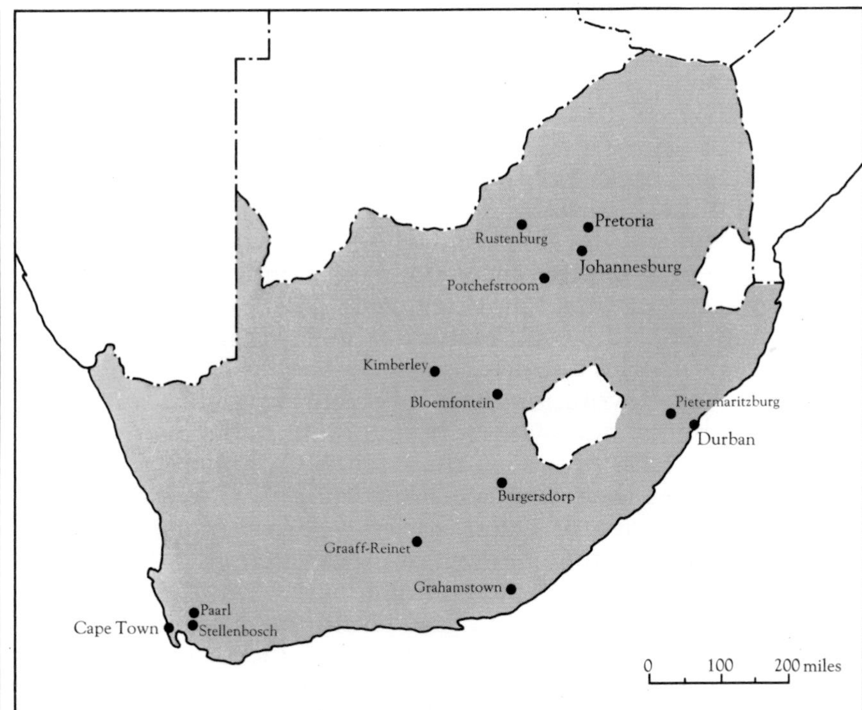

South Africa, showing some of the towns most closely associated with Afrikaner nationalism.

theologians who repudiated the theology of the Frenchman Calvin, and instead sought to rebuild Dutch Christianity on the basis of the medieval Dutch writer Thomas a Kempis.[2]

A Calvinist revival occurred that glorified the seventeenth century and proclaimed itself the source of the triumphs of the Dutch Republic. This revival, which defined Calvinism in terms of the theology of the Synod of Dort (1618–19), had two sources, one aristocratic, the other working class. Each of these groups felt their lifestyle threatened by the new liberalism of the bourgeoisie. The aristocratic movement was led by Willem Bilderdijk (1756–1831), whose poetic works were crucial in the revival of the Dutch language. Encouraged by Bilderdijk, a literary-cultural and a political movement developed united by their Calvinism. The cultural leader was Isaak da Costa (1798–1860); the political leader, Groen van Prinsterer (1801–1876).[3]

The working class Calvinist movement found expression in a church secession during 1834. The Dutch government persecuted the seceders, who were granted religious liberty only in 1849, by which time they were convinced that the liberal state was committed to the destruction of Calvinism. Henceforth liberalism was seen as the enemy of Calvinism. Although van Prinsterer never joined the secession of 1834, he became the political theorist and spokesman of the Calvinist movement, and it was he who coined the dictum, later to be taken up by Calvinists in South Africa, 'in isolation is our strength'.

One of the major preoccupations of van Prinsterer was the need for 'Christian' schools that would preserve what he looked upon as the Dutch Protestant spirit by teaching children to take a pride in their Calvinist heritage. The name he used to describe this type of education was 'Christian-National Education', another theme that was to be picked up in South Africa.

After van Prinsterer's death his mantle fell upon Abraham Kuyper (1837–1920). In Kuyper the aristocratic and populist elements of the Calvinist movement merged to produce a powerful social and political force. Kuyper founded the first modern political party in the Netherlands, the Anti-Revolutionary Party, and developed a Calvinist social theory that was to influence profoundly both Dutch and South African society. The climax of his life's work came in 1901 when he became prime minister at the head of a government that made many of his political theories a reality.[4]

The Anti-Revolutionary Movement brought into being Calvinist schools, newspapers, trade unions and a host of other institutions. It also provoked the Roman Catholics and liberals into establishing their own social institutions, thus creating the *verzuiling*, or pillars, of Dutch society. These pillars cut across class divisions, creating ideological blocks that give the Netherlands a social structure that is unique.[5]

Kuyper theorized about these developments in terms of the Calvinist doctrine of the sovereignty of God. The state, he argued, was a mechanical imposition on the organic nature of society. Each area of social life, or sphere, had its own calling to serve God and develop in an organic unity without interference from other social spheres. Thus the family, the church, education, business, the arts and science were all separate spheres that owed their existence to God. No sphere had the right to dominate another, and the proper function of the state was to protect the weak by maintaining a social pluralism that enabled each sphere to fulfil its God-given calling. In his view the education of children was a task allotted by God to parents, who had the duty to raise their offspring according to their religious beliefs. Neither the state nor the church had the right to control schools, which should be free to develop according to their own nature under the guidance of parents and teachers.[6]

S. J. du Toit

The influence of Anti-Revolutionary ideas was first felt in South Africa through the creation of the *Genootskap van Regte Afrikaners* (Fellowship of True Afrikaners). This society was founded in 1875 by S. J. du Toit and a group of friends inspired by the Dutch Calvinist literary movement and the theology of the Synod of Dort. The foundation of the Fellowship led to the publication of *Di Afrikaanse Patriot*, a magazine devoted to establishing as a literary medium the spoken language of the descendents of the Dutch settlers in South Africa. A number of books were published in an early form of Afrikaans, including in 1876 S. J. du Toit's *De Christelijke School in hare verhouding tot Kerk en Staat* (The Relationship of the Christian School to Church and State). This work called for the establishment of Christian-National schools in South Africa. The most influential of these publications was another book by du Toit, *Di geskiedenis van ons land in di taal van ons volk* (The history of our land in the language of our people), which shows the influence of Calvinist interpretations of Dutch history applied to South Africa.[7]

S. J. du Toit also founded South Africa's first political party in 1880, the *Afrikaner Bond*, modelled on Kuyper's Anti-Revolutionary Party. His debt to Kuyper can clearly be seen in his *Program van Beginsels* (Programme of Principles) published in 1882, which he described as

> 'the Programme of the anti-revolutionary or Christian historical party in the Netherlands . . . changed according to our circumstances'.

At its foundation the *Bond* was a Calvinist political party, but it soon fell under the control of Jan Hofmeyr, who cooperated closely with Cecil Rhodes until 1896, the *Bond* becoming a secular party in the process.

Although du Toit introduced and vigorously propagated a nationalism involving cultural, educational and political aspects based upon Calvinism, before the war he gained few true converts, although at times he attracted a substantial popular following in the Cape Colony. Interest in du Toit's ideas reached a peak during the war of 1880–1, but declined steadily afterwards. To understand his failure it is important to realize that the type of Calvinism that provided a basis for the development of Afrikaner nationalism was not popular in South Africa during the nineteenth century. From the early 1870s to the end of the 1920s the largest reformed church in South Africa, the Dutch Reformed Church (DRC), was dominated by an evangelicalism that rejected the Calvinist theology of the Synod of Dort. Evangelicals were concerned to 'save souls' and perfect the inner 'spiritual' man, not to reform this world. Their leaders, such as John and Andrew Murray, stressed that religion and politics should be kept separate, and they rejected Kuyper's theories as a sub-Christian return to the worldly involvement of medieval Catholicism. Only members of the small Gereformeerde Kerk (Reformed Church), which had been founded with the help of Paul Kruger in 1859, shared du Toit's vision of Calvinism, and it was in this circle that Kuyper's theories took root.[8]

Legacy of the war

Without the intervention of the South African War, and the social chaos it produced, it seems unlikely that Afrikaner nationalism would have developed within a Calvinist framework. The defeat of the republics severely strained the ability of Boer society to survive. Everywhere there were homeless people, widows and orphans, the sick and dying. British efforts to relieve distress were badly coordinated and totally inadequate. Nevertheless, the military leaders of the Boer community tended to leave repatriation and recuperation to the British while they worked for the political revival of their people. As a result they used the funds at their disposal to purchase newspapers and establish their own school system in opposition to the British administration's schools.[9]

Afrikaner women and their African servants pose beside an ox-waggon, a traditional symbol of the Afrikaner way of life.

Role of the churches

Because of these failures to relieve the sufferings of the people the burden of ameliorating the hardship created by the war fell upon the churches. They organized collections wherever they could raise money to help the poor, and appealed to friendly churches in the Netherlands and the United States for financial aid. With the funds they received they were able to act as welfare societies performing many of the functions of a welfare state. This ability to dispense aid gave their officers, the elders and pastors, great influence within local communities.[10]

Elders were assigned to every area served by the local congregation and made responsible for the people in those areas. Their duty was to discover spiritual and material needs through regular pastoral visits. They kept a close watch over the morals of their charges and reported any who violated accepted Christian standards to the Church Council. They also acted as mediators in marital disputes and in arguments between parents and children, or in any other situation that might disturb the unity of the community. Refusal to obey the instructions of the elders led to disciplinary action by the Church Council, with excommunication as the ultimate weapon. Because of their standing in the community and their power to dispense welfare, the elders and pastors were in a strong position to impose their will on the community. The efforts made by the churches at this time seem to have done a great deal to prevent the disintegration of Boer society, and after an initial period of decline lasting until about 1910, they were remarkably successful in reducing illegitimacy, drunkeness, broken marriages and other social ills resulting from the war.

Given the chaos created by the war it comes as no surprise to discover the emergence of millenial movements among the Boers. One such movement, known as the Swanepoels, migrated from the Transvaal to a remote part of the Cape Colony to escape the doom that they believed would be visited upon that modern Sodom, Johannesburg. Prophetic leaders also had an influence in shaping the lives of Boers during these years of uncertainty. One man, Niklaas van Rensburg, known as the Prophet of Lichtenburg, had a considerable following, including the former Boer general, J. H. de la Rey, who is said to have placed implicit trust in his visions. Van Rensburg's most famous prophecy came as part of a series of visions he experienced early in 1914. These included a battle between a red and a grey bull in which the red bull was killed. This vision was interpreted as foretelling the defeat of the British empire by Germany. Belief in this interpretation caused many Boers to join the rebels during the civil war of 1914. Another sign of tension after the war was the outbreak of that which church leaders described as 'witchcraft' among members of their congregations. In most cases this seems simply to have involved the consultation of African traditional healers instead of European doctors. But sometimes it appears to have involved cursings and a form of sorcery.

Biblical interpretations of the Boer experience

Post-war Boer society was defeated and demoralized. It was the churches that held the people together by providing something they needed even more than material aid: they gave them an understanding of their plight. The ministers of religion, the *predikants*, provided answers to the questions of why God had allowed the British to triumph and the republics to be destroyed; why he had allowed the horrors of the concentration camps, in which over 27 000 women and children had died, and an explanation for their suffering and defeat.

In their sermons they reminded the people of the sufferings of Israel and of Christ. They taught that God refines His people 'as by fire' (1 Peter 1.7) and that out of suffering comes the joy of serving God (1 Peter 4.12–19). They used examples drawn from the Old Testament to illustrate their arguments, and frequently preached on themes from the books of Isaiah, Ezra and Nehemiah, in which God's judgement upon Israel and the ordeals of the Babylonian exile are interpreted theologically. The Psalms also provided a source of great inspiration with Psalms 85, 97 and 126 proving to be particularly popular for sermon material. Through the consideration of the sufferings of Israel and the way in which God had led Israel to bring about his purposes despite apparent disaster, the Boer people were taught to see their own sufferings in a theological perspective that held out hope for the future. At the same time, the very nature of these sermons reinforced an implicit identification between the people of Israel and the Boers.[10]

Christian leaders taught that deliverance would come from God. For many Boers a worldly deliverance came about through the acceptance of the material benefits consequent upon anglicization. The British dominated economic life; therefore, for many, anglicization brought work and economic advancement. Long before the war a process of anglicization through economic pressure had been visible in Boer society. After the war it became one of the keys in Lord Milner's imperial policy. To consolidate British control of South Africa, Milner believed it necessary to secure the loyalty of the majority of Boers through a policy of denationalization linked with economic progress. He believed that his greatest hope for success lay in the education of Boer children so that they would come to appreciate the benefits of imperialism and British rule.[11]

Christian-National Education Movement

To carry out his scheme, Milner made E. B. Sargant the Director of Education for the two new colonies and erected hundreds of schools. To staff these he then recruited teachers of 'imperial sympathies' from all parts of the British empire. Like Milner, Sargant saw education as an extension of imperial policies. Writing to Milner shortly after his arrival in South Africa in 1901, he spoke of the 'golden opportunity' provided by the concentration camps to teach Boer children to speak English. In appointing teachers he sought

> 'women, thoroughly good teachers of patriotic mind . . . in order that they may teach the children of the burgers [*sic*] our language and ideals'.

He repeatedly reminded his teachers of their political task as agents of the empire, with the mission of pacifying the Boers and uniting all white South Africans under British rule.

Not unnaturally, such explicit and well publicized sentiments caused a strong reaction among many Boers. This consolidated around an organization formed during the war to help unemployed teachers in the Transvaal with funds from the Netherlands. In October 1902 a meeting was held between representatives of this teachers' organization, Boer military leaders and several churchmen. As a result the Commission for Christian-National Education was inaugurated on 30 October 1902. Within a short time the Commission had established fifty Christian-National schools with financial support from the Netherlands. The number of these schools continued to grow until they reached over two hundred in 1906 at a cost of over £5 000 per month.

From the minutes of the Christian-National Education Commission it is clear that for political leaders like Smuts and Botha the schools were a device to bring pressure upon the British authorities. It is also clear, however, that other members of the Commission supported the schools because they believed in the ideals of Christian-National Education as developed in the Netherlands. Throughout the short period of their existence the Transvaal Christian-National schools relied very heavily upon funds from supporters in the Netherlands. These supporters were Dutch Calvinists who sought to propagate their theory and practice of Christian education in South Africa. Their efforts were coordinated by H. J. Emous, the headmaster of the Christian High School in The Hague, who raised thousands of pounds from Dutch Calvinists who saw in the South African situation a repetition of their own long struggle for Christian-National Education.

Although Dutch funds helped establish the Christian-National schools and were essential for their continued existence, they covered only about a quarter of their running costs. As a result the remaining funds had to be raised in South Africa, and the movement consequently was always under strong financial pressure. This situation led the Boer leaders to negotiate with the British authorities about state aid for the schools, but the British refused to cooperate. The leaders of the movement naturally assumed that when a Boer government eventually came to power it would support Christian-National Education.

But to Botha and Smuts, and other politicians of their persuasion, the Christian-National schools were simply a political tool. Once their political party, *Het Volk* (The People), came to power in February 1907, they were prepared to modify their educational policy by abandoning Christian-National Education in an attempt to gain support among British voters for their policy of conciliation. Smuts explained his new education policy to a disappointed and disillusioned meeting of the Commission in April 1907. He argued that he was preparing a new Education Bill that would embody all that was good in Christian-National Education and that, in fact, he was acting on the basis of Christian-National principles. However, the Dutch language would not be given equal status with English, nor would all the tenets of Christian-National Education be incorporated. His arguments failed to convince his former colleagues, who regarded him as a traitor. Smuts was unmoved; unlike British officials, he knew the financial weakness of the Commission and the fact that in 1906 they had been told by their Dutch supporters that they could no longer expect regular gifts from the Netherlands and must therefore rely upon their own resources. As a result, by the end of 1907 almost all of the former Christian-National schools had been absorbed into the state system.

The situation in the Orange River Colony and the Cape was rather different from that in the Transvaal following the war. In these areas the Christian-National Education Movement did not expand to the same extent as it did in the Transvaal. This lack of growth was due to several factors. In the Transvaal the political organization of the *bittereinder* generals was a unifying force that gave the Christian-National schools the backing they needed. But no similar organization existed outside the Transvaal. Most important of all, the Dutch supporters of the Christian-National Movement specifically stated that the funds they were sending to South Africa were for use in the Transvaal. This restriction on the use of funds can be explained by the close ties between the Netherlands and the Transvaal republic, where many Dutch teachers had been employed before the war.

J. C. Smuts, whose Education Act of 1907 was a source of profound disappointment to the supporters of Christian-National Education. Because of lack of funds, almost all the Christian-National schools had been integrated into the state' system by the end of 1907. The few that remained became a symbol of hope and a focal point for the movement.

The situation was also affected by the agreement reached in the Orange River Colony between the leaders of the Dutch Reformed Church and the Director of Education, Hugh Gunn. This avoided most of the tensions that plagued the Transvaal. As a result the majority of Christian-National schools in the Orange River Colony were absorbed into the state system in 1905 without encountering any great difficulties.

From a Christian-National viewpoint educational provision in the Orange River Colony was further improved in 1908 with the passing of an Education Act introduced by Hertzog. This Act gave equal status to the Dutch and English languages and allowed for the teaching of religious education from a doctrinal position when and where parents desired it. The Act also increased the power of local school boards, and therefore of parents, by giving them a far greater say in the running of local schools. In addition, it allowed for the provision of grants-in-aid to private schools under certain circumstances.

The appeal of the Act to supporters of Christian-National Education is clear. Equally obvious is the way in which it appalled the English-speaking community throughout South Africa. For the English press, Hertzog became the epitome of 'Krugerism' and his Act was attacked in the English-language press for its 'racialism'.

Whereas before 1907 Botha and Smuts themselves were sometimes portrayed as representatives of 'Krugerism' by the English-language press, once in power they transformed themselves with an undignified speed into angels of light, to the dismay of many of their old colleagues. Their abandonment of the Christian-National schools convinced many that they had been deliberately misled, and their action turned the majority of South African Calvinists who espoused the theology of the Synod of Dort solidly against them. The Calvinists, however, managed to continue to maintain a small number of their own schools and kept up a constant stream of propaganda for Christian-National Education. The surviving schools became symbols of hope, thus providing a focus for the continuing movement.

A series of conferences were held and numerous booklets published advocating Christian-National Education. The head of the Reformed Church Theological School in Potchefstroom, Jan Lion-Cachet, published an attack on the Smuts Education Act in a pamphlet *Niet om te Twisten, maar . . . om des Gewetens wil* (A Matter of Conscience), which presented a strong argument for Christian schools in the Dutch Calvinist tradition. In addition to materials produced in South Africa, a number of Dutch works on Christian-National Education were widely circulated. The most popular of these seems to have been by a professor at the Free University of Amsterdam, J. Woltjer, *Wat is Het Doel van het Christelyk Nationaal Schoolonderwys?* (What is the meaning of Christian-National Education?), which also was the basis of an Afrikaans booklet, *De School Behoort aan de Ouders* (The School Belongs to the Parents), published in 1912.

The cartoonist David Wilson's caricature of Louis Botha, shown here standing guard in determined posture over 'British South Africa'. As Botha and Smuts were looked upon after 1907 with progressively more favour by English-speaking South Africans, many Afrikaners became more and more disillusioned with their politics and failure to give expression to Afrikaner nationalist aspirations.

In these books the role of the state in education was attacked, and the actions of the authorities in South Africa in particular were criticized.

Thus, as in the Netherlands, the educational theories developed by Calvinists led to conflict with the state. In the Netherlands the national element in Christian-National Education meant the common Calvinist heritage of all Dutchmen. In South Africa it became identified with the heritage of the Boers, and because of this, helped to consolidate their awareness of their distinct national identity, which was seen as a product of Calvinism. Therefore, while in the Netherlands Christian-Nationalism had simply created a Calvinist bloc within Dutch society, in South Africa it reinforced the differences between the English and the Boers. The Dutch preserved their religion through Christian-National Education; South Africans pre-

M. T. Steyn, the former President of the Orange Free State and founder in 1906 of the Women's Monument organization.

served both their religion and their identity as Afrikaners, which they believed their religion had helped to create. In this way an identification was made between being an Afrikaner and being a Calvinist, and the belief created that an attack upon either national identity or Calvinism was equally destructive of Christianity.

In fact, until about 1906, the majority of South Africans who would later identify as Afrikaners considered themselves to be either Cape Dutch, Freestaters, Transvalers, or, more probably, simply Boers. Sometime between 1906 and 1910 an awareness of being one people, Afrikaners, caught the imagination of a much larger number of South Africans than ever before. In the Transvaal the Christian-National schools helped foster this recognition of an Afrikaner identity. In other parts of South Africa support for the school struggle helped create a national consciousness. The two major factors that created and spread this new awakening of an Afrikaner identity were the Second Afrikaans Language Movement and the organization of a fund to erect a National Women's Monument to commemorate those who had perished in the British concentration camps. Neither of these were directly connected with the emergence of political nationalism, but a combination of elements from both of them led directly to the creation of the National Party.[12] In political terms, however, it must be recognized that while this emerging nationalism served to legitimate the creation of a new political organization, other social factors were at work that served to promote acceptance of its ideology, such as the failure of the Botha government to deal with rural poverty, rapid and unplanned urbanization, and increasing black-white racial tension brought about by competition for jobs in the towns.

Second Afrikaans Language Movement

In itself the development of Afrikaans as a written language after the war was not of political significance. The majority of writers who created Afrikaans were supporters of the conciliation policies of Botha and Smuts. J. F. E. Celliers, whose sentimental poem *Dis Al* (That's All) encapsulated the pathos of the people immediately after the war, wrote his *Unie Kantate* (Union Cantata) in 1910 as a joyous celebration of the Act of Union, which some nationalists were already regarding as an act of betrayal. Louis Leipoldt, who with Celliers and 'Totius' formed the celebrated Triumvirate of Second Language Movement poets, was also a close friend and supporter of Smuts, as was the author and publisher Gustav Preller. Of these men, Totius stood alone as a leading member of the Second Language Movement who was also a creator of Afrikaner nationalism.

It was the poetry of Totius, particularly those works produced in conjunction with the Women's Monument organization, that caused the Second Language Movement to become identified with the nationalist cause. Totius, J. D. du Toit (1877–1953), was the son of S. J. du Toit and a minister in the Gereformeerde Kerk (Reformed Church). He had studied in

Amsterdam under Abraham Kuyper at the Free University, where he wrote his doctorate on Methodism, which he regarded as sub-Christian. It was, however, the relationship between Totius and the organization formed by ex-president Steyn in 1906 to erect the National Women's Monument that gave his poetry its great power and social significance.

When Steyn announced his monument project, Botha and Smuts attempted to discourage him for fear of opening old wounds alienating English-speaking South Africans whom they were hoping to win over to their policies. But Steyn persisted, insisting that the future could only be built on the inspiration of the past, which was to be found in the sacrifice of the people. The monument caught the public imagination and was eventually unveiled on 16 December 1913. The timing of the opening of the monument was significant, for 16 December had great emotional connotations for Afrikaners. It was the anniversary not only of the Battle of Blood River, but also of the proclamation of independence that marked the outbreak of the first Anglo-Boer war of 1880–1, which eventually freed the Transvaal from British rule. It was also the day on which President Kruger had been buried in 1904. The choice of this date gave the nationalist cause a symbolic victory over the advocates of conciliation, who had unwisely chosen 31 May as the day to celebrate the Act of Union in 1910,[13] thereby for

Below left: a detail from Anton van Wouw's Women's Monument near Bloemfontein, dedicated to 'Our heroines and dear children'. It was through the poetry of Totius produced in conjunction with the Women's Monument organization that the Second Afrikaans Language Movement became closely associated with the nationalist cause.

Below right: S. J. P. Kruger, buried amid scenes of national grief on 16 December 1904. Significantly, 16 December was the date of the Voortrekkers' victory over the Zulu at the Battle of Blood River in 1838, the date of the outbreak of the Anglo-Boer War of 1880–1 and the date chosen for the official opening of the Women's Monument in 1913.

some identifying their cause forever with the humiliating Peace of Vereeniging, the anniversary of which was also 31 May. So the nationalist cause was strengthened by symbols of Afrikaner triumph while their opponents were seen in the light of defeat and British domination. Although Smuts and Botha attended the ceremonies by which the monument was officially opened, it was known that their hearts were not in the project and that they would have preferred to court the English.

To help raise funds for the erection of the monument, Totius published his first collection of poems in 1908 with the title *By Die Monument* (At the Monument). In the poems Totius depicted the tragedy of the concentration camps and gave in a simple way a theological interpretation of the suffering of the people. God had not deserted the people, as it seemed, but through their shared grief had bound them together as a covenant people. The poems were far more than literary pro-

Afrikaner women being transported to a concentration camp during the war. In his collection of poems published in 1908, By Die Monument, *Totius provided a theological interpretation of the sufferings experienced in the camps.*

Totius

ductions; they were a profound statement of national identity and political intent based upon a living faith in God's providential care. Like the biblical prophets, Totius gave an interpretation of historical events that transcended the sufferings of the present in terms of their ultimate significance. To the individual the agony of the concentration camps was inexplicable; but for the people it held a significance that provided a hope for the future, and gave each sufferer a share in the destiny of the nation. Through these poems the readers were able to experience a catharsis that made sense of the past: at last they could know that the sacrifice of their loved ones was not in vain, but formed part of the greater purposes of God.

This cycle of poems was supplemented by another collection in 1909 that took as its theme the Great Trek of 1836, which had opened the interior of southern Africa to white settlement. In these poems, which were entitled *Potgieter's Trek*, the trek of the Boer leader A. H. Potgieter was seen as a religious pilgrimage in search of freedom from the oppression of British rule. The message of the collection was summarized in the final section, simply headed *Potgieter*, which contains the following verse:

> But see! The world becomes wilder;
>   the fierce vermin worsen,
> stark naked black hordes,
>   following tyrants.
> How the handful of trekkers suffer,
>   the freedom seekers, creators of a People.
> Just like another Israel,
>   by enemies surrounded, lost in the veld,
> but for another Canaan elected,
>   led forward by God's plan.[14]

The message is clear and the identification with Israel explicit. Here we have the basis for the development of a form of civil religion as well as a justification for Afrikaner attitudes towards Africans. It then comes as a surprise when two of the poems in this section take an understanding and sympathetic attitude toward Africans, whom Totius sees as having legitimate grievances against the settlers. It is also important to realize that in these poems, which draw so heavily upon religous themes to illuminate the history of the Afrikaners, that history is also used to point the reader to God. This is done through a comparison of the life of the trekker with the transient nature of life itself. Taking up the biblical imagery of life as a pilgrimage, Totius used the longing of the trekker for new horizons to direct his readers' thoughts to the everlasting peace of God. In this way he created a feeling of religious awe that, in the context of the whole cycle of poems, had the effect of drawing the reader closer both to God and Afrikaner tradition. Thus the deeply religious passages reinforced the authority of those verses that spoke of the identity of the Afrikaner nation.

In 1912 Totius published a series of meditations upon the nature of life and death entitled *Wilgerboomboogies* (In Praise of

Weeping Willows), which established his reputation as a gifted and deeply religious poet. His next major collection of poems, *Ragel* (Rachel), which appeared in 1913, marked a return to the theme of Afrikaner identity. Like *By Die Monument* these were also published in conjunction with the National Women's Monument and contained a foreword by Steyn.

Ragel takes the biblical character of Rachel, the mother of Joseph, as its inspiration, and reflects on her significance for Israel and Afrikanerdom. The poems are rich in symbolism and portray Rachel as an archetypal mother. Her suffering and the suffering of her people, Israel, are seen in the light of the suffering of Christ, and by implication are linked with the suffering of Afrikaners. Totius does not simply interpret Afrikaner history by comparing historical events. Instead he gives Afrikaner experience a soteriological value by making it a redemptive fact. Like Israel, and following the example of Christ, the salvation of the Afrikaner people comes through suffering, making the poem a type of psalm to national deliverance.

Through his poetic exegesis of biblical themes, Totius used the scriptures as the prophets of Israel and writers of the New Testament used them. He applied scripture in a living and vital way to the experience of his contemporaries. Unlike the modern biblical scholar, he did not ask questions about the original meaning of the sacred text, but rather let it speak to his time. Thus he reveals himself as an extraordinary exegete who was encapsulated by the ethos of the Hebrew scriptures. And like the Hebrew prophets he concluded his work with a challenge to obedience. In his case it was a call to follow what he believed to be the calling of God for the Afrikaner people, and to keep apart from the peoples around them by maintaining their national identity. Towards the end of *Ragel* he alludes to the faithlessness of the people of Israel and the way in which they were tempted to ignore God's call and follow other gods. Then he issues the following challenge:

> Shall we forget our tearful past?
> Foolish, faithless people,
> let the hills bear witness:
> The faithful reply: No! Never!
> We will remember![14]

What more appropriate challenge could have been issued to Afrikaners on the eve of the founding of the National Party?

Willem Postma

Totius' influence as a supporter of Afrikaner nationalism was reinforced by the prose writings of his brother-in-law, Willem Postma (1874–1920). Postma wrote under the pen-name Dr O'kulis. He began his literary efforts with a regular column of political commentary in the Bloemfontein newspaper *De Vriend des Volks* (The Friend of the People). This column began in 1905 and continued until 1914, when the editor dropped it because of Postma's strong advocacy of the nationalist cause. Postma's writing was witty and to the point. He rejected conciliation and advocated nationalism long before Hertzog had begun to think of forming his own party. In 1909 his views gained a wide audience and great popularity through the publication of his book *Die Eselskakebeen* (The Ass's Jawbone), one of the earliest Afrikaans novels. It is the story of the struggle of a young Afrikaner for identity and his final resolve to serve his people as a teacher and advocate of Christian-National Education. The book was highly amusing and made many telling points of social criticism. It quickly established itself as an Afrikaans classic, and was used as a basic school textbook for three generations.

While Postma and du Toit were developing their cultural nationalism and a sense of identity based upon Afrikaner traditions and the Calvinist religion, they and others like them were active in propagating both Christian-National Education and the political theories of the Anti-Revolutionary Movement. All of these worked together to produce the ideological base out of which the National Party grew. General Hertzog is said to have been agnostic. Certainly he was not a Calvinist, but he recognized the strength of the Calvinist ideology and was willing to incorporate it into his own political arsenal. In this way he gained a solid core of support without which his party would not have survived. General Botha realized what was happening but rejected the Calvinists because he repudiated what he called their 'principle of isolation'.[15]

Political ideology

Calvinist political principles found expression in several small books published between 1909 and 1913, in addition to articles in Christian magazines and in Postma's column. J. D. du Toit (Totius) argued for them in 1909 in his book *Het Calvinism en ons Volk* (Calvinism and our People) and also in *Johannes Calvijn* (John Calvin), a biography that he wrote later in the same year with Dr T. Hammersma. The most systematic treatment of Calvinist political theory written after the *Principles* of S. J. du Toit in 1882 was a long chapter by Hammersma that appeared in a book to celebrate the opening of a new Reformed Church in Burgersdorp in 1913. This had the title *De Roeping van de Gereformeerde Tegenover de Staat* (The Political Calling of the Reformed) and expounded the theories of Kuyper.

In all of these writings, political and cultural, we find the basis of the intellectual justification of *apartheid*. It is often said that the theory of *apartheid* did not come into being until the 1940s when D. F. Malan first used the word to describe the policies of the National Party. In fact, all the elements of later developments, including the use of the word *apartheid* itself, can be found among the writings of Calvinists who advocated nationalism during this period. In 1905 students at the Reformed Theological College in Potchefstroom were writing about Afrikaners as 'a nation apart' and saying that their language separated them from other peoples. In 1907 Willem Postma propounded a fully fledged theory of separate development for Africans in *De Vriend des Volks*:

> 'give the Black nations a piece of land where they can establish their own schools, churches, prisons, parliaments. . . .'

J. B. M. Hertzog, founder of the National Party in January 1914.

And in 1912 Hammersma argued in the theological journal *De Jong Kalvinist* (The Young Calvinist) that the only solution to South Africa's racial policies that was consistent with Calvinism was 'separation' or 'segregation'. Finally, in 1913 Jan Kamp, a Dutchman who had been an editor working for Kuyper's newspaper, was reported in *Het Westen* (The Westerner) on 24 June 1913 as speaking of *apartheid* to describe the basic principle of Calvinist political theories in South Africa. He used *apartheid* in essentially the same way as it is used today.

Before the foundation of the National Party Willem Postma worked very closely with General Hertzog. On 13 December 1913 Postma heralded the birth of the new party by publishing a Programme of Principles for a National Party in *Het Westen.* When Hertzog called a special congress to found the National Party in January 1914 Postma's programme became the basis for discussion, and was eventually adopted with minor alterations as the *Programme of Principles of the National Party of South Africa.* The party was described as 'Christian-National', acknowledged the 'guidance of God' and 'calling' of the state, and had a theoretical framework that strongly reflected Kuyper's thought.[16]

Thus the National Party was launched on a tide of Calvinist sentiment that had been created in the years between 1902 and 1914. It is strange to discover at the second congress of the party in 1915 that Hertzog was in undisputed control of what had become virtually a secular political party. The change in the political fortunes of the Calvinists can be accounted for by the ill-health of their major theorist Willem Postma, which forced him to withdraw from active politics, and by the effects of the 1914 civil war, which weakened the Calvinist movement by removing many of its leaders from public life.

Conclusion

Many factors worked together to create Afrikaner nationalism following the second Anglo-Boer war, and these require a complex social and economic analysis. But the ideology that gave the Nationalists their intellectual legitimation and popular appeal was the result of the interaction between the experience of suffering and the interpretation of that experience by a small group of committed Calvinists. Through the Christian-National schools, the Second Language Movement and their support for the National Women's Monument, the Calvinists gained an influence that far outweighed their numbers. In using that influence they sought to revive a demoralized people and create hope for the future. Against the injustices of British imperialism and the ever present threat of anglicization, they pitted a vision of a pluralist society based upon the Dutch model and theories of Kuyper. In doing so, they were children of their time who, in reacting primarily against the English, laid the basis for contemporary Afrikaner justifications of their policies towards black people.

Without the creation of this ideology, a form of nationalism might well have grown up in South Africa, but it would have been very different from the one that did emerge. Alternatively, Marxism might have taken root among Afrikaner workers, when, in fact, as the Simons point out,[17] Afrikaner nationalism created an effective barrier to the communist penetration of Afrikaner society. To understand later developments of Afrikaner nationalism it is important to appreciate the significance of the period before 1914 that gave it birth. Only by seeing its background in the emotional experience of Afrikaners and its ideological roots in Dutch Calvinism can one begin to distinguish the contours on which later politicians have built.

In the final analysis any understanding of Afrikaner nationalism may be academic. Forces have been unleashed in southern Africa that many believe have taken the initative away from white society and given it to the blacks. But by attempting to gain an insight into Afrikaner nationalism we may at least begin to understand why South African political leaders so often act in ways that outsiders see as lacking in pragmatic value and the political wisdom of contemporary society. We may also begin to understand why outsiders also find it so difficult to communicate with Afrikaner nationalists.

References

1. Very little has been written about the Dutch Anti-Revolutionary Movement in English. The fullest treatment available is in an unpublished Ph D thesis by James William Skillen, 'The Development of Calvinistic Political Theory in The Netherlands', Duke University, 1973. It is also discussed by E. L. H. Taylor in *A Christian Philosophy of Law, Politics and the State*, Nutley, New Jersey, 1966.
2. These issues are discussed by James Hutton Mackay in *Religious Thought in Holland During the Nineteenth Century*, London, 1911, and by Simon J. de Vries in *Bible and Theology in the Netherlands*, Wageningen, 1968.
3. There is no biography of van Prinsterer in English.
4. The only biography of Abraham Kuyper in English is of poor quality – F. Vandenberg, *Abraham Kuyper*, Grand Rapids, 1960.
5. Cf. D. Moberg, 'Social Differentiation in the Netherlands', *Social Forces*, 39, 1961, 333–7.
6. A good outline of Kuyper's views may be found in his book *Lectures on Calvinism*, first published in English in 1898 and republished in various editions by Wm. B. Eerdmans of Grand Rapids.
7. A good treatment of the life and work of S. J. du Toit is to be found in T. R. H. Davenport, *The Afrikaner Bond*, Cape Town, 1960.
8. Very little is available in English on the differences between the various Dutch Reformed Churches. Probably the best source at present is T. Dunbar Moodie, *The Rise of Afrikanerdom*, Berkeley, 1975.
9. Donald Denoon in his book *A Grand Illusion*, London, 1973, makes a valuable study of post-war social conditions. He is weakest in his understanding of Christian-National Education and the role of the various Dutch Reformed Churches.
10. The information given here is based upon a study of church publications and documentary sources. See I. R. Hexham, 'Totalitarian Calvinism: the Reformed ("Dopper") Community in South Africa, 1902–1919', Ph D thesis, University of Bristol, 1975.
11. This section is based upon a study of Education Department Reports and the Minutes of the Christian-National Education Commission as well as related publications. See Hexham, *op. cit.*
12. Various dates have been suggested for the emergence of Afrikaner nationalism and a consciousness of a distinct Afrikaner identity. I find it difficult to support arguments for such awareness prior to the war. But see F. A. van Jaarsveld, *The Awakening of Afrikaner Nationalism*, Cape Town, 1961.
13. For an Afrikaner view see D. W. Kruger, *The Making of a Nation*, Johannesburg, 1969.
14. My translation.
15. Archive of the Secretary to the Department of the Prime Minister (1910–22), Pretoria Archives, Botha to Englebrecht, 18 January 1913.
16. See D. W. Kruger, *South African Parties and Policies: 1910–1960*, Cape Town, 1960.
17. See H. J. and R. E. Simons, *Class and Colour in South Africa, 1850–1950*, London, 1970.

The following books and articles provide further information about the subjects dealt with in the preceding chapters. Most of the items will be available in good civic libraries or in university libraries. The place of publication is London unless otherwise stated.

General books

T. R. H. Davenport, *South Africa: A Modern History*, 1977.
Byron Farwell, *The Great Boer War*, 1977.
Rayne Kruger, *Good-bye Dolly Gray*, 1959.
G. H. L. Le May, *British Supremacy in South Africa, 1899–1907*, 1965.
Johannes Meintjes, *The Anglo-Boer War 1899–1902: A Pictorial History*, 1978.
Thomas Pakenham, *The Boer War, 1979.*
S. B. Spies, *Methods of Barbarism? Roberts and Kitchener and Civilians in the Boer Republics, January 1900–May 1902*, Cape Town, 1977.
Monica Wilson and Leonard Thompson eds., *The Oxford History of South Africa*, Vol. II, 1971.

The Gold Mining Industry in the Transvaal 1886–99

Marcello de Cecco, *Money and Empire: The International Gold Standard, 1890–1914*, 1974.
Frederick H. Hatch and J. A. Chalmers, *The Gold Mines of the Rand*, 1895.
F. A. Johnstone, *Class, Race and Gold: A Study of Class Relations and Racial Discrimination in South Africa*, 1976.
A. Jeeves, 'The Control of Migratory Labour on the South African Gold Mines in the Era of Kruger and Milner', *Journal of Southern African Studies*, 2, 1 (1975).
Charles van Onselen, 'Randlords and Rotgut, 1886–1903', *History Workshop Journal*, 2, 1976.
Stanley Trapido, 'Landlord and Tenant in a Colonial Economy: The Transvaal, 1880–1910', *Journal of Southern African Studies*, 5, 1 (1978).
J. J. Van-Helten, 'German Capital, The Netherlands Railway Company and the Political Economy of the Transvaal, 1886–1900', *Journal of African History*, 19, 3 (1978).

British Imperial Policy towards South Africa 1895–99

A. H. Duminy, *The Capitalists and the Outbreak of the Anglo-Boer War*, University of Natal, 1977.
J. E. Flint, *Cecil Rhodes*, 1974.
J. A. Hobson, *The War in South Africa, Its Causes and Effects*, 1900.
J. S. Marais, *The Fall of Kruger's Republic*, 1961.
R. E. Robinson and J. Gallagher, *Africa and the Victorians*, 1961.
J. Van der Poel, *Railway and Customs Policies in South Africa, 1885–1910*, 1933.

A. Atmore and S. Marks, 'The Imperial Factor in South Africa in the Nineteenth Century: Towards a Reassessment', in E. F. Penrose ed., *European Imperialism and the Partition of Africa*, 1975.
G. Blainey, 'Lost Causes of the Jameson Raid', *Economic History Review*, 2nd series, 18, 2 (1965).
N. Garson, 'British Imperialism and the Coming of the South African War', *South African Journal of Economics*, 30, 1962.
A. N. Porter, 'Lord Salisbury, Mr Chamberlain and South Africa, 1895–9', *The Journal of Imperial and Commonwealth History*, 1, 1972.
A. N. Porter, 'Sir Alfred Milner and the Press, 1897–9', *The Historical Journal*, 16, 1973.
E. Stokes, 'Milnerism', *The Historical Journal*, 5, 1962.

Military Aspects of the war

L. S. Amery ed., *The Times History of the War in South Africa*, 7 vols., 1900–9.
J. B. Atkins, *The Relief of Ladysmith*, 1900.
C. R. De Wet, *Three Years War*, 1902.
K. Griffith, *Thank God We Kept the Flag Flying*, 1974.
J. F. Maurice and M. H. Grant eds., *History of the War in South Africa, 1899–1902*, 8 vols., 1906–10.
Deneys Reitz, *Commando, A Boer Journal of the Boer War*, 1929.
Count A. W. Sternberg, *My Experiences of the Boer War*, 1901.
B. Viljoen, *My Reminiscences of the Anglo-Boer War*, 1902.
W. H. Waters trans., *The German Official Account of the War in South Africa*, 1904.

Life on Commando

J. H. Breytenbach, *Die Geskiedenis van die Tweede Vryheidsoorlog in Suid-Afrika, 1899–1902*, Vol. 1, Pretoria, 1969.
C. R. De Wet, *Three Years War*, 1902.
H. C. Hillegas, *With the Boer Forces*, 1901.
O. Hintrager, *Met Steijn en de Wet op Kommando*, Rotterdam, 1902.
S. Izedinova, *A Few Months with the Boers: The War Reminiscences of a Russian Nursing Sister*, Johannesburg, 1977.

J. D. Kestell, *Through Shot and Flame*, 1903.
C. Plokhooy, *Met den Mauser: Persoonlijke Ervaringen in den Zuid-Afrikaanschen Oorlog*, Gorinchem, 1902.
H. Ver Loren van Themaat, *Twee Jaren in den Boerenoorlog*, Haarlem, 1903.

Tommy Atkins in South Africa

L. E. Du Moulin, *Two Years on Trek*, 1907.
'Linesman', *Words by an Eyewitness*, 1901.
James Milne, *The Epistles of Atkins*, 1902.
Trooper Cosmo Rose-Innes, *With Paget's Horse to the Front*, 1901.
Richard Price, *An Imperial War and the British Working Class*, 1972.
J. Ralph, *Towards Pretoria*, 1900.
P. T. Ross, *A Yeoman's Letters*, 1901.
A Subaltern's Letters to His Wife, 1901.
John Gooch, 'Attitudes to War in Late Victorian and Edwardian England', in Brian Bond and Ian Roy eds., *War and Society*, 1975.
Anne Summers, 'Militarism in Britain before the Great War', *History Workshop Journal*, 2, 1976.

The Siege of Mafeking

F. D. Baillie, *Mafeking: A Diary of the Siege*, 1900.
J. L. Comaroff ed., *The Boer War Diary of Sol T. Plaatje*, 1973.
B. Gardner, *Mafeking: A Victorian Legend*, 1966.
J. A. Hamilton, *The Siege of Mafeking*, 1900.
J. E. Neilly, *Besieged with B-P*, 1900.
Sol T. Plaatje, *Native Life in South Africa*, 1916.
E. E. Reynolds, *Baden-Powell*, 1942.
B. Roberts, *Churchills in Africa*, 1970.

Women and the war

J. Brandt, *The Petticoat Commando*, 1913.
J. E. De la Rey, *A Woman's Wanderings and Trials during the Anglo-Boer War*, 1903.
J. Fisher, *That Miss Hobhouse*, 1971.
A. R. Fry, *Emily Hobhouse: A Memoir*, 1929.
E. Hobhouse, *The Brunt of the War and Where It Fell*, 1902.
E. Hobhouse ed., *Tant Alie of Transvaal: Her Diary 1880–1902*, 1923.
E. Hobhouse, *War Without Glamour*, Bloemfontein, 1924.
L. Marquard ed., *Letters from a Boer Parsonage*, Cape Town, 1967.
A. C. Martin, *The Concentration Camps 1900–1902: Facts, Figures and Fables*, Cape Town, 1957.
J. C. Otto, *Die Konsentrasiekampe*, Cape Town, 1954.

J. L. Hattingh, 'Die Irene Konsentrasie-kamp', *Archives Year Book for South African History*, 30, 1 (1967).

Black People and the war

Sol T. Plaatje, *Native Life in South Africa*, 1916.

Donald Denoon, 'Participation in the "Boer War": People's War, People's Non-War or Non-People's War?', in B. A. Ogot ed., *War and Society in Africa*, 1972.
L. D. Ngcongco, 'Jabavu and the Anglo-Boer War', *Kleio* (UNISA), 2, 1970.
L. W. Truschel, 'Nation-building and the Kgatla: The Role of the Anglo-Boer War', *Botswana Notes and Records* (Gaborone), 4, 1972.
Peter Warwick, 'The African Refugee Problem in the Transvaal and Orange River Colony, 1900–02', *Southern African Research in Progress, Collected Papers 2*, University of York, 1977.
Peter Warwick, 'Black Industrial Protest on the Witwatersrand, 1901–02', in E. Webster ed., *Essays in Southern African Labour History*, Johannesburg, 1978.

British Society and the war

V. E. Chancellor, *History for their Masters*, 1970.
K. Griffith, *Thank God We Kept the Flag Flying*, 1974.
C. MacInnes, *Sweet Saturday Night*, 1967.
R. McKenzie and A. Silver, *Angels in Marble*, 1968.
H. Pelling, *Popular Politics and Society in Late Victorian Britain*, 1968.
Richard Price, *An Imperial War and the British Working Class*, 1972.
R. Roberts, *The Classic Slum*, Penguin ed., 1973.
J. A. Schumpeter, *Imperialism and Social Classes*, 1957.
B. Semmel, *Imperialism and Social Reform*, 1960.

F. Bealey, 'Les Travaillistes et la Guerre des Boers', *Le Mouvement Social*, 45, 1963.
Brian Bond, 'Recruiting to the Victorian Army, 1870–92', *Victorian Studies*, June 1962.

The Pro-Boers in Britain
Stephen Koss ed., *The Pro-Boers*, Chicago, 1973.
Henry Pelling, *Popular Politics and Society in Late Victorian Britain*, 1968.
Bernard Porter, *Critics of Empire*, 1968.
Richard Price, *An Imperial War and the British Working Class*, 1972.

J. W. Auld, 'The Liberal Pro-Boers', *Journal of British Studies*, 14, 2 (1975).
J. O. Baylen, 'W. T. Stead and the Boer War: The Irony of Idealism', *Canadian Historical Review*, 40, 1959.
F. Bealey, 'Les Travaillistes et la Guerre des Boers', *Le Mouvement Social*, 45, 1963.
J. S. Galbraith, 'The Pamphlet Campaign on the Boer War', *Journal of Modern History*, 24, 2 (1952).
I. Sellars, 'The Pro-Boer Movement in Liverpool', *Transactions of the Unitarian Historical Society*, 12, 2 (1960).

Collaborators in Boer Society
J. P. Brits ed., *Diary of a National Scout: P. J. du Toit, 1900–02*, Pretoria, 1974.
Donald Denoon, *A Grand Illusion*, 1973.
C. R. De Wet, *Three Years War*, 1902.
J. D. Kestell and D. E. Van Velden eds., *The Peace Negotiations*, 1912.
J. M. Spaight, *War Rights on Land*, 1911.

Donald Denoon, 'Participation in the "Boer War": People's War, People's Non-War or Non-People's War?', in B. A. Ogot ed., *War and Society in Africa*, 1972.
N. G. Garson, '"Het Volk": The Botha-Smuts Party in the Transvaal, 1904–11', *The Historical Journal*, 9, 1966.
V. E. Solomon, 'The Handsuppers', *Military Historical Journal* (Pretoria), 3, 1 (1974).

The Anglican Church during the war
John H. Bovill, *Natives Under the Transvaal Flag*, 1900.
Edwin Farmer, *The Transvaal as a Mission Field*, 1900.
Peter Hinchliff, *The Anglican Church in South Africa*, 1963.
Peter d'A. Jones, *The Christian Socialist Revival 1877–1914*, Princeton, 1968.
W. J. Knox Little, *Sketches and Studies in South Africa*, 1899.
A. Theodore Wirgman, *Life of James Green*, 2 vols., 1909.
Michael H. M. Wood, *A Father in God: The Biography of Archbishop West Jones*, 1913.

Poetry of the war
Alice M. Buckton, *The Burden of Engela: A Ballad-Epic*, 1904.
Coldstreamer (Harry Graham), *Ballads of the Boer War*, 1902.
T. W. H. Crosland, *The Five Notions*, 1903.
A. P. Grove and C. J. D. Harvey eds., *Afrikaans Poems with English Translations*, Cape Town, 1962.
Thomas Hardy, *Poems of the Past and Present*, 1901.
A. E. Housman, *Last Poems*, 1922.
Rudyard Kipling, *The Five Nations*, 1903.
Mome (G. Murray Johnstone), *The Off-Wheeler Ballads*, 1910.
H. D. Rawnsley, *Ballads of the War*, 1900 (enlarged 2nd ed., 1901).
Songs of the Veld (New Age), 1902.
Edgar Wallace, *Writ in Barracks*, 1900.
William Watson, *For England*, 1904.
M. van Wyk Smith, *Drummer Hodge, The Poetry of the Anglo-Boer War (1899–1902)*, 1978.

The United States and the war
Kenton C. Clymer, *John Hay: The Gentleman as Diplomat*, Michigan, 1975.
Richard H. Davis, *With Both Armies in South Africa*, New York, 1900.
John C. Ferguson, *American Diplomacy and the Boer War*, Philadelphia, 1939.
Elting E. Morison and John M. Blum eds., *The Letters of Theodore Roosevelt*, Vol. II, Harvard, 1951.
Bradford Perkins, *The Great Rapprochement: England and the United States, 1895–1914*, New York, 1978.

Paul Addison, 'Churchill and the United States', *New Edinburgh Review*, 38-9, 1977.

Reconstruction in the Transvaal
Donald Denoon, *A Grand Illusion*, 1973.
C. Headlam ed., *The Milner Papers (South Africa) 1897–1905*, Vol. II, 1933.
G. B. Pyrah, *Imperial Policy and South Africa, 1902–10*, 1955.
M. Streak, *Lord Milner's Immigration Policy for the Transvaal, 1897–1905*, Johannesburg, 1970.

Donald Denoon, 'Capitalist Influence and the Transvaal Government during the Crown Colony Period, 1901–6', *The Historical Journal*, 11, 1968.
Donald Denoon, 'The Transvaal Labour Crisis, 1901–6', *Journal of African History*, 7, 3 (1967).
Alan Jeeves, 'The Control of Migratory Labour on the South African Gold Mines in the Era of Kruger and Milner', *Journal of Southern African Studies*, 2, 1 (1975).
A. Mawby, 'Capital, Government and Politics in the Transvaal, 1901–7 : A Revision and a Reversion', *The Historical Journal*, 17, 1974.
Peter Richardson, 'Coolie and Randlords : The North Randfontein Chinese Miners' Strike of 1905', *Journal of Southern African Studies*, 2, 2 (1975).
E. Stokes, 'Milnerism', *The Historical Journal*, 5, 1962.

British Imperial Policy Towards South Africa 1905–10
W. K. Hancock, *Smuts*, Vol. I, *The Sanguine Years 1870–1919*, 1962.
W. K. Hancock and J. van der Poel eds., *Selections from the Smuts Papers*, Vol. II, *1902–10*, 1966.
R. Hyam, *Elgin and Churchill at the Colonial Office 1905–08*, 1968.
N. Mansergh, *South Africa 1906–61: The Price of Magnanimity*, 1962.
L. M. Thompson, *The Unification of South Africa 1902–10*, 1960.

R. Hyam, 'African Interests and the South Africa Act, 1908–10', *The Historical Journal*, 13, 1970.
R. Hyam and G. W. Martin, 'The Myth of the "Magnanimous Gesture" : The Liberal Government, Smuts and Conciliation, 1906', in *Reappraisals in British Imperial History*, 1975.
G. W. Martin, 'The Canadian Analogy in South African Union, 1870–1910', *South African Historical Journal*, 8, 1976.

Afrikaner Nationalism 1902–14
T. R. H. Davenport, *The Afrikaner Bond*, Cape Town, 1966.
Donald Denoon, *A Grand Illusion*, 1973.
D. W. Kruger, *The Making of a Nation*, Johannesburg, 1969.
D. W. Kruger, *South African Parties and Policies, 1910–60*, Cape Town, 1960.
Abraham Kuyper, *Lectures on Calvinism*, Grand Rapids, 1960.
T. Dunbar Moodie, *The Rise of Afrikanerdom*, Berkeley, 1975.
H. J. and R. E. Simons, *Class and Colour in South Africa, 1850–1950*, 1969.
Theo Sundermeir ed., *Church and Nationalism in South Africa*, Johannesburg, 1975.
F. Vandenberg, *Abraham Kuyper*, Grand Rapids, 1960.
F. A. Van Jaarsveld, *The Awakening of Afrikaner Nationalism*, Cape Town, 1961.

N. G. Garson, ' "Het Volk" : The Botha-Smuts Party in the Transvaal, 1904–11', *The Historical Journal*, 9, 1966.
L. Salomon, 'The Economic Background to the Revival of Afrikaner Nationalism', in J. Butler ed., *Boston University Papers in African History*, Vol. I, Boston, 1964.

The publishers gratefully acknowledge permission to reproduce the following illustrations: Africana Museum, Johannesburg 113, 188*b*, 190, 191, 202, 203, 206, 343, 350, 352, 355, 359; Courtesy of Birmingham Public Libraries, Local Studies Department 233; Bodleian Library, Oxford 27*bl*, 29*tr*; The Librian, University of Bristol 364; BBC Hulton Picture Library 18, 24, 27*br*, 40, 41*br*, 44, 49, 73*t*, 81, 84, 89*b*, 105*t*, *bl*, 117, 127, 130, 134, 135*b*, 136, 178, 182*r*, 200, 208, 218*l*, 230, 234, 277, 280, 284, 319, 324, 328, 367, 379; By Permission of the British Library 221, 231*tl*, *tr*, 245, 246, 316, 317, 330; Cape Archives Depot 41*t*, 71, 75, 76, 78, 82, 99*tl*, *b*, 105*br*, 129, 151, 163, 179*b*, 195*t*, *bl*, 197*b*, 199, 204, 261, 306*t*, 390; The Earl of Elgin 365, 368; Mary Evans Picture Library 181; The Evening News, London 254; Illustrated London News 32, 195*br*, 231*b*, 243; Dr S. E. Katzenellenbogen 358; Mafeking Museum 143, 145, 149, 152, 153, 154, 155; Mansell Collection 45, 50, 57, 146, 181, 220, 259, 263*r*, 268, 318, 320, 323, 363, 393, 395, 396, 402; National Army Museum 68*b*, 69, 88, 89*t*, 99*tr*, 100, 126, 128, 131, 135*t*, 137, 198, 285, 347, 398; National Film Archive 68*t*, 87, 218*r*, 226, 228, 232; National Portrait Gallery 39, 382; Prince Consort Army Library, Aldershot 286; Transcript of Crown Copyright Records in the Public Record Office by Permission of the Controller of H.M. Stationery Office 372; Punch Magazine 54, 55, 241, 248, 249, 370; Courtesy of the Royal Commonwealth Society 142, 147; The Scout Association 156, 158; Director of Sheffield City Libraries 223; South African Defence Force Archives, Pretoria 164*bl*, 167; John Topham Picture Library 47, 70, 96, 140, 188*t*, 219; Transvaal Archives Depot, Pretoria 73*b*, 109, 111, 114, 115, 116, 119, 120, 163, 164*tl*, *br*, 165, 166, 168, 169, 170*l*, 174, 175, 179*t*, 182*l*, 183, 197*t*, 397*l*; United Society for the Propagation of the Gospel 282, 287, 289; U.S. Library of Congress 321, 325; Dr M. Van Wyk Smith 11, 94, 150, 177, 212, 213, 251, 293, 295, 297, 300, 301, 303, 306*b*, 311, 312, 333, 397*r*; The War Museum of the Boer Republics, Bloemfontein 170*r*, 263*l*, 266, 270, 273, 275; Brian Willan 157.

Jacket, front: BBC Hulton Picture Library; back: Cape Archives Depot, top; Africana Museum, centre; M. Van Wyk Smith, bottom left; BBC Hulton Picture Library, bottom right.

Maps by Art Services.